"Days of Joy, Years of Recovery."

By

Carol Morfitt Welch

Presented by:

Brede Publishing

Helping Aspiring Authors Self-publish On Amazon &
Kindle

109 Hialeah Street, Osceola, Wisconsin 54020
715-417-3027
Email brede.publishing@aol.com

https://www.createspace.com/6934453

Publication Date: Feb 13 2017
ISBN/EAN13:   1543116477 / 9781543116472

"Days of Joy, Years of Recovery."

By

Carol Morfitt Welch

Edited by,

Joanne Bass

Acknowledgments

I'm thankful to my family, parents and siblings, for the life and relationships I have been able to draw on to tell my story.

I especially want to thank my daughter, Joanne Bass, who has tirelessly reviewed and edited my writing with perception and thoughtfulness.

I am also grateful to my other four children who have encouraged me in writing and who also shared with me the joys and throes of dysfunction and recovery.

Clarence and Grace Snyder, who have passed on, are deeply deserving of my gratitude for the mutual recovery of our family.

AA and Al-Anon have given us tools to work through our recovery and to reach others with whom we can share that fellowship.

Lastly, and most importantly, I am eternally grateful to a loving Father God, who saw fit at our extremity of dealing with life, to touch us with His love and healing strength.

Carol Morfitt Welch

Introduction

No addict's story began right where they are today. Or last week. Or last year.

And no story of the life of one affected by an addict began with the addiction or even with the relationship.

We are all a part of where we have been—the time, the place, the people. We are a part of our upbringing and our parents' upbringing. Those factors influence our perceptions and our responses. They even influence who and how we meet.

And, of course, there is the original plan of our Creator, who designed the continuation of human life by the drawing of men and women together.

Days of Joy, Years of Recovery is a story of how families through generations prepare a couple to affect the lives of each other. How the couple learns to enjoy, cope, endure, and sometimes find their way, if not early, sometimes deeply.

It's a story of how a powerful and loving God, who, when sought and received, can, and did, bring the healing solution.

This is a story of hope—hope in an awesome God, who brought sanity out of insanity, and healing to wounded and shattered hearts. A God who meets you right where you are when you look to Him.

You will see through this couple's story that very often the difficult times trigger the seeking and healing. Is that where you are—in a difficult time? This story can become yours—your story of hope.

And like the ripples in a pond, as the recovered people have shared their story with you, you will be able to spread the good you have received and put the positive effect in motion.

Carol and Dale

Their lives had a lot of ups and downs together, and through God's grace, they both came out on top.

Table of Contents

1 Merlin

The balmy glowing dawn in eastern sky,
gives way to wind on drying prairie grass.
With corn shock leaves turning brittle dry,
Another Iowa harvest comes to pass.

"Merlin, is there any way to tear you away from that spinning rope long enough to plan the day's work?" The tall slender teenage boy-turning-man, with a hint of bow of his legs, twisted around to bring the swinging lasso down the length of his frame, only to guide it whirling over his head again. Laughing, he let the coil fall at his feet, ready, finally, to talk.

"Well, the wheat is in, corn in shocks and ready to shred, and new seeding of alfalfa ready to survive the winter. Pearl and Walter are planning a pig roast. Then I'll bet we get down to fall plowing pretty steady. Rodeo circuit's moving up this way, and I have my bid in a couple of events."

Homer, the dad of Merlin and his brothers, Millard, Wayne, and Elmer, commented, "I imagine so, if you can hold up your end of the plowing. You've got a couple of good work horses broken besides your rodeo stock."

"Well, they're work horses too, if you value handling cattle." That was Merlin. No argument from Millard, who valued all aspects of farming—grain, cattle, and good horses to work each part.

So Homer went to tell Mary, "No cooking tomorrow. We'll let Pearl and Walter host the pig roast, and we'll form the clean-up crew." The younger boys, Wayne and Elmer, were more than happy for a family outing and break from harvesting and general field work.

Merlin trilled in his beautiful signature whistle a western melody as he got ready for the coming day. Checking on the horses, tack, ropes, and lassos were tasks that had to be done in addition to the mandatory farm work. So, with twirling and whistling out of the way, the fellows joined Ma for supper, a simple meal to end the day.

2 North English Girl

From North English, clear across the state,
the little lady caught the young man's eye.
Her papa called to aid the local magistrate,
as constable, keep law and order high.

Only a couple of years had passed since teen-
aged Merlin qualified for rodeo events, and changes
had taken place in the two older boys' lives—both
matters for satisfaction and for concern. Millard
continued to be a staunch and steady producer of
grain and cattle and was becoming influential in the
community. He was also courting a well-liked teacher
in the community. Merlin's skill, both at training farm
horses and performing in rodeo contests was
increasing, but with a barb of worry on the part of his
parents.

"Well, another good showing at roping and riding," Homer praised his son. (There was a bit more bow to Merlin's his legs and his feet shaped to the arch of the cowboy boots, when he returned from his latest contest in high spirits in more ways than one.) "You know, though, Son, you shouldn't be wasting your success on moonshine and such."

Merlin's Dad, Homer, didn't mention the tragedy of Merlin's brother, Wayne, who had too recently lost his life to pneumonia while incarcerated in a nearby jail. "You aren't setting a good example for young Elmer. You know, your younger brother practically idolizes you."

"Well. Tomorrow's another day." Merlin remarked as he did his usual routine, tending the horses and the tack before laying his exhausted bones in bed.

As sleep began to close the doors on the past day, the echoes of the cheers, the back slapping, the muttered remark of an opponent he had bested, began to slide together with other vague recollections of life as it was turning. He knew he should have seen his parents' grief at the seemingly shameful death of their son, Wayne; but he felt a creeping bitterness that they may have allowed it. (Wayne's lawless behavior during a drinking bout had led to his arrest, and his parents, angry and ashamed of his behavior, had refused to see him until they were notified of his critical condition too late to save his life.) Mixed with these feelings he couldn't have spoken, was the feeling that Millard, so good and stable, seemed to be preferred. Well, darn! He did have the purse awarded today. "Yeah, tomorrow is another day."

"Ooh, yeah, another day," Merlin groaned next morning as he reflected on how the jubilation and abandoned hilarity could carry with it the down and throbbing morning-after consequence.

Suddenly, the morning did an about-face. Homer and Mary knew it was coming, but with all the preparation and excitement of the rodeo, they had either forgotten to mention it to Merlin, or he simply hadn't heard. The new constable had arrived. Millard paged Merlin with a knock on the door. "If I know you, brother, I think you will want to look different when you meet the constable's family. He has a couple of young daughters."

Well, Millard couldn't have been more right. Suddenly, cold water, a comb, and a clean change of clothes were important; and these important alterations made the impression Merlin had hoped for. It wasn't only that he felt freshened up with great quickness, but the object for which he prepared was much more than he expected.

As Merlin entered the dining room, there was the new constable William Harkness, along with his wife, two sons, and two daughters. Evelyn, or Maude (her given first name), was the youngest daughter—a petite brunette with sparkling brown-black eyes and a modest smile. She immediately caught Merlin's eye, and that young cowboy had met his match. Merlin later heard that a local ministry student near North English had hoped to court her, but she felt she was not sufficiently outgoing to consider being a pastor's wife. "My good fortune," Merlin remarked.

Roadside grass, turned brittle and brown by the chill wind, rustled and flitted across the country road in front of the broad, low Morfitt house. Throughout the countryside sheds with the cupolas so characteristic of the day sheltered the gas-driven elevators, bins bulged with grain, and sturdy lean-tos sheltered the growing livestock. Northern Iowa seemed buttoned up for the long, windy winter months.

Inside the house, Homer and his sons reviewed the past year's production and plans for the next. Evenings by lamplight were often spent with the gathering of neighbors, including getting acquainted with the new constable's family and introducing them around. Merlin, usually restless in these times of quiet visiting, itching to be out with the rodeo guys or practicing his skills, took a different attitude during these visits with the constable's family. His only tendency to elude the circle of discourse was his directing of subtle witticisms with a sidelong grin toward Evelyn, who acknowledged with a lady-like smile.

Before many weeks, Merlin had asked the good constable Harkness if walking Evelyn to or from events was permissible, and soon Homer's Model-T gained the privilege of transporting sweet Maude Evelyn to local events. Of course, providing a ride for the two sisters was a good reason for more frequency in the use of the car.

Spring comes quickly in Northwestern Iowa, and the ground thawing for field work comes at much the same time as the break in weather that is favorable for training horses and practicing roping skills. Although cold weather had not deterred Merlin from working horses and roping during the winter months, it was a race in time to accomplish the training necessary for rodeo competition before he was needed to work steadily in the field.

A young man's fancy expands in spring on what has been occupying his mind through the winter. This year, as the crocus emerged and the lilac showed signs of budding, Merlin was most attentive to his sweetheart. But still, he was also very drawn to the hearty company of rodeo friends, and some of his social outings with the men who loved the sport of rodeo left Merlin with a hangover that left his folks in a dilemma: "Do we share this with Maude? She's so sweet and moral-minded. Or do we protect Merlin from the disapproval he would face if we told her?"

As it turned out, the decision was unnecessary. A shadow over the sparkling brown eyes told them that she was aware. In the manner of sweethearts, it was worked out quietly. Apparently the alcohol-augmented sociability was reduced to an infrequency that was less troubling to her, and before the coming of Christmas, Merlin and Maude were engaged.

3 Jackson County, Minnesota or Iowa

County lines seem arbitrary,
where addresses are concerned.
It's the village or the city,
the location can be learned.
A county is in a given state,
post office may differentiate.

The 1930's were not an easy time in rural Iowa. Maude Harkness, born and raised in North English, a southern Iowa town, was the youngest of policeman William Harkness' four children. During her early life, Maude missed about a year of grade school due to very poor eyesight and heart trouble, which was later thought to have been the result of rheumatic fever. Maude and her sister Olive, who were rather inhibited in their adult life, expressed some sense of adventure as young teens; and once lined up huge planks and directed and drove their dad's Model-T across a small creek.It was at approximately this juncture in Maude's life that her dad was called upon to take the office of city constable in Sibley, a small city in northern Iowa. So, the Harkness family—mother and dad, brothers Harold and James, and sisters Maude and Olive—moved to northern Iowa.

It was here that the Harkness family met the Morfitts; and quiet, but cheerful, little Maude finished high school and met a rather flamboyant young farmer, Merlin Morfitt, who was becoming a competent rodeo performer.

Attracted to one another, and both hoping to combine the farm and rodeo life, Merlin and Maude married and settled down near the Morfitt farm. To supplement their income, Maude and Merlin took jobs at a local dairy plant. Within the first year, they discovered they were going to be parents.

The birth of little Billy, named after Maude's father, was a joy to all the family, and as weeks went by, he became smiley and alert. Maude and Merlin prepared to take him to see cousins in their open Model-T sedan. To protect little Billy from the wind, they thoroughly bundled him in blankets, checking from time to time that he was comfortable.

When the happy moment arrived to present little Billy to Merlin's oldest sister and cousins, Maude gently unwrapped his covers and found him unresponsive. They tried everything they could to revive him; but the awful realization engulfed them: their baby was dead. Maude screamed hopelessly and seemingly endlessly, until others carried the lifeless baby into the house.

4 Hope Renewed

Days are long with empty arms,
and hope seldom comes if ever,
work filling time as likelihood,
with melancholy, whispers, never.

"Five years passed, Merlin and Maude working at the dairy, and no sign of a baby appeared to fill the empty arms. Then Maude began to notice some nausea and inability to get up in time for her duties at the dairy. With a mixture of joy and apprehension, they awaited the new baby's arrival. There was always conjecture as to whether the baby was born in Iowa or Minnesota, as the mailing address was Iowa, but the farm was in Jackson County, Minnesota, on the border.

When the doctor arrived to assist with the home birth, he asked Merlin to hold the lantern so he could have light for the task at hand. Someone noticed Merlin growing pale, and a family member grabbed the lantern from him before he sank to the floor. Fortunately a nurse was with the doctor, and he was able to see to deliver the baby as she held the lamp.

A healthy though tiny boy was born at the Morfitt home, filling the family with happiness. They named him Dale and took turns comforting his colicky times and reveling in his smiles and cooing. "Oh, may this baby live!" Their apprehensive hearts settled in stages as he developed from creeping to walking, and another remedy was needed.

Maude still had her job at the dairy, and she had no means to keep toddling Dale contained as she worked. The dairy owner's wife offered to watch over Dale during Maude's work time, and she took her up on the offer. It seemed like a good answer to the problem, until Maude found that the owner's wife had Dale fastened to the clothesline post with a leash while she did her own work.

For Maude, this must have been the last straw. Naturally reticent to stand up for herself, the welfare of her son was another matter. The family was already in a mode of planning to move to Wisconsin, where Maude's oldest brother had bought a farm. They looked around the area and found a farm that could be rented. The deal was made, and the Morfitts moved to a rather hilly but tillable farm near Amery, Wisconsin. Merlin, a horseman and horse trader, soon had the farm stocked with horses and a moderate herd of dairy cows.

5 Wisconsin

The shining days, sometimes with clouds,

as life, with problems facing,
the love of children, neighbors, friends,
worries, sometimes, erasing.

      Some of Merlin's brothers were drinkers, and others not; but Merlin's own alcohol consumption increased markedly. The rodeo life contributed to the social drinking, and, by the time they settled in Wisconsin, Maude became increasingly concerned. Would Merlin be home for chores on time? Safe on the road? In a good frame of mind?

Merlin's engaging personality and quick humor opened doors for him. He soon became well acquainted in the neighborhood and in demand when skilled horsemanship and roping was needed

A daughter, Marlys, came along, a new joy to the family. Here on the Wisconsin farm, Maude couldn't work away from home because, although she had been a competent driver as a teen, she never got a driver's license. Neighbors exchanged work for such things as threshing and corn shredding, but daily farm work was up to Merlin, with Maude's help.

When Dale started first grade a couple of miles away at Flanagan School, there was a bit of humor: as he was the only first grader, he was the smartest kid in his class, also the dumbest.Dale was slender in stature, with black hair, good looks, and a ready enthusiasm. His uncle cautioned Maude, "Watch that boy's temper!" Most people, however, found him good-natured, except, perhaps, his sister Marlys who once was left counting to a large number for "Hide and Seek" while Dale sneaked off to play with a neighbor boy.

With Merlin's proficiency with horses and skill at horse trading, there was always plenty of horsepower available on the farm, although in different stages of performance and dependability. By the time Dale was eight, Merlin had shown him the ropes with driving the horses. It happened, at times, that Merlin would harness the horses and hitch them to the machinery for the day's work, get Dale started with the driving, and leave for town.

Terrified, Maude would run out to the field, stop Dale and the horses mid-task, unharness them if they were tame enough, and prepare to face the music. This pattern continued to a great extent as years went by.

Dale, being an enterprising sort, had various farm projects going and became proficient in 4-H activities.

6 Future Farmer and Sisters

A bright new world,
seen brighter still,
a fan in his corner
spurs hopes and will.

As time to enter high school approached, the agriculture instructor, Mr. Niccum, came to visit the family and introduce Dale to the Future Farmers of America (FFA) program. Dale was flanked by his two sisters—smiley and enthusiastic Marlys, four years younger than Dale, and Sally, a charming brunette toddler. Before a word was said, Marlys, ever Dale's "booster," began to point out the projects Dale already had going. Blushing, Dale agreed that, yes, he did have some projects going—pigs, a few chickens, a neat garden plot, and a Guernsey calf he was raising.

Merlin chuckled, "Yeah, he's pretty good at handling horses too." Having alluded to what was really important to him, Merlin shook Mr. Niccum's hand and nodded, listening to what the class and club was all about.

Even with all of Dale's agricultural pursuits, his highest goal was to be on the football team. Passing, catching, running—any part of football he could practice with friends would fill most of his non-working time.

When the time came, Dale's relatively small stature was outdone by his enthusiasm and hard work. He was allowed to try out for freshman football, made the team, and was called to play on the field by mid-season—a huge reward for his efforts.

Football season over, the ongoing farm endeavors continued, and by spring Dale was elected to an office in the FFA club. FFA trips led by Mr. Niccum were a highly sought-after opportunity, and finding a replacement on the farm for a week-long trip was a major hurdle.

But each year Dale was able to go, a replacement was found. The group would travel around sections of the United States by bus, camping, visiting points of interest, and taking part in state and national activities. Those were highlights of Dale's life.

7 Turn Around

Just when you think
you can move ahead and earn, chin up,
life may take an unexpected turn.

Sophomore year, another fall, another football season, the county fair with awards in 4-H and FFA. Something was wrong though. The boy that had always bounded into his tasks and new opportunities was dragging along. Home remedies did no good. Dale seemed only to lose strength. As strength waned, so did his hand control. The family became alarmed.

One day while she was in town, Maude happened to meet Dr. Cornwall on the street. He motioned toward Dale, who was trying to keep up with friends as they made their way across the street. "That boy has rheumatic fever," Dr. Cornwall remarked simply.

Dr. Cornwall and Maude hurried over to Dale and guided him to the clinic. An exam and blood tests confirmed rheumatic fever, and calls to hospitals resulted in Dale's admittance to the state hospital in Madison, Wisconsin. There was some deliberation as to which department he should be admitted to due to his multiple symptoms. He had a heart murmur, extreme weakness, and loss of muscle control, diagnosed as St. Vitus dance, which sometimes accompanies severe rheumatic fever.

During the few days of testing and preparation to go to the hospital, Dale's condition declined rapidly, alarming his family and doctors with his rapid loss of strength. The St. Vitus dance increased so drastically that he could barely pull his clothes on and could not pick up an object with any measurable amount of control. When they arrived at the hospital, Dale was admitted to the youth psychiatric ward—a shock to the whole family, not only in the strange surroundings of the ward itself, but also in the distance from home.

"How will we afford a long hospital stay?" Merlin asked worriedly. Representatives of the state hospital were encouraging, alluding to programs available to help financially. Merlin recoiled at the idea of taking charity.

He had paid off the mortgage on the farm and wasn't about to take charity. Little did he know that such a decision, if carried out, would be a very great and unnecessary setback, to say the least. So Merlin, pride intact, paid the initial hospital fee, inquired about the length of stay, and took the rest of the family home with promises to see his young son soon.

8 Isolation and Communication

"I'll be home for Christmas,"
song fell on a heavy heart.
Cutting and bitter, the prospect,
Christmas alone and apart.

If you were acquainted with Maude, you would know that, though she worried a good deal, her enthusiasm for Christmas and desire to bring joy to her family overrode any misgivings she might have, and preparing for the holiday took precedence. She wasn't willing, come hell or high water, to allow Dale to have Christmas alone in a state hospital.

In the midst of the weakness and loneliness, Dale began to feel a little hope. The change from total helplessness and lack of control of his limbs to becoming able to weakly guide a spoon to his mouth gave a noticeable lift to his hope for life and allowed him to turn some of his thoughts and attention to fellow patients, most with emotional illness and some with physical symptoms as well.

Dale ached for the quadriplegic fellow patient whose dreams brought him shame as well as an acute consciousness of his physical incapacity. Confusion and fear were voiced among the fellow patients, while one or two expressed concern for others—concern that was courageous in view of their own problems.

As the days passed with ever so slight evidence of gaining strength or muscle control, the constant, regular cheery messages from home accompanied at least alternate days' mail delivery. Notes from classmates and get well cards helped to speed the days. Checking off days until Christmas brought a lump in his throat, but with reminding himself of the suffering of others in his hospital ward, he endured.

The scene back on the farm was quite a different story. News of Dale's minor signs of recovery spurred the family to prepare the house to be comfortable for him. Maude's sister-in-law, known for a bit of tartness in her tongue, left a memorable quote for the family to repeat ironically. After Merlin and the family had stretched plastic storm covering over the windows to draft proof the house, they came in shivering from the cold, slapping their hands, and getting hot drinks. Auntie remarked, "Well, it's just like this—if you don't prepare while the weather is nice, you do it when it's miserable."

Dale's high school class took up a collection to cheer him and, perhaps, provide for some needs because of his illness. The cards and gift were to be taken to Madison when his parents went to visit.

Making haste with everything they could, Dale's family prepared to make the trip to bring Christmas to their son. The arrival of the family was thrilling and emotional to a lonely boy, although he still needed some recovery time before returning home. The cards from classmates were a special treat, and everyone looked forward with heightened anticipation to Dale's advancing recovery and homecoming.

9 Recovery and Acceptance

This was not the path I chose,
but along the way,
new challenges to be met and lived out,
day by day.

Christmas came and went. Marlys was excited to show Dale how she had cared for his calves and fixed up his room. Meanwhile, Dale was gaining confidence in feeding himself, touching his feet to the floor, and setting up paper on which to write. Control of his hands was major, but to step on the floor to walk was still excruciating. The sensation of needles and pins radiated through his legs with the feeling that it might never leave.

Day by day, strength came. Doctors proclaimed the heart stronger and encouraged mild exercise. Soon, the preparations paid off, and the car was made ready for the trip to Madison to bring Dale home. Little sister Sally was full of news—new kittens, the naming of the baby calves, and greetings from friends. What an occasion, to be among family and home! A few weeks passed, and soon it was time for Dale to return to school.

Wins Highest Local Future Farmer Honor

The honor of being named the "outstanding Future Farmer" during his high school career, went to Dale Morfitt, senior FFA member and presiding president.

Made by popular vote, the selection is based upon the individual's farming program, FFA activities engaged in, services rendered, offices held, scholarship, awards won, character and personality.

Dale's farming program now consists of four cows, one grade yearling, one purebred yearling, one purebred calf, three grade calves, one baby beef, 200 hens, 100 pullets, 200 broilers, 25 ducks, farm accounts, dairy herd testing, three sows and litters, 13 acres of oats, six acres of corn, five acres of pasture renovation.

School prospects looked different now. "Sorry, son, competitive sports are out of the question." What of team mates with whom friendships had been formed? Mr. Niccum, the Ag teacher visited, recalling the efforts and results Dale had in his freshman year and how he could move forward with his 4-H and FFA projects. Dale began going to neighbors' homes to recruit 4-H members. The possibility of the FFA trip come summer grew prominent in his thoughts. Spring election resulted in an office in the local FFA.

A little time passed, and Dale realized that athletic team mates were not only athletes, but Ag students and close friends as well. As the boys began to get their driver's licenses and

sometimes took part in drinking parties and such, Dale became the "designated driver" because he had no interest in drinking after the bad experiences with his dad's drinking.

The following years of high school and farm work brought more accomplishment in agriculture related efforts, including FFA trips, judging contests, and leadership activities. The award of State Farmer in his FFA efforts was lauded by the community and prized by his family.

Wisconsin Department of Vocational Rehabilitation came on the scene during Dale's later high school years. "Son, it was a bad break that your dad mortgaged the paid-up farm to pay your state hospital bill in full instead of accepting state funds, but we hope to make that up to you as much as possible by awarding you a paid college education in agriculture."

Hopes soared in the Morfitt family and among Dale's supporters. The formalities of receiving the grant, being accepted into the University of Wisconsin, River Falls, were highlights of the senior year, along with finding housing and promises of siblings to help cover Dale's duties on the farm. Dale saw the heaviness of the farm debt as a result of his illness, but hopes of an education to prepare for a career as an instructor gave him a feeling of great hope.

10 A Send Off & Preoccupation

When hearts are high and future bright,
an unexpected turn,
may raise the hope or dim the light,
heat, comfort bring, or burn.

Summer following graduation was busy and hot. Partying with high school buddies who regarded him as their designated driver were less frequent due to heavy duties on the farm, but the camaraderie remained high.

One hot July night, a different neighbor, who had been an upper classman, joined him in relaxing after the hard day. They stopped in a nearby town to see who was around, and his older friend ribbed him a bit about his hard work and encouraged him to try a beer.

"A cold beer will do you good on a hot night like this," he suggested. Dale had avoided any alcohol like the plague because his father's drinking had brought much pain to the family. With mixed feelings, missing what others do as a self-reward, and reluctance to seem immature to the friend, Dale gave in to the one drink, his first ever, that ended in a blackout and a very sick morning, wondering how he got home.

To Dale's amazement, no sooner had the severe vomiting and headache let up than he was eager to get more. Thus began the downward spiral of jeopardizing those things most valuable to him.

He ended his first quarter in college by dropping out because, as was plausible for the family to explain, "He was needed on the farm. "The following three years were spent in farm work, day jobs, and closing the taverns. One of his buddies' parents threatened to have him and his friends black listed, forbidden in any taverns. An aspect that would have been a little amusing if it had not been so troubling, was his manner of coming home late without disturbing the family. Whoever might be awake would hear him quietly open the door, take off his shoes and walk upstairs in his stocking feet to avoid being heard.

As soon as he would open the door to his room, he would drop the shoes, inadvertently loudly alerting everyone in the house.

11 Growing Up

They told us it was growing pains,
that made legs ache, feet drag.
Someone said that when one complains,
busy hands help hearts that lag.

The very same year that Dale began his first year of high school, Carol, a little girl just twenty miles away, started the fifth grade. Clover Leaf School, a rural school about six miles from the closest town, had a new teacher—a man who rented the house on the Watruds' second farm, about a quarter of a mile from the school.

Carol was preoccupied that fall with the upcoming birth of a brother or sister. It was a big concern, because her mother Ida's health was precarious, and her doctor ordered bed rest about a month after school started. Carol and her next older brother, LeRoy, were assigned to keeping the house clean, waiting on Mama, and preparing passable meals. Carol had to be reminded that this was teamwork and not playtime, but they were both eager to help Mama in any way they could. Excused from farm chores while caring for Mama, the two shared homework and message-carrying.

Thanksgiving was pleasant with Aunts Edna, Christine, and Agnes visiting Mama and bringing food to share with the family. Aunt Adeline and Uncle Oscar visited too, with Loretta, Carol's close cousin, adding cheer to the occasion.

Within a week or two, Ida's daily condition was slipping and required a call from the doctor. In early December, Ida took the children to her side and said she would have to go to the hospital. Day by day, Daddy would bring home reports. After being monitored at the hospital for over a week, Ida began losing consciousness and soon lost the baby, too premature to survive.

Sunday night following the loss of the baby, there were prayers for Ida in the church. Carol's fear was that it would end like the prayer vigil for an older neighbor—who had died. "My heart hurts," she said as she huddled close to the wood heater to get warm. Her brothers held her and acknowledged her pain.

Monday morning, Aunt Agnes came to Carol's bedroom with tears in her eyes. Wanting to comfort her aunt, believing she was thinking about the baby, Carol said, "It's all right. I know about the baby."

Aunt Agnes said kindly, "Mama's gone to Heaven."

Carol was allowed to go with her aunts to choose a dress for Mama to wear to go to Heaven. Neighbors came to help put the house in order for a visitation, and Mama's body was brought to the house until time for the funeral.

Having the very person whose comfort Carol craved lying cold and stiff in the coffin was very stressful. And then, adding to the pain, one of those who had lent a hand to the family by helping with cleaning saw Laddie, the family's beloved dog, lying near the casket.

"Go on—get out of here," they commanded, seemingly without an ounce of feeling. All Carol's gratitude for their efforts melted away.

On Wednesday morning, the hearse came and loaded up Mama. An uncle brought a car—nicer than the Watrud's old '37 Ford—for the family to ride in; and they made their way out the long driveway and out the hilly, icy road in the freezing rain. Men had to help push cars and spread sand on some of the hills. Dane and Jimmy offered to help push. Carol and LeRoy, directed to stay in the car, were thankful to be in a warm Buick with an under-seat heater.

The comforting words of the pastor, Aunt Pearl's singing "Does Jesus Care," and Anita Eldon's fervent playing of the organ were a help; and the kids saw those things as a tribute to their mother. The cold, slippery walk and clinging together in the cemetery were softened by the hands and hugs of friends and neighbors.

"I wonder if people think I should be sadder— that I don't care as much as I should," Carol wondered. And so she made herself cry harder. "Oh, no!" she thought." I'm a phony."

Thursday morning was an experience of a totally different sort. Jimmy, LeRoy, and Carol held hands as they made their way into the school with their lunch pails and buckets. Dane had stayed behind to help finish chores, as it had been decided that he would stay home to help on the farm for a year before entering high school. Mr. Heinecke, perhaps meaning well and intending to prepare her for reality, took Carol aside. "Now you need to know there will be no special treatment because your mother died.

You will be treated like everyone else." Feeling as though salt was being rubbed into a wound, the chatty little girl kept her silence and longed for the day to be over.

Well, that was December 17, just over a week until Christmas. Neighbors stopped over on the weekend to cheer up the kids. Although Carol welcomed the loving gifts they brought, she privately shared her heart with her brothers: "Gifts won't bring Mama back for Christmas."

One little girl among the visitors announced, "My mom says you will be the mother now."

Carol spoke what her heart cried out: "No! I'm just a little girl." Little did she know how she would try vainly to mother Daddy and those big brothers.

12 We Keep On

Just clinging close, they try to cheer,
the family with same ache as mine.
With grit to face the coming year,
make the best, refuse to whine.

There was indeed little whining as the children strove to raise one another's spirits. It helped that dear Aunt Agnes agreed to stay for a few days to help the family get stabilized. Four children, ages ten through fifteen, were really too much; and she was severely crippled with arthritis, needing to rest up herself. Clarence found a young pregnant woman and her husband to be housekeeper and hired man.

These were the first in a series of few and far between, short-lived household helpers. Clarence had high expectations, and, in this case, there was strife between Carol's teen-age brothers and the young man who wanted more authority.

Three months into their bereavement, Carol's eleventh birthday was coming up. On a very cold night—too cold for Carol to be out—her brothers were going to a wonderful sledding hill about three miles away. Carol hated to miss such a fun event with her brothers, and she cried until time for bed. As she lay in her bed in tears, she began to vomit and was found to be running a temperature.

As things played out, the die was cast. Clarence and the young man had angry words, and the couple left. Throwing up and high temperatures did not alter the passage of events.

Carol woke the next morning with a peppering of chicken pox and was quarantined for two weeks. Having both Daddy and Dane home enabled the family to eat, Carol to be cared for, and the home fires to be kept burning for the boys who walked to and from school.

Even in the midst of sadness and chicken pox, Carol's eleventh birthday brought with it a good memory. To brighten things up a little, Daddy purchased a record player with long play records, and the whole family enjoyed it for many days to come.

The chicken pox ran their course, and the local health officer checked Carol over to affirm that she had recovered and could attend school. Less than a month passed, and Jimmy and LeRoy both woke up with headaches and high temperatures—red measles! Another quarantine, and Dad had only one boy to help with chores. Next in line were Dane and Carol. The one bright spot in this turn of events was that, after the first few days, they could, between the two of them, keep the fires going in the wood heater and cook stove and have some semblance of meals ready.

About two weeks later, Clarence hired a widow named Mary to keep house and cook. She lasted about a month, then needed to go back home to help her son on the farm. Carol did not grieve her leaving, as she had been very turned off when Mary euthanized a nest of baby mice by dropping them into the hot wood stove.

Teamwork, walking the mile to school together, and a certain amount of levity in meeting their challenges helped the kids through the last months of school. Summer came, and Clarence hired an older cousin to help with the housework. Between keeping ahead of the boys and keeping Carol dressed modestly, she found herself overwhelmed to try to fit housekeeping into the mix. After an early summer church camp, she found a less trying position.

Late summer, Clarence hired an elderly lady named Bessie, hoping she would be able to keep up the cooking and domesticate Carol a little. Probably the fact that she burned most of the meals accounted for the fact that there were always leftovers.

Those same burnt meals were then reheated and re-served the next day. On top of this, Bessie talked baby talk to Carol, and Carol reacted by becoming a little belligerent. Bessie's diabetes flared up, and she wasn't able to keep up the job.

As Carol took on more of the household responsibility, she developed the habit of strolling in the nearby hills or going up into the attic to read privately when her duties were mostly completed. On a low day, leaning on a warm tree was a comfort.

During fall and winter, the children kept up rather well, everyone being tolerant of Carol's cooking attempts and being tired of the alternatives. Much to their relief, Thanksgiving and Christmas were spent at aunts' and uncles' houses, so the family was spared that attempt at meal planning. However, Carol did cook a meal on New Year's Day for one of the aunt's families. It actually was passable, and her spirits were marred only by her brothers' teasing that she couldn't do it and her fear of tattling to Daddy, which might have lessened her place in their acceptance. All in all it was a special day, and oh, but are grown-ups ever wonderful about doing up those dishes!

As Carol's twelfth birthday approached, Clarence answered a position-wanted ad in the St. Paul paper for a house keeper—a widow with a young son two years younger than Carol. She was an outstanding cook and housekeeper, and for two enjoyable years they were a part of the Watrud's lives.

Tommy became like a little brother to Carol and a friend of the children in Clover Leaf School. Taking part in 4-H with a dairy calf and sharing his Morgan horse with the family were special activities they all enjoyed. And Beauty, the horse, was trained to pull a sleigh that the Watrud boys had fixed up.

Sadly however, this happy time ended in another parting as Clarence and Tommy's mother Maebelle had considered a romance and marriage, and this did not work out. So ended the playing in the hay mow, climbing trees all the way to the top with the exhilarating sensation that comes as the whole tree sways under you, and memorable times with the Clover Leaf School kids.

13 Growing Up or Apart

Acquaintances just come and go;
they may be fun or not.
But when dear friends apart may grow,
"What happened?" troubling thought.

The student body of Clover Leaf School consisted of the established families of mostly German descent, families of renters who moved from different areas, and families of established residents who moved in and set up farming. Marion and Carol were in the same class from first grade on through the end of high school. The three boys that started with them did not advance on schedule and were held back in second or third grade. This may have been a result of the teacher who followed Mrs. Plahn not being inclined to give individual attention and not being skilled or experienced in working with learning difficulties.

In any case, Marion and Carol continued in their grade, occasionally joined by a child of a renting family; but all through the years, Marion and Carol were the core in their grade. A large family moved in from Indiana, bringing changes in the friend combinations among children of several ages.

Carol went into her maturing years without her loving and understanding mother as the instructor and confidant she had always been; and Carol felt the need to confide in someone. It was natural that she would turn to her close friend Marion as confidant; and Carol shared the sensitive, confusing-to-a-young-girl issues in maturing with her.

Marion didn't likely mean to hurt Carol, and it was perhaps just an incidental remark, but Marion shared these highly personal, sensitive confidences with the girls one grade behind them. Carol was hurt and angry, and she shared her pain with Marion in the presence of the girls who now knew her innermost secrets: "Hurting your friend causes a lot of pain!"

The group laughed and changed their derision, "Heap big smoke but no fire."

The pain of being the brunt of disloyalty and mockery ran deep in Carol's already wounded heart. She didn't want to continue day after day, year after year in such close quarters with the one who had carelessly opened her tender secrets to others. She had always made straight A's in school, except for the few months following her mom's death. "I could skip a grade and go directly into high school," she pleaded with her dad. "I have straight A's, and I know I wouldn't have any trouble doing the work. Daddy sympathized, but he wouldn't make the request for Carol to skip a grade.

Carol's dad lovingly gifted her with a two year old riding horse, and she turned her interest to caring for and training that horse. There were still activities with Marion, but her horse and 4-H interests opened up opportunities for her to connect with other girls close to her age, including her next door neighbor, Joan.

Grade eight came and went: confirmation class, more advanced social studies including panel discussion, and spelling bees. An incident that Carol regretted happened when their school hosted one of the social studies panel discussions. There were students from other schools taking part, and Carol ignored a boy who had been special to her in favor of a new boy she found interesting. This lesson in the difficulty of altering what is done stuck, though not always observed perfectly. "If only I had some social sense," she mourned, but the lack of seeking good guidance in social issues plagued her.

Starting high school was a fresh experience, with an abundance of "new" to navigate. Some of the students knew each other well, having attended town school through all the lower grades. Other students from country schools shared her experience in needing to get acquainted with most of the students.

Carol soon became known as everybody's friend. She felt accepted and was eager to get to know her fellow students. She got involved in everything she could and showed care and concern for her classmates. She sat between pleasant students, boy and girl, in almost all of her classes, and daily life settled into a routine. By the first class meeting, Carol was nominated as a class officer. She was encouraged to try out for cheerleader, but she felt apprehensive. Dad probably wouldn't be willing to drive to all the athletic games; and, as she wasn't overly well-coordinated, she backed away from the opportunity. She wanted to let a couple of her classmates know she cared about them, and she attended their confirmation services.

Mama had told her at a younger age that chorus and glee club can be such fun. She joined, but it didn't turn out for her quite like it had for Mama. She had no experience singing in a group, and her background of singing on the farm left her unprepared for these activities. Sadly, she found herself frequently criticized, especially by her long-time friend. Classes were otherwise wonderful, and she took part in an opportunity to work on the school lunch program. Through this, she became very good friends with another Marian, and the two of them, along with Saundra and other girls, enjoyed many high school experiences together.

Midway into their freshman year, it was leaked out that the results of the recently administered IQ test were known by some students, who shared with the class members the highest and lowest scores. Carol cringed as she was pointed out as the highest scorer. The fear that classmates would think she felt superior and would possibly reject her weighed heavy on her. Her closest friends paid no attention, but Carol began to lose confidence, questioning her already shaky social skills.

Although her fears weren't totally unrealized, there were bright spots. Her old seatmate Chuck teased her, calling her "Professor," and Dad had always told her that those who tease you usually like you.

Homecoming was a highlight that year. A couple of the girls who weren't in band (Carol being one of them) were asked to ride the float in the parade, and it won first place.

Some of the freshmen girls had started dating, but Carol felt her dad wouldn't permit it. She enjoyed mixed parties, but she turned down the invitations she got for exclusive dates. The following summer, her neighbors talked her into going to free drive-in movies that were shown at one of the local lakes. There she met a popular boy named Jack, and they hit it off. For once, Carol felt confident in a social decision and, without being unfriendly, she let him know she wasn't into advanced necking. He became very fond of her, and they dated for a while. He, like her, managed the work at home. His responsibility was farming with his sister while their mom boarded away from home as a practical nurse.

Jack invited Carol to a Billy Graham movie. Carol was filled with a strong desire to go forward at the end of the movie and commit her life to the Lord. But her lack of social confidence crippled her, and she still regrets having stayed in her seat, afraid going forward would be taken as a commitment to Jack.

Their dating time ended on a sad note, as Carol responded to the flirting of one of Jack's friends. She knew she had caused hurt, and she became very cautious who she dated, not wanting to cause more pain. Dating several different boys briefly through her high school years, she was in for a surprise.

She had been writing to a young army man, and was very happy when he came home. While he applied for jobs in the city, Carol's girlfriend introduced her to Dale, a fellow who was her boyfriend's friend. It was a blind date, and when the couple of friends came with him to get her for the date, she was more than impressed. His black hair was combed attractively, and he wore a dark sport shirt over a contrasting t-shirt, and engineer boots. With a winning smile and engaging hazel eyes, his presence made her forget anyone else. Carol absolutely fell for him.

What was so wonderful was that he seemed to be just as interested in her. She had dreamed of someone she could share her thoughts with, and he seemed to really appreciate that and shared many feelings with her too. He told her how when they were apart he would laugh at her comical sayings and views on things; and she could hardly wait to tell him everything she saw or thought.

The fine young man just home from the army took her on their last date. Carol just could not think of being interested in someone else after meeting Dale.

That summer was the happiest of Carol's life. Her dream had been that when a man to love would come, they would put each other first and no longer have to contend with the possible unkindness of others. They celebrated Dale's birthday at Excelsior Amusement Park, had breakfast out, rode a speedboat, and spent long hours sharing their views on life.

One night, after about a month of dating, her friends came to see her along with Dale. He had been drinking, and she was very turned off, sure all her illusions had been wrong. She told him she couldn't stand drinking and, if that was his way, she wasn't ready to follow through with the romance or consider a life together in the future.

Dale declared his love and intention to leave alcohol alone. He confessed past escapades, including one with his uncle involving a night in jail and the uncle being forbidden back in the county. Dale's candor prompted her to consider their value to one another and keep an open mind about the possible drinking, knowing that, should it continue, it would mean the end on her part.

Carol was reassured, for the most part, and she was so fond of Dale that she looked for the best outcome. The best outcome seemed to be happening, and day by day, week by week, their time together was wonderful. Their time apart was spent anticipating time together. Amazingly, this girl who had never felt romantic love was so drawn to Dale, and he seemed to be that way toward her.

They spent the summer days visiting each other's homes and special uncles and aunts' homes. Uncle Clarence and Aunt Olive's lake was a deciding point—a beautiful summer day with so many hopes and dreams shared. The attraction for one another became stronger than ever. Determined to resist their impulses until marriage, they began to plan for a day they would be together for always.

The county fair was always a favorite time for Carol, and this year it offered an event never to be lived down. The cattle and horses had always been her special interest, but now all her attention was on Dale. They took Dale's youngest sister Sally to the fair with them, and Carol asked her brother LeRoy, who was exhibiting cattle, to keep Sally with him while she and Dale did some shopping. They got so involved in the shopping and planning that they started for home without going back to get Sally. They got home right on schedule, and Dale's mother asked, "Where is Sally?"

The couple drove the hour back to the fairgrounds and apologized to good-natured LeRoy. They hurried back to very late chores at Dale's house and then headed to Carol's home where she was expected.

Late summer, as school opening loomed, Carol was within weeks of beginning her senior year. Dale came to pick her up as usual, always a joyful time. This time, he was deeply troubled, not knowing which way to turn. His dad had apparently run up his bill at the bars past his ability to pay. Dale and his dad farmed on shares, so each of them had a part of the recently harvested grain. Dale's dad had taken Dale's share and sold it to pay his bills.

In Dale's eyes, this was a tangled thing. He felt the guilt of the farm being mortgaged because of his illness and the college grant wasted through his past drinking. How could he hold his dad responsible? Through their very torn and upset emotions and their desire to be together, they decided to elope and start a new life of their own. With a little planning, Carol had her suitcase packed and stowed near the end of the driveway.

Then she dressed in a pretty dress and walked a mile cross country to the old school where Dale was to pick her up. It happened that her old grade school classmate was walking up there too. In her excitement, Carol shared her secret.

A few minutes later, Dale met her there with her suitcase, and they headed for Pine City, Minnesota, where they could get their license with no waiting period. Her other friend, Marian, rode with them, and they completed the paper work for the license. They bought the rings and waited for Marian's boyfriend to arrive to be their witness.

A couple of unexpected people arrived first. Carol's brother James, on leave from the army, and her dad met them in the court building. Confronting them with the fact that Carol was under age and did not have permission, her dad insisted she come home. With much sadness, Carol rode back home with Dale, promising to meet her dad and James at the farm. Marian's boyfriend drove her home, and the wedding was temporarily off. The following Monday, Carol started her senior year, met by the information that her old class mate had shared the news of the failed elopement with the school. The years-old schism widened, as Carol felt the bitter sting.

She had kept many confidences for this girl, even after the seventh grade betrayal. Carol could honestly understand the girl warning her dad about the planned elopement. That could have been construed as kind—helping her to avoid a mistake. But to have the story told around school was a bitter pill to swallow.

In later years, Carol again was able to admire her old friend as a good and loving wife and mother, a beloved grandmother as well. But those school years were sure painful.

14 Senior Year

A phase in life now culminates.
The horizon unfolds new scenes,
more meaning now to talks and dates,
life's plans, too soon for teens?

The school bus now came down the mile driveway and picked Carol up in her yard. Dane and Jimmy were in college, and LeRoy was farming with Dad, planning to enroll in the university farm short course for the winter quarter.

After the first week or two of school, things again seemed normal. Marian and Saundra, dear friends, along with most of the class, shared thoughts and activities. When Homecoming time came, Marian, Saundra and Carol were again asked to ride on the float. This year the winning float—their float again—was to circle around in the football field during the halftime show. The weather had changed suddenly and, even though it was only mid-October, there was a heavy snowfall. Consequently Dale and Howard, Marian's boyfriend, got stuck on the country road in deep drifts, and arrived late. The float had to be pulled back into the garage where it had been sheltered. The girls laughed, "Well, our class float won again anyway."

Some minds quickly return to the same track whenever possibility presents itself. Carol's brother Jimmy (James) was to have his leave from the army over Thanksgiving. Now, wouldn't it be nice to have the wedding while he is at home? There were many reasons not to, but the time since the interrupted elopement had been difficult. Date less, and miss each other. Date more often, and invite temptation?

"Dad would be short on help with LeRoy at short course if I left home for marriage now," Carol thought with a twinge of guilt. "But—he has hired help before." So the guilt of selfishness was pacified.

In the end, it was decided that it may be best, if not wisest, to allow the marriage. Carol's aunts got together and helped plan. The ladies' aid would serve at the reception.

Dale's employer at his plumbing/heating job offered the entire bride and attendants' attire—and all the dresses fit! So, plans moved forward, and with a cousin and classmates as attendants, and Carol's brothers and a dear friend as best man and groomsmen, the wedding party was established. An oversight in the rehearsal, directed by the church organist, led to a blushing incident.
The pastor arrived early and sat with Dale as they waited for the music, the processional, etc. Assuming that all instructions had been given by the organist Anita, the pastor just chatted with Dale about life plans, but not the issue that would soon cause the blush.

As the bride and groom knelt side by side at the altar, Carol glanced up and was treated to a warm and intimate smile in sparkling hazel eyes. The prayers were prayed, candles were lit, the lovely solo sung, and vows repeated. The pastor pronounced them man and wife. Dale turned to embrace and kiss Carol, and she said, "We're not supposed to." Carol had learned that their church did not have the bride and groom kiss at the altar, but Dale had not. Laughter sounded through the church and accompanied the recessional as the bride and groom hurried out to take their place in the receiving line, laughing and blushing.

Many relatives and classmates and most of the church's congregation attended the wedding, and loving good wishes were spoken. One of the loveliest good wishes was offered to Carol from Dale's mother, "You can call me Mother now."

Dale's mother had been a sincere and kind participant in many ways. For one thing, she had seen the rings tucked away in one of Dale's drawers in August, and had even suspected there might have been a secret marriage. But she had kept quiet. For another thing, she was plagued with severe eczema, aggravated by all the dust and fumes of harvest time and was praying her face would be clear for the wedding. So November was better. Hurrah, Mother!

Dale and Carol moved into the house on the farm, and Dale's family moved to an apartment in Amery. The place was less spacious, but Maude was very happy to get away from many of the allergens that kept her troubled with eczema. She was also in a more convenient location to do baby sitting and other day work that she could use for extra expenses. It was a beloved trait she had that her money would be tucked away to provide a plentiful Christmas for the children.

Carol transferred to Amery High School and was in the same class as Dale's sister Marlys. Those first weeks in the new school were exciting. Dale would wave as she walked down to the bus if he hadn't left for his off-farm job yet. Everything was new, with the bus rides, getting acquainted with the students, and finding her place in class work and activities. It was so near Christmas vacation that school was probably busier than usual.

After a wonderful Christmas with both families—Carol and Dale still joined the Hanson (Mama's family) Christmas Eve as well as Christmas with Dale's family—there was time to put their belongings in order in the family house, which was now their home.

So Christmas vacation was a time for Carol and Marlys to help Mother and Sally move household goods to the apartment and for Dale and Carol to set up their housekeeping on a more permanent plan.

As Christmas vacation came to an end, Carol woke up very sick. "Oh, no, I'll have to miss more school!" When most of the week had passed, and nothing seemed to help her keep any food down, they decided to see the doctor.

After some testing, Dr. Whitlark advised Carol that her thyroid was low. She also seemed to have a condition fairly common with young married women. A test was done to see if there was a baby on the way, and the doctor prescribed medicine to ease her nausea and told to come back in a week.

There wasn't much relief from the nausea, but Carol tried to attend school again, only to end up in the nurse's office. Next week's doctor call was positive, both with the need for a thyroid supplement and that it was a pregnancy. She was advised to exercise lightly and encouraged to continue her activities as she could.

As weeks went by with prolonged vomiting, there were few days she was even able to stop by the school to get make-up work. She finally decided to try finishing these last few months by correspondence whenever she felt well enough to work on it. Mr. Hanson, the guidance counselor was a very helpful encourager.

Carol felt pretty sick a good deal of the time, and the couple looked for ways to make the time more pleasant. As the months passed, she began to feel life, and they started to call the little baby who was softly kicking, "Thumper." The school year passed by, punctuated by several stays in the hospital, and she hadn't completed her studies necessary for graduation.

Crops and garden were planted; and Dale took a summer job at the pea vinery. Continuing his chores and harvesting hay and oats, Dale was hard put to catch his early morning rides to the vinery. But he always did. On the nineteenth of August, Carol suggested that he call and see if he could go later. She was pretty sure she was having contractions. As they seemed a little more intense, she called the doctor, and he directed her in how to time them.

A little uneasy about how to pass the time, Carol took out cookie dough she had started and began to bake the cookies. It would be easy to keep track, as the cookies would take ten minutes for each pan.

When she noticed that a contraction was occurring a little before the cookies were done, Dale called the doctor and then drove her to the hospital. Checking to see that the birth was not imminent, Dr. Whitlark said Dale would have time to do his milking and come back. In the meantime, the doctor more thoroughly examined her and found that there was no heartbeat. Gently he suggested she have Dale summoned and then told them that the baby was not alive and would deliver naturally within a couple of hours.

The greatly anticipated delight of meeting little "Thumper" became the ordeal of getting it over with. Still, when the birth occurred, Carol asked, "Is it really...?" Dr. Whitlark said kindly, "Your little girl didn't make it. So Sorry."

Little Nancy weighed only three and one half pounds, although she was full term. The severe illness that Carol experienced—toxemia—was a result of toxins affecting both her and the baby. She had suspected something was amiss when she hadn't enlarged as expected. Again, Dr. Whitlark kindly encouraged her as he assured her that this was rare, and she could have other babies later.

Dale's good friend Duane, who had been his best man in the wedding, sat with her through the baby's funeral. The bubble gum cigars Mother Morfitt had bought to joyfully pass out to fellow workers went quietly to friends' children instead.

15 Empty Arms

Little firstborn she never held,
in a snow white box was laid.
Beneath a burning August sun,
with rosebuds, "Good-bye" was said.

How many, many people have had to pick up when a life is gone and go on. A wonderful custom in those years was the exchange of farm work at harvest time. The neighbors got together and threshed the oats for Dale and Carol, and the ladies helped cook the meal. Carol, not wanting to appear weak, poured the coffee. Unfortunately, she poured it right onto one neighbor's arm! Gallantly, he stated that he was tough, and it didn't hurt. Dale and Carol appreciated those neighbors and their life-lightening ways so much.

Carol felt almost guilty that the endless nausea was gone, but routines were easier, and the emotional heaviness lifted from time to time, making progress possible. They were thankful for the relief, as new opportunities that required teamwork were presented. Teamwork—right up Carol's alley! As she had dreamed of their mutual farm projects, looking across the fields at their cows and crops, the suggestion that came through the agricultural agent in the next county seemed attractive.

"Do you think work as a boarding milk tester would work out for me?" Dale presented the proposition to her. "If you could milk the cows the nights I need to stay over on other farms to weigh milk and take butterfat samples, I would do the heavier work—cleaning the barn and moving feed. We could use the milk house as the testing lab." Carol wondered if she could do the routine of testing while Dale did the heavier chores.

Within the month, they had set up their system and schedules, and then began a very meaningful year. Dale had to go to training at Madison for a week, and his dad agreed to check and see that things were going all right for Carol. While he was in Madison, Carol had some uncomfortable symptoms that prompted a doctor call. The news was bad and good. There was a bladder infection and, possibly, a pregnancy.

She again experienced morning sickness, but less than last year, when it had been all day sickness; and this time it responded to a change in schedule and diet. When Dale got back from the training, things were looking up. The first night he stayed away, he called home more than once to make sure Carol was all right. It was surprising how well they could each handle their tasks.

When the inspector came out, he was highly complementary on the condition of the milk house lab. So the fall and winter went, changing off turns milking, testing the milk, learning, and doing accurate record-keeping. Carol's milk testing and record preparation gave Dale time to haul in silage for feed and keep the barn cleaned.

There were times when the cold weather challenged their backward water system, overhead pipes from the pump to a gravity tank in the barn. At times, Carol needed to dismantle the outside pipes and bring them in so the heat of the cows in the barn could thaw them. Then, Dale could restore the water when he got home. All in all, they managed very well, and Carol was so pleased to have the energy, after the last year of sickness, to have the house ship-shape as well. It was an answer to her dream of working together as a team to make the farm work out.

As summer progressed, Carol began to see that her condition in late pregnancy didn't allow her to keep up the heavier work, so Dale asked for a leave of absence from work for the delivery and recovery.

To make ends meet and provide for the expense of the new baby, Dale was able to get a part time job at a local filling station.

It appeared to be a Godsend, as it was close, and Dale could do the milking between the times the owners changed off for supper. It was fun to fix up a temporary nursery near the bedroom and furnish it with a borrowed crib and gifts from relatives and friends. When the day came, just four days before the due date, there was great excitement.

Dale sat in the labor room with Carol for a while, but as things were not moving quickly, he went to report the progress to his mother. In the meantime, baby got eager to come and was there to meet Daddy when he returned to the hospital. Carol was so excited with the beautiful, healthy boy that she couldn't stop talking.

Aunt Marlys, who was married and now had a five month old baby boy and Aunt Sally, now just ready to enter junior high, were on hand. Sally saw little five month old Jimmy as a prospective playmate for the new baby, named Dale Eugene, Jr. and immediately nick-named Gene. What a happy time!

Immediately on the heels of Gene's birth, Carol came down with a severe kidney infection accompanied by a high fever. This kept her from breastfeeding, which was never restored. That was a great disappointment to Carol.

It was soon a joke with Carol's brothers, "You have to boil your hands to touch him," as Carol was strict about hygiene with the baby and his food. By the next summer, when Gene could walk and was playing in mud puddles, those tough standards had relaxed considerably.

16 Behind the Silver Lining

Diapers waving on the line,
flapping and billowing in sunshine,
always make me feel so good,
little banners of motherhood.

The joy of having the new baby, who was growing by leaps and bounds, was dearly shared by Dale and Carol and their relatives.

But things didn't go so smoothly. Following the kidney infection, Asiatic flu further decreased Carol's ability to keep up her end of the chores. When she was able to leave the house for an hour or so during Gene's early bedtime, Carol would do at least part of the feeding and milking of cows.

Dale decided to celebrate his wife's restored strength with a night out with his co-workers. Carol immediately noticed the signs of drinking, which had not been part of their life together, and worried, but felt bound to keep her part of the agreement.

That night was the beginning of a marked change. Dale began staying out very late after these drinking nights. The couple groped for solutions and tried different approaches. Should we just have a moderate drink at home on an evening or day off? So, beer and smoked cheese were tried a time or two, but by the third time, Dale's going out to pick up the beer extended into time to close the bar. Well, maybe going out together occasionally would be the solution. But it was very unpleasant for a non-drinker or very moderate drinker, and the budget did not handle it either.

Consequently, Carol stayed home, hoping for Dale's company for supper; but supper came and went, and she hoped he would join her by Gene's bedtime. Night sounds and the aftermath of doing chores when it wasn't her turn wore on her. Was this the man who helped her through that year of severe sickness—the man who was a team-worker as they established the milk testing operation? Different remedies came to mind. Barron County was still interested in having Dale as a boarding milk tester and could offer housing. That was not acceptable to Dale, as he was very attached to the farm.

It became more and more difficult for Carol to enjoy keeping a clean and organized house. Both tired from the work and feeling unloved, Carol's response was self-defeating. Dale saw her less effective housekeeping as a reason to go out and drink. Alarmed and at a loss for other answers, Carol tried to reflect on the happy times when they were so loving. "Wouldn't it be nice if we could spend more time together?" she suggested.

Dale retorted, "I'm not going to be hen-pecked."

As Carol looked out the window at the darkness, her eyes rested on a pretty decorated flower pot on the windowsill. Recalling Mother's telling of how she had received it, Carol felt a tenderness for the man whose words had just cut her so deeply. At about age nine, Dale had saved up his pennies and asked his dad if he could go along to town. Before going into the tavern, his dad told him when he finished at the store to wait in the car. Dale found this charming little flower pot with a pretty green plant in it, paid for it with his pennies, and went to the car to wait for his dad.

It wasn't long before it got very cold sitting in the car. Dale sheltered the little plant in the front of his jacket, then curled up around it to keep warm himself. It was getting dark when his dad came back to the car, and in the light of the dome light, Dale could see that the plant had become dark at the edges. Dale gave the plant to Mother, not as proudly as he had planned, but with hopes that she could revive it.

That plant didn't make it, but she later planted another plant in the pretty pot.

Carol swallowed past the heavy weight in her chest, and with teary eyes she told herself, "No wonder he drinks and gets thoughtless, with all the misery he has had."

Little did she know that the man who had rejected her request for more of his company was also picturing her as he envisioned her low point—a little girl standing in an icy cemetery. Why wasn't he bringing her some happiness?

A confusing aspect of escalating drinking behavior is that from time to time, there can be deep remorse. These times can be a cause for renewed hope, and indeed, the tenderness Dale showed also did extend to daily life at times. It was so beautiful to see him with his darling son and to enjoy occasional extra attention and a gift on special occasions. These infrequent instances helped to revive Carol's battered hope.

Having overextended himself financially, Dale found it necessary to sell the herd of cows, thankfully for enough money to clear himself of major difficulty. Breathing space was short-lived and they soon had to sell Carol's beloved saddle horse, which they had taught to do farm work when one of Dale's horses was disabled. Carol began to swallow the setbacks as part of the pain of life, not seeing a way out.

Through this painful time of drinking, interaction between the couple changed measurably. Dale would verbally lash out in unresolved anger of a lifetime, usually punctuated with choice curse words. Carol would react with loud defensive outbursts. This would become a pattern that only escalated over the next many years.

A new opportunity presented itself. A part time bookkeeper was needed for the Farmers Union feed mill. It seemed perfect to fill their needs. It was only half days, and the current bookkeeper would train her to use the business machine. Dale's sister Marlys was willing to babysit, so it could work. Without the cows, it might work out for the best.

Just a few weeks into the job, Carol found out she was pregnant again and the baby was in trouble. A brief stay in the hospital revealed an ended pregnancy. "You can go home and miscarry," Dr. Whitlark said. "Then come back to the hospital to be checked." Although the test indicated no life, Carol continued to have a little morning sickness and soon noticed her size was increasing. Doctor Whitlark said she had indeed defeated the frog that was used for the test. She continued the job at the feed mill until time to deliver the baby.

An unfortunate side issue of this employment was that the company had a credit union. Dale asked her from time to time to use that to make up their shortfall in bill paying. Over months, it was just too handy, and their debt grew.

The darling baby was born, a little pink and white doll—Joanne Carol, middle name for her mother. She was an easy-going baby, which made the babysitting situation easier. Daddy was there to welcome her, and that made home life seem better.

The nights had not changed. Supper would come, with hopes that Daddy would join them. By this time, he had taken a sales job with a delivery route. Bedtime would come. It would be so nice to have him to help put little ones to bed. A car would be heard on the road. Was that Dale? No. An appliance motor came on. Was that him? Torn between giving up on caring and looking for a way out, she would fall asleep. "Strange…" she would think as she drifted off to sleep. "How can drinking be worth the miserable hangover?"

17 Blessings in Disguise

Through remorse and new hope,
we tried to find good;
the years found increasing our precious brood.
Insidious element, please go away;
to make the world right, there must be a way.

"Straightening out the corners" was the term Dale used to describe some of his returns home. On one of these nights, he had gone off a road that was under construction, sinking the wheels deeply in the fill in the ditch area.

Carol woke to a ringing phone at 2:30 am. "The Buick is in the ditch. I need you to help me pull it out." Dale spoke in a whisper. He was at a home miles north. The family was sleeping, and he had gone in to use the phone.

"I can't come out in the middle of the night; the kids are sleeping." Allowing herself to be convinced that it was safe, she took her little Plymouth sedan to the appointed place and saw Dale walking toward it. Expecting him to get into the car to ride home, she opened the door.

"We can't leave the car here," he snapped. And the young wife and mother soon found herself trying to push that big Buick with her little Plymouth. It didn't work, and Dale got out and tried ramming it a little to move it. On the drive home, Carol burned with guilt at leaving the children in the house and grim disgust over being in this situation. The Buick was moved later.

There is a label used to the displeasure of a dysfunctional person—Carol had heard and rejected it: insanity. The definition is sometimes given as "repeating the same action and expecting a different result." Suddenly, a little sanity crept in. Many run-ins with the police, more than one wrecked vehicle...this just may be the thing that will help him see the harm in his drinking.

Even with this enlightenment, however, the situation persisted. Baby number three arrived. What a darling little Connie was—and so smiley. Having Daddy home with this new one would be so special too.

But it was the same as it had been. Suppertime—no Dad, bedtime—no Dad, cars on the road—no Dale. That was it! Once and for all he was going to see what his behavior was causing.

Carol marched resolutely to the closet, and took out the suitcase; to his drawers, and took out his clothes. She stuffed them in the boxes and the suitcase and set them outside the door. There! He would have a taste of what rejection felt like. She went to bed, feeling that settled it.

As she lay there, she thought of the many times she had feared a car accident. What if this was the time? Someone would come to the door saying, "Something terrible has happened to Dale." And she didn't even care.

She rolled out of bed, went out onto the porch, brought in the boxes and the suitcase, put all of the clothes back in the closet and the drawers, and Dale didn't even know of the incident until years later. Pacing and chafing had done no good. She compared herself to a cat hit on the road—a victim, the driver, a villain, the owner, an innocent bystander. She was each of them. Was there an answer anywhere?

The blessing in disguise showed its face once more, and it was incredibly well-disguised. The results would be a while in coming, though. A call in the middle of the night. The Barron County police had Dale in custody, arrested for a hit and run accident. This was another in a string of driving infractions involving liquor, but, as disillusioned as Carol had become with his behavior, she was shocked that he would be irresponsible about an injury he had caused.

So, Carol called her dad, who recommended that leaving him in jail would do him the most good. Past worrying about causing bad feelings, she agreed; it might be best. Two days later at the jail, among grim faces and painful pronouncements, one tiny person, six month old baby Connie squealed in glee and waved her arms joyfully at seeing her daddy. He later said that if anything could have brought about a resolve to change, that would have been it.

The time, however, was not yet. A fine, loss of the occupational license that had been issued to allow him to work after the loss of his driver's license, loss of income, as his work was sales work with a route, and still, the drinking went on, maybe less for a few days, but on.

True to form, the spouse Carol did her part. She arranged babysitting for little Connie whom she had been so happy to be home with, and drove Dale around on his sales route. Maybe it was the assurance of knowing where he was all day. A nagging feeling that the insanity was persisting hung on. Still, she had made a commitment, so she continued into the spring.

The situation became ludicrous. Because of the repossession of their dependable, newer car, they were driving a long station wagon that burned oil and would only start on a hill unless jumped. Carol would wait in the car with a window open to keep from breathing the exhaust smoke while he made his calls. They had to keep it parked on a hill so it could be started if the motor killed. "Try not to be conspicuous," Dale urged, as he walked off to his call or delivery. It would have been actually funny if it weren't so real.

After months of this, Dale again became eligible for a very limited occupational license. One of his very well respected customers was a long-time AA member who shared his story with Dale. Dale didn't say much about the conversation to Carol, but he began leaving literature from Barron County AA on the coffee table. Dale became ill with severe symptoms assumed to be leukemia. After testing and a stay in the hospital, he was diagnosed with mono, and it was some time before he could work at his normal pace.

When he was able to resume work, Dale got a part time job learning the insurance business and covering a route as a representative. He worked in different areas, at first with an experienced agent and then on his own.

Carol comforted herself that, although he was gone, he was with the other agent or staying with relatives; therefore, she believed, he was not drinking.

Carol had gotten a second shift job at a new computer plant in town. It was a hard winter for Carol, catching a ride to work, dealing with frostbite, and keeping wood fires going. It was her belief that Dale was sober during the time he was away for ten days at a time that gave her hope to keep going. When the finance company sent a representative to appraise their furniture, she said in desperation that they could take it. However, they offered her the choice of making half payments.

Thinking working closer to home might allow Dale to balance the home life, income-producing work, and having some fun in his life, he checked out what was available locally. A trial experience with the Fuller Brush Company seemed to be working out, and hearing that Fuller Brush had been the start for many successful salesmen, he had hope of a new start at making a living. The drawback was that unscheduled time led to a repeat of the downward slide into heavy drink.

At this time, Dale began to talk about how nice it would be to have another boy. Carol remarked that the gender is unpredictable. However, by Thanksgiving, there was another baby on the way. Following the usual morning sickness, Carol continued to have dizziness, and her doctor recommended walking a mile a day.

With the youngest two children not yet in school, Carol would take them for walks, flying a kite to keep it interesting.

Friends would see the kite in the air that fall and know Carol was walking with those children, sometimes meeting Gene's school bus.

Christmas came and went. Mother had done day work and saved for gifts. Dale had celebrated with drinking friends, much to Mother and Carol's sorrow. He was on hand, though, for the Christmas Eve with Carol's family and Christmas dinner with his family.

That happy occasion passed, and Dale spent the following week closing the bars. On the day of New Year's Eve, he appeared at about 3:00 am, and slept a few hours. Getting up to his coffee, he announced, "We're going out tonight."

Explosion. After the terrible week and late night! Having resolved not to upset the house over the frequent nights, Carol had settled into a sort of grim tolerance of the situation. However, the outrageous suggestion of New Year's Eve out after the late hour and all that went with it was too much.

"I will not go out on New Year's Eve with you," Carol yelled. "I've been in that scene before. Besides. I think you have celebrated enough last night—and this morning!

An unexpected calm from Dale surprised Carol, as he said, "Even if it's AA?"

"What?!" Carol thought of all the reasons why it couldn't work. "Baby sitters aren't available at the last minute on New Year's Eve, and besides it's twenty below zero, and that car never starts when it's this cold."

With the pleasing possibility of the evening, Carol called the babysitter they would get occasionally. Her family had canceled their party, and she could babysit. The car did start, and there was a hill at the meeting place if worse came to worst. Dale had spent the afternoon with a member of AA at the club where AA met and felt it would help. The man's story of the changes he had experienced, his acceptance of Dale, and the reassuring words posted on the walls, which included God, led him to feel the fellowship might be helpful.

As for Carol, who was very apprehensive, she was to meet the most accepting people she had ever met, and happy attitudes reached out to her with hope that things really could be better. Feeling hope as a really tangible thing, she didn't dare to acknowledge it, rode home in the car that actually did start, and silently held on to the intense feeling, lest it slip away.

18 More Disguise

A new year, could it be truly new?

'guess not, we've fallen every time.

But hope, though faint, quietly slipping through,

may lift enough to motivate the climb.

Hope seemed to be the fortifying element in the coming weeks. As Dale picked up his sales case in the morning, Carol chose to trust that he would return for supper—remember awaited suppers—and he really did. The AA clubhouse became a stopping place when he felt shaky. He could actually be reached there, if it was a break time or with a message to be passed on at a later stop. If you asked Dale what he hoped to get from this program, he explained later, it would be to feel free and loved.

Experienced members helped him pick a sponsor, actually a man who also needed a purpose, a man to help and a companion. Carol began to go to Al-Anon, and a sponsor was suggested for her. She began to learn for real that she wasn't the cause, cure, or controlling force in this alcoholic situation, and she could learn to live a better way. She learned to leave past mistakes for a confident present—big step. Meeting only monthly at that time, Carol had to wait a whole month to share with these open, accepting people. But they recommended materials to read that brought to life the experiences of others who had things as bad, or worse, than she did, who were finding effective ways of living.

Did the bed of roses suddenly bloom? Well, inwardly, things were looking up, but outwardly, life still threw curve balls. After a month, Dale's group manager could see that Dale's vehicle was a hindrance to him, as it was both unsightly and unreliable. He graciously offered the use of a car that he wasn't using until Dale could produce some income. Dale's parents loaned him their car, one they prized as a used car, good-looking and a great find for them, to go and get the borrowed car. So Dale and Carol drove to Dick, the sales manager, and picked up the car.

As they were returning to Amery on rather slippery roads, Dale led with Dick's car, and Carol followed with his parents' car. As Dale crossed the Somerset bridge, preceded by a sharp curve, Carol entered the bridge. An oncoming car in her lane on the bridge struck her head on. There was no place to veer, and she believed she would be dead.

Dale heard the crash and turned back. Carol was bleeding from her mouth and nose. No policeman was near, and Dale walked her to a nearby gas station until help would come. Carol sat and waited in shock, blotting blood. A customer who came into the shop asked her what happened. Probably affected by her shocked condition, she quipped, "I was in a fight."

Dale stammered, wishing she would behave appropriately. There was a lot at stake. She was three months pregnant, besides the loss of his parents' car. Now what? No money to pay for a tow. The need to take Carol to a doctor. Dale had been told to call the AA club if he had trouble, so he swallowed his pride and called. One of the men helped him get the car to a garage and helped him with the accident report. It was like a solid support under his feet, and he made it through the day. Carol was doing better and almost due for her monthly checkup, so they followed through with that.

Out on the route again in Dick's car, Dale was making better than adequate sales and had his first weekly delivery to make. With all their bills so much in arrears, they got a notice that the telephone was disconnected. Half a mile to the neighbor allowed for a message in most cases. Within the week, they got a warning that the electricity would be disconnected in two days. Carol agreed to take out some of Dale's orders for early delivery to get enough money to cover the late bill. With three little children, including a very unhappy baby in the car, Carol navigated the muddy roads to make those deliveries. By one o'clock on the final day she had the money in her hand; and with three little children in tow, she went into the electric company office. She laid the hard-gathered money on the desk, only to be told that the power had already been turned off. Not even the end of the final day?

"This should cover it," she said hopefully. No, was the answer. Now she would have to pay a penalty and a reinstatement charge. Carol protested that it was impossible, and the receptionist called the manager who decisively stated that there would be no exceptions. Carol, in exasperation threw the money on the counter and said, "He can take this and go wherever!"

She walked out with the children, wracking her brain to think how they could get along without electricity until the scheduled delivery three weeks away, when, neglecting everything else, they could pay the penalty and the re-connection fee. They did make it, using their wood stove to keep warm, and were glad that it was spring with a little more daylight in the evenings.

In the meantime, as Dale was out doing his sales work one evening, Carol was getting the children's supper. Little eighteen month old Connie was sitting on a kitchen chair, waiting for her dish. She lost her balance and fell backward onto the rocking horse rocker. As Carol picked her up, she could see Connie's movements were not normal. Carol set the little girl down to observe her, and Connie tumbled around. With no one to help her and no phone, Carol bundled up the three little ones and walked the half mile to the neighbors' house. The doctor was called, and Connie was taken to the hospital, where she, indeed, did have a concussion. Connie recovered and the incident caused her to grow closer to the neighbors who had helped. Were these three difficult months? Yes. Did Dale go back to drinking? No! How's that for hope rewarded?

Life finally settled into a routine. AA meeting each week, with regular contact with his sponsor and the clubhouse. Dale continued his sales route, and Carol's father offered to restock their dairy herd on a creamery assignment on the condition that Dale and Carol could keep their resolution to divide the labor. Carol connected with the Al-Anon group and learned to stand on her own feet, not blaming or demanding. A good life seemed to be emerging out of the chaos. Baby number four arrived the morning before Gene's birthday, with Gene being awakened to two realizations. One, stated plaintively:|"Now, I won't have my birthday party!" The other was that the tooth fairy had left money under his pillow—in pennies—and he had to count them before getting dressed to go to Grandma's so Mom could go to the hospital.

They did get to the hospital in time, and Gene was rewarded with a bright and cute blond baby brother they named Russell—and he did get his seventh birthday party. When Grandma brought the kids back home after Mom's hospital stay, Mom had his friends hiding to surprise him—and a big birthday cake. Little Russell slept through all the romping and laughing of games.

About two years down the road, dissension began to set in. Carol was very careful with spending, determined not to extend their obligations. Dale, on the other hand, began to express the feeling that this attitude was holding him back. He considered taking a sales job on the road that he thought offered more money. He would be gone two to three weeks at a time. Carol objected, knowing that taking care of all the cows and four children by herself was too much.

"I don't like it, Daddy."

Little two and a half year old Joanne with her tiny face and sparse baby-like hair, with a little ringlet gracing the nape of her neck, just reaching the last straw in going along with Dale's kidding, voiced her protest. On a rare day when Dale was home for a meal and cheerful, he was kidding Joanne about a piece of pickled herring he was coaxing her to try.

"It's so good, isn't it?"

Enthusiastic nod, then taking it out of her mouth.

"But, isn't it tasty?"

A little forced nod and then a puckered face, and the truth came out. It was so cute that both Dale and Carol hugged her, laughing.

Times of fun and laughter were rare. Babies and toddlers really appealed to Dale—when he was home.

When they began to have minds of their own and share their thoughts, the reaction was quite impatient and angry. As one Liz R. shared about drinking addiction. "It's like have a rattlesnake loose in the house; you never know when he will appear and strike out.

Early into the time that drinking behavior had curtailed the kind and humorous way of meeting problems in working together, Carol took a stand that she would not work with anyone who cursed at her. She struggled miserably that she could not make that work to protect the children.

"Let's do it again." Words came from Gene when the activity took on a fun side. Very likely the response was forbidding.

There were times after visiting the relatives in Iowa once a year that fun activities would take the fore, lasting a few days, as when Dale made stilts, and those big enough to catch on learned to walk on them. Another time big spools from electric cables became a balancing feat.

Those rare times were held in the memories of all. Soon, it was back to normal, and Daddy was scarce, either working every hour to farm and carry on a sales job or out too late to have energy to take part.

Children in 4-H or softball or band seldom had a dad at their event. Working together on home projects would be, "Can't you do it right?" Track meets and band performances went on with only Carol attending. Gymnastics and Ballet were also missed by Daddy.

Carol often reminded the children that Daddy was good at fixing appliances and fences and had a long commute to work, so we need to be thankful.

Gene's dream of having his dad take him fishing happened once. Excited over having his dad with him as other boy were gathered at the lake, Gene ran to tell them his dad was taking him fishing. Seeing that Gene went to them, Dale saw it as a rejection of him, fished for a short time and never took him fishing again. Carol, however, shivered through several opening days of fishing.

Russell and Connie both had the misfortune of having an overbite, plus having had front teeth knocked

out and coming back crooked. While waiting for a way to have them straightened, they were the object of much teasing. Russell struggled over the idea that his appearance didn't appeal to his dad, and that was why Daddy was angry and short on time with him. Connie was blessed with a helpful tendency that helped spare her of much of the disapproval.

Joanne and Connie became adept at sewing, but it was often the object of scolding that they should be doing other things. Carol's correcting of the children in Dale's presence often brought on a rage both toward Carol and the children.

Taking turns doing chores continued to be an issue. One evening, when it was Dale's turn, Carol suggested to Gene he could surprise his dad and have his chores started. Dale stayed in the house and left Gene to do the milking alone. Efforts at bringing family closer were discouraging.

The AA meetings regularly attended were a blessing in that there was no drinking, and he was helping others as well. The "dry drunk" behavior, though, was so painful one of the children suggested that if he would drink, perhaps he could go to treatment and get better. Occasionally they would pray that we would find a parking spot when driving anywhere and avoid a rage. Who would think that an answer lay ahead?

Their conversations were tense, punctuated by outbursts of, anger, cursing, and frustration on Dale's part and loud disagreement, defensiveness and reaction from Carol.

As it turned out, Dale did take the job, leading to much dissatisfaction and a virtual separation. Carol's dad talked them into another try, even if temporary. This began years of varying degrees of tension. Dale, rightly, put his recovery first, attending meetings and helping others. During this time, the friends who had been helping Carol with machinery and heavier work while Dale was on the road ran across a pony that their friends would sell at a low price. So, now the kids had a pony—black with a white blaze—and they named her Trixie.

Dale had a hard time making time for the children, especially as they got old enough to state their opinions. He commuted sixty-plus miles to St. Paul, Minnesota as a salesman and estimator for Sears.

Carol's priority was, along with a healthy recovered life, to raise their children well and give them a loving home. They were not always effective at having both time with the children and the many recovery connections. Dale was a hard worker, and there was little time for play, although he was always trying to make improvements. The fun was to come when all these goals would be met.

For now, there wasn't much agreement on anything. Dale's anger often led to out-of-control discipline (at least that's what Dale thought it was) of the children that was really a type of abuse—a kick behind a heavy engineer boot, a jerk, a slap, an angry, heavy-handed whipping with his belt, verbal abuse. Carol reacted by yelling at Dale for the abuse, often berating herself that she allowed her children to go through this.

Everything became tense, and Carol would in frustration with Dale's spending and his almost non-existent relationships with the children, lash out in angry frustration to the children when she really wanted to just encourage them.

And so it went. The children also learned to lash out or react as the situation warranted. Home life was at times very difficult.

Carol had a chance to attend college very economically when their fourth child went into kindergarten. This limited Carol's availability to work, but she did day work at times to help with expenses. This was Polk County Teachers' College, which qualified one for a teaching certificate. She had a wonderful mentor in the high school guidance counselor who had advised her. He helped arrange for a Title 3 program, which provided part time employment for three years as a career advisor to junior high and high school students. It was great too, as the schedule allowed her to be home when their kids were home from school.

Following the wonderful experience and opportunity, Carol continued at the school as an aide and tutor and attended summer school to work toward her BS degree in education. Again, she would hurry home to be with Dale, and he would be with other friends. Again, she would determine to avoid complaining, as she knew he needed the AA association.

Carol enrolled in the University of Wisconsin, River Falls with a full year of courses with student teaching. For her graduation the children celebrated by putting on an open house. What a glad day!

Dale went all out to make a celebration for Carol's big accomplishment. He purchased a van that they remodeled into a conversion van. His plan was to take it on a trip to California in commemoration of the graduation. Carol determined to overcome her resistance to buying the van, and it helped to realize they could sleep in it and eat many meals on the fold-out table and benches that made up into a bed.

However, as Carol looked for a campground, Dale looked for a hotel. What about the savings?

Add to this disappointment the fact that Dale had made the mistake of having his upper teeth pulled just before the graduation and trip, and he was very uncomfortable much of the time. That put a considerable damper on the hoped-for vacation feeling. (At a later date, in a time such as this, one of their daughters said, "It's the pain speaking.") Visiting and spending nights in the homes of relatives in San Jose and San Diego cut expenses and allowed for some relaxation. The connection was also special, and families on both sides were kind and gracious.

During this time, Gene got involved in alcohol and drugs. This was a painful time for the family, with the only mitigating part being the knowledge of the disease and the Al-Anon principles. Dale and Carol had to remind themselves to let go and allow Gene to find his way while being cognizant of legal issues. They had a new opportunity to extend the unconditional love they had already experienced. Gene attended a treatment program at Hazelden and Prescott, Wisconsin. When Mr. Krueger, Gene's counselor, bid Gene farewell, he turned to Dale and Carol and said, "I can't make any guarantees, but he knows where to come for help."

19 As We Understood

Again the roller coaster goes,
not always staying at the top.
Just when you pick the sweetest rose,
you see its petals gently drop.

Just prior to the California trip, a wonderful couple visited at the Morfitt's home. A fellow AA member who had heard him speak at the Florida convention told Dale about this man—Clarence Snyder—who was in the first forty group in AA. Clarence had a different view of the AA program, mainly because he had been there from the very beginning, when the Big Book was being written and the recovery rate was very high. Clarence's wife Grace was a charming southern lady who influenced many with her wise and loving ways. As Dale listened to Clarence talk about the early days, he began to see that much of the original program was being watered down. Clarence spoke at the AA banquet in Amery, and many members wondered at the difference, especially the couple's close relationship with the Master of Recovery—God.

Clarence and Grace encouraged Dale to come to a retreat in Florida to help him really become immersed in recovery. It didn't seem likely. Money was tied up in payments and very tight, so every work day was important. Carol still felt an empty place in her heart—a place that longed for family togetherness. After a pattern of Dale putting others in the group ahead of her plans, Carol felt all her efforts for a happy marriage were over.

Carol was doing some substitute teaching and taking advanced classes as she awaited responses to some of her teaching applications and interviews. In the meantime, the opportunity for a temporary factory job came up, and she decided to take it. The family situation had been so stressful to her that she found the factory job, where she could relax her mind as she worked, immensely helpful. It freed her attention so she could think through her relationship with God and practice at an easier pace to apply what she was learning about living. At one point, she remarked, "Now I can see what David meant when he said in the Psalms, 'He restoreth my soul.'"

Joanne, who at age sixteen had married an irresponsible man who abused and did not support her, had been deserted. That year, she trusted Jesus Christ as her savior from sin, and He gave her a new life. On one of Joanne's visits home, Carol shared her discouragement with her daughter. Joanne shared some Bible passages she thought would be helpful, and with a non-committal response from her mom, she left with a hug and a prayer.

Later in the week, Carol felt extremely low and decided to read the passages Joanne had shared. Sure enough, she should ask the Lord, even if she had believed as a child. She got on her knees and told Father God that she couldn't handle her life on her own, and would He please take it over. She believed Jesus died for her, and the Father raised Him from the dead, and she added, "Even if You don't do it the way I think, You can't do worse than I have." She got up and saw herself as a loved child—with all these faults—but loved. The Bible stories she had enjoyed from childhood now made sense. God, in His love, would bring good out of it all. She was ready to live a new life and let go and let God.

One of the very helpful facets of this trusting God was that when Gene's problems became public, instead of feeling shame Carol was able to pray that this incident might be the one that would lead to his finding help and trust in God.

One unprepared recipient of blessings in disguise was in line for another one. That fall, Dale received a flyer for the Camp Florida Retreat led by Clarence Snyder. Soon after Christmas, Dale developed a severe case of flu that he couldn't shake, and even after most of the respiratory effects were gone, a severe fatigue plagued him, and he just couldn't rally enough energy to go back to work. He was on sick leave with Sears, where he had been employed for some time, and Dale asked his doctor if a short trip to Florida would be helpful. The answer, "If you can handle the travel, it might do you good" was the go-ahead cue he needed.

When he told Carol about his plans, she said she would like to go too. He said it was for AA members only, and he would ride with the friend who had first recommended for Clarence to speak.

"Well, I think I should have an equal value purchase," Carol challenged. "It's only fair. I've been wanting a potter's wheel, and I think I should be able to spend money on myself for a change." She prepared to drive Dale over to his friend's, but he was evasive, suggesting that running into his friend's girlfriend might be awkward. That didn't feel right to Carol—there was no real reason given. She felt confused and later found out that the girlfriend had gone to the retreat with them. They didn't need to have any bad feelings, as Dale's spiritual condition may be bettered through the retreat, so she held her opinion to herself.

Dale was welcomed at Clarence and Grace's home, they shared a very informative and loving view of the original AA program with him, and then rode together to Camp Florida. When they arrived at the retreat, some older fellows were sitting around, and Dale, thinking with his fourteen years dry in AA he would have something to add, remarked, "It's nice to hear something about the spiritual side of the program."

Retelling the incident later, Dale said. "That old man stuck his long finger in front of my face and said, "There is no spiritual side of the program," and circling with his finger, "The whole circumference of the program is spiritual!"

It was a learning process. Many of the supposed ideas of AA were dispelled, as the freshness of the original program came forth. Through members having tried to adapt it to fit their "easier, softer way" as it is described in the Big Book of Alcoholics Anonymous, Chapter Five, "How it Works," had been watered down. Many had tried to find recovery through this watered down way, "but they could not."

Bedrock for Dale was seeing. Clarence and Grace treated each other, as well as those attending the retreat, with love and consideration. Number one: they quickly and firmly explained how they understood God, the God of the Bible, Creator, Redeemer, and Holy Spirit, and their faith showed in their actions.

Camp Florida was not a luxury place—outdoor privies, bring your own bedding and towels, and be ready to listen. And listen he did. During the return from camp to the Snyder's home Grace, a lovely, elderly lady, led Dale through his Fifth Step, where the member shares all his or her character defects, and he was able to pour out all the wrong actions and attitudes he felt so ashamed of and really start life on a new footing.

Upon arriving home in Wisconsin, Dale focused on the Big Book and the Bible, comparing the two to find out if all these unfamiliar ideas proved compatible. Carol edited cassette tapes of the Big Book for him that he had received at the retreat to be sure they were complete. It was a learning process for both of them, as they had previously talked more about the Big Book than actually read it.

Now, Al-Anon is a separate group, using the same steps and traditions, but focusing on the addict's loved one's own personal recovery, which, if applied sincerely, can benefit both people. Dale had always been a bit apprehensive about Carol getting too close to his AA group, and this had added to her feeling of rejection. However, helping him as he studied both the AA book and the Bible seemed to be a benefit toward both their programs.

One morning, just before Easter, Dale tested his physical stamina a little by going out to do errands in Amery. He stopped at a popular cafe, where he found the usual coffee break people gathered. As he entered, he noticed the only open place was near Pastor Adams, who had officiated at both Dale's parents' funerals. He had also prayed with Joanne just a year earlier to receive Jesus as Savior and had been helpful to the family. Dale decided to bring up the uppermost subject on his mind. "What is all this 'saved or born-again' you Baptists are always talking about?"

Pastor Adams said, "I have some time right now. Come over to the church." The church was right down the block, and over the course of the next hour, Pastor Adams repeated most of the message that had been shared with Dale at retreat: Surrender to God, believe He can restore you, and receive Him as your Lord.

Pastor Adams showed Dale a pamphlet that, through Bible verses, explained that God loves us and wants to give us eternal life, but our sin has separated us from God. As a result of our sin, we have a death sentence on us—both physical and spiritual. The death sentence has to be paid for the gap that separates us from God to be closed, and Jesus paid that death penalty for us. That's why He died on the cross. The pamphlet showed a picture of a man on one side of a great chasm and God on the other side, with nothing to bridge the gap—no way for the man to get to God. The next illustration showed the same chasm, but this time with a cross bridging the gap between man and God. Jesus died on the cross to pay the penalty for our sins and end the separation between us and God and to give us eternal life.

"I am the way the truth and the life," Jesus said in John 14:6. "No man cometh unto the Father, but by me." Dale bowed his head and trusted in the death, burial, and resurrection of Jesus as the substitutionary payment for his sins. That day, Dale felt a preview of the freedom and love he craved and began to pour himself into the God-given program that could restore his life.

One of the most noticeable outward things that changed immediately in Dale's life was his language. Whereas his conversations had previously been heavily punctuated with cursing, those words quickly dropped out of his speech.

Trusting Christ was a wonderful decision, but still not a guarantee of a rose garden. You might say that roses take a lot of care and patience, and there were a lot of weeds to dig out. One of these problem "weeds" was the lack of balance. Of course, recovery had to come first, but Carol felt, and expressed often, that it wasn't right for every person in recovery to come before every person in the family. It was a difficult issue, but the same people who shared how they understood God were also willing to share how they had achieved marital harmony, which change could only come with turning it over to God. More wisdom was needed.

Established ways die hard, and it was still a steep climb if harmony was to be achieved. Carol needed to understand that the disease of alcoholism tends to put alcohol ahead of relationships, and this can overlap into the recovery program as well. Although the reason for the neglect of emotional things can be understood, it can be difficult to endure. Carol, finally realizing how sick at heart she still was, went to a family program, which applied the same approach as AA treatment. She was so determined to get healthy that she was willing to accept a counselor that everyone said was harsh. She wanted so badly to hear the truth.

At this time, a smokers' clinic became available evenings, so Carol decided to attend it with Dale. Every night he met with the other participants, including girls she considered her friends, before she arrived and they all met together. She finally said that if she came last, she wanted out. Dale continued meeting with the others before she could arrive.

Having had him go out with these people rather than being home to enjoy the birthday cake she had planned with him and the kids—and the same thing for every other occasion she could bring to mind—Carol felt she couldn't go on. The next morning, she told him life had become too painful and asked him to leave. It was a sad time, and she felt cruel; but she held her ground.

As days passed, and Dale found a place to stay, they discussed the length of time this informal separation would last and how they would carry it out. Dale would come home weekly to see Russell, who was the only child still living at home, since Connie had enrolled in a Christian high school in St. Paul, sixty miles away.

That fall, Dale planned to attend the retreat again. "The taxes have to be paid first," Carol argued when she heard his plans. As it turned out, he went anyway. Carol changed her mind, since she couldn't change his and decided to go too; but it was too late to get a reservation.

"I'm not trying to break the marriage," Carol explained to Clarence, the founder of the retreat. "But the gaps between us are not about alcoholism." Clarence kindly remarked that a lot of recovery was still needed, and she accepted the advice and situation.

20 The Only One

If God is the only One you have,
You will find He is all you need.
You may even find yourself,
  a treasure great indeed.

So it was, those fall evenings, Carol would lift her eyes up to the top of the lordly white pine tree in the yard, and say, "God doesn't make junk." Hadn't He accepted her when she had surrendered to Him? That had been a decision, to be sure, but there were so many more to follow. She thought through things she had heard. "If it's supposed to be, it will be." "Another person can't make you happy. Unless you bring happy you into the relationship, it can't be happy."

Janelle, the dragon-type counselor, told her many things she did not like to hear, spotted her whining, and told her she couldn't expect to be sought-after. As she thought through these hard-gotten bits of information, Carol remembered that she had told her young daughters," Expect others to include you, and take part." Bingo! "I don't have to wait for permission to be included," she told herself. "I can kindly include myself where I want to be. If I can't take part, I have other interests I can apply myself to." Another bingo—she needed to have some real interests.

At one of the weekly "see Russ" evenings, she noticed that Dale was mentioning some of his own short-falls. Carol had to check herself not to mentally belittle the very behaviors she was trying to learn herself. Hmm, try not to build up expectations.

Carol was meeting with a group of Christian ladies, all of whom had some marital problems, and they would pray for each other.

At one of the counseling sessions, a man substituted for Janelle the counselor. He asked Carol a simple question about Dale. Whatever it was, God opened Carol's mind about what Dale must be experiencing. She could recognize the feeling of being put on the spot, being seen as wrong when much of his efforts are for the good.

This was not a "putting on a pedestal" view, but a look at the possible reality of another person. It was still a matter of waiting to see what God's will was, though it seemed it was for saving marriage. However, after being so sure she could see God's instructions, Carol had committed herself to allow for guidance from day to day. Their November anniversary day found her giving a small gift and a card that said you are loved even if you are not in the marriage, and you are wished happiness.

Dale continued to keep his weekly visits with Russ and sometimes talks with Carol. Each time he related some of the things he didn't like in their relationship he would seem to become more relaxed and open. He helped the kids decorate the Christmas tree, though this was not comfortable.

"I don't want a band aid on the marriage," Dale stated. If it was to continue, it would only be through God's will and healing.

One night, as Carol sat alone while Dale was at an AA meeting, it occurred to her that there was no way in the present situation to see if their relationship could work. However, since Dale was the one who had been distancing himself, it seemed it could only change if he suggested it. As Carol prayed, the words came clearly to her. From God? "Ask him if he would want to try." Carol recoiled.

"No, it can only work if he says he wants it." Again, "Ask him if he would want to try."

"No, it's like betraying myself."

The tap came at the door. Dale was back from his meeting. "Our six month trial separation is over. Would you want to try again?" It was Carol who spoke, and it was like the words were coming from someone else. Now she would never know if he would have asked.

"I'm afraid," Dale said.

"I'm afraid, too," Carol responded simply.

Dale stayed that night, and they began to try a new way, seeking to love with the love of Father God.

Carol had been thinking long and hard, even while she still did not believe getting back together was possible. The only way this can work at all is if she would totally let go. See what sort of things Dale would decide to do. Even with her strong resolve, it took relearning and self-discipline to state her feelings simply without demands or expectations.

Al-Anon has so much supportive sharing—not advice—to help a person adopt healthier ways of living and leave behind some of the behaviors that defeat them. Trusting in God was essential.

Although she had felt being together every day was the best thing, as they discussed plans, Carol accepted as possible that Dale stay in St Paul where he worked—say, three nights a week. As it unfolded, it actually seemed to be a benefit to have a day or two apart to process what was going on.

Because Carol had struggled with feeling that what she said wasn't accepted or understood, she had often reworded and restated things in hopes of getting a response. As she prayed about this situation, she saw that this repeating and rewording could be seen as an attempt to control and perhaps only served to make the idea she was presenting less appealing to Dale. It surprised her after she diligently applied the practice of expressing an idea or a feeling simply and letting go of it, that sometimes Dale would refer to it later. Later in the game, she sometimes would comment on how much better a person can do when they don't have our urging to resist.

21 Starting Over

A new life can be wondrous;
Hope, gradual, arises.
But, bowling us over,
amazing surprises.

Walking cautiously, praying for courage, Carol firmly decided to live by the principles she had embraced. Knowing that so many people in an alcoholic's family get caught up in trying to fix the addicted person, or in some way to manage the other person's life, Carol was determined to apply the wisdom she had learned in dealing with her own problem. In Al-Anon, people learn to lead and improve their own life and let go of the other people and let them take their own responsibilities.

Trusting God and her connection with Him was absolutely necessary, as she daily prayed for knowledge of His will and the power to carry that out. As she applied what she was learning from day to day, she was confronted with a new reality to face.

The alternate days of Dale and Carol being together allowed for a good amount of thinking and helped the weeks pass quickly. It seemed only days since they had resumed their life together, and Carol noticed a change in her body, a little filling out, mild nausea, and—shock! How could this be? She wouldn't discuss it until she saw her doctor. This was the day and age of contraceptives, and she had been cautious. Maybe her thyroid was out of balance or something. The appointment was made immediately.

Positive. How could this be? We want to be positive in our approach to life, but this was ridiculous. She would have to tell him. Their baby Russ was fifteen years old now, and she didn't even know if she and Dale would continue to live together. She was not going to have Dale suspect that she had planned it. She prepared herself and gave her well-planned out announcement:

"I have something to tell you, and it won't bind you to anything. I have learned to get along on my own and can, if I have to. Actually, Dr. Whitlark says there is a baby on the way, but you don't have to feel obligated."

As Carol attempted to continue her disclaimer, Dale, looking pale, said, "I kind of feel like Father Abraham." And, like Carol, not knowing what the future held for them, he mentioned apologetically that he had thought this would be the time of life they were going to be able to travel.

Not ready to commit themselves to the obvious requirements of the situation, they agreed to continue taking a day at a time. They were considerate of one another and tried to discuss their views and feelings, but a declaration of lasting love had not really been restated.

As weeks passed, Carol experienced extremely painful digestive problems but was able to endure with medicine and exercise. One night, when it was Dale's day to go back to St. Paul after his meeting, Carol had a painful attack and was admitted to the hospital. As Dale returned to the city that evening as planned, Carol believed this was the final sign that there would not be a continuation of the marriage. When Dale came home after the usual two days, he had been informed that the pregnancy was intact, and Carol was home, so he was prepared for what he wanted to discuss.

Not being a man of great preliminaries to a subject, he told Carol he'd like to be in the delivery room this time, as he had never been able to for the other babies. This seemed to be a result of his own prayers and soul searching. It was a turning point that Carol would not have imagined. Not only was he very interested in being part of the family, but he wanted to see how they could include each other in their recovery programs.

Since recovery was so central in Dale's life, this was a big step. One of the touchy places for Carol was that Dale seemed to put every person in AA ahead of her and not to include her. Now he began to show awareness that Al-Anon dealt more with the family problems caused by addiction and began to ask her about cases where that intervention might be helpful. Even more encouraging was that he, contrary to his earlier approach, acknowledged that her presence, with the agreement of the person sponsored, would be appropriate if the sponsored person was a female. This had been an issue that developed especially because some of the young female AA members felt so comfortable with Dale.

Surprisingly, with Carol's new involvement, not only did these young women become special to Carol, but the sharing between her and female recovering alcoholics helped her better understand her own program. The knowledge that alcoholics are addicted to a chemical, and people who need Al-Anon are addicted to people makes the same program work very well for both, if they have turned their lives over to God and thoroughly follow the steps.

It was a time of growth—in their relationship, in their programs, and in Carol's circumference.

Connie had finished high school in the Christian school and was accepted into a Christian college. Joanne was freed from the man who had abused her and deserted her, and she had lived as a single mother for almost three years. Having been counseled through teaching from the Bible that she could marry again, she was engaged to a Christian man from her church.

Connie was about to leave for college with her parents' new baby due in another month. In tears, after having Connie spend two precious weeks with her, Carol saw her off to college via Carol's brother LeRoy, who lived a few hours away at Urbana, Illinois.

Twenty-three years old now, Gene was still in the bonds of addiction, though he had been through treatment at age sixteen and was the subject of many prayers. Russell had two years remaining at Amery High School and was a right hand to his mother and dad.

Fall Festival weekend at Amery, Wisconsin. Dale and Carol's niece Ranae was to ride on one of the parade floats, and they were excited to see the parade. As Carol dressed to join Dale to find a parking place where they could watch the parade, she began to feel that she was losing her water. It was just little by little, but too much to plan on sitting an hour or more at the parade. Dale's sister Sally called a couple of times to see if they would make it in time to watch the parade. Mother Nature won out, and Carol had to go directly to the hospital. But it was almost four weeks early, and Dale and Carol were both apprehensive.

An exam at the hospital indicated everything was all right. It was a fairly long labor. "Out of practice," she joked. Dale sat with her through the labor, recording the time and duration of the contractions, and when they were close enough, Dr. Schroeder had her brought to the delivery room. In the early morning hours, Carol was finally directed to stop holding back, and little Scott, dark haired and very healthy-looking, greeted the world.

What a tender and precious time. Carol's dad was very relieved to have her well and with a healthy baby. Her own mother had died in a middle-age pregnancy, so it was a particular relief to him to see her come through safely.

The realization that all the childhood stages would now be repeated struck Carol, and Dale expressed that, with dependence on the Lord, they could be better parents.

Quite a change had taken place in the Morfitt home. The college degree that Carol had hoped would provide a better income to finance college for the children was now not available, at least for the time being. "I need to arrange child care for Scott so I can look for a teaching job to help pay your college expenses," Carol informed Connie and Russ.

"No. You need to stay home with the baby," they both answered with selfless resolve. They sought work-study and merit scholarships and made it through college mostly on their own.

22 Singular Silver Celebration

Such a happy day,
who would think by now,
we would with celebration
life avow.

Scott was born just a little over two months before their twenty-fifth wedding anniversary. Carol anticipated the fun of taking their new baby boy out, shopping for him, and showing him off as an anniversary celebration. It was perfect. She found a crib mobile that would flutter when he moved in his crib. Just what she wanted. It could respond to him.

She called her dear friend Carol Jeanne and told her what a happy day it was. Dale had gone to work in the morning and was due home shortly. Carol had a simple dish ready in the refrigerator and was so excited to show him what she had bought for Scott.

Dale came through the door, a gift in his hand—pretty little box. Her usual tie and socks were wrapped for him.

"You open your first," he said. "I'll open my socks later"—laughing. They both laughed. Tentatively, she smiled, as if asking if it was all right.

She carefully undid the beautiful curled ribbon and read the sweet, lacy card. Dale seemed very eager to see his gift opened. Cautiously, she peeled the tape, then the pretty paper to reveal a little box. A ring? It was—not only a ring, but a diamond! Carol had lost the diamond from her engagement ring nearly a year earlier. Here was the ring back, with a sparkling new diamond. This really was a happy day!

"This is perfect. I have supper in the fridge ready to eat." Carol said.

"I have the car warmed up and a reservation at The Terrace [a nice restaurant a few miles away in Somerset]. The Terrace has always been special to us." Determining that the food could be eaten later, Carol put on the pretty dress she had laid out—and her new ring. She saw in Dale's eyes the special intimate sparkle that she had treasured at their wedding and the two very early happy years. Scott bundled in his car seat was good company, and the food was marvelous. End of story? Oh, no, Joanne had invited her in-laws and Dale's sister's family; and Joanne's sister-in-law had made and decorated a beautiful fall cake, with mums and daisies reminiscent of Dale and Carol's wedding flowers. Joanne's husband Dave supplied a photo shoot with Scott, so it turned out to be a silver anniversary weekend.

The following spring, Clarence and Grace Snyder were again invited to speak at the annual banquet. However, Grace had a coronary procedure and couldn't travel, so Clarence came alone, leaving her in the hands of beloved friends. Clarence spent a little extra time, and Dale showed him some of the treatment facilities the area had become known for.

Clarence had talked with Dale so much about retreats that Dale had been trying to think of a way to get Amery people to Florida where they would have opportunity to receive the same healing he had found through the retreat. Clarence glanced at the barn on the Morfitt farm and remarked that it might be a place to hold a retreat.

That was Dale's cue to take the next step. Not only did the area have growing treatment centers, but within a mile of the Morfitt farm were two retreat center/Bible camps that might be considered. Before Clarence's week long stay ended, the decision was made along with an agreement to use the Wapogassett Bible camp that very fall. Well, that looked like quite a challenge, but Clarence, the founder of these retreats, offered to be on hand along with his wife to help them conduct the first retreat in early October.

July rolled around, and Gene was still a big item on the prayer list. He stopped in on a weekend and remarked that "if everything works out," he might consider going back to Croixdale at Prescott, Wisconsin, where he had gone through treatment seven years earlier. It turned out that "if everything works out" entailed him using alcohol and drugs without limit, and if he was still here, he would give it a try. A week later, he came by. He had a basket of laundry and himself. His mom said she could run his laundry through before he went.

Apprehensive that he would not go if he waited, Gene suggested she put Scott in the car seat and take him to the treatment center. So began his second treatment. As soon as families were allowed to come and visit, his mom and dad came. His dad sat down by him ready to listen to a speaker. Dad leaned over and said quietly, "You can put your old life behind you. The Seventh Step (Humbly asked God to remove our shortcomings) really works." Having had many rocky times in their relationship, it was definitely an encouragement. When treatment was finished, Gene had completed his steps:

1. We admitted we were powerless over alcohol—that our lives had become unmanageable.

2. Came to believe that a Power greater than ourselves could restore us to sanity.

3. Made a decision to turn our will and our lives over to the care of God as we understood Him.

4. Made a searching and fearless moral inventory of ourselves.

5. Admitted to God, to ourselves, and to another human being the exact nature of our wrongs.

6. Were entirely ready to have God remove all these defects of character.

7. Humbly asked Him to remove our shortcomings.

8. Made a list of all persons we had harmed, and became willing to make amends to them all.

9. Made direct amends to such people wherever possible, except when to do so would injure them or others.

10. Continued to take personal inventory and when we were wrong promptly admitted it.

11. Sought through prayer and meditation to improve our conscious contact with God as we understood Him, praying only for knowledge of His will for us and the power to carry that out.

12. Having had a spiritual awakening as the result of these steps, we tried to carry this message to alcoholics, and to practice these principles in all our affairs.

Many of the issues involving amends had to be completed after leaving treatment, and the last three steps that embody the first nine steps are a lifelong process.

23 Life Goes On

How to direct my gratitude
To One who gave, then life renewed,
Principles by which to live,
one day at a time as He will give.

Visiting with his dad from time to time following treatment, Gene expressed his desire to take part in the upcoming spiritual retreat. It was named "Spiritual Program Retreat" in response to the deep impression left on Dale by the man who clearly indicated that the whole circumference of the program was spiritual. The emblem for the retreat was the circle containing the title, affirming that message.

There they all were at the Morfitt house with sheets, blankets, pillows, and towels ready for the retreat weekend. The new leaders, Dale and Carol, had eyes and ears open, receiving instructions and observing how the experienced leaders conducted it. The new retreatants were greeted with hugs and warmth, and it was a learning experience for everyone. Gene was all ears and had an open heart to receive whatever the retreat had to offer. He only had to recall the exuberance of Dale at his returns from the Florida retreats, so full of new life and eager to change for the better, to have a pretty good idea of what was possible.

Dale had been so on fire for others to experience the freedom and love he had experienced—and now here it was, practically in their own back yard, with the retreat center a mile away.

As Gene mingled and listened and shared, everyone thought he had had his born again experience. However, he struggled through the night, praying, reflecting on the times he had felt the call and moved on. This time he purposed that if it was to be, it would stick. By morning, he was on his knees receiving God's love and acceptance, and he rose up a new person. "Oh, this is it! "If any man is in Christ, he is a new creation." That is written in the Bible—2 Corinthians 5:17.

Imagine the joy and affirmation for Dale and Carol that at their first attempt at leading a retreat, their precious son could declare he was a new creation. What kind of wonderful is that? As Grace Snyder put it with his young face between her hands, "Sweet baby, you are a new creation."

That was the first of many retreats that were held at Lake Wapogassett. Spiritual Program Retreats expanded to two a year, spring and fall. The spring retreat became late winter, and a spring retreat in Minnesota was begun.

Many wonderful friendships developed through the retreats because of the mutual fervent desire and effort to make available the opportunity that brought about such wonders in the early members. As enthusiastic members attended, some developed the strong desire to carry on the work. These surrounded themselves with followers who shared the benefits and opportunity for service, and they started retreats in other parts of the country and overseas as well.

They discovered the profound truth that "alcoholism is a family disease." Each individual applying his or her program and faith in God can bring recovery not only to the alcoholic but to the affected family.

As Dale and Carol and their children were experiencing this renewal and relationship healing, their local AA participation was ongoing. In the beginning of discovering sobriety, all is not a bed of roses—but it is worth it.

Some AA members who had been very adamant that religion was not a part of the program resisted to the point of breaking into their own groups. It isn't so easy to convey that while everyone is welcome, regardless of their religion or lack of it, each person is free to express his or her experience, strength, and hope and the source of it—but not to impose it on others.

A strong point that those who had a chance to know cannot deny is that those early members who depended on a God with a name and power and followed the teachings of the Big Book had a much higher percentage of recovery than those who simply went to meetings, though that was a good practice.

The recovery of the family and those sponsored by retreat people made the whole change worthwhile, and new people often came into AA with the background of retreat, adhering to Big Book beginnings. Through the years, while Dale worked on amends with the older children and learned to parent the younger one, commuting to work in St Paul always required extra planning for family events.

The ponies had been sold, as the children had become too big for them. When Scott was four or five, his older cousin rode his darling paint pony over to the farm and gave him to Scott. He was called Tony (Tony the Pony) and was fun for Scott and the grandchildren who were a little older and a little younger than Scott.

Graduations and marriages happened: the prayers of those who had lives committed to the Lord went out for one another and others. The year that Scott finished first grade, Dale had a heart incident that required an angiogram. Scott was left with his special Aunt Sally and Uncle Gary while Dale and Carol went to St Paul to Regions Hospital, most likely for the day, to have the test. As it turned out, for some reason a bit of plaque from the artery had lodged in the entrance to his intestines, resulting in a serious condition that required several days in intensive care. Because the whole time of the ICU was shaky, Carol stayed with Dale the entire time. For seven year old Scott, just a phone call didn't reassure him adequately, and he feared for his Dad's life. The emergency resulted in a condition that kept Dale from work for many weeks.

Reports of good results from a non-conventional treatment called chelation drew Dale to try the treatment. He experienced good results as well, and he was able to go back to a normal work schedule. He was able to continue his job in St. Paul, Minnesota, for Sears as an estimator for installed home improvements. With his physical condition remaining stable for several years, Dale dropped the chelation therapy, since it had to be paid for with their own funds because insurance didn't cover it.

When Scott was about eleven, Dale noticed an ad in the paper for a yearling filly, quarter horse and Belgian cross. Dale had grown up with work horses, and between the two of them, he thought, they might train her for both riding and driving. Carol's brother helped her train Mandy for riding, and Dale worked with her regularly to make her into a safe driving horse. The first time Carol drove Mandy out on the field alone, she felt so free, on top of the world.

Riding out there, Carol reflected on the painful selling of her first horse, Jeanie—due, mostly to changes caused by drinking. Carol had hidden her tears through that whole aching process, as she said to herself, "That's the way it goes."

Now, she looked over the fields they had dreamed of farming and thought of how much of life had gone by. As she marveled at the ease of handling the precious horse Dale had worked so hard to train, the tears spilled. "All that I have lost has come back," she said to the Lord. "Like it says in the book of Joel in the Bible, You have given back the years the locust has eaten." Mandy, whose name means "lovable" didn't seem upset in the least over Carol's emotional experience.

24 No Hiding in the Sand

So, you or I may start the trail,
Knowing only the Guide, and not the end.
Giving up fear we be mocked or fail,
go, trusting, forth, our Guide a faithful friend

During these years, Dale and Carol were involved in the Florida retreats and in assisting with other new retreats. The fall that one of the next challenges showed up, Carol had stayed home in Wisconsin, as she was teaching in a Christian school. Early the second morning Dale was away he called home, telling Carol about what seemed to be a heavy bladder hemorrhage. She suggested he follow the advice of his hosts and call a walk-in clinic. The bleeding stopped, and the medical team advised an examination when he returned to Wisconsin unless an emergency occurred.

For the next year, Dale had his bladder scraped at intervals, and the doctors discussed the continuum of the bladder condition. Perhaps it was because she simply had not faced reality, but Carol was shocked when Dale was referred to an oncologist.

A new retreat had opened near Terra Haute, Indiana; and Carol was scheduled to drive there and speak. As she drove through the varying landscapes and thought about where life was heading, a song came on the radio. "Since I met you baby," the lyrics said, and then continued to declare a lasting and life-changing love. Deeply touched in her heart, Carol met the lady who headed up the retreat with tears, and shared how deeply the words of the song—repeated at least three times during the drive—had touched her.

Her resolve to do everything loving in their relationship was uppermost in Carol's mind when she arrived home.

We often say, "It's a God thing," and this certainly was. The most recent report indicated a more extensive surgery was necessary, and Dale needed moral support more than ever.

Through the next eight years, crises and relief from crises followed one another—the removal of the bladder, infections that turned septic, a heart attack that kept him mostly unconscious for more than a week. Carol, who helped care for the urostomy after the bladder removal, was horrified with the fear that her procedures may have caused the life-threatening infection. To her relief, Dale's doctor said her care had not in any way contributed to the infection, and she resumed helping him with the condition.

Later, more tissue had to be removed, and during this procedure his heart stopped, but he was revived. Between these major physical situations, Dale worked as an estimator for a residential fence company. One week when Connie was visiting at home, she took him to one of his appointments. As he finished his measuring, he collapsed. The homeowner and Connie prepared to call an ambulance. In the meantime, Dale regained consciousness and proceeded to finish writing the sale.

During the later years of his cancer battle, Dale had several short-term healing events, to the joy of his praying friends. Dale used many natural remedies during these last years and reported to his doctor.

After a very good year, when he had been able to speak at a retreat in Scotland, the cancer hit with a vengeance. Use of radiation on his brain seemed to weaken him, even while reducing tumors. In the end, it was the septic infection that took him. The family had always dreaded his painful episodes with septic infection but, in the end, it may have saved him much suffering, shortening the final stages of his cancer.

25 Golden Wedding

Today

Another Fall rolls 'round again,
with brilliant leaves ablaze.
Frogs think of sleep, and birds fill up
for a trip of many days.

On silver hair-- maybe touched up,
wind ruffles, or sun shines.
The richness all around us
affirms the passing time.

We haven't quite crossed over
to days of winter's breeze,
but, coming after color,
is the magic of frost-trimmed trees.

The joys and hurts of rolling years
leave memories, some sublime.
So we live the joys and tears,
just one day at a time.

A year earlier, they hadn't been at all sure that their fiftieth anniversary would be reached. But here they stood, at the threshold of that golden day, with a restored life and marriage. Faith, use of unconventional supplements with overseeing by his doctor, and huge motivation to bring help to every suffering alcoholic it was possible to reach seemed to uphold Dale. He had made an effort to make amends to family and he said, "While I'm living, I intend to live."

The support of the believing AA family was major, extending the message that a life changing experience carried out in our way of living can bring a life of spiritual health and usefulness to others.

The five children and their families put on a beautiful golden wedding celebration for Dale and Carol, with many of Dale's friends in the program giving testimony of his help to them and to the lives of their families through recovery and faith.

Through the following year, Dale requested that Carol sing the Christmas song she had written in the church service, followed by some songs at his request in later services. As their daughter Joanne mentioned later on, having him enjoy her composing and singing was a great joy to Carol.

Carol often reflected how good it was that their earlier six-month separation did not end in divorce, and how thankful she was to be there for him in those difficult times of fighting cancer.

As the year neared its end, Dale said, "Let's have a nice, big family Christmas, and give this house we have put so much into a last hurrah." It was a good Christmas with all the children and grandchildren present.

Within weeks, Dale had to go into the hospital. While he was there, he told his doctor, "I've heard that when you're ready to live, you're ready to die; and I'm ready." There in the hospital he prayed with and anointed Gene to be the leader of the retreats.

Shortly after that, Dale came home on hospice care. As we helped Dale up the porch steps because he wasn't able to put any weight on his feet, Gene spoke through tears," This isn't the way he wanted to come home."

The hospice nurses were very kind, and his daughter-in-law Sheila, also a nurse, was a great help to the family, even helping to shift him around in his hospital bed so Carol could lie beside him. On Sunday after church, the children and many of the grandchildren, along with Dale's sister Sally and her husband Gary, gathered around in the bright living room where the bed sat near the picture window, so Dale could see the land if he opened his eyes.

Carol lay beside him and sang songs they used to sing in the car—Side by Side, You are My Sunshine, Moon River, Jesus, Like a Shepherd Lead Us. Noticing that one of the grandchildren who had helped Dale construct a dulcimer was strumming it, Carol said, "Why don't you sing Amazing Grace? Grandpa likes it so much."

The family joined in and sang with them. Dale appeared to be breathing irregularly, and he raised up his hands and exhaled. Carol breathed, "Oh, Dale, You're with Jesus."

Little Susie, their tiny dog that adored Dale jumped up on his bed, looked in his face, turned away crestfallen, and went to the door. The kids cried, held their mom and their children, and then called the hospice people.

26 Gone Home

Only God's grace can ease the pain,
the contradiction of our plans,
allow enough of letting go,
that we can glimpse His loving hand.

The going home was announced around the country and beyond to all the people who led or participated in retreats and AA and Al-Anon recovery.

The setting for the celebration of Dale's life was very fitting and beautiful. The Wapogassett Bible Camp and Retreat Center had recently built an awesome new building high above the lake, with windows extending along the whole side of the meeting room overlooking the lake. They called it Crossfire, and it was a focal point of the camp.

Spiritual Program Retreat had held their fall retreat in that new building. The setting would have pleased Dale, and it pleased his friends and family.

As the crowd gathered, huge, soft snowflakes drifted by these windows, over the evergreen trees, and out over the lake.

As the service was about to begin, the funeral director asked Carol if she would like to come forward and view Dale one last time. She had been contemplating placing one of the roses (his favorite) and one of the daisies (her favorite) in his hand. Not wanting to draw attention to herself, she declined and later placed the flowers at his graveside.

The worship team from Living Word Chapel of Forest, Wisconsin provided the music and led the singing, besides special numbers by Dale's grandchildren. The pastor sang one of Dale's favorite songs, What a Wonderful World. A special request Come to Jesus with a verse, "Dance with Jesus—and Live," was sung, as well as If You Could See Me Now. Dale was dancing before Jesus now, freed from his pain-filled body. Finally, Carol, the children and grandchildren, and any family who were there stood around the casket and sang Amazing Grace.

Leaders among the retreats in Florida and other parts of the country attended. Steve S. spoke, declaring that Dale, not having great material possessions, gave so much more—he gave himself.

Dale's children shared.
- Gene, who had inherited the leadership of the retreat with Dale's blessing, honored his dad and his life.
- Joanne revered him and her parent's lasting and renewed love and shared that Christ had made him a new person.

- Connie, always the purveyor of love and appreciation, exulted over his spiritual victory.
- Russell praised his legacy of giving and amends he had made real.
- Scott, sixteen years younger than the second youngest sibling, gave everyone a smile with his reference to himself as the Morfitt's remedy for the "empty nest syndrome."

Many local and visiting AA program and retreat members expressed their appreciation for a life shared to help others. A grandson spoke of how he would like to emulate a life for whom the parting tears were of such love and gratitude.

When the time was running late, it was suggested that more love expressions could be shared over lunch when they returned from the interment.

As the procession was assembled, as planned, Mandy, the horse that Dale had trained, and his beautiful hand-built passenger wagon that had given so many pre-Christmas rides in different towns, was the leader of the procession.

Decked out in its plushy red velvet cushions Joanne had made, and driven by Dale's dear brother-in-law Gary, it led out the long, curving driveway and road from the retreat center. Still, the huge snowflakes drifted down, sustaining the winter beauty.

Carol reflected on the many people in the procession. Especially dear was a young man who had kept her waiting past midnight as she sat in the family van while he poured out his heart to Dale and surrendered his life to God.

Many families that showed the solidarity of recovery surrounded the graveside at the end of the journey.

Carol recalled Dale quoting Clarence, retreat founder, as saying, "When I leave this world, I'll be in the ground. The grass over the grave will wave in the breeze, but it is the spirit that has been shared that will live on in healed lives."

27 Torch Passed

Blessing, as we do, the farewell road,
assured, as the horizon drops from sight,
of the welcome on the other side,
open arms and unbounded love.

There are two meaningful quotes for such a time as this. One is from a hymn, "Count your blessings; name them one by one." The other quote is from The Twelve Steps, "Took a searching and fearless moral inventory."

At such a junction in life's road, there is much for which to be thankful. It's a double-edged blessing—you get to be thankful for not only the good things that have happened, but also that you have developed a grateful heart.

In her own words paraphrased from 2 Corinthians 1, Carol says, "The help that God has given me in my difficulties is there for me to be of help to others."

Carol and Dale lived a lot of ups and downs together, and through God's grace, they both came out on top in many ways.

Carol learned that another person's best, when joined with God, was way beyond what she could have hoped for him. Following a joining of purposes, with God's guidance and provision, they even had their material needs covered. Spiritual and emotional healing was revealed in all its brightness when Carol was able to lie beside Dale and sing him home to Heaven at his last moments.

Dale found what he had always wished for—he became free and loved in many ways, joyfully freed by Father God to be himself. He became loved by many whom he had helped, and in the fellowship of shared humor and loyalty.

Gene got to love his dad as a fellow human and spiritual brother and was trusted and enthusiastically anointed to carry on his dad's work in the Spiritual Program Retreat to bolster the recovery of alcoholics and their families.

Joanne, in her pain, found Jesus and helped her parents to come to know Him personally, and she became a loving wife and mother of a Christian family.

Connie got her mom and dad as Christian brother and sister through example and sharing, became a fellow worker with Dale at Sears, and became a loving wife and mom.

Russell became big brother to Scott, the late gift in their born again life. With the Serenity Prayer principles, Russ took part with his Dad in unresolved hurts, became loving friends with his dad, and became a Christian husband and dad himself.

Scott got to grow up in a Christian home with parents still very fallible, but willing. Beginning a youth ministry venture in Colorado, he came home to be near his Dad in his illness. That was a tender blessing for both of them, which Scott will never regret.

God blessed them through many recovered addicts and recovered families—and the effect goes on, snowballing and mushrooming through the U.S. and beyond, through the efforts of those who have gone from being "hurt people who hurt people" to "helped people who help people."

Made in the USA
Columbia, SC
26 October 2018

Internal Medicine

Correlations and **C**linical **S**cenarios

Internal Medicine

Correlations and Clinical Scenarios

Conrad Fischer, MD
Residency Program Director
Department of Medicine
Brookdale University Hospital Medical Center
Brooklyn, New York

Associate Professor of Physiology,
   Pharmacology and Medicine
Touro College of Medicine
New York, New York

 Medical

New York   Chicago   San Francisco   Athens   London   Madrid
Mexico City   Milan   New Delhi   Singapore   Sydney   Toronto

1 2 3 4 5 6 7 8 9 0   CTP/CTP   19 18 17 16 15 14

ISBN 978-0-07-182698-3
MHID 0-07-182698-X

This book was set in Arno Pro by Thomson Digital.
The editors were Catherine A. Johnson and Harriet Lebowitz.
The production supervisor was Richard Ruzycka.
Project management was provided by Saloni Narang, Thomson Digital.
China Translation and Printing Services, Ltd. was the printer and binder.
This book is printed on acid-free paper.

Library of Congress Cataloging-in-Publication Data

Fischer, Conrad, author.
  Correlations and clinical scenarios. Internal medicine / Conrad Fischer.
    p. ; cm.
  Internal medicine
  Includes index.
  ISBN-13: 978-0-07-182698-3 (paperback : alk. paper)
  ISBN-10: 0-07-182698-X (paperback : alk. paper)
  I. Title. II. Title: Internal medicine.
  [DNLM: 1. Internal Medicine—Examination Questions. WB 18.2]
  RT48.6
  616.07'5—dc23
                                                    2013044220

McGraw-Hill Education books are available at special quantity discounts to use as premiums and sales promotions or for use in corporate training programs. To contact a representative, please visit the Contact Us pages at www.mhprofessional.com.

International Edition ISBN 978-1-259-25519-9; MHID 1-259-25519-0.
Copyright © 2014. Exclusive rights by McGraw-Hill Education, for manufacture and export. This book cannot be re-exported from the country to which it is consigned by McGraw-Hill Education. The International Edition is not available in North America.

Dedication

This book is dedicated to decreasing suffering.

*Everyone who takes an action to ease the burden of suffering on our planet,
no matter how small, is my brother or sister. I send you my love.*

CONTENTS

PREFACE

Why did we go to medical school? What was the beautiful vision of yourself in the future, when you set out to challenge obstacles, conquer barriers and commit yourself to medicine?

Hold On! You are ALMOST DONE!

The energy you need for your final push lies in the sacred vision you had of yourself when you started. Go back. Go back in time and remember your MCAT and medical school application essay and your personal statement for your residency application. I still have mine.

I wrote in flowery words about compressing all the desire of thousands of years of human history in the single moment of cosmic understanding that allows us to heal the world, grow an immortal soul, have a heart perfumed by love and bring into existence by our own constant work a better civilization where there are no separate groups, and people live with hope, peace, art, music, science and freedom from fear and pain.

My faculty advisor said, "Conrad, aren't you weird enough already? Take that out of your statement."

I kept it in.

Go back to beginning. Don't stop five minutes too soon. What you have in your hands will help you.

Save the world. Save the world outside you with medicine. Save the world inside you with hard work and eternally fragrant love.

Conrad Fischer, MD

INTRODUCTION AND HOW TO USE THIS BOOK

Look for the precise sequence through time to manage the computer-based case simulation (CCS) portion of the exam. That is the primary purpose of *Correlations and Clinical Scenarios: Internal Medicine.* You will find direction on exactly how long to move the clock forward in time and the precise sequence of which text or treatment should be done first in managing a patient. This will cover the order in which to give treatments, order tests and how to respond to test results. All CCS-related instructions appear in RED TYPE.

If you have never seen a particular case or you are a physician in a specialty other than internal medicine, this book is especially for you. It never has statements about "using your judgment" because you basically do not have any in these areas. If you want a cookbook that says, "Do this, do that, do this", then you have the right book in your hands. All initial case presentations and their continuing scenarios appear in yellow boxes.

This book will prepare you for the multiple choice questions that comprise the majority of the exam as well as the computer-based case simulations and the new basic science foundations that have just been added to the exam.

USMLE Step 3 or COMLEX Part 3 is the last phase in getting your license. Most of you are in residency and have no time to study. *It's totally uncool that they changed the exam just before YOU are about to take it! I am 100% sure it was not meant personally to torture you alone.*

Here is how to best use this book:

First read the disease or subspecialty in any standard text book. I personally suggest either my own *Master the Boards Step 3,* or *Current Medical Diagnosis and Treatment.*

The cases in this book are meant to further interrogate your understanding of the subject. There are hundreds of new multiple choice questions that are not in anyone's Q bank.

Every single case has numerous basic science foundations (which appear in blue boxes) added to it so you will have a solid understanding of it simply by following along in the case. You do not have to search through any of your old step 1 books or basic science texts. If I thought a basic science correlate was important, I have put it in. If I did not think it was important I left it out.

Finally, I always wanted to write something specifically for CCS. This is it. Because new test changes are frightening and the basic science questions are new for step 3, I decided to make one book to cover both things.

Bon appetite!

LIST OF ABBREVIATIONS AND ACRONYMS

AAA—Abdominal aortic aneurysm

ACh—Acetylcholine

AChR—ACh receptor

AFB—Acid-fast bacillus

AIDS—Acquired immunodeficiency syndrome

aPTT—Activated partial thromboplastin time

ACS—Acute coronary syndrome

ARDS—Acute respiratory distress syndrome

ATN—Acute tubular necrosis

ARB—Add angiotensin receptor blocker

ADP—Adenosine diphosphate

ATPase—Adenosine triphosphatase

ATP—Adenosine triphosphate

ACTH—Adrenocorticotropic hormone

ALT—Alanine aminotransferase

A-a—Alveolar-arterial

AA—Amino acids

AT1—Amino acid transporter

NH_3—Ammonia

NH_4+—Ammonium

ACE—Angiotensin-converting enzyme

ANGII—Angiotensin II

ARBs—Angiotensin receptor blockers

AE1—Anion exchanger 1

ABI—Ankle-brachial index

AS—Ankylosing spondylitis

AWMI—Anterior wall myocardial infarction

anti-CCP—Anti-cyclic citrullinated peptide

ADH—Antidiuretic hormone

APC—Antigen-presenting cell

ANCA—Antineutrophil cytoplasmic autoantibody

ANA—Antinuclear antibody

APL—Antiphospholipid

ART—Antiretroviral treatment

ASCA—Anti-*Saccharomyces cerevisiae* antibody

TNF—Anti-tumor necrosis factor

AR—Aortic regurgitation

AS—Aortic stenosis

ABG—Arterial blood gas

AV—Arteriovenous

AST—Aspartate aminotransferase

AFib—Atrial fibrillation

ANP—Atrial natriuretic peptide

AV—Atrioventricular

ASCT—Autologous stem cell transplant

BPH—Benign prostatic hyperplasia

HMG-CoA—Beta-hydroxy-beta-methylglutarylcoenzyme A

BiPAP—Bilevel positive airway pressure

BP—Blood pressure

BUN—Blood urea nitrogen

BMT—Bone marrow transplant

BRCA—Breast cancer antigen

BAL—Bronchoalveolar lavage

BNP—B-type natriuretic peptide

CREST—Calcinosis cutis, Raynaud phenomenon, esophageal motility disorder, sclerodactyly, and telangiectasia

CCBs—Calcium channel blockers

CO_2—Carbon dioxide

CA II—Carbonic anhydrase II

CO—Carbon monoxide

COHg—Carboxyhemoglobin

CMC—Carpometacarpal

COMT—Catechol-*O*-methyltransferase

CDC—Center for Disease Control and Prevention

CDI—Central diabetes insipidus

CNS—Central nervous system

CSF—Cerebrospinal fluid

CT—Chest computed tomography

CLC-5—Chloride channel 5

CLC-Kb—Chloride channel Kb

CHF—Congestive heart failure

COPD—Chronic obstructive pulmonary disease

CAP—Community-acquired pneumonia

CBCs—Complete blood counts

CHEM-20—Comprehensive metabolic panel

CT—Computed tomography

CCS—Computer-based case simulation

CURB—Confusion, uremia, respiratory distress, BP low

CPAP—Continuous positive airway pressure

BP—Control blood pressure

CRH—Corticotropin-releasing hormone

CRP—C-reactive protein

CK—Creatine kinase

CK-MB—Creatine kinase myocardial band

CPK—Creatine phosphokinase

CK—Creatinine kinase

CJD—Creutzfeldt-Jakob disease

CD—Crohn disease

cAMP—Cyclic adenosine monophosphate

cGMP—Cyclic guanosine monophosphate

CMV—Cytomegalovirus

cANCA—Cytoplasmic antineutrophil cytoplasmic antibody

DAF—Decay-accelerating factor

DTRs—Deep tendon reflexes

DVT—Deep venous thrombosis

DHEA—Dehydroepiandrosterone

DM—Dermatomyositis

DDAVP—Desmopressin acetate

D5W—Dextrose 5% in water

DI—Diabetes insipidus

DLCO—Diffusing capacity of the lungs for carbon monoxide

DSA—Digital subtraction angiography

DPP-IV—Dipeptidyl peptidase IV

DM—Disease management

DMARDs—Disease-modifying antirheumatic drugs

DCT—Distal convoluted tubule

DIP—Distal interphalangeal

dsDNA—Double-stranded DNA

EF—Ejection fraction

ECG—Electrocardiogram

EMG—Electromyography

ED—Emergency department

ERCP—Endoscopic retrograde cholangiopancreatography

EUS—Endoscopic ultrasound

ESRD—End-stage renal disease

ENaC—Epithelial sodium channel

EBV—Epstein-Barr virus

ESR—Erythrocyte sedimentation rate

EPO—Erythropoietin

ER—Estrogen receptor

FSPs—Fibrin split products

5-FC—5-Flucytosine

FTA—Fluorescent treponemal antibody

FTA-ABS—Fluorescent treponemal antibody absorption

FSH—Follicle-stimulating hormone

FEF25–75%—Forced expiratory flow 25% to 75%

FEV_1—Forced expiratory volume at 1 second

FiO_2—Forced inspiratory oxygen

FVC—Forced vital capacity

Fab—Fragment antigen binding

FFP—Fresh frozen plasma

GABA—Gamma-aminobutyric acid

GGTP—Gammaglutamyl transferase

ZES—Gastrinoma

GERD—Gastroesophageal reflux disease

GI—Gastrointestinal

GFR—Glomerular filtration rate

GLP—Glucagonlike peptide

GIP—Glucose-dependent insulinotropic peptide

G6P—Glucose-6-phosphate

G6PD—Glucose-6-phosphate dehydrogenase

HbA$_1$c—Glycated hemoglobin

GSK3—Glycogen synthase kinase 3

GPI—Glycosylphosphatidylinositol

GnRH—Gonadotropin-releasing hormone

GH—Growth hormone

GBS—Guillain-Barré syndrome

HEENT—Head, ears, eyes, nose, throat

HFE—Hemochromatosis

Hb—Hemoglobin

HgBart—Hemoglobin Bart's

HUS—Hemolytic uremic syndrome

HIT—Heparin-induced thrombocytopenia

HMP—Hexose monophosphate

HDL—High-density lipoprotein

HCG—Human chorionic gonadotropin

HIV—Human immunodeficiency virus

HLA—Human leukocyte antigen

HLA-B27—Human Leukocyte Antigen B27

HD—Huntington disease

HCTZ—Hydrochlorothiazide

11-HSD—11-Hydroxysteroid dehydrogenase

HOCM—Hypertrophic obstructive cardiomyopathy

ITP—Idiopathic thrombocytopenic purpura

IgA—Immunoglobulin A

IgE—Immunoglobulin E

IgG—Immunoglobulin G

IgM—Immunoglobulin M

IVC—Inferior vena cava

IBD—Inflammatory bowel disease

IDU—Injection drug use

IGF—Insulinlike growth factor

IRSs—Insulin receptor substrates

ICU—Intensive care unit

IFN—Interferon

IGRA—Interferon gamma release assay

IL—Interleukin

INR—International normalized ratio

ISUP—International Society of Urological Pathology

IM—Intramuscularly

IV—Intravenous

IVIG—Intravenous immunoglobulin

IVIG—IV immunoglobulin

JAK2—Janus kinase 2

JVD—Jugulovenous distention

LDH—Lactate dehydrogenase

LA—Left atrium

LBBB—Left bundle branch block

LV—Left ventricle

LVESD—Left ventricular end-systolic diameter

LVH—Left ventricular hypertrophy

LAP—Leukocyte alkaline phosphatase

LFTs—Liver function tests

LATS—Long-acting thyroidstimulator

LOC—Loss of consciousness

LDL—Low-density lipoprotein

LES—Lower esophageal sphincter

LMWH—Low molecular weight heparin

LP—Lumbar puncture

LH—Luteinizing hormone

MRCP—Magnetic Resonance Cholangiopancreatography

MRI—Magnetic resonance imaging

MH—Malignant hyperthermia

MCV—Mean corpuscular volume

MAC—Membrane attack complex

6MP—6-Mercaptopurine

mRNA—Messenger RNA

MCP—Metacarpophalangeal

MTP—Metatarsophalangeal

MetHb—Methemoglobin

MRSA—Methicillin-resistant *Staphylococcus aureus*

MTX—Methotrexate

MMA—Methylmalonic acid

MAP—Mitogenactivating protein

MR—Mitral regurgitation

MS—Mitral stenosis

MRM—Modified radical mastectomy

MAO—Monamine oxidase

MGUS—Monoclonal gammopathy of unknown significance

MALToma—Mucosa-associated lymphoid tissue lymphoma
MUGA—Multigated angiogram
MEN—Multiple endocrine neoplasia
MuSK—Muscle specific kinase
MG—Myasthenia gravis
MI—Myocardial infarction
NAC—N-acetylcysteine
NG—Nasogastric
NDI—Nephrogenic diabetes insipidus
NCV—Nerve conduction velocity
NMS—Neuroleptic malignant syndrome
NADP—Nicotinamide adenine dinucleotide phosphate
NO—Nitric oxide
NMDA—N-methyl-D-aspartate
NHL—Non-Hodgkin lymphoma
NSAIDs—Nonsteroidal anti-inflammatory drugs
NSTEMI—Non-ST segment elevation MI
NE—Norepinephrine
NS—Normal saline
NAAT—Nucleic acid amplification test
OA—Osteoarthritis
GSSG—Oxidized glutathione
Pap—Papanicolaou
PTH—Parathyroid hormone
PD—Parkinson disease
PNH—Paroxysmal nocturnal hemoglobinuria
PCO_2—Partial pressure of carbon dioxide
PO_2—Partial pressure of oxygen
PCI—Percutaneous coronary intervention
PAD—Peripheral arterial disease
PIGA—Phosphatidylinositol glycan anchor biosynthesis class A
6PG—6-Phosphogluconate
P-32—Phosphorus
PE—Physical examination
PCP—Pneumocystis jiroveci pneumonia
PAN—Polyarteritis nodosa
PCR—Polymerase chain reaction
PMNLs—Polymorphonuclear Leukocytes

PMR—Polymyalgia rheumatica
PM—Polymyositis
PM-DM—Polymyositis-dermatomyositis
PET—Positron emission tomography
PGY1—Postgraduate year 1
PGY3—Postgraduate year 3
PHN—Postherpetic neuralgia
KOH—Potassium hydroxide
PVCs—Premature ventricular contractions
PR—Progesterone receptor
PSA—Prostate specific antigen
PT—Prothrombin time
PPIs—Proton pump inhibitors
PIP—Proximal interphalangeal
PA—Pulmonary artery
PE—Pulmonary embolus
PFTs—Pulmonary function tests
PPD—Purified protein derivative
RPR—Rapid plasma reagin
RANKL—Receptor activator of nuclear factor kappa B ligand
RBC—Red blood cell
RDW—Red blood cell distribution width
RBCs—Red blood cells
GSH—Reduced glutathione
rBAT—Renal basic amino acid transport glycoprotein
RTA—Renal tubular acidosis
RV—Residual volume
RA—Rheumatoid arthritis
RF—Rheumatoid factor
RhoGAM—RhO(D) immune globulin
RV—Right ventricle
RL—Ringer lactate
SI—Sacroiliac
SERCA—Sarcoplasmic-endoplasmic reticulum calcium adenosine triphosphatase
SERMs—Selective estrogen receptor modulators
SSRI—Selective serotonin receptor inhibitor
SPEP—Serum protein electrophoresis

STD—Sexually transmitted disease
SS—Sickle cell
SA—Sinoatrial
NaK ATPase—Sodium- and potassium-activated adenosine triphosphatase
SAH—Subarachnoid hemorrhage
SVT—Supraventricular tachycardia
SIADH—Syndrome of inappropriate secretion of antidiuretic hormone
SLE—Systemic lupus erythematosus
SBP—Systolic blood pressure
TCR—T-cell receptor
Th1—T helper 1
NCCT—Thiazide-sensitive Na-Cl co-transporter
TAL—Thick ascending limb
TTP—Thrombotic thrombocytopenic purpura
TBG—Thyroid-binding globulin
TFTs—Thyroid function tests
TSH—Thyroid-stimulating hormone
TSH—Thyrotropin
TSH-R—Thyrotropin G-protein-coupled receptor
TRH—Thyrotropin-releasing hormone
T_4—Thyroxine
TPA—Tissue plasminogen activator
TIBC—Total iron-binding capacity
TLC—Total lung capacity
TEE—Transesophageal echocardiography
TIA—Transient ischemic attack

TRPM6—Transient receptor potential cation channel, subfamily M, member 6
TIPS—Transjugular intrahepatic portosystemic shunt
TTE—Transthoracic echocardiogram
TCAs—Tricyclic antidepressants
T_3—Triiodothyronine
TMP-SMZ—Trimethoprim-sulfamethoxazole
TB—Tuberculosis
TNF—Tumor necrosis factor
TNF-alpha—Tumor necrosis factor alpha
UC—Ulcerative colitis
US—Ultrasound
UA—Urinalysis
UTI—Urinary tract infection
UAG—Urine anion gap
VZIG—Varicella-zoster immune globulin
VZV—Varicella-zoster virus
VEGF—Vascular endothelial growth factor
VIP—Vasoactive intestinal peptide
VDRL—Venereal Disease Research Laboratory
VBGs—Venous blood gasses
VQ—Ventilation-perfusion
V:Q—Ventilation-to-perfusion ratio
VT—Ventricular tachycardia
vWD—Von Willebrand disease
vWF—Von Willebrand factor
WBCs—White blood cells
WPW—Wolff-Parkinson-White
ZES—Zollinger-Ellison syndrome

Internal
Medicine

Correlations and **C**linical **S**cenarios

CHAPTER **1**

CARDIOLOGY

CASE 1: Pulmonary Edema

Setting: *emergency department (ED)*

CC: *"I can't breathe."*

VS: *R: 28 breaths/minute; BP: 150/98 mm Hg; P: 118 beats/minute; T: 97°F*

HPI: *A 63-year-old woman presents to the ED with shortness of breath that started earlier in the day and worsened over several hours. She says the dyspnea is "like swimming a whole pool underwater." It is worsened by exertion and relieved by sitting up.*

She has a history of hypertension and a myocardial infarction 2 years ago. She takes "a bunch of pills" every day, which she cannot remember the name of. Her physician does not have privileges at your hospital, so the record is not available.

ROS:
• *No chest pain*
• *No history of valve disease*

PE:
• *Chest: rales 2/3 up bilaterally*
• *Cardiovascular: jugulovenous distention (JVD), an extra sound on auscultation*
• *Extremities: bilateral pitting edema up to the knees*

What is the mechanism of the finding on the heart examination?

a. Rapid filling of the ventricle during diastole

b. Rupture of the chordae tendineae

c. Fibrinous exudate in between the heart and the pericardium

d. Aberrant conduction tract at the atrioventricular (AV) node

e. Increased gradient of pressure between the left ventricle (LV) and the aorta

Answer a. Rapid filling of the ventricle during diastole

An S_3 gallop is most likely in pulmonary edema from congestive heart failure (CHF). When the mitral valve opens in diastole, the massive fluid overload in the lungs rapidly spills into the ventricle making a "splash" of fluid called an "S_3 gallop."

Rupture of the chordae tendineae (choice b) happens acutely as a complication of myocardial infarction 1 to 2 weeks after the muscle dies and necroses. Fibrinous exudate (choice c) is the cause of a rub in pericarditis. Aberrant conduction (choice d) is from short PR or preexcitation syndromes such as Wolff-Parkinson-White (WPW) syndrome. The

1

auscultatory finding of WPW is a loud S_1 from early closure of the mitral valve. Increased gradient of pressure is from aortic stenosis. The stenotic valve blocks flow out, so that in severe disease, the pressure in the LV is 50 to 70 mm Hg greater than what is found in the aorta.

> Orthopnea is venous pooling in the chest when lying flat.

Edema is found on examination. What is the mechanism?

a. Decreased hydrostatic pressure of the interstitial fluid

b. Decreased oncotic pressure

c. Alteration of the diffusion coefficient (K_F) of the capillary

d. Increased hydrostatic pressure in the peripheral capillaries

e. Increased hydrostatic pressure in the glomerular capillaries

Answer d. Increased hydrostatic pressure in the peripheral capillaries

Peripheral edema of CHF is from back pressure from the heart resulting in increased hydrostatic pressure in peripheral capillaries. Because of gravity, the lowest, or most "dependent" areas of the body have the highest hydrostatic pressure. This increases filtration across the capillary membrane. There is no change in the oncotic pressure in CHF, and the intrinsic nature of the capillary wall, or K_F, does not change.

The patient is moved from the stretcher in the triage area of the ED already wearing a face mask for oxygen set at 50% forced inspiratory oxygen (FiO_2). The nurses sit her upright.

Initial Orders:

- *Oxygen*
- *Oximeter continuously*
- *Furosemide and morphine IV*
- *Nitroglycerin (paste cutaneously)*
- *Chest x-ray, electrocardiogram (ECG), arterial blood gas (ABG) analysis*
- *B-type natriuretic peptide (BNP) for equivocal cases when diagnosis is uncertain*

As you move the clock forward 15 to 30 minutes, the patient begins to feel better. If a loop diuretic such as furosemide is effective, urine will be made within 30 minutes. If not, give an additional IV dose of a loop diuretic at least every 30 minutes until urine is made. Make sure you repeat vital signs in acutely ill patients every 15 to 30 minutes especially when giving medications that can lower blood pressure (BP) such as diuretics, nitrates, morphine, and angiotensin-converting enzyme (ACE) inhibitors. On a single-best-answer question, never consult a cardiologist for pulmonary edema management. You are expected to manage cases like this on your own. The majority of patients with acute pulmonary edema will respond to preload reduction alone.

> Nitrates:
> • Mainly venous dilators
> • Decrease preload more than afterload

If furosemide is not in the choices, which drug should you choose as an alternative that has the same mechanism of action?

a. Spironolactone

b. Acetazolamide

c. Bumetanide

d. Chlorthalidone

e. Conivaptan

Answer c. Bumetanide

The loop diuretics are furosemide, bumetanide, torsemide, and ethacrynic acid. They inhibit the $Na^+/K^+/2Cl^-$ pump in the thick ascending limb of the loop of Henle. This is the site where 25% of sodium is reabsorbed in the kidney. Spironolactone blocks aldosterone's effect at the late distal tubule and early collecting duct. Spironolactone and eplerenone specifically block the epithelial sodium channel (ENaC). Acetazolamide inhibits carbonic anhydrase. It is effective at the proximal tubule and is rarely used as a diuretic and never for acute pulmonary edema. Chlorthalidone is a thiazide diuretic inhibiting approximately 6% to 7% of total sodium absorption at the distal tubule. Conivaptan inhibits the V_2 receptor of the collecting duct. V_2-receptor antagonists are replacing demeclocycline in the treatment of the syndrome of inappropriate secretion of antidiuretic hormone (SIADH). Conivaptan and tolvaptan exclusively block water reabsorption by blocking antidiuretic hormone (ADH).

> *After a second dose of furosemide, the patient fails to produce urine in significant amount and her shortness of breath worsens. Her respiratory rate increases from 26 to 36 breaths/minute. Her BNP level is markedly elevated, but it is of marginal value in a person who comes in with an obvious presentation of pulmonary edema.*

Which test will make the most difference in the management of acute pulmonary edema?

a. BNP

b. Chest x-ray

c. ABG

d. ECG

e. Echocardiogram

Answer d. ECG

If the ECG shows an arrhythmia such as ventricular tachycardia (VT) or atrial fibrillation (AFib) or flutter, you may be able to quickly restore cardiac output by performing immediate synchronized cardioversion. In a healthy person, atrial systole provides only a small amount to the overall LV filling and cardiac output, on the order of 10% to 15%. In a person with dilated cardiomyopathy or valve disease, atrial systole or "kick" is essential to providing a much greater percentage, such as 30% to 50%. With cardiomyopathy, AFib can propel the patient into flash pulmonary edema. Echocardiography does not change acute management. It is essential to long-term treatment to know if there is systolic or diastolic dysfunction, but this has no effect on acute pulmonary edema management.

You move the clock forward 10 to 20 minutes, and the results of the test are automatically sent to you. You will receive the notice, "report available."

- *ECG: Sinus tachycardia*
- *ABG: pH 7.48; partial pressure of carbon dioxide (PCO_2) 28 mm Hg; partial pressure of oxygen (PO_2) 58 mm Hg on 50% face mask*
- *Chest x-ray: Pulmonary vascular congestion, cardiac enlargement, and pleural effusion*

Pleural effusion in CHF is from increased pulmonary capillary hydrostatic pressure. The mechanism is the same as in peripheral edema (Figure 1-1).

Atrial stretch creates BNP production. BNP excretes water and salt through the kidney.

Additional doses of diuretic and morphine are given. IV nitroglycerin is given with no effect. As you move the clock forward, oxygen saturation on 50% or 100% face mask hovers near 90%. Always recheck vital signs every 15 to 30 minutes in patients as unstable as this.

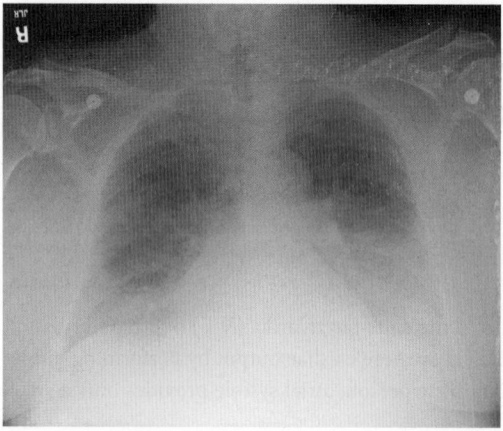

Figure 1-1. Pulmonary edema. Note indistinct vasculature, perihilar opacities, and peripheral interstitial reticular opacities. Although this is an anteroposterior film, making cardiac size more difficult to assess, the cardiac silhouette still appears enlarged. (Reproduced with permission from Loscalzo J. *Harrison's Pulmonary and Critical Care Medicine*, 2nd ed. New York: McGraw-Hill Education; 2013.)

On the computer-based case simulation (CCS), you should order a consultation with cardiology and critical care on a patient not responding to preload reduction. Consultants on CCS will never give specific treatment or testing advice.

**Maximum Preload Treatment + Persistent Hypoxia
= Intensive Care Unit Placement**

Morphine works by dilating pulmonary veins and decreasing hydrostatic pressure in capillaries.

What is the mechanism of the medication you should try next?

a. Dilation of afferent arteriole of glomerulus

b. Beta-hydroxy-beta-methylglutaryl-coenzyme A (HMG-CoA) reductase inhibition

c. Vasoconstriction of arterioles

d. Positive inotrope and vasodilation

e. Venodilation

Answer d. Positive inotrope and vasodilation

Dobutamine acts as both a positive inotrope, increasing contractility, and as a peripheral vasodilator. This allows greater forward flow of blood. Dopamine will increase contractility but is a vasoconstrictor on peripheral vessels. Dopamine increases afterload.

The patient in placed on dobutamine and transferred to the intensive care unit (ICU). Many patients in these circumstances are intubated for mechanical ventilation. If your case describes a failure to improve with dobutamine or the phosphodiesterase inhibitors milrinone or inamrinone, then intubation is correct. Continuous positive airway pressure (CPAP) or bilevel positive airway pressure (BiPAP) can be tried to keep the patient from being intubated. Ventilators have frequent complications with pneumonia, and CPAP or BiPAP can save a person from this complication.

On Step 3 CCS, it is unlikely to combine the details of acute pulmonary edema management with long-term treatment issues such as ACE inhibitors, angiotensin receptor blockers (ARBs), beta-blockers, spironolactone, and digoxin. These issues are addressed in separate cases.

The final point of management addressed is why a patient develops acute pulmonary edema. Less than 0.1% of patients with CHF are admitted in this condition. If someone presents with acute pulmonary edema, the most likely precipitants of decompensation are

- *Nonadherence to medication*
- *Ischemia*
- *Arrhythmia*
- *Infection*

If you see patients who are taking their medications but still develop pulmonary edema, the most important first step is to exclude arrhythmia. If there are no arrhythmias, you must exclude ischemia as a cause of decompensation. People do not develop pulmonary edema for no reason. Exclude coronary artery disease when you have no clear reason for the acute episode of pulmonary edema.

Pulmonary Edema Precipitants
• Ischemia
• Arrhythmia
• Infection
• Nonadherence to medications

CASE 2: Congestive Heart Failure

CC: *"I've been short of breath off and on for a few months."*

VS: *R: 18 breaths/minute; BP: 142/92 mm Hg; P: 78 beats/minute; T: 97°F*

HPI: *A 54-year-old man with a history of hypertension for the last 5 years presents to the ambulatory care center with intermittent episodes of dyspnea. These episodes are worse with exertion, particularly walking up stairs.*

ROS:
• *No chest pain*
• *No palpitation*
• *No syncope*
• *Occasional orthopnea and paroxysmal nocturnal dyspnea*

PE:
• *Cardiovascular: no JVD, 2/6 murmur at the apex radiating to the axilla, S_4 gallop*
• *Extremities: 2⁺ pitting edema*

What is the mechanism of the S_4 gallop on examination?

a. Rapid ventricular filling in diastole

b. Calcification of the mitral valve

c. Atrial systole into the noncompliant ventricle

d. Shunt from left to right

Answer c. Atrial systole into the noncompliant ventricle

Normally, the atrium should contract and the blood will easily enter the ventricle without a sound. This is because the ventricle should relax to receive the blood. Hypertension causes thickening of the LV. Compliance = volume change/pressure change. A *noncompliant* ventricle exhibits a *large change in pressure* with only a small change in volume.

Calcification of the mitral valve (choice b) is from mitral stenosis. Mitral stenosis gives a diastolic murmur. Shunt from left to right (choice d) is a ventricular septal defect, which gives a continuous "machinery murmur."

Initial Orders:
- *ECG*
- *Chest x-ray*
- *Transthoracic echocardiogram*

On a CCS case, as you move the clock forward, results of tests will automatically be sent to your screen. You will see the notice "report available." **In a relatively stable office or ambulatory case, you do not have to see the patient each time a result comes back. You can let the test results accumulate and see the patient in 1 to 2 weeks for a case such as this.**

Test Results:
- *ECG: left ventricular hypertrophy, SV_1 and RV_s >35 mm*
- *Chest x-ray: left ventricular hypertrophy*
- *Echocardiogram: dilated left ventricle; 32% ejection fraction (EF); modest mitral regurgitation (MR)*
- *Some segmental wall motion abnormalities present*

Because of dilated cardiomyopathy, you start an ACE inhibitor, such as lisinopril or enalapril. CCS does not allow you to test doses, and you cannot order medications by class name. You must enter "lisinopril" on a CCS case, and are not allowed to order just "ACE inhibitor." In a single-best-answer question, never order a cardiology consultation in a CHF case. You are expected to manage CHF without consultation. **The only way to know if this person had systolic or diastolic dysfunction is with echocardiogram. Hypertension initially gives hypertrophic cardiomyopathy, but over time, the heart tires and begins to dilate. This can eventually lead to a dilated cardiomyopathy.**

What is the main difference between ACE inhibitors?

a. Efficacy in lowering mortality in CHF
b. Usefulness in hypertension
c. Dosing
d. Propensity to cause cough
e. Propensity to cause hyperkalemia

Answer c. Dosing

The only major difference between ACE inhibitors is dosing. All lower mortality in systolic dysfunction and all cause cough and hyperkalemia.

ACE increases bradykinin, which causes cough.

ACE inhibitors increase potassium by blocking aldosterone release.

Which of the following is most likely to lower this patient's mortality?

a. Metoprolol
b. Digoxin
c. Furosemide

d. Spironolactone
e. Hydrochlorothiazide

Answer a. Metoprolol

Beta-blockers lower mortality in systolic dysfunction. The effect of beta-blockers is not ubiquitous to the entire class of medications. Beta-blockers useful for CHF are:

- Metoprolol
- Carvedilol
- Bisoprolol

Digoxin does not lower mortality in CHF. Spironolactone is most useful in severe class III and IV CHF in which there is dyspnea with minimal exertion or at rest. Loop diuretics such as furosemide are frequently used to decrease fluid overload, but they do not lower mortality. Thiazide diuretics are used for hypertension, but the effect in CHF is not beneficial beyond just controlling BP.

The patient returns a week after starting the ACE inhibitor and beta-blocker. He denies having a cough, but his dyspnea is not improved. You increase the dose, and on follow-up a week later, he is still symptomatic. Spironolactone is added orally. Although spironolactone was invented as a potassium-sparing diuretic, the dose used in CHF is well below the diuretic dose. Like most medications in CHF that lower mortality, it is used to inhibit the rennin-angiotensin-aldosterone system. Loop diuretics such as furosemide are used to control symptoms of fluid overload such as edema. Two weeks later, the patient's symptoms of dyspnea are well controlled.

Which should you test for?

a. Potassium level
b. Sodium level
c. Repeat echocardiogram

d. Holter (24-hour) ambulatory ECG monitor
e. Urine electrolytes

Answer a. Potassium level

All the medications the patient is on can alter the potassium level. ACE inhibitors, beta-blockers, and mineralocorticoid-receptor blockers such as spironolactone can increase potassium levels, and furosemide can lower potassium levels. Although CHF and a number of the medications used can alter sodium levels, there is no point in routinely monitoring the blood or urine sodium level because there is nothing you will do different therapeutically. In the absence of symptoms, neither the Holter monitor nor echocardiogram are useful. To assess intermittent arrhythmia, such as nonsustained VT or AFib, 24-hour ambulatory ECG or Holter monitoring is useful. If there is severe hyperkalemia with the use of ACE inhibitors or ARBs, the solution is to switch to hydralazine and nitrates. This combination both dilates arterioles directly with hydralazine and dilates coronary arteries so blood is not "stolen" away from the coronary arteries.

> Furosemide inhibits potassium reabsorption at the thick ascending limb of the loop of Henle.

> *If there are persistent symptoms despite the use of ACE inhibitors, beta-blockers, spironolactone, and loop diuretics, the next medication to add is digoxin. Digoxin does not lower mortality. This is the most commonly tested point about digoxin. It decreases symptoms and decreases rates of hospitalization, but does not lower mortality.*

Which of these is most likely to inhibit androgens?

a. Enalapril
b. Losartan
c. Carvedilol
d. Spironolactone
e. Digoxin
f. Furosemide
g. Indapamide
h. Hydrochlorothiazide

Answer d. Spironolactone

Spironolactone is a direct antagonist of the androgens (dehydroepiandrosterone [DHEA] and androstenedione) that originate from the adrenal gland as well as an inhibitor of the gonadal androgen testosterone. It inhibits *both* the receptor as well as androgen production. When this occurs, switch spironolactone to eplerenone. Eplerenone has a proven mortality benefit without the antiandrogenic adverse effects. Spironolactone is so antiandrogenic that it is used with the specific therapeutic intent of inhibiting androgens in women with acne, hirsutism, and male pattern hair loss.

> *The vast majority of cases of CHF are controlled with ACE inhibitors, beta-blockers, spironolactone, diuretics, and digoxin. If the patient is still short of breath, and the QRS interval is wide, resynchronization with a biventricular pacemaker is very useful in getting both ventricles to contract together. An implantable defibrillator will decrease mortality, but because its only function is to restart the heart if the person actually has sudden death, it will not decrease symptoms.*
>
> *Ultimately, cardiac transplantation is sometimes needed if there are persistent symptoms despite maximum medical therapy.*

Do not combine ACE with ARB medication. Combining will not improve morbidity or lower mortality.

Which decreases mortality in diastolic dysfunction?

a. Metoprolol

b. Digoxin

c. Furosemide

d. Enalapril

e. Eplerenone

f. Valsartan

g. Nothing is proven to lower mortality in diastolic dysfunction.

Answer g. Nothing is proven to lower mortality in diastolic dysfunction.

Diastolic dysfunction is also called "heart failure with preserved EF" because there is a normal EF. There is no medication that is clearly proven to lower mortality in this diastolic dysfunction. We use beta-blockers, diuretics, and sometimes calcium channel blockers (CCBs), but that does not mean they are proven to lower mortality.

The most accurate method for assessing EF is nuclear ventriculogram or multigated angiogram (MUGA). Nucleotide angiography surpasses echocardiogram for accuracy of EF measurement.

CASE 3: Acute Coronary Syndrome

Setting: *ED*

CC: *"My chest hurts, Doc."*

VS: *R: 23 breaths/minute; BP: 144/94 mm Hg; P: 104 beats/minute; T: 99.8°F*

HPI: *A 68-year-old man who has had crushing, substernal chest pain for the past 15 to 20 minutes arrives at the ED. He immediately called 911 for an ambulance right after the pain began. He has had "chest discomfort" a few times before when walking up stairs in his home, but it was a "vague soreness" that lasted 1 to 2 minutes and stopped right after he got to the top of the stairs. Today, the pain was more severe in intensity and did not stop.*

PMI:

- *Hypertension*
- *Tobacco smoking—quit 5 years ago*
- *Hyperlipidemia*

Medications:

- *Nifedipine*
- *Vitamins*

PE:
- *Cardiovascular: normal*
- *Lung sounds normal*
- *Head, ears, eyes, nose, throat (HEENT): normal*

On the CCS, choose parts of the physical examination based on what *could be* abnormal.

Initial Orders:
- *ECG*
- *Creatine kinase myocardial band (CK-MB)*
- *Troponin*
- *Myoglobin*
- *Aspirin*
- *Nitroglycerin sublingual*
- *Morphine*

All patients admitted to the hospital need complete blood counts (CBCs), urinalysis (UA), basic metabolic panels, and chest x-rays.

As the clock is moved forward 15 to 20 minutes, the CK-MB, troponin, and myoglobin levels all revert to normal. The ECG shows ST-segment elevation in leads V_2 through V_4. The patient describes his pain as "sore, squeezing, and pressure-like." He is somewhat short of breath.

What test becomes abnormal first?

a. CK-MB

b. Troponin

c. Myoglobin

Answer **c.** Myoglobin

Myoglobin level increases as early as 1 to 4 hours after the onset of myocardial damage. Elevation of myoglobin level is absolutely *not* specific to cardiac muscle. You do *not* see an elevated myoglobin level because of its specificity to heart tissue. You order a myoglobin test because a normal test at 4 hours strongly excludes a current infarction. CK-MB and troponin levels do not begin to increase until 4 to 6 hours after the onset of damage.

What is the mechanism of the drug you should add?

a. Blockade of $P2Y_{12}$ adenosine diphosphate (ADP) receptor

b. Potentiation of antithrombin III

c. Thrombin inhibition

d. Plasmin inhibition

e. Dihydropyridine receptor inhibition

Answer a. Blockade of $P2Y_{12}$ ADP receptor

All patients with unstable angina (acute coronary syndrome [ACS]) need two antiplatelet medications. A second drug is added to aspirin. Clopidogrel, prasugrel, and ticagrelor work through inhibiting the ADP receptor on the platelet. Heparin is not as useful in an acute ST-segment elevation myocardial infarction (MI) as it is in unstable angina or non-ST segment elevation MI (NSTEMI).

• Potentiation of antithrombin III = heparin

• Thrombin inhibition = argatroban, lepirudin

• Plasmin inhibition = aminocaproic acid (This is *always* wrong in coronary syndromes.)

• Dihydropyridine receptor inhibition = CCB

> *Aspirin and clopidogrel are started. Nitroglycerin, morphine, ACE inhibitor, metopro-*
> *lol, and a statin are given as well.* Medications on CCS are considered to be administered
> as soon as you verify them on the electronic order system. There is no time delay to drug
> administration on CCS. *There is a modest improvement in pain and no change in vital*
> *signs. Angioplasty is superior to thrombolytics in terms of outcomes such as mortality, inci-*
> *dence of CHF, and recurrences of chest pain. Only 20% of hospitals in the United States*
> *can do urgent angioplasty with intervention.* Your question will clearly tell you if the cath-
> eterization laboratory is close enough to get the balloon inflated within 90 minutes of the
> patient with chest pain arriving at the ED.

Up to how long after the onset of chest pain should thrombolytics be given?

a. 30 minutes

b. 90 minutes

c. 3 hours

d. 4.5 hours

e. 12 hours

Answer e. 12 hours

Thrombolytics are useful for an ST-segment elevation MI for 12 hours after the onset of pain. They do not work for NSTEMI. Use them for 3 to 4.5 hours for a stroke. It is very easy to confuse the question "how long after *onset of pain*" with "how long after *coming to the*

ED" should thrombolytics be used. Once in the ED, you should have thrombolytics in the patient's needle within 30 minutes of coming to the door.

Tissue plasminogen activator (TPA) is good for 12 hours after onset of chest pain.

TPA is used *only* for chest pain with ST elevation and new left bundle branch block (LBBB).

The patient is at a hospital with an interventional cardiac catheterization laboratory. Percutaneous coronary intervention (PCI) is performed. A sirolimus-coated stent is placed and the vessel diameter is increased in size from 2 mm to 4 mm.

What is the increase in the amount of flow with this increase in vessel size?

a. 2×

b. 4×

c. 8×

d. 16×

Answer d. 16×

Use Poiseuille's equation: Flow is proportional to the radius raised to the fourth power. So a doubling in radius or diameter will increase flow by $2 \times 2 \times 2$ or 16 times. Flow is inversely proportional to the length of the tube and the viscosity of the liquid. Length and viscosity cannot be changed in coronary syndromes.

This equation explains why interventions that increase the interior lumen diameter are the ones that improve flow and mortality. Beta-blockers such as metoprolol lower mortality, but they are not as dependent on time. In other words, although it is urgent to deliver anticoagulants and PCI, you are not pressed for time in administering beta-blockers.

Mortality Benefit in Myocardial Infarction
- Aspirin
- Second antiplatelet drug
- Angioplasty
- Thrombolytics
- Beta-blockers
- Statins

CASE 4: Aortic Stenosis

Setting: *office or ambulatory care*

CC: *"I feel short of breath when I push myself."*

VS: *R: 12 breaths/minute; BP: 108/72 mm Hg; P: 64 beats/minute; T: 99.8°F*

HPI: *A 78-year-old man, who was a long-term patient of your partner, presents with exertional dyspnea. Shortness of breath has been occurring for several months. It is slowly getting worse, and he can count the number of steps he must take into his two-storey house before it happens. He now feels light-headed as well.*

ROS:
- *Denies chest pain*
- *Denies loss of consciousness*

PMHx:
- *Hypertension*
- *Hyperlipidemia*
- *Osteoarthritis*

Medications:
- *Enalapril*
- *Hydrochlorothiazide*
- *Ibuprofen*
- *Atorvastatin*

PE:
- *Cardiovascular: systolic murmur, crescendo-decrescendo heard best in the second right intercostal area*

Where will the murmur radiate to?

a. Axilla   **c.** Carotids
b. Lower left sternal border

Answer c. Carotids

Aortic stenosis (AS) murmur will project up the aorta toward the direction of the carotid arteries. MR radiates to the axilla. MR is pansystolic (or holosystolic) and will obscure hearing either S_1 or S_2. Aortic regurgitation (AR) radiates down the lower left sternal border. AR is a diastolic decrescendo murmur.

Why is there a delay between the closure of the mitral and tricuspid valves (S_1) and the beginning of the murmur?

a. Insufficient backflow of blood   **d.** Isovolumetric relaxation
b. Rapid aortic filling   **e.** Shunt circulation
c. Isovolumetric contraction

Answer c. Isovolumetric contraction

At the start of ventricular contraction, blood does not move across the aortic valve. It takes time for actin and myosin filaments to shorten and to increase LV pressure to the point where blood moves. Blood does not move until it exceeds diastolic pressure, which is usually around 80 mm Hg. When LV pressure exceeds diastolic pressure, the aortic valve will open and blood will exit the LV and enter the aorta. This is when the murmur occurs.

The murmur of AS is delayed after S_1 until LV pressure increases enough to open the aortic valve.

No Blood Movement = No Murmur

On auscultation, maneuvers are performed in the office to see what the diagnosis is, before an echocardiogram is performed. Squatting and leg raise increase venous return to the heart. Standing suddenly and the Valsalva maneuver will decrease venous return to the heart. This patient's murmur of AS will become louder with squatting and leg raises and quieter with standing and Valsalva maneuvers.

AS narrows the aortic valve. According to the Reynolds number, as diameter decreases, turbulence should decrease. Why does the narrowing caused by AS provide turbulence enough to produce a murmur, if the total flow is decreased?

a. Viscosity increases.

b. Viscosity decreases.

c. Velocity increases more than diameter decreases.

d. Increased filling actually increases total flow in AS.

e. Dilated cardiomyopathy compensates.

Answer c. Velocity increases more than diameter decreases.

Velocity is inversely proportional to surface area. As the surface area decreases, velocity increases. However, the velocity increases with the value of πr^2. Hence, you have less blood moving through the aortic valve, much faster. Flow is down, velocity is up. This is what creates the turbulence that produces a murmur that you can hear.

$$\text{Reynolds number} = \frac{\rho d v}{\eta}$$

where

ρ = density of blood

d = diameter of the blood vessel

v = velocity of blood flow

η = viscosity of blood

$v = Q/A$

And $A = A$ is the area, or πr^2

Initial Orders and Results:

• *Chest x-ray: left ventricular hypertrophy, clear lung fields*
• *ECG: left ventricular hypertrophy*
• *Echocardiogram: aortic stenosis, symmetrical ventricular hypertrophy*
• *Oximeter: normal*

The patient returns to discuss the findings with you after several weeks. His symptoms of breathlessness are about the same.

Which therapy will decrease the progression of AS?

a. Diuretics
b. ACE inhibitors
c. HMG-CoA reductase inhibitors (statins)

d. Beta-blockers
e. CCBs
f. None

Answer f. None

No medication has ever been shown to decrease the rate of progression of AS. AS is an idiopathic disorder of increasing fibrosis, sclerosis, and calcification of the aortic valve (Figure 1-2). None of these medications will decrease progression, and some, such as diuretics, can be dangerous in terms of decreasing LV filling pressure.

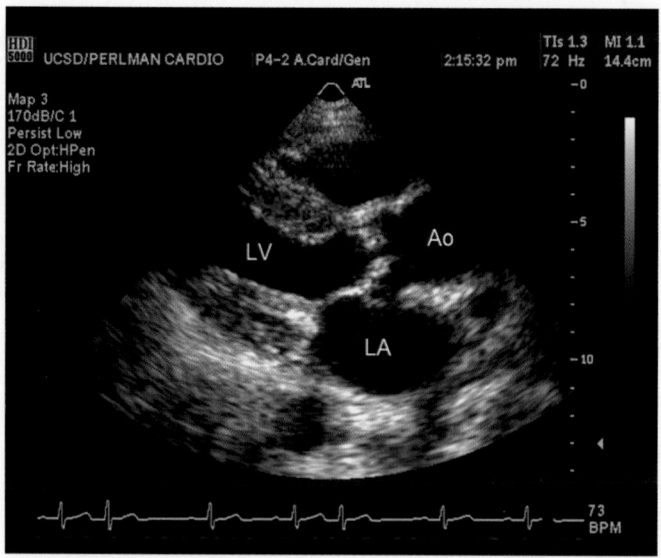

Figure 1-2. Parasternal long-axis plane demonstrating a thickened, stenotic aortic valve. Ao, aorta; LA, left atrium; LV, left ventricle. (Reproduced with permission from Fuster V, et al., ed. *Hurst's The Heart*, 13th ed. New York: McGraw-Hill; 2011.)

> *You move the clock forward 3 to 6 months on a CCS case.* The patient reports worsening dyspnea and he has had an episode of syncope. You recommend valve repair. He is now 79 years old.

Which is best for this patient?

a. Balloon valvuloplasty
b. Open aortic valve commissurotomy
c. Replace with metal valve
d. Replace with bioprosthetic valve

Answer d. Replace with bioprosthetic valve

Balloon valvuloplasty is not a good choice for stenotic aortic valves. The valve will only restenose and worsen. In addition, the procedure may simply create aortic regurgitation. The same is true of an open commissurotomy.

Replacement of aortic valves is clearly the best choice when symptoms of shortness of breath or syncope develop. A bioprosthetic valve is preferred because it does not need anticoagulation with warfarin. On average it will last 10 years, but in an elderly, relatively sedentary person, it may last 15 years. Metal valves need an international normalized ratio (INR) higher than 2 to 3 because metal valves are so thrombogenic. This puts an elderly person at very high risk of bleeding.

> *The patient refuses to undergo valve replacement surgery. He says, "I'm too old," and leaves the office. He comes back a few months later. His exercise tolerance has decreased, and he becomes dyspneic even walking across his own living room. He had two more episodes of syncope. He is now ready for valve replacement.*

What test should you do prior to surgery?

a. Holter monitor
b. Troponin or CK-MB
c. Arterial blood gas
d. Cardiac catheterization
e. Positron emission tomography (PET) scan

Answer d. Cardiac catheterization

There is a very high incidence of coronary artery disease in those with AS. Frequently, simultaneous coronary bypass surgery is done in 50% to 70% of patients. Troponin and CK-MB testing are only for ACS. A PET scan measures the uptake of 18-fluorodeoxyglucose. It is useful to tell the content of solid lesions to see if there is cancer inside. Cancers generally have an increased metabolic rate of glucose, and the PET scan will light up with a cancer.

Which has the shortest survival in AS?

a. Syncope
b. Angina
c. CHF
d. Left ventricular hypertrophy

Answer c. CHF

By the time the heart dilates in size, nothing can be done to restore it to normal size and shape. This is why replacement of the aortic valve should occur before cardiac dilation has occurred. Angina is the most common and earliest finding of AS and can be easily reversed by coronary bypass surgery.

CASE 5: Mitral Stenosis

Setting: *office or ambulatory clinic*

CC: *"I get short of breath."*

VS: *R: 26 breaths/minute; BP: 108/72 mm Hg; P: 104 beats/minute; T: 99.8°F*

HPI: *A 26-year-old woman comes to the office with increasing shortness of breath and palpitations over the last several months. She also has hemoptysis. She emigrated from South America several years ago. She has no fever.*

PMHx: *rheumatic fever as a child*

Medications: *none*

PE:
Cardiovascular:
• *Third heart sound in diastole just after S$_2$*
• *Diastolic rumbling murmur*
• *All heard best at apex*
• *Loud S$_1$*

What is the basis of the loud S$_1$?

a. Calcium is crunchy.
b. Fibrous bands are being broken.
c. The mitral valve is still open when LV pressure becomes high.
d. AFib eliminates atrial systole.
e. There is left ventricular noncompliance.

Answer c. The mitral valve is still open when LV pressure becomes high.

S$_1$ is created by the sound of the mitral valve closing. The loudness is created by a delay in closure from fibrous tissue delaying its movement. This means LV pressure builds to a much higher level before it closes than it would in a healthy person. It is like "slamming" a stuck door.

The sound is not caused by breaking either calcium or fibrous tissue. AFib does not impair mitral closure in anyone. The LV has normal compliance in mitral stenosis (MS). MS is a problem with emptying the atrium that has nothing to do with LV compliance.

Rheumatic fever is by far the most common cause of MS.

Loud S_1 is a "slam of the door."

What causes the hemoptysis?

a. Tricuspid stenosis
b. Left-to-right shunting
c. Right-to-left shunting
d. Pulmonary hypertension
e. Atrial septal defect

Answer d. Pulmonary hypertension

Stenosis of the mitral valve causes pulmonary hypertension. This "stretches" the vessels of the pulmonary vasculature until they burst. It is a kind of super-exaggerated increase in the hydrostatic pressure of the pulmonary veins to the point where the integrity of the delicate pulmonary capillaries bursts.

The majority of the symptoms of MS can be related back to the pulmonary hypertension.

• Dyspnea and orthopnea

• Ascites, edema, and hepatosplenomegaly if right heart failure occurs

Besides obstruction of flow, which of these contributes to create pulmonary hypertension?

a. Increased carbon dioxide (CO_2) content
b. Decreased pH
c. Hypoxia
d. Respiratory alkalosis

Answer c. Hypoxia

Hypoxia constricts pulmonary blood vessels. Pulmonary vasculature has profound auto-regulatory controls that shunt blood flow away from the hypoxic parts of the lung. This is because flow in the lungs is supposed to *collect* oxygen, therefore, vasoconstriction in hypoxic areas is to *decrease* flow away from those areas. If the whole lung has hypoxic flow, there will be a global vasoconstriction of the pulmonary vessels.

Pulmonary hypertension is the root of all MS symptoms.

The patient has been getting progressively more short of breath. Although dyspnea used to occur only with significant exertion, it is now interfering with the patient's ability to walk up stairs. She occasionally has palpitations. An ECG in the office shows normal sinus rhythm.

Initial Orders:

• *Chest x-ray*
• *Echocardiogram*

- *Basic metabolic panel (CHEM-7)*
- *Sodium-restricted diet*
- *Furosemide orally*

As you move the clock forward 3 to 4 days, the results come back as:

Chest x-ray:
- *Straightening of left heart border, elevation of left mainstem bronchus, second density behind the heart*

Echocardiogram:
- *Moderate MS with marked dilation of left atrium (LA)*
- *Valve diameter 1.2 cm²*
- *No thrombi in atrium*
- *Mild calcification of mitral valve*

Chemistry:
- *Sodium 129 mEq/L (normal 135–145 mEq/L)*
- *Blood urea nitrogen (BUN) 24 mg/dL (normal 6–14 mg/dL)*

On chest x-ray, what elevates the left mainstem bronchus?

a. The LV pushes it up.

b. The LA pushes it up.

c. The pulmonary artery is enlarged.

d. The right ventricle (RV) is hypertrophic.

Answer b. The LA pushes it up.

The LA is the most posterior structure in the heart. It sits behind the heart and can appear as a "double density" behind the heart. LA enlargement obliterates the aortopulmonary knob or window on the left-hand side (Figure 1-3).

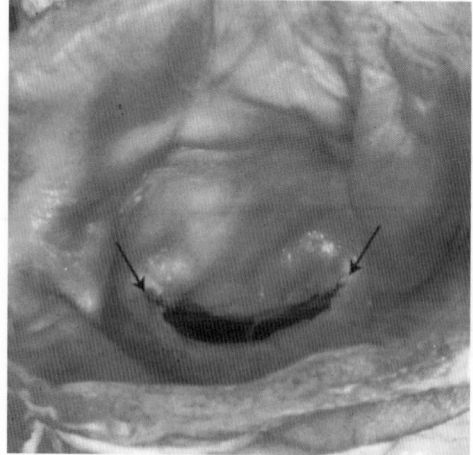

Figure 1-3. The typical fish-mouth appearance of rheumatic mitral stenosis is shown. (Reproduced with permission from Otto CM, ed. *Valvular Heart Disease*. Philadelphia, PA: Saunders; 1999:13–42.)

What is the mechanism of hyponatremia and high BUN?

a. From sodium-restricted diet
b. Atrial natriuretic peptide
c. Decreased aldosterone level

d. Decreased permeability of collecting duct
e. Decreased stimulation macula densa

Answer b. Increased ADH and atrial natriuretic peptide

Stretching of the atrium releases atrial natriuretic peptide (ANP) as it does in all forms of CHF or anything that increases fluid in the heart. It is very hard to decrease serum sodium levels just from a sodium-restricted diet. Low tissue perfusion and decreased sodium load to the kidney should increase stimulation of the macula densa and increase renin and not decrease it. Both low perfusion of the juxtaglomerular complex and stimulation of the macula densa will increase aldosterone levels, not decrease them in any form of CHF.

Low perfusion pressure of the carotid body will signal the brain to make more ADH in the hypothalamus. Increased ADH increases the permeability of the collecting duct; it does not decrease it. Increased permeability of the collecting duct will reabsorb free water into the body, not lose free water.

Decreased renal perfusion results in prerenal azotemia and an elevation of BUN. This is true of cirrhosis, nephrotic syndrome, or CHF.

Which finding will be present on ECG?

a. $SV_1 + RV_5 > 35$ mm
b. Enlarged P wave in V_1

c. Biphasic P wave in V_1
d. aVL > 13 mm

Answer c. Biphasic P wave in V_1

A biphasic P wave in V_1 is a sign of left atrial hypertrophy. The LA is the most posterior structure in the heart. Enlargement will pull electrical forces away from the anterior chest wall. The first deflection will be upright from the right atrium. The second deflection will be sharply posterior from the enlarged LA, pulling the electricity backward.

$SV_1 + RV_5 > 35$ mm or aVL > 13 mm = Left Ventricular Hypertrophy

Enlarged P wave in V_1 = Right Atrial Hypertrophy

Muscle = Electricity on Electrocardiogram

More Muscle = More Electricity

The patient comes back in 2 weeks to discuss her test results. Her symptoms are not better despite diuretics and salt restriction. Palpitations are more frequent. An in-office ECG shows AFib. You offer the patient balloon valvuloplasty, but she declines it. Metoprolol is started to control her heart rate. The patient does not return for 6 months. She is pregnant and her obstetrician has referred her to you because of markedly worse dyspnea, palpitations, and the new onset of dysphagia (Figure 1-4).

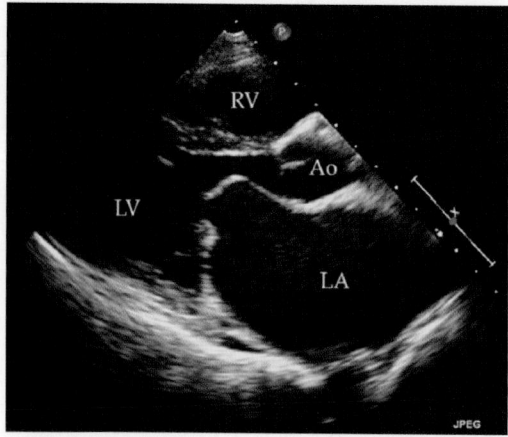

Figure 1-4. Parasternal long-axis view of mitral stenosis. The LA is enlarged, mitral opening is limited, and doming of the anterior mitral leaflet is present. Ao, aorta; LA left atrium; L, left ventricle; RV, right ventricle. (Reproduced with permission from Fuster V, et al., ed. *Hurst's The Heart*, 13th ed. New York: McGraw-Hill; 2011.)

Dysphagia in MS is from an enlarged LA pressing on the esophagus.

Plasma volume increases by 50% in pregnancy, worsening fluid overload in MS.

What is the mechanism of the increase in plasma volume in pregnancy?

a. Red blood cell production decreases.
b. Aldosterone level increases.
c. The maximum osmolarity of urine decreases.

d. Hypothalamic osmoreceptors reset and ADH level increases.
e. Glomerular filtration rate decreases.

Answer d. Hypothalamic osmoreceptors reset and ADH level increases.

Pregnancy changes the level at which the osmolarity receptors in the hypothalamus would shut off ADH production. ADH secretion continues at an osmolarity of 280 mOsm when a nonpregnant person would have it shut off. Pregnancy increases the glomerular filtration rate (GFR) and increases permeability of the collecting duct, thereby increasing free water reabsorption.

The patient agrees to balloon valvuloplasty in the sixth month of her pregnancy, which markedly relieves symptoms. To control her heart rate, metoprolol is continued.

Beta-blockers and calcium channel blockers are safe in pregnancy.

Endocarditis prophylaxis is *not* used for MS.

CASE 6: **Atrial Fibrillation**

Setting: *ED*

CC: *"I feel a fluttering in my chest."*

VS: *R: 32 breaths/minute; BP: 118/88 mm Hg; P:128 beats/minute, irregularly irregular; T: 98.1°F*

HPI: *A 42-year-old gastroenterologist comes to the office with 1 single day of palpitations and fluttering in his chest. He has never had this before. He denies chest pain, lightheadedness, or shortness of breath. He is very anxious. He drinks a large amount of vodka at night four to five times a week and frequently travels to present papers at international meetings.*

PMHx: *none*

Medications: *none*

Each part of the physical examination on CCS takes the same amount of time, no matter the case.

PE:
- *Neurological: normal*
- *Cardiovascular: no murmurs, rubs, or gallops*
- *Abdomen: normal*
- *Extremities: no edema*

Initial Orders:
- *ECG*
- *CHEM-7*
- *Chest x-ray*
- *Oximeter*
- *CBC*

As you move the clock forward 10 to 20 minutes, all the laboratory results come back as normal except for the ECG. The ECG shows AFib at a rate of 125 to 130 beats/minute. The QRS duration is normal (Figure 1-5).

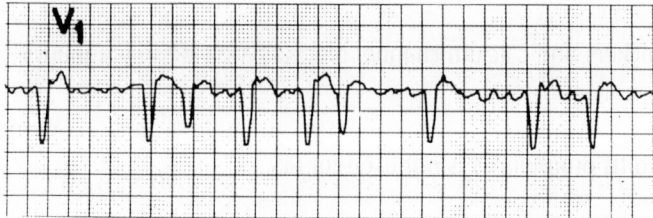

Figure 1-5. Atrial fibrillation. (Reproduced with permission from Tintinalli JE, et al. *Tintinalli's Emergency Medicine, A Comprehensive Study Guide*, 7th ed. New York: McGraw-Hill; 2011.)

When is immediate electrical cardioversion for AFib correct?

a. Palpitations not improved
with medication

b. Severe anxiety

c. Pallor, sweating, and decreased
capillary refill

d. BP 78/50 mm Hg and chest pain

Answer d. BP 78/50 mm Hg and chest pain

Electrical cardioversion is indicated for tachyarrhythmias when there is life-threatening hemodynamic instability, such as chest pain, CHF caused by the arrhythmia, decreased systolic BP, or hemodynamically related confusion.

Although uncomfortable, none of the other symptoms described here are severe enough to put the patient through the risk and discomfort of electrical cardioversion. Pallor, anxiety, sweating, and palpitations are all subjective, hard to measure, and not life-threatening.

> Cardioversion works by causing the simultaneous depolarization of all the myocytes in the heart.

What is the most common cause of AFib?

a. Caffeine

b. Cocaine

c. Hypertension

d. Hyperthyroidism

e. Ischemia (coronary disease)

Answer c. Hypertension

AFib occurs most commonly as a result of structural abnormalities of the heart caused by hypertension, cardiomyopathy, or valvular heart disease.

Although it is commonly believed that caffeine causes AFib, this has not been shown to be true. Caffeine and cocaine can speed up rate-controlled atrial arrhythmia, but it is unlikely that caffeine alone can cause AFib in a normal heart.

Hyperthyroidism can cause AFib, but it is a far less common cause than hypertensive heart disease. It is rare for ischemia or coronary disease to present with AFib in the absence of other structural heart disease.

The patient is uncomfortable from palpitations but is hemodynamically stable. What treatment is first?

a. Quinidine
b. Heparin
c. Warfarin

d. Metoprolol
e. Depends on results of the echocardiogram

Answer d. Metoprolol

Rate control with either a beta-blocker, CCB, or digoxin is the first step in managing rapid AFib. Rate control is more important than trying medications such as quinidine, amiodarone, flecainide, or propafenone to chemically convert AFib into normal sinus rhythm. Anticoagulation is not needed for AFib present for <48 hours. The echocardiogram results may help tell who needs anticoagulation, but controlling the rapid ventricular response is not dependent on echocardiogram findings.

What is the mechanism of rate control in AFib or flutter (Figure 1-6)?

a. Inhibition of "Funny" sodium channels in the sinoatrial (SA) node
b. Stimulation of outward potassium channels

c. Inhibition of conduction in the AV node
d. Blocking Purkinje fibers

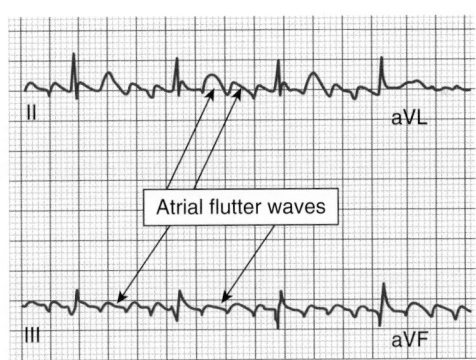

Figure 1-6. Atrial flutter. (Reproduced with permission from Conrad Fischer.)

Answer c. Inhibition of conduction in the AV node

Any beta-blocker will work to slow AV nodal conduction in atrial arrhythmias. Only the CCBs diltiazem or verapamil slow conduction to control rapid rate.

Alcohol intoxication causes atrial fibrillation.

After metoprolol or diltiazem, the patient's heart rate reduces to 80 beats/minute. All symptoms resolve. Admittance to the ICU is not necessary and the patient is placed on a regular hospital ward. Heparin is not necessary. The echocardiogram shows a normal heart size and shape with no significant valvular disease and no thrombi. The AFib does not stop, but the rate remains controlled and there are no symptoms.

What is the best therapy?

a. Aspirin

b. Warfarin

c. Dabigatran

d. Rivaroxaban

Answer a. Aspirin

CHADS is an acronym for risk factors for stroke in AFib. If the CHADS score is 0 or 1, aspirin alone is sufficient. If the CHADS score is 2 or more, use warfarin, dabigatran, or rivaroxaban.

> C = Congestive heart failure
> H = Hypertension
> A = Age >75 years
> D = Diabetes
> S = Stroke or transient ischemic attack (TIA) (Either of these alone is worth 2 points and indicates automatic anticoagulation medication.)

This patient has a CHADS score of zero, and aspirin alone is sufficient.

Dabigatran is a direct thrombin inhibitor. No INR monitoring is needed.

Rivaroxaban is a factor Xa inhibitor. No INR monitoring is needed.

CASE 7: Supraventricular Tachycardia, Ventricular Tachycardia, and Wolff-Parkinson-White Syndrome

Setting: *ED*

CC: *"I think I have palpitations."*

VS: *R: 34 breaths/minute; BP: 138/88 mm Hg; P: 160 beats/minute; T: 99.8°F*

HPI: *A 19-year-old woman presents to the ED complaining of palpitations. She is anxious and her chest is uncomfortable from the rapid heart rate. She is not confused, and there is no "chest pain." She is a generally healthy person, and this is the first time she has been to an ED. She drank four Red Bull energy drinks today.*

PMHx: *none*

Medications: *none*

Initial Orders:
- CHEM-7
- CBC
- Echocardiogram

- ECG
- Calcium and magnesium levels

What does the ECG show (Figure 1-7)?

a. AFib

b. Atrial flutter

c. Supraventricular tachycardia (SVT)

d. VT

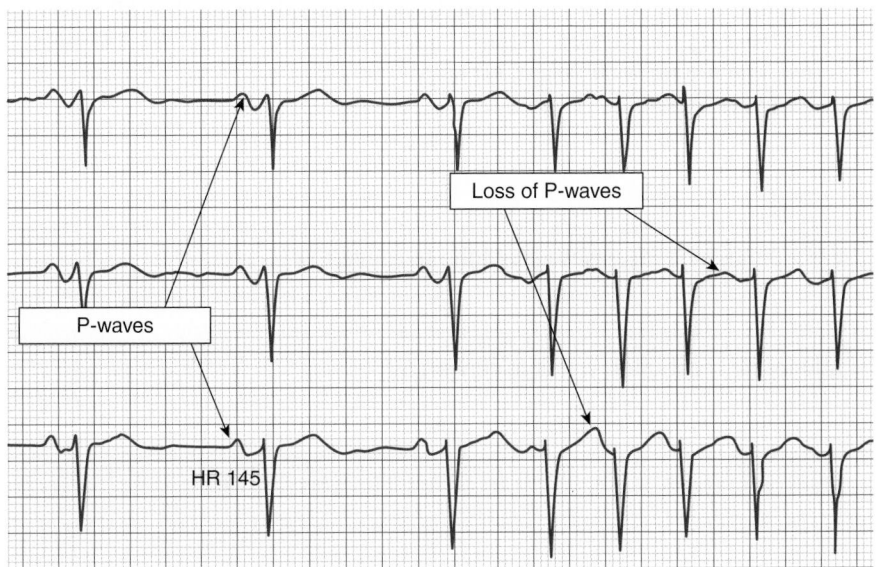

Figure 1-7. Supraventricular tachycardia. (Reproduced with permission from Conrad Fischer.)

Answer c. Supraventricular tachycardia (SVT)

The first part of the ECG reading, on the left, shows sinus rhythm because of the presence of P waves and a normal QRS duration <100 msec. On the right, there is a narrow complex (<100 msec) tachycardia with no P waves, no fibrillatory waves, and no flutter waves. That is the definition of SVT. If there are clear P waves, then it is not SVT.

SVT and atrial flutter are regular in rhythm. Fibrillation is irregular.

What is the mechanism of the patient's SVT today?

a. Caffeine

b. Ischemia

c. Abnormal conduction pathway at the
AV node

d. Ectopic focus in the ventricle

e. Thrombus in the atrium

Answer c. Abnormal conduction pathway at the AV node

The vast majority of SVT is based on abnormal "wiring" at the AV node or an AV nodal reentry. Caffeine does not create SVT. Ischemia is a prominent cause of ventricular arrhythmias but, virtually never, atrial arrhythmias. Ectopic ventricular foci create VT, not SVT. AFib leads to stasis in the atrium that creates thrombi, but thrombi do not create SVT.

The patient is lying on her stretcher continuing to feel palpitations. Her BP is now 112/82 mm Hg. Carotid sinus massage is attempted, but it is not effective. Adenosine is given with two sequential boluses, but the SVT persists. Move the clock forward 5 to 10 minutes on CCS after vagal maneuvers and adenosine administration.

Carotid massage increases vagal tone to convert SVT.

Adenosine most often works to convert SVT.

If you are uncertain about patient status, click on "Interval History" to get an update.

Because the patient is hemodynamically stable, there is no indication for cardioversion. Palpitations do not count as hemodynamic instability. BP remains at 118/80 mm Hg. Diltiazem or verapamil is given as an IV bolus, and you move the clock forward 5 to 10 minutes. All IV agents that may potentially affect the cardiac conduction system should

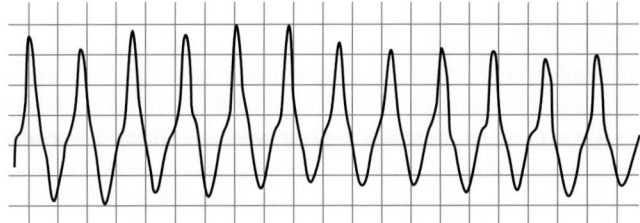

Figure 1-8. Ventricular tachycardia. (Reproduced with permission from Stern SDC, et al. *Symptom to Diagnosis: An Evidence-Based Guide.* New York: McGraw-Hill; 2010.)

be given under telemetry or continuous cardiac monitoring. *The telemetry monitor now shows VT (Figure 1-8).*

What should you do first?

a. Consult cardiology.
b. Transfer the patient to the ICU.
c. Check vital signs.
d. Perform synchronized cardioversion.
e. Perform unsynchronized cardioversion.

Answer c. Check vital signs.

Any change in a patient's cardiac rhythm requires the BP to be checked immediately. If VT results in hypotension, you need immediate synchronized cardioversion. If VT persists, but BP stays normal, use amiodarone first, possibly followed by lidocaine or procainamide if there is no response to amiodarone.

Do not *ever* order consultations for a person who is unstable and needs immediate help. The CCS Step 3 examination expects you to help the patient, not to defer responsibility. On CCS, consultants never tell you what to do. They just say "I saw your patient; I have no specific recommendations. Do what you think is right."

Do not *ever* transfer an unstable or potentially unstable patient to another part of the hospital without first starting treatment and ordering tests. Both a transfer and a consultation are inappropriate first responses on the Step 3 examination because they make you look like an idiot who cannot care for a sick patient.

Shock Unstable Ventricular Tachycardia
Unstable =
• Chest pain
• Systolic <90 mm Hg
• CHF
• Confusion from hypoperfusion

> *As you order vital signs, the clock will automatically move forward 2 minutes. If you have not already done so, order calcium, magnesium, oxygen, and potassium levels. Low levels of all of these are associated with developing arrhythmias, particularly ventricular arrhythmias. Do not wait for the results to give magnesium. Giving magnesium can help correct ventricular arrhythmia. Do not give calcium or potassium without being sure the level is low.*
>
> *When the clock is moved forward 2 minutes, the patient's BP is 140/90 mm Hg. Palpitations are the only symptom. VT persists.*

What should you do?

a. Perform synchronized cardioversion.   **c.** Give amiodarone.
b. Perform unsynchronized cardioversion.   **d.** Give quinidine.

Answer c. Give amiodarone.

Use amiodarone first for hemodynamically stable VT. Amiodarone is a clear first choice as an antiarrhythmic for both VT and ventricular fibrillation. Although lidocaine is a second-line drug, Step 3 does not put you in "hairsplitting" decisions where lidocaine *could be* a choice. The wrong answers are clearly wrong. Quinidine is a rarely used class Ia agent for atrial arrhythmias, and there is no point in cardioverting VT until medications have been tried and failed.

> *After amiodarone, the rhythm converts to normal sinus at a rate of 70 beats/minute. Symptoms of palpitations resolve.*

What most likely led to this situation in which SVT deteriorates to VT after the use of verapamil?

a. Dilated cardiomyopathy   **c.** WPW syndrome
b. Hypertrophic cardiomyopathy   **d.** Brugada syndrome

Answer c. WPW syndrome

WPW is notorious for worsening after the use of CCBs (Figure 1-9). WPW is one of the only syndromes to alternate SVT with VT. Dilated cardiomyopathy may have worsening systolic function with the use of a prominent negative inotrope such as verapamil, but neither dilated nor hypertrophic cardiomyopathy alone will result in an arrhythmia just from use of a CCB.

Brugada syndrome is a genetic disorder leading to syncope and sudden death in association with a right bundle branch block pattern on an ECG. It is more common in persons of Asian ethnicity.

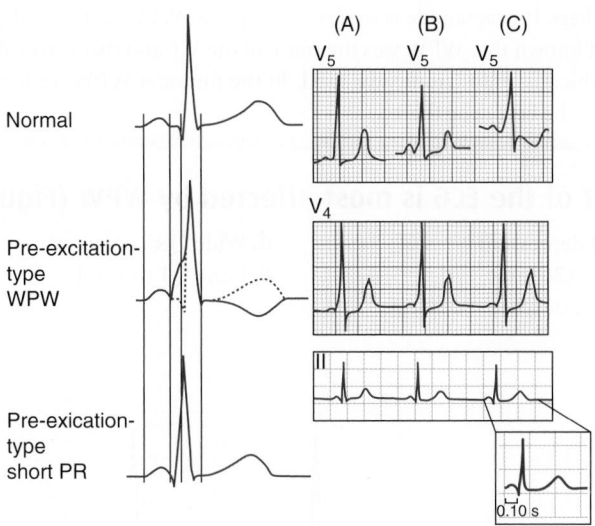

Figure 1-9. **Left:** Wolff-Parkinson-White (WPW)-type preexcitation and short PR-type preexcitation. **Right:** (*top*) Delta waves of different magnitude: (A) minor preexcitation and (B, C) significant preexcitation; **middle:** three consecutive QRS complexes with evident preexcitation; (*below*) short PR-type preexcitation. (Reproduced with permission from Fuster V, et al., ed. *Hurst's The Heart*, 13th ed. New York: McGraw-Hill; 2011.)

What is the mechanism of arrhythmia formation in WPW?

a. Elimination of normal AV node

b. Bundle branch block in ventricles

c. Accessory bundle of Kent

d. Loss of normal calcium channel in the AV node

Answer c. Accessory bundle of Kent

WPW is an anatomic defect in the conduction system of the AV node. An abnormal accessory pathway is present. Calcium channel blocking medications produce blockade in the normal AV nodal tissue forcing cardiac conduction down the abnormal accessory pathway in the bundle of Kent. This can lead to either SVT or VT, although SVT is more common.

Besides the CCBs that were used in this patient, what is the medication most dangerous in WPW?

a. Digoxin

b. Beta-blockers

c. Procainamide

d. Sotalol

Answer a. Digoxin

Digoxin has a strong blocking effect on normal AV nodal conduction tissue. This effect forces conduction down the abnormal pathway. This occurrence is much less common with beta-blockers. Procainamide is the best therapy for WPW during arrhythmia. In this case, it was not known that WPW was the cause of the VT and that is why the standard of care for VT, which is amiodarone, was used. In the future, if WPW leads to SVT or VT, procainamide is the best drug therapy.

Which part of the ECG is most affected by WPW (Figure 1-10)?

a. PR segment depression

b. PR interval <120 msec

c. PR interval >200 msec

d. Wide QRS complex

e. Long QT interval

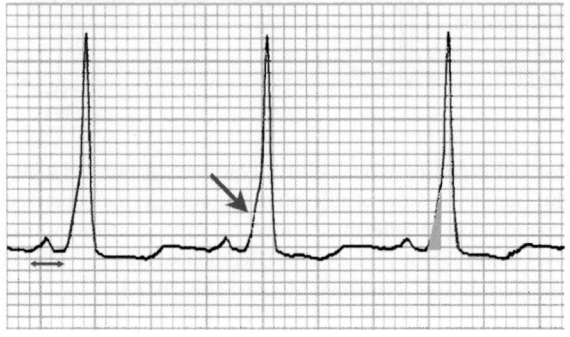

Figure 1-10. The PR interval is shortened (*double arrow*) and a delta wave (upsloping initial QRS segment) is seen (*arrow, shaded area*). (Reproduced with permission from Knoop KJ, et al. *The Atlas of Emergency Medicine*, 3rd ed. New York: McGraw-Hill; 2010.)

Answer b. PR interval <120 msec

The accessory bundle of Kent conducts faster than the normal AV node. This make the PR interval shorter than the lower limit of normal, which is 120 msec.

> The slowest conduction in the normal heart is the AV node.

> *The patient is admitted to the ICU, which is appropriate for patients with WPW presenting with VT. Patients with asymptomatic WPW or just SVT can be sent to the regular hospital ward. Order an echocardiogram if not already done. Now that the patient is stable, consult cardiology and electrophysiology. The patient needs evaluation for a permanent repair with radiofrequency catheter ablation.*

WPW syndrome is readily cured with catheter ablation.

Case 8: Pericardial Tamponade

Setting: *ICU*

CC: *His blood pressure is low.*

VS: *R: 26 breaths/minute; BP: 102/52 mm Hg; P:110 beats/minute; T: 100.4°F*

HPI: *It is 2 o'clock in the morning on July 2 during your postgraduate year 2 (PGY-2). The intern finished medical school about an hour ago and is looking to your expert leadership with a patient admitted to the hospital a week ago for an anterior wall myocardial infarction (AWMI). The patient developed hypotension and lightheadedness a few hours ago and was moved to the ICU. He is a 67-year-old man with recurrent episodes of chest pain during this hospital stay. He was treated with thrombolytics on admission. An echocardiogram on hospital day 3 showed EF at 34% and decreased anterior wall motion.*

PMHx: *hypertension, diabetes, and hyperlipidemia*

Medications:
- *Aspirin*
- *Prasugrel*
- *Metoprolol*
- *Ramipril*
- *Cerivastatin*

PE:
- *Cardiovascular: bilateral JVD, no murmurs*
- *Chest: clear to auscultation*
- *Extremities: small amount of edema*
- *Skin: diaphoretic*

What is the mechanism of response to this hypoperfusion?

a. Increased beta-1-stimulation of peripheral vessels

b. Increased beta-2-stimulation of peripheral vessels

c. Decreased vagal stimulation of arterioles

d. Increased alpha-1-stimulation of peripheral vessels

e. Central alpha-2-stimulation

Answer d. Increased alpha-1-stimulation of peripheral vessels

α_1-Stimulation is a vasoconstrictor of peripheral vessels. This will shunt blood from the skin, which is approximately 5% of blood flow into the central circulation, such as the heart and brain. Alpha-1-stimulation also constricts muscle vessels resulting in more shunting of blood to central organs. Beta-2-stimulation dilates skeletal muscle, which is undesirable with cardiac pump dysfunction.

Acetylcholine and parasympathetic stimulation do not touch peripheral vessels. Alpha-2-stimulation prevents the release of norepinephrine from nerves. Alpha-2-stimulation will result in vasodilation and will lower BP.

Acetylcholine neither constricts nor dilates skin and muscle arterioles.

Norepinephrine is an alpha-1-agonist.

After moving the clock forward 10 to 15 minutes, repeat vital signs: R: 28 breaths/minute; BP: 96/58 mm Hg; P:118 beats/minute.

What is the right step?

a. Bolus dextrose 5% in water (D5W)
b. Bolus half normal saline (NS)
c. Bolus NS
d. NS and dopamine
e. Ringers lactate and levarterenol

Answer c. Bolus NS

It is inappropriate to try to increase BP with D5W. The best initial fluids to raise BP are either NS or Ringer lactate (RL). Do not start pressors such as dopamine or levarterenol without first trying fluids. This is particularly true of dopamine in a patient with myocardial ischemia. Dopamine can worsen myocardial ischemia and oxygen consumption.

Initial Orders:
- *Bolus NS*
- *ABG*
- *Chest x-ray, portable*
- *CBC*
- *CK-MB*

Why does the mechanism of NS make it the best fluid for hypotensive patients?

a. Lactate is converted to bicarbonate by the liver.
b. NS has higher tonicity compared to other fluids.
c. D5W increases free water loss at the kidneys.
d. NS increases oncotic pressure of the capillaries.

Answer b. NS has higher tonicity compared to other fluids.

NS has considerably higher osmotic content compared with that of D5W or half NS. This increases its tonicity and is more likely to keep the fluid in the vascular space. The majority of D5W and half NS will leave the vascular space and enter the interstitial fluid space. Although this may increase the overall volume status of the patient, it will not increase the BP as much as either NS or RL. NS does not contain lactate; RL has the lactate that is converted to bicarbonate by the liver. Because NS has no protein, it will not increase the oncotic pressure of the vascular space.

> If two to three fluid boluses with NS do not raise BP >90 mm Hg, then use levarterenol or pseudoephedrine.

> Levarterenol and pseudoephedrine are pure alpha-1-agonists.

> *After each fluid bolus, move the clock forward 5 to 10 minutes, and recheck BP. This patient's BP stays at 94/60 mm Hg and his pulse rate remains 120 beats/minute. His neck veins are increasingly distended. His lungs remain clear. ABG results show PO$_2$ 68 mm Hg on room air with respiratory alkalosis. A chest x-ray reveals a cardiac shadow slightly enlarged bilaterally. His CK-MB level is elevated.*

> Monitoring CK-MB level is better than monitoring troponin level at detecting reinfarction.

What can be done *first* to detect the etiology?

a. Cardiac catheterization
b. Coronary angiography
c. A >10 mm Hg decrease in BP on inhalation
d. Transesophageal echocardiogram
e. Holter monitoring

Answer c. A >10 mm Hg decrease in BP on inhalation

Hypotension + JVD + Tachycardia = Pericardial Tamponade

Pulsus paradoxus is a >10 mm Hg decrease in BP on inhalation. Pulsus paradoxus can be checked at the bedside and is a good way to tell if the heart is being compressed. On inhalation, venous return to the right side of the heart increases. Normally, the heart expands in external diameter. When compressed by tamponade fluid, the heart cannot enlarge in total size. What happens when there is right-sided heart enlargement when the total cardiac size cannot increase? The RV enlarges from venous return on inhalation and compresses the LV. The right side of the heart expands in size; the left side of the heart is "squished" smaller. This decreases BP.

Tamponade seen on ECG has "electrical alternans," which is alternating large and small QRS complexes.

NS is continued and pulsus paradoxus is found on examination. It is far more important to perform pericardiocentesis to remove fluid than to wait for an echocardiogram or cardiac catheterization. Removing as little as 50 mL of fluid will allow the heart to expand and increase BP. On CCS, order the procedure you need. Because you do not know which procedures will need a consultation on the computer program, just order the procedure and the program will tell you when a consultation is needed first.

What will be found on echocardiogram as the first sign of cardiac tamponade?

a. LV compression in systole
b. LV compression in diastole
c. RV compression in diastole
d. Opening of ventricular septal defect
e. LA dilation

Answer c. RV compression in diastole

The right side of the heart collapses first because the walls are thinner and more easily compressed (Figure 1-11). All compressions from pericardial effusion happen in diastole when the heart is trying to fill (Figure 1-12).

Cardiac catheterization shows equalization or pressures in all chambers in diastole.

With bedside needle pericardiocentesis, the BP immediately increases after withdrawing 100 mL of straw-colored, nonbloody fluid. As you move the clock forward, the BP drops again the following day. Management of a recurring pericardial effusion is with surgical placement of a "window" or hole through which the fluid can drain into the pleural space (Figures 1-13 and 1-14). Once the fluid drains into the pleural space, it can easily be reabsorbed there. The most likely cause of pericardial effusion in the patient is the recent series of myocardial infarctions. Dressler syndrome, or post-MI pericardial inflammation is a rare event because of the routine use of aspirin in all patients. Despite this, the most likely explanation is the inflammation created by the multiple MIs.

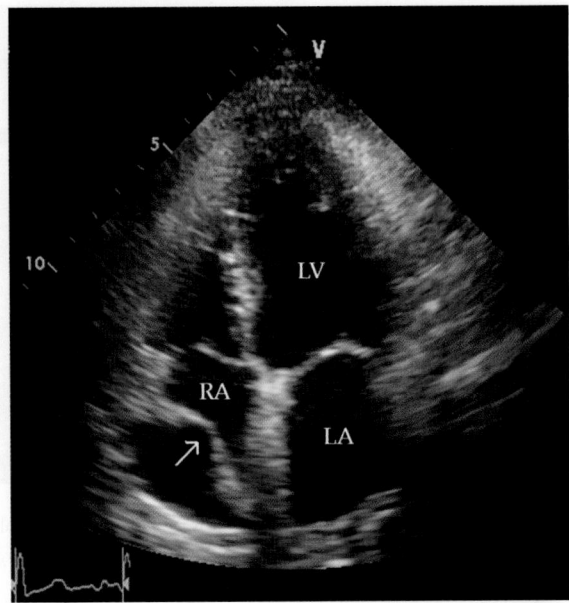

Figure 1-11. Right atrial collapse (*arrow*) in a patient with a small pericardial effusion. LA, left atrium; LV, left ventricle; RA, right atrium. (Reproduced with permission from Fuster V, et al., ed. *Hurst's The Heart*, 13th ed. New York: McGraw-Hill; 2011.)

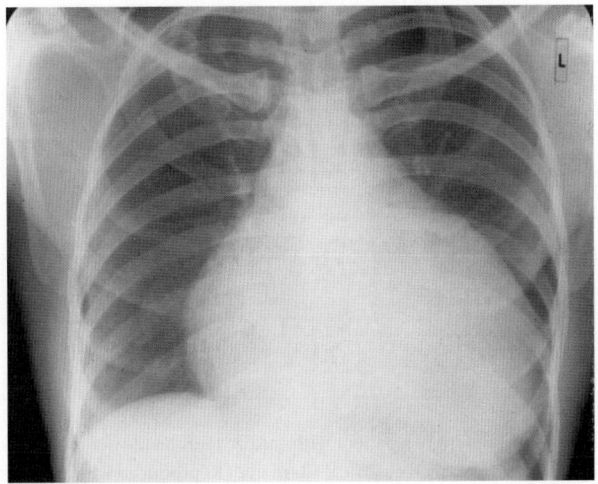

Figure 1-12. Pericardial effusion on posteroanterior film radiography. Chest radiogram (anterior) of a patient with rapidly increasing pericardial effusion and hemodynamic evidence of cardiac tamponade. Note how the cardiac silhouette is rounded in its lower portion and tapers at the base of the heart, resembling a plastic bag filled with water sitting on a table. (Reproduced with permission from Belenkie I. Pericardial disease. In: Hall JB, et al: *Principles of Critical Care*, 3rd ed. New York, McGraw-Hill; 2005).

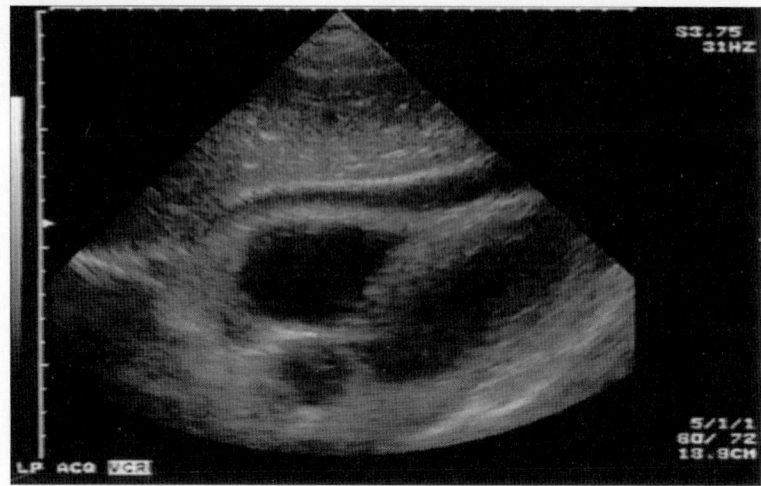

Figure 1-13. Subxiphoid pericardial ultrasound reveals a large pericardial fluid collection. (Reproduced with permission from Brunicardi FC, et al: *Schwartz's Principles of Surgery*, 9th ed. New York: McGraw-Hill; 2010.)

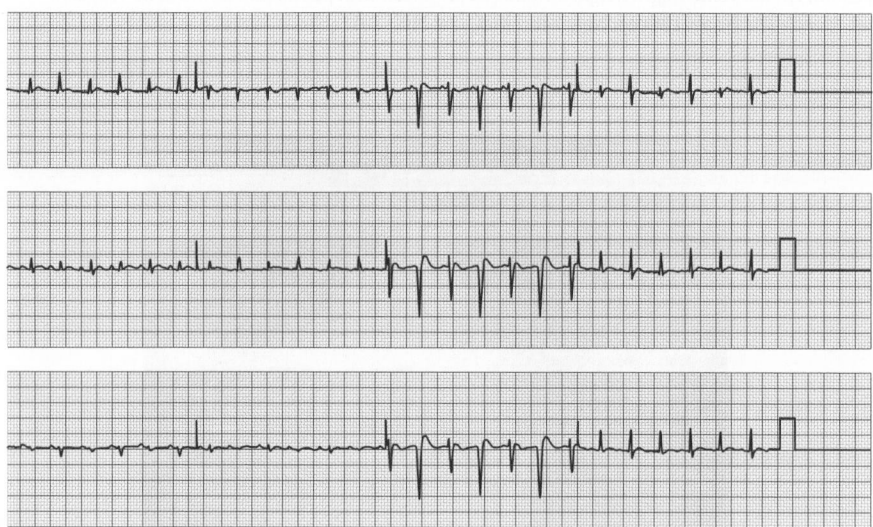

Figure 1-14. Electrocardiogram of a patient with cardiac tamponade demonstrates low voltages in the limb leads and marked electrical alternans. (Reproduced with permission from Hall JB, et al. *Principles of Critical Care*, 3rd ed. New York: McGraw-Hill; 2005.)

CASE 9: Complete Heart Block

Setting: *ICU*

CC: *Confusion*

VS: *R: 24 breaths/minute; BP: 70/40 mm Hg; P: 40 beats/minute; T: 97.4°F*

HPI: *You are called to see a 64-year-old woman admitted last night with an acute MI. She underwent angioplasty and was started on aspirin, ticagrelor, atorvastatin, metoprolol, enalapril, and nitroglycerin, and placed in the ICU. You are now called because the nurse found the patient to be suddenly confused.*

PMHx:
- *Hypertension*
- *Tobacco use*
- *MR*

Outpatient Medications:
- *Nifedipine*
- *Hydrochlorothiazide*

PE:
- *General: pale, uncomfortable*
- *Cardiovascular: cannon A waves in neck*
- *Cardiovascular: 2/6 pansystolic murmur found*
- *Neurological: confusion, examination incomplete secondary to confusion*
- *Chest: clear to auscultation*

Which is most important?

a. Atropine

b. Transcutaneous pacemaker

c. Transvenous pacemaker

d. Epinephrine

e. Levarterenol

Answer a. Atropine

Bradycardia with symptoms needs atropine to speed up the heart rate and raise BP. All of the treatments listed will raise BP, but atropine is most appropriate. Atropine works faster than either form of pacemaker and is considerably more comfortable than the transcutaneous pacemaker. Epinephrine will both speed the heart rate and raise BP, but it is a disaster to use in acute MI. Epinephrine will provoke ischemia that can be fatal. It is wrong to use the alpha-1-agonist levarterenol without first using atropine, fluids, and a pacemaker. Alpha-agonists are used to raise BP when you cannot correct or control the underlying cause.

Initial Orders:
- *Atropine IV*
- *NS bolus*
- *ECG*
- *CK-MB, troponin*
- *CHEM-7 (electrolytes), calcium, magnesium*

Atropine and NS are given. Remember that on CCS, treatments are considered "administered" the instant you confirm them. However, unless you move the clock forward, you cannot detect an effect of the treatment. As you move the clock forward 5 minutes, recheck the vital signs. If atropine is going to be effective, it will work instantly, but this cannot be detected on CCS unless there is a movement forward in time.

In symptomatic bradycardia, atropine is more important than etiology.

Atropine blocks the effect of acetylcholine at the SA and AV nodes. Acetylcholine slows heart rate.

How does atropine increase heart rate in bradycardia?

a. Decreases potassium efflux
b. Increases the rate of I_F or "Funny" sodium channels
c. Prolongs phase-2 calcium entry
d. Increases the velocity in Purkinje fibers
e. Increases the conduction speed at the Bachmann bundle in the atria

Answer b. Increases the rate of I_F or "Funny" sodium channels

Phase 4 in nodal tissue is flattened or slowed by acetylcholine. Atropine makes it rise faster. Phase 4 is created by "Funny" sodium channels or I_F. Faster I_F channels equate to faster depolarization in nodal tissue. Atropine speeds the rate at which both the SA and AV nodes depolarize. This is identical to the effect norepinephrine has.

On Nodal Tissue:

Atropine = Decreased Acetylcholine = Increased Norepinephrine Effect

Decreased Acetylcholine = Faster Phase 4 = Faster I_F = Faster Heart Rate

Phase 4 depolarization in nodal tissue is the site of the vagal effect on heart rate.

As you move the clock forward, the pulse rate increases from 40 to 50 beats/minute; BP rises from 70/40 to 84/50 mm Hg. You give an addition stat dose of atropine and another bolus of NS and move the clock forward 5 minutes. Repeat the vital signs, which takes 2 minutes of "simulated time" on CCS. The pulse rate is now 55 beats/minute and BP is 106/60 mm Hg. If the BP had not risen to a systolic above 90 mm Hg, the answer would have been, "transcutaneous pacemaker." *The stat ECG report returns 10 minutes after ordering it indicating third-degree (complete) heart block at a rate of 40 beats/minute.*

How can the ECG report show the heart rate at 40 beats/minute, when the heart rate has increased at the time of the report?

a. Any test ordered on CCS is done instantly. It was ordered when the rate was 40 beats/minute.

b. CCS is not based on time.

c. ECG cannot be done stat on CCS.

Answer a. Any test ordered on CCS is done instantly. It was ordered when the rate was 40 beats/minute.

When writing original orders, the heart rate was 40 beats/minute. All test are considered "done" at the instant you confirm the order. The report comes up later as you pass the time on the clock with the notice "report available." You can cancel any order you do not want by double clicking on the order before the report comes back. You will always be asked to confirm everything on CCS two to three times before it is implemented. It is critical that you understand that tests are done instantly, otherwise you will give extra treatment the patient does not need, thinking "Hey, why is the heart rate still low? I should give more atropine!" No. The ECG report is delayed, and the patient has improved since the test was done.

Test reports on CCS always list the exact time they were ordered.

You ask for an "Interval History" at the physical examination tab. The patient reports feeling much better and the confusion has resolved. BP is 106/60 mm Hg. Cannon A waves are still present. Lungs are clear. You order a temporary transcutaneous pacemaker to be placed on the patient's chest wall. It will not fire if you set the low limit of the heart rate to 50 beats/minute and the patient's heart rate continues higher than that.

What is the mechanism of the cannon A wave?

a. Atrial systole against a closed tricuspid valve

b. Shunt through a patent foramen ovale

c. Ventricular systole

d. Back pressure from the ventricle when the mitral valve opens

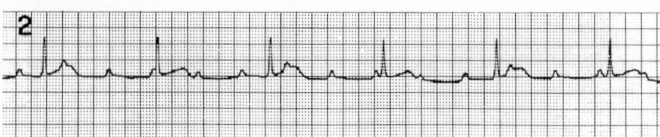

Figure 1-15. Third-degree atrioventricular block. (Reproduced with permission from Tintinalli JE, et al. *Tintinalli's Emergency Medicine, A Comprehensive Study Guide,* 7th ed. New York: McGraw-Hill; 2011.)

Answer a. Atrial systole against a closed tricuspid valve

The A wave is a sign of atrial systole in the jugular vein. It is normal to have an A wave. It is abnormally large in complete heart block because the atrium is often contracting when the tricuspid valve is closed. *Complete* or third-degree heart block means that the atria and ventricles are contracting with no relationship to each other (Figure 1-15). Normally, the tricuspid valve is always open when the atrium is contracting. Now it will sometimes be closed, and the blood will rush backward into the neck veins like a person bouncing up on a trampoline. "Boing" and the blood moves backward into the neck veins.

Bradycardia + Hypotension + Cannon A Waves = Complete Heart Block

Cannon A waves indicate third-degree AV block.

When BP normalizes (systolic >100 mm Hg) in an ICU patient, you can move the clock forward at greater intervals such as 2 to 4 hours. On CCS, you can never tell in advance precisely when the case will end in "simulated" time. You have 10 to 25 minutes of "real" time, which is your time for each case. It can be disconcerting when you suddenly see a screen that says, "This case will end in 5 minutes of real time." Test takers often become anxious because there is no objective way to verify whether the case is ending. It could be because you achieved the objectives and the test has run its course, or because you made a mistake. Make liberal use of the "interval history" button, which is the only means of obtaining a status report on your patient. In a patient such as one with complete heart block, the emphasis will be on initial management.

You move the clock forward 2 hours and BP remains at 108/70 mm Hg. A repeat ECG shows persistent complete heart block. Order a transvenous pacemaker. Make sure you have discontinued the beta-blockers. CCS will not send you a message saying, "Hey, you idiot! Stop giving drugs that slow the heart rate in symptomatic bradycardia."

Which wall of the heart is most likely to have infarcted in this patient?

a. Anterior

b. Inferior

c. Lateral

d. Posterior

Answer b. Inferior

An inferior wall infarction is most frequently associated with AV nodal block and bradycardia. When it is accompanied by nausea and vomiting, it is from direct inflammation of the diaphragm related to the infarction. When associated with bradycardia, it is from increased vagal tone inhibiting the SA node. This is sometimes called the Bezold-Jarisch reflex.

Inferior MI stimulates vagal tone.

What coronary vessel led to AV block in this patient?

a. Left main

b. Left circumflex

c. Right coronary

d. Left anterior descending

e. Septal perforators

Answer c. Right coronary

The right coronary artery is the most frequent source of the blood supply to the AV node. If there was just a vagal reflex, it would produce sinus bradycardia. This is why a permanent pacemaker is so frequently necessary in patients with ischemia-induced complete heart block. The damage is often permanent.

Later the same day, a transvenous pacemaker is placed. An ECG is obtained, showing functioning pacer spikes and a wide QRS complex. The heart rate is 70 beats/minute and BP is 118/70 mm Hg. Mentation is normal, and there is no chest pain.

What is the mechanism of wide QRS complex in this case?

a. Pacer impulses travel slowly from myocyte to myocyte instead of down the normal His-Purkinje system.

b. The pacer lead is in the atrium.

c. Smooth muscle junctions are not functioning in paced rhythm.

d. The pacer lead is overly fibrosed, blocking impulse propagation.

e. Intercalated discs do not function between myocytes with pacemakers.

Answer a. Pacer impulses travel slowly from myocyte to myocyte instead of down the normal His-Purkinje system

All pacemakers placed in ventricles produce a wide complex. You cannot put the lead in the atrium because in this case, the AV node is injured, and the impulse would not conduct to the ventricle.

> An echocardiogram confirms an inferior wall MI. The pacemaker is functioning normally. Metoprolol and enalapril are restarted. Chemistry is normal including calcium and magnesium levels. CK-MB level is elevated. Several hours later, BP suddenly drops to 80/40 mm Hg. Pulse rate is 70 beats/minute, which is the set rate of the pacemaker, and pacemaker spikes are seen. Chest is clear to auscultation. Neck vein distention is visible.

What is the most likely cause of the hypotension?

a. Free wall rupture

b. Valve rupture

c. Septal rupture

d. Right ventricular infarction

Answer d. Right ventricular infarction

Right ventricular infarction accompanies inferior wall MI in 30% to 40% of patients. This is because they both have the same arterial supply, which is the right coronary artery. The test is to flip the ECG leads to the right side of the chest and get a right ventricular ECG. There is no specific therapy except to load fluids.

> After a bolus of NS, BP rises and symptoms resolve.

CASE 10: Mitral Regurgitation

Setting: *office*

CC: *"Here to check my pressure, Doc."*

VS: *R: 12 breaths/minute; BP: 125/82 mm Hg; P: 75 beats/minute; T: 98.4°F*

HPI: *A 54-year-old woman with long-standing hypertension visits your office for her routine evaluation every 6 months. She generally feels well. She feels okay with ordinary efforts such as walking on flat surfaces or housecleaning. She has just transferred her care to you from one of your partners who retired.*

PMHx:
- *Hypertension*
- *MR*

Medications:
- *Chlorthalidone*

What murmur would you expect with the history of MR?

a. Pansystolic
b. Crescendo-decrescendo systolic
c. Diastolic decrescendo
d. Midsystolic extra sound with late murmur
e. Continuous "machinery" murmur

Answer a. Pansystolic

MR obscures both S_1 and S_2 sounds and can also be described as "holosystolic." The crescendo-decrescendo murmur is either aortic stenosis or hypertrophic obstructive cardiomyopathy. A diastolic decrescendo murmur (choice c) is aortic regurgitation. The midsystolic extra sound with murmur is mitral valve prolapse. A continuous machinery murmur (choice e) is patent ductus arteriosus.

PE:
- *Chest: normal, no rales*
- *Extremities: no edema*
- *Cardiovascular: II/VI pansystolic murmur radiating to the apex*

Initial Orders:
- *Echocardiogram*
- *ECG*
- *Chest x-ray*
- *CHEM-7*

As an office-based case of someone who is generally asymptomatic, you can bring your patient back to the office on CCS in 2 to 4 weeks after the initial visit. Nonacute chronic cases do not have precise parameters to guide the time interval between visits because it is not clear and therefore, you will not be graded on it.

Test Results:
- *Echocardiogram: moderate MR, EF 62%, LV end-systolic diameter 35 mm*
- *Chemistry: normal*
- *ECG: LV hypertrophy*

What is the mechanism of LV hypertrophy?

a. Increasing wall thickness decreases wall tension according to the Laplace law.

b. Increasing wall thickness generates hypertension.

c. Wall thickness has no impact on the Laplace law.

d. Increasing radius will decrease the wall tension.

Answer a. Increasing wall thickness decreases wall tension according to the Laplace law. Increasing LV wall thickness decreases wall tension.

Law of Laplace: Radius × Pressure = Wall Tension
Wall Thickness

This is why decreasing BP will decrease wall tension as well. This is also why the radius of the LV chamber increases its rate of dilating once dilation begins. The bigger or wider the LV, the faster it will dilate. This is why BP has to be controlled before LV dilation occurs.

The wider a chamber is, the faster it widens.

Which is more accurate for assessing LV hypertrophy?

a. Transthoracic echocardiogram

b. MUGA (nuclear ventriculogram)

c. ECG

d. Catheterization

Answer a. Transthoracic echocardiogram

An echocardiogram is far more accurate than ECG for LV hypertrophy. The MUGA or nuclear ventriculogram assesses EF and does nothing to assess LV thickness. A nuclear ventriculogram is the single most accurate method of assessing EF. Catheterization looks at valve function and pressure gradients but does not evaluate LV wall thickness.

Chlorthalidone inhibits sodium uptake in the distal tubule.

When the patient is lying on a table and you lift the patient's legs in the air, the murmur of MR increases in intensity. What is the mechanism?

a. Increasing afterload

b. Increased myocardial oxygen consumption

c. Decreased atrial filling pressure

d. Pooling blood in abdomen

e. Increased venous return/preload

Answer e. Increased venous return/preload

Leg raises and squatting from a standing position will increase venous return to the heart and increase filling pressure. MR, AR, MS, and AS will all increase in loudness or intensity with maneuvers such as these, which put more blood in the heart.

What is the best medical management of the MR?

a. No changes are needed; continue chlorthalidone.

b. Use endocarditis prophylaxis when bloody dental work is planned.

c. Add a beta-blocker.

d. Switch chlorthalidone to lisinopril.

e. Add spironolactone.

f. Switch chlorthalidone to furosemide.

Answer d. Switch chlorthalidone to lisinopril.

Regurgitant cardiac lesions, such as MR and AR, are best managed with vasodilators such as ACE inhibitors, ARBs, or nifedipine. We think there is some benefit in decreasing the rate of progression of regurgitation.

None of these valvular lesions has sufficient turbulence to need endocarditis prophylaxis. Beta-blockers and spironolactone would offer no benefit for a person with a normal EF. There is no fluid overload, so switching to a loop diuretic offers nothing for this patient.

You stop chlorthalidone and start lisinopril. Advance the clock 1 to 2 weeks to check BP and for adverse effects of ACE inhibitors such as cough, angioedema, and hyperkalemia. On return 2 weeks later, the patient feels well and her BP is 118/78 mm Hg. You schedule an appointment 3 months into the future. BP is again well controlled. After another 3 months, you repeat the echocardiogram with these results: EF 55%, left ventricular end-systolic diameter 45 mm.

What is the effect on handgrip as an ausculatory maneuver on this patient?

a. It decreases venous return, softening the murmur.

b. It increases venous return, improving or softening the murmur.

c. It increases afterload, worsening the murmur.

d. Handgrip has no effect on regurgitant lesions.

Answer c. It increases afterload, worsening the murmur.

Handgrip is based on the patient squeezing the examiner's hand. This increases afterload by compressing the arteries of the arm. This has an effect the opposite of that of an ACE inhibitor and will, therefore, worsen regurgitant lesions such as AR and MR. The volume of blood in the arm is too small to make a meaningful increase in venous return.

You schedule the patient to return for repeat echocardiogram in 3 months. On return, EF decreases from 55% to 50% and LV end-systolic diameter increases from 45 mm to 48 mm. The patient has no symptoms at rest or with usual exertion. She has been fully adherent to the lisinopril.

What is the right action?

a. Institute no change and instruct the patient to return for follow-up in 3 to 6 months.

b. Switch the ACE inhibitor to an ARB.

c. Add an ARB to the ACE inhibitor.

d. Refer the patient for catheter or surgical valve repair or replacement.

e. Add metoprolol to the patient's medication regimen.

Answer d. Refer the patient for catheter or surgical valve repair or replacement.

Surgical repair or replacement of the mitral or aortic valve must be done for regurgitant lesions before the patient develops symptoms. Once the ventricle dilates, there is no way to reverse the dilation and that is why anatomic correction must be done when the EF starts to drop. Vasodilators cannot reverse LV dilation, they can only prevent it from occurring.

Criteria for Surgical Repair or Replacement

	MR	AR
EF	<60%	<55%
LVESD	>40 mm	>55 mm

AR, aortic regurgitation; EF, ejection fraction; LVESD, left ventricular end-systolic diameter; MR, mitral regurgitation.

CASE 11: Peripheral Arterial Disease

Setting: *ambulatory care center*

CC: *"My legs hurt when I walk."*

VS: *R: 14 breaths/minute; BP:145/86 mm Hg; P: 70 beats/minute; T: 99.8°F*

HPI: *A 74-year-old man comes to your clinic with pain in his left leg that he says he has felt for the past few months. The pain localizes predominantly to the calves and is related to walking and is relieved when he sits down to rest. The pain is described as "soreness" and "aching" or "like being punched." He is able to walk for three to four blocks before it occurs and until recently, has not been overly limited in his mobility.*

PMHx:
- *Hypertension*
- *Diabetes*
- *Tobacco smoking*

Medications:
- *Metformin*
- *Nifedipine*

PE:
- *Cardiovascular: S_4 gallop*
- *Extremities: pale, pulses are palpable in dorsalis pedis area*

Which physical finding should you check for?

a. Enlarged liver
b. Loss of hair and sweat glands in legs
c. Enlarged spleen
d. Ascites and hemorrhoids

Answer b. Loss of hair and sweat glands in legs

Peripheral arterial disease (PAD) predisposes to loss of skin appendages such as hair follicles and sweat glands. Pulses are lost in very late disease.

S_4 is heard with atrial systole into a noncompliant left ventricle.

What is the best initial step?

a. Angiography
b. Ankle-brachial index (ABI)
c. Refer to vascular surgery
d. Doppler ultrasounds of lower extremities

Answer b. Ankle-brachial index (ABI)

ABI is the clear first choice in the evaluation of PAD. It serves to establish a diagnosis, although it does not determine the precise location of the lesion. An ABI <0.9 indicates vascular disease.

It is premature to go straight to angiography. Angiography is the most accurate test, but it is not the one to establish an initial diagnosis of PAD. It can reveal the anatomic location to determine the site of repair.

Doppler ultrasounds are not needed if you can feel a pulse. They are also not as important as determining the difference in BP between upper and lower extremities. You should not refer to vascular surgery for a simple diagnostic procedure such as ABI, which you can do.

In the upright position, where is BP the highest?

a. Brain
b. Carotid
c. Brachial
d. Legs

Answer d. Legs

BP is greater in the legs than the arms when standing because of the effect of gravity. The difference is based on a patient's height, but it would be expected to be at least 60 to 80 mm Hg greater in the lower extremities. When lying flat, BP should be equal in the arms and legs. If, when lying flat, BP is more than 10% less in the legs than in the arms (ABI <0.9), obstruction to flow is present. Severe PAD is an ABI <0.6.

Initial Orders:

- *ABI*
- *Lipid panel (low-density lipoprotein [LDL], total cholesterol)*
- *CHEM-7*
- *CBC*
- *ECG*
- *Glycated hemoglobin (HbA₁c)*

The patient returns the following week to discuss the results of the ABI. His value is 0.7. His symptom of pain when walking several blocks is the same.

Laboratory Test Results:

- *CBC: normal*
- *CHEM-7: normal*
- *LDL: 145 mg/dL*
- *ECG: LV hypertrophy*
- *HbA₁c: 7%*

Which BP medication is best for PAD?

a. ACE inhibitor
b. Beta-blocker
c. CCB
d. Diuretic
e. Alpha-1-antagonist

Answer a. ACE inhibitor

ACE inhibitors have some impact in modifying the progression of disease in PAD. CCBs are not particularly effective in PAD. The benefit of a CCB, alpha-antagonist, and diuretic are not more than the benefit of simply controlling BP. There is no disease-modifying effect of the medications listed above on PAD.

CCBs do not benefit the atherosclerotic plaque in the intimal lining of vessel.

Smooth muscle in arteries is exterior to the intimal lining; relaxing it does not open the vessel in PAD.

You switch the nifedipine to lisinopril and add aspirin. You begin the discussion of tobacco cessation by asking if the patient has a goal to stop smoking and try to arrange follow-up to set a quit date. On CCS, remember to always do patient counseling on all lifestyle issues such as weight loss, exercise, diabetic diets, and tobacco cessation. All "population health" issues are major concerns of the Step 3 examination. This can be very difficult to remember for residents trained to focus only on current symptoms in a patient.

Which medication is most effective in PAD?

a. Ticlopidine
b. Cilostazol
c. Pentoxifylline
d. ACE inhibitors

Answer b. Cilostazol

The single most effective medication in PAD is cilostazol. This is a medication that is used for only this single indication. It is not used for coronary, carotid, or cerebrovascular disease. Ticlopidine is a nearly extinct drug to inhibit platelets. It is a P2Y ADP receptor antagonist like clopidogrel, but should rarely be used because of neutropenia and thrombotic thrombocytopenic purpura (TTP). Pentoxifylline is an older medication for PAD that has been replaced by cilostazol.

> Ticlopidine can be offered as a wrong answer choice on the Step 3 examination. Ticlopidine causes neutropenia and TTP.

What is the mechanism of cilostazol?

a. Thrombin inhibition
b. Decrease cyclic adenosine monophosphate (cAMP)
c. Increases plasmin activation
d. Phosphodiesterase inhibition
e. Inhibits calcium activation of clotting cascade

Answer d. Phosphodiesterase inhibition

Cilostazol inhibits phosphodiesterase. This increases cAMP. There is both inhibition of platelet activation and some inhibition of vascular smooth muscle. It both prevents platelet aggregation and has some vasodilatory effect.

> Pentoxifylline increases "rheology" or diapedesis of red blood cells— great mechanism, no clinical benefit.

> Metformin is fine in PAD. No disease management (DM) regimen is superior to another in PAD.

End all ambulatory cases with education, counseling, or advising on lifestyle issues:
• Obesity: weight loss
• Diabetes: diet and exercise
• Hypertension: diet and sodium restriction
• Hyperlipidemia: weight loss

The results of the repeat LDL test is 142 mg/dL. The patient has started lisinopril and aspirin and continued his metformin.

What should be done about his LDL level?

a. Diet and exercise alone for 3 to 6 months and repeat
b. Statin
c. Niacin
d. Ezetimibe

Answer b. Statin

PAD is equivalent to coronary disease, so it is important to lower the LDL to <100 mg/dL in patients with PAD. With an LDL of 142 mg/dL, diet, exercise, and weight loss are insufficient to control the level. Statins are therapeutically equivalent for use on Step 3. Niacin is not as effective as a statin. Niacin is relatively contraindicated in diabetes because it can cause glucose elevation.

Ezetimibe lowers LDL, but has no proven mortality benefit or proof that it alters the natural history of any form of vascular disease.

Get LDL cholesterol <100 mg/dL in PAD—the same as in coronary disease.

Which is most effective to help stop smoking?

a. Education methods
b. Nicotine gum
c. Nicotine patch
d. Bupropion

Answer d. Bupropion

Nicotine patches and gums are more effective than education alone, but bupropion or varenicline is more effective than nicotine replacement.

Advance the clock 2 to 4 weeks. The patient returns using an ACE inhibitor, cilostazol, metformin, and aspirin. He wants to try to stop smoking and agrees to start bupropion and return for follow-up in 2 weeks. The pain is unchanged. Over the next 6 months, the patient stops smoking. Repeat LDL is 85 mg/dL and BP 124/78 mm Hg. On CCS, you never know where the case will stop. Keep advancing the clock. Your case may not have the happy ending this one does. If symptoms worsen in your case despite maximum medical therapy, do an angiogram in preparation for revascularization angioplasty or bypass.

BP goal with PAD is <130/80 mm Hg.

Which of these is a standard preventive measure in this patient?

a. Abdominal aorta ultrasound
b. Chest computed tomography (CT)
c. Exercise tolerance test
d. Renal artery stenosis screening
e. Prostate specific antigen (PSA)

Answer a. Abdominal aorta ultrasound

All men who were ever smokers need an ultrasound to exclude aneurysm. This should be done once between the ages of 65 and 75 years. This is *not* true for women or nonsmokers. PSA is not recommended for any group. There is no lung cancer screen with chest CT for smokers that is clearly effective or recommended.

Exercise tolerance testing is not a screen for asymptomatic patient. Abdominal aortic aneurysm (AAA) screening is standard for asymptomatic persons.

For statins, liver function tests are standard, not creatinine kinase (CK) levels.

CASE 12: **Syncope**

Setting: *ED*

CC: *"She passed out!"*

VS: *R: 14 breaths/minute; BP:124/75 mm Hg; P:76 beats/minute; T: 97.5°F*

HPI: *A 65-year-old woman is brought to the ED by ambulance after losing consciousness in church. The patient was in her usual state of health until she woke up lying on her back in church. She was transferred to a stretcher and brought to the ED. The onset of loss of consciousness (LOC) was sudden. She cannot recall how long it lasted, but friends say it was only for a few minutes. When she awoke, she knew where she was immediately. Currently, she feels fine.*

PMHx:
- *Osteoarthritis*
- *Diverticulosis*

Medications:
- *Acetaminophen one to two times a day*

PE:
- *General appearance: older woman sitting up on stretcher looking her stated age; comfortable; not diaphoretic*
- *Cardiovascular: no murmur*
- *Neurological: normal*

ROS:
- *Denies chest pain, dyspnea, headache*
- *Denies bowel or bladder incontinence*
- *She "felt shaky and sweaty" before the episode. She "felt very hot."*

As you move the clock forward 5 to 10 minutes and take an interval history, you will find that the vast majority of cases of syncope do not change. Syncope is extremely common, and in the majority of patients, the etiology is never found. The most important part of syncope evaluation is the history.

Why do atrial arrhythmias generally not lead to syncope?

a. The rate is not fast enough.
b. Atrial systole eventually occurs.
c. Stroke volume remains intact.

d. Vasoconstriction compensates.
e. α_1-Receptors upregulate.

Answer c. Stroke volume remains intact.

Only 10% to 15% of cardiac output is dependent on the atrial contribution to ventricular filling. Loss of atrial systole leaves stroke volume intact in most cases. VT markedly decreases cardiac output and ventricular fibrillation eliminates it.

Here are the two key questions and the examination for syncope:
1. *Was the **loss** of consciousness gradual or sudden?*
   *If **gradual** (patients are shaky, sweaty, lowering themselves to the ground or to a seated position),*
   - *Hypoglycemia*
   - *Hypoxia*

   - *Drug toxicity or alcohol*
   - *Vasovagal*

   *If **sudden** (patients feel fine, then wake up on the floor),*
   - *Neurological or seizure*
   - *Cardiac: arrhythmia or obstructive disease*

2. *Was* **regaining** *of consciousness gradual or sudden?*
   If **gradual**,
   • *Seizure: Patients are "post-ictal" in that they need time to become normal over a few minutes to hours.*
   If **sudden** *("like a light switch turned off and on"),*
   • *Cardiac: arrhythmia, ischemia, structural*

3. ***Examination***
   • *Arrhythmia rarely reveals an abnormality on cardiac examination.*
   • *Murmurs: hypertrophic obstructive cardiomyopathy (HOCM) versus aortic stenosis versus mitral stenosis*

Initial Orders:

• *ECG*	• *Head CT*
• *Telemetry monitoring*	• *CHEM-7*
• *CK-MB, troponin*	• *Urine toxicology screen*
• *Echocardiogram*	*(some cases)*

Patients with syncope do not need to be placed in the ICU just for syncope. They only need the ICU if ventricular arrhythmia is found. Admit the patient to the regular hospital ward but order telemetry. Ninety percent of mortality with syncope is from a cardiac problem. You can view your syncope case as (exclude MI and arrhythmia) for those patients with no clear etiology at the beginning. If your case presents a person who is shaky and sweaty with a documented low glucose (<60 mg/dL), then you do not have to place the person on telemetry or order echocardiography. If your case is clearly hypotensive from pulmonary embolus, they need TPA and should be admitted to the ICU.

Syncope can be either considered one of the most complicated conditions with a broad differential or one of the simplest with the same list of tests for almost everyone.

If there is no clear etiology from the patient's history, order
• ECG and telemetry   • CK-MB, troponin
• Echocardiogram   • Head CT

It is very unlikely to have a significant obstructive lesion with no murmur on examination.

As with many patients with syncope, as you move the clock forward 2 to 4 hours, there is no change in status, no new symptoms, and the tests return as normal.

• *ECG: normal sinus rhythm with no ST- or T-wave abnormalities*

• *Echocardiogram: mild MR, no wall motion abnormalities*
• *CK-MB, troponin, head CT: normal*

> *Continue to advance the clock on CCS until the tests are all normal.* **Keep the patient in the hospital for 24 hours of telemetry monitoring.**

Do not order any consultations for syncope patients unless a cardiac abnormality is found.

Regurgitant lesions do not cause syncope.

Do not order carotid Doppler ultrasounds in syncope.

Why does carotid stenosis not cause syncope?

a. It is too gradual in onset.

b. The posterior circulation supplies the brainstem.

c. Anterior circulation flows to the reticular activating system.

d. Vertebrobasilar circulation comes straight off the carotid.

Answer b. The posterior circulation supplies the brainstem.

The "sleep–wake" center for the brain is in the brainstem. Anterior or carotid circulation does not supply the brainstem. A patient can have a 100% occlusion of both carotid arteries and not lose consciousness. The patient may develop a stroke of the middle and anterior cerebral artery circulation, but will not lose consciousness.

Only posterior circulation (vertebral and basilar artery) occlusion causes syncope.

Stenosis lesions rapidly decrease stroke volume and cardiac output.

CHAPTER 2

HEMATOLOGY

CASE 1: Iron Deficiency Anemia

Setting: *office*

CC: *"I feel tired."*

VS: *R: 18 breaths/minute; BP: 110/70 mm Hg; P: 87 beats/minute; T: 97.8°F*

HPI: *A 32-year-old woman with several weeks of increasing tiredness and fatigue visits your office. She says she feels worse after walking up stairs and improves with rest. Her menstrual periods last 5 days and are regular.*

PE:
- *General appearance: normal*
- *Cardiovascular: normal*
- *Chest: clear to auscultation*

Initial Orders:
- *Complete blood count (CBC)*
- *Thyroid function tests (thyroxine [T$_4$], thyroid-stimulating hormone [TSH])*
- *Oximeter*

The patient does not return for her scheduled office visit the following week. She comes 2 months later because her fatigue has worsened and now interferes with functioning. She is now dyspneic with significant exertion, such as walking two flights of stairs.

Previous Laboratory Test Results:
- *Thyroid function: normal*
- *Oximeter: 98%*
- *CBC:*
- *Hematocrit: 28%*
- *Hemoglobin: 9 g/dL*
- *Mean corpuscular volume (MCV): 74 fL*
- *White blood cells (WBCs): 7000/µL*
- *Platelets: 378,000/µL*

Which of these does *not* cause this patient's type of anemia?

a. Sideroblastic

b. Folic acid deficiency

c. Iron deficiency

d. Chronic disease

e. Thalassemia

Answer b. Folic acid deficiency

Folic acid deficiency is associated with macrocytosis and large cells. The others all cause microcytic anemia. Expect an MCV >100 fL in folic acid deficiency.

Orders:
- CBC
- Iron, total iron-binding capacity (TIBC), ferritin level
- Reticulocyte count
- Peripheral smear
- Schedule an office visit for the following day (laboratory test results should be back by then)

The computer-based case simulation (CCS) always tells you precisely when the results of the laboratory tests return. It will say "Report Available" and give a precise time.

Which of these *can be* associated with target cells?

a. Autoimmune hemolysis

b. Iron deficiency

c. Folic acid deficiency

d. Vitamin B$_{12}$ deficiency

Answer b. Iron deficiency

Any of the microcytic anemias *can* be associated with target cells. The *most likely* of all the anemias to cause target cells is thalassemia. Both alpha- and beta-thalassemia can cause target cells and thalassemia can also be caused by thalassemia trait. Autoimmune hemolysis causes spherocytes, not target cells.

What is the mechanism of target cell formation?

a. Precipitation of hemoglobin in the red blood cell (RBC) membrane

b. Excess cell membrane bunching up on the surface

c. Loss of membrane from protein loss

d. Cellular dehydration

e. Ankyrin and spectrin deficiency

Answer b. Excess cell membrane bunching up on the surface

Target cells are formed exclusively from excess RBC membrane. The amount of hemoglobin is too small for the size of the covering. The excess membrane "bunches up" on the cell surface.

The patient returns the following day. You never have to be uncertain about the time to have the patient come back on CCS, because when you order the tests, it will tell you when the report will be back.

CBC:
- *Hematocrit: 23%*
- *Hemoglobin: 7 g/dL*
- *MCV: 70 fL*
- *WBCs: 7,400/μL*
- *Platelets: 578,000/μL*
- *Iron: low*
- *TIBC: elevated*
- *Ferritin level: low*
- *Reticulocyte count: 1%*
- *Peripheral smear: microcytic, hypochromic cells; no target cells; no schistocytes or fragmented cells*
- *Red blood cell distribution width (RDW): elevated*

What is the mechanism of elevated TIBC?

a. Decreased saturation of the transferrin transport protein
b. Decreased saturation of transferring in storage in marrow
c. Increased hepcidin
d. Iron is locked in macrophages

Answer a. Decreased saturation of the transferrin transport protein

Transferrin transport two iron atoms on each molecule. This is the fast transporter in plasma of iron to be incorporated into hemoglobin and into cells. A high *capacity* on a protein such as transferrin means that it is empty or unoccupied. Iron locked in macrophages is the mechanism of the anemia of chronic disease.

Ferritin is a hollow ball of proteins that stores iron in tissue. Free iron is toxic.

What is the significance of the high platelet count?

a. None, it is an expected part of iron deficiency anemia.
b. It is a marker of additional disease and needs investigation.
c. Essential thrombocytosis will develop. Order a Janus kinase 2 (JAK2) mutation test.

Answer a. None, it is an expected part of iron deficiency anemia.

Platelet elevation is an expected feature of iron deficiency anemia. The etiology may be that erythropoietin has some stimulatory effect on megakaryocytes. No further evaluation is needed.

Thrombocytosis in iron deficiency needs no further investigation.

RDW is found to be elevated. What is the mechanism?

a. In iron deficiency, new cells are larger.

b. In iron deficiency, new cells are smaller.

c. Microcytosis becomes stable.

Answer b. In iron deficiency, new cells are smaller.

As you run out of iron, the cells become smaller. The RBC is a "bad of hemoglobin." If there is no iron to make hemoglobin from, then the cells become smaller. It is like making smaller sandwiches when you run low on food.

The patient returns feeling tired. Her stool is heme negative. The presumed mechanism of her iron deficiency anemia is menstruation in a woman. Her menstrual periods do tend to be somewhat heavy. Oral ferrous sulfate is started, and you ask her to return in 2 weeks.

What will change first in response to iron replacement?

a. MCV

b. Reticulocyte count

c. Hemoglobin level

d. RDW

Answer b. Reticulocyte count

Reticulocytes are the measure of new cell formation. Reticulocyte concentration has to increase first for any of the other features of a CBC to change.

Reticulocytes: Methylene blue stains ribosomal RNA from residual endoplasmic reticulum.

The patient returns in 2 weeks. The repeat hematocrit test shows that the level rose from 23% to 25%. The reticulocyte count rises only from 1% to 2.5%.

Which of the following over-the-counter substances may be impeding the absorption of iron?

a. Cimetidine

b. Vitamin C

c. Vitamin D

d. Carbonated beverages

Answer a. Cimetidine

Anything that raises the gastric pH will inhibit iron absorption. H_2-blockers, proton pump inhibitors, and liquid antacids can all impair iron absorption. Carbonated beverages and vitamin C can increase iron absorption because they acidify the stomach.

> High pH (basic) inhibits iron absorption. Acid, like vitamin C, increases iron absorption.

> *The patient admits to taking both liquid antacids and H_2-blockers. She did not think to tell you because she did not consider them important, saying, "Well, I don't need a prescription for them, so I didn't think of them as a medication." You ask her to stop taking them and start taking vitamin C. She continues the oral ferrous sulfate. Move the clock forward another 2 weeks. She returns feeling better except that her stool, she says, is black and she is constipated.*

> Oral ferrous sulfate causes constipation and black stool.

> Everyone on iron should be given a stool softener, such as docusate.

How can you differentiate the effect of oral ferrous sulfate from gastrointestinal bleeding?

a. Iron is stool-guaiac negative.
b. Iron is stool-guaiac positive.
c. Upper endoscopy is needed to be sure.
d. Colonoscopy is needed to be sure.

Answer a. Iron is stool-guaiac negative.

Oral ferrous sulfate, or elemental iron, causes constipation because only 1% to 2% of it is absorbed. The remaining iron in the bowel lumen causes constipation. It is also guaiac or heme negative. Colonoscopy would not be useful even if there was upper gastrointestinal (GI) tract bleeding.

> FerroUS iron is normal in the U.S.

What is the normal function of hepcidin?

a. Stores iron in the liver

b. Stores iron in the marrow

c. Master regulator of the rate of iron absorption in the bowel

d. Liver regulator of excretion bilirubin

e. Transports iron from destroyed RBCs to the liver for recycling

Answer c. Master regulator of the rate of iron absorption in the bowel

Hepcidin is made by the liver to stop excess iron absorption in the bowel. Hepcidin prevents hemochromatosis by blocking iron transport from enterocytes in the bowel wall into the portal system. Hepcidin keeps iron in the bowel.

Iron is absorbed in the duodenum.

Eight weeks after the starting iron and stopping antacids, the patient returns. Her symptoms are resolved and her hematocrit is 36%.

CASE 2: Thalassemia

Setting: *office*

CC: *"I didn't know my blood count was low."*

VS: *normal*

HPI: *A 28-year-old woman comes for preemployment screening tests prior to her first job as a fellow in orthopedic surgery. She has never had a CBC before and did not know her hematocrit was low.*

- *Hematocrit: 28%*
- *Hemoglobin: 10 g/dL*
- *MCV: 65 fL*
- *Smear: target cells*

Which is most likely to be found in this patient?

a. Her RBC count is elevated.

b. Her platelet count is elevated.

c. Her TIBC is elevated.

d. Her iron level is elevated.

Answer a. Her RBC count is elevated.

Thalassemia is associated with an increase in the RBC count. This patient most likely has thalassemia because it is a microcytic anemia with a very low MCV and no symptoms. This is because the RBC count goes up, which maintains the hematocrit. Also, target cells are most likely in a person with thalassemia. Platelet count elevation (choice b) is found in iron deficiency anemia.

Iron studies are ordered and the patient returns in 2 days to discuss the results. Which of the following is most likely to be found?

	Iron	TIBC	Ferritin
a.	High	NL	NL
b.	NL	NL	NL
c.	Low	Low	NL
d.	Low	High	NL

NL, normal; TIBC, total iron-binding capacity.

Answer b. Normal (iron, TIBC, ferritin)

Iron studies are normal in thalassemia. High circulating iron (choice a) level indicates sideroblastic anemia. The most accurate test for sideroblastic anemia is a Prussian blue stain. Low iron level with a low iron-binding capacity is the anemia of chronic disease. Choice d is iron deficiency anemia. Up to one-third of those with iron deficiency anemia can have a normal ferritin level. This is because ferritin is an acute phase reactant and its level increases with infection, cancer, and stress in the same way a white count or sedimentation rate would.

> Prussian blue is an iron stain. Sideroblastic anemia has iron built up in RBC mitochondria.

> Target Cells = Low Hemoglobin (Hb) in the Large RBC Membrane

> *The patient comes back to discuss her CBC and iron study results. She does not understand how her RBC count can be up, and her hematocrit level can be down.*

What else besides thalassemia can do this?

a. Hypoxia and polycythemia vera
b. Leukemia and essential thrombocytosis
c. Hereditary spherocytosis
d. Autoimmune hemolysis

Answer a. Hypoxia and polycythemia vera

Besides thalassemia, hypoxia causes an increased RBC count. These patients and those with polycythemia vera will have an excessively high hematocrit concentration. Thalassemia is a cause of anemia. It is easy to confuse hypoxia with polycythemia vera because both have supranormal high hematocrit levels.

> The repeat CBC and iron studies are normal. You inform the patient that she likely has thalassemia trait. You do not offer an electrophoresis because it will not change your management of this patient's medical care. She is requesting the electrophoresis because she "just wants to know."

What do you tell her?

a. You refuse because you do not want to be manipulated by another doctor.

b. You refuse, because it will not change her treatment.

c. You agree because you should do any test that is not harmful or expensive.

d. You agree because she has a right to know what type of thalassemia she has.

Answer d. You agree because she has a right to know what type of thalassemia she has.

The patient does not know if she has alpha-thalassemia or beta-thalassemia and she wants to know. Patients do *not* have a right to "any test they want." This is true even if they are paying cash and the test is uncomplicated. For example, I do not have a right to demand an abdominal computed tomography (CT) "just because I want to know." The physician is *not* obligated to perform tests unless they have direct medical benefit.

> You perform the hemoglobin electrophoresis and reschedule the patient in a week to discuss results.

Which electrophoresis result is most likely in this patient?

	HbA	HbA$_2$	HbF	HbH
a.	96%	2%	2%	0
b.	60%	1%	1%	38%
c.	2%	33%	65%	0

Answer a. Normal

This person has thalassemia trait. Alpha-thalassemia trait will give a normal electrophoresis. This is very hard for most people to understand. The electrophoresis does not tell the total amount of hemoglobin. It tells the relative percentages of each subtype. In alpha-thalassemia trait, all the types of hemoglobin are decreased, but they are decreased in normal proportions.

Choice b is more severe alpha-thalassemia. This would present with a lower hematocrit level and symptoms. Choice c is beta-thalassemia major, not beta-thalassemia trait.

> HbH = Tetrads of Four Beta-chains

> Four genes are needed to fully produce alpha-chains.

How many genes are deleted in this patient?

a. 1

b. 2

c. 3

d. 4

Answer b. 2

Alpha-thalassemia trait is defined at the deletion of two of the normal four genes responsible for alpha-chain production. One gene deletion is clinically normal. One gene deletion is a "silent carrier" in which the CBC is normal. Four gene deletions is not compatible with life. The fetus would die in utero of heart failure. You cannot survive without any alpha-chains.

> • Hemoglobin Bart's (HbBart) = Four Genes Deleted
> • HbH = Three Genes Deleted
> • Silent Carrier = One Gene Deleted

> *The patient is informed that she has alpha-thalassemia trait with two genes deleted. She is always asymptomatic. There is no treatment for her to correct the disorder.*

What benefit is there in knowing she has alpha-thalassemia trait?

a. There is no benefit except for her own knowledge.

b. The trait progresses to thalassemia major in some cases.

c. The patient can have genetic counseling for reproductive purposes.

Answer c. The patient can have genetic counseling for reproductive purposes.

For a person considering reproduction, thalassemia trait has enormous significance. A person may choose not to reproduce with a person who also has a thalassemia trait to avoid a risk of thalassemia major. The couple may choose to have amniocentesis or other testing done during pregnancy to assess a baby that has been conceived.

What is the most precise method of determining this patient's type of thalassemia?

a. Genetic testing

b. Bone marrow

c. Electrophoresis—as precise as it gets

Answer a. Genetic testing

The only way to be certain of the number of genes deleted is by genetic testing. Bone marrow shows nothing specific.

Which form of thalassemia has high reticulocytes?

a. Alpha-thalassemia trait

b. Three-gene-deleted alpha-thalassemia

c. Beta-thalassemia trait

d. Beta-thalassemia major

Answer b. Three-gene-deleted alpha-thalassemia

The deletion of three genes results in a much lower hematocrit that needs periodic transfusion. The RBCs are made in increased number, but they have a very short survival.

CASE 3: Vitamin B$_{12}$ Deficiency (Alcoholism, Peripheral Neuropathy)

Setting: *office*

CC: *"I have numbness and tingling in my feet."*

HPI: *A 78-year-old man comes to your office with several weeks of progressive weakness and fatigue. He easily tires when exerting himself. Over the last 1 to 2 weeks, he has developed a "tingling" in his feet that he describes as a "pins and needles" sensation.*

PMHx:
- *Alcoholism*
- *Hypertension*
- *Diabetes*

Medications:
- *Enalapril*
- *Metformin*

PE:
- *General: tired older man*
- *Cardiovascular: 2/6 murmur at apex radiating to axilla*
- *Chest: clear*
- *Neurological: decreased sensation symmetrically over the lower extremities bilaterally; normal position and vibratory sensation*

How can you tell the difference between peripheral neuropathy from alcohol, diabetes, or vitamin B$_{12}$ deficiency by symptoms alone?

a. Duration

b. Intensity

c. Location

d. Impossible to tell

Answer d. Impossible to tell

Peripheral neuropathy is indistinguishable based on the etiology. All etiologies cause bilateral symptoms, which are more noticed in the feet, slowly progressive, and defined as "pins and needles" sensations. The precise mechanism of the damage to myelin in vitamin B$_{12}$ deficiency is not precise. Diabetes and alcohol can *also* cause deficits of position and vibratory sense.

All peripheral neuropathy is from damaged myelin.

Discuss the patient's alcohol use with him. Use the CAGE questions:
- *Are you trying to* **C**ut down *the amount of alcohol you use?*
- *Does it make you* **A**nnoyed *when asked about your drinking?*
- *Do you feel* **G**uilty *after drinking?*
- *Do you start your day with an* **E**ye opener *in the morning?*

Initial Orders:
- *CBC*
- *Basic metabolic panel (CHEM-7)*
- *Calcium and magnesium levels*
- *Glycosylated hemoglobin (HbA$_1$c)*
- *Vitamin B$_{12}$ and folate levels*

Although the most accurate test of peripheral neuropathy is the electrodiagnostic test (i.e., nerve conduction studies), this test should not be done routinely for either diabetes or vitamin B$_{12}$ deficiency. It should be a clinical diagnosis.

The precise mechanism of myelin damage in vitamin B$_{12}$ deficiency is not clear.

You advance the clock 1 week.

CBC Results:
- *Hematocrit: 28%*
- *MCV: 118 fL*
- *WBCs: 2800/μL*
- *Platelets: 120,000/μL*

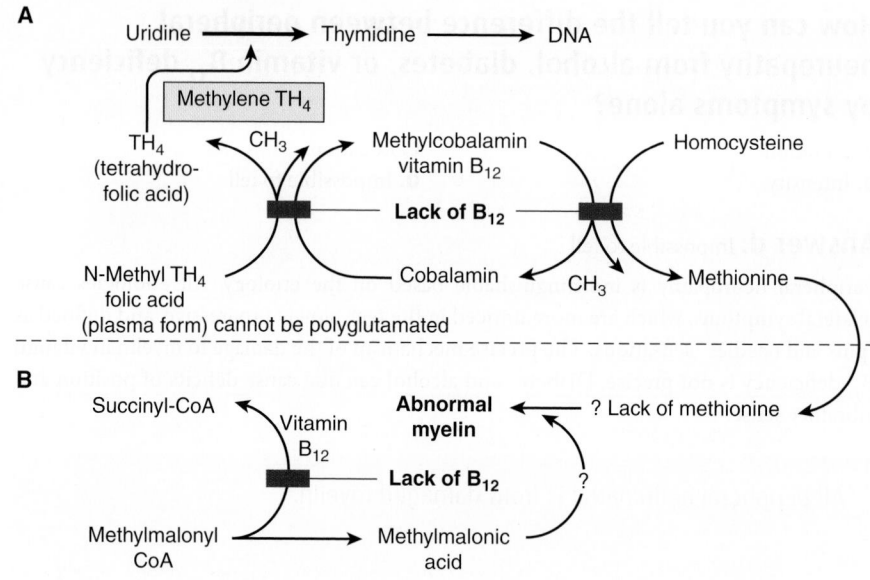

Figure 2-1. Role of cobalamin (vitamin B_{12}) and folic acid in nucleic acid and myelin metabolism. Lack of either cobalamin or folic acid retards DNA synthesis (**A**) and lack of cobalamin leads to loss of folic acid, which cannot be held intracellularly unless polyglutamated. Lack of cobalamin also leads to abnormal myelin synthesis, probably via a deficiency in methionine production (**B**). CH_3, methylium cation; CoA, coenzyme A; ?, possible. (Reproduced with permission from Chandrasoma P, Taylor CR. *Concise Pathology*, 3rd ed. New York: McGraw-Hill; 1998.)

- *Vitamin B_{12} level: borderline low*
- *Folate: normal*
- *Calcium, magnesium: normal*

- *Glucose: 185 mg/dL*
- *HbA_1c: 8.5%*

Vitamin B_{12} is essential for methyl transfer in DNA production (Figure 2-1).

Vitamin B_{12} deficiency can cause pancytopenia or anemia alone.

What is the goal of glucose in a diabetic?

a. It depends on whether it is type 1 or 2 diabetes.
b. The goal is between 80 and 110 mg/dL.

c. The goal is HbA_1c <6.5%.
d. The goal is HbA_1c <7%.
e. The goal is HbA_1c <10%.

Answer d. The goal is HbA_1c <7%.

You should add medications until the HbA_1c is <7%. The initial diagnosis of diabetes is a HbA_1c >6.5%.

With a HbA$_1$c >7%, you should add a second oral hypoglycemic. Which second agent to add is not clear. Metformin is first. As a second, you can add a sulfonylurea, rosiglitazone, nateglinide (or repaglinide), or a dipeptidyl peptidase IV (DPP-IV) inhibitor such as sitagliptin, saxagliptin, or linagliptin.

What test should be done to confirm the presence of vitamin B$_{12}$ deficiency?

a. Methylmalonic acid level

b. Anti-intrinsic factor/antiparietal cell antibodies

c. Schilling test

d. Homocysteine level

Answer a. Methylmalonic acid level

Methylmalonic acid levels build up in vitamin B$_{12}$ deficiency. Homocysteine level increases in both vitamin B$_{12}$ and folate deficiency. Vitamin B$_{12}$ deficiency can have a low normal level in 10% to 20% of patients routinely. Anti-intrinsic factor, antiparietal cell antibodies, and the Schilling test are not used to discover whether there is a vitamin B$_{12}$ deficiency. They are used to identify the etiology of the deficiency.

Orders:
- *Second oral hypoglycemic agent*
- *Methylmalonic acid level*
- *Dilated eye examination*

Advance the clock to get the results of the methylmalonic acid (MMA) level, which turns out to be elevated. The point of doing the anti-intrinsic factor and antiparietal cell antibody tests is to determine the etiology of the vitamin B$_{12}$ deficiency, which is particularly important in this case.
    Both antibodies are negative.

What is the most likely cause of the vitamin B$_{12}$ deficiency?

a. Blind loop syndrome

b. Pernicious anemia

c. Metformin use

d. Angiotensin-converting enzyme (ACE) inhibitor use

e. Dietary deficiency

Answer c. Metformin use

Metformin decreases intestinal absorption of vitamin B$_{12}$ in 10% to 30% of patients.

Metformin causes decreased ileal absorption of vitamin B$_{12}$. Calcium supplementation corrects it.

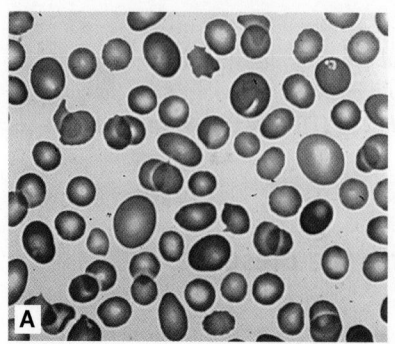 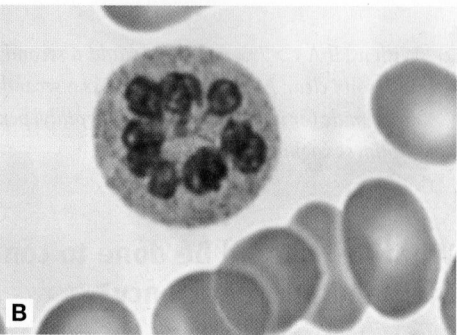

Figure 2-2. Peripheral blood smear from a patient with vitamin B_{12} deficiency showing oval macrocytes (**A**) and hypersegmented neutrophil (**B**). (Reproduced with permission from Lichtman MA, et al. *Lichtman's Atlas of Hematology.* 2007, www.accessmedicine.com.)

What is the difference between megaloblastic and macrocytic anemia?

a. MCV

b. Vitamin B_{12} etiology

c. Folate deficiency etiology

d. Hypersegmented neutrophils

Answer d. Hypersegmented neutrophils

Macrocytic just means an MCV >100 fL. Vitamin B_{12} and folate deficiency both cause macrocytosis and megaloblastosis. They are indistinguishable based on hematologic findings (Figure 2-2).

> Folate is not needed for myelin formation.

> *Vitamin B_{12} is given orally. Two weeks later, laboratory test results show an elevated lactate dehydrogenase (LDH) and indirect bilirubin. The smear still shows hypersegmented neutrophils.*

Why did the hematologic picture not improve?

a. Vitamin B_{12} is malabsorbed and needs to be given by injection.

b. It needs more time to recover.

c. Diabetes prevents cell formation until it is corrected.

Answer a. Vitamin B_{12} is malabsorbed and needs to be given by injection.

Whether the malabsorption is caused by calcium-dependent ileal malabsorption or pernicious anemia, you need to give vitamin B_{12} by intramuscular injection. Step 3 does not test dosing, but does test route of administration. The LDH and indirect bilirubin are elevated because there is an "ineffective erythropoiesis." Cells are made in the marrow, but destroyed just after production.

Reticulocyte count is low in vitamin B_{12} deficiency from early cell destruction.

Expect a hypercellular bone marrow in vitamin B_{12} deficiency.

Intramuscular vitamin B_{12} is given. Reticulocytes are expected to be produced in 2 to 3 days.

What should you test for immediately after replacement?

a. Potassium level

b. Calcium level

c. LDH and bilirubin

d. Hematocrit

Answer a. Potassium level

The potassium level can suddenly drop after giving vitamin B_{12}. Changes in LDH and bilirubin are of no clinical significance. You have to wait 1 to 2 weeks to see a meaningful change in hematocrit. Potassium is "packaged up" into an enormous number of new cells. If rapid cell breakdown causes hyperkalemia, then vitamin B_{12} replacement is one of the only things in which rapid cell formation can cause low potassium.

Potassium is 95% intracellular.

Neuropathy can improve if it is minor and of short duration.

CASE 4: Sickle Cell

Setting: *emergency department (ED)*

CC: *"I have really bad pain in my legs, back, and chest."*

VS: *R: 28 breaths/minute; BP: 152/88 mm Hg; P: 110 beats/minute; T: 101.8°F*

HPI: *A 28-year-old man with a history of sickle cell (SS) disease arrives at the ED with recurrence of a pain crisis. This is the same as his usual crisis. He has been noncompliant with hydroxyurea. Besides pain, he has had fever. At home, it was 102°F.*

PMHx:
- *Gallstones*
- *Osteomyelitis*
- *Skin ulcers*
- *Pneumonia*
- *Priapism episode in past*

Gallstones in SS disease are from an aggregation of chronically high indirect bilirubin levels.

The mechanism of skin ulcers is not clear, but poor flow is likely.

Medications:
- *Folic acid*
- *Hydroxyurea (not taking)*
- *Oxycodone*

What is the most important step at this time?

a. Perform physical examination.
b. Draw blood cultures and start antibiotics.
c. Begin intravenous (IV) fluids.
d. Restart hydroxyurea
e. Obtain old records to confirm SS in this patient.

Answer b. Draw blood cultures and start antibiotics.

Because doing the physical examination advances the clock and moves "Simulated Time," this is a "Save-a-Life Point." Infection in SS is easily fatal unless rapidly treated. Start antibiotics immediately. *Pneumococcus, Haemophilus, Klebsiella,* and *Salmonella* can all be growing in the blood at the time of the *first* temperature elevation.

Sickle Cell + Fever = Blood Cultures + Ceftriaxone NOW!

Sickle cell anemia eliminates the spleen through the process of autoinfarction.

No Spleen = Encapsulated Organisms Kill the Patient

PE:
- *Chest: some rales at left base; decreased excursion from splinting*
- *Extremities: ulcer with superficial purulent material over anterior shin; scarring from old ulcers scattered on legs*
- *Heart: 1/6 systolic murmur*
- *Neurological: nonfocal*
- *Genitals: normal*

What causes priapism in SS disease?

a. Stasis in penis

b. Arterial insufficiency

c. Stasis and infarction of prostatic plexus of veins

d. Decreased hemoglobin concentration

Answer c. Stasis and infarction of prostatic plexus of veins

The same stasis and infarction of flow that cause chest syndrome, retinal lesions, skin lesions, and stroke, also diminishes flow out of the penis as veins pass through the prostate.

SS disease is associated with decreased nitric oxide, causing priapism, which is similar to how pulmonary hypertension develops.

The patient is very uncomfortable. Because you will be treating patients unfamiliar to you in an ED setting, you will be confronted with people you are not sure have SS crisis. Ethically, it is better to treat everyone as having a genuine event and give pain medications. The most important part of this case is to give oxygen, fluids, and antibiotics before all other considerations. Stopping the crisis and preventing septic death from an autosplenectomized adult with SS disease is the most important task.

Initial Orders:
- *Oxygen*
- *Normal saline (NS) continuously*
- *Ceftriaxone (if febrile)*
- *Hydromorphone (Dilaudid) IV*
- *CBC and peripheral smear*
- *Liver function tests (LFTs)*
- *Reticulocyte count*
- *Chest x-ray*
- *Electrophoresis (if patient is unknown to you)*
- *Urinalysis (UA) and blood cultures (if not done)*
- *Folic acid*

Any patient in pain can have hypertension and tachycardia. Treat the pain first and recheck blood pressure and heart rate.

SS disease originates from a single amino acid substitution. Valine replaces glutamic acid at position 6

You move the clock forward 1 hour and check to see that the pain has improved with "Interval History." Rechecking oxygen saturation is always a good idea because the root cause of SS crisis is an abnormal crystallization of sickle hemoglobin at low oxygen states.

Test Results:
- *CBC and peripheral smear: hematocrit 28%; smear: sickled cells, WBCs 18,000/μL (Figure 2-3)*
- *LFTs: indirect bilirubin elevated 2.5 mg/dL*
- *Reticulocyte count: 15%*
- *Chest x-ray: left lower lobe infiltrate*
- *UA: no WBCs*

Why are there high levels of bilirubin and bilirubin stones in SS disease?
- Normal RBCs live 90 to 120 days.
- Sickle RBCs live only 10 to 20 days.

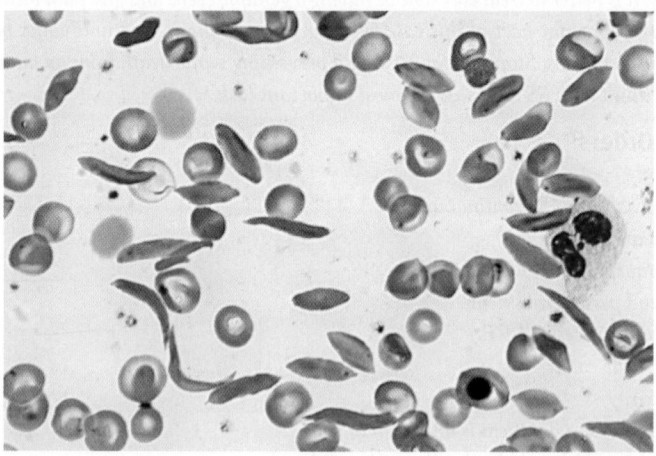

Figure 2-3. Sickle cells. Homozygous sickle cell disease. A nucleated red blood cell and neutrophil are also in the field. (Reproduced with permission from Longo DL, et al. *Harrison's Principles of Internal Medicine*, 18th ed. 2012, www.accessmedicine.com.)

Everyone with SS disease has a reticulocyte count 5 to 10 times higher than normal because cells are rapidly destroyed.

SS disease is a chronic, partially compensated hemolytic anemia.

Although the chest x-ray shows an infiltrate, the patient is already on antibiotics for fever. Other antibiotic choices are levofloxacin, moxifloxacin, or adding vancomycin to the ceftriaxone. This is all to cover pneumococcus. WBC counts are routinely elevated in SS disease. This is an expected finding and is part of the chronic hyperactivity of the marrow.

Expected Abnormalities in Sickle Cell Disease
• Reticulocyte count 5% to 25%
• High indirect bilirubin level
• Elevated WBC count

Salmonella is the most common documented cause of osteomyelitis in SS disease.

Pulmonary hypertension is common in SS disease from deficient nitric oxide (NO).

You move the clock forward 1 day after the initial laboratory test results are checked and oxygen, fluids, pain medications, and antibiotics are ordered. On hospital days 2 and 3, the hematocrit levels drop from 28% to 25% to 20%.

What is the most likely cause?

a. Folic acid insufficiency

b. Parvovirus

c. Sepsis

d. Sickle cell crisis itself

Answer b. Parvovirus

Parvovirus can "freeze" the marrow in SS disease. It has a predilection for infecting those with hemoglobinopathy. Folic acid deficiency can definitely lead to a sudden stop in RBC production, so you should check to see if you remembered to order a folic acid test. Sepsis can stop marrow production but should not work this fast. You should not ascribe sudden drops in hematocrit levels to the SS crisis alone. Pain crises are not the same as hemolytic events. The etiology of pain in SS crisis is not precisely clear, but it is definitely not the same as seeing a drop in hematocrit.

Orders:
- *Reticulocyte count*
- *Repeat CBC*
- *Folic acid if not ordered*

The reticulocyte count comes back as 2%. This is far too low for SS disease especially in a person on folic acid.

Orders:
- *Parvovirus polymerase chain reaction (PCR) for DNA*
- *IV immunoglobulin (IVIG) if the hematocrit level continues to drop*
- *Transfusion*

The most accurate test for SS disease is hemoglobin electrophoresis.

Sickle cell trait is increased in certain countries because it stops the spread of malaria by destroying the first infected cells.

Despite giving oxygen and adding vancomycin to ceftriaxone and hydration, the patient's chest pain and hypoxia worsen. What is the next step?

a. Change antibiotics.

b. Provide continuous positive airway pressure (CPAP).

c. Perform exchange transfusion.

Answer c. Perform exchange transfusion.

Exchange transfusion is the fastest way to terminate a pain crisis. It involves replacing the majority or the patient's blood. This effectively eliminates the sickling. Indications for exchange transfusion are:

- Acute chest syndrome not responding (hypoxia worsens)
- Central nervous system (CNS) events or stroke
- Priapism
- Retinal infarction

Order a hematology consultation for a patient with severe sickle crisis, especially for one needing an exchange transfusion. Move the clock forward a few hours. After the transfusion, the patient's symptoms resolve. Cultures do not grow an organism. Move the clock forward 6 to 12 hours at a time.

On hospital day 7, the patient is ready to leave. You get the message "This case will end in 5 minutes of real time."

What are your final orders?
- *Folic acid test*
- *Pneumococcal vaccine (if not previously given in last 5 years)*
- *Hydroxyurea*
- *Follow-up office visit in 1 week*

Hydroxyurea increases levels of fetal hemoglobin.

Sickle cell disease predisposes to dehydration by impairing renal tubular concentrating ability.

CASE 5: **Autoimmune Hemolysis**

Setting: *ED*

CC: *"I feel very weak and my skin has turned yellow."*

VS: *R: 26 breaths/minute; BP: 102/64 mm Hg; P: 118 beats/minute; T: 99.8°F*

HPI: *A 43-year-old woman recently treated for a dental abscess with amoxicillin presents to the ED with 2 days of progressively worsening weakness, fatigue, and yellow skin. She says that her friends told her that her eyes have turned yellow.*

PMHx:
- *Dental abscess*
- *Root canal performed 4 days ago*

Medications:
- *Amoxicillin for last 4 days*

PE:
- *Skin: jaundiced*
- *Head, ears, eyes, nose, throat (HEENT): scleral icterus*
- *Abdomen: soft, nontender, no spleen felt*

Initial Orders:
- *LFTs*
- *CBC*
- *UA*
- *LDH*

Move the clock forward only enough time to obtain test results. There is no way to tell from the jaundice and icterus whether this is from a biliary source or is hepatic or hemolytic in nature. You can only tell once you know whether it is direct bilirubin or indirect bilirubin.

Which form of hemolysis produces bilirubin in the urine?

a. None
b. Spherocytosis
c. Hemolytic uremic syndrome (HUS)

d. Autoimmune
e. Paroxysmal nocturnal hemoglobinuria (PNH)

Answer a. None

Only direct bilirubin goes into the urine. Indirect bilirubin does not go into urine. Hemolysis produces indirect bilirubin, which is not water soluble. There are two ways to get tests. One is: "Hey, I will order a bunch of tests because I do not know what is there!" The other is: "Direct bilirubin from hepatitis or obstructive jaundice goes into the urine. Indirect bilirubin from hemolysis does not go into the urine. I am getting the UA to *prove* or *disprove*, whether there is bilirubin in the urine, so I can establish a diagnosis."

Move the clock forward 30 to 50 minutes.

Laboratory Test Results:
- *LFTs: normal aspartate aminotransferase (AST) and alanine aminotransferase (ALT); total bilirubin 8 mg/dL, direct bilirubin 0.8 µmol /L*
- *CBC: hematocrit 26%; MCV 105 fL; platelets normal; WBCs 7400/µL*
- *UA: no urobilinogen; no RBCs*
- *LDH: elevated*

These results exclude a liver source of jaundice. Drug-induced hepatitis elevates AST, and viral hepatitis elevates ALT.

Why is MCV elevated?

a. Reticulocytes are larger than mature cells.
b. Lipids stick to RBCs making them look larger.

c. Myelodysplasia has developed.
d. Folic acid deficiency developed.

Answer a. Reticulocytes are larger than mature cells.

New cells or reticulocytes are slightly larger than mature RBCs. You should expect a slightly elevated MCV with hemolysis. Although lipids do sometimes stick to cells making them larger, this has nothing to do with this case. It is unlikely folic acid deficiency can develop in 1 to 2 days and change MCV like this.

LDH level increases with any form of cell destruction.

Orders:
- Repeat CBC
- Haptoglobin
- Reticulocyte count
- Coombs test
- Peripheral smear

Which of the following is most likely to give spherocytes on smear?

a. Autoimmune hemolysis
b. Glucose-6-phosphate dehydrogenase (G6PD) deficiency
c. PNH
d. Cold agglutinin disease

Answer a. Autoimmune hemolysis

Immunoglobulin G (IgG) antibodies grab onto a piece of the RBC membrane. Macrophages and the spleen remove pieces of the membrane. This produces a tighter, smaller cell with less membrane but the same amount of hemoglobin. This produces a cell that is small and round—a *spherocyte*.

Move the clock forward 1 hour.

- CBC: hematocrit 24%
- Haptoglobin: decreased
- Reticulocyte count: 8%
- Coombs test: positive IgG warm antibody
- Smear: no schistocytes; no fragmented cells; spherocytes are seen

Hereditary spherocytosis is most likely to enlarge the spleen.

What is the difference between a direct and indirect Coombs test?

a. There is no difference in vitro.
b. A direct Coombs test detects IgG attached to RBCs; an indirect Coombs test detects antibodies in circulation.
c. A direct Coombs test leads to cell destruction; an indirect Coombs test does not.

Answer b. A direct Coombs test detects IgG attached to RBCs; an indirect Coombs test detects antibodies in circulation.

In a direct Coombs test, antibodies attach to RBCs. The antibodies are used against Fc receptors to detect clumping. In an indirect Coombs test, neutral sheep RBCs are introduced into patient serum. Antibodies then attach to the RBCs. Although an indirect Coombs test implies a higher level of antibody than a direct Coombs test, the clinical implications are negligible.

> Splenic enlargement needs time. Autoimmune hemolysis is too acute to enlarge the spleen.

> *When the Coombs test result is positive and you see a clear decrease in haptoglobin and elevation in reticulocyte count and jaundice, you know this is autoimmune hemolysis. You should add glucocorticoids, such as prednisone or methylprednisolone, and repeat the CBC in 4 to 6 hours.*

> Penicillins destroy RBCs with a hapten mechanism. Antibodies are made to both the RBC membrane and penicillin.

Where are the RBCs being destroyed?

a. Spleen
b. Liver
c. Intravascular

Answer a. Spleen

Warm IgG antibodies lead to destruction of RBCs in the spleen. Cold immunoglobulin M (IgM) antibodies destroy RBCs in the liver. IgG antibodies can be treated with steroids. IgM antibodies do not respond to steroids.

> IgM cold agglutinins originate from mycoplasma and Epstein-Barr virus.

> IgM-induced hemolysis does not respond to steroids or splenectomy.

> *Methylprednisolone and folic acid are started. You move the clock forward 8 hours and then 24 hours. The repeat CBC shows a dropping hematocrit from 24% to 22% to 20%,*

and a transfusion of two units of packed RBCs is given. The hematocrit stays at 20%. Two more units raise the hematocrit concentration from 20% to 21%.

Each unit of packed red blood cells should increase the hematocrit concentration by 3 points.

What should you do to increase the hematocrit concentration?

a. Remove the spleen today.
b. Start IVIG.

c. Add dexamethasone to methylprednisolone.
d. Perform plasmapheresis.

Answer b. Start IVIG.

IVIG can help rapidly interrupt immune-mediated hemolysis if it is from a drug such as penicillin or on an autoimmune basis. There is no benefit to using multiple glucocorticoids. Plasmapheresis only removes circulating antibodies and does not work in hemolysis from a hapten mechanism. It will work with HUS or thrombotic thrombocytopenic purpura (TTP).

Removing the spleen is effective in preventing recurrences of immune-mediated cell destruction, but should not be done first.

IVIG saturates Fc receptors on macrophages.

IVIG prevents the macrophage from "grabbing" the IgG on the RBC and dragging it off to be destroyed in the spleen.

Azathioprine and cyclophosphamide are effective, but take a month to work.

Rituximab works for both cold agglutinins (IgM) and warm (IgG) by inhibiting CD20 cells.

Death from autoimmune or warm IgG hemolysis is very rare. If steroids do not control the disease and transfusions do not increase the cell count, IVIG can work acutely. Azathioprine, cyclophosphamide, and rituximab are immunosuppressives but take several weeks to work. Splenectomy prevents recurrences in 70% of patients.

CASE 6: Glucose-6-Phosphate Dehydrogenase Deficiency

Setting: *ED*

CC: *"My urine is dark."*

VS: *R: 25 breaths/minute; BP: 110/70 mm Hg; P: 105 beats/minute; T: 101°F*

HPI: *A 23-year-old man comes to the ED with complaints of a few hours of dark urine and fatigue. He had been having a cough with sputum and fever for the past 2 days. His condition suddenly got worse after his temperature went up early today. He has not started any new medications recently.*

PE:
- *Chest: rales at right base*
- *Abdomen: nontender liver*
- *Neurological: normal*
- *Skin: yellow*

Initial Orders:
- *CBC*
- *Chest x-ray*
- *LFTs*
- *UA*
- *Oximeter*

Fever, cough, and sputum are clearly a respiratory infection. The question is: Why is the patient suddenly fatigued and why the jaundice?

Laboratory Test Results:
- *CBC: hematocrit 30%; MCV 90 fL; WBC and platelet counts normal*
- *Chest x-ray: right lower lobe infiltrate*
- *LFTs: total bilirubin 6.8 mg/dL; direct bilirubin 1.2 mg/dL; LDH elevated, AST and ALT normal*
- *UA: dipstick positive for blood, but no RBCs seen*
- *Oximeter: 92% on room air*

High indirect bilirubin, high LDH, and anemia are clear for hemolysis. The chest x-ray and hypoxia on oximeter indicate pneumonia.

Orders and Results:
- *Reticulocyte count: 4%*
- *Coombs test: negative*
- *Repeat hematocrit: 29%*
- *Start ceftriaxone and azithromycin*

Reticulocytes can take several days to increase to their full range. The negative Coombs test only really excludes autoimmune hemolysis. Lack of chronicity excludes PNH. The absence of splenomegaly and recurrences excludes hereditary spherocytosis.

Always do a peripheral smear on cases of hemolysis.

Order and Results:

• *Peripheral smear: bite cells, no schistocytes, no fragmented cells*

As you move the clock forward to get results, you will never lose points by reviewing the chart too much if you are uncertain. Bite cells are indicative of G6PD deficiency.

G6PD catalyzes the initial step in the hexose monophosphate (HMP) shunt.

Which of the following should be tested first to find G6PD deficiency?

a. G6PD level

b. Complement levels

c. Brilliant cresyl blue stain for Heinz bodies

d. Genetic studies

Answer c. Brilliant cresyl blue stain for Heinz bodies

Heinz bodies are not visible on routine peripheral blood smear. You can clearly miss G6PD deficiency by missing Heinz bodies unless you specifically look for them (Figure 2-4). G6PD levels are normal on the day of an acute hemolytic event because only older, deficient cells are destroyed.

After acute hemolysis, only cells with a normal G6PD level are left behind.

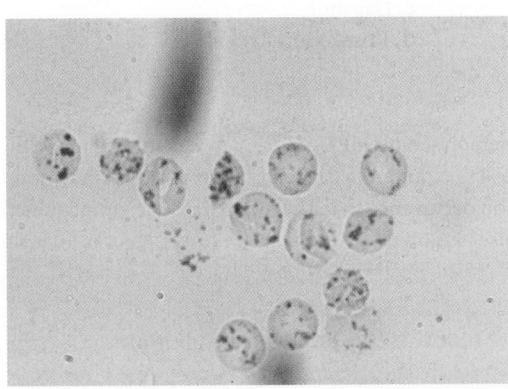

Figure 2-4. Heinz bodies. Supravital stain. These bodies are particles of denatured hemoglobin, usually attached to the inner face of the red blood cell membrane. (Reproduced with permission from Lichtman MA, et al. *Lichtman's Atlas of Hematology.* 2007, www.accessmedicine.com.)

Why are there *no* fragmented cells in G6PD deficiency?

a. Cells are taken to the spleen for destruction.

b. Cells "dissolve" or melt rather than fragment.

c. Cell destruction happens in the spleen.

Answer b. Cells "dissolve" or melt rather than fragment.

In G6PD, deficient cells are destroyed by oxidant stress in the vessels, but they do not "fragment" into pieces.

G6PD reduces nicotinamide adenine dinucleotide phosphate (NADP) to coenzyme nicotinamide adenine dinucleotide phosphate (NADPH).

Oxidants, such as superoxide anion (O2⁻) and hydrogen peroxide, are formed within RBCs, thereby oxidizing Hb.

Move the clock forward until you have the result of Heinz body stain. **The presence of Heinz bodies and bite cells are the best you can do to establish a diagnosis of G6PD deficiency on the day of the acute hemolytic event.**

Heinz bodies are precipitated oxidized hemoglobin in the RBC membrane.

Which of the following is the most common cause of acute hemolytic events in G6PD deficiency?

a. Fava beans

b. Infection

c. Dapsone

d. Primaquine

Answer b. Infection

Although the original description of hemolysis in G6PD deficiency was in patients with malaria who get primaquine, this is far less common a cause of hemolysis than infection. Infections are simply a far more common occurrence than the use of dapsone, primaquine, and fava beans although all of these cause hemolysis.

NADPH is needed for glutathione reductase to protect the cell from oxidant stress.

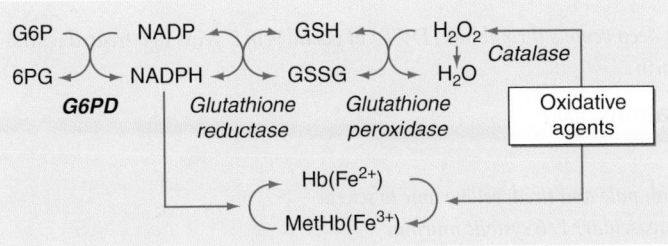

Figure 2-5. Diagram of redox metabolism in the red blood cell. G6P, glucose-6-phosphate; 6PG, 6-phosphogluconate; G6PD, glucose-6-phosphate dehydrogenase; GSH, reduced glutathione; GSSG, oxidized glutathione; Hb, hemoglobin; MetHb, methemoglobin; NADP, nicotinamide adenine dinucleotide phosphate; NADPH, reduced nicotinamide adenine dinucleotide phosphate. (Reproduced with permission from Longo DL, et al. *Harrison's Principles of Internal Medicine*, 18th ed. 2012, www.accessmedicine.com.)

The follow-up CBC the next day shows no significant change in hematocrit. What is the treatment?

a. Supportive, no specific therapy

b. Steroids

c. Intravenous G6PD

d. IVIGs

Answer a. Supportive, no specific therapy

Nothing reverses the oxidant stress of infection on cells deficient in G6PD. The most deficient cells are destroyed immediately. The ones with borderline levels will survive with bite cells and Heinz bodies. You have to wait 2 months and recheck the G6PD level.

G6PD deficiency is an X-linked recessive disorder (Figure 2-5).

X-linked recessive inheritance expresses almost exclusively in male patients.

CASE 7: Paroxysmal Nocturnal Hemoglobinuria

Setting: *office*

CC: *"My urine is dark when I get up in the morning."*

VS: *R: 24 breaths/minute; BP: 110/70 mm Hg; P: 78 beats/minutes; T: 97.8°F*

HPI: *A 24-year-old man with intermittent episodes of dark urine in the morning comes to your office. He has been feeling "weak and tired" for months. He gets short of breath when he is walking up stairs and is easily fatigued. He does not have a fever and has not had any infections in the past.*

PMHx: *deep venous thrombosis (DVT) of portal vein 2 years ago treated with 6 months of warfarin*

Medications: *none*

PE:
- *General: pale and tired, yellow tone to sclerae*
- *Cardiovascular: 1/6 systolic murmur*
- *Extremities: no edema, no tenderness*
- *Neurological: normal*

Initial Orders:
- *CBC*
- *UA*
- *CHEM-7*
- *LFTs*

What is the most common cause of hematuria?

a. Infection

b. Stones

c. Trauma

d. Neoplasia

Answer a. Infection

By far, the most common cause of dark urine from hematuria is infection, although dysuria (frequency, urgency, burning) should also be present and is not in this patient. Renal and bladder stones can certainly be the cause, but would usually be accompanied by flank pain. Although 2% to 5% of patients with renal cell cancer have polycythemia from excess erythropoietin production, it is far more common for renal cancer to present with hematuria and anemia.

There is no point in discussing dark urine without first excluding infection.

Move the clock forward only 1 to 2 days. Even though the test results may come back in just 2 to 4 hours if ordered "Routine," do not keep a patient waiting for hours in the office for these test results. Have the patient go home and come back to receive the results.

Reports:
- *CBC: hematocrit 28%; WBCs 2,800/μL (low); platelets 94,000/μL (low)*
- *UA: dipstick positive for hemoglobin, no urobilinogen; no WBCs*
- *CHEM-7: potassium (K) 5.3 mEq/L; otherwise normal*
- *LFTs: indirect bilirubin 4.2 mg/dL (elevated); LDH elevated*

Rapid hemolysis causes hyperkalemia.

Intravascular hemolysis gives hemoglobin in urine, with no RBCs.

Orders:
- *Peripheral smear*
- *Reticulocyte count*
- *Haptoglobin level*
- *Coombs test*

Have the patient return the following day to discuss laboratory test results:
- *Smear: schistocytes, fragmented cells*
- *Reticulocytes: 14%*
- *Haptoglobin: decreased*
- *Coombs test: negative*

Haptoglobin binds and transports newly released hemoglobin from destroyed RBCs to spleen and liver for recycling.

Free Hb and iron are damaging to the kidneys. Haptoglobin grabs it before it "burns" the kidney.

Hb is oxidized in the kidney to hemosiderin.

What is the mechanism of renal damage from hemoglobin?

a. Glomerulonephritis
b. Nephrotic syndrome
c. Acute tubular necrosis
d. Syndrome of inappropriate secretion of antidiuretic hormone (SIADH)
e. Obstruction

Answer c. Acute tubular necrosis

When haptoglobin is used up, free hemoglobin filters in the kidney and oxidizes the tubules potentially leading to renal failure from acute tubular necrosis (ATN). Hemosiderin in the urine is an indication of this severe oxidative toxicity to the kidney. Cells in the tubules and macrophages pick up discarded iron and store it in tissue as hemosiderin. When seen on UA, **hemosiderin is a *bad* thing**. It means enough free iron and hemoglobin have been released to overwhelm the haptoglobin, and now the macrophages are grabbing it to store it in tubule cells. The tubule cells then die, slough off, and end up in the patient's urine as hemosiderin.

Steps in Hemosiderin Production and Renal Injury
1. Macrophages scavenge bad iron.
2. Macrophages make hemosiderin in tissue.
3. Hemosiderin "cooks" the tubule cells.
4. Dead cells fall into the urine.

Hemosiderin in Urine = Zombie Tubule Cells

On the Step 3 examination, prognosis questions are often asked. They are phrased as: "What can the patient expect?"

The patient has hemolysis with pancytopenia. The presence of schistocytes and fragmented cells indicates intravascular hemolysis. The Coombs test is negative. Haptoglobin is more likely to be low in intravascular hemolysis. There is the DVT in an unusual site.

Pancytopenia + Intravascular Hemolysis + Clots = PNH

What is the most accurate test to establish a diagnosis of PNH?

a. Sugar water (sucrose hemolysis) test
b. CD55 and CD59 by flow cytometry
c. Ham test
d. Complement levels

Answer b. CD55 and CD59 by flow cytometry

CD55 and CD59 are the markers for complement-removing proteins indicating the deficiency of glycosylphosphatidylinositol (GPI), a protein that characterizes PNH. Normally, complement attaches to cells, but is removed by certain proteins before they are able to destroy the RBC. These proteins act as complement-removing factors and are sometimes called *decay-accelerating factors*. They anchor to the RBC on GPI. PNH is a genetic defect in GPI. The complement-removing proteins do not attach. Cells are then destroyed by complement.

The mutation-damaging GPI is on the stem cell.

PNH Stem Cell Defect = Pancytopenia

Which of these is *not* in the prognosis of PNH?

a. Iron deficiency anemia
b. Myelodysplasia
c. Polycythemia vera

d. Recurrent DVT
e. Acute myeloid leukemia

Answer c. Polycythemia vera

As a clonal stem cell defect, PNH can transform into a number of hematologic malignancies, such as acute leukemia. Aplastic anemia and myelodysplasia are routine findings. The only way to cure PNH, therefore, is with a bone marrow transplant to remove the underlying stem cell defect. Because of the morbidity and mortality associated with the bone marrow transplant procedure, treatment with chronic transfusion and iron replacement is often preferred.

> The only way to cure PNH is bone marrow transplantation.

What is the original root cause defect of PNH?

a. The mutation is in the phosphatidylinositol glycan anchor biosynthesis, class A (*PIGA*) gene.
b. There is a failure to produce the anchoring protein, GPI.

c. Decay-accelerating factor (DAF) or CD55 and CD59 cannot attach.
d. The complement stays attached to the RBCs.
e. RBCs are destroyed.

Answer a. The mutation is in the phosphatidylinositol glycan anchor biosynthesis, class A (*PIGA*) gene.

The sequence of events in PNH starts with choice a (*PIGA* is defective). Without *PIGA*, the GPI anchor is not made. Without the GPI anchor, DAF and CD59 do not attach to the RBC membrane. Without DAF and CD59, the complement stays attached and destroys cells. The root cause of everything, however, is the defect or mutation in the *PIGA* gene (Figure 2-6).

> Why is there more hemolysis at night?
> Lower respiratory rate increases the partial pressure of carbon dioxide (PCO_2), which makes slight acidosis, in turn, activating more complement.

The patient's low cytometry shows a deficiency of CD55 and CD59. You get the message, "This case will end in 5 minutes of real time." Your final orders should be:
* *Supplement with iron and folic acid.*
* *Transfuse as needed.*
* *Give steroids when the transfusion requirement is large.*
* *Give eculizumab to decrease transfusion dependence.*

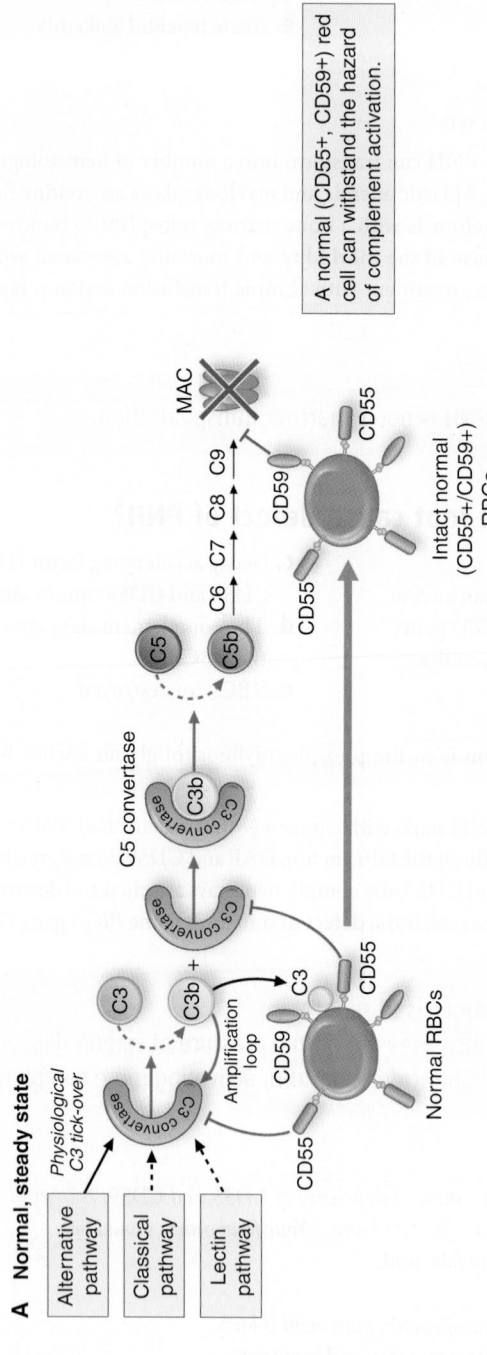

Figure 2-6. The complement cascade and the fate of red blood cells (RBCs). **A.** Normal red blood cells are protected from complement activation and subsequent hemolysis by CD55 and CD59. These two proteins, being glycosylphosphatidylinositol (GPI)-linked, are missing from the surface of paroxysmal nocturnal hemoglobinuria (PNH) red blood cells as a result of a somatic mutation of the X-linked *PIGA* gene that encodes a protein required for an early step of the GPI molecule biosynthesis.

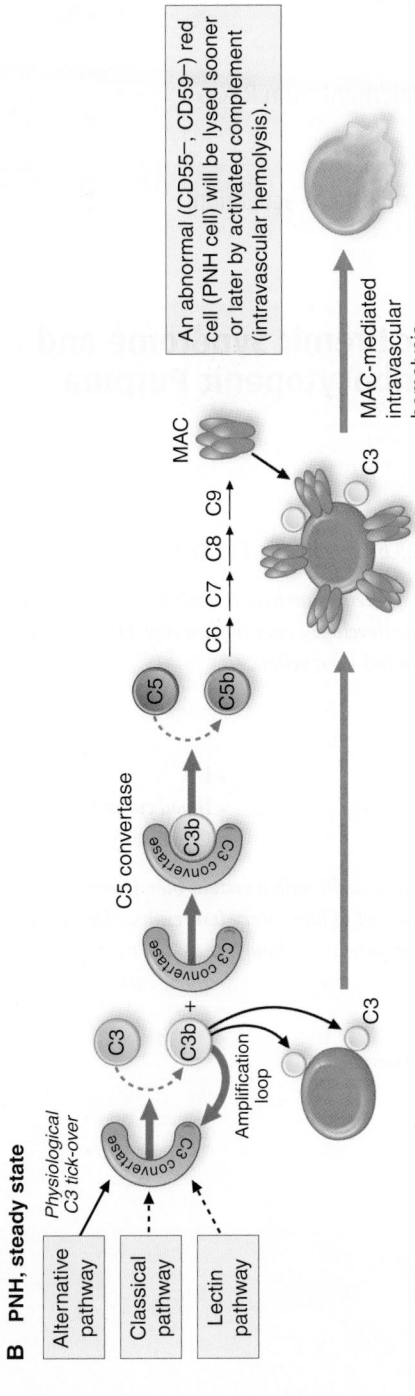

B PNH, steady state

Alternative pathway — *Physiological C3 tick-over*

Classical pathway

Lectin pathway

C3 convertase

Amplification loop

C3   C3b +

C5 convertase

C3 convertase   C3 convertase   C3b

C5   C5b

C6 C7 C8 C9

MAC

C3

C3

MAC-mediated intravascular hemolysis

An abnormal (CD55–, CD59–) red cell (PNH cell) will be lysed sooner or later by activated complement (intravascular hemolysis).

Figure 2-6. (*Continued*) **B.** In the steady state, PNH erythrocytes suffer from spontaneous (tick-over) complement activation, with consequent intravascular hemolysis through formation of the membrane attack complex (MAC); when extra complement is activated through the classical pathway, an exacerbation of hemolysis will result. (Reproduced with permission from Luzzato L, et al. Paroxysmal nocturnal hemoglobinuria and eculizumab. *Haematologica* 210;95(4):523–526.)

Eculizumab is an antibody against C5 complement.

Eculizumab removes complement from RBCs.

Steroids may diminish complement activation.

CASE 8: Hemolytic Uremic Syndrome and Thrombotic Thrombocytopenic Purpura

Setting: *ED*

CC: *"My urine is dark."*

VS: *BP: 92/50 mm Hg; P: 125 beats/minute; T: 102°F*

HPI: *A 43-year-old man with a recent diarrheal episode for 5 days arrives at the ED. He says that dark urine and fatigue developed over the last day. He has been febrile. There is some blood in the stool. His skin has been yellow.*

Initial Orders:
- *Normal saline*
- *CHEM-7*
- *LFTs*
- *CBC*
- *UA*
- *Blood cultures*
- *Chest x-ray*

When a patient is febrile and tachycardic with a systolic blood pressure <100 mm Hg, give fluids while waiting for the initial set of laboratory test results. Nothing is more important than hydration in a hypotensive patient. Although there are no respiratory symptoms, on CCS it is acceptable to order a chest x-ray on every patient with a fever.

PE:
- *Abdomen: mild diffuse tenderness*
- *Chest: clear*
- *Neurological: normal*

Fever =
- UA
- Blood cultures
- Chest x-ray

Move the clock forward to get laboratory test results:
- *CHEM-7: blood urea nitrogen (BUN) 34 g/dL; creatinine 1.8 mg/dL*
- *CBC: hematocrit 32%; platelets 78,000/μL*
- *UA: hemoglobin present; no bilirubin*
- *Blood cultures: normal*
- *Chest x-ray: normal*
- *Liver: bilirubin 5 mg/dL, 80% indirect; LDH elevated*

What is the most appropriate next step for this patient?

a. Check the laboratory test results for hemolysis, hydrate, and observe.

b. Start ciprofloxacin.

Answer a. Check the laboratory test results for hemolysis, hydrate, and observe.

Do not start antibiotics in this patient. With hemolysis, thrombocytopenia, and renal insufficiency, HUS is possible. Antibiotics can worsen HUS.

When antibiotics kill organisms, they release toxin, potentially worsening HUS.

Orders:
- *CBC*
- *Renal and LFTs*
- *Peripheral smear*
- *Stool culture on sorbitol MacConkey agar*

Sorbitol MacConkey agar is the specific test for *Escherichia coli* O157:H7.

Escherichia coli O157:H7 slowly ferments sorbitol.

Repeat laboratory test results come back in 30 minutes in the ED:
- *CHEM-7: BUN 44 g/dL; creatinine 2.1 mg/dL*
- *CBC: hematocrit 30%; platelets 52,000/μL*
- *Peripheral smear: schistocytes, fragmented cells*

Do not order either antibiotics or platelets. Platelets in HUS and TTP can worsen the disorder by creating more clumping out of platelets in small blood vessels.

Escherichia coli 0157:H7 elicits a Shiga toxin.

HUS and thrombotic thrombocytopenic purpura (TTP) originate from a deficiency of a disintegrin and metalloprotease with thrombospondin domain 13 (ADAMTS 13) (Figure 2-7).

You move the clock forward 12 hours and recheck the laboratory test results because rising BUN and creatinine levels, as well as a dropping platelet count, are very distressing. You will want to give platelets as the count drops, especially if it goes below 50,000/µL, but do not do it. They clump out and precipitate in the brain and kidney.

vWF and Platelet Adhesion

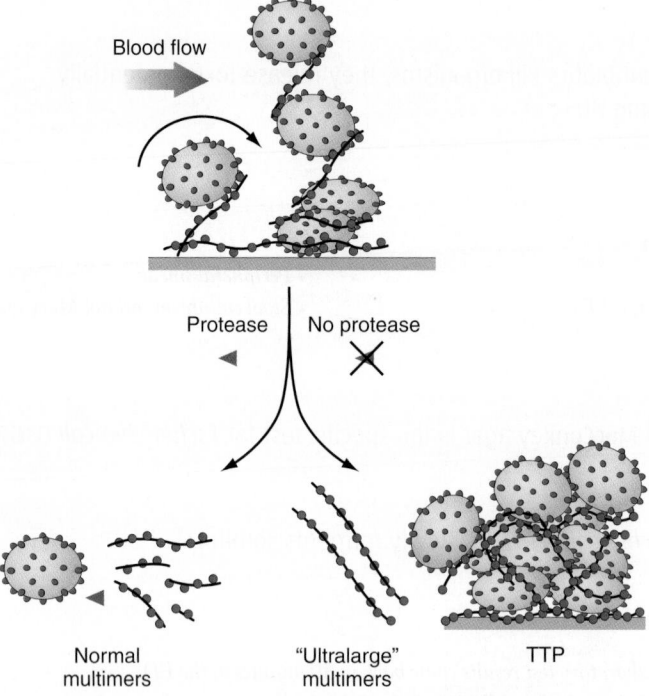

Figure 2-7. Pathogenesis of thrombotic thrombocytopenic purpura (TTP). Normally, the ultra-high-molecular-weight multimers of von Willebrand factor (vWF) produced by the endothelial cells are processed into smaller multimers by a plasma metalloproteinase called ADAMTS 13. In TTP, the activity of the protease is inhibited, and the ultra-high-molecular-weight multimers of vWF initiate platelet aggregation and thrombosis. (Reproduced with permission from Longo DL, et al. *Harrison's Principles of Internal Medicine,* 18th ed. 2012, www.accessmedicine.com.)

On the second hospital day, do an "Interval History." The patient is reported as developing confusion. You review the repeat laboratory test results:
- *CHEM-7: BUN 58 g/dL; creatinine 2.4 mg/dL*
- *CBC: hematocrit 26%; platelets 44,000/µL*

ADAMTS 13 dissolves von Willebrand factor (vWF). Without it, platelets stay excessively aggregated and adherent.

With worsening renal function, confusion, fever, and intravascular hemolysis, and decreasing platelet concentration, the patient is now defined as having TTP. You must not give platelets. Instead, order plasmapheresis when TTP is severe, or as in this case, worsening.

Plasmapheresis in TTP is not done to remove something from the patient's blood; it is done to add ADAMTS 13 from normal plasma.

Orders:
- *Move the patient to the intensive care unit (ICU).*
- *Repeat CBC, BUN, and creatinine tests.*
- *Consult hematology (remember, consultants on CCS never tell you what to do).*
- *Order plasmapheresis.*

ADAMTS 13 cleaves vWF, freeing platelets from each other.

Plasmapheresis adds ADAMTS 13 back to the patient.

In the ICU after plasmapheresis, the patient's confusion resolves. The platelet count starts to rise and the BUN and creatinine levels stop decreasing. Sorbitol MacConkey culture grows Escherichia coli O157:H7.

The case ends with the patient still in the ICU. If your case continues, transfer the patient back to the hospital floor 1 to 2 days after the BUN, creatinine, and platelet counts improve.

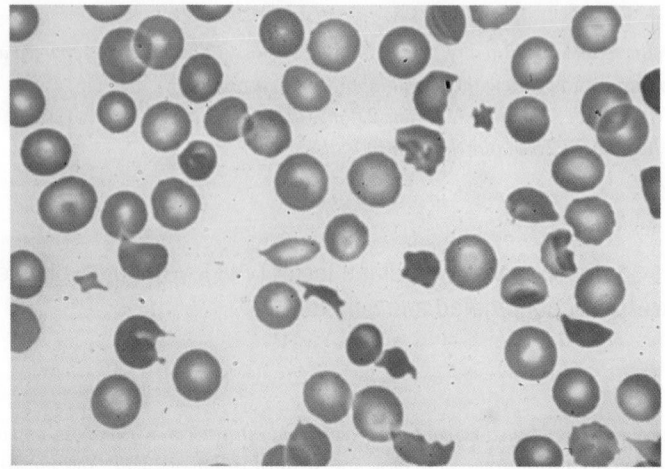

Figure 2-8. Thrombocytopenia, Thrombotic Thrombocytopenic Purpura (TTP). Blood film. Markedly decreased platelets (absent in this field) and red blood cell shape changes characteristic of TTP. (Reproduced with permission from Lichtman MA, et al. *Lichtman's Atlas of Hematology.* 2007, www.accessmedicine.com.)

In TTP, 100% of patients have low platelet counts and hemolysis, but only 50% of the patients have neurologic problems (Figure 2-8).

CASE 9: Immune Thrombocytopenic Purpura

Setting: *office*

CC: *"I have bleeding from my nose."*

HPI: *A 32-year-old woman with epistaxis for the past few days visits your office. The patient says she has a lifelong history of bleeding, but cannot remember precisely what the problem is that she bleeds from. She says "they always give me some pills for a week and it all gets better." She has some "dark spots" on her legs as well. Her menstrual periods can be very heavy at times.*

Medications: *none regularly*

PE:
- *General: healthy appearing*
- *HEENT: moderate epistaxis*
- *Skin: petechiae on bother lower extremities*

Initial Orders: *(done stat)*
• *CBC*
• *Prothrombin time (PT), activated partial thromboplastin time (aPTT), international normalized ratio (INR)*

Many offices and large practices have the ability to do laboratory tests on-site and can order the tests and request immediate results. On CCS, if you are uncertain what you can order, just place the order and the program will tell you if there is anything else you must do to get the results.

Report Available:
• *CBC: platelet count 27,000/μL*
• *PT, aPTT, INR: all normal*

Patients who are unstable can be sent to the hospital ED. You can order initial tests and treatments from the office and then send the person to the higher level of care.

You move this patient to the ED of the hospital. Every time you move a patient, all the original orders go with them unless you specifically stop them. In the ED, orders are:
• *Repeat CBC*
• *PT, aPTT, INR*
• *Prednisone*
• *Abdominal ultrasound*
• *Hematology evaluation*

As you advance the clock, the laboratory test results return:
• *CBC: platelets: 22,000/μL; hematocrit 40%*
• *PT, aPTT, INR: all normal*
• *Abdominal ultrasound: normal spleen size*
• *Hematology evaluation: "Your patient has been seen. We have no specific recommendations. Please order any tests or treatments you feel are indicated."*

Prednisone decreases the affinity of macrophages for platelets.

Antiplatelet antibodies are too nonspecific to be worthwhile.

One hour after transfer to the ED, the patient's bleeding worsens. There is melena, more petechiae, and hematuria. A repeat CBC shows platelet level at 8000/μL.

Which is the fastest way to raise the platelet count in idiopathic thrombocytopenic purpura (ITP)?

a. Prednisone

b. Dexamethasone

e. Platelet transfusion

d. IVIG

e. Romiplostim or eltrombopag

Answer d. IVIG

IVIG works faster than any other method of increasing the platelet count and is more effective. Steroids work by inhibiting the affinity of the macrophage for the Fc end of the antibodies attached to platelets. Platelet transfusions do not work because as soon as the platelets enter the body, they are covered with antiplatelet antibodies and rapidly destroyed.

What is the mechanism of IVIG in increasing platelet count?

a. Inhibition of neutrophils

b. Stimulation of megakaryocyte growth

c. Supersaturation of Fc receptors on macrophages

d. Inhibition of leukotrienes

e. Inhibition of interleukin

Answer c. Supersaturation of Fc receptors on macrophages

Antiplatelet antibodies cover the surface of platelets. Macrophages attach to the Fc receptor and "grab" the platelets and bring them to the spleen for destruction.

Megakaryocytes are produced in very high amounts in ITP.

No test can diagnose ITP. Bone marrow is sometimes evaluated to exclude a production problem by finding large numbers of megakaryocytes.

IVIG is ordered. Move the clock forward 1 to 2 hours and recheck the platelet count. If there is severe, life-threatening bleeding 6 hours after the start of steroids and IVIG, you may have to consider platelet transfusion. Platelet transfusion is rarely done for three reasons:

1. *Bleeding is rarely severe enough to need platelets.*
2. *Steroids are usually quite efficacious, starting within hours.*
3. *Platelets are consumed as soon as you infuse them into the patient.*

No one knows why ITP occurs.

New platelets have an increased size or "mean platelet volume."

As you move the clock forward, the platelet count stabilizes. If this problem recurs, send the patient for evaluation for splenectomy. If you move the clock forward, and ITP recurs after removing the spleen, start romiplostim or eltrombopag.

What is the precise location of platelet destruction in ITP?

a. Intravascular
b. Spleen

c. Kupffer cells of liver
d. Tissue

Answer b. Spleen

After being covered with antiplatelet antibodies and grabbed by macrophages, the platelets are actually destroyed in the spleen. This is why splenectomy is so effective in controlling ITP.

No Spleen = No Platelet Removal

Rh_0(D) immune globulin (RhoGAM) or anti-D antibodies have nothing to do with platelets. They stuff up the macrophages.

Romiplostim and eltrombopag are thrombopoietin. They stimulate megakaryocyte growth.

Rituximab removes CD20 lymphocytes, which make antibodies against platelets.

ITP cases end when the platelet counts start to rise and bleeding stops. The platelet count does not have to increase to normal levels. It just has to start rising. Steroids for initial therapy and adding IVIG for life-threatening bleeding remain the standard of care. The most likely fundamental of the basic science question on the Step 3 examination for ITP will be to know the mechanism of how IVIG works. The fragment antigen binding (Fab) *end of IVIG has nothing to do with platelets. IVIG mechanism is involved entirely with blocking the macrophage. If the macrophage is fully saturated with Fc ends of IVIG or $Rh_o(D)$ immune globulin (RhoGAM) (anti-D antibodies), there is no room to bind the Fc ends of the immunoglobulins attached to platelets.*

Rituximab works by removing the lymphocytes that make the antibodies that attack platelets. You know that rituximab removes CD20-positive lymphocytes. This is the same mechanism for how it works in cold agglutinin disease and how it works in rheumatoid arthritis.

Romiplostim and eltrombopag are stimulants of megakaryocytes. They are thrombopoietin. These medications are used when splenectomy does not control the disease. It seems that ITP is not entirely a "destruction problem" and that stimulating production seems to help.

CASE 10: Von Willebrand Disease

Setting: *office*

CC: *"I took aspirin, and when I cut myself shaving I bled for 2 days!"*

VS: *normal*

HPI: *A 23-year-old woman who is generally healthy comes to your office because of abnormal bleeding after a minor cut. It stood out because she usually never takes aspirin, but this time after using aspirin for a headache, the skin kept oozing blood for more than 2 days.*

PMHx: *prolonged bleeding after dental extraction in past*

Medications: *none*

PE:
• *Skin: bleeding from skin nick/cut when shaving; some petechiae of lower extremities*

Initial Orders:
• *CBC*
• *PT and aPTT*
• *CHEM-7*
• *LFTs*

Move the clock forward until the time that says "Report Available" for the CBC, PT, and aPTT. All bleeding problems need at least these tests. LFTs are done because most clotting factors are made in the liver.

Which of these is *not* made in the liver?

a. Factor VIII and vWF

b. Factor IX and X

c. Fibrinogen

d. Factor II, VII

e. Albumin

Answer a. Factor VIII and vWF

Factor VIII and vWF are made under the endothelial cell lining of the vasculature. That is precisely where they are needed when a person is cut and that is where they are both made and stored. All of the other clotting factors are made in the liver. That is why the PT and aPTT tell more about liver function than the transaminases AST and ALT. You can damage a tiny part of the liver (<5%) and have a huge bump up in AST/ALT levels, but you need to damage 70% to 80% of the liver before you even begin to see a synthetic abnormality of the clotting factors.

Platelet-Related Bleeding
- Skin—petechiae
- Nasal—epistaxis
- Gums and gingiva
- Vaginal

Factor-Related Bleeding
- Joints—hemarthrosis
- Muscles and hematoma

Move the clock 30 to 60 minutes to get the stat laboratory test report.

- *CBC: hematocrit 38%; MCV 88 fL; WBCs 8000/μL; platelets 225,000/μL (normal)*
- *PT: 12 seconds (normal)*
- *aPTT: 70 seconds (abnormally prolonged)*
- *Chemistry and LFTs: normal; normal LDH*

Causes of prolonged aPTT
- Deficiency of factor VIII, IX, XI, XII
- Acquired inhibitors of these factors
- von Willebrand disease (vWD)
- Antiphospholipid syndromes

Why can this not be hemophilia A?

a. Would not present first at this age
b. Wrong type of bleeding

c. Expressed only in men
d. All of the above

Answer d. All of the above

Hemophilia A should present as delayed bleeding into a joint in a male child.

Hemophilia A is an X-linked recessive disorder:
• Men only
• Y chromosome does not count
• Homozygous females are rare

The patient's bleeding stops. You send her home. The "bleeding time" test is not necessary. You already know she has prolonged bleeding. Also, the bleeding time test is too nonspecific to be useful. Any platelet disorder will give a prolonged bleeding time.

Orders:
• *vWF antigen level*
• *vWF activity (ristocetin cofactor and collagen activity) level*

vWD is autosomally transmitted, either dominant or recessive based on subtype.

Which cell in marrow makes vWF?

a. Neutrophils
b. RBCs

c. Megakaryocytes
d. Lymphocytes

Answer c. Megakaryocytes

Besides endothelial cells and the connective tissue of the vessel wall, vWF is also made by megakaryocytes.

Why is the aPTT level increased in vWD?

a. vWF is in the clotting cascade.
b. Factor VIII is bound to vWF.

c. vWD has an antiphospholipid antibody.

Answer b. Factor VIII is bound to vWF.

When vWF level is decreased, it is not there to bind factor VIII. This elevates the aPTT, but the function of factor VIII, which is a coagulant factor (the antihemophilic factor A), is not impaired. The other name for vWF is "factor VIII antigen." You should expect to see an elevated aPTT in half of patients with vWD.

The vWF antigen level is low. The ristocetin cofactor activity level is markedly impaired. You repeat the test the patient off aspirin and it persists. There is no active bleeding. This is likely type I vWD, which is seen in about 80% of cases. The patient needs her wisdom teeth removed. You are planning to give desmopressin acetate (DDAVP) or desmopressin prior to the procedure.

What is the mechanism of DDAVP?

a. Increased production of vWF

b. Increased expression of vWF receptors

c. Inhibition of ADAMTS 13

d. Release of subendothelial stores of vWF and factor VIII

e. Inhibition of plasmin

Answer d. Release of subendothelial stores of vWF and factor VIII

DDAVP releases what has already been made under endothelial stores. Aminocaproic acid and tranexamic acid work by inhibiting plasmin.

Type I vWD is a deficiency of vWF or antigen.

vWF acts in two ways:
1. Platelet to platelet IIb/IIIa (aggregation)
2. Platelet to vessel wall Ib/IX (adherence)

DDAVP is given and the dental extraction is performed. Bleeding persists and a subsequent dose of DDAVP is ineffective.

At this point, what medication should you use?

a. Aminocaproic acid

b. Factor VIII replacement

c. Protamine sulfate

d. Steroids

Answer b. Factor VIII replacement

Factor VIII and vWF (antigen) travel bound together. That is why you can use DDAVP for hemophilia treatment and you can use factor VIII replacement of vWD. Thrombin splits factor VIII off vWF. Aminocaproic acid is a plasmin inhibitor of marginal value. Protamine reverses heparin.

Type I vWD is autosomal dominant—half of children inheriting the gene mutation will be affected.

After giving factor VIII replacement, the bleeding stops. Counsel the patient not to use aspirin or aspirin-containing products. Advance the clock until you get the "Case will end in 5 minutes of real time" screen. No additional orders are necessary.

CASE 11: Clotting Factor Deficiency

Setting: *office*

CC: *"My surgeon told me to see about my bleeding risk before surgery."*

HPI: *A 50-year-old woman comes to see you about an elevated aPTT that her surgeon found prior to a planned lumpectomy for breast cancer. She had her screening mammogram at age 50 years and a small abnormality was found. Needle biopsy showed infiltrating ductal carcinoma. Bleeding was not excessive at the time of the biopsy. The patient is perimenopausal now and her menstrual periods have always been modest in intensity, lasting 3 to 4 days.*

PMHx: *normal vaginal delivery for children; no additional bleeding*

Medications: *none*

PE: *normal*

Initial Orders:
- *CBC*
- *PT, aPTT, INR*
- *LFTs*

Hemophilia is not expressed in women.

Hemophilia does not present at this age without abnormal bleeding.

Move the clock forward 1 week to get test results. This is a preoperative clearance case and is not an emergency. In preoperative clearance cases, never write the phrase "cleared for surgery." If there is nothing to do, write "Medically optimal for procedure. No further medical management needed prior to procedure."

Laboratory Test Results:
- *CBC and LFTs: normal*
- *PT and INR: normal*
- *aPTT: prolonged to 65 seconds*

Order a mixing study first when evaluating clotting factor deficiencies. Any clotting factor deficiency will correct to a normal aPTT when mixed 50:50 with normal plasma. This is because the clotting factor level has to be decreased by 70% to 80% before the aPTT will even begin to elevate. Often, the coagulation test will not be abnormal until the clotting factor deficiency is as much as 85% to 90%.

*If the aPTT does **not** correct or attain a normal level when mixed with normal plasma, it likely means the presence of a clotting factor inhibitor. Acquired inhibitors of factor VIII and IX can occur with aging and may not have serious pathologic significance. However, factor inhibitors can be caused by cancer.*

Deficiencies correct aPTT to normal.
Inhibitors do *not* correct to normal.

The mixing study shows a normalization of aPTT. Order a hematology consultation to show that you "know when to get help," but remember that consultants will never tell you concretely what to do.

Because this is a clotting factor deficiency, you should order specific clotting factor levels. The patient's gender and age eliminate the possibility of hemophilia.

Orders:
• *Factor XI level*
• *Factor XII level*

Factor XII deficiency is never associated with bleeding and never needs treatment.

Factor XIII deficiency does cause bleeding, but it is not in the clotting cascade, so aPTT is normal.

Factor XIII is "clot stabilizing factor" and may make fibrin permanently resistant to the effects of plasmin.

Reports:
• *Factor XI 15% of normal level*
• *Factor XII 90% of normal level*

Because the patient does not bleed under normal activity, there is no regular therapy to use. With a lumpectomy, the patient is about to undergo a serious operative procedure. You should tell the surgeon to give her fresh frozen plasma (FFP) an hour prior to the procedure. Factor XI replacement is not available in the United States. The value of aminocaproic acid and tranexamic acid for surgical procedures with factor XI deficiency is not clear. Both agents inhibit plasmin and prevent the breakdown of fibrin. The basic science mechanism question is clear. Whether to use them before operative procedures in factor XI deficiency is not clear.

Give FFP before operative procedures to patients with factor XI deficiency.

FFP has all clotting factors *except*:
• Factor VIII
• vWF

CASE 12: Thrombophilia (Hypercoagulable States): Deep Venous Thrombosis and Heparin-Induced Thrombocytopenia

Setting: *ED*

CC: *"My leg is swollen."*

VS: *R: 14 breaths/minute; BP: 126/86 mm Hg; P: 84 beats/minute; T: 100.8°F*

HPI: *A 34-year-old woman comes to your hospital ED by taxicab after getting off a plane from Gujarat, India. She developed pain in her leg that she noticed when disembarking from the plane. Her leg feels tight and "swollen." She denies dyspnea, chest pain, or light-headedness.*

PMHx: *tobacco smoker*

Medications: *oral contraceptives*

PE:
• *Cardiovascular: normal*
• *Chest: normal*
• *Extremities: swelling of left leg, warm to touch*

Homans sign (pain in calf on dorsiflexion) has limited accuracy.

A pain in the leg after a long flight and immobility is a clear risk for DVT. But even a long plane ride should not be enough to make a normal person clot. Plane rides unmask underlying thrombophilia (hypercoagulable state). This history, however, is enough to warrant therapy without waiting for results of duplex ultrasound.

Initial Orders:
- *Lower extremity duplex ultrasound*
- *Enoxaparin (low molecular weight heparin [LMWH])*
- *Chest x-ray*
- *Oximeter*
- *CBC, INR, PT, aPTT*

Clots, such as DVT or pulmonary embolus, give fever.

Results:
- *The duplex ultrasound shows a large clot in the femoral vein.*
- *The chest x-ray, CBC, and oximeter results are all normal.*

Even though the patient denies dyspnea, on CCS you can order "extra" tests that are reasonably related to the chief complaint. You will not lose points for getting an x-ray or oximeter for someone at risk of pulmonary embolus (PE). You will not lose points for getting a baseline CBC in someone you are potentially going to anticoagulate.

Orders:
- *Enoxaparin to continue subcutaneously*
- *Warfarin with target INR 2 to 3*

You do *not* have to order a thrombophilia evaluation for the first clot.

Warfarin inhibits factors II, VII, IX, and X.

The patient should not be admitted to the hospital just for a DVT. The patient can inject her own LMWH and be discharged with follow-up by her own doctor or an ambulatory care clinic. It takes at least 2 to 3 days for the INR to change in response to warfarin. Warfarin only stops production of new clotting factors, it does not alter the effect of clotting factors already present.

Make sure you advise the patient to stop smoking!

Warfarin causes skin necrosis with protein C deficiency because protein C is an anticoagulant.

Protein C:
• It has the shortest half-life of any factor.
• It is vitamin K dependent.
• Warfarin removes the anticoagulant.

*The patient is moved to the "Home" location. Move the clock 3 days forward for a visit in the office location. Perform "Interval History" to check symptoms. **You will need to check the INR every 1 to 2 days until the patient reaches a "steady state" on her warfarin dose.***

Which form of thrombophilia should be tested for this patient?

a. None
b. Protein C
c. Protein S
d. Antithrombin III
e. Antiphospholipid (APL) syndrome
f. Factor V Leiden mutation
g. Homocysteine

Answer a. None

It is an attractive choice to want to test for a form of thrombophilia in this patient. It just does not matter on the first clot. The intensity of warfarin to an INR of 2 to 3 is the same whether there is a thrombophilia or not. The duration of anticoagulation is the same at 6 months. None of these thrombophilias is proven to need lifelong anticoagulation with a single clot. In this patient's case, the main management is to tell her to stop smoking and stop using oral contraceptives.

Orders:
• *CBC*
• *INR*

The patient's CBC is normal. After 3 days on warfarin, the patient's INR is 1.5. You advise the patient strongly to stop smoking and stop using oral contraceptives as a form of contraception. She needs to continue enoxaparin (LMWH) for several more days until her INR is <2.

Protein S is a vitamin K-dependent anticoagulant just like protein C.

You have a daily check of the INR with the patient coming to the office each day. Three days later (after 6 days of warfarin), her INR is 2.1 and you stop enoxaparin. Advise the patient that she will need 6 months of therapy and that she should come in every 2 to 3 days for INR monitoring until you know the level is stable.

Factor V Leiden mutation is the most common genetic cause of thrombophilia.

Mechanism of Factor V Mutation
• Factor V does not respond to protein C.
• Protein C usually inhibits factor V.
• When mutated, factor V is resistant to protein C.
• The mechanism is the same as that in protein C deficiency.

Over the next 6 months, the patient's INR stays in the range of 2 to 3 and she is asymptomatic. Warfarin is stopped. A year later she develops shortness of breath over a few hours.

Which form of thrombophilia is most likely to have a recurrent clot?

a. All are equal
b. Protein C
c. Protein S
d. Antithrombin III

e. APL syndrome
f. Factor V Leiden mutation
g. Homocysteine

Answer e. APL syndrome

APL is most likely to recur and it is the only form of thrombophilia in which you may consider lifelong therapy with warfarin from the first clot. Because this patient does not have lupus or any other sign of autoimmune disease, there was no point in testing her. The most likely cause of this person's clot was smoking in a person on oral contraception.

The patient in the ED is markedly hypoxic and tachycardic. A CT angiogram shows a clot. Her blood pressure is normal and thrombolytics are not used. She is given a bolus of IV unfractionated heparin. The follow-up aPTT shows little elevation. A second IV bolus of heparin is given with only a slight rise in aPTT.

What is the reason for lack of response to IV heparin?

a. All are equal

b. Protein C

c. Protein S

d. Antithrombin III

e. APL syndrome

f. Factor V Leiden mutation

g. Homocysteine

Answer d. Antithrombin III

When a patient is resistant to the effects of IV heparin, it is most likely from antithrombin deficiency. Heparin works through potentiating the effects of antithrombin. Antithrombin is a misnomer in that it inhibits the effect of not only thrombin, but also the effect of all the clotting factors in the whole cascade. You recognize it when you bolus with IV heparin and there is no response.

APL Syndromes
- Lupus anticoagulant
- Anticardiolipin antibodies
- May raise aPTT, but cause clotting

The Russell viper venom test is the most accurate test for lupus anticoagulant.

The patient becomes stable by the end of the first hospital day. Heparin is continued. Warfarin is started. On the third hospital day, the platelet count begins to drop from 170,000/μL to 120,000/μL to 100,000/μL.

After stopping heparin, what is most appropriate course of action?

a. Give antiplatelet factor IV antibodies

b. Order serotonin release assay

c. Start argatroban

d. Start enoxaparin

Answer C. Start argatroban

Argatroban is a direct-acting thrombin inhibitor. There is no cross-reaction with heparin. Enoxaparin is a type of heparin. You must stop all forms of heparin when faced with heparin-induced thrombocytopenia (HIT).

It is not appropriate to wait for confirmatory laboratory testing for HIT. Although antiplatelet factor IV antibodies and serotonin release assay are the most accurate tests, it is more important to switch therapy.

HIT presents with thrombosis, not bleeding. Platelets "clump out."

CHAPTER 3

ENDOCRINOLOGY

CASE 1: Diabetes—Initial Diagnosis and Treatment

Setting: *office*

CC: *"I get thirsty a lot."*

VS: *R: 12 breaths/minute; BP: 144/92 mm Hg*

HPI: *A 53-year-old man comes for evaluation of his borderline high blood pressure (BP) and some intermittent sense of increased thirst. The patient has had BP readings of 134/86 mm Hg, 148/96 mm Hg, and 142/90 mm Hg on the last three visits. He has been reluctant to start antihypertensive medications and, instead, has been trying to correct it with exercise and weight loss. He has been trying for 9 months. His weight has increased by 4 lb.*

PMHx: *obesity*

ROS: *increased frequency of urination, no burning, no urgency, no hesitancy*

Medications: *none*

PE:
- *General: comfortable*
- *Heart, Lung, Abdomen: normal*

Initial Orders: (obtained fasting)
- *Basic metabolic panel (CHEM-7)*
- *Complete blood count (CBC)*
- *Urinalysis (UA)*
- *Glycated hemoglobin (HbA₁c)*
- *Lipid panel (low-density lipoprotein [LDL], high-density lipoprotein [HDL], triglycerides, total cholesterol)*

If the case gives the option for examining laboratory test results on the same day as the original visit, do so. If not, then reschedule the patient for the following week on the computer-based case simulation (CCS).

Always do an "Interval History" on any patient returning for a new office appointment.

There is no change in the patient's symptoms of intermittent thirst and inability to control his weight with diet and exercise.

Laboratory Test Results:
- *CHEM-7: glucose 218 mg/dL; blood urea nitrogen (BUN) 22 g/dL; creatinine 0.7 mg/dL; bicarbonate 24 mEq/L; potassium (K) 4.0 mEq/L*
- *CBC: normal*
- *UA: mild glucose (100 mg/dL); no white blood cells, no red blood cells*
- *HbA$_1$c: 8.4%*
- *Lipid panel (LDL, HDL, triglycerides, total cholesterol): LDL 145 mg/dL, others normal*

Obesity increases annually and so does diabetes.

Adipose tissue must have insulin for glucose to enter.

More Obesity = More Tissue Resistance = More Insulin Need

Insulin uses a tyrosine kinase receptor (Figure 3-1).

Lifestyle modifications of weight loss and exercise have already failed in this patient. You should still order "Advise," "Educate," and "Counsel" for both as well as a diabetic diet. However, given the increase in weight despite 6 months of previous efforts, you need to start medications. The same is true for hyperlipidemia. Metformin is the best initial therapy for obesity-related type 2 diabetes. It will not cause hypoglycemia and it will not increase weight. Sulfonylurea medications will do both of these things.

If people could do it, weight loss and exercise would eliminate 25% of diabetes immediately.

Exercising muscle does not need insulin.
Resting muscle does need insulin.

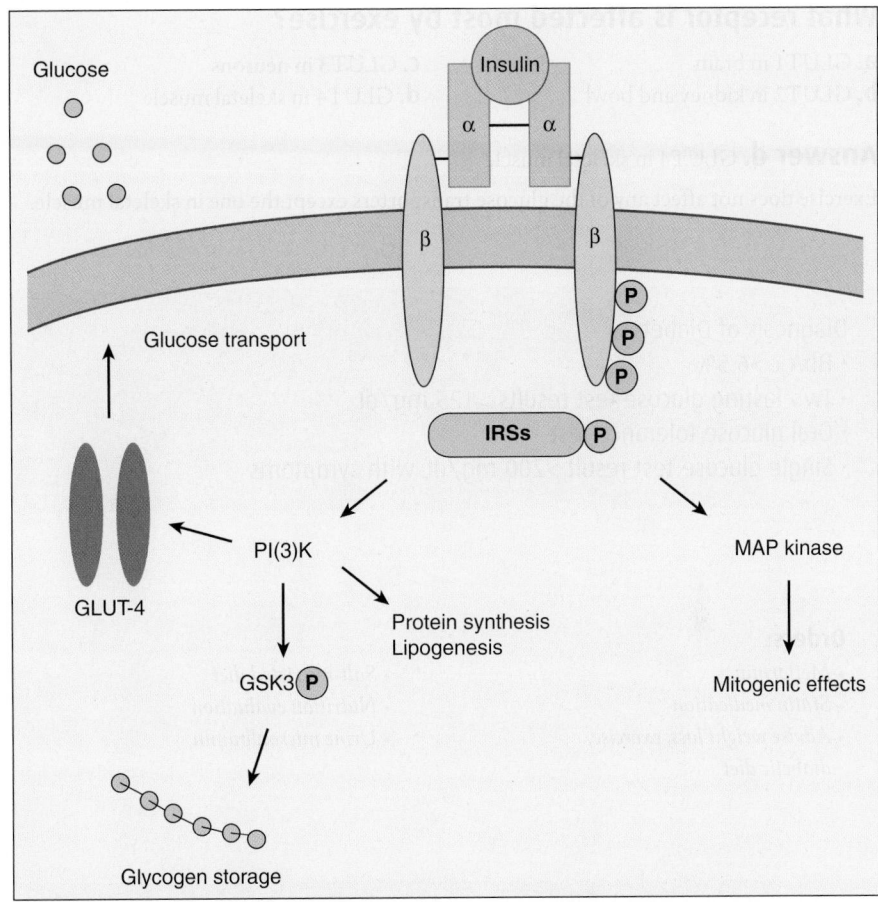

Figure 3-1. Model of insulin receptor signaling. The insulin receptor is composed of two and two subunits linked by disulfide bonds. Binding of insulin to the extracellular subunits activates a tyrosine kinase present in the cytoplasmic domain of the subunit. The activated kinase autophosphorylates specific tyrosine residues in the subunit. Receptor kinase activation is also the critical first step in a cascade of intracellular events that begins with phosphorylation of multiple docking proteins (insulin receptor substrates [IRSs]). Once activated, these multifunctional proteins initiate complex intracellular signaling pathways. Binding of IRS to phosphatidylinositol 3'-kinase (PI3-K) initiates one of the major pathways effecting carbohydrate, protein, and lipid metabolism, including translocation of the glucose transporter, GLUT-4, to the cell surface and the inactivation, by phosphorylation, of glycogen synthase kinase 3 (GSK3) and subsequent dephosphorylation and activation of glycogen synthase, thus stimulating glucose storage. In contrast, mitogenic effects of insulin are mediated by a mitogen-activating protein (MAP) kinase pathway. (Reproduced with permission from McPhee SJ, Hammer GD. *Pathophysiology of Disease: An Introduction to Clinical Medicine*, 6th ed. New York: McGraw-Hill; 2010.)

What receptor is affected most by exercise?

a. GLUT1 in brain

b. GLUT2 in kidney and bowl

c. GLUT3 in neurons

d. GLUT4 in skeletal muscle

Answer d. GLUT4 in skeletal muscle

Exercise does not affect any of the glucose transporters except the one in skeletal muscle.

Diagnosis of Diabetes

- $HbA_1c >6.5\%$
- Two fasting glucose test results >125 mg/dL
- Oral glucose tolerance test
- Single glucose test result >200 mg/dL with symptoms

Orders:

- Metformin
- Statin medication
- Advise weight loss, exercise, diabetic diet
- Salt-restricted diet
- Nutrition evaluation
- Urine microalbumin

Neural tissue does not use insulin for glucose transport.

What is the mechanism of the patient's polyuria?

a. Saturation of SGLT2 in the proximal tubule

b. Insufficient insulin at the kidney tubule

c. Deficient antidiuretic hormone (ADH) effect at the collecting duct

d. Deficient ADH release from the posterior pituitary

e. Saturation of glucose transporters in the distal tubule

Answer a. Saturation of SGLT2 in the proximal tubule

The threshold for beginning to spill glucose into urine is a serum glucose level above about 180 to 200 mg/dL. This level drops with age and older people will spill glucose into urine at a lower blood level. The receptor for glucose on the tubule lumen side is the SGLT2. This is a cotransporter with sodium. Transport maximum for the tubule is about 375 mg/dL. This means all glucose reabsorption is fully maximized at all the tubules at a serum glucose level of 375 mg/dL. Between 200 and 375 mg/dL, you can still increase glucose reabsorption because not all the nephrons hit 100% saturation at the same blood level.

Nephrons are a "parallel circuit." Not all saturate at the same glucose level.

SGLT2 receptors in the kidney are in the proximal tubule.

The patient returns in 1 week. His symptoms of thirst and polyuria have already improved. He had been getting up three times a night to urinate and now it is only once. He is fully adherent to metformin and statin. His BP is 138/92 mm Hg, and microalbumin is present in his urine.

Metformin works by blocking gluconeogenesis.

Drugs that increase insulin level drive glucose and lipids into cells, including adipose tissue cells.

Because metformin does not increase insulin level, it does not increase weight gain.

Because the patient has microalbuminuria, an angiotensin-converting enzyme (ACE) inhibitor should be started. All ACE inhibitors are totally identical therapeutically in terms of their benefit. The only difference is dosing, which is not covered on CCS. The BP goal in a diabetic patient is <130/80 mm Hg, so this patient needs to start an ACE inhibitor to control BP as well. There is no point in checking the HbA_1c level so soon after starting oral hypoglycemic medications. It takes 1 to 2 months for HbA_1c to have a meaningful change.

Red blood cells live 90 to 120 days. HbA_1c measures average glucose over this time.

> **Orders:**
> • *ACE inhibitor (enalapril, lisinopril, ramipril)*
> • *Serum glucose*

What is the mechanism of ACE inhibitor benefit for microalbuminuria?

a. Dilation of afferent arteriole increases glomerular filtration rate (GFR).

b. Dilation of efferent arteriole decreases glomerular hypertension.

c. Decreased BP protects the tubules.

d. Aldosterone inhibition affects the kidney.

Answer b. Dilation of efferent arteriole decreases glomerular hypertension.

Angiotensin II (ANGII) normally constricts the efferent arteriole. ACE inhibitors inhibit ANGII and dilate the efferent arteriole. This will have a brief effect on decreasing GFR, but overall, decreasing intraglomerular pressure protects the kidney vasculature from damage. This is similar to how decreasing hypertension decreases the risk of stroke or coronary disease. Briefly, there is decreased perfusion pressure, but in the long term, it protects the vasculature of both the brain and the heart.

ACE inhibitors decrease hydrostatic pressure in the glomerular capillary.

Metformin is contraindicated in renal insufficiency to avoid lactic acidosis.

The patient is given prescriptions for lisinopril, metformin, and a statin. A prescription is also given for a home BP monitor and fingerstick glucose monitoring. He returns in 2 weeks and his BP is 132/84 mm Hg. His home glucose test results are: 182 mg/dL, 170 mg/dL, 184 mg/dL, 165 mg/dL.

Because the patient's glucose levels are not fully controlled on metformin, add a second agent. It is not clear which one to use and the Step 3 examination will not ask you unless there is a specific contraindication to one of them.

Everyone on a statin should have aspartate aminotransferase (AST) and alanine aminotransferase (ALT) checked.

Orders:
• *Add a second oral hypoglycemic medication.*
  ◊ *Sulfonylurea (e.g., glyburide, glipizide, glimepiride)*
  ◊ *Thiazolidinedione (e.g., rosiglitazone)*
  ◊ *Dipeptidyl peptidase IV (DPP-IV) inhibitor (e.g., sitagliptin, saxagliptin, linagliptin)*
• *Order liver function tests (LFTs)*

Bring the patient back in 1 week to the office. The second agent will have started to work, but sulfonylureas may not have a peak effect for 2 to 3 weeks. If your case presents a person 2 to 3 months after the start of treatment, obtain an HbA$_1$c measurement.

Mechanism of Action
• Sulfonylurea increases insulin release from the pancreas.
• Thiazolidine increases peripheral insulin sensitivity.
• DPP-IV blocks the metabolism of incretins and increases the level of glucagonlike peptide (GLP) and glucose-dependent insulinotropic peptide (GIP).

Incretins (GIP and GLP) increase insulin and decrease glucagon release from the pancreas.

The patient returns in 2 weeks and he is on two oral hypoglycemic medications. His BP is 124/78 mm Hg. His home glucose test results are: 124 mg/dL, 136 mg/dL, 120 mg/dL, and 128 mg/dL. The goal of LDL is <100 mg/dL in diabetes because it is an equivalent of coronary disease. Keep moving the clock forward doing vaccinations and health maintenance in diabetes until you get the screen that says, "Case ends in 5 minutes of real time." The complication of diabetes and routine preventive medicine will be covered in the next case.

CASE 2: Diabetes—Prevention of Complications

Setting: *office*

CC: *"I am here to follow up on my medication."*

VS: *blood pressure: 134/94 mm Hg; pulse rate: 84 beats/minute*

HPI: *A 54-year-old man, who was diagnosed with diabetes last year, comes to your office for a follow-up appointment. He was placed on metformin and a sulfonylurea, which controlled his glucose levels for most of the last year. Currently, he has started to have some episodes of nocturia one to two times a night. He insists he is fully adherent to his medications.*

PMHx:
- *Hypertension*
- *Hyperlipidemia*
- *Microalbuminuria*

Medications:
- *Metformin, atorvastatin, lisinopril, glimepiride*

Initial Orders:
- *HbA₁c*
- *CHEM-7*
- *LFTs*
- *UA, urine microalbumin*
- *Lipid panel (LDL, HDL, triglycerides, total cholesterol)*

The patient returns 1 week later to receive the results of his laboratory tests:

- *HbA₁c: 7.8%*
- *Serum glucose: 195 mg/dL*
- *UA negative for protein, small glucose found; positive urine microalbumin*
- *Transaminases normal*
- *LDL: 80 mg/dL, others normal*

Microalbuminuria is caused by a loss of negative charges on the glomerular basement membrane.

Statins cause LFT elevation much more often than causing creatinine kinase level elevation.

The HbA₁c goal level is <7%.

Although the patient's HbA$_1$c concentration is not much above the target, he is having a recurrence of his symptoms of polyuria. Also, the goal of BP in a diabetic is <130/80 mm Hg. You have to add an additional agent. It is not clear which medication to add as the second drug in a diabetic.

Where is the majority of glucose absorbed in the nephron?

a. Proximal tubule

b. Loop of Henle

c. Distal tubule

d. Collecting duct

Answer a. Proximal tubule

One hundred percent of glucose should be absorbed by the end of the proximal tubule. There should be no glucose entering the loop of Henle. Some nephrons begin to saturate the SGLT transporter at a serum glucose level of 200 mg/dL. This is "threshold." All are saturated at glucose level 375 mg/dL. Any rise in serum glucose level above 375 mg/dL will go straight into the urine.

Insulin has no effect on the secondary active transport of the proximal tubule.

Any Glucose in Urine = Some Blood Glucose Levels >200 mg/dL

The transport maximum for the tubule 375 mg/dL.
No further increase in reabsorption is possible.

You add a calcium channel blocker or beta-blocker as the second antihypertensive agent. Never combine an ACE inhibitor and an angiotensin receptor blocker (ARB). Even though the mechanisms are different, there is no efficacy in combining them. Besides BP control, there is nothing more you can do to prevent proteinuria when a patient is on an ACE inhibitor.

Orders:
- Amlodipine
- Sitagliptin
- Continue lisinopril, atorvastatin, metformin, glimepiride

Thiazolidinediones (rosiglitazone)
• Increase peripheral insulin sensitivity
• Contraindicated in congestive heart failure (CHF) and fluid overload

Glucose reabsorption is by secondary active transport with sodium.
It is the same mechanism in the small bowel.

DPP-IV breaks down incretins (GIP and GLP).

The patient does not return for 2 months. He says, "I am fine; my fingersticks are all 110 to 135 and my home BP monitor shows 110 over 70 to 125 over 75." His nocturia has resolved. His weight is 7 lb less than the last visit, which you ascribe to the DPP-IV inhibitor, sitagliptin. He is sometimes constipated by it, but it does not bother him.

What is the mechanism of weight loss with DPP-IV inhibitors?

a. GIP slows gastric motility.

b. Lower glucose slows motility—glucose is cathartic.

c. GLP stimulates motilin release.

d. DPP-IV drugs decrease acetylcholine.

Answer a. GIP slows gastric motility.

Gastric motility is directly slowed by incretins such as GIP. The old name for GIP was "gastric inhibitory peptide." Motilin does increase gastric motility, but GLP does not stimulate it. The other gastrointestinal (GI) tract hormones secretin and cholecystokinin also decrease gastric motility. DPP-IV inhibitors block the metabolism of incretins. Exenatide and liraglutide on injectable medications that are long-lasting synthetic incretins.

Exenatide (synthetic GIP produces significant weight loss by slowing stomach motility.

Calcium channel blockers also cause constipation by inhibiting intestinal smooth muscle.

The patient's current vital signs and laboratory test results are:

- *BP <130/80 mm Hg*
- *LDL <100 mg/dL*
- *HbA$_1$c <7%*

On CCS, if you are moving the clock forward and if the case does not end, it may mean it is waiting for you to do routine health maintenance and preventive medicine.

Orders:
- *Dilated ophthalmologic examination (refer to ophthalmology)*
- *Monofilament examination of the feet*

The eye examination shows nonproliferative retinopathy at this time. The foot examination is normal. The patient is maintained for a long time on the same medications. If your case shows complications on a return visit much later, the responses are:

- *Neuropathy: Start gabapentin, lamotrigine, or pregabalin.*
- *Constipation or diabetic gastroparesis: Start erythromycin or metoclopramide.*
- *Proliferative retinopathy: Inject vascular endothelial growth factor (VEGF) inhibitors or do laser photocoagulation.*

Mechanism of Complication of Diabetes

Neuropathy:
- Peripheral nerves have blood vessels feeding them or "vasonervorum." Diabetes damages this microvasculature and starves peripheral nerves.

Gastroparesis:
- Diabetics have a decreased ability to sense gastric and intestinal distention, which is a part of neuropathy that also affects GI tracts.
- Motilin is decreased; erythromycin increases motilin release.

Proliferative Retinopathy:
- Blood flow to the retina is decreased from microvascular insufficiency.
- Distal vessels release humoral factors that stimulate vessel growth.
- Overgrown vessels in the retina block vision (Figure 3-2).
- VEGF inhibitors stop the abnormal new vessels from growing and blocking vision.
- Ranibizumab and bevacizumab are VEGF inhibitors that stop macular degeneration and inhibit diabetic retinopathy.
- Laser photocoagulation decreases production of these growth factors (Figure 3-3).

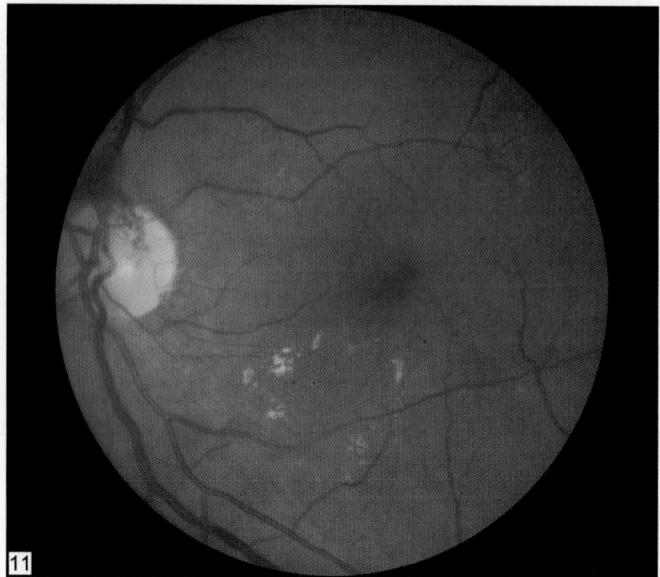

Figure 3-2. Diabetic retinopathy. Neovascularization of the disc. (Reproduced with permission from LeBlond RF, et al. *DeGowin's Diagnostic Examination*, 9th ed. New York: McGraw-Hill; 2009.)

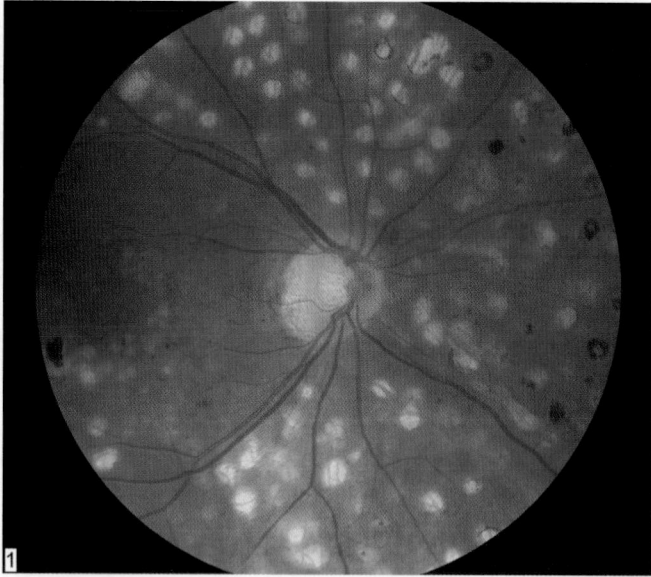

Figure 3-3. Panretinal photocoagulation is the application of laser burns to the peripheral retina. The ischemic peripheral retina is treated with thousands of laser spots to presumably eliminate vasogenic factors responsible for the development of neovascular vessels. Laser spots cause scarring of the retina and choroid, and scars may be hypotrophic (white spots) or hypertrophic (black spots). (Reproduced with permission from Paul D. Comeau.)

CASE 3: Diabetic Ketoacidosis

Setting: *emergency department (ED)*

CC: *"He is confused and breathing fast."*

VS: *R: 34 breaths/minute; BP: 106/68 mm Hg; P: 122 beats/minute; T: 99.8°F*

HPI: *A 34-year-old man with a history of type 1 diabetes is brought to the ED by his family for confusion and lethargy for the last day. The patient has been a lifelong diabetic who also has some unclear psychiatric issues. The family says he stopped taking his insulin a few days ago for unclear reasons—he may have just run out of his medications.*

PE:
- *General: lethargic, disoriented, rolling around in bed, respiratory distress*
- *Chest: clear to auscultation*
- *Abdomen: soft, nontender*
- *Cardiovascular: no murmur, no gallop*
- *Neurological: unable to determine whether there are focal deficits*

Initial Orders:
- *CHEM-7*
- *Normal saline (NS) bolus*
- *Arterial blood gas (ABG)*
- *UA*
- *Acetone, beta-hydroxybutyrate levels*
- *Electrocardiogram (ECG)*

What is the single most important test in diabetic ketoacidosis (DKA)?

a. Glucose level

b. pH

c. Ketone and/or acetone levels

d. Serum osmolarity

Answer b. pH

The glucose level is not as important as knowing if the patient is acidotic. Glucose levels can fluctuate wildly from high to medium, but if the patient's pH on an ABG or serum bicarbonate on chemistry is near normal, it does not matter. The same is true of ketones, acetone, beta-hydroxybutyrate, or acetoacetate. The level of these ketone bodies is not as important as the level of accumulated acid.

Glucose, ketones, and osmolarity are not as important as pH and bicarbonate levels.

Move the clock forward the absolute minimum amount of time needed to get results of the ABG. Recheck vital signs and consult the intensive care unit if it has not already been done. Re-bolus with intravenous (IV) fluids. Use NS or Ringer lactate. More than half the problem in DKA is inadequate amounts of fluid.

Laboratory Test Results:

CHEM-7:
- *Glucose 725 mg/dL*
- *Bicarbonate 12 mEq/L*
- *Chloride 100 mEq/L*
- *K 6.4 mEq/L*
- *Sodium 126 mEq/L*

ABG: pH 7.12; partial pressure of carbon dioxide (PCO_2) 28 mm Hg; partial pressure of oxygen (PO_2) 95 mm Hg

- *UA: glucose 1000 mg/dL; ketones +++*
- *Acetone, beta-hydroxybutyrate levels: markedly elevated*
- *ECG: sinus tachycardia, normal T wave, no ST abnormalities*

Glucose 100 Up = Sodium 1.6 Down

For every 100 mg/dL above normal glucose level, sodium level is decreased by 1.6 mEq/L.

What is the mechanism of the artificial decrease in sodium?

a. It is a laboratory artifact.
b. Acid interferes with sodium measurement.

c. Hyperglycemia pulls water out of cells, diluting out the sodium.
d. Ketone bodies bind sodium, removing it from circulation.

Answer c. Hyperglycemia pulls water out of cells, diluting out the sodium.

Knowing the numerical relationship between sodium and glucose is indispensable to accurately assessing the anion gap. In addition, because hyponatremia causes confusion and hyperglycemia causes confusion, it is important to be able to address and correct the proper abnormality. When glucose levels markedly increase, it pulls water out of cells. Because the total number of sodium molecules do not change, the extra water in the vascular space drives the sodium level down.

Insulin uses a tyrosine kinase receptor.

Acid stimulates hyperventilation at the brainstem.

What is the mechanism of hyperkalemia?

a. Transcellular shift (exchange) for acid (H^+)

b. Failure of renal excretion

c. Cell lysis

d. Potassium bound by ketone bodies

Answer a. Transcellular shift (exchange) for acid (H^+)

When acid or hydrogen ions (H^+) build up in the blood, the majority of live cells in the body buffer the acid by absorbing it. To maintain electrical neutrality, the cells will release a K^+ for each H^+ it picks up. In addition, insulin drives potassium into cells with glucose. If there is no insulin, the cells will not receive potassium. Also, insulin has a direct stimulatory effect on sodium-potassium adenosine triphosphatase (Na^+/K^+-ATPase). Without insulin, the cells will not pick up insulin by stimulation of Na^+/K^+-ATPase.

Did you know insulin stimulate Na^+/K^+-ATPase to drive K^+ into cells?

Two liters of NS were given in the first hour. A meaningful fluid bolus is 20 mL/kg. Repeat the chemistry level every 1 to 2 hours to guide fluid and insulin dosing and to determine the need for IV bicarbonate. It is not precisely clear when IV bicarbonate is needed, but for most cases, when the pH is <7.2, it is acceptable to use.

Orders:
- *IV insulin continuous drip*
- *NS bolus*
- *CHEM-7*
- *Venous blood gas*
- *Move the patient to the intensive care unit (ICU) if not done*

Hyperkalemia is expected in all patient's with metabolic acidosis with an increased anion gap.

Why is the K^+ level increased?
There is a transcellular shift with H^+.
There is no insulin to drive Na^+/K^+-ATPase.

What is the difference between venous pH and arterial pH?

a. Venous < Arterial

b. Arterial > Venous

c. Equal

Answer c. Equal

If there is no respiratory disease, arterial and venous pH should be essentially equal. A difference of a few hundredths of a point is clinically irrelevant. This is why you can use venous blood gasses (VBGs) to monitor DKA response to management. There is no reason to torture patients with the pain of an arterial puncture for no reason when you can do a venous puncture.

> Use venous blood gasses to monitor DKA response to therapy.

> *Move the clock forward every 15 to 30 minutes for the first hour or two. Use "Interval History" to see if there is a clinical response to the use of fluids and insulin. There should be a measurable effect within 30 minutes to IV insulin and massive volume replacement. If there is no improvement, repeat the "bolus NS" and "IV insulin" orders.*
>
> **Orders:**
> * *VBG*
> * *CHEM-7*
> * *NS bolus*
> * *IV insulin*

What is the mechanism of lethargy and confusion in DKA?

a. Acid inhibits neural transmission.

b. Hyponatremia is the mechanism.

c. Hyperosmolarity dehydrates brain cells.

d. Hyperkalemia interferes with neural transmission.

Answer c. Hyperosmolarity dehydrates brain cells.

Serum osmolarity is usually dependent entirely on serum sodium content. In severe hyperglycemia, the extremely high glucose level acts as an osmotic draw on brain cells. This dehydrates them, and central nervous system (CNS) neural function, especially for cognitive purposes, is worse when dehydrated.

$$\text{Serum Osmolarity} = (2 \times \text{Serum Sodium [mEq/L]}) + (\text{Glucose [mg/dL]}/18)$$
$$+ (\text{BUN [g/dL]}/2.8)$$

> The brain does not think well with high osmolarity sucking out the water.

The brain switches to using ketones for fuel.

After 2 hours, the patient's lethargy resolves, and normal mentation returns. The repeat laboratory test results are:
- *Glucose 245 mg/dL*
- *K 4.8 mEq/L*
- *Serum bicarbonate 18 mEq/L*
- *pH 7.32*

What is the biggest change you must make in management?

a. Stop IV insulin; switch to subcutaneous delivery.

b. Switch to oral fluids.

c. Add potassium to fluids.

d. Move the patient out of ICU.

Answer c. Add potassium to fluids.

As the potassium starts to drop into the normal range, add potassium replacement. This is because the body becomes massively depleted of potassium because of the metabolic acidosis. Acidosis takes potassium out of cells. High blood potassium is excreted at the kidney to protect the heart from fatal arrhythmia. When acidosis corrects, potassium shifts back into cells and blood levels will drop *below* normal.

During acidosis, potassium is excreted from kidneys.

The body becomes massively depleted of potassium during metabolic acidosis.

Potassium is added to routine IV fluids. Repeat the VBG every 2 hours until the pH nears the normal 7.4.

You do not have to wait for the ketones to disappear to transfer the patient out of the ICU. The ketone bodies are like garbage that needs time to clear away.

When serum bicarbonate level rises above 20 to 22 mEq/L and pH is above 7.35, you can transfer the patient out of the ICU.

When cells cannot take up glucose because of a lack of insulin, they switch to lipids and free fatty acids as an alternate fuel source. Free fatty acids, unfortunately, come with a toxic end product called *ketones*. This is why:
• No insulin ensures no glucose uptake.
• Cells eat fatty acids and make ketones.
• Ketones create acid.

Ketones are acid end products of lipid metabolism.

CASE 4: Hypothyroidism

Setting: *office*

CC: *"I just feel so weak and tired."*

VS: *R: 10 breaths/minute; BP: 135/94 mm Hg; P: 56 beats/minute; T: 96.8°F*

HPI: *A 48-year-old woman with progressively worsening fatigue and tiredness developing over the last several months comes to your office. She says she, "has gotten to the point where everything is a struggle." She has also been gaining weight and suffering from constipation.*

PMHx:
• *Depression*
• *Dry skin*

Medications:
• *Selective serotonin receptor inhibitor (SSRI)*
• *Bupropion*
• *Stool softeners*

PE:
• *General: sad appearing, modestly obese, slumping on examination table*
• *Cardiovascular: normal*
• *Abdomen: no organomegaly, decreased bowel sounds diffusely*
• *Neurological: decreased relaxation phase of reflexes*
• *Skin: course, thick hair*

Initial Orders:
• *CBC*
• *CHEM-7*
• *Thyroid function tests (TFTs): free thyroxine (T_4), thyroid-stimulating hormone (TSH)*
• *Calcium, magnesium levels*

In office-based cases, advance the clock to the time and day when the test results all list "Report Available."

Advance the clock 1 week to have the patient revisit.

Laboratory Test Results:
- CBC: *hematocrit 34%; mean corpuscular volume (MCV) 90 fL*
- CHEM-7: *normal except sodium 132 mEq/L*
- Free T*$_4$*: *low*
- TSH: *high*
- Calcium, magnesium levels: *normal*

Low T$_4$ + High TSH = Hypothyroidism

Normocytic anemia is part of hypothyroidism.

T$_4$ is anabolic. Without it, things do not grow—like red blood cells.

Low T$_4$ causes low sodium level.
Low T$_4$ impairs free water clearance.

The patient is certainly very happy to know she has a clear medical reason for her tiredness and possibly her depression.

The patient asks why she feels cold all the time, and why her temperature is low?

a. Pituitary insufficiency

b. Concomitant adrenal insufficiency

c. Because T$_4$ directly stimulates heat production in cells

d. From the hyponatremia and anemia

Answer c. T$_4$ directly stimulates heat production in cells

The metabolic rate of all mature cells in the body is under the direct control of thyroid hormone except for the adult brain, the spleen, and the uterus. We are 98.6°F even when the ambient temperature is lower than that because the rate of Na^+/K^+-ATPase in almost all bodily tissues is under the control of thyroid hormone. T$_4$ controls the "thermostat" for the body. The patient's inability to generate a faster rate of metabolism lowers her temperature and makes her feel colder.

> Low T_4: Bowels slow = Constipation
> High T_4: Bowels fast = Frequent bowel movements

> Coarse, thick hair and dry skin are a routine finding in hypothyroidism.

Which of the following acts as a steroid hormone?

a. T_4

b. TSH

c. Thyrotropin-releasing hormone (TRH)

d. Reverse triiodothyronine (T_3)

Answer a. T_4

T_4 is produced from the amino acid tyrosine, but it has a steroid hormone mechanism of action. Steroid hormones have a receptor in the cytosol or the nucleus and work by creating new mRNA and new proteins. They are not stored in vesicles and they have protein carriers. T_4 follows all these pathways in its mechanism of action. Reverse T_3 is metabolically inactive, so it has no steroid effect. TSH and TRH are peptide hormones.

> Peptide Hormones
> • No protein carrier
> • Short half-life
> • Cell surface receptor
> • Work through G-proteins and second messengers

> Steroid hormones do not use G-proteins.

> **Orders:**
> • Vital signs
> • Synthroid (levothyroxine) replacement
> • CHEM-7
> • Lipid panel (LDL, HDL, triglycerides)
>
> Repeat vital signs only take 2 minutes to do and will automatically advance the clock.
>
> **VS:** R: 12 breaths/minute; BP: 142/94 mm Hg; P: 54 beats/minute; T: 96.8°F

What is the mechanism of bradycardia in hypothyroidism?

a. T_4 is needed for myocardial contractility.

b. T_3 speeds conduction at the atrioventricular (AV) node.

c. T_4 has a permissive effect on catecholamines.

d. Hypothyroidism causes involution or loss of sinoatrial (SA) node tissue.

Answer c. T_4 has a permissive effect on catecholamines.

The root cause of bradycardia in hypothyroidism is the combined effect on catecholamines with T_4. Without T_4, there is a decreased effect of both norepinephrine and epinephrine at both the SA and AV node. In addition, hypothyroidism leads to a decreased metabolic requirement of almost all the cells in the body. Low T_4 and low T_3 levels mean the muscles use less oxygen and need less perfusion (Figure 3-4).

Hypothyroidism causes bradycardia because of loss of catecholamine stimulation on the heart as well as decreased demand from a "slower" running body. This is the same reason people gain weight with hypothyroidism.

T_4 is converted to T_3 in tissues.

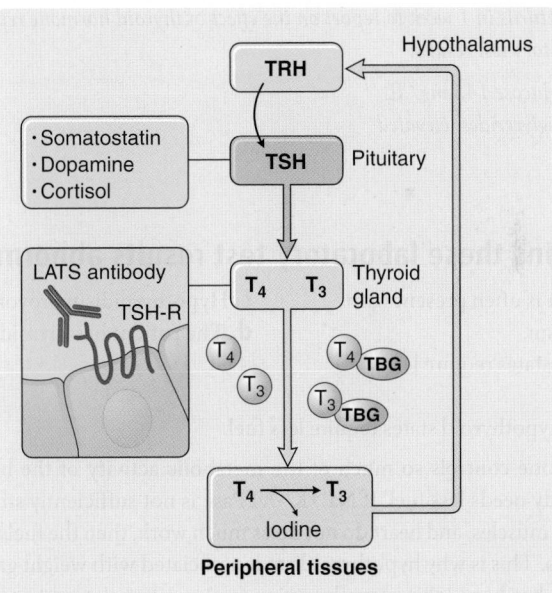

Figure 3-4. The hypothalamic–pituitary–thyroid axis. LATS, long-acting thyroid-stimulator; T_3, triiodothyronine; T_4, thyroxine; TBG, thyroid-binding globulin; TRH, thyrotropin-releasing hormone; TSH, thyrotropin; TSH-R, thyrotropin G-protein-coupled receptor. (Goldsmith LA, et al. *Fitzpatrick's Dermatology in General Medicine*, 8th ed. [online] New York: McGraw-Hill; 2012.)

T_3 is much more active than T_4.

Why is T_3 more active than T_4?

a. T_3 is more protein bound.
b. T_3 leaves plasma and enters the cell much more easily.
c. T_4 has a shorter half-life.

d. Reverse T_3 directly inhibits T_4 tissue effect.
e. Reverse T_3 is converted to T_4.

Answer b. T_3 leaves plasma and enters the cell much more easily.

T_4 is converted to T_3 by 5-iodinase at the level of the tissues peripherally to increase the metabolic activity of those tissues. T_3 is less protein bound and therefore can enter the cell and be more active. This also gives T_3 a shorter half-life. T_4 is more protein bound and is therefore less active.

More Protein Binding = Less Activity

The patient returns in 1 week to report on the effect of thyroid hormone replacement and discuss laboratory test results:

- *CHEM-7: glucose 145 mg/dL*
- *LDL and triglycerides: elevated*

What explains these laboratory test results abnormalities?

a. Glucagonoma is often present with hypothyroidism.
b. Hypothyroid states require less fuel.

c. Hypothyroidism provokes diabetes.
d. The patient has thyroid hepatopathy.

Answer b. Hypothyroid states require less fuel.

If thyroid hormone controls so much of the metabolic activity of the body, it is logical that a slower body needs less fuel. If Na^+/K^+-ATPase is not sufficiently stimulated and the patient's bowels, muscles, and heart do not do as much work, then the fuels, such as glucose and fats, build up. This is why hypothyroidism is associated with weight gain.

The patient has been taking levothyroxine for 1 week and reports a slight increase in energy and a brighter mood. There is no change in weight, skin, or BP. You schedule a 1-month follow-up appointment because changes with thyroid hormones are very slow. T_4 needs time to take effect and changes in the levothyroxine dose should not be done more frequently than every 6 to 8 weeks.

Rapid increases in thyroid hormone dosing is dangerous in which of these?

a. Diabetes

b. Coronary disease

c. Stroke

d. Renal insufficiency

Answer b. Coronary disease

Thyroid hormone controls metabolic rate. Rapid increases in thyroid hormone increase metabolic activity and myocardial demand. Hyperthyroidism can provoke myocardial ischemia by increasing total body oxygen consumption rates.

> Go slowly when increasing thyroid hormone replacement in patients with coronary disease.

> Low thyroid hormone levels cause polysaccharides to accumulate in vessel walls, making them stiff. Stiff vessels cause hypertension.

The patient returns 6 weeks later feeling much improved. She feels more energetic and her constipation has resolved. Her weight has decreased by 6 lb (2.7 kg); her pulse rate is 65 beats/minute; her BP is 134/78 mm Hg; and her temperature is 97.4°F.

Orders:

• T_4 and TSH

Long-term hypothyroidism management is easy. If T_4 is low and TSH is high, continue to increase the levothyroxine dose every 6 to 8 weeks. All symptoms will resolve.

CASE 5: Hyperparathyroidism

Setting: *ED*

CC: *confusion, lethargy, and constipation*

VS: *R: 12 breaths/minute; BP: 145/94 mm Hg; P: 86 beats/minute; T: 97.8°F*

HPI: *A 34-year-old man is brought to the ED by his family because of lethargy. He lives alone and was not answering the phone for several days. His father has to have the lock* *broken to get into the house. He was found on the floor disoriented and awake only enough to say he is constipated and has abdominal pain.*

PMHx: *none*

Medications: *none*

"Altered mental status of unclear etiology": These orders should be written even before doing the physical examination because the physical examination moves the clock forward. Legal drugs (e.g., opiates) kill far more people than illegal drugs, so immediately give the patient naloxone as an opiate antagonist.

- *Give naloxone (it is always safe in patients with acute altered mental status).*
- *Give thiamine.*
- *Start dextrose.*
- *Order calcium, sodium, glucose, magnesium levels; oximeter; computed tomography (CT) of the head; urine toxicology screen.*

Acute opiate withdrawal will not kill the patient!

PE:
- *Neurological: lethargic, unable to follow commands*
- *Cardiovascular: normal*
- *Abdominal: decreased bowel sounds*
- *Extremities: decreased skin turgor*

Do not give flumazenil! Benzodiazepine withdrawal causes seizures.

Initial Orders:
- *Naloxone, thiamine, dextrose IV stat*
- *NS bolus, then continuous*
- *CHEM-7*
- *CBC, UA, head CT scan*
- *LFTs*
- *Urine toxicology screen*

Sodium alters brain neural transmission; potassium does not.

Both renal and liver failure cause encephalopathy.
Order BUN, creatinine, and transaminases levels.

With acute confusion, move the clock forward only 5 to 10 minutes. On CCS, although everything you order is considered to be done instantly, you cannot see the effect of it unless you move the clock forward. For example, if you order naloxone, it is given instantly, but you cannot determine on CCS that it is effective unless you move the clock and do an "Interval History" or occasionally get a spontaneous nurse's note telling you an update on the status.

You move the clock forward 5 minutes. There is no effect from either the glucose or the naloxone. The bolus of NS is given because the patient is extremely dehydrated. You move the clock forward another 15 minutes to get the results of the serum chemistry, CT, and UA.

One of the great magical things about the Step 3 examination on CCS is that the patient can be in multiple places at the same time. The blood tests, CT, and urine sample will all be listed as obtained at the exactly same time.

Laboratory Test Results:
- *Total calcium: 16 mg/dL (normal 9–10.5 mg/dL)*
- *BUN: 70 g/dL (normal 7–20 g/dL)*
- *Creatinine: 2.2 mg/dL (normal 0.7–1.2 mg/dL)*
- *Bicarbonate: 21mEq/L*
- *CBC, transaminases, head CT, and urine toxicology: normal*

What is the mechanism of altered mental status in this patient?

a. Dehydration

b. Hypokalemia

c. Sepsis

d. Metabolic acidosis

Answer a. Dehydration

Severe hypercalcemia is routinely associated with massive volume depletion. This is why the BUN-to-creatinine ratio is so high. Potassium does not alter CNS neural activity. Potassium will alter cardiac conduction, but not neural conduction. Although there is a slight metabolic acidosis, it does not cause altered mental status.

Acidosis can be caused by renal insufficiency or parathyroid hormone (PTH) inhibiting bicarbonate absorption at the proximal tubule.

Reorder a fluid bolus and run IV fluids continuously. The most important management of severe hypercalcemia is restoring fluid balance. NS by itself increases calcium excretion from the kidney.

Do NOT give furosemide before giving liters of fluid!

Never use thiazides in hypercalcemia: Thiazides increase calcium levels.

What is the mechanism of thiazides in increasing calcium levels?

a. They increase calcium reabsorption at the distal tubule.

b. They decrease calcium filtration at the glomerulus.

c. They increase PTH effect at the bone.

d. They block phosphate metabolism.

Answer a. They increase calcium reabsorption at the distal tubule.

Calcium is reabsorbed at the distal tubule. Phosphate is usually absorbed at the proximal tubule.

As soon as you confirm the presence of hypercalcemia, you should hydrate the patient and give bisphosphonates, as well as look for the cause.

Orders:
- *PTH level*
- *Phosphate level*
- *Pamidronate*
- *Re-bolus NS*

You move the clock forward 1 hour. Move this patient with acute, unresolving mental status changes to the ICU and give him more fluids. Bisphosphonates, such as pamidronate or zoledronic acid, will take 1 to 3 days to work, so any effect you see on improvement of the calcium level in the first few hours is entirely due to NS increasing the excretion of calcium at the kidney.

What is the mechanism of massive volume depletion in hypercalcemia?

a. Blockage of ADH production in the hypothalamus

b. Blockage of ADH release from the posterior pituitary gland

c. Blockage of ADH effect on the collecting duct in the kidney

d. Constriction of the afferent arteriole

Answer c. Blockage of ADH effect on the collecting duct in the kidney

ADH stimulation of the kidney needs normal calcium and potassium levels. Hypercalcemia causes nephrogenic diabetes insipidus (NDI).

Hypokalemia and hypercalcemia cause nephrogenic NDI.

After 2 hours, the patient wakes up somewhat but is still lethargic. He complains of abdominal pain.

Laboratory Test Results:
- *Calcium: 14.7 mg/dL*
- *Phosphate: 1.5 mg/dL (normal 2.4–4.1 mg/dL)*
- *PTH: elevated*

Bisphosphonates inhibit osteoclasts in the bone.

What is the mechanism of high calcium causing lethargy and constipation?

a. Inhibition of acetylcholine reuptake at the neuromuscular junction

b. Somatostatin release

c. Raising the threshold for depolarization of neural tissue

d. Blockade of β-receptors

Answer c. Raising the threshold for depolarization of neural tissue

High calcium levels inhibit neural hyperexcitability. High calcium levels move the threshold for depolarization higher and farther away from the resting membrane potential.

High Calcium Level = Short QT on ECG

Low Calcium Level = Prolonged QT on ECG

Because of the continued high calcium level and the persistence of symptoms despite hours of hydration, you give calcitonin. Calcitonin works much faster than bisphosphonates, but will wear off.

Calcitonin rapidly inhibits osteoclast activity.

After giving calcitonin, move the clock forward 2 to 4 hours. Continue to give NS in large volumes. You will only give furosemide if the person is not producing urine. This is entirely possible because hypercalcemia can create severe prerenal azotemia. It can also be associated with CHF.

Loop diuretics increase calcium excretion at the loop of Henle.

By the second hospital day, massive volume replacement of 4 to 8 L should have improved the patient's mental status. His abdominal pain has improved and he is able to have a bowel movement. Hyperparathyroidism is confirmed again.

Orders:

• *Consult endocrinology.*
• *Move the patient to a hospital ward.*
• *Continue hydration and bisphosphonates.*
• *Order a nuclear sestamibi parathyroid scan.*
• *Repeat calcium, BUN, creatinine, and phosphate levels.*

A nuclear sestamibi scan is to localize which of the four parathyroid glands has to be removed.

Hyperparathyroidism—85% occurs from a solitary adenoma.
Remove it!

PTH:
• Reabsorbs calcium from bone
• Reabsorbs calcium at the distal tubule
• Increases activation of vitamin D
• Blocks phosphate absorption at the proximal tubule

When asymptomatic, you do not need to remove the parathyroid gland *unless*:
• There is bone disease (osteoporosis).
• There are kidney stones.
• There is decreased renal function.
• Calcium levels are more than 1 point above normal when the patient is younger than 50 years old.

Your case may go as far as rechecking the calcium and phosphate levels after removal of the adenoma. Most cases of hyperparathyroidism present as asymptomatic elevation in the calcium level. This case was to help you understand the key basic science foundations of severe hypercalcemia.

CASE 6: **Hypercortisolism**

Setting: *office*

CC: *"My face is getting fat and hairy."*

VS: *BP: 153/98 mm Hg; P: 74/minute; T: 97.2°F*

HPI: *A 27-year-old woman comes to your office concerned that her face is getting "fatter and rounder" despite the fact that she exercises and restricts her diet. She has an increasing* *acne problem. She was referred to you by her dermatologist who she was seeing for the acne and thinning hair on her scalp.*

PMHx:
- *Infertility, irregular menstruation*
- *Borderline hypertension*
- *Vertebral compression fracture*

Medications: *none*

PE:
- *General appearance: somewhat obese abdomen*
- *Skin: striae on flanks, bruises on thin arms*
- *Head, ears, eyes, nose, throat (HEENT): excess hair over lip and at chin*
- *Cardiovascular: normal*

Hypertension in Young People

Clue in History or Physical	Diagnosis
Hypokalemia	Conn syndrome (hyperaldosteronism)
Truncal obesity, bruising, striae	Cushing syndrome (hypercortisolism)
Upper extremity blood pressure > lower extremity blood pressure	Coarctation of aorta
Hirsutism, irregular periods	Congenital adrenal hyperplasia
Episodic	Pheochromocytoma
Bruits or murmur at flanks	Renal artery stenosis

History has enough clues to guide initial testing.

What is the best initial test to look for hypercortisolism?

a. A 24-hour urine cortisol
b. Adrenocorticotropic hormone (ACTH) level
c. Magnetic resonance imaging (MRI) of the head
d. High-dose dexamethasone suppression
e. Random serum cortisol

Answer a. A 24-hour urine cortisol

Cortisol levels have tremendous fluctuation during the day. Randomly testing for blood or urine cortisol is useless and always the wrong answer. Every time you get anxious or get a parking ticket, your cortisol level goes up. The 24-hour urine cortisol test tells the average cortisol level over the past day.

The "1-mg overnight dexamethasone suppression test" is too nonspecific. If the morning cortisol level remains elevated, it can be from anxiety, depression, or alcoholism. A normal test result excludes hypercortisolism.

> Never start with a head MRI in endocrine disorders.

> **Initial Orders:**
> • *Comprehensive metabolic panel (CHEM-20)*
> • *Lipid panel*
> • *UA*
> • *24-hour urine cortisol collection*

Which of the following is the only hormone made continuously?

a. Cortisol

b. Testosterone

c. T_4

d. Growth hormone (GH)

e. ACTH

Answer c. T_4

All hormones are made in pulsatile fashion except for T_4 and T_3, which are made continuously. They are all subject to feedback inhibition—after production, they go back and shut off their own stimulatory hormone. Cortisol does feedback inhibition on the pituitary and hypothalamus to shut off ACTH and corticotropin-releasing hormone (CRH).

> Cortisol is glucuronidated or "sugar coated" to come off the binding protein and be excreted in the urine.

> *Move the clock forward 1 to 2 weeks to have the result of the 24-hour urine test.*
>
> • *CHEM-20: potassium borderline low; bicarbonate elevated; glucose 185 mg/dL*
> • *Lipid panel: LDL and triglycerides elevated*
> • *UA: normal*
> • *24-hour urine cortisol collection:* **elevated**

What is the mechanism of low potassium and high bicarbonate?

a. Volume depletion

b. Mineralocorticoid effects of cortisol

c. 11-Deoxycorticosterone elevation

d. ACTH effect on kidney

Answer b. Mineralocorticoid effects of cortisol

Adrenal hormones are not purely of one single effect. Cortisol has some mineralocorticoid or aldosterone-like effect. That is also why the potassium level is low. Aldosterone levels are likely low in hypercortisolism. This is because cortisol raises BP.

1. High BP shuts off renin.
2. No Renin = No ANGII
3. No ANGIII + Low Potassium = No Aldosterone Synthesis

> Mineralocorticoid (aldosterone) effect
> • Potassium (K⁺) excretion
> • Hydrogen (H⁺) excretion
> • Sodium reabsorption

> *The patient is relieved to know that she has a diagnosis that can explain her facial fatness and truncal obesity.*

The patient wants to know if the acne and hirsutism are also related to this same problem. What do you tell her?

a. Yes, she is secreting more testosterone.

b. Yes, adrenal androgen excess accompanies Cushing syndrome.

c. Yes, cortisol suppresses estrogen production.

d. No, unfortunately you must find a second tumor.

Answer b. Yes, adrenal androgen excess accompanies Cushing syndrome (Figure 3-5).

Dehydroepiandrosterone (DHEA) and androstenedione are cosecreted with hypercortisolism. In addition, there is some androgen-like effect of cortisol. Acne, male pattern hair loss, and excess hair on the face in women is part of hypercortisolism. This is the same reason this patient is infertile. Excess androgens are interfering with her ovulatory cycles.

> Excess androgen levels cause acne. Sebaceous glands have testosterone receptors.

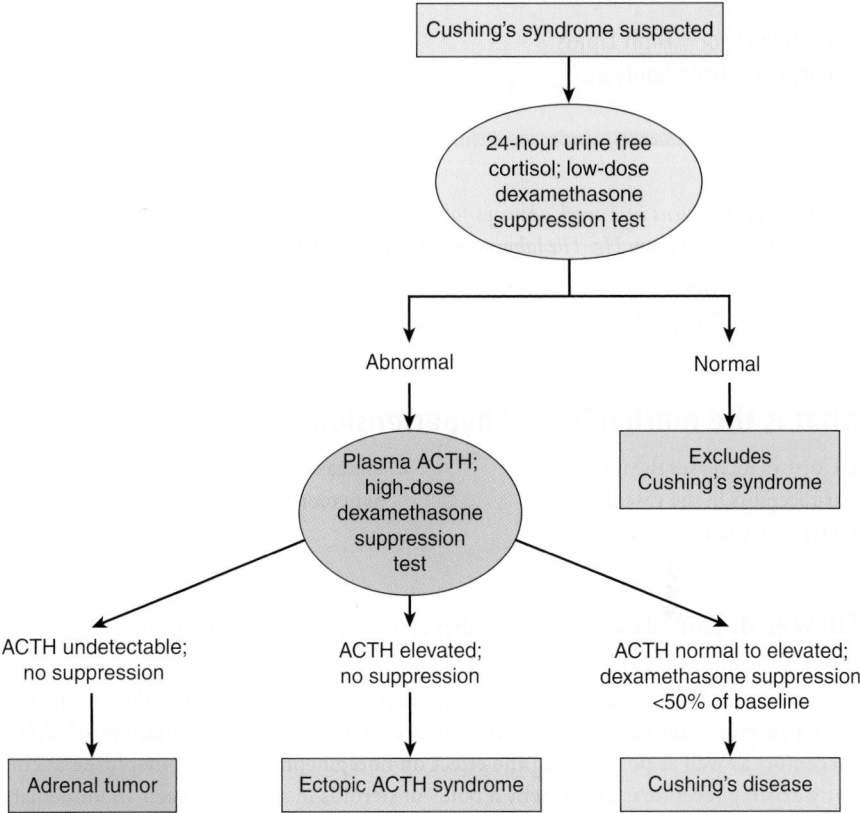

Figure 3-5. Diagnostic evaluation of Cushing syndrome and procedures for determining the cause. Boxes enclose clinical diagnoses, and ovals enclose diagnostic tests. ACTH, adrenocorticotropic hormone. (Reproduced with permission from Felig P, Baxter JD, eds. *Endocrinology and Metabolism,* 2nd ed. New York: McGraw-Hill; 1987, as redrawn in McPhee SJ, Hammer GD. *Pathophysiology of Disease: An Introduction to Clinical Medicine,* 6th ed. New York: McGraw-Hill; 2010.)

The patient is delighted that she can get "one stop shopping" to fix her fat face, obese trunk, acne, and restore her periods and fertility. She wants to know where the lesion is.

What test do you order next?

a. ACTH level

c. CT of adrenals
b. MRI of head

Answer a. ACTH level

If the ACTH level is high, then the source is the pituitary or an ectopic focus, such as the lungs. If the ACTH level is low, then the source is the adrenal glands.

High Cortisol = High Lipids
Cortisol causes lipolysis.

The patient returns in 1 week. Always follow BP in any person who was hypertensive. Her BP is 148/94 mm Hg. The laboratory test results show:

- *ACTH: elevated*
- *Glucose: 176 mg/dL*

What is the mechanism of hypertension?

a. Cortisol increases the number of α-receptors in the vasculature.

b. Hyperglycemia increases osmotic pressure in vessels.

c. Increasing norepinephrine accompanies hypercortisolism.

Answer a. Cortisol increases the number of α-receptors in the vasculature.

There is an increased *effect* of catecholamines, not an increased level. Cortisol has a permissive effect on catecholamines in the vasculature. This is by the direct effect of alpha-1-receptors on vasoconstriction. Glucocorticoids increase the number of alpha-1-receptors as well as potentiating the effect on norepinephrine and epinephrine at currently existing receptors. This is why a bolus of steroids in sepsis has such an immediate effect in raising BP. There is a slower aldosterone-like effect at the kidney, increasing sodium reabsorption.

Hypercortisolism causes striae and easy bruising.

Skin is made of collagen protein.
Cortisol breaks down proteins to use the amino acids for gluconeogenesis.

After you have established the presence of hypercortisolism with a 24-hour urine cortisol collection, use the ACTH level to determine the location. When the ACTH level is proven elevated, then do a high-dose dexamethasone suppression test to distinguish between a pituitary source and an ectopic source.

Order:
- *High-dose dexamethasone suppression test*

Response to high-dose dexamethasone:
• The pituitary gland will suppress the ACTH level.
• Ectopic foci will *not* suppress the ACTH level.

The patient has suppression of the ACTH level. You now order an MRI of the head to find a lesion. All of this testing is so that you will remove the correct part of the body. Because 10% of the population has an abnormal pituitary on MRI, you must never start with a scan. You might end up removing the pituitary inappropriately if the source is really elsewhere.

Cortisol causes osteoporosis by directly breaking down bone.

Cortisol increases osteoclast activity.

The MRI shows a lesion in the pituitary. You consult a neurosurgeon for removal.

What is the most likely histology?

a. Hyperplasia
b. Adenoma
c. Neoplasia

Answer b. Adenoma

Most functional pituitary tumors are adenomas. They retain the ability to be suppressed by feedback inhibition but only with high-dose dexamethasone administration.

Bone matrix is protein and is broken down to amino acids for gluconeogenesis.

Which of the following is the *greatest* or *major* mechanism of how cortisol increases serum glucose level?

a. Increasing gluconeogenesis
b. Decreasing glucose excretion at kidney
c. Having a permissive action on glucagon
d. Blocking uptake into tissues like muscle and adipose

Answer d. Blocking uptake into tissues like muscle and adipose

Although cortisol does increase gluconeogenesis and breaks down glycogen by permissive action on glucagon, the major mechanism is blocking uptake into peripheral tissues.

Move the clock forward to follow up after removal of the pituitary lesion. Make sure you replace thyroid hormone and sex hormones in addition to giving prednisone or hydrocortisone. Recheck the patient's chemistry looking for a normal glucose, potassium, sodium, and bicarbonate levels.

CASE 7: Acromegaly

Setting: *office*

CC: *"I'm sleepy all day long, and my wife says I snore."*

VS: *R: 12 breaths/minute; BP: 158/98 mm Hg; PR: 78 beats/minute; T: 97.8°F*

HPI: *A 48-year-old man with hypertension and diabetes comes to the office because he has daytime somnolence and his wife complains that he snores. He is also here for routine management of diabetes and hypertension.*

ROS:
- *Shoe, hat, and ring size started increasing over the last 1 to 2 years*
- *Body odor*
- *Erectile dysfunction*

PMHx:
- *Diabetes and hypertension*

Medications:
- *Lisinopril*
- *Metformin*

PE:
- *General appearance: soft, sweaty, mushy handshake; rather unattractive*
- *HEENT: large nose, lips, and jaw; teeth widely spaced*
- *Cardiovascular: 3/6 pansystolic murmur radiating to axilla*

Initial Orders:
- *HbA$_1$c*
- *CHEM-7*
- *Lipid panel*

What is the best initial test?

a. Insulinlike growth factor (IGF)
b. GH

c. MRI head
d. Glucose suppression test

Answer a. Insulinlike growth factor (IGF)

IGF has a longer half-life than GH. Because GH has a shorter half-life, elevated levels are harder to detect. Never start with a scan of the head in endocrinology. Do the MRI of the brain only after the disorder has been biochemically confirmed.

IGF is protein bound, giving it a long half-life.

When is GH release maximal?

a. On waking
b. 30 minutes before waking

c. Middle of the night
d. Before sleep

Answer c. Middle of the night

Deep sleep is the stimulant for the normal diurnal variation in GH level. Cortisol level increases 30 minutes before waking.

Move the clock forward 1 week.

Laboratory Test Results:
- *HbA₁c: 7.2%*
- *CHEM-7: glucose 145 mg/dL; BUN and creatinine: normal*
- *Lipid panel: elevated LDL and triglycerides*
- *IGF: markedly elevated*

Acromegaly grows sweat glands!

Growth Hormone Mechanisms
- Acts as antiinsulin
- Raises serum glucose
- Raises free fatty acid level

Acromegaly causes hypertension.

You increase the dose of metformin and discuss possibly adding a second oral hypoglycemic agent to get the HbA₁c concentration under 7%. You inform the patient that both his diabetes and hypertension may be from acromegaly, but you need to confirm the etiology.

Orders:
• *Glucose suppression test*

IGF causes obstructive sleep apnea by growing neck tissues.

Erectile Dysfunction Etiology
• Diabetes
• Hypertension
• Vascular disease
• Associated with sleep apnea

IGF and GH fail to suppress with glucose loading. This is a failure of the normal feedback inhibition mechanism. You order an MRI and ask the patient to return to discuss the results. The patient comes back the following week and you inform him that the scan does show a pituitary lesion, and transsphenoidal surgery is needed to remove it. You also tell him that his diabetes may resolve when you remove the lesion.

If GH is an *antiinsulin* that raises glucose and free fatty acid levels, why does it produce another hormone call *insulinlike growth factor*? What is insulinlike about it?

a. Effect on hormone sensitive lipase   **c.** Effect on lipids
b. Effect on protein synthesis

Answer b. Effect on protein synthesis

GH is an antiinsulin in terms of its glucose and lipid effect. GH stimulates production of IGF at the liver and skeletal muscle. IGF is *insulinlike*, not GH. IGF increases protein synthesis, amino acid uptake into cells, and DNA synthesis.

Both IGF and insulin use a tyrosine kinase receptor.

The patient is frightened by the idea of "brain surgery" and does not come back to see you for a year. Order an "Interval History." His erectile disfunction, body odor, and sleep apnea have all worsened. In addition, his numbness and tingling in the first three fingers of both hands have worsened by use. He has become immobile because of knee pain.

Physical Examination:
- *Facial features coarsened*
- *Knees enlarged and abnormally shaped*
- *New 3/6 pansystolic murmur radiating to the axilla*

Uncontrolled IGF leads to misshapen joints and arthropathy.

IGF expand proteins abnormally.

Orders:
- *Glucose, HbA₁c, lipids*
- *Repeat MRI of head*
- *Echocardiogram*

What is the mechanism of the carpal tunnel syndrome?

a. Abnormal protein growth in the canal   **c.** Potassium alteration
b. Sodium alteration

Answer a. Abnormal protein growth in the canal

Acromegaly results in a protein expansion in the canal that the median nerve travels through. This compresses the nerve. Carpal tunnel syndrome is the most common neuropathy in acromegaly.

One week later the patient returns. He is becoming short of breath with exertion. His test results show that his glucose level is 195 mg/dL; his HbA₁c concentration is 8.4%; his MRI shows an enlarging pituitary lesion; and his echocardiogram shows moderate mitral regurgitation with an ejection fraction of 32%.

Mechanism of Cardiomyopathy
- IGF causes abnormal cardiac shape.
- Hypertension, diabetes and hyperlipidemia cause coronary disease.

What cancer should you test the patient for?

a. Colon

c. Prostate

b. Lung

d. Gastric

Answer a. Colon

IGF leads to excess colonic polyp formation. This increases the risk of colon cancer.

Which of the following will most likely resolve after removing the pituitary gland?

a. Hyperlipidemia

c. Cardiomyopathy

b. Carpal tunnel

d. Joint abnormality

Answer a. Hyperlipidemia

Because the high lipid level results from the antiinsulin effect of GH, it will likely resolve after the GH is decreased. The other problems are from a permanent growth of protein and will not "resorb" after the GH and IGF levels drop. You have to remove the pituitary gland before these problems advance.

The most common cause of death from acromegaly is cardiomyopathy from coronary disease.

A month later you are seeing the patient at a follow-up appointment after the removal of his pituitary gland. He has been started on thyroid hormone replacement and prednisone.

Additional therapies to lower GH and IGF levels:
- Pegvisomant
- Octreotide (somatostatin)
- Cabergoline

Pegvisomant is a direct GH receptor antagonist.

Move the clock forward another 2 to 4 weeks. Recheck glucose and HbA₁c levels because the patient may have a decreased need for diabetes medication. Treat the mitral regurgitation with ACE inhibitors as you would for any person with mitral regurgitation.

CASE 8: **Hyperaldosteronism**

Setting: *ambulatory care center*

CC: *"My legs feel like lead."*

VS: *BP: 168/98 mm Hg; P: 72 beats/minute*

HPI: *A 43-year-old man comes to clinic because his "arm and legs feel like they weigh 100 pounds each." There is a progressive slowness for muscle weakness. It is equal in all four extremities, started 6 months ago, and is slowly progressive and uncomfortable.*

ROS:
- *No visual problems; no diplopia*
- *No respiratory problems*
- *No dyspnea*
- *Yes to significant polyuria*

PMHx:
- *Hypertension: difficult to control*

Medication:
- *Nifedipine*

PE:
- *General: tired, slumped posture while sitting on table*
- *Cardiovascular: S₄ gallop*
- *Musculoskeletal: decreased strength throughout*
- *HEENT: no ptosis*

S₄ from hypertension

S₄: atrial systole into stiff noncompliant ventricle

Initial Orders:
- CHEM-7, CBC
- ECG
- UA
- Calcium, magnesium, phosphorus
- Thyroid function (T_4, TSH)

Generalized weakness is hard to evaluate. It has to be distinguished from the fatigue or tiredness of anemia versus decreased motor strength from thyroid, calcium, potassium, or magnesium abnormalities. This patient has actual muscle weakness, not fatigue and shortness of breath after exertion. Because it is generalized and continuous, it is hard to say that it is myasthenia.

- Myasthenia: worse at end of day
- Guillain-Barré: acute, several days, ascends from legs upwards
- Botulism: acute, descends from face
- Tick paralysis: diffuse, overwhelming, sudden
- Hypokalemia: diffuse, can be chronic if undetected; rare with K >2.5 mEq/L

Move the clock forward to get the blood chemistry results immediately. The patient should be brought back no later than the following day.

- CHEM-7: sodium normal; K: 2.4 mEq/L
- ECG: S wave deep in leads V_1 and V_2; R wave tall in leads V_5 and V_6; U waves present
- Magnesium: slight decrease
- T_4, TSH, CBC, UA, calcium, phosphorus: normal

Hypokalemia: U waves from Purkinje fiber repolarization

ECG:
$SV_1 + RV_5$ >35 mm = Left Ventricular Hypertrophy (LVH)

The most urgent step is to replace the potassium. The route of administration is dependent on the setting of your case. The setting or location of treatment is an essential feature of the Step 3 examination. Because this is an ambulatory care patient who has been living like this for months, you do not need to hospitalize the patient. Use oral potassium replacement for outpatients. If the patient is hospitalized, you should never discharge a patient with an abnormal potassium level—either high or low.

What is the mechanism of the patient's muscle weakness?

a. The resting membrane potential is excessively low.

b. The Na$^+$/K$^+$-ATPase pump is inactive.

c. The ungated potassium channel is closed.

d. The voltage gate potassium channels stay open.

Answer a. The resting membrane potential is excessively low.

Resting membrane potential is based on potassium levels. The threshold for depolarization is about −45 mV. When you move the resting membrane potential down from −70 to −80 or to −90 mV you are moving further *away* from threshold. There is no effect on Na$^+$/K$^+$-ATPase. The ungated channels have more potassium leaving the cell.

Potassium Replacement Rates
• Oral: No maximum rate of replacement
• IV: <10 to 20 mEq/h

Muscles cannot contract if they cannot depolarize.

You order potassium tablets and instruct the patient to take them with a lot of water. Ask the patient to return the following day to recheck the potassium level. It is completely possible to replace the potassium over 1 to 2 days.

The Interval History shows that the patient reports much greater mobility and strength and his potassium level is now 3.1 mEq/L.

Low serum potassium (K) pulls potassium ions (K$^+$) out of cells. Hitting the threshold for depolarization is harder when cells have low K$^+$.

Further potassium replacement continues over the next 2 to 3 days. Bring the patient back frequently to recheck his levels. You should also see a resolution of U waves on the ECG.

Both high and low potassium levels cause arrhythmia.

Low K levels decrease conduction through the His-Purkinje system.

By the following week, the potassium level has normalized. All muscle weakness has resolved. The polyuria has resolved as well.

Hypokalemia causes nephrogenic diabetes insipidus.

ADH does not work effectively with low K or high calcium (Ca) levels.

The patient's repeat blood pressure level is 168/100 mm Hg.

What is the mechanism of hypertension?

a. ANGII constricting arterioles
b. Excess ADH acting as vasopressin
c. Aldosterone increasing sodium absorption at late distal or early collecting duct

d. Smooth muscle hyperplasia of arteries
e. Catecholamine excess
f. Renin excess

Answer c. Aldosterone increasing sodium absorption at late distal or early collecting duct

High BP with low serum potassium level is most likely hyperaldosteronism. Although all the features listed cause hypertension, none of them is particular to this case. The main feature of basic science correlates for the Step 3 examination is not just to know something is happening, but to know precisely why it is happening. Aldosterone works by increasing sodium reabsorption at the cortical portion of the collecting duct. That is the early part of it, where it meets the distal convoluted tubule (DCT).

Hypertension + Hypokalemia = Hyperaldosteronism

What is the difference between ADH and vasopressin?
a. Production site

b. Storage site

c. Chemical structure

d. Amount and target organ

Answer d. Amount and target organ

ADH is made in the hypothalamus at the paraventricular and supraoptic nuclei. It is not made in the posterior pituitary. ADH is transported down the pituitary stalk to the posterior pituitary where it is stored. ADH works at the kidneys on the V2 receptor of the collecting duct. ADH inserts aquaporin to increase permeability to water so it can be reabsorbed. Vasopressin is the same substance, but stimulates the V1 receptor in the vasculature to cause vasoconstriction.

ADH absorbs water.
Vasopressin constricts vessels.

A 1% osmolarity change increases ADH.
A 10% volume change increases ADH.

High ADH levels constrict vessels at high levels and we call it *vasopressin.*

The patient has persistent hypertension. Because potassium is normal, muscle weakness has resolved, but you need to investigate the diagnosis of primary hyperaldosteronism or Conn syndrome.

Orders:
- *Plasma aldosterone*
- *Plasma renin*
- *CHEM-7*

Which of the following is consistent with primary hyperaldosteronism?

	Aldosterone	Renin
a.	High	High
b.	High	Low
c.	Low	Low
d.	Low	High

Answer b. Aldosterone high and renin low

When aldosterone is being produced autonomously, the ratio of aldosterone to renin is 20:1. Any cause of dehydration or renal artery stenosis can raise both the renin and aldosterone levels.

The patient returns in 1 week.

Report:
- *Aldosterone level high, renin level low (ratio 25:1)*
- *Serum bicarbonate level elevated*

Metabolic alkalosis is from aldosterone increasing hydrogen ion (H+) excretion.

What is the precise location and mechanism of H+ loss?

a. Proximal tubule

b. Epithelial sodium channel (ENaC)

c. α-Intercalated cells

d. Aquaporin

Answer c. α-Intercalated cells

In the late distal tubule and early collecting duct, there are two cells on which aldosterone has its primary effect (Figure 3-6). The alpha-intercalated cells reabsorb sodium and excrete an H+. The ENaC reabsorbs sodium and excretes potassium. ENaC is the precise site of potassium loss from hyperaldosteronism.

Intercalated: H+

ENaC: K+

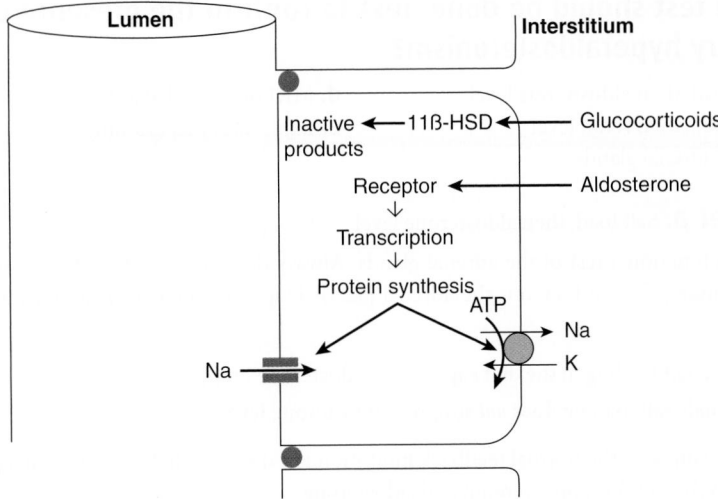

Figure 3-6. Mechanism of aldosterone action. Aldosterone enters principal cells and interacts with cytosolic aldosterone receptors. The aldosterone-bound receptors interact with nuclear DNA to promote gene expression. The aldosterone-induced gene products activate sodium channels and sodium pumps to increase sodium reabsorption. Glucocorticoids, such as cortisol, are also capable of binding to the aldosterone receptor. However, they are inactivated by 11-hydroxysteroid dehydrogenase (11-HSD). ATP, adenosine triphosphate; K, potassium; Na, sodium. (Reproduced with permission from Eaton DC, Pooler JP. *Vander's Renal Physiology*, 8th ed. New York: McGraw-Hill; 2013.)

What is the most common cause of primary hyperaldosteronism?

a. Unilateral adenoma
b. Bilateral adenoma
c. Unilateral hyperplasia
d. Bilateral hyperplasia
e. Cancer or neoplasia

Answer a. Unilateral adenoma

Unilateral adenoma accounts for 60% to 80% of cases. Only 3% is unilateral hyperplasia. Most of the rest is bilateral hyperplasia. Only 1% to 2% is cancer or neoplasia.

Normal Stimulants to Renin
• Low sodium level
• Beta-1-stimulation
• Low pressure at juxtaglomerular complex

Which test should be done next to confirm the presence of primary hyperaldosteronism?

a. Salt load, then aldosterone level

b. Salt load, then renin level

c. CT of adrenal glands

d. MRI of adrenal glands

e. Exploratory laparotomy

Answer a. Salt load, then aldosterone level

This is a functional test of the adrenal glands. Always do functional tests before scans in endocrinology. If you take out the adrenal glands inappropriately, you cannot put them back in.

• Normal: Salt loading in the diet suppresses aldosterone level.

• Abnormal: Salt loading does *not* suppress aldosterone level.

The failure of the normal feedback inhibition is a disease. High salt levels in a person with high BP should suppress renin and aldosterone.

The zona glomerulosa makes aldosterone.

The following week the patient's salt loading test shows a persistent high aldosterone level despite 5000 mEq/day in the diet. The adrenal CT shows a bilateral hyperplasia.

What is the treatment?

a. Open surgical removal

b. Laparoscopic removal

c. Spironolactone

d. Prednisone

e. Removal of pituitary gland

Answer c. Spironolactone

Adenomas and cancer are removed by laparoscopic surgery. Bilateral hyperplasia is treated with the aldosterone receptor antagonist spironolactone. Removing the pituitary gland will do nothing because the pituitary exerts no control on aldosterone production. Aldosterone is controlled by renin.

Direct Stimulants to Aldosterone Synthesis
• Angiotensin II
• Hyperkalemia

There is no edema with hyperaldosteronism because of "sodium escape" at the kidney.

After 1 week on spironolactone, the patient's BP has lowered to 134/84 mm Hg. He feels less tired.

What do you have to monitor for?

a. Low sodium

b. High sodium

c. High potassium

d. Metabolic alkalosis

Answer c. High potassium

Because spironolactone is an aldosterone receptor antagonist, some people develop high potassium levels. Spironolactone blocks the ENaC and the intercalated cells.

Two months later the patient comes because of pain in his chest. The discomfort is bilateral. There is enlargement of breast tissue consistent with gynecomastia.

What is the mechanism?

a. Spironolactone inhibits androgens.

b. Prolactin levels have increased.

c. Estrogen release has increased.

d. Progesterone level has increased.

Answer a. Spironolactone inhibits androgens.

Spironolactone inhibits androgens. This causes enlargement of breast tissue or gynecomastia. In polycystic ovary syndrome, spironolactone treats hirsutism and helps restore menstruation.

Spironolactone is stopped and eplerenone is started. Eplerenone is an alternate mineralocorticoid receptor antagonist that does not inhibit androgen receptors. Move the clock forward 1 month at a time until the CCS program ends the case. Monitor the patient's CHEM-7 looking for potassium, sodium, and bicarbonate abnormalities.

CASE 9: Prolactinoma

Setting: *office*

CC: *"I'm making breast milk, but I'm not pregnant."*

HPI: *A 34-year-old woman comes to office with abnormal milk production from her breasts for the last few weeks. She did three home pregnancy tests and all are negative. She has been unsuccessfully trying to get pregnant for 2 years. Her menstrual periods are irregular.*

PMHx:
- *Depression*

Medications:
- *Fluoxetine*

PE:
- *Normal except galactorrhea*

Initial Orders:
- *Urine beta-human chorionic gonadotropin (HCG)*
- *Prolactin level*

The patient's repeat urine beta-HCG level is normal. Bring the patient back in a few days to discuss the results of the prolactin level. Of all the endocrinopathies, prolactin is unique in that so many medications and mechanical problems like nipple stimulation can cause hyperprolactinemia and galactorrhea (Figure 3-7).

Which of the following is *not* clearly associated with hyperprolactinemia?

a. Antipsychotic medications
b. Tricyclic antidepressants
c. SSRIs
d. Cimetidine
e. Verapamil
f. Opiates

Answer c. SSRIs

SSRIs are just not clearly associated with increased prolactin levels.

- Dopamine inhibits prolactin release.
- Antipsychotics decrease dopamine levels.

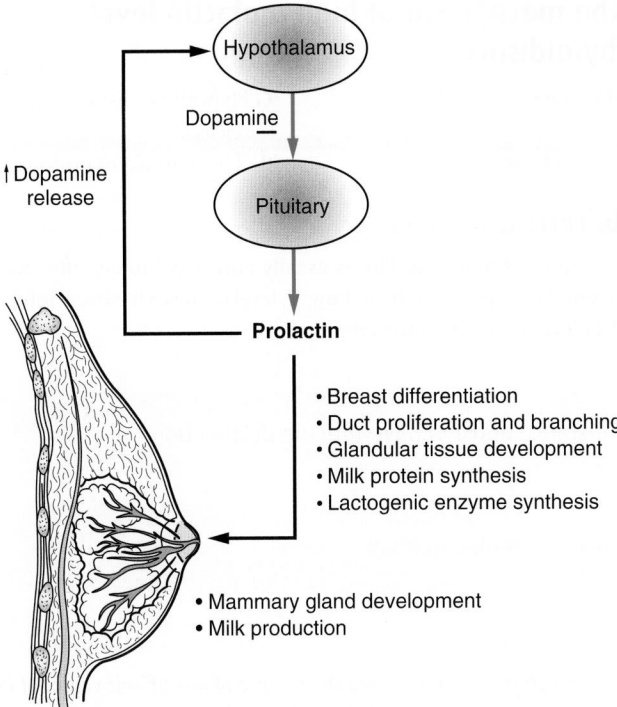

Figure 3-7. Physiologic effects of prolactin. Prolactin plays an important role in the normal development of mammary tissue and in milk production. Prolactin release is predominantly under negative control by hypothalamic dopamine. Suckling stimulates the release of prolactin. Prolactin inhibits its own release by stimulating dopamine release from the hypothalamus. (Reproduced with permission from Molina PE. *Endocrine Physiology*, 3rd ed. New York: McGraw-Hill; 2010.)

The patient returns and her prolactin level is elevated.

Which of the following endocrinopathies is associated with high prolactin level?

a. Estrogen deficiency
b. Addison disease
c. Cushing syndrome or hypercortisolism

d. Hypothyroidism
e. GH deficiency

Answer d. Hypothyroidism

It is reasonable to exclude hypothyroidism in any person with hyperprolactinemia. Increased estrogen directly stimulates the pituitary to release prolactin. This is the mechanism in pregnancy of how breast glands normally grow. The placenta makes estrogen. Estrogen makes prolactin. Prolactin makes the breast glands grow.

What is the mechanism of high prolactin level in hypothyroidism?

a. T_4 normally suppresses prolactin release.

b. TRH level is increased.

c. Hypothyroidism decreases dopamine release.

d. TSH stimulates prolactin.

Answer b. TRH level is increased.

TRH stimulates prolactin release. This is usually only at pathologically increased levels of TRH such as found in hypothyroidism. Low T_4 level removes feedback inhibition on TRH. Very high TRH level stimulates prolactin.

> Opiate substance abusers have erectile dysfunction.

> Opiates increase prolactin level.

> *Because of the high prolactin level and the absence of identifiable causes of hyperprolactinemia, you send the patient for an MRI of the head.*

What functional biological test is there of prolactin?

a. Metoclopramide stimulation test

b. Dopamine suppression test

c. Estrogen stimulation test

d. Naloxone stimulation test

e. None

Answer e. None

High Prolactin + Exclude Correctable Causes = Brain MRI

> *An MRI is done. The patient returns for the results and is told she has a 5-mm lesion in the pituitary gland.*

What is the next best step?

a. Refer to neurosurgery

b. Radiation treatment

c. Octreotide

d. Cabergoline

e. Pergolide

Answer d. Cabergoline

Cabergoline is an oral dopamine receptor antagonist that causes less nausea and vomiting than bromocriptine. This is clearly the first line of therapy for all microadenoma. Surgery is done if the lesion is larger than 3 cm or the dopamine agonist has failed. Radiation is a third or fourth attempt at treatment. Octreotide is a somatostatin analogue. There is no significant efficacy with a somatostatin analogue. Prolactinomas are managed exactly opposite to acromegaly. Surgery is the first-line treatment in acromegaly.

Cabergoline is an ergot derivative.

Transsphenoidal surgery is performed. Prednisone, T_4, and sex hormones replacement therapy is started. Follow up with the patient until the program ends the case.

CHAPTER **4**

NEUROLOGY

CASE 1: Stroke

Setting: *emergency department (ED)*

CC: *"My arm is weak."*

VS: *BP: 188/115 mm Hg; P: 90 beats/minute; T: 100.1°F; R: 14 breaths/minute*

HPI: *A 58-year-old man with half an hour of right arm and leg weakness was sent to the ED in an ambulance by his family. His family noticed the arm and leg weakness immediately because it happened while at dinner when it looked like he got up and tripped. On lifting him up, they found the whole right side of his body weak and his speech had become garbled.*

PMHx:
- *Hypertension*
- *Tobacco smoking*

Medications:
- *Nifedipine*
- *Lisinopril*

PE:
- *Neurological: clear weakness on right side 2/5 power, right facial droop*
- *Cardiovascular: normal*
- *Abdominal: normal*

Grading of Power on Neurological Examination
- 0/5: Flaccid, completely paralyzed.
- 1/5: Muscle twitch, no movement.
- 2/5: If examiner lifts extremity, patient can move it side to side.
- 3/5: Patient can hold up extremity against gravity only. No load bearing.
- 4/5: Weak.
- 5/5: Normal.

What is the most urgent step?

a. Control blood pressure (BP).

b. Order computed tomography (CT) of head.

c. Give aspirin.

d. Give thrombolytics.

Answer a. Control blood pressure (BP).

All of these are important in a stroke, but the point of this question is that you cannot give any form of anticoagulation without first excluding hemorrhage. You must not send someone off to a CT without giving the first dose of antihypertensive medication.

Initial Orders:
- *Labetalol intravenously (IV)*
- *Head CT without contrast*
- *Complete blood count (CBC), prothrombin time (PT), activated partial thromboplastin time (aPTT), electrocardiogram (ECG)*
- *Neurology or stroke team evaluation*

CT with contrast is used to look for cancer or infection.

Blood does not need contrast to be visible.

You move the clock forward 5 minutes. It is expected that the stroke team evaluation will occur within 5 minutes after the initial physician evaluation. More than any other disease, stroke evaluation is on a precise expectation of time frame. The head CT or magnetic resonance imaging (MRI) is expected to occur within 15 minutes of the initial physician evaluation with a reading by an expert in 20 minutes.

Why is stroke more sensitive to time than any other tissue or organ damage?

a. Brain tissue has no glycogen stores.

b. Carbon dioxide accumulation is more damaging to central nervous system (CNS) tissue.

c. Acid (hydrogen ion [H^+]) accumulation is more damaging to CNS tissue.

d. Ketones cannot supply energy to cerebral tissue.

Answer a. Brain tissue has no glycogen stores.

Your brain wants 100% glucose. Because there is no glycogen storage in the brain, it needs all its food to be brought in continuously by blood flow. This is perhaps the single most important "basic science fundamental" to know for a stroke: The brain has no glycogen stores. Brain tissue uses glucose as a fuel almost exclusively. Ketones can be used, but it takes time for them to be produced and for the brain to switch the biochemistry to be able to consume them. Carbon dioxide and acid dilate cerebral vasculature to increase flow to hypoxic brain tissue, but they are not damaging.

> Cerebral tissue lives mostly on glucose.

> *Move the clock forward 5 minutes and recheck the patient's BP. Acute BP control with labetalol, nitroprusside, enalaprilat, or nimodipine will start to have an effect instantly if the drug is working. You cannot give thrombolytics if the BP is >180/110 mm Hg, so controlling BP is indispensable to proper management.*

> You must practice the computer-based case simulation (CCS) cases before entering the examination.

> **Orders:**
> • *Vital signs (under the "Physical Examination" tab on top)*
>
> *Two to five minutes later, the repeat BP level is 180/112 mm Hg.*
>   *Give another dose of IV labetalol. The most important thing to remember about using acute BP-lowering medications on CCS is that the route of administration be IV. The specific agent is not as important. However, you cannot order medications by class on CCS; you must write orders by name of medication. You cannot order "BP drug" or "beta-blocker." You have to order "labetalol."*

> The onset of action for IV labetalol is 2 to 5 minutes.

> *Two to five minutes later, the repeat BP level is 170/104 mm Hg.*

What is the mechanism of action of labetalol?

a. Beta-1, central alpha-1

b. Beta-1, peripheral alpha-1

c. Beta-1 and 2, peripheral alpha-1

d. Beta-1 and 2, central alpha-2

Answer c. Beta-1 and 2, peripheral alpha-1

Labetalol and carvedilol are the two combined alpha/beta-blockers. They are nonspecific beta-blockers and also block peripheral alpha-1-receptors. Peripheral alpha-1-receptors are the mechanism of how norepinephrine raises BP. Alpha-1-constriction is a rapid and powerful way to alter BP.

> Do not lower BP more than 25% on first day.

Move the clock forward 10 to 15 minutes until the CT report is available. **Because hemorrhages cause 15% of strokes, you have to exclude bleeding before any anticoagulation medications can be given.**

- Head CT: no blood, no masses
- Repeat BP 158/98 mm Hg
- ECG: left ventricular hypertrophy, unchanged from previous ECG
- CBC, PT/aPTT: normal

What should you do next?

a. Lower BP further.

b. Give aspirin.

c. Give thrombolytics.

d. Give clopidogrel.

e. Give heparin.

Answer c. Give thrombolytics.

Thrombolytics are the standard of care for acute nonhemorrhagic stroke within the first 3 to 4.5 hours after the onset of symptoms. Most clinicians would use it up to 4.5 hours after onset, but the Step 3 examination will avoid all potential controversy and will make it either clearly less than 3 hours or more than 4.5 hours from the time of onset.

Repeat the neurological examination to confirm the findings.

Which of the following is most likely to be found?

a. Unilateral blindness

b. Bitemporal hemianopsia

c. Homonymous hemianopsia

d. None

Answer c. Homonymous hemianopsia

When you have a patient with a stroke causing loss of motor strength on one half of the body, you should expect the visual field to be lost on the same side. Half of each eye's visual field will be lost.

Right side weakness: right visual field loss

When are the other choices correct?
· Aspirin: Use if presenting after 4.5 hours.
· Clopidogrel: If the patient is already on aspirin, switch from aspirin after 4.5 hours.
· Heparin: Never give for stroke.
· Dipyridamole: If the patient is already on aspirin at the time of a stroke, add to aspirin.

Never combine aspirin with clopidogrel for stroke!

Combining aspirin with dipyridamole is **good**.
Combining aspirin with clopidogrel is **bad**.

Thrombolytics are given. Move the patient to the hospital ward. The intensive care unit (ICU) is not needed. On CCS, there is no way to physically move the patient to a place called "stroke unit." The stroke unit is not one of the five places you have to choose from on CCS locations.

• *All of the previous orders will follow the patient in any location.*
• *Vital signs are done on CCS with each move.*
• *Unless you see it on your screen under "Orders," it is not being done.*

CBC, PT, and aPTT prior to thrombolytics:
· Thrombocytopenia and coagulopathy are contraindications.

Which best describes the mechanism of thrombolytics?

a. Prevents fibrinogen activation
b. Cleaves fibrin into D-dimers

c. Removes fibrin split product from fibrin
d. Increases action of plasmin on factor XIII

Answer b. Cleaves fibrin into D-dimers

Thrombolytics activate plasminogen into plasmin. Plasmin cleaves newly produced fibrin strands into their breakdown product, which is D-dimers. Fibrin split products (FSPs) are liberated from fibrinogen to activate it into fibrin. Thrombin is what cleaves off the FSPs. Factor XIII is a clot-stabilizing factor that solidifies a clot.

The patient has been moved to the hospital ward after the use of thrombolytics. His repeat BP is 156/96 mm Hg. There is a slight improvement in his right-sided weakness during the repeat neurological examination.

You will never get in trouble on the CCS by reviewing charts or examining patients too often!

Once thrombolytics are given and the follow-up neurological examination is done, you should explore reasons for the emboli going to the brain.

Orders:
- *Echocardiogram*
- *Telemetry*
- *Carotid artery duplex Doppler ultrasound*

Where is the source site of the clot or stroke in this patient?

a. Anterior cerebral
b. Middle cerebral
c. Posterior cerebral

Answer b. Middle cerebral

Upper and lower extremity hemiparesis, facial droop, and expressive aphasia are classic for middle cerebral artery stroke.

Anterior Cerebral Stroke:
- Cognitive and psychiatric deficit
- Lower extremity weakness > upper extremity weakness
- Urine incontinence

Posterior Circulation (Vertebral or Basilar):
- Loss of consciousness
- Dysarthria, diplopia, dysphagia, dizziness
- Bilateral defects

Do not order carotid artery Doppler ultrasound for posterior circulation defects!

Carotid arteries do not anatomically supply the vertebral or basilar artery.

As you move the clock forward to get the results remember to order:
- *Physical therapy and rehabilitation evaluations*
- *Restart aspirin 24 hours after thrombolytics*
- *If the patient was on aspirin, switch to clopidogrel or add dipyridamole*

Echocardiograms, telemetry, and carotid artery Doppler ultrasounds are often unrevealing in a stroke. If there is >70% stenosis on the affected side, refer the patient to vascular surgery for endarterectomy. We do not know what to do about asymptomatic carotid artery stenosis.

CASE 2: Parkinson Disease

Setting: *office*

CC: *"My walking is getting really slow."*

HPI: *A 74-year-old man with progressive inability to walk over the past year comes to your office. He also has a hard time getting up from a seated position and he becomes lightheaded when he tries.*

PMHx: *ostearthritis*

Medications: *acetaminophen*

PE:
- *General: immobile, seems very "grim-faced"*

Neurological:
- *Tremor at rest at 3 cycles/second, cogwheeling present*
- *Slow gait; significant retropulsion. He cannot easily turn.*

Initial Orders:
- *MRI of head*
- *CHEM-20*

The patient's diagnosis of Parkinson disease (PD) is obvious on examination. There is no test to specifically diagnose PD. An MRI of the head can be used to see if there are previous strokes that led to the PD. All of your Step 3 examination questions on PD will concern drug therapy, and the basic science fundamental questions will be on the mechanisms of these treatments.

Which should be tested for on examination?

a. Hyperreflexia

b. Orthostatic hypotension

c. Spasticity of muscles

d. Decreased papillary reflexes

Answer b. Orthostatic hypotension

Patients with PD frequently have orthostatic hypotension. This is why they cannot easily get up from a seated position. When rising, the autonomic nervous system is slow to respond. The normal increase in pulse rate and vasoconstriction is not occurring. When a normal person stands, the baroreceptors in the carotid sinus and atria sense the decrease in pressure or stretch. Because these are mechanoreceptors, firing is decreased. The medulla does not perceive the change in posture and there is no output to the sinoatrial (SA) node to increase firing or to the arterioles to contract. Hence, BP is abnormally low when standing and patients can experience syncope. This is like "cogwheel rigidity" of the autonomic nervous system.

Response to Standing
• Normal: vasoconstriction and tachycardia
• PD: inappropriately low pulse rate

In PD, phase 4 depolarization of the SA node stays abnormally flat.

The patient has orthostasis on examination as well as decreased facial movements (hypomimia). The main thing that bothers him is slow gait and general immobility. He is not as bothered by the tremor because it stops when he reaches for something.

Orders:
• *Anticholinergic agent (benztropine, trihexyphenidyl)*

The mechanism by which anticholinergics improve PD is unknown.

Why does decreasing acetylcholine increase dopamine?
We do not know!

Instead of the previously scheduled 2-week follow-up appointment, the patient is brought back in 4 days by his wife. He has abdominal pain, dry mouth, and urine retention.

Which of the following should you also ask about or examine for?

a. Bradycardia

b. Memory difficulty

c. Diarrhea

d. Constricted pupils

Answer b. Memory difficulty

Acetylcholine helps with memory formation. Inhibition of acetylcholine (ACh) will provoke dementia. This is why anticholinergic medication like benztropine is hard to use in those older than 65 to 70 years old. It worsens Alzheimer disease. This is why we use drugs like donepezil, rivastigmine, and galantamine for Alzheimer disease. They increase ACh and improve memory. In addition, inhibiting ACh should cause tachycardia, constipation, and dilate pupils.

> More ACh = More Memories
> Less ACh = Less Memories

> Anticholinergics worsen glaucoma.
> Dilated Pupils = Blocked Canal of Schlemm

> *You stop the benztropine and start amantadine. When you see the patient again in 2 weeks, there is no significant improvement.*

What is the next step to try?

a. Catechol-*O*-methyltransferase (COMT) inhibitor (tolcapone, entacapone)
b. Ropinirole or pramipexole
c. Bromocriptine
d. Selegiline

Answer b. Ropinirole or pramipexole

These medications are direct-acting dopamine receptor agonists. They have less efficacy than levodopa/carbidopa, but they have less adverse effects as well. The standard of care in most PD is to try a dopamine receptor agonist at the beginning of treatment.

Bromocriptine is a dopamine agonist but is a derivative of ergot, and thereby has more adverse effects, such as nausea and vomiting. In choosing treatment, if two medications have the same efficacy, use the one with less adverse effects.

Selegiline is a monamine oxidase (MAO) inhibitor. This class of drugs decreases the metabolism of dopamine, but the efficacy is unclear.

> Amantadine efficacy is limited.

> Amantadine may increase dopamine release from the substantia nigra.

You start ropinirole and see the patient again in 2 weeks. He has modest improvement in mobility and orthostasis. Over the next year, he is stable then begins to deteriorate again. You now add levodopa/carbidopa, and he markedly improves.

What is the mechanism of carbidopa?

a. Direct dopamine agonist

b. Inhibition of dopamine decarboxylase

c. Decreased urinary excretion of dopamine

d. Synergistic with dopamine at substantia nigra

Answer b. Inhibition of dopamine decarboxylase

Levodopa normally has a very short half-life. It, therefore, will decompose and not allow transfer across the blood brain barrier into the brain. Carbidopa is a peripheral dopamine decarboxylase inhibitor. This allows a greater level to enter the brain.

You see the patient at 2-week intervals and increase the dose of levodopa/carbidopa. Perform a neurological examination and check for orthostasis at each visit. The patient is not fully controlled after 2 months.

What should you do?

a. Nothing more can be done.

b. Add tolcapone or entacapone.

c. Order deep brain stimulation.

Answer b. Add tolcapone or entacapone.

Tolcapone and entacapone are COMT inhibitors. They block the metabolism of dopamine in the brain. They enhance activity of dopamine at the substantia nigra. They have definite efficacy but are exclusively an add-on therapy to levodopa/carbidopa. They will not work by themselves.

After a few days on the new medications, the good news is, the patient has much better mobility. The bad news is, he has started to develop visual hallucinations and sees "bugs coming out of the walls."

What is the mechanism of the hallucinations?

a. It is the direct toxicity of the COMT inhibitor.

b. The patient has decreased serotonin levels.

c. Dopamine increases psychosis.

d. Decreased ACh increases psychosis.

Answer c. Dopamine increases psychosis.

The difficulty of medicating patients with PD is that the massive increase in dopamine can cause psychosis in some patients. The dose needed to control PD may mean that the only way to get the PD controlled is to give enough dopamine even though it may lead to the adverse effect of psychosis. The treatment is quetiapine, which is an antipsychotic medication with the lowest amount of parkinsonian adverse effects.

Anti-Parkinson disease (PD) medications cause psychosis.
Antipsychosis medications cause PD.
Anti-PD medications cause dementia.
Anti-dementia medications cause PD.

CASE 3: Myasthenia Gravis

Setting: *office*

CC: *"I feel so weak at the end of the day."*

VS: *BP: 112/72 mm Hg; P: 90 beats/minute; T: 99.8°F (37.7°C); R: 18 breaths/minute*

HPI: *A 54-year-old woman comes to the office with increasing muscle weakness and tiredness over the past few months. She feels "totally spent" at the end of the day and her "arms and legs feel like lead." She feels so tired that she has a hard time finishing meals.*

ROS:
• *Double vision*
• *No fever, no headache, no weight loss*

PMHx: *none*

Medications: *none*

PE:
• *General appearance: tired, but fully alert*
• *Neurological: decreased muscle strength in all four extremities equally; normal deep tendon reflexes (DTRs); normal pupillary response*
• *Head, ears, eyes, nose, throat (HEENT): bilateral ptosis*

Initial Orders:
• *Anti-ACh receptor antibodies*
• *Anti-muscle specific kinase (MuSK) antibodies*
• *Chest x-ray*

Edrophonium (Tensilon) test is neither as sensitive or specific as antiacetylcholine receptor antibodies.

Myasthenia gravis (MG) is not a disease you start to treat empirically unless the patient experienced an acute, overwhelming presentation of weakness threatening breathing. MG is generally a disease that progresses over months.

Report:
- *Anti-ACh receptor (AChR) antibodies positive*
- *Anti-MuSK antibodies present*
- *Chest x-ray: normal*

Anti-AChR antibodies are positive in 90% of those with MG. If patients present with MG limited to the eyes with diplopia, the sensitivity falls to 50%. Anti-MuSK antibodies are generally used in patients whose anti-AChR antibodies are negative.

Anti-MuSK is for those with false negative AChR antibodies.

What is usually the most common presentation of MG?

a. Proximal muscle weakness
b. Diaphragm and respiratory muscle weakness
c. Difficulty chewing and diplopia
d. Upper extremity and hip girdle weakness
e. Four-limb paralysis

Answer c. Difficulty chewing and diplopia

MG usually presents with diplopia and decreased ability to chew because they are the only two muscles used regularly. Because MG is a decremental decrease in strength on repetitive use, the patient must be using the muscles in order for it to be noticed.

What is the difference between pyridostigmine, neostigmine, and edrophonium?

a. Dosing and duration of effect
b. Mechanism of action
c. Adverse effects
d. Site of action

Answer a. Dosing and duration of effect

Acetylcholinesterase inhibitors are all essentially identical except for how long they last and therefore how frequently they are dosed. Acetylcholinesterase inhibitors all block the metabolism or breakdown of ACh at the neuromuscular junction. This increases the level and the clinical effect.

ACh receptors on muscle are nicotinic.

ACh receptors in the lung, bladder, bowel, saliva, and eye are muscarinic.

The patient is started on pyridostigmine. Move the clock forward 2 days. Do an "Interval History" to confirm the effectiveness of the medication. The patient reports a moderate improvement with pyridostigmine. You decide to confirm the diagnosis with additional testing before just increasing the dose.

What is the most accurate test for MG?

a. Biopsy
b. Single-fiber electromyography (EMG)

c. Creatine phosphokinase (CPK) and aldolase
d. ACh level

Answer b. Single-fiber electromyography (EMG)

EMG involves the placement of a needle into the muscle, and repetitive stimulation is sent through it. In MG, there is a clear decrease in muscle strength and frequency of contraction in response to nerve stimulation. More electrical jolts produce fewer muscular contractions.

Single-fiber EMG confirms the diagnosis as MG. You increase the dose of pyridostigmine. Do a chest CT as soon as the diagnosis of MG is confirmed. This is to exclude thymic hyperplasia and thymoma associated with MG. If it is found, it will need to be removed.

In children, the thymus gland "programs" T lymphocytes for action.

The thymus gland has little residual function in adults and can be removed without major adverse effect.

Move the clock forward and see the patient every month. Perform a neurological examination at each visit to assess the effectiveness of your medications. The patient is lost to follow-up for a few months and runs out of medications. When she returns, the patient has an overwhelming weakness and respiratory distress.

What is the treatment that will have the fastest effect for this acute myasthenic crisis?

a. Start intravenous immunoglobulin (IVIG).

b. Give steroids.

c. Remove the thymus gland.

d. Give anti-tumor necrosis factor drugs (e.g., etanercept).

e. Give cyclosporine.

Answer a. Start intravenous immunoglobulin (IVIG).

Acute myasthenic crisis is treated with IVIG or plasmapheresis. IVIG is much easier to use. Plasmapheresis has the same difficulty as setting up dialysis. The presumed mechanism of IVIG is that the Fc portions of the immunoglobulins will "stuff up" or fully saturate the Fc receptors on the macrophage. The macrophage then can no longer remove ACh receptors at the neuromuscular junction (Figure 4-1). Anti-tumor necrosis factor (TNF) medications have no benefit in MG. Steroids, cyclosporine, azathioprine, and cyclophosphamide take weeks or months to work.

MG will impair the patient's ability to inhale.

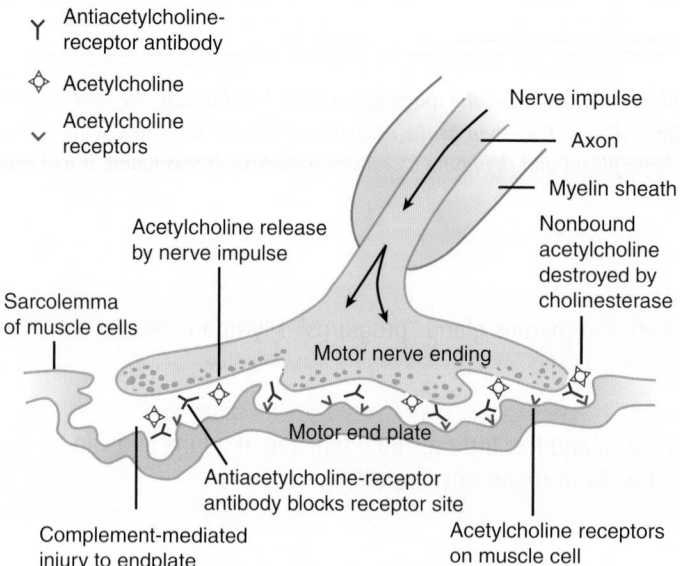

Figure 4-1. Pathogenesis of myasthenia gravis. Acetylcholine released at the nerve ending by the nerve impulse normally binds with acetylcholine receptors. This evokes the action potential in the muscle. In myasthenia gravis, antiacetylcholine receptor antibody binds to the acetylcholine receptor and inhibits the action of acetylcholine. Bound antibody evokes immune-mediated destruction of the endplate. (Reproduced with permission from Chandrasoma P, Taylor CE. *Concise Pathology*, 3rd ed., New York: McGraw-Hill; 1998.)

Acute myasthenic crisis = IVIG or plasmapheresis

Plasmapheresis removes antibody that attacks ACh receptors.

IVIG blocks macrophages that attack ACh receptors.

IVIG and pyridostigmine are started. The patient is moved to the ICU. After 24 hours, she starts to improve. After 2 days, she is breathing normally and able to walk. Move the patient to the ward and advance the clock. After another day, send the patient home.

Never send the patient home directly from ICU.

After the patient is discharged, she does well for a few months, and then the disease starts to progress. See the patient on CCS at 1-month intervals and do an "Interval History" and neurological examination each time. The patient's symptoms worsen on maximal pyridostigmine.

What is the next step?

a. Give IVIG.

b. Perform a thymectomy.

c. Add neostigmine.

Answer b. Perform a thymectomy.

The thymus gland programs the T cells that attack the neuromuscular ACh receptor. Removing the thymus gland in MG is like removing the spleen in a person with idiopathic thrombocytopenic purpura (ITP). Thymectomy markedly improves neuromuscular function in the majority of patients. It will not have much effect in those who are older than 60 to 70 years of age in whom T-cell function is already set and thymus removal will alter little.

You cannot move to a place called "Operating Room."

Order the procedure you need. CCS will tell you if a consultation is required.

The patient undergoes thymectomy. Over the next few weeks symptoms have mild improvement, but the patient cannot function normally. There is additional drug therapy to consider in patients with MG:
- *Cyclosporine*
- *Azathioprine*
- *Tacrolimus or sirolimus*

What is the mechanism of these medications?

a. Neutrophil inhibition
b. Interleukin-1
c. Leukotriene inhibition
d. Decrease of T-cell activation
e. Prostaglandin activation

Answer d. Decrease of T-cell activation

Cyclosporine is a calcineurin inhibitor. Azathioprine, its metabolite 6-mercaptopurine (6MP), and tacrolimus all inhibit activation of T cells. The major defect in MG is abnormal T-cell activation directed against the ACh receptor. Sometimes glucocorticoids can be used in the short term for control of MG over a few weeks. These other medications are then used to get the patient off steroids.

Make sure you exclude thymic hyperplasia and thymoma in MG.

MG is always progressive on acetylcholinesterase inhibitors. They do not interrupt the disease process.

Order each of the immunosuppressive drugs and advance the clock 1 month. It takes 2 to 3 months to see a maximal effect of these medications. They are slow in action. It is impossible to be sure which one will work in advance.

Check the renal function of patients on cyclosporine.

CASE 4: Subarachnoid Hemorrhage

Setting: *ED*

CC: *"My head hurt real bad, then I passed out."*

VS: *BP: 154/94 mm Hg; P: 110 beats/minute; T: 100.8°F; R: 18 breaths/minute*

HPI: *A 34-year-old woman with no significant past medical history is brought by ambulance to the ED after passing out in the nave of Le Parker Meridien hotel. She was sitting at lunch with her mother and suddenly developed an excruciating headache. She woke up a few minutes later while being loaded into the ambulance.*

Medications: *none*

PE:
- *General: uncomfortable, shielding her eyes*
- *HEENT: photophobia and neck stiffness present*
- *Neurological: no focal deficits*

Why is this *not* meningitis?
- Sudden in onset
- Loss of consciousness

Initial Orders:
- Head CT

What is "special" about the CT to order?

a. Use contrast.
b. Order thin cuts through the base of the brain.

c. Wait 24 to 48 hours for greater sensitivity.

Answer b. Order thin cuts through the base of the brain.

Because blood is heavier than cerebrospinal fluid (CSF), you should do thin cuts through the base of the brain to detect small bleeds. The blood will have settled to the base of the brain by gravity. Contrast is used to detect abscess and neoplasia. Waiting markedly decreases the sensitivity of the CT for blood.

Any adult admission to hospital should have:
- CBC
- Basic metabolic panel (CHEM-7)
- ECG
- Chest x-ray
- Urinalysis (UA)

You will not lose points by ordering these tests on CCS and you may "trip" over the diagnosis by accident.

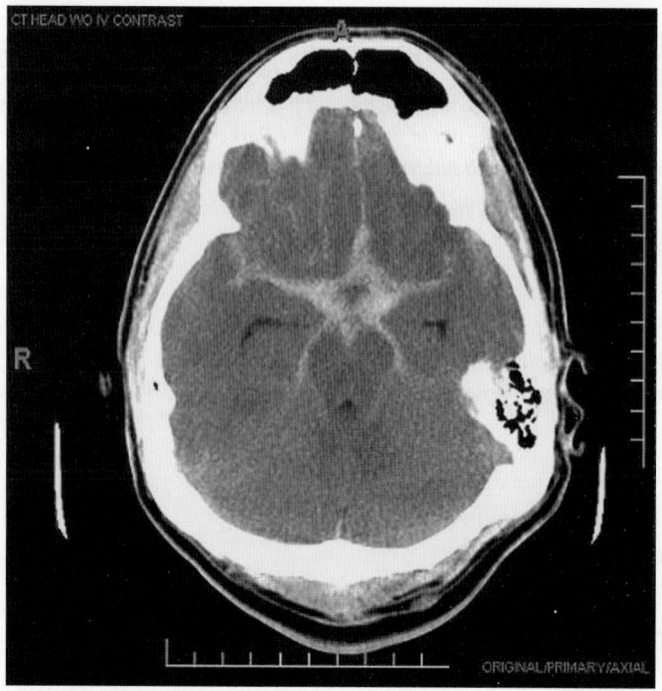

Figure 4-2. Classic appearance of a large subarachnoid hemorrhage. Notice the hemorrhage pattern fills the cerebrospinal fluid spaces at the base of the brain and around the brainstem. (Reproduced with permission from Doherty GM. *Current Diagnosis & Treatment: Surgery*, 13th ed. New York: McGraw-Hill; 2010.)

The maximum sensitivity of a CT is within the first 12 hours after the bleed.

Advance the clock just enough to get the results of the CT scan. **You cannot initiate therapy until you know if there is blood.**

Report:
• *Head CT: subarachnoid hemorrhage (SAH) diffusely surrounding brain (Figure 4-2)*

If the CT were negative, what test would have been next?

a. Lumbar puncture (LP)

c. Digital subtraction angiogram

b. MRI

Answer a. Lumbar puncture (LP)

The sensitivity of CT in SAH is 92% to 95% on the first day and approaches 100% in the first 6 to 12 hours. MRI is not as useful to detect blood. The key points on LP in SAH are:
- There is a high opening pressure.
- There is no change in cell count from tube 1 to tube 4.
- Xanthochromia starts in 2 hours.
- Spectrophotometry detects bilirubin 12 hours after a bleed.

> *The patient's BP is 146/92 mm Hg. She is awake and uncomfortable, shading her eyes.*

What should you do about the patient's elevated BP?

a. No therapy is indicated.

b. Give IV fluids and phenylephrine to raise it further.

c. Give labetalol to lower it further.

Answer a. No therapy is indicated.

Modest hypertension probably helps cerebral perfusion in SAH. It is clear that attempting to decrease BP to a low pressure, for example, <120/80 mm Hg, in this patient is likely dangerous. This would represent a >25% drop from the original BP of 154/94 mm Hg and might impair cerebral perfusion. There is no clear benefit to using fluids and phenylephrine or dopamine to raise BP more.

What is the mechanism of loss of consciousness in SAH?

a. Increased intracranial pressure suddenly decreases CNS perfusion.

b. Vasospasm.

c. Potassium alteration.

Answer a. Increased intracranial pressure suddenly decreases CNS perfusion.

Bleeding into the brain increases the intracranial pressure and decreases the ability of blood to get into the brain. This is why hypotension is so dangerous after an SAH. Therapeutic hypertension with fluids and pressors (phenylephrine or dopamine) is not clearly beneficial. Vasospasm occurs after SAH in response to the bleeding. Vasospasm is not the cause of the loss of consciousness. It is a reaction to it.

> - *Move the patient to the ICU.*
> - *Consult neurosurgery.*
> - *Repeat vital signs every 2 hours, especially watching for extremes of BP.*

Which is the best method to find the location of the bleed?

a. Digital subtraction angiography (DSA)   **c.** Repeat CT
b. MRI

Answer a. Digital subtraction angiography (DSA)

DSA is the best method to determine the location of the aneurysm. You need to find the site of the lesion and repair it as soon as possible. Do not delay the DSA. The greatest chance of rebleeding is on the first day of the bleed. Half of people who rebleed will die.

> Get a move on! Get the DSA.

What is the most common cause of SAH?

a. Sudden hypertension   **c.** Trauma
b. Spontaneous rupture of a saccular   **d.** Vasculitis
aneurysm of the circle of Willis

Answer b. Spontaneous rupture of a saccular aneurysm of the circle of Willis

As much as 2% to 5% of the population has saccular aneurysm of the circle of Willis at autopsy. Almost all remain unruptured at the time of death. It is not clear why some rupture and others do not. Although cigarette use and hypertension are associated with rupture, this is not a direct temporal relationship such as "I was fine until I smoked that cigarette."

> *The DSA shows the location of the aneurysm to be the anterior communicating artery. The patient's BP is 142/90 mm Hg.*

What is the best way to fix it?

a. Craniotomy and open repair   **c.** Laparoscopy
b. Endovascular coiling and embolization   **d.** Nimodipine
with platinum wire

Answer b. Endovascular coiling and embolization with platinum wire

Endovascular coiling clots off the site of the bleed and does not require craniotomy. Laparoscopy is for the pelvis and abdomen. Nimodipine is used to prevent subsequent stroke but does not fix the site of the aneurysm.

> Platinum wire
> • Does not oxidize
> • Is biologically inert

Nimodipine
• Is a calcium channel blocker
• Prevents vasospasm
• Decreases risk of "downstream" stroke
• Does *not* prevent rebleeding

Once the DSA shows the location of the aneurysm, order the endovascular repair procedure with coiling and embolization. If this is a multiple choice question and the stem says "Coiling is not available at your hospital," the answer is "Transfer to a hospital that does coiling/embolization." Do not alter the proper care of a patient around the logistics at your hospital. Move hospitals rather than do a procedure that is not ideal.

Get patients what they need.
Never do an inadequate procedure because it is not available at your institution.

Alter logistics to get right care.
Do **not** alter right care around logistics.

The patient undergoes the platinum wire coiling procedure and the site of the aneurismal bleed is repaired. Nimodipine is ordered and the patient's BP is 134/88 mm Hg.
    The following treatments are not *clearly beneficial and we* **do not** *recommend their routine use:*
• *Hypothermia*   • *Steroids*
• *Antiepileptic drugs*   • *Statins*

CASE 5: Guillain-Barré Syndrome

Setting: *ED*

CC: *"My legs are weak."*

VS: *BP: 110/70 mm Hg; P: 110 beats/minute; T: 97.8°F; R: 12 breaths/minute*

HPI: *A 43-year-old man comes to the ED with bilateral leg weakness, which he has been experiencing for the past 2 days. For the first day it was minor and did not interfere with function. On the day of admission, he has become unable to walk. He is brought by ambulance.*

PMHx: *none*

Medications: *none*

PE:
- *General: awake and alert*
- *Neurological examination: bilateral leg weakness, equally on both sides; absence of ankle jerk and knee jerk reflexes*

Chest: *clear*

Cardiovascular: *normal*

HEENT: *normal pupil reflexes; no ptosis*

Initial Orders:
- *Forced vital capacity (FVC)*
- *Peak inspiratory capacity*
- *Oximeter*

Which of the following will lead to the patient's death?

a. Sepsis

b. Respiratory failure

c. Seizure

d. Encephalitis

Answer b. Respiratory failure

When weakness ascends up to the diaphragm, it will potentially impair breathing. Guillain-Barré syndrome (GBS) is ascending weakness with the loss of reflexes. MG is weakness that is slowly progressive and distinctly worsens with repetitive use.

There is a slight decrease in FVC and a peak inspiratory pressure of –24 cm H_2O. There is no fever. Because there is impairment of respiratory functioning, the person should be placed in the ICU. You do not want the patient to develop respiratory failure unobserved on a regular hospital ward.

Which of the following will stay intact in this patient?

a. Elastic recoil

b. Ability to cough

c. Total lung capacity

d. Inspiratory reserve volume

Answer a. Elastic recoil

Elastic recoil is not based on muscular exertion. GBS only impairs muscular exertion. It has no effect on tissue characteristic, such as elastic fibers or the flexibility of the chest wall. Total lung capacity is decreased because it is based partly on the inspiratory reserve volume, which will be markedly reduced in this patient.

What is the most accurate diagnostic test?

a. Nerve biopsy
b. Nerve conduction velocity (NCV) testing
c. Serum anti-nerve immunoglobulin G (IgG)
d. LP
e. Lumbosacral spine CT/MRI

Answer b. Nerve conduction velocity (NCV) testing

A needle is placed at one end of the nerve and an electrical impulse is administered. A positive test shows decreased F-wave transmission. There is no such test as a "serum anti-nerve IgG." Although LP is often done, it is more useful for excluding other diseases than it is to specifically show something pathognomonic for GBS.

Orders:
- Start IVIG.
- Do LP.
- Test NCV.
- Move the patient to ICU.

Which of the following is most likely found on LP in GBS?

a. Moderate elevation of lymphocytes
b. High protein with normal cell count
c. Low glucose and neutrophils
d. High protein and high lymphocyte count

Answer b. High protein with normal cell count

The LP is done to exclude CNS infection. You should find a normal CSF cell count in GBS. There is no specific finding on LP that confirms GBS.

IVIG should be ordered stat without waiting for a laboratory confirmation of the diagnosis. GBS can result in permanent neurological disability and there is no reason to delay therapy although it does not work overnight.

CSF shows normal cell count and elevated protein. NCV testing takes more time to perform and receive results.

Ask anyone with GBS about the following:
- Recent vaccinations
- Diarrheal episodes or gastrointestinal (GI) tract infections

Campylobacter infection is the most common identifiable event causing GBS.

IVIG = Plasma Exchange (Plasmapheresis) for Efficacy

What is the mechanism underlying GBS?

a. Interleukin elevation

b. Antibodies attacking CNS white matter

c. Antibodies attacking peripheral nerve myelin

d. Infarction of vasonervorum

Answer c. Antibodies attacking peripheral nerve myelin

In GBS, antibodies attack the myelin, stripping it off and damaging conduction. Without myelin, NCV is slow. Campylobacter provokes the production of these antibodies for an unknown reason. The vasonervorum is damaged in diabetes peripheral neuropathy and vasculitis. Multiple sclerosis damages CNS white matter.

"Molecular mimicry" means something in myelin seems to "mimic" the cell surface of campylobacter.

In the ICU, the patient is reported as "looking fine" and the postgraduate year 3 (PGY3) resident wants to transfer the patient out immediately. He says "the saturation is normal."

How would you best follow the patient's respiratory condition?

a. Serial arterial blood gas (ABG) measurements

b. Peak inspiratory flow

c. Pulse oximetry

d. Forced expiratory volume at 1 second (FEV_1)

Answer b. Peak inspiratory flow

You want to know if the respiratory muscles are weakening before the patient's oxygen saturation level drops. You cannot wait for the partial pressure of carbon dioxide (PCO_2) to rise before determining that the patient needs intubation. It will be too late. The same is true of oxygen saturation. The PCO_2 and oxygen saturation do not change until there is outright respiratory failure. Peak inspiratory pressure predicts who is *about to* have respiratory failure before it occurs.

**Peripheral Nerves/
Roots/Ganglia**

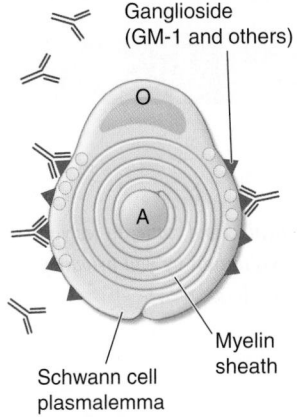

Ganglioside
(GM-1 and others)

O

A

Schwann cell
plasmalemma

Myelin
sheath

Figure 4-3. Antibodies attack and remove myelin from peripheral nerves. (Reproduced with permission from Longo DL, et al. *Harrison's Principles of Internal Medicine,* 18th ed., Vol. 2. New York: McGraw-Hill; 2012.)

Do *not* wait for desaturation or respiratory acidosis!
Use peak *inspiratory* pressure to follow GBS!

Thirty percent of patients with GBS need intubation.

GBS is a demyelinating disease decreasing muscle strength (Figure 4-3). The diaphragm is a muscle.

Peak inspiratory pressure starts to improve as does the FEV₁ on bedside spirometry. You transfer the patient out of the ICU. Consult medical rehabilitation, physical therapy, and the hospital social worker. The Step 3 examination is also very big on asking "what will you tell the patient?" in terms of prognosis. Twenty percent of patients will not recover muscle strength and it will take months for full recovery in the patients who do recover.

Ineffective Therapy in GBS
• Glucocorticoids
• Combining IVIG and plasmapheresis
• Cyclosporine

- IVIG blocks macrophages.
- Blocked macrophages cannot attack myelin.

CASE 6: Dementia

Setting: *office*

CC: *"My memory is getting bad."*

HPI: *A 77-year-old former chairman of medicine at your medical school comes to see you for initial testing for memory loss. He wants to get an initial evaluation by you privately before his wife and children find out he may have serious memory loss.*

PMHx:
- *Localized prostate cancer surgically resected 10 years ago*
- *Sober alcoholic; last drink 2 years ago*

Medications: *none*

PE:
- *General: charming older gentleman; no abnormalities noted*
- *Neurological: no focal deficits, able to remember only two of three objects at 5 minutes. No cogwheel rigidity. No myoclonus. No movement disorder.*

Initial Orders:
- *Head MRI*
- *Vitamin B$_{12}$ and methylmalonic acid level*
- *Thyroid function tests (thyroid-stimulating hormone [TSH], thyroxine [T$_4$])*
- *Rapid plasma reagin (RPR) Venereal Disease Research Laboratory (VDRL) test*

Alzheimer disease: neurofibrillary tangles, amyloid plaques

Vivid hallucinations with exquisite detail are characteristic of

a. Alzheimer disease

b. Lewy body dementia

c. Creutzfeldt-Jakob disease (CJD)

d. Multiinfarct (vascular) dementia

Answer b. Lewy body dementia

Lewy body dementia is characterized by parkinsonism and extremely vivid hallucinations with great detail. There is no specific test and no treatment beyond the dopamine agonists and dopamine replacement that you would use for Parkinson disease.

The patient returns a week later to discuss the laboratory test results. He feels the same. He loves what he is doing, but just gets forgetful.

Reports:
• *Head MRI: normal*
• *Vitamin B$_{12}$ and methylmalonic acid levels: normal*
• *TSH and T$_4$: normal*
• *VDRL: normal*

Which of these is characterized by rapid progression and myoclonus?

a. Alzheimer disease
b. Frontotemporal dementia (Pick disease)
c. CJD
d. Multiinfarct (vascular) dementia

Answer c. CJD

CJD can take a person from normal function to death in 3 to 6 months. There is no effective therapy for CJD. CSF shows the 14-3-3 protein, which spares the patient a need for brain biopsy for definitive diagnosis.

CJD is associated with prions. They are
• Transmissible
• Cause spongiform encephalopathy
• Do not grow or replicate in the laboratory

You explain to the patient he might have early Alzheimer-type dementia or mild cognitive impairment. He wants to start therapy. You order donepezil.

Donepezil, rivastigmine, and galantamine increase CNS ACh level.

Which of these is characterized by choreiform movement and emotional lability?

a. Huntington disease
b. Frontotemporal dementia (Pick disease)
c. CJD
d. Normal pressure hydrocephalus

Answer a. Huntington disease (HD)

HD is characterized by
- Dementia at an early age
- Emotional lability
- Movement disorder or chorea

HD has CAG trinucleotide repeat genetic sequences.

HD Treatment
- Tetrabenazine
- Increases dopamine
- Improves movement disorder

Over the next 6 to 12 months, the patient's memory loss continues to progress. You add memantine to his donepezil. Get a neurology consultation, but do not expect them to tell you anything.

Memantine Mechanism
- *N*-methyl-D-aspartate (NMDA) receptor antagonist
- Neuroprotective

Combine
Acetylcholinesterase inhibitor (donepezil)
and
Memantine

The patient's memory stabilizes over the next 6 months.

CASE 7: Meningitis

Setting: *ED*

CC: *"My head hurts."*

VS: *BP: 145/92 mm Hg; P: 108 beats/minute; T: 102.8°F; R: 23 breaths/minute*

HPI: *A 31-year-old man comes to the ED with 1 day of severe fever, headache, and neck stiffness. He is very uncomfortable and is lying on the stretcher with a pillow over his face. He has been nauseated and vomited several times.*

PMHx: *none*

Medications: *none*

What should you do next?

a. Perform a physical examination.
b. Give ceftriaxone and vancomycin IV.
c. Give ceftriaxone, vancomycin, and
   dexamethasone IV.

d. Order a head CT.
e. Order blood cultures.

Answer e. Order blood cultures.

If this is "real life," order blood cultures, antibiotics, and the steroids even before you do the physical. This is because the presentation of a chief complaint with fever, headache, stiff neck, and what seems to be photophobia is so clear for meningitis that getting the antibiotics ready in the shortest period of time is the most important thing you can do. However, remember that on CCS, the instant you order a test or a treatment, it is considered "administered" by the program. That means you just want to get the blood cultures to determine the specific organism involved rather than having the antibiotics given before an LP.

The "instant" you order something on CCS, it is considered "Administered."
Ordered = Administered on CCS

Timing is critical with meningitis! Move fast!

PE:
• *General: very uncomfortable man. Trying not to move.*
• *Neurological: no focal deficits; cranial nerves intact*
• *Musculoskeletal: neck inflexible*
• *HEENT: photophobia present*

Initial Orders:
• *LP*

What do you expect to see on CSF if this is viral meningitis?

a. Protein extremely high, lymphocytes
elevated

b. Glucose low, neutrophils elevated

c. Protein mildly elevated, lymphocytes
elevated

d. Thousands of white cells with 90%
neutrophils

Answer c. Protein mildly elevated, lymphocytes elevated

You should know what you expect to see on the test you order before it is done. Viral meningitis has an elevated white blood cell (WBC) count that is mostly lymphocytes. The CSF protein can be normal or mildly elevated. Bacterial meningitis has a predominance of neutrophils.

Head CT Before LP
- Focal neurological findings
- Papilledema
- Severe confusion (makes neurological examination incomplete)

As soon as the LP is done, advance the clock just a few minutes and order the antibiotics. Your whole aim in meningitis should be to give the antibiotics as soon after the LP as possible. You do the head CT before an LP in some patients because of the possibility that the intracranial pressure is increased unevenly in the skull. Focal findings and papilledema indicate a possible mass lesion and an LP may lead to herniation. Meningitis increases intracranial pressure, but it is increased evenly throughout the brain and that is why herniation does not occur just from the elevated intracranial pressure of meningitis.

Orders:
- *Ceftriaxone, vancomycin, and dexamethasone IV*
- *Droplet isolation*

What class of medication does vancomycin belong to?

a. Glycopeptide
b. Penicillin

c. Aminoglycoside
d. Vancomycin

Answer a. Glycopeptide

Glycopeptides are glycosylated cyclic nonribosomal peptides. The glycopeptides are vancomycin, teicoplanin, and telavancin.

What is the mechanism of action of vancomycin?

a. Ribosomal
b. Cell wall

c. Protein synthesis
d. DNA gyrase

Answer b. Cell wall

Vancomycin inhibits the backbone polymers of the cell wall of gram-positive bacteria. Because gram-negative bacteria form through a different mechanism, vancomycin has no effect on gram-negative organisms. Macrolides (e.g., azithromycin) inhibit ribosomes. Quinolones inhibit DNA gyrase, which is the enzyme needed to unwind DNA so it can be replicated.

> Vancomycin inhibits the cell wall through a different mechanism than do cephalosporins and penicillin.

Blood cultures were obtained and the LP performed. Move the clock forward to obtain results. *Patients are placed on droplet isolation until you are sure the organism is not Neisseria meningitidis.*

Report:
- CSF: 2400 WBCs; 87% neutrophils
- Protein: 89 mg/dL (elevated)

Gram Stain Characteristics of Organisms
- Positive diplococci: Pneumococcus
- Negative diplococci: Neisseria
- Positive cocci in clusters: Staphylococcus
- Pleomorphic gram-negative coccobacilli: Haemophilus
- Positive rod: Listeria

The Gram stain shows gram-positive diplococci.

What would you do differently based on this finding?

a. Stop ceftriaxone.
b. Stop vancomycin.
c. Stop droplet isolation.
d. Add penicillin.
e. Stop dexamethasone.

Answer c. Stop droplet isolation.

Droplet isolation is only needed for *Neisseria meningitidis.* You should not alter the antibiotics until the results of culture and sensitivity are known. If the organism is fully sensitive, a penicillin or cephalosporin is superior in efficacy to vancomycin. If the organism if penicillin resistant, vancomycin is needed.

Dexamethasone must be continued because it decreases both neurological injury from meningitis as well as mortality.

For which organism do steroids give the greatest mortality benefit?

a. Pneumococcus

b. Neisseria

c. Staphylococcus

d. Haemophilus

e. Listeria

Answer a. Pneumococcus

The reason for the benefit being greatest with pneumococcus is not clear. Steroids decrease inflammation in general.

Move the clock forward 6 to 12 hours and reexamine the patient. You know it is bacterial meningitis from the thousands of neutrophils on CSF as well as the Gram stain. Bacterial meningitis is profoundly damaging to the brain and it is important to be sure there is no neurological damage.

PE:

• *Neurological examination: nonfocal, more comfortable*

• *HEENT: photophobia and neck stiffness still present*

What is the most common neurological sequela from meningitis?

a. Memory loss

b. Hearing loss

c. Respiratory distress

d. Visual disturbances

Answer b. Hearing loss

The most common neurological effect of meningitis is hearing loss. Patients on initial presentation can have ocular problems such as double vision. Untreated meningitis can result in hydrocephalus. It is not clear why there is more damage to the eighth cranial nerve than the other parts of the system.

Which site of the brain is most involved in this patient?

a. Parenchyma

b. Arachnoid

c. Dura

d. Ventricles

Answer b. Arachnoid

The part of the brain most affected by meningitis is the leptomeninges or immediate covering of the brain. The arachnoid is under the dura and this is the main part affected. Encephalitis infects the brain parenchyma. None of these infections is in the ventricles.

Move the clock forward another 6 and then 12 hours. Once the patient is stable, you should look for a source of the meningitis.

Order:
- *Head CT/MRI*
- *Chest x-ray*

Sources of Pneumococcal Meningitis
- Sinusitis
- Mastoiditis
- Pneumonia

Why is intracranial pressure up in meningitis?
- Vasogenic edema
- Cytotoxins from neutrophils
- Inflammation of arachnoid villi

What is the mechanism of hydrocephalus developing as a complication of meningitis?

a. Inflamed arachnoid villi cannot drain CSF.
b. Granuloma forms.
c. Cells undergo coagulation necrosis.
d. Fibrinoid necrosis occurs.

Answer a. Inflamed arachnoid villi cannot drain CSF.

CSF normally drains out of arachnoid villi. When they are inflamed by infection or blocked by red blood cells, hydrocephalus can develop. This is the mechanism of developing hydrocephalus from subarachnoid hemorrhage.

On the second hospital day, you are called by the nurse because the patient has suddenly turned bright red. On examination his skin is red. Vancomycin is infusing.

What is the mechanism of this "red man syndrome?"

a. Allergy
b. Histamine release from mast cells
c. IgE
d. Neutrophil dysfunction

Answer b. Histamine release from mast cells

Vancomycin provokes a histamine release from mast cells when infused rapidly. The solution is to slow the rate of infusion.

On the following day, the CSF and blood cultures are reported as growing Streptococcus pneumonia *that is sensitive to penicillin. A head CT shows no sinusitis and no mastoiditis.*

Orders:
- *Stop vancomycin.*
- *Continue ceftriaxone (or ampicillin).*
- *Continue steroid.*
- *Keep the patient in the hospital for at least 10 days of IV antibiotics.*

Routine repeat LP is not needed.

CASE 8: Head Trauma-Subdural

Setting: *ED*

CC: *"Hit in head playing football"*

VS: *BP: 144/92 mm Hg; P: 54 beats/minute; T: 100.8°F; R: 18 breaths/minute*

HPI: *A 20-year-old college student was hit in the head when he was tackled in a football game. The patient had just received a thrown ball and was immediately tackled and knocked into a nearby wall striking his head. He lost consciousness. The patient awoke about 10 minutes later and was disoriented when loaded into the ambulance.*

Cushing Reflex
- Increased intracranial pressure
- Hypertension
- Bradycardia

PMHx: *none*

Medications: *none*

PE:
- *General: groggy, somewhat lethargic*
- *Neurological examination: no focal deficits detected*
- *HEENT: pupils equally round and reactive*

Initial Orders:
- *Head CT without contrast*

What is the mechanism of dilated pupil in intracranial bleeding?

a. Hypertension from any cause

b. Brainstem stroke

c. Compression of third cranial nerve

d. Meningeal irritation

Answer c. Compression of third cranial nerve

Large bleeds that cause uncal herniation will compress the third cranial nerve. The parasympathetic fibers are on the outside of the nerve and will be damaged first. Parasympathetic fibers normally constrict a pupil. If you compress the parasympathetic fibers on the outside of the third cranial nerve, the pupil will dilate.

The dilation of a pupil is on the same side as a bleed.

Advance the clock. The CT scan is performed and you are waiting for the report. Repeat the physical examination after 15 to 30 minutes in severe head trauma.

PE:
• *General: more lethargic, difficult to arouse*
• *Neurological examination: hard to assess because of altered mental status; some weakness of left side of body*
• *HEENT: dilation of right pupil only*

What is the mechanism of the "lucid interval" in which the patient awakens, then loses consciousness?

a. Constriction of cerebral vessels

b. Accumulation of blood in skull decreasing perfusion

c. Cerebellar dysfunction

d. Decreased myocardial contractility

Answer b. Accumulation of blood in skull decreasing perfusion

Both subdural and epidural hematoma can cause a "lucid interval." The initial loss of consciousness (LOC) is from the shock of head trauma. This is the same as in a concussion. After the patient awakens, there can be an accumulation of blood in the skull. This accumulation of blood increases intracranial pressure and decreases cerebral perfusion. The decrease in perfusion causes a second loss of consciousness. This is the reason we must observe people who have had head trauma. We are observing for an increase in intracranial pressure from blood that subsequently alters mental status.

As soon as the mental status and neurological examination start to deteriorate, you should immediately intubate and hyperventilate the patient. If the CT results are not back, you should still do this.

Indication for Intubation after Head Trauma
• Worsening mental status
• New focal neurological deficits
• Unilateral dilated pupil

Pupil dilates = *Herniate* = Do *not* wait = INTUBATE + *hyperventilate!*

What is the mechanism of a beneficial effect in hyperventilating intracranial hemorrhage?

a. Decreased PCO_2 constricts cerebral vessels.

b. Increased oxygen constricts cerebral vessels.

c. Raising pH increases cerebral perfusion.

d. Bicarbonate improves perfusion.

Answer a. Decreased PCO_2 constricts cerebral vessels.

Cerebral vasculature is very sensitive to concentrations of carbon dioxide (CO_2). When CO_2 is high, cerebral vessels dilate to remove this metabolic waste product. When CO_2 is low, the blood vessels will constrict and perfusion decreases. In a normal person, this small change in overall intracranial volume will not have a meaningful impact on cerebral perfusion, but when you have a massive increase in intracranial pressure a small change in volume can result in a big drop in pressure. This decrease in pressure is to help slow down uncal herniation until you have time to surgically decompress the skull and drain the blood out. Hyperventilation is a bridge to surgical decompression.

Low compliance creates big changes in pressure with small changes in volume.

The skull has low compliance:
Small Decrease in Volume = Big Decrease in Pressure

Move the clock forward to allow the intubation and to get results of the CT scan. Hyperventilation is a temporary bridge to the definitive procedure, which is surgical decompression.

Report:
• *Head CT: large subdural hematoma on right side, midline shift present (Figure 4-4)*

Vasoconstriction from hyperventilation wears off rapidly.

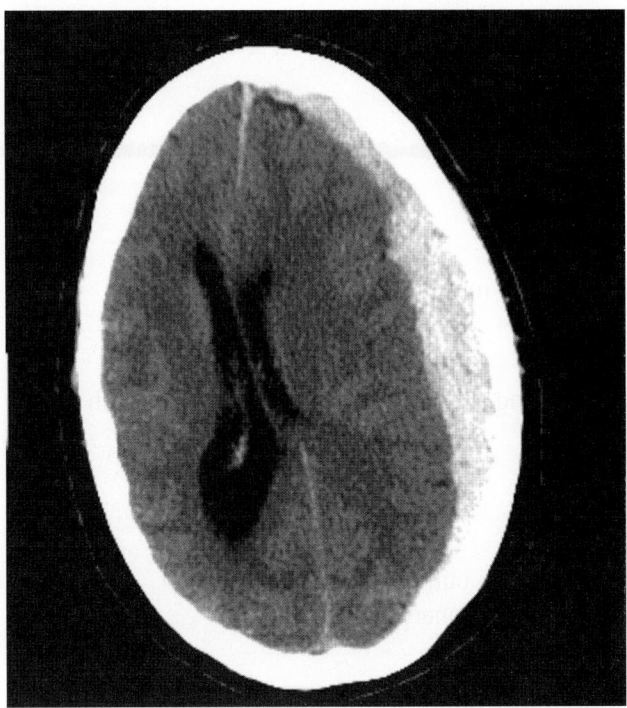

Figure 4-4. Acute subdural hematoma is white. The midline is shifted. (Reproduced with permission from McKean SC, et al. *Principles and Practice of Hospital Medicine*. New York: McGraw-Hill; 2012.)

Blood in brain causes fever.
Any clot or collection of blood causes fever.

Orders:
- *Mannitol IV*
- *Neurosurgery evaluation*
- *Craniotomy and drainage*
- *Move to ICU if not already done*
- *ECG*

You cannot move the patient to a location called "Operating Room."
Order the procedure the patient needs (e.g., craniology/drainage).

Move the clock only 15 to 30 minutes in a rapidly developing case such as this. **Reexamine the neurological system each time.**

Report:
• *ECG: deeply inverted T waves*

Target PCO_2 25 to 30 mm Hg with hyperventilation

Intracranial bleeding and head trauma are associated with T-wave inversion on ECG.

"Cerebral T waves"
• Massive sympathetic outflow
• Vasoconstriction of coronary arteries

Leave the patient in the ICU after the craniotomy and drainage. Place a ventriculostomy tube for both drainage and pressure monitoring. Do not move the patient out of the ICU until the ventriculostomy is removed and the neurological examination stabilizes. On CCS, a case of massive intracranial bleeding with herniation and the need for emergency surgical decompression will emphasize initial management.

Which of the following is proven to benefit this patient?

a. Methylprednisolone (steroids)   **c.** Antiepileptic drugs
b. Pantoprazole (proton pump inhibitors)

Answer b. Pantoprazole (proton pump inhibitors)

Stress ulcer prophylaxis with proton pump inhibitors (PPIs) is indicated in head trauma, burns, and those undergoing mechanical ventilation.

CHAPTER 5

GASTROENTEROLOGY

CASE 1: Gastrointestinal Bleeding

Setting: *ED*

CC: *"My stool is black."*

VS: *BP: 96/56 mm Hg; P: 108 beats/minute; T: 98.8°F; R: 22 breaths/minute*

HPI: *A 76-year-old man with a history of aortic stenosis (AS) comes with 3 days of multiple red, black stools. He had five episodes just today. He is dyspneic on exertion and comes now because of tiredness.*

PMHx:
- *AS*
- *Hypertension*
- *Former tobacco smoker*
- *Hyperlipidemia*

Medications:
- *Atorvastatin*
- *Nifedipine*

PE:
- *Cardiovascular: 3/6 murmur radiating to carotid arteries*
- *Abdomen: soft, nontender*

What is the most important first step to take with this patient?

a. Check for orthostasis.

b. Start normal saline (NS) bolus.

c. Order a colonoscopy.

d. Order an upper endoscopy.

Answer b. Start normal saline (NS) bolus.

Fluid resuscitation is by far the most important thing you can do for a person with a large gastrointestinal (GI) tract bleed. It is far more important to restore perfusion pressure than to look for the precise etiology of the bleed. Also, a tachycardia (pulse rate >100 beats/minute) at rest or systolic blood pressure (SBP) <100 mm Hg indicates a 30% blood volume loss. For an average-sized person, this is 1.5 to 2 L of volume lost. Orthostasis implies the loss of about 15% to 20% of blood volume. This person's current blood pressure (BP) (96/56 mm Hg) and pulse rate (108 beats/minute) imply that more volume has been lost than would occur with mere orthostasis. When intravascular volume is low, there should be an increase in heart rate and a vasoconstriction of peripheral vessels to fully correct BP.

Orthostasis:
Check BP and pulse rate when the patient is laying down, then sitting up or standing:
· Increase in pulse rate >10 beats/minute
· Decrease in systolic BP >20 mm Hg

Orthostasis: 15% to 20% volume lost
SBP <100 mm Hg or pulse rate >100 beats/minute = 30% blood volume lost

Orthostasis is detected by:
· Decreased firing of mechanoreceptors
· Carotid, aortic arch

Where is the information processed that detects decreased firing of carotid and aortic baroreceptors resulting in vasoconstriction and tachycardia?

a. Frontal lobes
b. Medulla oblongata
c. Hypothalamus
d. Thalamus
e. Internal capsule

Answer b. Medulla oblongata

The medulla receives information from the stretch or mechanoreceptors of the carotid artery, atria, and aortic arch. Decreased pressure in peripheral pressure or mechanoreceptors results in decreased firing. The medulla will respond with a peripheral vasoconstriction and tachycardia. Norepinephrine will stimulate alpha-1-receptors in arterioles causing vasoconstriction. This compensation is incomplete when changing position if there is >15% to 20% blood volume loss.

Initial Orders:
• NS or Ringer lactate bolus
• Complete blood count (CBC), prothrombin time (PT), activated partial thromboplastin time (aPTT), type and cross, CHEM-20
• Electrocardiogram (ECG)
• Pantoprazole IV
• GI consult

Move the clock forward 15 minutes and recheck both blood pressure and pulse rate. If the SBP is <100 mm Hg, reorder a bolus of intravenous (IV) NS. If after two boluses, the SBP is still low, transfer the patient to the intensive care unit (ICU).

On the computer-based case simulation (CCS), the consultant does not tell you what to do, but in this case, getting a GI consultation implies you know they are needed for serious GI tract bleeding.

Report:

- CBC: hematocrit 32%; mean corpuscular volume (MCV) 82 fL; platelets 185,000/μL
- PT, aPTT: normal
- Chemistry: blood urea nitrogen (BUN) 32 g/dL (elevated); creatinine 1.1 mg/dL
- ECG: no ST-T or T-wave abnormalities

The first CBC is not accurate in acute bleeding. You must always repeat it to see the trend.

If the PT or aPTT is prolonged (elevated), what is the best way to correct it?

a. Fresh frozen plasma (FFP)

b. Vitamin K orally

c. Vitamin K IV

d. Cryoprecipitate

Answer a. Fresh frozen plasma (FFP)

The fastest way to correct a coagulopathy is with FFP. Vitamin K needs at least 12 to 24 hours to work in order to generate clotting factors. If there is liver insufficiency, then FFP will not work at all. Cryoprecipitate is a condensation of clotting factors from pooled multiple donors. You will collect 50% of the clotting factors in 10% of the volume of fluid. Cryoprecipitate is best when you need enormous amounts of clotting factors and FFP is not enough or the volume of FFP required to provide that amount of clotting factor would be too great.

Which of the following is in highest concentration in cryoprecipitate?

a. Fibrinogen, von Willebrand factor

b. Factor II, VII

c. Factor XI, X

d. Factor XII

Answer a. Fibrinogen, von Willebrand factor

Cryoprecipitate is especially high in fibrinogen, von Willebrand factor (vWF) and factor VIII. The reason we *never* use cryoprecipitate first for anyone is that we use desmopressin acetate (DDAVP) for vWF and recombinant factor VIII for hemophilia and those with von Willebrand disease (vWD) not responding to DDAVP.

Cryoprecipitate is a pooled product.
Pooled products transmit more viruses.

The patient's repeat BP is 100/64 mm Hg and pulse rate is 102 beats/minute.

Orders:
- *Bolus NS*
- *CBC*

BUN level rises with decreased renal perfusion or prerenal azotemia.

Why does the BUN level rise in prerenal azotemia?

a. Angiotensin breaks down proteins.
b. Catecholamine release breaks down proteins.
c. Antidiuretic hormone (ADH) increases urea absorption at the collecting duct.
d. ADH decreases urea excretion at proximal tubule.

Answer c. Antidiuretic hormone (ADH) increases urea absorption at the collecting duct.

When ADH increases the permeability of the collecting duct to water, it also stimulates urea transporters that increase urea reabsorption. This helps maintain the high osmolarity of the renal medulla so that water can be reabsorbed. Although urea is a metabolic end product of protein metabolism, neither angiotensin nor catecholamines has any effect on protein production or destruction. Angiotensin does increase urea levels.

ADH stimulates UT1 or "urea transporter 1" in the collecting duct to absorb urea.

More ADH = More Urea Reabsorbed

Blood in the *upper* GI tract increases BUN level.

With major GI tract bleeding, move the clock forward 15 to 30 minutes. IV fluids and proton pump inhibitors (PPIs) should be running continuously.

Which therapy has a definite benefit in acute upper GI tract bleeding?

a. PPI
b. H$_2$-blocker
c. Sucralfate
d. Nasogastric tube
e. Iced saline lavage

Answer a. PPI

PPIs do have a benefit in stopping and controlling acute upper GI tract bleeding. This has never been shown with the H$_2$-blockers or sucralfate. The nasogastric (NG) tube has extremely little benefit. There is no therapeutic intervention with an NG tube. The iced saline lavage is useless.

> *Move the clock forward to get CBC results:*
> *The repeat CBC shows hematocrit level at 29% and platelet count at 165,000/µL.*

What mechanism explains the drop in hematocrit concentration from 32% to 29% in this patient?

a. Continued upper GI tract blood loss
b. Continued lower GI tract blood loss
c. Dilution from hydration

Answer c. Dilution from hydration

It is expected that patients will have a decrease of 3 to 4 points in hematocrit concentration just from hydration of fluids. You should only consider a decrease more than this amount to be significant.

> Black Stool or Melena = Upper GI Tract Source
> Upper GI Tract Source = Proximal to Ligament of Treitz

Which of the following is a definite benefit of an NG tube?

a. Decreases mortality
b. Can help determine source of bleeding
c. Stops rate of blood loss
d. Eliminates need for endoscopy

Answer b. Can help determine source of bleeding

If you are going to do upper endoscopy in a patient, NG tube placement is useless and painful. If you do not know whether to scope from above or below, an NG tube is occasionally useful to help localize the source of bleeding to the upper GI tract. The problem with the NG tube, besides its discomfort, is that a negative lavage misses 30% of bleeding especially if it is in the duodenum. Red blood from the NG tube indicates an upper GI tract source. Only the use of an NG tube definitively excludes an upper GI tract source if you see bile in the aspirate.

An NG tube misses 30% of upper GI tract bleeds.

A CBC after 2 hours of hydration shows the following:
• Hematocrit 23%
• Platelets 145,000/μL

What would be the likely cause of death in a patient with GI tract bleeding?

a. Stroke
b. Myocardial infarction
c. Congestive heart failure (CHF)

d. High output cardiac failure
e. Renal failure

Answer b. Myocardial infarction

Decreased oxygen-carrying capacity to the myocardium leads to ischemia. Myocytes in the heart cannot distinguish between hypoxia, coronary stenosis, or anemia. Ultimately, with severe bleeding and anemia, the patient will infarct his heart. This patient has AS. That implies a 50% to 70% chance of coronary disease as well. An older person needs to keep the hematocrit concentration >25% to 30%. A young, healthy person can easily tolerate a hematocrit level of 20% or 25% until his or her bone marrow recovers in 2 to 3 weeks.

Older people or those with coronary disease die at hematocrit levels that just make a younger person tired.

After several hours, do an "Interval History." Also do an Interval History if there is a change in laboratory values such as this drop in hematocrit concentration.

The patient reports feeling light-headed and short of breath. This is an absolute indication for transfusion in addition to a dropping blood count on CBC.

Orders:
• *Packed red blood cells*
• *CBC*
• *Upper endoscopy*

Hematocrit should increase by 3 points for each unit of packed red blood cells given.

On CCS, treatments like transfusion are considered done or "administered" immediately, but you cannot detect the effects of them until after you move the clock forward and get a repeat test.

After an hour post transfusion, you repeat the CBC and see the following:
- *Hematocrit: 25%*
- *Platelets: 132,000/μL*

At what platelet count should you order a platelet transfusion?

a. <150,000/μL
b. <100,000/μL

c. <50,000/μL
d. <10,000/μL

Answer c. <50,000/μL

Give platelets when the level drops below 50,000/μL when patients are bleeding or going for surgery. If a patient is not bleeding, you never need to keep the count that high.

Death from GI tract bleed is from inadequate fluid resuscitation.

The upper endoscopy was performed and no varices were found, but there is an ulcer in the duodenum with a visible bleeding vessel. The vessel was injected with epinephrine and electrical diathermy or cautery was applied and the bleeding has ceased.

What would be done differently if there were esophageal varices?

a. Octreotide and banding
b. Octreotide and sclerotherapy
c. Propranolol
d. Blakemore tube

e. Surgical shunt
f. Transjugular intrahepatic portosystemic shunt (TIPS)

Answer a. Octreotide and banding

Octreotide decreases acute variceal bleeding. Banding stops bleeding vessels. Sclerotherapy is only done if banding cannot be performed for a technical reason. Sclerotherapy has far greater risk of ulceration and stricture later. Propranolol prevents subsequent bleeding. Beta-blockers have no effect in acute GI tract bleeding.

A Blakemore tube is rarely ever used. It is a temporary procedure to tamponade bleeding vessels until surgery or the TIPS procedure can be done.

Octreotide is a somatostatin.
Somatostatin decreases portal hypertension.

After the procedure, repeat the CBC several times every few hours. Continue the PPI. When the CBC shows the hematocrit level has stabilized, the patient can be transferred out of the ICU.

CASE 2: Achalasia

Setting: *ambulatory care center*

CC: *"Food gets stuck when I eat."*

HPI: *A 37-year-old woman with difficulty swallowing over the past few months comes to the ambulatory care center. She says that the difficulty has been with solid food as well as liquids. It has continued to worsen. She now wakes up with undigested food particles on her pillow. There is no pain on swallowing.*

ROS:
• *No tobacco use*
• *Minimal alcohol consumption*
• *Twelve-pound weight loss over 3 months*

PMHx/Medications: *none*

PE:
• *General: no visible distress*
• *Abdomen: normal*
• *Chest: normal*
• *Rectal: stool heme negative*

Initial Orders:
• *Comprehensive metabolic panel (CHEM-20)*
• *Chest x-ray*

Barium is okay to start with for dysphagia cases.

Esophagus: Barium is useful.
Stomach: Barium is not useful.

Ambulatory cases should be moved forward a week at a time if there is a new diagnosis to make. Chronic, long-term disease is moved forward at 1-month to 3-month intervals. Any patient with GI tract bleeding should have a GI consultation ordered.

A week later, the patient feels the same. Dysphagia for solid food and liquid continues. Food particles continue to be found on her pillow in the morning.

Reports:
• *CHEM-20: BUN 4 g/dL (slightly low); albumin 3.6 g/dL*
• *Chest x-ray: widening at the top of the mediastinum*

Wide Mediastinum
+ Chest pain = Dissection
+ Dysphagia = Esophagus

Dysphagia with pain on swallowing is odynophagia. In a person with acquired immunodeficiency syndrome (AIDS) and a CD4 cell count <100 cells/mm³, what is the first step?

a. Endoscopy
b. Fluconazole
c. Stool candida culture

d. Serum candida antigen
e. Chest computed tomography (CT)

Answer b. Fluconazole

AIDS with a CD4 cell count <100 cells/mm³ plus odynophagia indicates esophageal candidiasis in 90% of patients. Because there is such a high likelihood of candida in AIDS, this is one of the few times you can use empiric therapy to confirm a diagnosis. There is no such test as serum candida antigen. If there is no response, then do an endoscopy.

Never culture stool for yeast! Everyone has yeast in their stool.

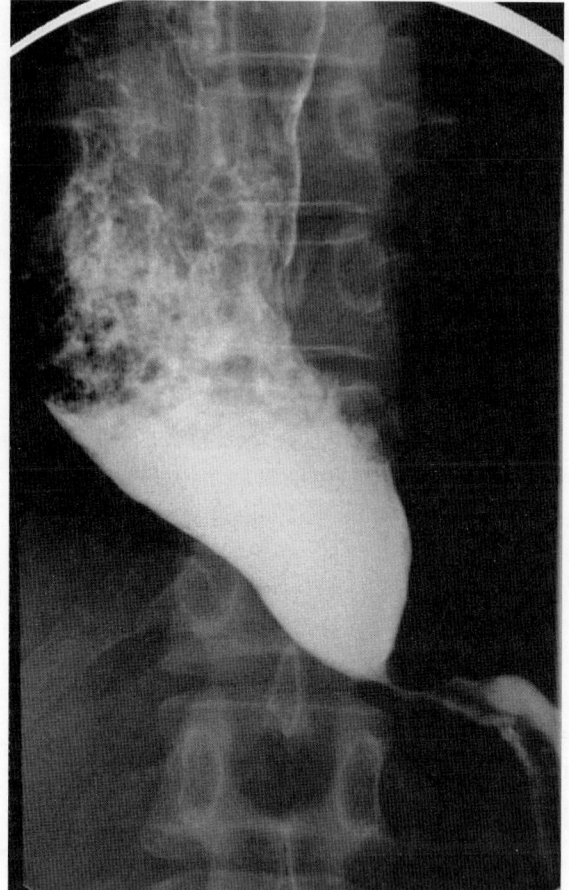

Figure 5-1. Esophageal achalasia. Note dilation of the esophageal body, retained barium, and distal esophageal narrowing (bird's beak). (Reproduced with permission from Doherty GM. *Current Diagnosis & Treatment: Surgery*, 13th ed. New York: McGraw-Hill; 2010.)

> *Schedule the patient to see a gastroenterologist and order a barium esophagram. There is no blood test for any form of dysphagia.*
>
> **Report:**
> • *Barium esophagram: wide at top, narrow at bottom (Figure 5-1)*
> • *Gastroenterologist: no specific recommendations; order what you think is necessary*

What is the most accurate diagnostic test?

a. Endoscopy

b. Manometry

c. Biopsy

d. Secretin stimulation test

Answer b. Manometry

The single most accurate test for achalasia is manometry. This is never a test that is done first. Manometry is the right answer when a patient has a swallowing disorder and no clear diagnosis after barium and endoscopy.

> Proximal esophagus: skeletal muscle.
> Distal esophagus: smooth muscle.

> Smooth muscle is connected by gap junctions. When stretched, it contracts as a syncytium.

Now consider the occurrence of intermittent chest pain in a man whose ECG and stress test are normal. The chest pain is brought on by cold drinks. It is prevented by calcium channel blockers and nitrates. What is the most accurate test?

a. Barium

c. Endoscopy

b. Manometry

Answer b. Manometry

Esophageal spasm is characterized by intermittent severe contraction of the smooth muscle of the esophagus. Manometry is most accurate. Calcium channel blockers and nitrates relax smooth muscle.

> Consultations on CCS will not tell you what to order. In this case, order the upper endoscopy yourself. If consultants told you what to order, then the Step 3 examination could not test your knowledge level.

> *Move the clock ahead until you see "Report Available" on the upper endoscopy. The report shows smooth mucosa with no lesions and narrowing at the distal esophagus.*

> Plummer-Vinson Syndrome
> • Iron deficiency without bleeding
> • Some transform to squamous cell cancer

Barrett Esophagus Histology
• Columnar metaplasia
• Becomes adenocarcinoma, not squamous

Why does the lower esophageal sphincter (LES) tighten in achalasia?

a. Loss of myenteric plexus

b. Loss of Auerbach plexus

c. Decrease in vasoactive intestinal peptide (VIP)

d. Excess vagal tone

Answer a. Loss of myenteric plexus

Achalasia is the loss or degeneration of the inhibitory neurons of the esophageal wall. There is incomplete peristalsis. Auerbach plexus is what is lost in Hirschsprung disease.

It is not known why the neurons degenerate in achalasia.

What causes the receptive relaxation that opens the stomach from 50 mL to 2000 mL on eating?

a. Epinephrine

b. VIP

c. Dopamine

d. Norepinephrine

e. Serotonin

Answer b. VIP

Stretch receptors in the stomach detect increased volume and through vagal stimulation release VIP. VIP is what opens the stomach for receptive relaxation.

VIP opens GI tract sphincters.

Now that achalasia is confirmed, a dilation procedure with an endoscope or surgical myotomy can be performed. Dilation procedures are less invasive, but also have a higher risk of perforation.

For those declining either procedure, botulinum toxin, or Botox, can be injected into the LES. These injections have less complications, but they also wear off after a few months or a year.

What is the mechanism of botulinum toxin?

a. Decreased release of acetylcholine from the presynaptic terminal

b. Blockade of acetylcholine receptor

c. Increased acetylcholine esterase

d. Blockage of the sodium channels

Answer a. Decreased release of acetylcholine from the presynaptic terminal

Botulinum toxin prevents the release of vesicles of acetylcholine in response to depolarization of the nerve. The nerve impulse hits the neuromuscular junction, but no neurotransmitter is released and the muscle relaxes.

Most people choose endoscopic dilation. This can be curative. See the patient immediately after the procedure to check for perforation. Then ask her to return several times over the next month to be sure the procedure is effective. If successful, it should be fully curative.

CASE 3: Gastroesophageal Reflux Disease

Setting: *office*

CC: *"Heartburn"*

HPI: *A 27-year-old man with several months of epigastric discomfort and a burning sensation in his chest comes to see you at your office. He says that the discomfort is worse after he lies down for a while. He often has a bad taste in his mouth like "I am sucking on a handful of coins."*

PMHx:
- *Recurrent pharyngitis*
- *Hoarseness*
- *Chronic cough*

Acid hits the back of the throat causing pain.

Twenty-five percent of patients with chronic cough have reflux disease.

Acid hits the carina causing cough.

> Medications:
> • Multiple short courses of antibiotics for pharyngitis and cough
> • Cimetidine intermittently

What physical finding is characteristic of gastroesophageal reflux disease (GERD)?

a. Epigastric tenderness

b. None

c. Loss of dental enamel

d. Parotid gland enlargement

Answer b. None

GERD is entirely a symptom complex. There is no physical finding. Loss of dental enamel and parotid gland enlargement are from vomiting in anorexia or bulimia, not GERD.

> • PE: normal
> • Abdomen: nontender epigastric area

GERD is often misdiagnosed as:
• Pharyngitis
• Laryngitis
• Bronchitis

Acid hits the vocal cords causing hoarseness.

> **Initial Orders:**
> • PPI, such as omeprazole

Why is cimetidine only effective in two-thirds of patients?

a. Incomplete inhibition of parietal cell

b. Increase in gastrin production

c. Tachyphylaxis (it wears off)

d. Helicobacter pylori

Answer a. Incomplete inhibition of parietal cell

Histamine is one of three stimulants to the production of acid at the parietal cell of the stomach. Because histamine potentiates the effect of acetylcholine from the vagus nerve as well as the effect of gastrin, there is a 60% to 70% reduction in acid production. At least one-third of patients will not have their acid production controlled by an H_2-blocker such as cimetidine, ranitidine, or famotidine.

> *The patient returns the following week. He has only partial improvement in his symptoms. The bad taste in his mouth persists.*

Which cranial nerve is responsible for the bad taste in his mouth?

a. V

b. VII

c. VIII

d. IX

e. XII

Answer d. IX

Acid hits the back of the tongue producing a bitter taste that is often described as "metallic." Cranial nerve IX (glossopharyngeal) and X (vagus) transport the sense of taste from the back of the tongue. The bitter taste receptors and perception are at the back of the tongue to inhibit the likelihood of aspiration into the airway. Sweet taste receptors are at the anterior portion of the tongue and are controlled by the facial nerve, cranial nerve VII.

> *After several more weeks of return visits, it is clear that the PPI is not completely controlling the patient's symptoms.*

GERD should be controlled by PPIs in 95% of patients.
Failure of PPI = Confirm the Diagnosis

What should you do to confirm the diagnosis?

a. Double the dose of the PPI.

b. Do an endoscopy.

c. Do a 24-hour pH monitor.

d. Put in an NG tube for acid output.

Answer c. Do a 24-hour pH monitor.

The most accurate test of GERD is the 24-hour pH monitor. Because PPIs are amazingly effective at 95% symptom control, the failure of PPI treatment means there is a 20:1 chance that the diagnosis is not really GERD. Endoscopy can show Barrett esophagus and erosive esophagitis, but you cannot tell that acid is refluxing by endoscopy alone.

Substances that dilate the LES
- Nicotine
- Alcohol
- Caffeine
- Chocolate
- Peppermint

> *The 24-hour pH monitor confirms the presence of GERD. The patient continues to be bothered by symptoms of heartburn. You are planning a surgical or endoscopic procedure to tighten the LES.*

What test should you do prior to a Nissen fundoplication or other LES-tightening procedure?

a. Esophageal manometry

b. Chest CT

c. Nuclear gastric emptying test

Answer a. Esophageal manometry

You have to be sure the ability of the esophagus to contract is normal prior to an LES-narrowing procedure. If you tighten the LES, and esophageal contractility is inadequate, you will create a blockade like achalasia.

> Nuclear gastric emptying using barium-soaked bread tests for diabetic gastroparesis.

> *After the procedure, symptoms resolve for 2 years. There is a recurrence of GERD-like symptoms and PPIs are now given regularly. PPIs control the symptoms. Upper endoscopy shows columnar metaplasia.*

What is the management?

a. Distal esophagectomy

b. Endoscopic mucosal resection

c. PPIs and repeat endoscopy in 2 to 3 years

d. Repeat surgical tightening

Answer c. PPIs and repeat endoscopy in 2 to 3 years

Barrett esophagus or columnar metaplasia of the distal esophagus is managed by doing surveillance endoscopy every 2 to 3 years.

> - Patients with Barrett esophagus have a 0.5% per year chance of esophageal cancer.
> - Patients with low-grade dysplasia need repeat endoscopy every 6 months.
> - Patients with high-grade dysplasia need endoscopic mucosal resection.

Most patients with GERD do not progress to Barrett esophagus and only a very few go on to cancer.

CASE 4: Peptic Ulcer Disease

Setting: *office*

CC: *"My stomach hurts."*

VS: *BP: 118/86 mm Hg; P: 84 beats/minute; T: 97.8° F; R: 16 breaths/minute*

HPI: *A 43-year-old infectious diseases doctor visits to your office complaining of epigastric pain over the past few weeks. The patient is extremely tense, undergoing a divorce, and has been having increasing epigastric pain despite the use of H_2-blockers and liquid antacids at first and now omeprazole.*

What is the most common cause of epigastric pain?

a. GERD

b. Nonulcer (functional) dyspepsia

c. Duodenal ulcer

d. Gastric ulcer

e. Gastritis

Answer b. Nonulcer (functional) dyspepsia

Fifty to ninety percent of epigastric pain is functional dyspepsia and no etiology is ever found. Ulcers make up only 10% to 15% of epigastric pain. Nonulcer dyspepsia is like a tension headache. It is, by far, the most common cause of the pain and nothing of the mechanism is clear.

PMHx: *none*

Medications: *omeprazole only*

"Alarm symptoms" indicating urgent endoscopy:
- Weight loss
- Blood in stool or anemia
- Dysphagia

ROS:
- *No weight loss*
- *No blood in stool*
- *No dysphagia*

Which is reliably associated with tenderness on examination?

a. Duodenal ulcer

b. Pancreatitis

c. Gastric ulcer

d. Nonulcer dyspepsia

Answer b. Pancreatitis

Only pancreatitis is routinely associated with epigastric tenderness. Ulcer disease is tender only about 10% of the time.

PE:
- *General: anxious, well-built muscular man*
- *Abdomen: soft, nontender*

Initial Orders:
- *Upper endoscopy*
- *Gastroenterology evaluation*
- *Continue omeprazole*

When is "scope" the answer for epigastric pain?
- Alarm symptoms
- Bleeding
- Age >45 to 55 years
- Symptoms not resolving with PPIs

Upper endoscopy shows a large gastric ulcer. A biopsy is obtained for H. pylori. *The rapid urease test is positive for* Helicobacter.

How is a gastric ulcer managed differently than a duodenal ulcer?

a. PPIs are not used.

b. Repeat the endoscopy and do a biopsy in 4 to 8 weeks.

c. Treat *H. pylori.*

Answer b. Repeat the endoscopy and do a biopsy in 4 to 8 weeks.

A gastric ulcer is associated with cancer. A duodenal ulcer is not associated with cancer. Re-scope the gastric ulcer to be sure it has resolved and there is no cancer. The indication for endoscopy in this patient was the failure of antisecretory therapy with PPIs.

Orders:
- *Continue PPI*
- *Start amoxicillin and clarithromycin*

Gastric ulcer: 4% cancer
Duodenal ulcer: 0% cancer

How does *H. pylori* survive in the acid of the stomach?

a. Flagella keeps it in the lumen of the stomach.

b. Bicarbonate production increases.

c. Urease makes ammonia to neutralize acid.

d. Urease inhibits the proton pump.

Answer c. Urease makes ammonia to neutralize acid.

Helicobacter has urease. Urease makes ammonia out of urea. Ammoni*a* (NH_3) binds acid (H^+) and turns it into ammoni*um* (NH_4^+). This is how acid is neutralized. That is the fundamental basic science you need to know about ulcers.

Helicobacter neutralizes acid with ammonia.

For which of the following is treatment for *Helicobacter* NOT indicated when found?

a. GERD

b. Duodenal ulcer

c. Gastric ulcer

d. Gastritis

e. Mucosa-associated lymphoid tissue lymphoma (MALToma)

Answer a. GERD

Helicobacter does not cause GERD. It is associated with all the others and is largely the causative organism.

Six weeks after therapy, the patient's symptoms have resolved. Repeat endoscopy does not reveal evidence of ulcer or cancer. All patients with evidence of Helicobacter *should be tested to confirm that it has been eradicated.*

When positive, these tests indicate a current infection
- Breath testing
- Stool antigen

CASE 5: Zollinger-Ellison Syndrome

Setting: *office*

CC: *"Why do my ulcers keep coming back?"*

VS: *BP:114/74 mm Hg; P: 88 beats/minute; T: 97.8°F; R: 14 breaths/minute*

HPI: *A 43-year-old man who was recently tested and treated for a gastric ulcer now comes to your office with recurrence of epigastric pain. The eradication of the last gastric ulcer was confirmed by repeat endoscopy several weeks after treatment. A biopsy showed no cancer at the time. Testing for active Helicobacter infection was negative as well. He restarted a PPI 2 weeks ago but still has epigastric discomfort. He took ibuprofen for a few days for the pain.*

ROS:
• *Diarrhea several times a day*

Medications:
• *Esomeprazole*
• *Ibuprofen*

Nonsteroidal antiinflammatory drugs (NSAIDs) are the second most common cause of ulcers.

1. NSAIDs inhibit prostaglandins.
2. Prostaglandins make gastric mucus.
3. Gastric mucus protects against acid.

PE:
• *Abdomen: soft, nontender, hyperactive bowel sounds*
• *Skin: vesicular lesions on extensor surfaces*

Which of these tests *cannot* determine if *H. pylori* infection is current and active?

a. Stool antigen

b. Breath testing

c. Serology

d. Biopsy

Answer c. Serology

The presence of immunoglobulin G (IgG) alone for serology for *H. pylori* cannot show that the infection is active. Serology cannot tell old versus new infection. We tend to use the stool antigen test more often for technical reasons—it is easier to do and no equipment is needed—in an office. Biologically, carbon-labeled urea and stool antigen testing are equal.

Breath Test Mechanism
1. The patient drinks urea that is labeled with radioactive carbon.
2. Urease splits off the ammonia.
3. Ammonia (NH_3) binds to acid and stays in the gut as NH_4^+.
4. Carbon dioxide (CO_2) with label (C_{13} or C_{14}) is exhaled and detected.

Initial Orders:
• *Do a* Helicobacter *stool antigen test.*
• *Continue esomeprazole.*
• *Stop ibuprofen.*

Exclude persistent *Helicobacter* infection as a cause of treatment failure first.

If *Helicobacter* was not eradicated with PPI, amoxicillin, and clarithromycin, what would be the first step?

a. Retreat with the same regimen.
b. Continue PPI; switch antibiotics to metronidazole, tetracycline, and bismuth subsalicylate.
c. Obtain sensitivity testing of the organism.
d. Repeat the endoscopy.
e. Add an H_2-blocker.

Answer b. Continue PPI; switch antibiotics to metronidazole, tetracycline, and bismuth subsalicylate.

Manage persistent *Helicobacter* infections as a failure of antibiotics and possible resistance to the original antibiotics. Switching the medications and trying that for 2 to 3 weeks is easier than waiting for sensitivity testing. Bismuth's effect is to suppress *Helicobacter* infection.

The Interval History shows that the patient says his pain persists. He saw another clinician, who ordered a serum gastrin level, which is elevated.

What is the meaning of the elevated gastrin?

a. Everyone on a PPI has an elevated gastrin, it means nothing at this time.

b. He has Zollinger-Ellison syndrome (ZES).

c. The patient must have a pancreatic lesion.

Answer a. Everyone on a PPI has an elevated gastrin, it means nothing at this time.

Gastrin levels should not be evaluated while patients are on PPIs. Every time you lower gastric acidity with a PPI, H$_2$-blocker, or liquid antacid, the gastrin level will rise. To diagnose ZES or gastrinoma, you need to evaluate the gastrin level after stopping PPI therapy.

Acid is feedback inhibition on gastrin.

NORMAL: *Low Acid = High Gastrin*

Have the patient return to discuss the results of Helicobacter testing.

> *Also, any time you have a complicated case that fails primary therapy, order a consultation in the area. This shows that you know when you need help.*

Report:

• *Stool antigen is negative for Helicobacter.*

Order:

• *Upper endoscopy*

Move the clock forward to get the endoscopy done. If pain persists after NSAIDs are stopped and persistent Helicobacter infection has been excluded, you need to scope the patient.

Report:

• *Upper endoscopy: multiple, large ulcers in second and third portions of duodenum*

Evaluate gastrin level after stopping PPI therapy when the patient has
• Large ulcers (>1 cm)
• Multiple ulcers
• A recurrence of symptoms after *Helicobacter* eradication
• Distal ulcers (past the first part of the duodenum)

Hold the PPIs for a day and recheck the gastrin level or measure gastric acid output with a tube.

High Acid + High Gastrin = ZES

The patient comes to the office after not taking a PPI for 2 days and has both the gastrin level and the gastric acid output measured. Both are elevated, but the gastrin level is only marginally elevated and not higher than 1000 pg/mL.

When gastrin levels are equivocally elevated, what test will confirm gastrinoma?

a. Ultrasound

b. CT

c. Magnetic resonance imaging (MRI)

d. Secretin suppression test

e. Endoscopic ultrasound (EUS)

Answer d. Secretin suppression test

Secretin should normally lower gastrin levels. Secretin decreases acid by releasing bicarbonate-rich fluid from the pancreas. Secretin also shuts off acid production by decreasing gastrin by a direct suppressive effect. In gastrinoma, the gastrin level will not go down with secretin.

Endocrine disorders must always be confirmed with a function test before an imaging test. You cannot tell the functional content of a lesion by ultrasound (US), CT, or MRI. EUS is an excellent test for locating lesions in the pancreas, but it cannot show the functional content of the lesion.

1. Gastrin stimulates parietal cells to make acid.
2. Acid in the duodenum makes secretin.
3. Secretin releases 2 to 3 L/day of bicarbonate-rich fluid from the pancreas.

Normal: Secretin suppresses gastrin to stop acid production.
Gastrinoma: Secretin cannot suppress gastrin.

The patient returns earlier than expected because of sudden worsening of diarrhea during the test for gastric acid output and gastrin levels while stopping the PPI. Both gastrin and acid levels were high. In addition, there was a change in stool "character."

What is the mechanism of the diarrhea?

a. Acid inactivates lipase.

b. Acid increases GI tract motility.

c. Gastrin opens sphincters.

d. It is caused by bacterial overgrowth from long-term PPI use.

e. Pepsin deactivation

Answer a. Acid inactivates lipase.

Lipase in the duodenum works at a pH >4. When acid is massively overproduced as it is in gastrinoma, you frequently get diarrhea. It is effectively a steatorrhea. Pepsin that is made in the stomach is inactivated by basic pH in the duodenum. This is why the physiologic effect of pepsin is limited and it is not necessary for life.

Acid in the duodenum actually decreases gastric motility. Gastrin directly stimulates stomach motility and growth. The acid the gastrin makes slows the small bowel motility.

Normal GI tract physiology:
- Acid in the duodenum slows stomach emptying.
- Acid inactivates lipase.
- Base inactivates pepsin.

Gastric acid output and gastrin level are high. The patient's diarrhea resolves with restarting a PPI. You can cure gastrinoma by surgical removal if the lesion is solitary. If it is metastatic, the patient will need lifelong PPIs and there is no cure.

Orders:
- *Abdominal CT*
- *Calcium level*

The abdominal CT and MRI do not show metastatic disease. The calcium level is normal. There was actually an increase in the gastrin level with the use of secretin. High calcium level with gastrinoma would have meant hyperparathyroidism. Hyperparathyroidism with gastrinoma means possible multiple endocrine neoplasia (MEN) syndrome.

When do you look for MEN?
- Hypercalcemia

High Calcium + Gastrinoma = Look for MEN

Why is there a paradoxical rise in gastrin with the use of secretin in gastrinoma (ZES)?

a. Secretin directly stimulates gastrin in gastrinoma.
b. Cholecystokinin level increases.

c. Bicarbonate release raises pH and removes any residual feedback inhibition on G cells.

Answer c. Bicarbonate release raises pH and removes any residual feedback inhibition on G cells.

Gastrinoma is an adenoma. Adenomas can return some residual normal feedback inhibition sensitivity. When secretin causes the ductal cells of the pancreas to release bicarbonate-rich fluid, there is loss of the normal feedback inhibition provided by acid.

If the abdominal CT does not show metastases, order an EUS and nuclear somatostatin scan. When using both modalities, you exceed 95% sensitivity in finding metastatic gastrinoma. You want to be sure the disease is local before you go in and resect it.

Orders:
- *EUS*
- *Nuclear somatostatin scan*

Both tests have negative results. The patient should undergo surgical resection of the gastrinoma and the disorder will resolve.

Gastrinoma leads to increased somatostatin receptors in the GI tract.

CASE 6: **Inflammatory Bowel Disease**

Setting: *ED*

CC: *"I have blood in my stool."*

VS: *BP:110/70 mm Hg; P: 84 beats/minute; T: 101.1°F; R: 12 breaths/minute*

HPI: *A 23-year-old medical student arrives at the ED with blood and mucus in her stool that she says has been going on for several weeks to months. She also has low-grade fever and weight loss. The frequency of bowel movements has increased and that is why she has come today to the ED.*

ROS: *joint pain, diffusely*

PMHx: *none*

Medications: *Patient tried ciprofloxacin for diarrhea with no effect.*

PE:
- *General: tired, weak, and angry appearing*
- *Abdomen: soft, nontender*
- *Skin: red-brown tender lesion below the knees*

Initial Orders:
- *CBC*
- *Stool studies: culture, ova/parasite examination*
- *CHEM-20*
- *IV NS*
- *Orthostatic BP assessment*

Which one of these is associated with blood?

a. Giardia   **c.** Cryptosporidia
b. *Entamoeba histolytica*

Answer b. *Entamoeba histolytica*

The only protozoan that gives blood in stool is *Entamoeba*. Infection of any kind is highly unlikely to be going on for "weeks to months." It is very rare for any infection to last more than a few days. Infections are generally all self-limited and last for <1 week.

> Forms of Diarrhea *Never* with Blood
> • Viral
> • *Staphylococcus aureus, Bacillus cereus*
> • Giardia
> • Cryptosporidia
> • Cholera

> *One hour later in the ED, the initial reports are ready:*
> • *CBC: hematocrit 32%; normal MCV; white blood cells (WBCs) 14,500/μL;*
>   *platelets 535,000/μL*
> • *CHEM-20: potassium normal; albumin 2.7 g/dL (low); calcium 7.2 mg/dL (low)*
> • *Stool studies: results pending for the culture, ova/parasite examination*
> • *Orthostatic BP: not present*

> Platelet and WBC level can be elevated from any inflammatory stress.

> *Low Albumin Level = Low Total Calcium Level*

> Albumin down 1 g/dL = Calcium down 0.8 mg/dL

> *This is chronic diarrhea and it is nearly impossible to have an infection such as Campylobacter, Salmonella, or Shigella going on for weeks or months. There is evidence of malnutrition or malabsorption with the low albumin.*

What test distinguishes between anemia of chronic disease and malabsorption with both iron and vitamin B$_{12}$/folate deficiency?

a. Reticulocyte count

b. Red cell blood distribution width (RDW)

c. MCV

Answer b. Red blood cell distribution width (RDW)

RDW is a measure of how similar all the cells are in size. If all cells are the same size, the RDW is low, because there is no "distribution" of width, they are all the same. If some cells are small and some are large, the "mean" corpuscular volume or MCV will be normal, but the RDW will be increased. This is because some cells will be small and some large, with a normal average.

All nutritional deficiencies give a low reticulocyte count.

For chronic diarrhea cases, hydrate the patient and move the clock forward to get stool study results. Once you have excluded infections, order endoscopy and GI evaluation.

Reports:
• *Stool culture: no growth*
• *RDW: Increased*

• *Stool ova/parasites: negative*

Several weeks of bloody diarrhea, mucus, fever, and weight loss are suggestive of inflammatory bowel disease (IBD) in general. There is no clear way to distinguish between Crohn disease (CD) of the colon and ulcerative colitis (UC) without endoscopy and sometimes biopsy.

What is the difference between UC and CD?

a. Joint pain
b. Iritis and uveitis
c. Sclerosing cholangitis

d. Skin symptoms: pyoderma gangrenosum and erythema nodosum
e. No difference

Answer e. No difference

The extraintestinal manifestations of both forms of IBD are identical. CD affects the large bowel in 40% of patients, and when this happens, CD can give sclerosing cholangitis. They can both give eye, skin, joint, and liver abnormalities.

Sigmoidoscopy reveals an inflamed mucosa consistent with IBD.

Orders:
• *Steroids IV*
• *Iron studies, vitamin B$_{12}$ level, methylmalonic acid level*

• *Mesalamine*

Mesalamine
- 5-ASA derivative
- Less adverse effects than sulfasalazine

Budesonide
- Oral steroid for IBD
- Extensive first-pass effect at liver
- Decreases systemic toxicity

Move the case forward 1 day. On the second hospital day, the frequency of diarrhea is reported as much decreased after the start of steroids and mesalamine.

- *Iron studies: low iron, high iron-binding capacity*
- *Vitamin B$_{12}$ level low, methylmalonic acid level high*

- Iron is absorbed in the duodenum.
- Vitamin B$_{12}$ is absorbed in the terminal ileum.

What is the greatest difference between CD and UC?

a. Response to mesalamine

b. Fistulae

c. Response to steroids

Answer b. Fistulae

CD causes fistulae, perirectal disease, and can affect any level in the bowel from mouth to anus. All IBD is treated with the 5-ASA medication mesalamine.

Transmural granuloma causes fistulae.

Which is consistent with CD?

a. Antineutrophil cytoplasmic autoantibody (ANCA) **positive,** Anti-*Saccharomyces cerevisiae* antibody (ASCA) **negative**

b. ANCA **negative,** ASCA antibody **positive**

Answer b. ANCA negative, ASCA positive

It can sometimes be difficult to distinguish between CD and UC especially when they both involve the large bowel. UC is ANCA positive/ASCA negative. The mechanism behind all of this is not clear.

By the third hospital day, the frequency of bowel movements and presence of blood is greatly decreased. Transfer the patient home. Every time you try to take the patient off steroids, her diarrhea, pain, bleeding, and mucus recur. Mesalamine is not enough to maintain them in remission.

Which therapy should you choose?

a. Azathioprine or 6-mercaptopurine
b. Methotrexate
c. Cyclophosphamide
d. Mycophenolate

Answer a. Azathioprine or 6-mercaptopurine

These agents are immunosuppressive agents that help wean a patient off steroids and prevent recurrence. Methotrexate is for rheumatoid arthritis, not IBD. Mycophenolate and cyclophosphamide are useful in lupus nephritis, but not IBD.

Perirectal Disease = Ciprofloxacin and Metronidazole

Rising Alkaline Phosphatase = Sclerosing Cholangitis
Magnetic Resonance Cholangiopancreatography (MRCP) = Best Test
Treat with cholestyramine or ursodeoxycholic acid.

- Cholestyramine binds bile in the bowel lumen.
- Ursodeoxycholic acid prevents bile formation.

Inflammatory bowel disease is a disorder that goes through intermittent periods of relative activity and inactivity. Several years later, the patient develops abdominal pain and a mass that is palpable. Despite mesalamine and steroids, a fistula develops between the bowel and the skin of the anterior abdominal wall.

What is the mechanism of the best therapy?

a. Interleukin inhibition
b. Inhibition of tumor necrosis factor (TNF)
c. Anti-CD20 antibody
d. Phospholipase inhibition

Answer b. Inhibition of tumor necrosis factor (TNF)

The anti-TNF medications are best used to close up fistulae in CD. Fistulae develop in the skin, vagina, and between bowel loops. Anti-TNF medications can reactivate tuberculosis (TB) and it is important to screen with a purified protein derivative (PPD) or interferon gamma release assay (IGRA) prior to using them. You do not have to complete all 9 months of therapy with isoniazid to safely use the anti-TNF drugs. These drugs are: infliximab, etanercept, and adalimumab.

What is the mechanism whereby TB is reactivated by anti-TNF medications?

a. They directly stimulate the growth of mycobacteria.

b. They suppress lymphocyte function.

c. TNF keeps granulomas intact.

d. No mechanism is known.

Answer c. TNF keeps granulomas intact.

TB is contained by the immune system and walled off in granulomas. TB can exist in a nonreplicative dormant state for many years inside a granuloma. TNF is the chemical signal the body uses to maintain the granuloma. When TNF is inhibited, the granuloma "unlocks" and TB starts to replicate again.

Starting the anti-TNF medication leads to resolution of the fistula over a few days. The medication also has an excellent effect on the primary disease, and the frequency of blood and diarrhea markedly improves.

Screening for Colon Cancer in IBD Patients
• Colonoscopy
• After 8 to 10 years of colon involvement
• CD patients also if the colon is involved

Features that do **not** change with disease activity:
• Sclerosing cholangitis
• Pyoderma gangrenosum

---

*Move the clock forward 1 to 3 months at a time. **Continue mesalamine chronically.***
On CCS, it can be confusing if you think you have done everything, but the case does not end. Remember to do healthy maintenance such as vaccinations and tobacco cessation.

CASE 7: Celiac Disease

Setting: *office*

CC: *"I've had diarrhea for months!"*

VS: *BP: 110/72 mm Hg; P: 76 beats/minute; T: 98° F; R: 14 breaths/minute*

HPI: *A 28-year-old woman with persistent diarrhea over several months visits you at your office. She has lost 15 lb in the last 6 months. She bruises easily and her menstrual periods are heavy. Her stool has a "greasy" quality and does not flush down the toilet easily because it floats at the top of the water. The entire bathroom is abnormally malodorous after bowel movements.*

PMHx:
* *Iron deficiency ascribed to heavy menstruation*

Medications:
* *Ferrous sulfate*

PE:
* *General: thin and tired*
* *Abdomen: soft, nontender, normal sized organs*
* *Lung, Heart: normal*
* *Skin: several bruises on legs*

Initial Orders:
* *Stool culture, WBCs, ova/parasites*
* *CBC*
* *CHEM-20*

Even though an infection is very unlikely to persist for several months, you must first exclude an infectious cause in diarrhea before going to other tests such as endoscopy. It is also very unlikely to have a 15-lb weight loss from an infectious diarrhea.

Report:
* *Stool Culture, WBCs, Ova/Parasites: negative*
* *CBC: hematocrit 30%; MCV 85 fL; WBCs 3,200/μL (low); platelets 118,000/μL (low)*
* *RDW 25% (markedly elevated)*
* *CHEM-20: albumin 4.5 g/dL; calcium 6.8 mg/dL (low)*

Some Iron-Deficient Cells + Some Vitamin B_{12}-Deficient Cells = Dimorphic or Two Distinct Cell Problems

Normal MCV + High RDW = Dimorphic Red Blood Cell Population

What is the fastest way to diagnose vitamin B₁₂ deficiency?

a. Vitamin B_{12} level
b. Peripheral smear
c. Methylmalonic acid (MMA) level

d. Schilling test
e. Anti-intrinsic factor antibody

Answer b. Peripheral smear

In vitamin B_{12} deficiency, the smear will show hypersegmented neutrophils. Vitamin B_{12} levels, if low, are very specific, but they can be in the normal range in 20% to 30% of those with vitamin B_{12} deficiency. MMA levels are elevated in vitamin B_{12} deficiency also. A Schilling test is never done—it is an old test to determine the etiology of vitamin B_{12} deficiency.

> Normal average number of WBC lobes = 3.5

> *The Interval History shows the patient continues to have diarrhea, has lost another 2 lb of weight in the last 3 weeks, and continues to have "oily" stool. The peripheral smears shows hypersegmented WBCs are present with target and hypochromic cells.*

What is the best initial test for the presence of fat in stool?

a. Colonoscopy
b. Sudan black stain

c. Maltese cross
d. A 72-hour fecal fat

Answer b. Sudan black stain

Sudan black is a fat stain. A 72-hour fecal fat is an antiquated test for fat malabsorption. Maltese crosses are for detecting fat in urine. Colonoscopy is not a good test for fat malabsorption. Fat is not absorbed in the colon. Water and salt are absorbed in the colon.

> The colon absorbs no fat.

> **Reports:**
> • *Sudan black stain of stool: fat globules*
> • *Vitamin B_{12} level: low*
> • *Stool heme: negative*
> • *Serum iron: low*
> • *Ferritin: low*
> • *Total iron-binding capacity: elevated*
> • *PT and aPTT: both prolonged*

What is the mechanism of iron deficiency?

a. Bleeding

b. Duodenal malabsorption

c. Gastric malabsorption

d. Colon malabsorption

Answer b. Duodenal malabsorption

The duodenum is the site of absorption of all divalent cations such as calcium, magnesium, and iron. The stomach does not absorb iron. This patient has no blood in the stool, so it is not bleeding. The reason the iron deficiency is not from menstruation is that the MCV is normal, not low.

Divalent cations absorbed at duodenum:
- Calcium (Ca^{++})
- Iron (Fe^{++})
- Magnesium (Mg^{++})

Vitamin K malabsorption can cause bruising.

The patient returns in a week to discuss her laboratory results, which show that she has fat malabsorption with iron and vitamin B$_{12}$ deficiency as well as hypocalcemia.

Low calcium etiology:
- Duodenal malabsorption
- Decreased fat-soluble vitamin absorption (vitamins A, D, E, and K)
- Decreased vitamin D

Low Vitamin D = Low Phosphate

Orders:
- *Antitissue transglutaminase*
- *Antiendomysial antibodies*
- *Antigliadin antibodies*

Which of these is safe to eat in this disorder?

a. Wheat
b. Rice
c. Oats

d. Barley
e. Rye

Answer b. Rice

Foods safe in gluten-sensitive enteropathy are rice, corn, soy, and potatoes. Flour based on these foods are safe.

All of the antibody tests (transglutaminase, endomysial, and gliadin) are positive. You explain to the patient that she has gluten-sensitive enteropathy or celiac disease. Iron deficiency is caused by destruction of villi in the duodenum. Calcium deficiency is caused both by loss from duodenal absorption as well as loss of vitamin D because of fat malabsorption. You advise the patient to remove all foods with gluten from her diet, such as wheat, rye, oats, and barley.

Vitamin B$_{12}$ is lost because of terminal ileum destruction.

Coagulopathy and bruising are caused by vitamin K malabsorption.

The Step 3 examination likes to ask you "what will you tell the patient about his or her prognosis?" They expect you to be able to communicate appropriately with patients about what will happen to them in the future.

The patient asks what she can expect after removing gluten (wheat, rye, oats, barley) from her diet.

What do you tell her about the future?

a. She will have instant symptom resolution in 24 to 48 hours.
b. She will experience a gradual resolution of symptoms and all malabsorption over a few weeks.

c. She will have no change in symptoms, but bruising and bone, iron, and vitamin B$_{12}$ abnormalities will resolve.
d. She can restart eating gluten-containing foods 6 to 12 months after abstention. It will all resolve permanently.

Answer b. She will experience a gradual resolution of symptoms and all malabsorption over a few weeks.

Celiac disease is based on circulating antibodies. It takes several weeks for them to resolve even after stopping exposure to gluten. The disorder, however, is permanent. If she begins to eat gluten again, it will all recur. There is no cure for celiac disease. Symptoms resolve with removing the gluten antigen over time, but the hypersensitivity will recur with reexposure.

What is the basis of the autoantibody?

a. IgA

b. IgG

c. IgM

d. IgE

Answer a. IgA

Most of the autoantibodies in celiac disease are IgA autoantibodies. Antitissue transglutaminase, antiendomysial antibodies, and antigliadin antibodies are all largely IgA antibodies.

> Bone loss is from secondary hyperparathyroidism in celiac disease.

> *The patient stops all gluten-containing food. On her return in 6 weeks, symptoms of diarrhea start to improve. The consistency of her stool stops being oily and floating. She gains 3 lb.*
>
> **Orders:**
> - *Repeat antibody titers*
> - *Calcium level*
> - *CBC*
> - *Small bowel biopsy*

> Antibody titers should improve with the elimination of gluten from the diet.

> *Repeat titers improve as does the calcium level and hematocrit. The small bowel biopsy must be done to exclude bowel wall lymphoma. Repeat small bowel biopsy is done after several months to check for restoration of the flattened villi.*

CASE 8: Hemochromatosis

Setting: *office*

CC: *"My joints hurt and my skin is turning dark."*

VS: *BP: 104/74 mm Hg; P: 76 beats/minute*

HPI: *A 54-year-old man with progressive arthralgia of the lower extremities, tiredness, and fatigue comes to the office because his wife says his skin is darkening. She also brought him for his erectile dysfunction.*

PMHx:
• *Type 2 diabetes*

ROS:
• *Dyspnea on exertion*

Medications:
• *Metformin, repaglinide*

What is the mechanism of the repaglinide?

a. Increased insulin release from the pancreas

b. Peripheral insulin sensitization

c. Decreased gluconeogenesis

d. Increased levels of incretins (glucose-dependent insulinotropic peptide [GIP], glucagonlike peptide [GLP])

Answer a. Increased insulin release from the pancreas

Repaglinide and nateglinide are insulin secretagogues that function in the same way as sulfonylureas. They increase insulin release from the pancreas. They can, therefore, cause hypoglycemia and weight gain.

PE:
• *General: tired, dark skin clearly obvious*
• *Extremities: no joint swelling, no deformity*
• *Abdomen: enlarged spleen*
• *Genitals: testicles small*

Initial Orders:
• *CBC*
• *Liver function tests*
• *CHEM-20*
• *Glycated hemoglobin (HbA₁c)*
• *Testosterone level*

Abnormal Reports:
• *Albumin 2.5 mg/dL (low)*
• *Aspartate aminotransferase (AST) 123 units/L, alanine aminotransferase (ALT) 145 units/L (both three times the upper limit of normal)*
• *HbA₁c 7.2%*
• *Free and total testosterone decreased*

Which is the best initial test for to give a specific diagnosis?

a. Liver biopsy

b. Iron, total iron-binding capacity (TIBC), ferritin

c. Hemochromatosis (*HFE*) gene test

d. MRI

Answer b. Iron, TIBC, ferritin

Iron and ferritin levels are elevated. TIBC is decreased. Hemochromatosis is a collection of information that can be difficult to put together. There is no single physical finding that is specific for the disorder. It is a collection of abnormalities that only in a pattern suggest iron overload.

- Liver disease
- Joint pain
- Hypogonadism
- Hypopituitarism
- Diabetes

The patient's diabetes may be from undiagnosed hemochromatosis.

Joint pain in hemochromatosis is from the calcium pyrophosphate deposition of pseudogout.

The patient's iron and ferritin levels are elevated and the transferring saturation is over 80%. The patient refuses liver biopsy.

Patients can refuse procedures on CCS. A spontaneous note will pop up as you move the clock forward saying "Patient declines procedure."

Orders:
- *HFE gene*
- *Liver MRI*

The HFE gene test is abnormal and the liver MRI shows markedly increased iron.

What is the best initial therapy?

a. Phlebotomy

b. Deferoxamine

c. Deferasirox

d. Deferiprone

Answer a. Phlebotomy

Phlebotomy is able to remove far more iron than a chelating agent. The chelating agents are used when someone receives frequent transfusions and you cannot treat with phlebotomy.

Deferoxamine is much harder to use than deferasirox or deferiprone because it must be given by subcutaneous injection. Deferasirox and deferiprone are administered orally.

What is the site of the fundamental defect that causes hemochromatosis?

a. Duodenum

b. Liver

c. Heart

d. Pituitary

Answer a. Duodenum

The genetic defect that leads to hemochromatosis causes the overabsorption of iron in the duodenum. Normally, hepcidin is made by the liver and stops iron absorption when the body has what is required. In hemochromatosis, there is persistent iron absorption. This leads to accumulation in the liver, heart, pituitary, pancreas, joints, and skin.

> Iron accumulation in the pituitary gland decreases levels of luteinizing hormone (LH) and follicle-stimulating hormone (FSH).

> *The patient is not enthusiastic about repeated episodes of phlebotomy.*

What do you tell him the most common cause of death is without phlebotomy?

a. Cirrhosis

b. Liver cancer

c. Cardiac failure

d. Diabetes

Answer a. Cirrhosis

Liver disease kills more people than heart failure in hemochromatosis. The causes of death in patients with hemochromatosis are as follows:

- Cirrhosis: 60%
- Hepatoma: 20%
- Cardiac failure: 15%

> Restrictive cardiomyopathy is the most common heart disease associated with hemochromatosis.

> *After telling the patient he will have progressive cirrhotic death or liver cancer without phlebotomy, he agrees to the phlebotomy.*

CASE 9: Pancreatitis

Setting: *ED*

CC: *"My stomach hurts and I am vomiting."*

VS: *BP: 92/60 mm Hg; P: 124 beats/minute; T: 101.5°F; R: 22 breaths/minute*

HPI: *A 45-year-old woman comes to the ED with 2 days of abdominal pain and 1 day of increasingly severe nausea and vomiting. She has never had this before. The pain makes it difficult for her to find a comfortable position in the bed and she is trying to hold herself still. Vomiting has bile but no blood. Pain is described as "sore," "dull," and very severe.*

PMHx: *obesity; denies significant alcohol use*

Medications: *none*

PE:
- *General: obese woman lying still, uncomfortable*
- *Abdomen: severe midepigastric tenderness; some guarding; not rigid*

Initial Orders:
- *Amylase, lipase*
- *CBC*
- *CHEM-20*
- *NPO (nil per os or no eating)*
- *IV NS: high volume*
- *IV hydromorphone (Dilaudid)*

- Pancreatitis causes fever.
- Most deaths from pancreatitis are from inadequate fluid resuscitation.

Which cause of pancreatitis is *increasing in incidence* the most?

a. Alcohol
b. Gallstones
c. Trauma
d. Drug induced
e. Cancer

Answer b. Gallstones

The incidence of gallstones is markedly increasing. Gallstones leave the gallbladder and get stuck in the ductal system at the point where they can block the pancreatic duct. Any stone, stricture, tumor, or obstruction can cause pancreatitis. Greater obesity increases the incidence of gallstones.

Obesity = Cholesterol = Gallstones

IV fluids are started in high volume. Pain medications are given and the clock is moved forward to obtain the laboratory test results.

On CCS, acute pancreatitis should be treated as an assessment for possible ICU placement until you know that BP and pulse rate are stable. Reexamine the patient and repeat the vital signs in 30 minutes and again in 1 hour until you know the patient is stable.

- Massive amounts of intravascular fluid leaks into tissues.
- Inflammatory mediators in pancreatitis cause a massive capillary leak.

Repeat VS in 30 minutes: BP: 96/62 mm Hg; P: 118 beats/minute; T: 101.5°F; R: 18 breaths/minute

- *Amylase 850 units/L (elevated)*
- *Lipase 754 units/L (elevated)*
- *CBC : WBC 15,500/μL*
- *CHEM-20: normal bilirubin; normal lactate dehydrogenase (LDH); normal AST*

Pain can cause tachycardia and hyperventilation.

Pancreatitis increases the WBC count because of inflammation.

An abdominal US is performed to determine the etiology of the pancreatitis. You do not need to do a US to prove there is pancreatitis. The presence of pain, nausea, vomiting, tenderness, and high amylase/lipase prove the presence of pancreatitis. The sonogram is to detect stones in the ducts and gallbladder.

Orders:
- *Abdominal US*
- *Triglyceride level*
- *Calcium*
- *Oximeter*

Pancreatitis causes hypoxia by capillary leak in the lungs
(acute respiratory distress syndrome [ARDS]).

Move the clock forward 4 hours.

VS: *BP: 100/70 mm Hg; P: 114 beats/minute*

Report:
- *Abdominal US: stones in gallbladder; dilated pancreatic duct, no stone in duct*
- *Triglyceride level: 445 mg/dL*
- *Calcium: normal*
- *Oximeter: 97% on room air*

Triglycerides >1000 mg/dL cause pancreatitis.

High calcium level causes pancreatitis.
Pancreatitis causes **low** calcium level.

1. Dead Pancreas = Malabsorption of Fat
2. Fat in the bowel binds calcium in the bowel.
3. Calcium bound in the bowel decreases blood calcium.

What is the utility of a CT scan in this patient?

a. Confirm the severity of the ductal obstruction.

b. Look for pancreatic necrosis.

c. Confirm the diagnosis of infected necrotic pancreatitis.

d. Determine the severity of disease.

Answer b. Look for pancreatic necrosis.

Pancreatic necrosis easily becomes infected. You must give antibiotics such as imipenem or meropenem if there is necrosis before it becomes infected. You are doing the CT scan to see if there is >30% necrosis. If there is >30% necrosis, give imipenem or meropenem and do a CT-guided biopsy. If there is necrosis that is already infected, the pancreas must be surgically debrided.

No test can determine the severity of pancreatitis disease in the first 48 hours of presentation of acute pancreatitis. No radiologic test can tell that the pancreatitis is infected. Only a needle biopsy by CT guidance can do that.

More than 30% Necrosis of Pancreas = Antibiotics and Needle Biopsy
Infected Necrotic Pancreatitis = Surgical Debridement

No radiologic test can determine infection.

IV fluids and pain medication continue for the patient. The abdominal CT shows pancreatitis and gallstones in the gallbladder. The CT does not show necrosis of the pancreas and no stones are seen in the ductal system. There is currently no ductal dilation.

By the end of the second hospital day, the patient's BP is 110/74 mm Hg and his pulse rate is 90 beats/minute.

Interval History:
• *Pain and nausea have improved considerably.*

Which of the following is most likely to benefit this patient?

a. NG tube placement
b. MRCP

c. Endoscopic retrograde cholangiopancreatography (ERCP)
d. Surgical evaluation for cholecystectomy

Answer d. Surgical evaluation for cholecystectomy

Even though the ducts are not currently dilated, the cause of pancreatitis in this patient is a stone that caused obstruction and passed. You need to get the rest of the stones out of there before another obstruction occurs.

An NG tube is useless in acute pancreatitis. MRCP and ERCP are not needed if there is no evidence of ductal dilation.

The obstruction is assessed and treated. After the acute episode of pancreatitis has resolved and the gallbladder is removed, you should expect the case to end.

CHAPTER **6**

NEPHROLOGY

CASE 1: Acute Kidney Injury, Prerenal Azotemia (Dehydration)

Setting: *emergency department (ED)*

CC: *Tired, weak, and short of breath*

VS: *BP: 168/106 mm Hg; P: 89 beats/minute; T: 97.8°F; R: 28 breaths/minute*

HPI: *A 62-year-old woman comes to the ED with 1 day of severe shortness of breath and cough. She says "it came on all of a sudden" when she was largely at rest. She is extremely obese and does not move most of the time. She is adherent to her medications most of the time.*

PMHx:
- *Congestive heart failure (CHF)*
- *Hypertension*
- *Obesity*

Medications:
- *Lisinopril, carvedilol, digoxin*

On the computer-based case simulation (CCS), dyspnea and serious blood pressure (BP) abnormalities are two of the main problems that need treatment and testing to be ordered before the physical is done. For dyspnea, order oxygen, oximeter, and chest x-ray (sometimes arterial blood gas [ABG]). For symptomatic hypertension, order labetalol, enalaprilat, or nitroprusside intravenously (IV).

PE:
- *General: morbidly obese; hard to examine*
- *Chest: incomplete examination because of obesity, possible rales at bases*
- *Extremities: edema; one leg more swollen than the other*
- *Cardiovascular: no murmurs heard; no gallops*

Initial Orders:
- *Chest x-ray*
- *Oximeter*
- *ABG*
- *Oxygen*
- *Basic metabolic panel (CHEM-7)*
- *Electrocardiogram (ECG)*

1. Hypertension increases myocardial work.
2. More work requires more oxygen (O_2) consumption.
3. More O_2 consumption leads to more ischemia.
4. More ischemia leads to a less mobile heart.
5. A less mobile heart exacerbates CHF.

Which medication is *missing* from this patient's treatment that would lower her risk of death from CHF?

a. Spironolactone
b. Furosemide

c. Nifedipine
d. Amiodarone

Answer a. Spironolactone

Although a diuretic is good to prevent fluid overload, mineralocorticoid receptor antagonists like spironolactone and eplerenone are superior for lowering mortality. Calcium channel blockers help to control BP, but do nothing for mortality benefit in CHF.

Move the clock forward 15 minutes and look at the Interval History: The patient feels better with the oxygen, but the diagnosis is not clear. There are no clear rales, jugulovenous distention (JVD), or S₃ gallop.

Report:

- *Chest x-ray: enlarged heart; no abnormalities, clear in lung fields; incomplete study from obesity*
- *Oximeter: 92%*
- *ABG (on room air): pH 7.49; partial pressure of carbon dioxide (PCO₂) 30 mm Hg; partial pressure of oxygen (PO₂) 64 mm Hg*
- *CHEM-7: blood urea nitrogen (BUN) 12 g/dL; creatinine 0.8 mg/dL*
- *ECG: sinus tachycardia, right bundle branch block*

The patient does not improve.

Order:

- *Furosemide IV*

What is the site of action of furosemide?

a. Tip of loop of Henle
b. Thick ascending limb (TAL) of loop of Henle

c. Na⁺/K⁺-ATPase
d. Inhibition of aquaporins at loop of Henle

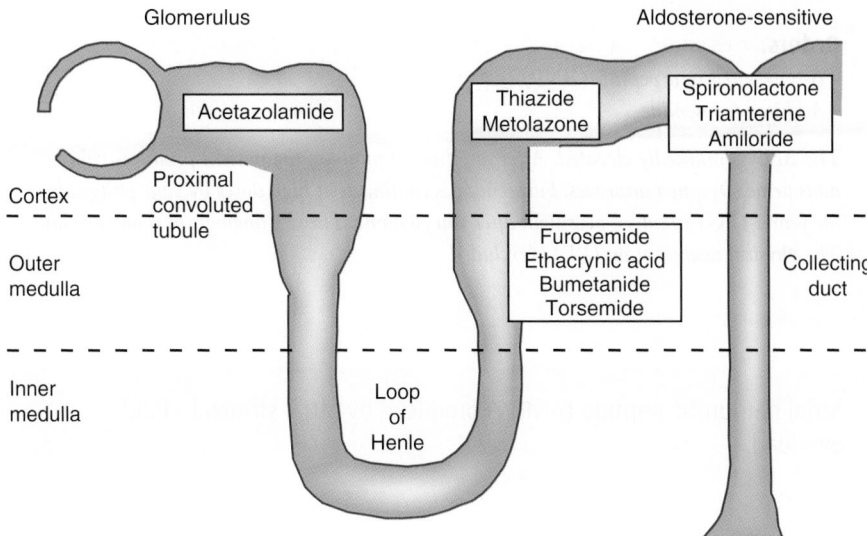

Figure 6-1. Tubular sites of action of the major diuretics used in clinical medicine. (Reproduced with permission from Fuster V, et al. *Hurst's The Heart*, 13th ed. New York: McGraw-Hill; 2011.)

Answer b. Thick ascending limb (TAL) of loop of Henle

Loop diuretics such as furosemide, bumetanide, and indapamide do not actually work at the tip of the loop. They work at the TAL of the loop (Figure 6-1). This is the site where 25% of sodium (Na) is absorbed at the nephron. Blocking absorption at the TAL cannot be compensated for by sodium absorption at the distal tubule. This is why loop diuretics are so effective at removing fluid from the body.

Furosemide inhibits the $Na^+/K^+/2Cl^-$ pump in TAL.

After two repeated doses and urine production, the patient is still dyspneic. Prior to your receiving the patient, the ED attending ordered a computed tomography (CT) angiogram with contrast. He was concerned about a pulmonary embolus in light of the dyspnea, incomplete examination, and relatively normal chest x-ray.

Sudden Dyspnea + Clear Lungs = Possible Pulmonary Embolus

You do not agree with the diagnosis of pulmonary embolus and think this is CHF.

Orders:
• B-type natriuretic peptide (BNP)
• Addition furosemide

The BNP is markedly elevated. After another 30 minutes, the patient produces voluminous urine. Dyspnea improves. Furosemide is continued at high doses by your postgraduate year 1 (PGY1) intern overnight after you go home. The CT angiogram shows no clot. The physical examination (PE) is excluded.

Atrial natriuretic peptide (ANP) is produced by atrial stretch in fluid overload.

Now that the dyspnea has improved, move the clock forward to the second day.

Orders:
• Echocardiogram
• CHEM-7
• Troponin

Report:
• Echocardiogram: decreased diastolic function; increased left ventricle (LV) thickness; 64% ejection fraction
• Troponin: normal
• Chemistry: BUN 28 g/dL; creatinine 1.8 mg/dL; potassium (K) 3.2 mEq/L

Loop diuretics inhibit absorption of potassium at TAL.

LV hypertrophy is from hypertension.

Later in the day, the chemistries are repeated.

• BUN: 37 g/dL
• Creatinine: 2.5 mg/dL

BUN-to-Creatinine Ratio
>20:1 = Prerenal Azotemia = Decreased Perfusion
<15:1 = Intrarenal Acute Kidney Injury = Acute Tubular Necrosis (ATN)

Which of the following laboratory values suggest ATN?

a. Creatinine level rising 5 points in a day
b. Urine sodium >40 mEq/L
c. Urine osmolarity >500 mOsm/kg
d. Fractional excretion of sodium (FeNa) <1%
e. Urine eosinophils

Answer b. Urine sodium >40 mEq/L

ATN is the death of kidney tubule cells. Tubule cells normally absorb sodium. If they are dead, sodium cannot be absorbed and the urine sodium level rises. Nothing raises creatinine 5 points a day. Even an anephric person with zero renal function does not increase the creatinine by 5 points in a day. High urine osmolarity is found in prerenal azotemia. A dehydrated person increases water reabsorption from the kidneys. Urine eosinophils are found in allergic interstitial nephritis.

Do not forget to move the patient out of the ED after the initial set of laboratory tests and treatments!

Contrast agents cause ATN. Look for:
• Urine sodium >40 mEq/L
• Urine osmolarity <350 mOsm/kg

The patient does not feel the rising creatinine. Her dyspnea has improved with BP control to 118/70 mm Hg.

Repeat Laboratory Test Results:

• *BUN: 48 g/dL*
• *Creatinine: 2.6 mg/dL*
• *Urine sodium: 12 mEq/L*
• *Urine osmolarity: 840 mOsm/kg*
• *Serum bicarbonate (HCO$_3$): 34 mEq/L (elevated)*

Which of the following do you expect in this patient?

a. Granular or muddy brown casts

b. Hansel stain positive

c. Urine specific gravity 1.001

d. Hyaline casts

e. Maltese crosses

Answer d. Hyaline casts

Hyaline casts are expected in prerenal azotemia. They are accumulated Tamm-Horsfall protein, which solidifies into a hyaline cast when the person becomes "dry." In this patient, it is very important to make a precise diagnosis. If it is overdiuresis, you may need to give a small amount of IV fluids.

Granular or muddy brown casts occur in ATN. They are dead tubular epithelial cells. Hansel and Wright stains are used to detect eosinophils in urine in allergic interstitial nephritis. Urine specific gravity is low (<1.010) in ATN. Dead tubule cells (ATN) cannot reabsorb water, so the urine is dilute. Maltese crosses are fat bodies in urine seen in hyperlipidemia.

What is the mechanism of elevated bicarbonate level in this patient?

a. Prerenal azotemia increases bicarbonate production at the distal tubule.

b. Proximal tubule absorption of bicarbonate is increased.

c. Acid excretion at the proximal tubule is increased.

Answer a. Prerenal azotemia increases bicarbonate production at the distal tubule.

Volume contraction increases renin and angiotensin II. Increased angiotensin II (ANGII) increases aldosterone production. Aldosterone excretes acid in the distal tubule and increases new bicarbonate production.

Decreased Body Volume = Metabolic Alkalosis or Contraction Alkalosis

Tubules absorb sodium and water. Dead tubules (ATN) result in:
- Dilute urine (<350 mOsm/kg)
- High sodium level (>40 mEq/L)

Urine specific gravity approximates urine osmolarity.
- Specific Gravity 1.001 = Osmolarity <100 mOsm/kg
- Specific Gravity 1.040 = Osmolarity >500 mOsm/kg

Sodium Absorption in the Kidney.
- It is the greatest energy-using step in the kidney.
- Sixty-seven percent is absorbed in the proximal tubule.

What was the most likely etiology of the patient's dyspnea on presentation?

a. Hypertension
b. Renal injury

c. Fluid overload

Answer a. Hypertension

Hypertension was likely the etiology of the shortness of breath in this person. Because the BUN-to-creatinine ratio later became clearly 20:1 with low urine sodium level and high urine osmolarity, it becomes clear that this is all prerenal azotemia from overdiuresis. At the beginning, it is often not clear. Contrast agents are most dangerous in those with decreased renal perfusion.

Stop medications and cancel tests on CCS by double clicking on them. CCS will always ask you to confirm everything you do two to three times.

Discontinue the diuretics and order IV fluids. Repeat the chemistry levels 12 and 24 hours later to be sure the patient is going in the right direction.

Contrast may have contributed to some kidney injury in this patient in addition to prerenal azotemia. What therapy *reverses* ATN?

a. Nothing
b. Bicarbonate

c. N-acetylcysteine
d. Low-dose dopamine

Answer a. Nothing

There is no therapy proven to reverse ATN. It is like sunburn. You cannot reverse ATN, you can only prevent it. Hydration, N-acetylcysteine, and bicarbonate all have some effect in preventing contrast-induced renal failure. They cannot reverse it once it has occurred. Low-dose "renal" dopamine is worthless. It is always a wrong answer.

Low-dose dopamine is useless for kidney injury.

Prevent contrast-induced renal injury:
• Give 1 to 2 L hydration.

What should be changed in chronic medications?

a. Continue spironolactone.

b. Stop digoxin.

c. Add angiotensin receptor blocker (ARB).

Answer b. Stop digoxin.

Digoxin and spironolactone have no benefit in diastolic dysfunction. There is no point in adding an ARB to an angiotensin-converting enzyme (ACE) inhibitor. The patient needs to have her BP controlled, which will avoid decompensated CHF. Use beta-blockers, ACE inhibitors, and possibly calcium channel blockers.

Repeat the chemistries to see that the BUN and creatinine levels have both started to decrease. Do it often so you know when you can stop hydration.

CASE 2: Acute Renal Failure (Rhabdomyolysis)

Setting: *ED*

CC: *"My muscles hurt and my urine is dark."*

VS: *BP: 112/70 mm Hg; P: 108 beats/minute; T: 98°F; R: 18 breaths/minute*

HPI: *A 27-year-old man arrives at the ED by ambulance after undergoing the physical fitness test for being a firefighter. He had to lift a 150-lb bag, run up a flight of stairs while carrying it, and proceed across a balance beam. He then had to do 50 pushups and 50 sit-ups. At the end, he developed dark urine and diffuse muscle pain.*

PMHx/Medications: *none*

PE:
• *General: weak, tired, and in pain*
• *Heart, Lung, Abdomen: normal*

What would be the most likely cause of death in this patient?

a. Dehydration

b. Renal failure

c. Hyperkalemia

d. Hyperphosphatemia

e. Hypocalcemia

Answer c. Hyperkalemia

The single most important fact about rhabdomyolysis is knowing that hyperkalemia causes death when it is severe. Everything in this list occurs, but the one that kills you is hyperkalemia.

- High Potassium Level = ECG
- Ninety-five percent of potassium in the body is intracellular.

Rapidly Destroyed Cells = Hyperkalemia

Initial Orders:

- *ECG*
- *CHEM-7*
- *Bolus IV saline*
- *Urinalysis (UA)*
- *Creatine phosphokinase (CPK)*
- *Calcium*
- *Phosphate*

Rhabdomyolysis is a case where timing is essential. Exclude hyperkalemia and cardiac toxicity immediately. Order potassium level and ECG even before the PE.

Peaked T Waves = Give Calcium Chloride (or Gluconate)

Reports:

- *ECG: peaked T waves*
- *CHEM-7: potassium 6.8 mEq/dL; BUN 26 g/dL; creatinine 1.5 mg/dL*
- *UA: dipstick + blood*
- *Calcium level: 6.8 mg/dL (low)*
- *Phosphate: elevated*

Why do we give patients calcium to protect the heart?

a. It drives calcium back into the cells.

b. It blocks norepinephrine release.

c. It raises the threshold for depolarization.

d. It decreases conduction velocity in His-Purkinje tissue.

Answer C. It raises the threshold for depolarization.

Calcium makes it harder for neural tissue to depolarize. This is a good thing if the myocardium might abnormally depolarize and lead to arrhythmia. This is sometimes referred to as "membrane stabilization." To depolarize, neural and muscle tissue must become more positive until it hits a "threshold" or trigger point to depolarize. Resting or baseline membrane potential is often at –70 to –90 mV. The cells must increase to –50 or –45 mV before the threshold for depolarization is reached. Calcium raises the level so the threshold is more "out of reach" and depolarization does not occur.

High Calcium = Harder to Depolarize
Low Calcium = Easier to Depolarize

There is no maximum rate of calcium infusion. Calcium channels are closed at baseline.

IV calcium is given and IV fluids are running. Now you must give medication to lower the blood potassium level.

Orders:
- *Insulin*
- *Glucose*
- *Repeat chemistry*
- *Urine myoglobin*

Insulin drives potassium into cells by stimulating Na^+/K^+-ATPase.

The type of fluids in rhabdomyolysis is not clear. Use normal saline (NS) for now.

Urine dipstick cannot distinguish between
- Red blood cells (RBCs)
- Hemoglobin
- Myoglobin

Move the clock forward 15 minutes.
- *Repeat potassium level: 6.2 mEq/L*
- *Urine microscopic: no RBCs seen*
- *CPK: 28,000 units/L*

CPK levels are not dangerous until above 5000 to 10,000 units/L.

What causes hypocalcemia?

a. Decreased parathyroid hormone (PTH).
b. Binding by sarcoplasmic-endoplasmic reticulum calcium adenosine triphosphatase (SERCA).

c. Urinary loss.
d. Suppression of vitamin D.

Answer b. Binding by sarcoplasmic-endoplasmic reticulum calcium adenosine triphosphatase (SERCA).

SERCA has calcium adenosine triphosphatase (ATPase) pumps that pull calcium into storage. When muscles are damaged by rhabdomyolysis, the exterior membrane becomes permeable to calcium in blood. The muscle then binds up all the calcium by pumping it into SERCA. Normally SERCA only has contact with the interior of the muscle cells. In rhabdomyolysis, the interior now contacts blood calcium.

Damaged muscle binds calcium.

Where in the hospital should this patient be placed?

a. Place the patient in the intensive care unit (ICU).
b. Keep the patient in ED for the first 24 to 48 hours.

c. Place the patient in the hospital ward.
d. Discharge the patient after his potassium level is corrected.

Answer a. Place the patient in the intensive care unit (ICU).

After initial administration of fluids and correcting the potassium level, you can move the patient to the ICU. The indication for ICU placement is hyperkalemia with ECG changes. Patients can go to a regular hospital ward just for hydration for rhabdomyolysis. Renal insufficiency is not an indication for ICU placement. Even in rhabdomyolysis, the creatinine level cannot rise more than 1 to 2 points a day.

What is the mechanism of hyperphosphatemia?

a. Binding to muscle

b. Release from muscle

c. Renal insufficiency

d. Hyperparathyroidism

Answer b. Release from muscle

The majority of phosphate is in muscles and inside cells. Destroyed cells and muscle release phosphate and potassium and bind calcium.

Continue IV fluids at high volume to "flush out" the kidneys. It is not clear if bicarbonate or mannitol make a clear difference in outcomes. The proposed mechanism of bicarbonate is that it prevents precipitation of CPK and myoglobin in the kidney tubule. The idea of mannitol is to decrease the duration of contact of myoglobin with the kidney tubule—like taking your hand off a hot stove.

Move the clock forward 4 hours and repeat the potassium and chemistry levels.

Keep the patient in the ICU until the potassium level is repeatedly normal and the ECG is normal. Move the patient to the floor. When on the floor, you do not need to do the chemistry more often than twice a day.

Move the clock forward until you see:

• No rise in creatinine level and no need for dialysis

• CPK levels drop below 1000 units/L

At that point you can discharge the patient from the hospital if the case has not ended already.

Do not be dismayed if many acute cases give you the "this case will end in 5 minutes of real time" screen before you can send the patient home. In those cases, the emphasis is simply on initial management.

CASE 3: Glomerulonephritis (Immunoglobulin A)

Setting: *office*

CC: *"I have blood in my urine."*

VS: *BP:143/92 mm Hg; T: 98°F*

HPI: *A 34-year-old man comes to your office after noticing what he thinks is blood in his urine off and on for the past few months. The first time he had it, his other physician gave him an antibiotic. Now it has recurred. He has a sore throat the day before each episode.*

PMHx/Medications: *none*

PE: *normal*

Initial Order: *UA*

Hematuria Causes
- Stones
- Infection
- Glomerulonephritis
- Tumor (renal or bladder cancer)
- Trauma

The UA can be done immediately. There can be no meaningful discussion about dark urine or blood in the urine without the UA results.

Report:
- *RBCs 100 to 200*
- *No white cells*
- *No protein*

Which is associated with necrotizing granulomas?

a. Wegener granulomatosis
b. Churg-Strauss syndrome
c. Goodpasture syndrome
d. Microscopic polyangiitis
e. Polyarteritis nodosa (PAN)

Answer a. Wegener granulomatosis

As the name Wegener granulomatosis implies, this disease is associated with granulomas. All of the listed disorders are systemic diseases and Wegener granulomatosis is a systemic vasculitis involving the skin, joints, eyes, brain, and gastrointestinal (GI) tract with special localization to the upper and lower respiratory tract.

Upper and Lower Respiratory Tract + Cytoplasmic Antineutrophil Cytoplasmic Antibody (cANCA) = Wegener = Steroids + Cyclophosphamide

PAN is associated with chronic hepatitis B and C.

With just some hematuria, but no protein, there is no immediate therapy needed. You can schedule the patient to follow up with you in a month to see if there is persistence and further evaluation is needed.

Which disease is associated with linear deposits in the glomerulus on biopsy?

a. Wegener granulomatosis
b. Churg-Strauss syndrome
c. Goodpasture syndrome
d. Microscopic polyangiitis
e. PAN

Answer c. Goodpasture syndrome

Only Goodpasture syndrome has linear deposits.

Lung + Kidney + Antibasement Membrane Antibodies = Goodpasture Syndrome

A month later the patient has a recurrence of hematuria. There is no pharyngitis this time.

Repeat UA:
• *RBCs 100 to 200*
• *Dysmorphic RBCs*
• *No protein*

Which of the following has "dysmorphic" RBCs?

a. Stones
b. Infection
c. Glomerulonephritis
d. Tumor (renal or bladder cancer)
e. Trauma

Answer c. Glomerulonephritis

RBCs can become misshapen or "dysmorphic" as they pass through an abnormal glomerulus in glomerulonephritis. Nevertheless, any persistent or recurrent hematuria needs evaluation with a culture and ultrasound of the urinary system. You must exclude stones and anatomic problems with the urinary system with hematuria.

Orders:
• *Urine culture*
• *Ultrasound of urinary system*

Polycystic kidney disease most commonly presents with recurrent hematuria.
• Stones
• Recurrent pyelonephritis

Move the clock forward a week. Recurrent episodes of hematuria need investigation.

Report:
• *Urine culture: no growth*
• *Ultrasound: normal; no stones; no hydronephrosis; no cysts*

Which is most likely to present with recurrent abdominal pain that is worse on eating?

a. Wegener granulomatosis
b. Churg-Strauss syndrome

c. Microscopic polyangiitis
d. PAN

Answer d. PAN

PAN is a systemic vasculitis that spares the respiratory system. There is no single clear feature because, like Wegener granulomatosis, it is a systemic vasculitis involving the skin, joints, eyes, brain, and GI tract. Because of the presence of narrow vessels in the arterial system of the bowel, pain related to eating, or "intestinal angina" occurs. Look for an abnormal GI angiogram or sural nerve biopsy. Treat with steroids and cyclophosphamide as you would Wegener granulomatosis and Churg-Strauss syndrome.

Vasculitis + Asthma + Eosinophils = Churg-Strauss Syndrome = Steroids + Cyclophosphamide

The patient returns in a month. The UA now shows (Figure 6-2) the following:
• *RBCs 100 to 200*
• *Dysmorphic RBCs*
• *RBC casts*
• *Mild proteinuria*

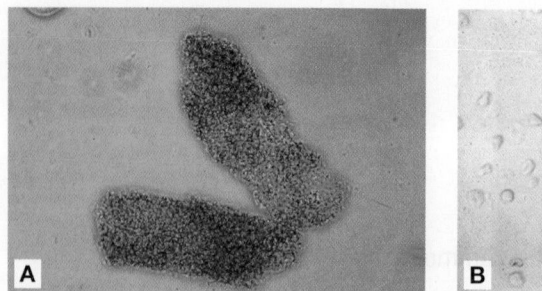
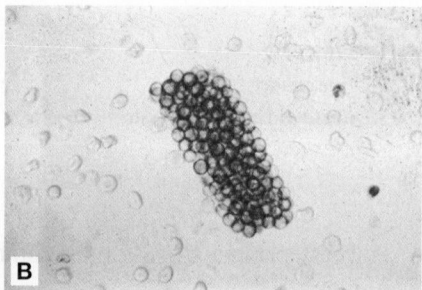

Figure 6-2. A. Fine granular casts. **B.** Red blood cell cast. (Reproduced with permission from Agnes B. Fogo, MD, Vanderbilt Collection.)

Immunoglobulin A (IgA) nephropathy is the most common glomerulonephritis.

What else besides the kidney is routinely involved in IgA nephropathy?

a. Nothing

b. GI tract

c. Joints

d. Skin

e. Lung

Answer a. Nothing

IgA nephropathy is monosymptomatic to the kidney alone. Henoch-Schönlein purpura involves the GI tract, joints, and skin. Oddly, although Henoch-Schönlein has a more serious systemic presentation at first, it nearly always resolves spontaneously and permanently in >95% of patients. It is IgA nephropathy that is much more dangerous. There is chronic and recurrent kidney disease in 60% to 70% of patients and a third will end up on dialysis with end-stage renal disease (ESRD).

A month later, the hematuria persists in the patient's urinalysis. The BUN and creatinine levels are normal but start to slightly elevate after a few months.

Which test can confirm IgA nephropathy?

a. Renal biopsy only

b. Skin biopsy

c. GI biopsy

d. IgA level in blood

Answer a. Renal biopsy only

The difficulty of IgA nephropathy diagnosis is that only the renal biopsy can establish a diagnosis. Checking IgA levels in blood is unreliable.

See the patient at 1 month, 3 months and 6 months. If hematuria persists or the creatinine level stays elevated, order the kidney biopsy. Also order a nephrology consultation.

On CCS, if a consultation is felt to be needed prior to a procedure, the test will tell you. Just order the procedure you feel is necessary. Never wait for a consultant to tell you to do anything, it will not happen.

Which form of IgA-mediated disease has treatment that will reverse it?

a. IgA nephropathy

b. Celiac disease

c. Henoch-Schönlein purpura

d. None

Answer d. None

Stopping gluten and wheat in the diet is not the same as having a treatment that will reverse it. There is no therapy that will allow a person with celiac disease to eat wheat. No therapy reverses IgA-mediated disease. We have steroids for IgG- and IgE-mediated disease.

The renal biopsy shows IgA deposition in the kidney and the diagnosis is confirmed. There is no definitive therapy for IgA nephropathy. Over time, about a third of patients progress and proteinuria worsens. When this happens, order prednisone and ACE inhibitors. There is a difference between the questions "What will you do?" and "What treatment stops the disease?"

There is no treatment that can stop IgA nephropathy.
Use ACE inhibitors and steroids.

If the case allows, move the clock forward 1 to 2 years. If the creatinine level starts to rise, refer the patient for renal transplant screening. There is no cure for IgA nephropathy. You have to transplant the kidney.

CASE 4: Nephrotic Syndrome (Membranous)

Setting: *office*

CC: *"Why are my legs swollen?"*

VS: *BP: 112/70 mm Hg; P: 92 beats/minute; T: 98°F; R:12 breaths/minute*

HPI: *A 34-year-old man comes to see you at your office for swelling of both of his legs developing slowly over several months. He has seen another physician who gave him a diuretic to decrease the swelling, but there was no improvement.*

PMHx:
• *Hyperlipidemia for 3 years*

Medications:
• *Simvastatin*

ROS:
• *Several colds and sinus infections over the past year*
• *Anxiety about swelling*
• *Denies pain, dyspnea*

PE:
• *General: emotionally distressed*
• *Chest: clear to auscultation*
• *Cardiovascular: no murmurs, no gallops*
• *Extremities: bilateral lower extremity edema to the knees*
• *Head, Ears, Eyes, Nose, Throat (HEENT): mild periorbital edema*

Initial Orders:
• *UA*
• *Echocardiogram*
• *Comprehensive metabolic panel (CHEM-20)*

Liver function tests
• *Lipid panel*

Periorbital edema is a main clue to low albumin as etiology.

Move the clock forward just enough to get the results. **The patient is described as visibly anxious and you need to discuss the results with him as soon as possible.**

Report:
• *Urinalysis: 4+ protein, oval fat bodies*
• *Echocardiogram: normal*
• *CHEM-20: albumin 2.1 mg/dL*

Liver function tests: normal
• *Low-density lipoprotein (LDL) 145 mg/dL; triglycerides 500 mg/dL (elevated)*

What is the best way to tell whether a patient's albumin level is low from liver disease or another cause?

a. Aspartate aminotransferase (AST) and alanine aminotransferase (ALT)
b. Lactate dehydrogenase (LDH)
c. Prothrombin time (PT)

d. Liver sonogram
e. Alkaline phosphatase and gamma-glutamyl transferase (GGTP)

Answer C. Prothrombin time (PT)

If the albumin level is low, but the PT is normal, the liver is definitely *not* the cause of the low albumin level. It is impossible for the liver to be synthetically normal enough to make clotting factors but not normal enough to make albumin. The liver does not selectively fail to produce one protein such as albumin, but still make other proteins such as clotting factors. The AST and ALT can be normal when the liver is nearly dead. You have to have live cells to make transaminases. Dead livers do not shed AST/ALT. Bald people do not shed hair.

A liver sonogram tells nothing about the synthetic capacity of liver. Alkaline phosphatase and GGTP assess the biliary system. Obstruction elevates the levels of both.

Binge drinking elevates GGTP first.

The world's best test of liver synthetic function is PT!

UA in hyperlipidemia
• Oval fat bodies
• Maltese crosses

Nephrotic Syndrome =
• Hyper albumin**uria** +
• Hyp**o**albumin**emia** +
• Edema +
• Hyperlipidemia

The patient is actually quite relieved to hear the results of the tests. He feels this explains why, as a young man, he had hard-to-control hyperlipidemia.

Edema = Low Oncotic Pressure + Increased Sodium Absorption

Why does this patient have frequent respiratory infections?

a. The function of the neutrophils is decreased.

b. IgG is lost in urine.

c. Antibodies are not made when the albumin level is low.

d. Lipids inactivate lymphocytes.

Answer b. IgG is lost in urine.

The precise etiology of infections in nephrotic syndrome is not entirely clear, but likely reflects loss of immunoglobulins in urine.

Keep BP under 130/80 mm Hg in nephrotic syndrome.

You tell the patient to increase the dose of his statin medication and to return to check his BP. Although nephrotic syndrome is not a coronary artery disease equivalent, the lower the triglycerides and LDL are, the better it will be for his nutritional status.

Orders:
• *Urine protein-to-creatinine ratio*
• *Nephrology evaluation*
• *Nutrition evaluation*
• *Low sodium diet*
• *ACE inhibitors*

Urine protein-to-creatinine ratio = 24-hour urine collection
• Ratio of 3:1 = 3 g/24 h excreted
• Ratio of 5:1 = 5 g/24 h excreted

Which of these medications should you ask the patient about having used?

a. Nonsteroidal antiinflammatory drugs (NSAIDs)

b. Lamotrigine

c. Proton pump inhibitors

d. Quinolone

Answer a. Nonsteroidal antiinflammatory drugs (NSAIDs)

NSAIDs have a clear association with the development of membranous glomerulonephritis and nephrotic syndrome. The other medications listed cause allergic interstitial nephritis, not nephrotic syndrome.

Cancer, especially lymphoma, causes nephrotic syndrome.

The patient comes back in 2 weeks. The swelling is worse in one leg than the other. Lower extremity Doppler ultrasound shows a deep venous thrombosis (DVT). The patient is started on enoxaparin and warfarin. His urine protein-to-creatinine ratio is 7:1.

Urine Protein-to-Creatinine Ratio >3.5 = Nephrotic Syndrome
>3.5 g of protein/24 h = Nephrotic Syndrome

Renal function varies with posture.
Matching protein with creatinine corrects for the alteration in renal function during the day.

What is the mechanism of DVT in nephrotic syndrome?

a. Urine loss of clotting factors (II, VII, IX, X).

b. Overproduction of clotting factors.

c. Urine loss of protein C, S, and antithrombin.

d. Low albumin level leading to stasis.

Answer c. Urine loss of protein C, S, and antithrombin.

Together with all the protein lost as albumin is also the loss of natural anticoagulants. Nephrotic syndrome is a hypercoagulable state. Protein C, protein S, and antithrombin are lost in the same way that albumin is lost. In addition, there is iron, zinc, and copper deficiency because the carrier proteins for these metals are lost as well.

Carrier protein loss leads to deficiency of
• Iron (transferrin)
• Copper (ceruloplasmin)
• Zinc

The patient declines a kidney biopsy that you order. The note says, "Patient declines biopsy because he does not understand what difference it will make in therapy."

Orders:
- *Antinuclear antibody (ANA), hepatitis B and C serology*
- *human immunodeficiency virus (HIV)*
- *Antineutrophil cytoplasmic autoantibody (ANCA)*
- *Cryoglobulins*

Chronic hepatitis causes vasculitis that can involve the kidney.

Hepatitis C causes cryoglobulins.
Treat with interferon, ribavirin, and either telaprevir or boceprevir.
(Three drugs for hepatitis C)

In 2 weeks, the patient's edema has only worsened. All the results of the tests ordered are normal. He agrees to kidney biopsy.

The loss of high density lipoproteins in the urine signals very low density lipoprotein (VLDL) and chylomicrons to increase lipid levels. Lipoprotein signals prompt the clearance of lipids from blood. Without lipoproteins, lipids build up.

The renal biopsy shows membranous glomerulonephropathy. The patient is placed on prednisone orally and returns every month, but after 3 months there is no improvement in urine protein excretion or serum albumin levels.

What should you add to therapy?

a. Add cyclophosphamide.
b. Add cyclosporine.
c. Add rituximab.

d. Add tacrolimus.
e. All are viable options.

Answer e. All are viable options.

It is not precisely clear as to which therapy to use. Although cyclophosphamide has been used for a long time, there is also significant risk of adverse effects.

> Mechanism of Action
> • Cyclosporine: calcineurin inhibition inactivating T cells
> • Tacrolimus: calcineurin inhibition
> • Rituximab: anti-CD20 antibody

Over the next several months, the nephrotic syndrome improves. It is not possible to give a definite answer as to which of these therapies is better than the other. All have fairly good efficacy. Many cases of nephrotic syndrome spontaneously resolve over time. ACE inhibitors and lipid-lowering therapy should be continued until that happens.

CASE 5: End-Stage Renal Failure and Dialysis

Setting: *office*

CC: *"My kidneys are failing, do I need dialysis?"*

VS: *BP: 152/92 mm Hg; P: 64 beats/minute; T: 98°F; R: 22 breaths/minute*

HPI: *A 67-year-old man with a history of hypertension and diabetes who has had renal insufficiency for several years now comes to the office for evaluation of his kidneys. The patient is obese and has had difficulty controlling both his diabetes and high BP. He is adherent to diet and tries to exercise.*

PMHx:
- *Hypertension for 12 years*
- *Diabetes for 8 years*
- *Tobacco in the past; quit 15 years ago*

Medications:
- *Lisinopril*
- *Nifedipine*
- *Sitagliptin*
- *Glyburide*

PE:
- *General: tired, but comfortable*
- *Extremities: edema present*
- *Chest: basilar rales bilaterally*
- *Cardiovascular: S₄ gallop; no murmurs*

Initial Orders:
- *CHEM-7*
- *UA*
- *Complete blood count (CBC)*

Which is *not* an indication for dialysis?

a. Fatigue
b. Hyperkalemia
c. Fluid overload

d. Encephalopathy
e. Metabolic acidosis
f. Pericarditis

Answer a. Fatigue

Everyone is fatigued or tired. This is too nonspecific a finding. All the others, potassium, fluid, pericarditis, acidosis, and encephalopathy are definitely indications for immediate dialysis. Despite control of BP and diabetes, many people have worsening renal dysfunction that will need dialysis. Your job is to detect who is having worsening creatinine clearance (<30 mL/minute) and will need dialysis before their condition gets bad enough to have metabolic acidosis and these other findings.

As usual, the patient returns in 1 to 2 weeks for evaluation of his laboratory test results.

Reports:

- CHEM-7: BUN 48 g/dL; creatinine 4 mg/dL; potassium 4.9 mEq/L; bicarbonate 19 mEq/L
- UA: protein 2+
- CBC: hematocrit 32%; mean corpuscular volume (MCV) 85 fL

Renal failure decreases erythropoietin level, resulting in anemia (Figure 6-3).

Orders:

- *Vascular access placement (arteriovenous [AV] graft)*
- *Phosphate level*
- *Calcium level*
- *Nephrology evaluation*

Acid production: 1 mEq/kg per day
There is no other way to excrete it than through the kidneys.

What is the most common cause of death with ESRD over time, even on dialysis?

a. Infection
b. Coronary disease

c. Sodium disorder

Answer b. Coronary disease

Renal insufficiency greatly accelerates the process of atherosclerosis.

> *The patient is seen by a vascular surgeon to place an AV graft. The patient is tired, but otherwise not significantly different than usual.*
>
> **Reports:**
> • *Calcium level low*
> • *Phosphate level high*

The calcium level is low from decreased levels of 1,25 dihydroxyvitamin D. Replace calcium and vitamin D in renal failure.

Hyperparathyroidism from low calcium levels damages bone.

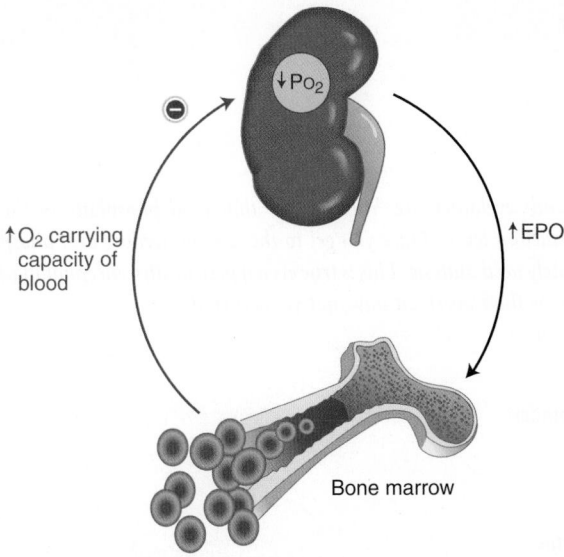

Figure 6-3. Regulation of red blood cell production by erythropoietin. If the ability of blood to carry oxygen decreases because of a fall in numbers of red blood cells (e.g., normal cell death, pathological destruction of red blood cells, bleeding, etc.), the kidney senses lower partial pressure of oxygen (PO_2) levels and increases the levels of erythropoietin (EPO). EPO then signals the bone marrow to increase production of red blood cells. (Reproduced with permission from Kibble JD, Halsey CR: *The Big Picture: Medical Physiology,* 1st ed. New York: McGraw-Hill; 2009.)

Orders:
- *Oral vitamin D and calcium carbonate replacement*
- *CBC*
- *CHEM-7*

Move the clock forward 4 to 6 weeks. It takes this long to place an AV fistula and to allow it time to epithelialize and "mature" enough to be usable for dialysis.

In ESRD, always get a chemistry level every time you see a patient. Nephrology is a laboratory specialty. There is no significant physical finding to follow.

Report:
- *Chemistry: BUN 54 g/dL; creatinine 4.5 mg/dL*
- *CBC: hematocrit 29%*
- *Phosphate: elevated*

Phosphate-lowering medications bind phosphate in the bowel:
- Calcium carbonate
- Lanthanum
- Sevelamer

Lanthanum and sevelamer are "rare earths" that bind phosphate in the bowel without affecting calcium levels. Once you get to the level of needing oral phosphate binders, patients definitely need dialysis. This is true even if pericarditis, encephalopathy, dangerous hyperkalemia, or fluid overload have not yet occurred. Do not wait for these dangerous developments on CCS.

Orders:
- *Phosphate binders*
- *Calcium*
- *Vitamin D*
- *Dialysis*
- *Erythropoietin*

The only anemia of chronic disease treated with dialysis is ESRD.

After 6 weeks, the graft of the AV fistula should be sufficiently mature to allow vascular access. You should expect every patient on dialysis to be on:
- *Calcium replacement*
- *Vitamin D*
- *Oral phosphate binder (calcium carbonate, sevelamer, lanthanum)*
- *Erythropoietin*
- *BP and lipid control*

This treatment should continue permanently.

CASE 6: Syndrome of Inappropriate Secretion of Antidiuretic Hormone

Setting: *ED*

CC: *"My husband has been really confused."*

VS: *BP:112/76 mm Hg; P: 98 beats/minute; T: 99°F; R: 22 breaths/minute*

HPI: *A 58-year-old man with lung cancer diagnosed several weeks ago is admitted to the ED. He has been undergoing a staging evaluation and has not started therapy. He is brought in by his wife because he has been increasingly confused over the past 2 days.*

PMHx:
- *Tobacco smoking for 30 years, quit 5 years ago*
- *Hypertension*

Medications:
- *Amlodipine*

If CCS describes "Acute mental status changes of unclear etiology," order naloxone, dextrose, and thiamine first. Acute confusion, like hypotension and dyspnea, is a reason to initiate therapy before PE.

PE:
- *General: visibly agitated and confused*
- *Neurological: lethargic, confused, only able to state his name; examination incomplete secondary to inability to follow commands*
- *Cardiovascular: normal*
- *Abdomen: normal*

Initial Orders:
- *CHEM-20*
- *Oximeter*
- *Calcium*
- *Head CT*

Which of these will *not* cause confusion?

a. Hyponatremia

b. Hypernatremia

c. Hyperkalemia

d. Hypercalcemia

e. Hypoxia

Answer c. Hyperkalemia

Potassium disorders do not cause altered mental status. Potassium disorders lead to cardiac conduction abnormalities by altering the resting membrane potential. Altered mental status and confusion are caused by:

• Any sodium or glucose disorder

• High calcium

• Hypoxia

• Anatomic abnormalities of the brain

• Intoxication

• Liver or renal failure

These are also the same things that cause seizures.

The worst form of confusion is a seizure!

Resting membrane potential is strongly based on ungated potassium channels.

If a patient can speak, but does not know his name, it is a psychiatric problem.

Advance the case the smallest amount of time to get the first test results. On CCS, you do not have to do anything to get the reports of tests as long as you advance the clock. There is no difference between the "On" and "In" types of time advance. If it is 9 a.m., it is the same to say advance "IN 15 minutes" or "ON 9:15 a.m."

Report:

• *CHEM-20: sodium 112 mEq/L; BUN 8 g/dL; creatinine 0.7 mg/dL*

• *Oximeter: 97% on room air*

• *Calcium: 9.2 mg/dL (normal)*

• *Head CT: no metastases*

Sodium kills with seizures.

Volume status is the key to diagnosing sodium disorders.
• High volume: CHF, cirrhotic, nephrotic
• Low volume: diuretics, Addison disease
• Normal: syndrome of inappropriate secretion of antidiuretic hormone (SIADH), pseudohyponatremia, psychogenic polydipsia

Depolarization is based on the rapid influx of sodium.

PE:
• *Extremities: no edema, no dehydration*
• *Neurological: lethargic, stuporous*

You will never lose points on CCS by examining a patient too much.

Orders:
• *3% hypertonic saline*
• *Conivaptan IV*
• *Repeat chemistry*
• *Urine sodium, urine osmolarity*
• *Uric acid level*
• *Transfer patient to ICU*

With hyponatremia, a *healthy* person would make:
• Maximally dilute urine (lowest possible osmolarity)
• Minimum urine sodium (<10 mEq/L)

Laboratory tests are always done first (before other procedures) on CCS. If a test (urine sodium) and a treatment (hypertonic saline) are ordered simultaneously, the test is always done first.

Low sodium level alters the depolarization of neural tissue.

What is the mechanism of conivaptan?

a. It resets the hypothalamic osmostat.

b. It is a V1-receptor antagonist.

c. It is a V2-receptor antagonist.

d. It is a V2-receptor stimulant.

e. It inhibits the posterior pituitary release of antidiuretic hormone (ADH).

Answer c. It is a V2-receptor antagonist.

Conivaptan and tolvaptan are peripheral V2-receptor antagonists. They inhibit the effect of ADH on the collecting duct. They inhibit permeability of the collecting duct so it cannot reabsorb water.

Normal minimum urine osmolarity: 50 mOsm

The distal convoluted tubule (DCT) is the site of the minimum osmolarity of urine.

Move the clock forward 30 to 60 minutes and reexamine the neurologic system and recheck the sodium level.

Report:
- *Urine sodium 64 mEq/L (high)*
- *Urine osmolarity 480 mOsm/kg*

Orders:
- *CHEM-7*

Each aquaporin passes 1,000,000 water molecules/second reabsorbing back into the body.

Conivaptan prevents placement of aquaporins in the collecting duct.

Advance the clock 1 to 2 hours at a time for the first 12 hours in severe hyponatremia. Severity in hyponatremia is based on the symptoms, not the number.

Severe Hyponatremia = Seizures, Coma, or Profound Confusion

Report:
- *Sodium 114 mEq/L after 2 hours of treatment*
- *Uric acid level low (diluted by excess free water)*

Increase sodium level by 6 to 12 points over 12 hours in patients with severe hyponatremia.

The sodium content of NS is 154 mEq/L, while this patient has a sodium level of 112 or 114 mEq/L. What will be the effect of giving NS to this person?

a. Too rapid an increase in serum sodium

b. Too slow an increase in serum sodium

c. No effect

d. Decrease in serum sodium

Answer d. Decrease in serum sodium

NS drops serum sodium levels in SIADH. This is one of the hardest things to understand about the disorder. It has to do with osmolarity. The osmolarity of NS is less than the patient's urine. NS osmolarity is 308 mOsm/kg (Na 154 mOsm/kg + chloride [Cl] 154 mOsm/kg). The urine osmolarity of this patient is 480 mOsm/kg. This means that NS is actually more dilute than the patient's urine. Although the sodium level of NS is greater than that in the patient's serum, the patient's urine is more dilute. Each liter of NS will give net free water compared with the patient's urine, and the serum sodium level will drop.

If you give a diuretic such as furosemide with the NS, you will improve the patient's serum sodium level. This is because loop diuretics will decrease the urine osmolarity.

Never give NS alone in SIADH! It makes it worse!

Furosemide drops urine osmolarity so net free water is lost.

After 4 hours, the serum sodium level rises to 117 mEq/L. Symptoms start to improve and the patient is less confused.

What happens when the sodium level is brought up too rapidly?

a. Monocular blindness

b. Central pontine demyelinization

c. Cerebral edema

d. Transverse myelitis

Answer b. Central pontine demyelinization

Remember to keep the rate of the rise of the sodium level slow. If a low sodium level is brought up too fast, there is central pontine myelinolysis, or osmotic demyelinization syndrome. This syndrome is delayed several days after the correction of the sodium. It looks like a brainstem stroke with dysarthria, dysphagia, diplopia, and mental status changes.

> *Increase the sodium 12 to 18 points over the first 24 to 48 hours. Once sodium is on the rise, there is no benefit to elevating it rapidly. For the long term, this patient has an uncorrectable cause of SIADH with his lung cancer. The patient will need either demeclocycline or tolvaptan to prevent a recurrence of symptomatic hyponatremia.*

Demeclocycline and tolvaptan
• Inhibit ADH effect on the collecting duct

CASE 7: Hypernatremia (Central Diabetes Insipidus)

Setting: *hospital ward*

CC: *"I feel tired and confused."*

VS: *BP:102/72 mm Hg; P: 104 beats/minute; R: 23 breaths/minute*

HPI: *A 27-year-old man came to the ED yesterday after head trauma and loss of consciousness from a motorcycle accident. The initial head CT was normal. He was visibly intoxicated from alcohol and it was unsafe to discharge him without reliable observation. After a few hours, he improved, but now he is confused again.*

PMHx/Medications: *none*

PE:
• *Neurological: lethargic, confused, and unable to name the date, the president, or the place where he is right now; focal neurological signs cannot be assessed because of patient confusion*
• *Heart, Lungs, Abdomen: normal*

Except for reflexes, the neurological examination is based on the ability of the patient to follow commands.

You cannot assess papilledema with a confused person. The head needs to be still.

Initial Orders:
- *Head CT*
- *CHEM-7*
- *Oximeter*
- *Liver function*
- *Urine toxicology screen*

Delirium tremens cannot start on the same day as the last drink.

Alcohol withdrawal is based on the stiffening of cell membrane, which is missing the "relaxing" effect of alcohol.

Report:
- *Head CT: no bleeding*
- *CHEM-7: sodium 165 mEq/L (normal 135–145 mEq/L); BUN 45 g/dL; creatinine 1.8 mg/dL*
- *Oximeter: normal*
- *Liver function: normal*
- *Urine toxicology screen: no opiates; cocaine and marijuana present*

Which of the following is most likely to kill a person who is in withdrawal?

a. Marijuana

b. Alcohol

c. Cocaine

d. Opiates

Answer b. Alcohol

Alcohol can kill a person who is intoxicated or in withdrawal with neurological toxicity. No one has ever died from marijuana intoxication or withdrawal. Marijuana is damaging to short-term memory. This is reversible after abstention for 1 month. This patient is confused because of dehydration.

> Dehydration
> • High sodium level
> • High BUN-to-creatinine ratio >20:1

> *Order dextrose 5% in water (D5W) as soon as you know that the patient has dehydration. NS will help as well, but because there seems to be a free water deficit, then give free water. The intake and output on the patient has not been recorded. There is no way to assess how much urine he has been putting out over the past day.*
>
> **Orders:**
> • *Bolus D5W and continuous*
> • *Repeat CHEM-7*
> • *UA*
> • *Urine sodium and urine osmolarity*
> • *Monitor input and output*

> D5W acts as free water replacement.

> One hundred percent free water would cause hemolysis.
> Dextrose prevents hemolysis.

What happens to the dextrose in D5W?

a. It enters the RBC.

b. It is metabolized.

c. Nothing, it stays in circulation in plasma.

d. It is converted into protein.

Answer b. It is metabolized.

D5W is, essentially, pure free water replacement. You cannot give water alone as IV fluids because it would lead to hemolysis in the veins through which it was being infused. The point of the dextrose is to keep the fluid from being so hypotonic or hyposmolar that cells would swell and burst. The pancreas senses the dextrose as sugar. Insulin will put the excess sugar into storage as glycogen or triglycerides (adipose), or the dextrose will simply be consumed as fuel for cells. No matter the metabolic pathway, to storage or consumption, the dextrose goes away, and only the water is left in the body.

Hypernatremia and Dehydration
· High Urine Output = Diabetes Insipidus
· Low Urine Output = Dehydration

Advance the clock 1 hour, then a second hour, and assess the urine output and urine laboratory test values. Nurses report two urinations over the next 2 hours with 400 mL in each one. Normal urine output is 0.5 to 1 mL/kg per hour so this is voluminous, especially considering hypernatremia.

Reports:
· *Sodium: 167 mEq/L*
· *UA: no white blood cells (WBCs); specific gravity 1.002*
· *Urine sodium: 12 mEq/L*
· *Urine osmolarity: 80 mOsm/kg*

Normally, where is the point of maximum osmolarity of the kidney?

a. Glomerular capsule
b. The tip of the loop of Henle
c. The TAL of the loop of Henle
d. DCT

Answer b. The tip of the loop of Henle

Maximum osmolarity should be 1200 mOsm/kg and should be at the tip of the loop of Henle. The ability of any species to survive in hostile environments facing dehydration is based on how high the osmolarity can be made at the tip of the loop of Henle.

Minimum concentration: distal tubule

Orders:
· *D5W bolus and continuous*
· *Desmopressin acetate (DDAVP) IV*

DDAVP can be given IV, by nasal spray, or subcutaneously.

On CCS, if you order a test and a treatment at the same time, the test is done first. So to see the effect of the DDAVP, you have to move the clock forward and repeat the testing. If you order both the urine osmolarity and the vasopressin at the same time, it will not reflect the effect of the drug. CCS does not have delays in the administration of drugs or obtaining tests and results as you would in real life.

Advance the clock 30 minutes. This should be enough time to see an effect of the DDAVP on the urine osmolarity, sodium, and volume. If the patient is severely confused, transfer the patient to the ICU.

After vasopressin administration, which values are consistent with central diabetes insipidus (CDI)?

	Urine Osm (mOsm/kg)	Urine Na (mEq/L)	Volume
a.	850	10	High
b.	700	60	Low
c.	120	12	High

Na, sodium; Osm, osmolarity.

Answer b. Urine osmolarity 700 mOsm/kg (rises), urine sodium 60 mEq/L (rises), urine volume drops.

CDI will normalize in response to vasopressin administration, nephrogenic diabetes insipidus (NDI) will not. You do not have to see a maximal increase in urine osmolarity (1200 mOsm/kg) in response to vasopressin. You just have to see a significant rise in urine osmolarity and a drop in urine volume. Patients with diabetes insipidus (DI) urinate so much that a decrease in volume in response to vasopressin should be obvious within 1 to 2 hours.

Nephrogenic DI results from hypercalcemia and hypokalemia.

Orders:
- *Urine sodium*
- *Urine osmolarity*
- *CHEM-7*

Do frequent neurological examinations on patients with severe DI. Rapid increases in serum sodium levels can lead to markedly worsening mental status and seizures.

Report:
- *Urine sodium: 48 mEq/L*
- *Urine osmolarity: 550 mOsm/kg*
- *CHEM-7: sodium 165 mEq/L*

What mechanism is responsible for the development of DI in this patient?

a. Alcohol effect on the kidney
b. Trauma to the hypothalamus
c. Undiagnosed electrolyte disturbance
d. Damage to the stalk of the pituitary gland

Answer d. Damage to the stalk of the pituitary gland

Head trauma most often produces a temporary CDI from damage to the pituitary stalk. When the stalk alone is damaged, the hypothalamus is still producing ADH. To have permanent CDI, there has to be loss of both storage of ADH in the posterior pituitary as well as the production of ADH. Electrolyte (calcium, potassium) disturbance and alcohol cause nephrogenic DI, not central DI.

How much fluid is missing or needs to be replaced in this patient?

a. Two liters
b. Five liters
c. Cannot be determined with present information

Answer c. Cannot be determined with present information

You must have the patient's weight to know. You must calculate the fluid deficit to know how much water to give. You cannot determine how much fluid is missing without the body weight.
- Men: 60% is water weight
- Women: 50% is water weight

This patient's sodium is 165 mEq/L, which is 25 points above the normal value of 140 mEq/L. There is about 20% of fluid missing (18% to be absolutely precise). (A man weighing 100 kg will have 60 L of water. Sixty percent of 100 kg is 60 L, and 20% of that is 12 L.) This person's fluid deficit is 10 to 12 L, but you cannot determine that without knowing the body weight.

Move the clock forward; hydration (D5W) and vasopressin continue to be given.
Repeat CHEM-7: sodium 154 mEq/L

> Do not lower the sodium more than 0.5 to 1 mEq/h or the patient will seize.

Why do seizures develop with a rapid decrease in sodium level?

a. Hemolysis
b. Cerebral edema

c. Myelinolysis
d. Renal failure

Answer b. Cerebral edema

When the plasma osmolarity is rapidly decreased, the cells of the brain are relatively hypertonic, or hyperosmolar compared to plasma. This will result in brain edema and seizures. All sodium level changes (up or down) must occur slowly.

> A high sodium level in brain cells results in osmotic draw into cells, causing edema.

> *Correct the sodium level over 2 to 3 days. When the neurological examination normalizes, the patient can be transferred out of the ICU. You cannot tell if the CDI will be permanent until you observe the patient over time.*

CASE 8: Hyperkalemia (Tumor Lysis Syndrome)

Setting: *hospital ward*

CC: *"I feel weak since my chemotherapy."*

VS: *BP: 112/72 mm Hg; P: 88 beats/minute; T: 100.2°F; R: 16 breaths/minute*

HPI: *A 32-year-old woman admitted for combination chemotherapy for non-Hodgkin lymphoma (NHL) is in the hospital the night after the administration of the medications. She had IV fluids started the morning of the chemotherapy. She received cyclophosphamide, doxorubicin (Adriamycin), vincristine, and prednisone. She is now feeling severe muscle weakness.*

PMHx: *stage IV lymphoma with widespread disease including bone marrow*

Medications:

- *IV NS*
- *Allopurinol*

Allopurinol
- Inhibits xanthine oxidase
- Inhibits production of uric acid

PE:
- *General: weak and tired*
- *Neurological: normal, no focal deficits*
- *Musculoskeletal: decreased motor strength in all four extremities*

Allopurinol is a hypoxanthine analog.

Initial Orders:
- *CHEM-20*
- *UA*
- *Uric acid level*
- *IV saline*
- *Continue allopurinol*
- *ECG*
- *Phosphate and magnesium levels*

Hydration and allopurinol are standard before chemotherapy to prevent tumor lysis syndrome.

Move the case forward the shortest amount of time to get the potassium level. The single most important thing is to exclude a dangerous level of hyperkalemia and cardiac toxicity from it.

Report:
- *Potassium 6.8 mEq/dL*
- *UA: normal*
- *Uric acid level: elevated*
- *ECG: widening of QRS, flat T wave*
- *Phosphate: elevated*

Hyperkalemia + ECG Changes = Calcium Chloride (or Gluconate) IV

- Calcium protects the heart from hyperkalemia.
- Calcium raises the threshold at which depolarization occurs.

What is the mechanism of a high phosphate level?

a. Muscle breakdown

b. Release from lymphocytes

c. Binding with potassium

d. Renal failure

Answer a. Muscle breakdown

Phosphate is released from intracellular storage. There is no direct effect of potassium on phosphate. Although renal failure is associated with high phosphate level from the inability to excrete it, this could not happen in just 1 day. Even if uric acid were to cause renal failure, it would not become evident on the same day.

- If the patient is allergic to allopurinol, use febuxostat.
- Febuxostat is a xanthine oxidase inhibitor.

Immediately after the hyperkalemia and ECG abnormalities are discovered, the patient is given calcium chloride, glucose, and insulin. Move the clock forward and recheck the potassium level. The potassium level should start to improve within 30 minutes.

Insulin stimulates Na^+/K^+-ATPase to drive potassium into cells.

How does hyperkalemia cause muscle weakness?

a. It inhibits acetylcholine release at the neuromuscular junction.

b. It prevents repolarization.

c. It interferes with the actin-myosin interaction.

d. It blocks calcium release from SERCA.

Answer b. It prevents repolarization.

Repolarization is based on potassium being extruded from cells to lower the cell to a negative polarity. In other words, the positively charged potassium ion (K^+) has to leave the cell so that it can go back to its resting membrane potential, which is −70 to −90. If the blood level of potassium is markedly increased, the potassium cannot leave the cell. In fact, potassium can go backwards into the cell through the ungated potassium channels.

Increased Blood K = K Cannot Leave Cells
K Cannot Leave Cells = No Repolarization
No Repolarization = No Depolarization
All This = Muscle Becomes Weak and Patient Dies of Arrhythmia

Several hours later, the potassium level has been normalized and the muscle weakness has resolved. Repeat chemistry shows the creatinine level rises from 0.8 to 1.5 mg/dL. Uric acid is still up. Six hours later, despite fluids and allopurinol, the creatinine goes to 1.7 mg/dL.

What is the mechanism of uric acid's damaging effect on the kidney?

a. Tubular damage
b. Vasoconstriction of afferent arteriole
c. Interference with TAL $Na^+/K^+/2Cl^-$ pumps

d. Vasa recta toxicity
e. Glomerular damage

Answer a. Tubular damage

Uric acid causes acute tubular necrosis. Uric acid and oxalic acid are two forms of crystals that both damage the kidney. You can see the crystals on a urinalysis. You must lose more than 50% of renal function before the creatinine will even begin to rise. When allopurinol damages the kidney, it is from allergic interstitial nephritis.

Diagnosing Etiology of Renal Failure
• Allopurinol: Hansel stain for eosinophils
• Uric acid: urine crystals

Report:
• *UA: no WBCs, uric acid crystals seen*
• *Hansel stain (urine eosinophils): negative*

As hydration and allopurinol have not been able to control the uric acid–induced renal failure, you add rasburicase. The following day, the uric acid level normalizes. BUN and creatinine levels come back down to normal 2 days later. Allopurinol and febuxostat do not decrease uric acid levels once it is formed. They only prevent formation.

Rasburicase dissolves uric acid into allantoin.
Allantoin benignly goes out through the kidneys.

Rasburicase "melts" uric acid. It is a uricase!
Increasing urate oxidase!

Case Summary:
Tumor lysis syndrome is a known entity after chemotherapy, particularly for lymphoma. Prevention with hydration and either rasburicase or allopurinol is standard. Rasburicase may be better than allopurinol and that is the lesson learned from this case. Elevations in potassium, phosphate, and uric acid levels are well known. There is no clear benefit of routine urinary alkalinization.

CASE 9: Renal Tubular Acidosis

Setting: *hospital ward*

CC: *"My head hurts and the light hurts my eyes."*

VS: *BP:152/92 mm Hg; P: 98 beats/minute; T: 102°F; R:18 breaths/minute*

HPI: *A 45-year-old man with acquired immunodeficiency syndrome (AIDS) is admitted to the hospital for fever, headache, and stiff neck. The head CT was done by the ED physician and was negative. Symptoms have been going on for 5 to 10 days. He is not adherent to his antiretroviral therapy. His CD4 count is "around 50 [cells/mm³]," but he has not seen a doctor for months.*

CT before lumbar puncture (LP):
• Focal findings
• Papilledema
• Severe confusion
• Possibly in immunocompromised persons

PMHx:
- *AIDS*
- *Oral thrush*
- *Herpes simplex*

Medications: *nonadherent*

PE:
- *General: uncomfortable, lying face down on stretcher*
- *HEENT: photophobia and nuchal rigidity are present; fully alert; no focal findings detected*

Initial Orders:
- *LP*
- *Serum cryptococcal antigen*
- *CD4 level*
- *Genotyping*

Genotype = HIV viral sensitivity testing

Advance the clock just enough to get the results of the LP. **Although the most common cause of meningitis is** Cryptococcus, **you want to get the LP to quickly exclude bacterial meningitis.**

What is the fastest way to tell the difference between bacterial and fungal meningitis?
- Cell count
- Thousands of Polymorphonuclear Leukocytes (PMNLs) = Bacterial Meningitis
- Ten to Hundreds of Lymphocytes = Fungal, Viral, Rickettsia

Report:
- *Cerebrospinal fluid (CSF): 117 × 10⁹/L WBCs, 94% lymphocytes*
- *Opening pressure elevated*
- *Gram stain negative*
- *Protein elevated*

Although this elevation of lymphocytes does not prove a patient has Cryptococcus, in the context of HIV, treatment for Cryptococcus is best. Do not wait for the results of cryptococcal antigen level.

The India ink capsule stain is 60% sensitive and an antiquated test. Use the cryptococcal antigen test.

The India ink capsule stain uses the large, sugary glycocalyx around *Cryptococcus* to repel the ink.

What is the best initial therapy for *Cryptococcus*?

a. Caspofungin   **c.** Amphotericin
b. Fluconazole   **d.** Itraconazole

Answer c. Amphotericin

Amphotericin, often combined with 5-flucytosine (5-FC) is the best therapy for *Cryptococcus*. Caspofungin does not cover *Cryptococcus*. Fluconazole does not have as much efficacy and benefit in mortality as amphotericin.

Caspofungin inhibits 1,3-glucan linkage in the fungal cell wall. *Cryptococcus* does not have this bond.

Amphotericin inhibits ergosterol in the fungal cell wall.

Amphotericin is started. The cryptococcal antigen comes back the next day markedly elevated. CD4 is 18 cells/mm³ and the genotype shows a fully sensitive virus. Antiretroviral drugs are started. After 5 days on amphotericin, the chemistry test results are:
- *Potassium 3.0 mEq/L (low)*
- *Creatinine 2.1 mg/dL*
- *Serum bicarbonate 18 mEq/L (normal 22–26 mEq/L)*
- *Sodium 140 mEq/L*
- *Chloride 112 mEq/L (elevated)*

What causes this change in laboratory results?

a. Sepsis

b. Lactic acidosis

c. Amphotericin effect on the distal tubule

d. 5-Flucytosine toxicity

Answer c. Amphotericin effect on the distal tubule

Amphotericin use has a clear association with distal renal tubular acidosis (RTA). The anion gap is normal (Na$^+$ 140 mEq/L) − (Cl$^-$ 112 mEq/L + HCO^{3-} 18 mEq/L) = 10 mEq/L.

Sepsis and lactic acid give an elevated anion gap metabolic acidosis. The two most common causes of normal anion gap metabolic acidosis are diarrhea and RTA.

> RTA and Diarrhea
> · High chloride level
> · Normal anion gap

Which test can be used to distinguish diarrhea and RTA as the cause of normal anion gap metabolic acidosis?

a. Serum bicarbonate level

b. Sodium level

c. Urine anion gap (UAG)

d. Response to antibiotics

Answer c. Urine anion gap (UAG)

$$UAG = Na^+ - Cl^-$$

Na$^+$ > Cl$^-$ = Positive UAG = RTA

Na$^+$ < Cl$^-$ = Negative UAG = Diarrhea

UAG is based on the kidney excreting acid or hydrogen ion (H$^+$) bound to ammonium chloride or NH$_4$Cl$^-$. In diarrhea, this mechanism works, because the kidney works. In RTA, the kidney does not work, so it cannot excrete acid.

> The urine anion gap is the hardest thing to understand in nephrology.

Report:
· *Urine sodium level is greater than urine chloride level*
· *Repeat potassium: 3.0 mEq/L*

Distal RTA on amphotericin is an expected event.
Everyone gets it after a few days.

Amphotericin inhibits the ability of the distal tubule to excrete acid.

Which of the following should be found with amphotericin?

	Urine pH	Response to Giving HCO$_3$	Serum K	Stones
a.	<5.5	Urine pH rises	Low	No
b.	>5.5	Urine pH same	Low	Yes
c.	>5.5	Urine pH same	High	No

HCO$_3$, bicarbonate; K, potassium

Answer b. Urine pH is high (>5.5), serum K is low, and stones can form.

Distal RTA is a defect in the ability of the kidney to excrete acid. This makes the urine pH alkalotic (Figure 6-4). In an alkalotic (pH > 5.5) urine, stones are more likely to form. In most types of distal RTA, you can treat with bicarbonate because the proximal tubule is where the bicarbonate is absorbed and it still works. This is why distal RTA can be treated with bicarbonate if you cannot reverse the cause.

In proximal RTA (choice a) the urine pH rises when bicarbonate is administered because the kidney is not able to absorb it. This is why proximal RTA cannot be fully treated with just giving bicarbonate. The patient will not be able to absorb it. Because the urine ends up being acidotic (pH < 5.5) after all the bicarbonate runs out of the body, stones are not formed. Stones more often form in a higher urine pH.

Replace potassium. Everyone on amphotericin for more than a few days develops a reversible distal RTA and will need potassium replacement. After 7 to 10 days, you can safely switch the amphotericin to oral fluconazole, and the RTA and increased creatinine should all spontaneously resolve.

Distal RTA of amphotericin is self-limited after stopping it.

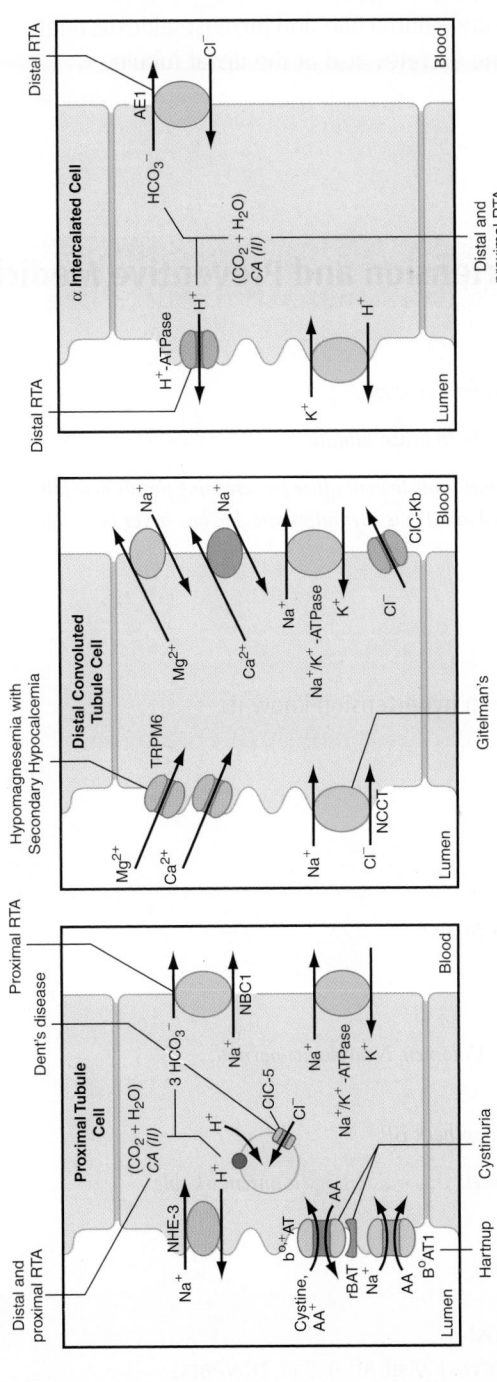

Figure 6-4. Schematic representation of channels, transporters, and enzymes associated with hereditary renal tubular disorders. AA, amino acids; AE1, anion exchanger 1; AT1, amino acid transporter; CA (II), carbonic anhydrase II; CLC-5, chloride channel 5; CLC-Kb, chloride channel Kb; NCCT, thiazide-sensitive Na-Cl co-transporter; rBAT, renal basic amino acid transport glycoprotein; RTA, renal tubular acidosis; TRPM6, transient receptor potential cation channel, subfamily M, member 6. (Reproduced with permission from Longo DL, et al. *Harrison's Principles of Internal Medicine,* 18th ed., Vol. 2. New York: McGraw-Hill; 2012.)

- Proximal RTA is treated with diuretics.
- Diuretics induce volume contraction and increase aldosterone.
- Increased aldosterone excretes acid at the distal tubule.

CASE 10: Hypertension and Preventive Medicine

Setting: *office*

CC: *"I'm here for screening for a new job."*

VS: *BP:148/94 mm Hg; P: 78 beats/minute*

HPI: *A 49-year-old man has come to your office for screening for his new job. He has some forms that need to be filled out. He is asymptomatic. He has never been told he had high BP before.*

Only half of people with hypertension know it.

PMHx:
- *Appendectomy 2 years ago*
- *Hernia repair 10 years ago*

Medications: *none*

PE:
- *HEENT, Heart, Lungs, Abdomen, Neurologic: normal*

Initial Orders:
- *Return in 1 to 2 weeks to recheck BP*

The patient returns in 1 week. Interval History is unremarkable.

Preventive medications!
Check patients' BP at *every* visit after age 18 years!

Orders:
- *Vital signs*
- *Cholesterol, LDL*
- *Influenza vaccination (if office visit occurs in the fall or winter)*

Influenza vaccination should be given to every adult yearly.

Only half of people who *know* they have hypertension have well-controlled BP!

On CCS, is it hard to remember to do preventive medicine on all patients? It is easy for BP, lipid, and cancer screening to be lost in the "drama" of the acute problem, but you must do it.

Report:
- *VS: BP 148/92 mm Hg; P: 72 beats/minute*

Twenty to thirty percent of mild elevations in BP are artifactual (not real). Repeat three to six times if the patient has no symptoms.

Cardiac Output × Peripheral Resistance = Blood Pressure

The amount of time between return visits in hypertension evaluation is not precise. You are safe at having the patient come back in 1 to 2 weeks.

Report:
- *BP 146/94 mm Hg*
- *Cholesterol and LDL: normal*

Besides screening for hyperlipidemia, what other screening tests are routine for this person at age 49?

a. ECG
b. Colonoscopy
c. Prostate specific antigen (PSA)
d. Chest x-ray
e. None

Answer e. None

Colonoscopy starts at age 50 in a person at average risk with no family history of colon cancer. PSA testing is not recommended: It does not lower mortality and only increases the morbidity of unnecessary procedures. A screening chest x-ray is neither sensitive nor specific for anyone, including smokers.

"Screening" means testing an asymptomatic population.

Which form of secondary hypertension should you test the patient for?

a. Pheochromocytoma

b. Hyperaldosteronism (Conn syndrome)

c. Renal artery stenosis

d. None

Answer d. None

In the absence of specific symptoms, physical findings, or laboratory abnormalities, you should *not* be routinely tested for any of these.

Advise, educate, and counsel the patient on weight loss, exercise, sodium restriction, and diet. Have him return at 1 month intervals to assess compliance. Nutrition evaluation should occur for every patient with hypertension, diabetes, or hyperlipidemia. The Step 3 examination will want you to vigorously pursue lifestyle modifications and not pursue unnecessary laboratory evaluation.

For hypertension, no laboratory test is "essential" in an asymptomatic person with hypertension. Do not forget to "Educate," "Advise," and "Counsel" every patient.

Weight loss and exercise decrease BP by decreasing peripheral resistance.

Move the clock forward at 1-month intervals for 3 to 6 months to assess the efficacy of lifestyle modifications.

VS: *BP 152/95 mm Hg*

Orders:

• *Hydrochlorothiazide (HCTZ)*

HCTZ
• Blocks sodium reabsorption at the distal tubule
• Can block only 6% to 7% of sodium
• Increases calcium reabsorption

Advance the clock only 1 week after introducing new medications. This is to check for both efficacy and adverse effects.

Repeat BP: *150/92 mm Hg*

Only 60% to 70% of patients with hypertension have their BP level controlled with one BP medication.

Without sufficient control, it is not clear which BP medication should be added as a second agent.

Orders:
• *Add an ACE inhibitor, beta-blocker, or calcium channel blocker.*

Angiotensin normally
• Increases aldosterone
• Increases ADH
• Increases thirst
• Increases sodium absorption at the proximal tubule
• Vasoconstricts peripheral vessels

Move the clock forward 1 week. If a BP medication works, it will be evident in 24 to 48 hours and the dose can be increased. If there is a "compelling indication" such as another disease, for example, diabetes (ACE, angiotensin receptor blocker [ARB]), myocardial infarction (MI) (beta-blocker), or osteoporosis (HCTZ), always start with the therapy that will also benefit the other compelling indication.

Beta stimulation normally
• Increases heart rate
• Increases stroke volume
• Increases renin release

ACE Inhibitor Cough
• From bradykinin increase

You do not have to investigate secondary hypertension unless BP is uncontrolled with the use of two to three medications. Once BP is brought under 140/90 mm Hg, do not add further medications unless the patient is diabetic or has end-organ damage. In those cases, continue to add medication until the BP is <130/80 mm Hg.

Calcium Channel Blocker Adverse Effect
• Constipation
• Edema

CHAPTER **7**

PULMONARY

CASE 1: Asthma

Setting: *emergency department (ED)*

CC: *"I can't breathe."*

VS: *BP: 124/76 mm Hg; P: 112 beats/minute; T: 97°F; R: 32 breaths/minute*

HPI: *A 32-year-old man comes to the ED with 1 day of severe shortness of breath after several days of cough. He has a long history of asthma, which is usually mild. He has only been hospitalized once before several years ago. He stopped using his inhalers 2 weeks ago because he ran out of medications.*

PMHx:
• *Asthma*
• *Allergies (ragweed, pollen)*

Medications:
• *Albuterol intermittently*
• *Fluticasone inhaler*

What is the best way to tell how severe the patient's asthma exacerbation is?

a. Pulmonary function test (PFT)
b. Respiratory rate
c. Wheezing on examination
d. Prolonged expiratory phase
e. Oximeter

Answer b. Respiratory rate

If the respiratory rate is low at 10 to 14 breaths/minute, it does not matter how much the patient says he feels short of breath or if there is wheezing. You can have wheezing but not be in severe distress. You can have extremely severe asthma, and wheezing can stop when all air movement stops. An oximeter can show a normal saturation or one that is >90% to 92% with very severe asthma. A person can be markedly hyperventilating to maintain a normal partial pressure of oxygen (PO_2) and oxygen saturation.

Respiratory rate is the fastest way to tell the degree of respiratory illness.

Effects of Hyperventilation
- Lower partial pressure of carbon dioxide (PCO_2) by 4 mm Hg
- Raise PO_2 by 5 mm Hg

For every 4-point DEcrease in PCO_2, the PO_2 should INcrease 5 points.

Acute asthma in the ED is a case when orders should be done even before the physical examination.

Orders:
- *Oxygen*
- *Oximeter*
- *Arterial blood gas (ABG)*
- *Chest x-ray*
- *Peak expiratory flow*

If tests and treatments are ordered at the same time on the computer-based case simulation (CCS), the test is always done first. If you order the oximeter and ABG at the same time as oxygen, the test will not reflect the treatment.

PE:
- *General: clear respiratory distress, sitting on edge of bed trying to catch his breath*
- *Chest: bilateral wheezing, prolonged expiratory phase*
- *Abdomen: soft, nontender*
- *Cardiovascular: no murmurs, no gallops*

What part of pulmonary function testing would wheezing correspond to?

a. Increased total lung capacity (TLC)
b. Increased residual volume (RV)
c. Decreased forced vital capacity (FVC)
d. Decreased forced expiratory volume at 1 second (FEV_1)
e. Decreased expiratory reserve volume

Answer d. Decreased forced expiratory volume at 1 second (FEV_1)

Wheezing is entirely an expiratory problem in which there is an abnormal narrowing of the airway decreasing the FEV_1. Wheezing is an audible decrease in FEV_1.

As soon as wheezing is detected on examination, inhaled or nebulized albuterol should be ordered. There is no contraindication to inhaled albuterol in anyone. In addition, glucocorticoids should be ordered as soon as possible because there is a delay of 4 to 6 hours in seeing a clinical effect of steroids.

Orders:
- *Albuterol nebulizer*
- *Methylprednisolone intravenously (IV)*

Albuterol is a beta-2-agonist.

Reports:
- *Oximeter: 94% saturation*
- *ABG: pH 7.52; PCO_2 24 mm Hg; PO_2 70 mm Hg*
- *Chest x-ray: no infiltrates, no pneumothorax*
- *Peak expiratory flow: 150 L/second*

WARNING! Next part is hard! Numbers ahead!

If a healthy person were to hyperventilate himself to a PCO_2 of 24 mm Hg, what should the expected PO_2 be?

a. 70 mm Hg
b. 80 mm Hg
c. 100 mm Hg

d. 120 mm Hg
e. 150 mm Hg

Answer d. 120 mm Hg

Because the PO_2 should go up if the PCO_2 goes down, a 16-point decrease in PCO_2 should result in a 20-point increase in PO_2. This is the "alveolar gas equation."

1. Atmospheric pressure 760 mm Hg minus 47 mm Hg for water = 713 mm Hg
2. 21% of this 713 is oxygen = 150
3. Inhaled alveolar air: PO_2 150
4. $150 - PCO_2/0.8 = $ expected PO_2
5. $24/0.8 = 30$
6. $150 - 30 = 120$

Hyperventilation should raise the PO_2 in a healthy person.

Which part of the PFTs does peak flow most closely correspond to?

a. FVC

b. FEV$_1$

c. Residual volume

Answer b. FEV$_1$

Peak flow is the maximum rate of exhalation. FEV$_1$ is a *volume* of air to move in 1 second, but the peak flow is the maximum *rate*. FEV$_1$ is similar to the distance you must drive. Peak flow is similar to the maximum speed of the car.

There is no maximum dose of albuterol inhaler.

Move the clock forward 15 minutes.

Order:

• *Interval History*

• *Vital signs (to recheck respiratory rate)*

• *Albuterol nebulizer*

Decreasing PCO_2 raises pH.

PCO_2 down 10 mm Hg = pH up 0.08

Report:

• *The patient is still very dyspneic and has difficulty speaking in complete sentences.*

• *The patient's respiratory rate is 30 breaths/minute.*

Which of the following will work as an acute rescue medication in asthma exacerbation?

a. Theophylline

b. Cromolyn

c. Ipratropium

d. Omalizumab

e. Montelukast

Answer c. Ipratropium

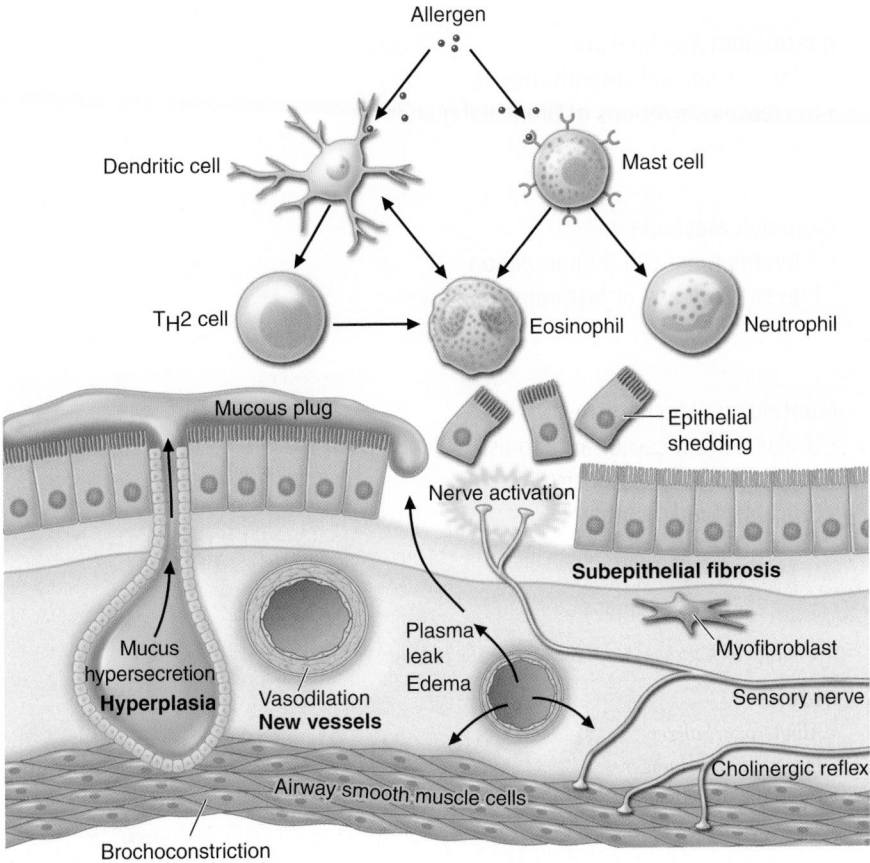

Figure 7-1. The pathophysiology of asthma is complex with participation of several interacting inflammatory cells, which result in acute and chronic inflammatory effects on the airway. (Reproduced with permission from Longo DL, et al. *Harrison's Principles of Internal Medicine,* 18th ed., Vol. 2. New York: McGraw-Hill; 2012.)

Ipratropium and tiotropium have some effect in asthma. They are quaternary amine anticholinergic agents. They inhibit acetylcholine effect and act locally in the lungs because they are not absorbed. The other medications are third-line drugs in the chronic maintenance of preventing asthma exacerbation. None of them works in acute circumstances. Theophylline is a phosphodiesterase inhibitor that increases cyclic adenosine monophosphate (cAMP) (Figure 7-1).

Omalizumab:
• Monoclonal antibody
• Inhibits immunoglobulin E (IgE)

Ipratropium Mechanism:
• Dilates bronchial smooth muscle
• Decreases secretions of bronchial glands

Cromolyn Mechanism:
• Prevents mast cell degranulation
• Prevents release of histamine

Montelukast Mechanism:
• Leukotriene receptor antagonist
• Decreases bronchospasm
• Does *not* work acutely

Move the clock forward and reexamine the patient.

Orders:
• *Albuterol nebulizer*
• *Ipratropium nebulizer*
• *Continue steroids*
• *Magnesium IV*

Magnesium has a mild relaxing effect on bronchial smooth muscle.

As you move the clock forward, use 15- to 30-minute intervals. This patient has now received multiple doses of albuterol, ipratropium, magnesium, and steroids. There is nothing more in terms of medications that can be done. Epinephrine adds nothing to albuterol. There is no greater efficacy of epinephrine compared to albuterol, but considerably more adverse effects particularly in those with a history of heart disease.

Orders:
• *Repeat ABG: pH 7.34; PCO$_2$ 46 mm Hg*

Transfer the patient to the intensive care unit (ICU) and consider intubating the patient because of the increased PCO$_2$ respiratory acidosis. When asthmatics become tired, respiratory failure can happen very suddenly.

Any respiratory acidosis in asthma is life-threatening.

With severe asthma, your patient may or may not be described as needing ICU care. The key issue for you is to know that even a slight respiratory acidosis or slight increase in PCO_2 is an indication for ICU transfer. If there is no respiratory failure, put the patient on the regular hospital ward until the respiratory rate normalizes to less than 20 breaths/minute and dyspnea decreases. If the patient is described as needing ICU and ventilator management, you can expect the stay to be brief, such as 1 to 2 days, and then the patient will go back to the floor.

After moving the clock forward and seeing the symptoms improve, switch steroids to oral prednisone. Once stable on oral medication and inhaled steroids and albuterol, the patient can be safely transferred home.

CASE 2: Chronic Obstructive Pulmonary Disease

Setting: *office*

CC: *"I get short of breath when I walk up a flight of stairs."*

VS: *BP: 110/70 mm Hg; P: 64 beats/minute; T: 98°F; R:12 breaths/minute*

HPI: *A 75-year-old long-term male smoker comes to the office with increasing dyspnea when walking, especially upstairs. The patient had been a smoker of one pack/day for 50 years. He quit 2 years ago. This is the first time he has had a decrease in exercise tolerance as he could walk two to three blocks before becoming short of breath.*

ROS:
• *No cough, no sputum, no fever*
• *No weight loss*

PMHx:
• *Diabetes: well controlled*

Medications:
• *Metformin, glyburide*

PE:
• *Chest: no wheezing, no rales, no rhonchi*
• *Cardiovascular: no murmurs*
• *Extremities: some clubbing, no edema*

Initial Orders:
• *Oximeter*
• *Chest x-ray*
• *PFTs*

There are no unique physical findings in chronic obstructive pulmonary disease (COPD).

At very late stages of the disease, patients can develop a barrel chest.

What is the physiologic basis of a barrel chest?

a. Increased fibrosis of lungs

b. Increased residual volume

c. Decreased compliance

d. Decreased FEV_1

Answer b. Increased residual volume

As air becomes trapped in the lungs, the diaphragm flattens and the chest enlarges. These increased volumes are all residual volume, or the part of the air that cannot be exhaled. This is all a sign of increased *total* lung capacity, but not usable lung. The usable part of lung volume, the FEV_1 and FVC, both diminish (Figure 7-2).

FEV_1/FVC Down + Residual Volume Up = COPD

Report:

• *Oximeter: 94% room air saturation*

• *Chest x-ray: clear lung fields, hyperaeration, some flattening of diaphragm*

Which of these becomes abnormal first in COPD?

a. TLC

b. FEV_1

c. Forced expiratory flow 25% to 75% (FEF25–75%) or peak mid-maximal flow

d. Forced vital capacity (FVC)

Answer c. Forced expiratory flow 25% to 75% (FEF25–75%) or peak mid-maximal flow

The FEF25–75% will become abnormal first in COPD. This is the middle part of the breath. FEF25–75% decrease will precede a decrease in the FEV_1.

FEF25–75% indicates a small airway.

Small airways collapse first.

As radius decreases, the pressure of collapse increases.

Law of Laplace

$$P = T/R$$

Where P is pressure, T is wall tension, and R is radius

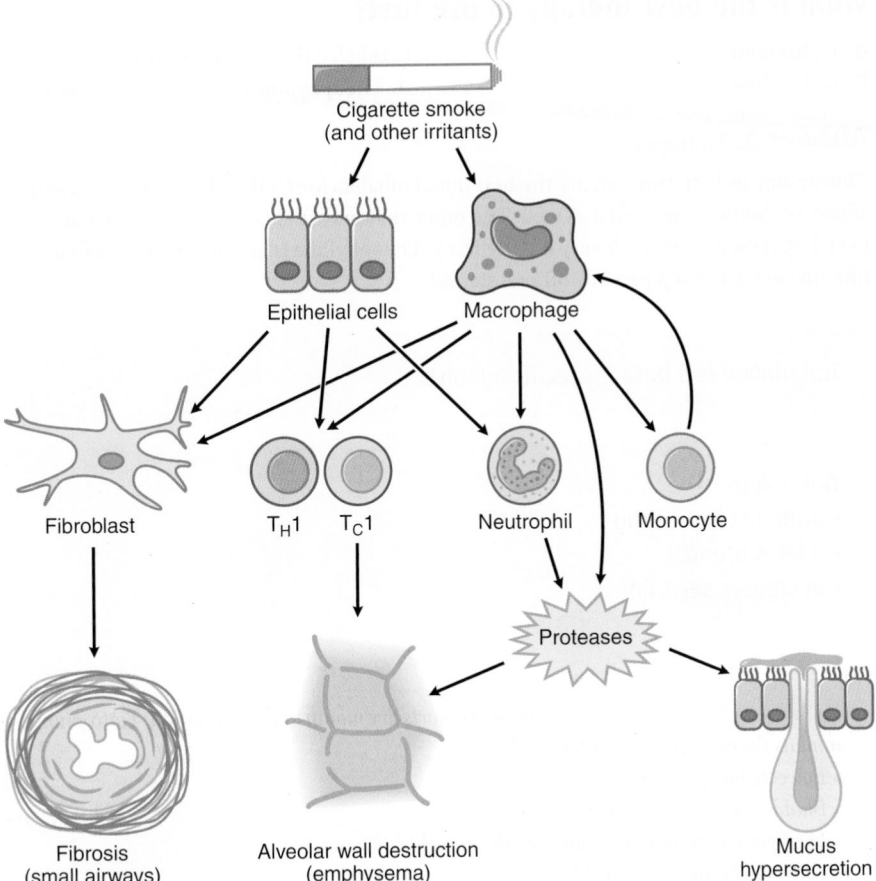

Figure 7-2. Cellular mechanisms in chronic obstructive pulmonary disease. Cigarette smoke and other irritants activate epithelial cells and macrophages in the lung to release mediators that attract circulating inflammatory cells, including monocytes (which differentiate to macrophages within the lung), neutrophils, and T lymphocytes (T helper [TH1] and TC1 cells). Fibrogenic factors released from epithelial cells and macrophages lead to fibrosis of small airways. Release of proteases results in alveolar wall destruction (emphysema) and mucus hypersecretion (chronic bronchitis). (Reproduced with permission from Brunton LL, et al. *Goodman & Gilman's The Pharmacological Basis of Therapeutics,* 12th ed. New York: McGraw-Hill; 2011.)

Move the clock forward 1 week. The patient still reports decreased exercise tolerance. The patient's PFTs show:
- *Decrease in FEF25–75%*
- *FEV$_1$ 65% of predicted*
- *FVC 80% of predicted*

What is the best therapy to use first?

a. Tiotropium

b. Terbutaline

c. Inhaled fluticasone (steroid)

d. Theophylline

Answer a. Tiotropium

Tiotropium and ipratropium are the best initial inhalers for COPD. It is not clear whether albuterol should be used first as well. The other answers are clearly wrong. Terbutaline is a beta-2-specific agonist with very little efficacy. Theophylline is an add-on drug as fourth or fifth line to try to keep patients off oral steroids.

Terbutaline is a beta-2-specific agonist.

Tiotropium
- Antimuscarinic drug
- Dilates bronchi
- Decreases secretions

You advance the clock 1 week. The patient reports dry mouth and constipation. Tiotropium inhibits the muscarinic receptors in the
- *Bowel (constipation)*
- *Bladder (urinary retention)*
- *Eye (worsens glaucoma by dilating the pupil)*
- *Salivary glands (dry mouth)*

The neuromuscular junction has nicotinic receptors for acetylcholine. It is not affected by tiotropium.

Stop the tiotropium. However, not all patients with COPD will respond to albuterol. Only half have asthma-like "reactive airways" disease. Do PFTs before and after the use of albuterol and see if there is an improvement.

Pre- and post-bronchodilation PFTs
- Do FEV_1 before and after albuterol administration.
- If there is a 12% increase in FEV_1, it indicates reversible airway disease.

There is a 20% rise in FEV₁ with albuterol. You start the medication and advance the clock. The patient is still not controlled and you add an inhaled steroid to therapy.

Inhaled steroids are all identical in efficacy
- Fluticasone
- Beclomethasone
- Triamcinolone

The patient returns in 1 week much improved with greater exercise tolerance. He is then lost to follow-up for a year during which time he does not return. The next time you see the patient he is much more short of breath with dyspnea starting at half-a-block exertion.

In severe COPD, which of these is most likely to be found on this patient's PFTs?

	FEV₁ (%)	FVC (%)	TLC (%)
a.	86	94	92
b.	42	64	124
c.	58	60	56
d.	96	53	78

FEV₁, forced expiratory volume at 1 second;
FVC, forced vital capacity; TLC, total lung capacity.

Answer b. FEV₁ and FVC both down

With severe COPD, FEV₁ and FVC go down, but FEV₁ decreases even more. TLC goes up, but it is not useful. It is all unusable residual volume.

COPD is from the loss of elastin fibers (Figure 7-3).

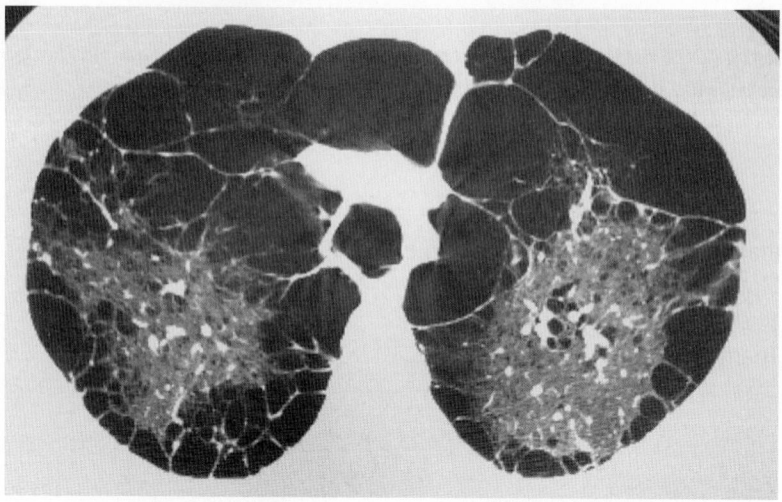

Figure 7-3. A computed tomography (CT) scan of a patient (at the level of the pulmonary veins) showing multiple large peripheral bullae; the patient was diagnosed with severe paraseptal emphysema. (Reproduced with permission from Miller WT, Jr. *Diagnostic Thoracic Imaging.* New York: McGraw-Hill; 2006.)

Orders:
- *ABG*
- *Restart albuterol, tiotropium, and inhaled steroids*
- *Basic metabolic panel (CHEM-7)*
- *Complete blood count (CBC)*

Which of the following is a feature of this patient's disorder?

a. Decreased lung compliance

b. Increased lung compliance

c. Hypersensitivity of central chemoreceptors

Answer b. Increased lung compliance

COPD is an increase in lung compliance. Patients can inhale, but cannot exhale. This is why they retain carbon dioxide (CO_2). They cannot move the air. There is an insensitivity of central chemoreceptors to CO_2 and acid. This is part of why there is a blunted respiratory drive.

Three drives for respiration
- Increased CO_2
- Acid (hydrogen ion)
- Decreased PO_2

Because of shortness of breath, have the patient return in just 1 to 2 days to see if there is improvement. He is somewhat improved, but exercise intolerance makes it impossible for him to walk the two flights of stairs in his own house.

ABG Report: *pH 7.37; PCO_2 60 mm Hg; PO_2 59 mm Hg; saturation 89%*

Central chemoreceptors are stronger than peripheral chemoreceptors.
- Central CO_2 and acid
- Peripheral oxygen

Report:
- *CBC: hematocrit (Hct) 55%; mean corpuscular volume (MCV) 78 fL*
- *CHEM-7: bicarbonate 36 mEq/L (elevated)*

Chronic Hypoxia = Increased Erythropoietin = High Hematocrit (Polycythemia)

Polycythemia from hypoxia gives small cells (low MCV).

The patient meets criteria for chronic home oxygen. Low-flow oxygen (1–2 L/minute) lowers mortality. Low-flow oxygen in hypoxic COPD lowers mortality. Criteria for home oxygen use are:
- *PO_2 <55 mm Hg or saturation <88%*
- *PO_2 <60 mm Hg or saturation <90% with polycythemia or pulmonary hypertension*

Peripheral chemoreceptors for oxygen
Detect PO_2 <60 mm Hg

The patient is started on oxygen and continued on tiotropium, albuterol, and inhaled steroids. Bicarbonate level is elevated in the kidney by carbonic anhydrase in response to the chronic elevation of PCO_2.

When CCS says, "Case will end in 5 minutes of real time," it does not mean you made a mistake. It does give you an opportunity to do any health maintenance you may have forgotten.

Final Orders:
- *Flu vaccine yearly*
- *Pneumococcal vaccination for anyone with COPD*

Chronic Respiratory Acidosis = Metabolic Alkalosis

Oxygen prevents fatal pulmonary hypertension.

CASE 3: Pneumonia

Setting: *ED*

CC: *"Cough, shortness of breath, and chest pain"*

VS: *BP: 108/72 mm Hg; P: 112 beats/minute; T: 102.8°F; R: 26 breaths/minute*

HPI: *A 68-year-old man with several days of increasing cough, discolored sputum production, and chest pain arrives at the ED. The pain is sharp, right sided, and worsens when he takes a deep breath. He has had a fever of 102°F at home. The dyspnea markedly worsened today, and that is what made him come to the hospital.*

PMHx:
- *Tobacco smoking in past; quit 15 years ago*

Medications:
- *Vitamins*

On CCS, for dyspnea, order oxygen, oximeter, and chest x-ray.

For routine fever evaluation, how much testing should you order just because of the presence of a fever?

a. Chest x-ray

b. Chest x-ray, urinalysis (UA)

c. Chest x-ray, UA, blood culture

d. Chest x-ray, UA, blood culture, stool culture

e. Chest x-ray, UA, blood culture, stool culture, urine culture

Answer c. Chest x-ray, urinalysis (UA), blood culture

These are the tests of fever evaluation just for a person with no other localizing symptoms. You can order this on CCS for any fever.

Initial Orders:
- *Oximeter, chest x-ray, oxygen*
- *Blood cultures, UA*

PE:
- *General: fatigued, tired*
- *Chest: right-sided crackles in lung field*
- *Abdomen: nontender, no organomegaly*
- *Cardiovascular: no murmurs, no gallops*

Which of the following is the greatest determinant of the need for hospital admission?

a. Hypoxia and hypotension
b. Number of lobes involved
c. Age and medication use
d. Organism type and previous intubation
e. Number of previous episodes of pneumonia

Answer a. Hypoxia and hypotension

Admission to the hospital is based on the severity of the disease. The severity of pneumonia is based on the presence of hypoxia, hypotension, altered mental status, and renal failure.

All the other features, such as age, the number of previous illnesses, and the number of lobes involved, are important, but not nearly so important as hypoxia and hypotension. If you have only one lobe involved in a young person, but the patient is hypotensive (systolic blood pressure [SBP] <90 mm Hg) or hypoxic, then the young patient needs to be admitted.

Mycoplasma pneumonia involves five lobes, but it is mild and does not cause hypoxia or hypotension. The same is true of Chlamydia pneumonia. So admission is not based on etiology, it is based on the severity.

Move the clock forward to the minute you need to get the results of the oximeter.

Because you ordered the oxygen and oximeter at the same time, the oximeter reading will not reflect the oxygen administration. Tests ordered at the same time as treatments do not reflect the treatments.

Results:
- *Oximeter: 91% saturation on room air*

Saturation <92% = PO_2 at least <70 mm Hg = Severe pneumonia

Pneumococcus
- Most common community-acquired pneumonia (CAP)
- Environmental source or reservoir unknown

You can repeat the oximeter reading now that the patient is on oxygen. It will reflect the use of oxygen now that you have moved the clock forward.

In pneumonia, it is key to
• *Assess oxygenation and blood pressure (BP) immediately.*
• *Get x-ray results and start antibiotics within 30 minutes of the patient's arrival in the ED.*

Advance the clock 10 to 20 minutes to get x-ray results.

Orders:
• *ABG*

ABG helps answer the question, "Ward or ICU?"

Hypotension + Severe Hypoxia (PO$_2$ <60 mm Hg) = ICU

Report:
• *Chest x-ray: right middle and right lower lobe infiltrates; effusion on right*
• *UA: no white blood cells (WBCs), no protein*
• *ABG: pH 7.46; PCO$_2$ 34 mm Hg; PO$_2$ 65 mm Hg*

Hyperventilation should mean respiratory alkalosis.
PCO$_2$ down 10 mm Hg = pH up 0.08

What test should you use first to detect pleural effusion?
a. X-ray
b. Computed tomography (CT)
c. Ultrasound
d. Thoracentesis

Answer a. X-ray
All detect a pleural effusion. Start with the x-ray.

Decubitus x-ray detects pleural effusion.
Effusions Move = Layer Out

Orders:
- *Ceftriaxone IV*
- *Azithromycin IV*
- *Decubitus x-ray*
- *Transfer patient to hospital floor*

What difference does it make if there is an effusion?

a. No difference in treatment

b. Placement of patient in ICU

c. Need for thoracentesis

d. Difference in antibiotic choice

Answer C. Need for thoracentesis

Thoracentesis is needed if there is an effusion to see if there is empyema. Empyema means an infection in the pleural space, not just that there is fluid transudatively moving into the pleural space. An empyema is infected exudate. If there is empyema, drainage with a chest tube is needed because it will act like an abscess. In addition, undrained empyema can also slow scar formation and tighten the lungs and destroy lung function.

The patient is moved to the hospital ward. All orders for decubitus films, oxygen, azithromycin, and ceftriaxone go with the patient. Move the clock forward to get results of the films.

Ceftriaxone inhibits cell wall production.

Azithromycin inhibits ribosomal production of protein.

Report:
- *Decubitus x-ray: layering out of effusion seen*

Orders:
- *Thoracentesis under sonographic guidance*
- *Pulmonary consultation*

Which quality of pleural fluid is the strongest indication for chest tube drainage?

a. Lactate dehydrogenase (LDH) >60% of serum

b. pH <7.2

c. Protein >50% of serum

d. WBC count 500/μL

Answer b. pH <7.2

Unquestionably, the strongest indication for chest tube drainage is a low pleural fluid pH. This is the greatest indicator of severe infection. LDH >60% of serum and protein >50% of serum indicate an exudative effusion, but not clearly an infection. WBC count in pleural fluid is strangely not as accurate an indicator of infection as it is in urine, cerebrospinal fluid (CSF), and ascites.

Normal pleural fluid pH is 7.6.

Pleural Fluid Report:

• *pH: 7.5*
• *Protein and LDH: slightly elevated*
• *WBCs: 486/mm³*

*The patient is on oxygen and antibiotics. Repeat the oximeter on oxygen to ensure adequate oxygenation. As soon as hypoxia, fever, and hypotension improve, the patient can be safely discharged home on oral azithromycin. The same criteria for admission (CURB)—**C**onfusion, **U**remia, **R**espiratory distress, **B**P low—are the same as for discharge. In the absence of CURB, the patient can leave.*

Pneumonia vaccine should be given to prevent infection with other serotypes.

CASE 4: Pneumocystis Pneumonia

Setting: *ED*

CC: *"I keep coughing and I can't breathe."*

VS: *BP: 108/72 mm Hg; P: 88 beats/minute; T: 101.4°F; R: 26 breaths/minute*

HPI: *A 54-year-old man with acquired immunodeficiency syndrome (AIDS) arrives at the ED with several days of increasing dyspnea and cough. The dyspnea is definitely worse on* *exertion and that is the main reason he has come to the ED. The cough is dry and nonpro-ductive: "Nothing comes up when I cough." He has not measured his temperature.*

PMHx:
- *AIDS: does not know his CD4 count*
- *Oral thrush*

Medications: *none for past 6 months; "I'm supposed to be taking something, but I don't know the name of it."*

ROS:
- *Inspiratory "catch"—sharp pain under sternum when he breaths in*

PE:
- *General: thin, wasted appearance*
- *Chest: clear bilaterally*
- *Abdomen: normal*
- *Cardiovascular: normal*

Initial Orders:
- *Oximeter, oxygen, ABG, chest x-ray*
- *CBC*
- *CD4 count*
- *LDH*

Pneumococcus is the most common CAP in patients with AIDS.

Reports:
- *Oximeter: 94% room air saturation*

Although the most common CAP in AIDS is pneumococcus, the patient has a dry cough and normal lung examination.

Interstitial pneumonia is associated with a nonproductive cough.

Reports:
- *ABG: pH 7.49; PCO$_2$ 32 mm Hg; PO$_2$ 70 mm Hg (on room air)*
- *Chest x-ray: bilateral interstitial infiltrates*
- *CBC: WBCs 3200/μL (low); Hct: 34%; MCV 88 fL*
- *LDH: 825 units/L (elevated)*

Interstitial Infiltrates
• Pneumocystis
• Mycoplasma
• Chlamydia pneumonia
• Viral
• Coxiella

"Empty" Alveoli = Dry Cough

What is this patient's alveolar-arterial (A-a) gradient?

a. 20 mm Hg
b. 24 mm Hg
c. 30 mm Hg

d. 40 mm Hg
e. 45 mm Hg

Answer d. 40 mm Hg

A-a gradient = $150 - (PCO_2/0.8 + PO_2)$
$150 - (32/0.8 + 70)$
$150 - (40 + 70)$
$150 - 110 = 40$ mm Hg

Any cell breakdown causes high levels of LDH.

Why does mycoplasma *not* appear on Gram stain?

a. No cell wall
b. Intracellular

c. Too small
d. No stainable DNA

Answer a. No cell wall

Mycoplasma does not have a true cell wall. Mycoplasma is encased in a cell membrane that does not pick up Gram stain. Chlamydia and viruses are intracellular. Gram stain does not stain DNA, it stains the cell wall.

Normal LDH strongly excludes *Pneumocystis jiroveci pneumonia* (PCP).

Once you have the results of the chest x-ray, you can order therapy. Unlike the other forms of pneumonia, PCP is not covered by the usual CAP drugs of ceftriaxone and azithromycin or a quinolone such as levofloxacin, moxifloxacin, or gemifloxacin.

What is the indication for giving steroids in PCP?

a. PO$_2$ <80 mm Hg or A-a gradient
>25 mm Hg

b. PO$_2$ <70 mm Hg or A-a gradient
>25 mm Hg

c. PO$_2$ <70 mm Hg or A-a gradient
>35 mm Hg

d. PO$_2$ <60 mm Hg or A-a gradient
>35 mm Hg

Answer C. PO$_2$ <70 mm Hg or A-a gradient >35 mm Hg

Glucocorticoids such as prednisone give a 50% decrease in mortality in a person with severe PCP. Use of steroids are absolutely lifesaving in severe disease. Never be worried about short-term steroid use in acutely ill patients even if they are immunocompromised.

Orders:
• *Trimethoprim-sulfamethoxazole (TMP-SMZ) IV*
• *Prednisone orally*
• *Pulmonary consultation*
• *Bronchoscopy and bronchoalveolar lavage (BAL)*

TMP-SMZ is a folate antagonist.

Advance the clock to get the results of the bronchoscopy. There should be an immediate improvement in respiratory status the same day with the use of steroids. Steroids will decrease fluids or swelling in the interstitial membrane and allow greater transfer of oxygen from the alveolus to the arteriole.

Reports:
• BAL: P. jiroveci found
• CD4: 18

Pneumocystis jiroveci (Figure 7-4)
• It is a fungus by DNA classification.
• Antifungal drugs do not work.

Over the next several days, there is no change to therapy. Decreasing the steroid dosage will happen after 5 days. Do an "Interval History" every day the patient is in the hospital to confirm improvement. Serum chemistry should be done at least every 2 days in a hospitalized patient undergoing active IV treatment.

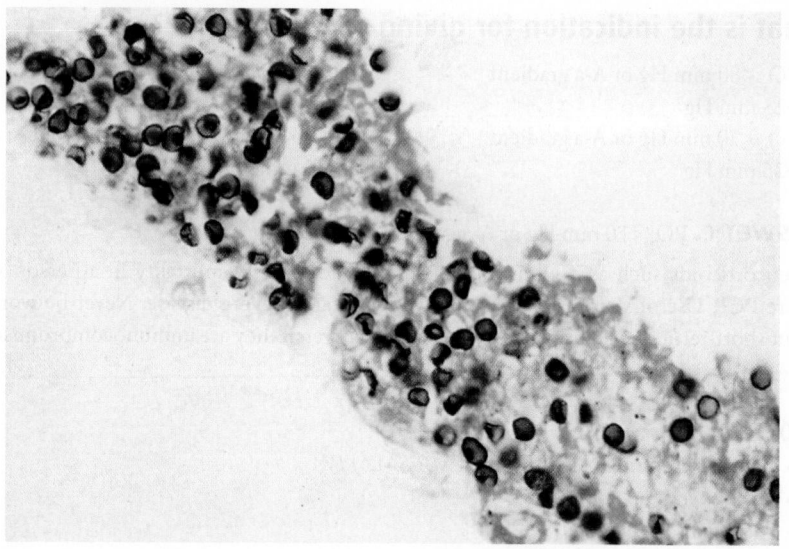

Figure 7-4. Pneumocystis pneumonia. A silver stain of this material from the lung reveals folded cysts, some of which contain comma-shaped spores. (Reproduced with permission from Connor DH, et al., eds. *Pathology of Infectious Diseases*, vol. 1. New York: Appleton & Lange; 1997.)

Pneumocystis jiroveci
• Formerly *Pneumocystis carinii*
• Does not grow on fungal media

Reports:
• *Interval History: "Improved shortness of breath"*
• *Chemistry:*
  ◦ *Creatinine 1.8 mg/dL (elevated)*
  ◦ *Blood urea nitrogen (BUN): normal*
  ◦ *Sodium: 130 mEq/L (normal 135–145 mEq/L)*
  ◦ *Glucose: 165 mg/dL*

TMP decreases the tubular secretion of creatinine.

All pneumonias cause the syndrome of inappropriate secretion of antidiuretic hormone (SIADH).

Steroids increase glucose:
• Decreased uptake by muscle
• Increase gluconeogenesis
• Permissive action on glucagon

What should you do about these laboratory abnormalities?

a. No action is needed.

b. Stop steroids.

c. Stop TMP-SMZ and switch to IV pentamidine.

d. Stop TMP-SMZ and switch to aerosolized pentamidine.

Answer a. No action is needed.

Move the clock forward and repeat the laboratory tests. You do not need to do anything for these laboratory abnormalities at this mild level. Prednisone is lifesaving in severe PCP and a glucose level of 165 mg/dL is clinically irrelevant for a short period of 2 to 3 weeks. A mild bump up in creatinine level has very limited clinical significance. You will be switching to oral TMP-SMZ at 10 to 14 days to complete the full 3 weeks orally if the patient is stable. Also, IV pentamidine is even more nephrotoxic than TMP-SMZ.

Aerosolized pentamidine is completely inadequate at acute therapy. It is a fourth-line choice used rarely, if at all for prophylaxis of PCP.

TMP decreases the tubular secretion of creatinine.

Advance the clock and recheck the laboratory test results. If there is no further deterioration in chemistry levels, just continue the same treatment. Start antiretroviral medications, such as efavirenz, emtricitabine, and tenofovir. When the patient is improved and ready for discharge, long-term prophylaxis with oral TMP-SMZ is used lifelong, or until the patient's CD4 count is brought up above 200 with antiretroviral treatment (ART). Steroids are tapered down so that they stop at the time the patient is switched from full-dose IV or oral TMP-SMZ to the prophylactic dose.

When the patient's CD4 level increases:
• Continue lifelong ART.
• Stop prophylactic medications when the CD4 count is above 200 cells/mm³.

CASE 5: Tuberculosis

Setting: *ED*

CC: *"Fever, cough, sputum, weight loss"*

VS: *BP: 112/70 mm Hg; T:101.4°F; R: 18 breaths/minute*

HPI: *A 34-year-old immigrant from Asia comes to the ED with fever, cough, and sputum with some hemoptysis developing over a few weeks. The patient has lost 15 pounds unintentionally over the past few weeks.*

PMHx: *alcoholism*

Medications: *none*

PE:
• *Head, Ears, Eyes, Nose, Throat (HEENT): normal, no adenopathy*
• *Chest: scattered rales, no consolidation*
• *Cardiovascular: no murmurs, rubs, gallops*

Initial Orders:
• *Chest x-ray*
• *Oxygen*
• *Oximeter*

A patient with these symptoms can also be put on isolation from the beginning. You will not lose points for doing so.

Report:
• *Chest x-ray: apical infiltrate (Figure 7-5)*
• *Oximeter: 95% saturation on room air*

Orders:
• *Respiratory isolation*
• *Sputum acid fast stain*
• *Mycobacterial culture*

Purified Protein Derivative (PPD) Skin Testing
• Not for acute diagnosis
• Not for symptomatic persons
• Not with fever, cough, sputum, abnormal x-ray

PPD screens asymptomatic groups.
PPD detects previous exposures in high-risk groups.

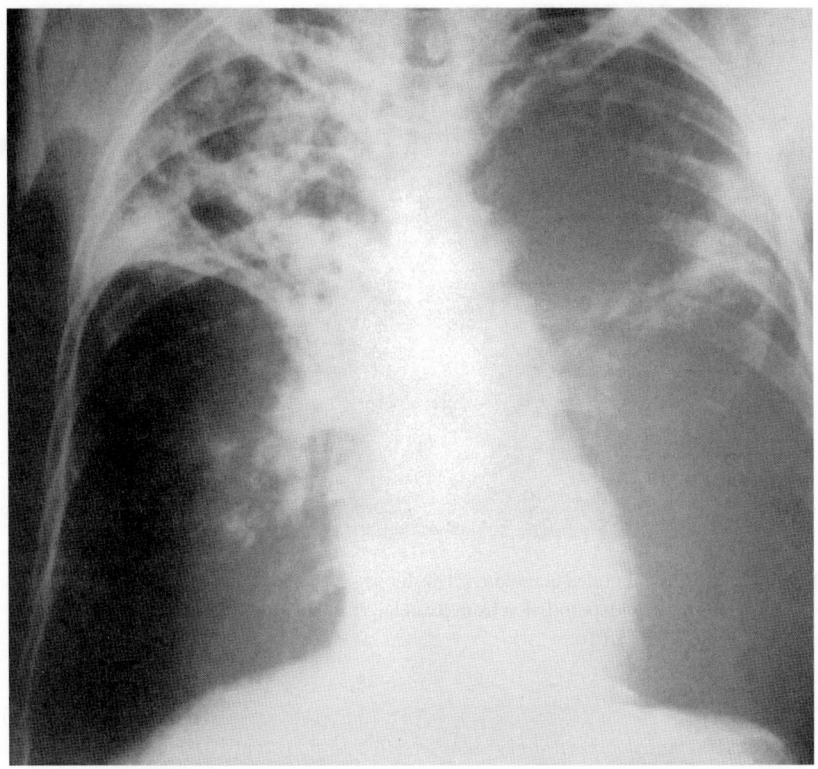

Figure 7-5. Advanced pulmonary tuberculosis involving the apex and upper lobe. (Reproduced with permission from Tintinalli JE, et al. *Tintinalli's Emergency Medicine, A Comprehensive Study Guide*, 7th ed. New York: McGraw-Hill; 2011.)

The patient is placed on respiratory isolation. Some providers, based on the x-ray and the clarity of the diagnosis, may choose to add ceftriaxone and azithromycin. Do not start empiric tuberculosis (TB) medication until you have obtained sputum acid-fast cultures. You will want to give the sample every chance to grow.

Obtain sputum acid-fast cultures before starting anti-TB medications.

Acid-fast culture is the only way to determine the sensitivity of an organism.

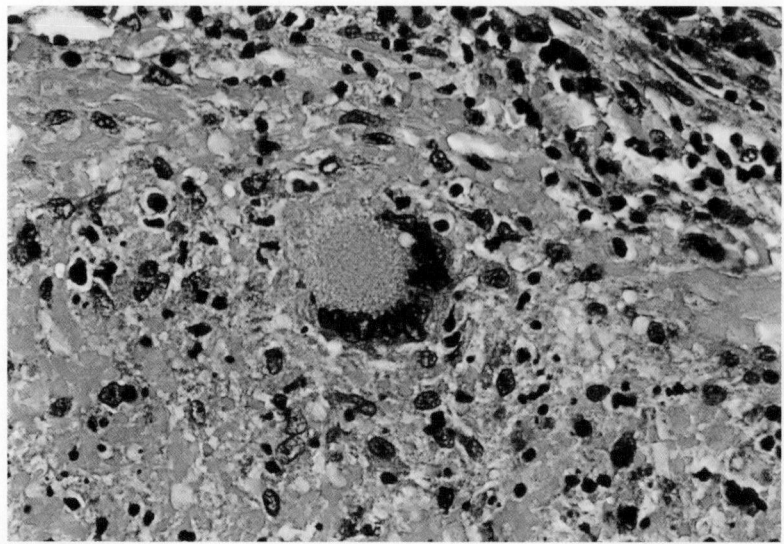

Figure 7-6. Note the rounded granuloma. This biopsy shows old tubercle bacilli walled off in the lung. (Reproduced with permission from Ryan KJ, et al. *Sherris Medical Microbiology*, 5th ed., New York: McGraw-Hill; 2010.)

The patient is placed on respiratory isolation. His fever persists at 101°F and then 101.5°F.

Report:
• *Acid-fast stain: positive (Figure 7-6)*

Once the acid-fast stain is positive, order four TB medications and vitamin B_6 (pyridoxine).

Orders:
• *Rifampin*
• *Isoniazid*
• *Pyrazinamide*
• *Ethambutol*
• *Vitamin B_6*
• *Liver function tests (LFTs) (aspartate aminotransferase [AST], alanine aminotransferase [ALT])*

Isoniazid increases urinary loss of pyridoxine (vitamin B_6).

Move the clock forward to get the results of LFTs and see if there is a change in them by the use of TB medication.

TB medications are eliminated by hepatic p450 systems.

The patient must remain on isolation until repeat acid-fast stains of sputum show that the TB has been cleared from the smear and the patient is not dangerous to others.

Results: *baseline LFTs are normal.*

What test will tell first if the acid-fast bacilli are the organism *Mycobacterium tuberculosis* or another species in the genus *Mycobacteriaceae*?

a. Culture

b. Polymerase chain reaction (PCR)

c. Response to therapy

d. No way to tell

Answer b. Polymerase chain reaction (PCR)

PCR takes infinitesimally small amounts of genetic material from an organism and multiplies it in order to detect the speciation of the organism before the cultures grow. Mycobacterial culture can take 4 to 6 weeks to grow. The PCR can speciate the organism in a day.

There is no difference in the appearance of mycobacteria on a smear.

The patient remains in the hospital on respiratory isolation. Respiratory isolation can be very lonely and depressing. Staff do not visit you as often, and when they do, it is briefer and there is much less discussion.

After 7 days in the hospital, you repeat the sputum smear because the patient states "I can't stand it in isolation. I have to get out of here as soon as possible."

Report:
• *The repeat acid-fast bacillus (AFB) stain at 7 days is positive.*

What test can be done to prove whether the mycobacteria on the stain are alive or dead?

a. Nothing can be done.

b. Use a PCR assay.

c. Wait for the results of the culture.

d. Do interferon provocation testing.

Answer c. Wait for the results of the culture.

You cannot do anything right away to tell if the AFB are alive or dead. PCR will tell the species, but cannot tell if they are viable AFB that can spread disease, or just dead, old AFB.

> *After 10 days in isolation, the patient says that he is walking out of the hospital: "You can't stop me!"*

What can you do to control this potential TB transmission problem?

a. Arrest him and put him in prison.

b. Place a guard at the door to enforce isolation.

c. Consult the ethics committee.

d. You can do nothing; he is an adult who is free to go.

Answer b. Place a guard at the door to enforce isolation.

He does not have the right to leave the hospital as long as he has AFB in his sputum that may be viable. As long as a patient can transmit TB, you have the right to incarcerate him in the hospital. Because you are not a police officer, you do not have the right to arrest or imprison him. There is no point in consulting an ethics committee for a clear, straightforward problem. It does not matter what they say. It is not an ethics problem. It is an *infection control problem*.

Active TB in Sputum = Mandatory Respiratory Isolation

From whom you mainly isolating the patient?

a. General unexposed public

b. Household contacts

c. Friends and family

Answer a. General unexposed public

Interestingly, the family is not the biggest concern. They have already been exposed. You are isolating the patient from other patients and the general public who has never been exposed to TB. The patient is already on TB medications and is much less infectious now than he was before he came to the hospital. You are isolating him from new contacts.

> *After another week, the repeat AFB stain is negative, and the patient is released from the hospital. He will get all four TB drugs for the first 2 months, then continue isoniazid and rifampin alone for another 4 months.*

Pulmonary TB
• Total therapy: 6 months

Bone, Central Nervous System (CNS), Miliary, or Pregnant Patient
• Total therapy: 9 months

Toxicity
• Pyrazinamide: hyperuricemia
• Rifampin: red secretions, body fluids
• Ethambutol: optic neuritis, color vision problems

When the final "Case will end in 5 minutes of real time" screen pops up, do not forget to order TB screening for the patient's contacts. Either the PPD skin test or the in vitro interferon gamma release assay is used. Both tests indicate the need for 9 months of treatment with isoniazid and vitamin B_6 to prevent possible reactivation of TB in those previously exposed.

CASE 6: Pulmonary Embolus

Setting: *ED*

CC: *"I'm having a hard time catching my breath."*

VS: *BP: 108/68 mm Hg; P:108 beats/minute; T: 101°F; R: 24 breaths/minute*

HPI: *A 42-year-old woman, coming from India, just deplaned at the airport, feeling very short of breath, and was brought immediately to the ED. She was on a flight from Mumbai, through Dubai to New York, and started feeling dyspneic about an hour before landing. The flight stewards thought she might be having a panic attack and had her lie down on the floor in the first class cabin, but saw no improvement in her symptoms. The woman is on a stretcher in your ED with oxygen in place, and she is feeling anxious.*

PMHx: *ovarian cysts*

Medications: *none*

As with most of the CCS pulmonary and dyspnea cases, order oxygen, oximeter, chest x-ray, and ABG.

PE:
• *General: anxious, sweating*
• *Chest: clear to auscultation, no rales, rhonchi, or crepitations*
• *Cardiovascular: normal*
• *Abdomen: benign*

Oxygen is considered to be administered immediately, but tests ordered at the same time are considered to be done first. It is much harder to interpret an oximeter or ABG while the person is on oxygen. It is never precisely clear how much oxygen patients are really getting except when they are on ventilator support.

Report:
- *Oximeter 90% room air saturation*
- *Chest x-ray: normal*
- *ABG: pH 7.47; PCO$_2$ 31 mm Hg; PO$_2$ 62 mm Hg*

CCS is designed to assess your ability to determine just the right timing of tests versus treatments or both.

What should you do next for this person?

a. Order a ventilation-perfusion (VQ) scan.

b. Give the patient heparin.

c. Move the patient to ICU and do a CT angiogram.

d. Perform and embolectomy.

e. Order an inferior vena cava (IVC) filter.

Answer b. Give the patient heparin.

This is enough information to indicate the need to start therapy. The acute onset of shortness of breath without wheezing on examination or the rales of congestive heart failure (CHF) has a high predictive value for pulmonary embolus (PE). The number one issue in PE management is, in fact, making sure you know *not* to wait for specific tests like a CT angiogram, VQ scan, or lower extremity Doppler ultrasound to start therapy.

Acute Hypoxia + Normal Lung Examination and Chest X-Ray = PE

Little else besides PE causes severe desaturation and clear lungs.

Peripheral chemoreceptors:
- Aortic arch hypoxia
- Stimulation PO$_2$ <60 mm Hg

How will you determine the need for thrombolytics?

a. Lower extremity Doppler ultrasound

b. Hypotension and right-sided heart strain on echocardiogram or electrocardiogram (ECG)

c. CT angiogram

d. VQ scan and D-dimer

Answer b. Hypotension and right-sided heart strain on echocardiogram or electrocardiogram (ECG)

Thrombolytics are used for the most severe, large clots. This question basically asks if you know how to assess the severity of the clot. Large clots block blood flow. Blocked blood flow decreases BP and causes back pressure in the heart. Clot size on CT is not as important as decreased heart function.

Severe Dangerous Clot = Hypotension and Abnormal Heart Pressure

With a large clot, which test gives the first abnormal result?

a. Right ventricular hypertrophy

b. Right bundle-branch block

c. Increased pulmonary artery (PA) pressure

d. Increased wedge pressure

e. ECG with $S_1 Q_3 T_3$ pattern

Answer c. Increased pulmonary artery (PA) pressure

Big clots block PAs. Blocked PAs give pulmonary hypertension, which is largely saying the same thing. Right ventricular hypertension happens later. ECG findings occur after that. Wedge pressure indicates left atrial pressure. Wedge pressure is measured on a right-sided heart catheter but has nothing to do with right-sided heart pressures.

Large clots cause pulmonary hypertension.

Orders:
- ECG
- Echocardiogram
- Activated partial thromboplastin time (aPTT), prothrombin time (PT), international normalized ratio (INR)
- CT angiogram

Low molecular weight heparin has equal efficacy to IV heparin.

Heparin works by potentiating antithrombin.
It prevents clot formation, but does not destroy old clots.

The patient is on oxygen and heparin. Repeat oximeter shows the saturation largely unchanged at 91% to 92%. On a 50% facemask saturation, it is still at 93% to 94%.

When the ECG does show an abnormality, what is the most common abnormality found?

a. $S_1 Q_3 T_3$ pattern
b. Nonspecific ST-T wave changes
c. Right bundle-branch block

d. Tall R waves in V_1 and V_2 (right ventricular hypertrophy)

Answer b. Nonspecific ST-T wave changes

The reason for the nonspecific ST- and T-wave changes is not precisely clear. The other findings going along with right-sided heart strain may have more specificity for a PE, but are much less common, being seen in <25% of patients.

Clots and hematomas give fever.

Coagulation Studies
Done at baseline for those patients who need anticoagulation therapy.

Reports:
• *ECG: sinus tachycardia with T-wave flattening in I, aVL, and V_5 and V_6*
• *aPTT, PT, INR: normal*
• *CT angiogram: large clot in PAs bilaterally*

With persistent hypoxia despite increasing administration of oxygen and signs of right-sided heart strain, the patient should be placed in the ICU and thrombolytics (tissue plasminogen activator [tPA]) given.

The ventilation-to-perfusion ratio (V:Q) mismatch prevents increased oxygenation despite giving oxygen to the patient.

Report:
• *Echocardiogram: PA pressure 54 mm Hg (elevated); decreased right ventricular motion; enlarged right atrium*

Which form of thrombophilia changes initial therapy?

a. None
b. Antiphospholipid syndrome

c. Protein C or S deficiency
d. Factor V Leiden mutation

Answer a. None

Thrombophilias make no difference in acute management. You use heparin followed by 6 months of warfarin initially with all of them. All of them get an INR of 2 to 3 with the first clot. That is why there is no point in testing for them with a first clot. They do not change management.

If a clot is found on CT, then Doppler ultrasounds of the legs do not matter.

If a clot is found on Doppler ultrasounds of the legs, then CT does not matter.

> All that matters is:
> Clot versus No Clot

> Doppler ultrasounds are 60% to 70% sensitive for the PE source.

What is the mechanism of thrombolytics?

a. Plasmin breaks fresh clots into D-dimers.

b. Fibrinogen is activated to fibrin split products.

c. They inhibit the cascade start (factor XII and VII).

d. They break up fibrinogen after factor XIII stabilizes it.

Answer a. Plasmin breaks fresh clots into D-dimers.

Thrombolytics activate plasminogen into plasmin. Plasmin dissolves recently activated fibrin into D-dimers. Plasmin will not specifically break up clotting that has been cross-linked and stabilized by factor XIII. It is thrombin that activates fibrinogen by splitting off fibrin-split products.

> Thrombin activates fibrinogen, creating split products.
> Plasmin destroys fibrin, creating D-dimers.

> *After administering thrombolytics, both oxygenation and BP improve in the patient.*
>
> **Repeat VS:** *P: 98 beats/minute; BP 118/74 mm Hg*
>
> **Repeat ABG:** *pH 7.42; PCO$_2$ 38 mm Hg; PO$_2$ 74 mm Hg*
>
> **Orders:**
> * *Transfer patient to ward.*
> * *Continue heparin.*
> * *Start warfarin.*
> * *Measure INR.*
> * *Do CBC.*

• If heparin-induced thrombocytopenia (HIT) develops, use argatroban.
• Argatroban is a direct-acting thrombin inhibitor.

After transferring the patient to the hospital ward, repeat the physical examination. Move the clock forward 1 day at a time after moving the patient to the hospital ward. Repeat the CBC and INR each day looking for HIT and to achieve a therapeutic INR of 2 to 3. You will not see an effect of warfarin for several days and should not expect to see a fully therapeutic INR for 5 to 7 days.

Use IVC filter:
• For bleeding
• When anticoagulation cannot be used
• When there is a recurrence while fully anticoagulated

Warfarin
• Inhibits factors II, VII, IX, X
• Needs 3 days to work

After 5 days, the patient's INR rises to 2.4. You can stop the heparin when the INR comes above 2 and discharge the patient. The length of therapy should be 6 months.

CASE 7: Sarcoidosis

Setting: *office*

CC: *"I get tired and winded when I walk."*

VS: *BP: 110/70 mm Hg; T: 98°F; R: 14 breaths/minute*

HPI: *A 32-year-old African American woman comes to the office complaining of intermittent episodes of shortness of breath. She has been told she has asthma and is intermittently placed on albuterol inhalers and oral steroids. Her shortness of breath clears up and she stops all medications until it recurs a few months later. She also has a cough that is not productive of sputum.*

PMHx:
- *Skin lesions intermittently: undiagnosed*

Medications:
- *None routinely; steroids and inhaled beta-agonists intermittently*

PE:
- *General: well-nourished*
- *Chest: some crepitations bilaterally*
- *Skin: dark lesion on face, reddish-brown tender lesions on shins*
- *Cardiovascular: loud P_2*

Initial Orders:
- *Chest x-ray*
- *Pulse oximeter*

Pulmonary hypertension causes a loud P_2.

The patient returns a week later to discuss the findings on the chest x-ray. There is no short-ness of breath acutely and no treatment is started.

New visits to the clinic or office should always start with an "Interval History" to see what has been going on since the last visit. In this way, you will assess both new symptoms and the response to new medications.

Interval History: "Patient has some mild decrease in exercise tolerance, but it has not changed recently. No dyspnea with household and work activities."

Report:
- *Chest x-ray: bilateral hilar adenopathy*

Hilar Adenopathy Etiology
- Lymphoma
- Thyroid
- Teratoma
- Sarcoid
- TB

With no fever, weight loss, or palpable peripheral adenopathy, it is hard to conclude that this is lymphoma or malignancy. Tuberculosis should give fever, cough, and sputum and

> would not give a "waxing and waning" presentation with intermittent episodes. Although there are no interstitial infiltrates, early sarcoid can present just with hilar adenopathy. The majority will never progress to having interstitial infiltrates.

Orders:
- PFTs
- Calcium blood
- Calcium urine
- Angiotensin-converting enzyme (ACE) level
- CHEM-20

Reports:
- Calcium: blood normal, urine elevated
- ACE: elevated

Granulomas in sarcoid produce vitamin D.

Calcium is freely filtered at the glomerulus.

Report:
- PFTs

Which of these is consistent with sarcoidosis?

	FEV$_1$ (%)	FVC (%)	TLC (%)
a.	86	94	92
b.	42	64	124
c.	58	60	56
d.	96	53	78

FEV$_1$, forced expiratory volume at 1 second;
FVC, forced vital capacity; TLC, total lung capacity.

Answer c. FEV$_1$ 58% [decreased], FVC 60% [decreased], TLC 56% [decreased]

Sarcoidosis is a pulmonary fibrosis that results in restrictive lung disease. All of the lung volumes are decreased, but they are down proportionately. The ratio of FEV$_1$ to FVC is

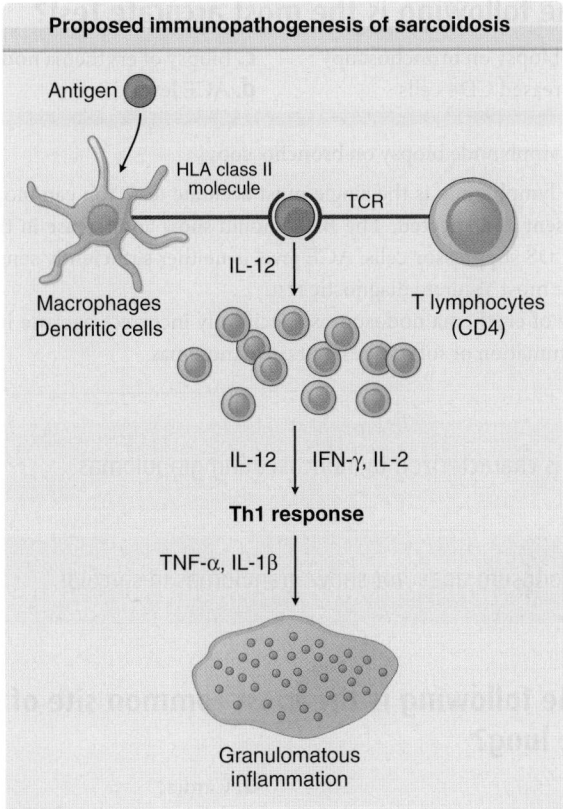

Figure 7-7. Proposed immunopathogenesis of sarcoidosis. An antigen, presently unknown, is engulfed and processed by an antigen-presenting cell (macrophage or dendritic cell). The processed antigen is presented to a T-cell receptor (TCR) of a T lymphocyte via an human leukocyte antigen (HLA) class II molecule. Once the HLA receptor and TCR have bound the processed antigen, numerous lymphokines and cytokines of the T helper 1 (Th1) class are released that lead to T-cell proliferation, recruitment of monocytes, and eventual granuloma formation. A few of these lymphokines and cytokines are shown, with those released by the antigen-presenting cells on the left and those released by lymphocytes on the right. IFN, interferon; IL, interleukin; TNF, tumor necrosis factor. (Reproduced with permission from Goldsmith LA, et al. *Fitzpatrick's Dermatology in General Medicine*, 8th ed. [online] New York: McGraw-Hill; 2012.)

normal. Restrictive lung disease is present in sarcoid even when there is only adenopathy visible on the chest x-ray. Early fibrosis will not be visible on the chest x-ray.

The patient is informed that she likely has sarcoidosis (Figure 7-7). The skin lesions are likely sarcoid as well. Only 10% of patients with sarcoidosis have an elevated blood calcium level, but 60% to 75% have elevated urine calcium levels.

Which of the following is the most accurate test?

a. Lymph node biopsy on bronchoscopy **c.** Biopsy of erythema nodosum on shins
b. BAL with increased CD4 cells **d.** ACE level

Answer a. Lymph node biopsy on bronchoscopy

The biopsy of a lymph node is the single most accurate test. You can biopsy a peripheral node if it is present and affected. The BAL should show an increase in the ratio of CD4 helper cells to CD8 suppressor cells. ACE level is neither sufficiently sensitive or specific enough to be the most accurate diagnostic test.

The biopsy of erythema nodosum is specifically incorrect because it will show panniculitis or inflammation of soft tissues, but no granulomas.

> Sarcoidosis is characterized by noncaseating granulomas.

> Erythema nodosum does *not* show granulomas in sarcoid!

Which of the following is the most common site of sarcoid outside the lung?

a. Liver **d.** Cardiac
b. Skin **e.** Salivary gland
c. CNS

Answer b. Skin

All of the listed sites can be involved in sarcoidosis, but the most common area outside the lung is the skin. The liver, spleen, and kidney are involved, but they are almost always clinically silent.

> Cardiac Sarcoid
> • Atrioventricular (AV) block
> • Restrictive cardiomyopathy

> Neurosarcoidosis
> • Hypothalamus
> • Pituitary
> • Bilateral facial palsy

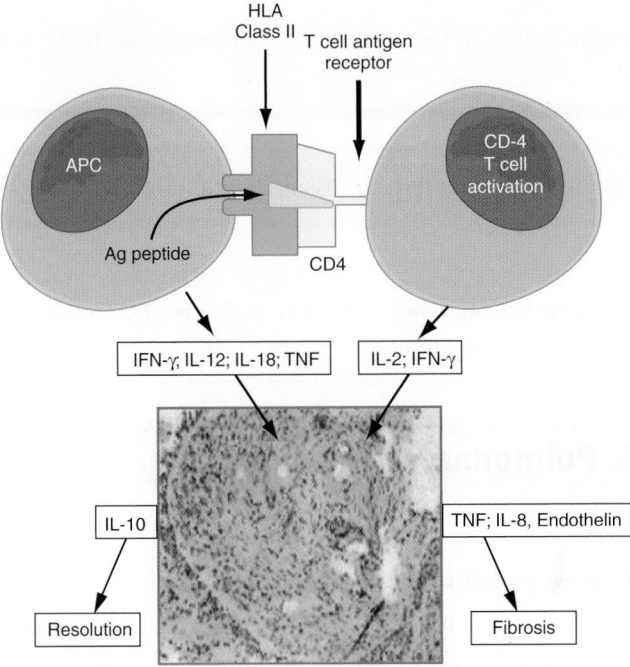

Figure 7-8. Schematic representation of initial events of sarcoidosis. The antigen-presenting cell and helper T-cell complex leads to the release of multiple cytokines. This forms a granuloma. Over time, the granuloma may resolve or lead to chronic disease, including fibrosis. APC, antigen-presenting cell; HLA, human leukocyte antigen; IFN, interferon; IL, interleukin; TNF, tumor necrosis factor. (Reproduced with permission from Longo DL, et al. *Harrison's Principles of Internal Medicine*, 18th ed., Vol 2. New York: McGraw-Hill; 2012.)

> *The patient undergoes transbronchial biopsy, which shows noncaseating granulomas (Figure 7-8) in the lymph nodes. Currently, she is not short of breath.*

What is your next step?

a. Treat with intermittent pulses of prednisone to prevent exacerbations.
b. Treat with cyclophosphamide.

c. Treat with prednisone when episodes of shortness of breath arise.
d. Treat with anti-tumor necrosis factor (TNF) medications.

Answer C. Treat with prednisone when episodes of shortness of breath arise.

Asymptomatic sarcoidosis needs no therapy. When symptoms arise, they should quickly resolve when treated with steroids. This is exactly what has been happening to the patient when she got labeled as asthmatic. Steroid doses would improve the sarcoidosis, but it would seem to the physician as improving asthma.

The diffusing capacity of the lungs for carbon monoxide (DLCO) is low in sarcoid.

Carbon monoxide diffuses through tissue 200 times easier than oxygen.

On CCS, this sarcoidosis case is to be seen "as needed" on the clock. If there are no symptoms, no treatment or testing is needed.

CASE 8: Pulmonary Hypertension

Setting: *office*

CC: *"I really get out of breath when I walk around."*

VS: *BP: 114/72 mm Hg; P: 90 beats/minute; T: 99.8°F; R:14 breaths/minute*

HPI: *You are visited at your office by a 34-year-old woman with recently diagnosed CREST (calcinosis cutis, Raynaud phenomenon, esophageal motility disorder, sclerodactyly, and telangiectasia) syndrome and with increasing dyspnea especially on exertion that has been slowly progressive over several months. She originally presented last year with triphasic color changes and pain of Raynaud phenomenon. Nifedipine partially controls this. Her skin has been tightening up, but she is still mobile. Her reflux disease is well maintained on omeprazole. She has no cough, fever, or sputum.*

PMHx/Medications: *as above*

PE:
- *General: thin woman*
- *Chest: no rales; no crepitations; no dullness to percussion*
- *Cardiovascular: loud P$_2$, no murmur*
- *Skin: immobile, sclerodactyly present; few telangiectasia*

Initial Orders:
- *Chest x-ray*
- *Echocardiogram*
- *Oximeter*
- *CBC*

Report:
- *Oximeter: 91% to 92% saturation on room air*

Because oxygen saturation is >90% on room air, you do not order supplemental oxygen. Clearly, the patient desaturates when walking around, as oxygen demand increases. Schedule a repeat visit in a few days after the test results are back.

What do you expect to find on the CBC?

a. Increased platelets
b. Hct increased, MCV decreased
c. Hct decreased, MCV decreased
d. Normal
e. WBC count increased

Answer b. Hct increased, MCV decreased

The body's response to chronic hypoxia is to increase erythropoietin and red blood cell (RBC) production. This decreases MCV. Erythropoietin is produced at the kidney, which is also the site of detection of chronic hypoxia.

What is the physiologic mechanism of a loud P₂?

a. Tricuspid stenosis
b. Pulmonic stenosis
c. Pulmonary hypertension
d. Aortic stenosis
e. Atrial septal defect

Answer c. Pulmonary hypertension

The P₂ is the second part of the S₂ heart sound. When there is pulmonary hypertension, the normal P₂ becomes like a "slammed shut door," and it is a sign of both increased pressure and decreased flow out of the pulmonary valve.

> **Reports:**
> - *Chest x-ray: enlarged right ventricle on lateral x-ray*
> - *Echocardiogram: pulmonary hypertension, increased right ventricular wall thickness, and right ventricular hypertrophy*

What is the mechanism of pulmonary hypertension in this patient?

a. CREST causes primary pulmonary hypertension with normal lung parenchyma.
b. The patient has pulmonary fibrosis.
c. Hypoxia led to vasoconstriction of the pulmonary vasculature, which led to pulmonary hypertension.
d. Right-to-left shunting through a patent foramen ovale puts desaturated blood in the lungs.
e. Carbon dioxide retention makes the pulmonary vasculature dilate.

Answer a. CREST causes primary pulmonary hypertension with normal lung parenchyma.

CREST syndrome includes primary pulmonary hypertension. It is called "primary" entirely because the lung parenchyma is normal. Anyone with lung fibrosis or COPD has pulmonary hypertension from decreased compliance of the lung and the greater work of the right ventricle. Primary pulmonary hypertension leads to hypoxia. Hypoxia further constricts pulmonary vessels. The origin of the defect, however, is the idiopathic narrowing of the PA.

CREST Pulmonary Hypertension
• Excess prostacyclin
• Excess endothelin

The patient returns in 3 months feeling worsening dyspnea.

PE:
• *Abdomen: enlarged liver*
• *Extremities: peripheral edema*

Pulmonary Hypertension = Decreased RV Filling

Decreased RV Filling = Increased Hydrostatic Venous Pressure

Increased venous hydrostatic pressure transudates edema into tissues.

Orders:
• *Furosemide orally is started.*

Over the next few weeks, the patient continues to have worsening dyspnea on exertion. Oxygen saturation hovers at 89% to 90%. Oxygen is started.

Oxygen vasodilates pulmonary vasculature.
Oxygen decreases pulmonary hypertension.

Progression of dyspnea continues. The patient feels fine at rest on oxygen but quickly desaturates on exertion. The repeat echocardiogram shows worsening PA pressure.

Orders:
• *Warfarin to INR 2 to 3*
• *Pulmonary consultation*
• *Evaluation for right-sided heart catheterization and vasoreactivity test*
• *Trial of calcium channel blockers*

Anticoagulation for:
- Sluggish blood flow +
- Intrapulmonary thrombosis +
- Dilated right side of heart

The patient returns in 2 weeks. There is no significant improvement in symptoms. Right-sided heart catheterization was equivocal for improvement with calcium channel blockers (e.g., diltiazem). Pulmonary consultation, as do all consultations on CCS, does not give specific advice.

Orders:
- *Continue home oxygen, warfarin, and furosemide.*
- *Begin trial of bosentan (or ambrisentan).*

Bosentan or Ambrisentan
- Endothelin-1 antagonists
- Decrease growth of PA

After 2 weeks, on return, the patient is no better. Her oxygen saturation hits 90% on a 3-L nasal canula and her exercise tolerance is deteriorating.

Orders:
- *Add epoprostenol.*
- *Add sildenafil.*

Epoprostenol
- Prostacyclin analogue
- Prostaglandin I_2
- Eicosanoid derivative
- Inhibits platelet activation
- Vasodilatory

Sildenafil
- Phosphodiesterase inhibitor
- Cyclic guanosine monophosphate (cGMP) inhibitor
- Prolongs nitric oxide effect
- Vasodilates pulmonary vasculature

Over time, severe pulmonary hypertension may need lung transplantation. The management of primary pulmonary hypertension is extremely difficult. There is no medical therapy to cure or permanently halt the disorder. Most treatment is a matter of trial and error.

CHAPTER 8

RHEUMATOLOGY

CASE 1: Rheumatoid Arthritis

Setting: *office*

CC: *"My hands hurt."*

VS: *normal*

HPI: *A 38-year-old woman with pain in her hands for the past year visits you at your office. She takes acetaminophen and over-the-counter nonsteroidal antiinflammatory drugs (NSAIDs) with some relief. The pain began in several metacarpophalangeal (MCP) joints of the hands with the thumb especially affected. Pain has started in the feet as well, affecting the metatarsophalangeal (MTP) joints. She has difficulty moving the joints when getting out of bed or after staying in one position too long. The pain is worse in the morning, but improves as she starts to move around over the course of the day over the next 1 to 2 hours.*

PMHx: *none*

Medications:
- *Ibuprofen*
- *Acetaminophen*

PE:
- *Musculoskeletal*
  - *"Boggy" swelling of several small joints in each hand and foot symmetrically*
  - *Decreased grip strength of hands*
  - *One elbow minimally involved*
- *Skin: no nodules in skin*
- *Chest: dullness and decreased breath sounds at left base*

Initial Orders:
- *Erythrocyte sedimentation rate (ESR)*
- *C-reactive protein (CRP)*
- *Anti-cyclic citrullinated peptide (anti-CCP)*
- *Rheumatoid factor (RF)*
- *X-ray of hands*
- *Chest x-ray*

The cause of rheumatoid arthritis (RA) is unknown.

Short-term steroid therapy can sometimes help acutely.

Chronic NSAID use: 20% chance of ulcer per year

The patient continues to use ibuprofen for pain with some relief.

Reports:
- *ESR: 68 mm/h*
- *CRP: elevated*
- *Anti-CCP: positive*
- *RF: positive*
- *X-ray of hands: normal joints*
- *Chest x-ray: effusion on one side*

What is the difference in the overall clinical value of CRP and ESR?

a. None
b. ESR is for diagnosis; CRP is for follow up.
c. ESR is more sensitive for RA.
d. CRP is better for predicting mortality.
e. ESR is more useful in response to therapy.

Answer a. None

There is no overall difference in the use of ESR or CRP in either diagnosis or the response to treatment. There is no clear area in which there is a definite benefit of one versus the other in testing, treatment, or prognosis.

Anti-CCP is the most *specific* of the tests for RA.

RF: immunoglobulin M (IgM) against the Fc portion of IgG

Which of these is essential to diagnose RA?

a. Abnormal x-ray
b. Nodules
c. Anti-CCP or RF positive
d. Anemia
e. Arthrocentesis

Answer c. Anti-CCP or RF positive

There *must* be *some* laboratory evidence of RA to establish a diagnosis. There is no one single test to establish a diagnosis of RA even though the anti-CCP is the most specific of the tests. An anti-CCP antibody result alone, without the involvement of multiple small joints, morning stiffness >1 hour, and a duration of several months is not RA. Normocytic anemia happens from the anemia of chronic disease and is completely nonspecific. Nodules are only present in 20% of patients, though they can be present in the lung and eyes. An abnormal x-ray is most certainly *not* essential for establishing a diagnosis of RA. The entire point of using disease-modifying antirheumatic drugs (DMARDs) is to prevent the development of an abnormal result shown on x-ray.

> The "bogginess" felt on palpation during the examination is overgrown synovial lining.

> RF is associated with
> • Hepatitis C
> • Cryoglobulins
> • Endocarditis
> • Tuberculosis
> • Age

Positive RF does *not* equal RA.
Positive RF *alone* does *not* equal anything.

What is unique about the pleural effusion of RA seen in this patient?

a. High white blood cell (WBC) count
b. Low glucose level
c. High protein level
d. Negative Gram stain

Answer b. Low glucose level

For unclear reasons (like everything in RA), the etiology of low glucose level in RA pleural effusion is unknown. RA effusions do, however, have the lowest glucose level of any pleural effusion.

The patient is started on low-dose prednisone and methotrexate (MTX). She returns the following week and has marked improvement in pain, mobility, and morning stiffness.

> • MTX takes 2 to 6 weeks to be effective.
> • MTX is a folate antagonist.

After 1 month, steroids are stopped and the patient remains on MTX weekly and NSAIDs for pain. You must advise the patient against becoming pregnant while on MTX because it is teratogenic.

**MTX-caused liver or lung fibrosis is a *must know*
for the Step 3 examination!**

MTX Folate Antagonism = Teratogenicity

Which of these should you use if MTX cannot be tolerated?

a. Leflunomide

b. Gold salts

c. Cyclosporine

d. Penicillamine

Answer a. Leflunomide

Leflunomide is an alternative to MTX as a DMARD in those who have liver or lung fibrosis. None of the others is *ever* the right answer. Gold salts are no longer used in RA.

The patient comes to the office a few months after the start of MTX and is feeling better. She would like to become pregnant, but knows that MTX cannot be used in pregnancy.

Which is the best therapy for RA in pregnancy?

a. Sulfasalazine and hydroxychloroquine

b. Tumor necrosis factor (TNF) inhibitors

c. Minocycline

d. Leflunomide

Answer a. Sulfasalazine and hydroxychloroquine

These are the safest in pregnancy. Minocycline is a tetracycline antibiotic and should be avoided in pregnancy. Leflunomide is both a teratogen and a carcinogen.

Leflunomide is a pyrimidine antagonist.

The mechanism of retinal toxicity with hydroxychloroquine is unknown.

The patient stops MTX therapy and switches to hydroxychloroquine for a few months while waiting for the MTX to wash out of her system.

What will happen to her RA activity during pregnancy?

a. Improve

b. Worsen

c. No change

Answer a. Improve

Most persons with RA improve during pregnancy. This was the original observation in the 1930s that led to the discovery of steroids.

In the ninth month of pregnancy, now off MTX, why is it important to tell the patient's anesthesiologist and obstetrician prior to delivery that the patient has RA?

a. So they can order an x-ray of her neck

b. So they can give her bolus intravenous (IV) steroids

c. So they will not do a cesarean section (C-section) delivery

d. So they will stop hydroxychloroquine and sulfasalazine therapy

Answer a. So they can order an x-ray of her neck

Always inform surgical and anesthetic colleagues about RA because intubation is potentially dangerous because of C1 to C2 cervical spine subluxation (Figure 8-1). C-section is almost always done under epidural anesthesia so this is not dangerous. RA generally does not involve the axial skeleton, which is the spine and sacroiliac (SI) joints, but endotracheal intubation is especially dangerous. The hyperextension that is usually done can lead to cord compression.

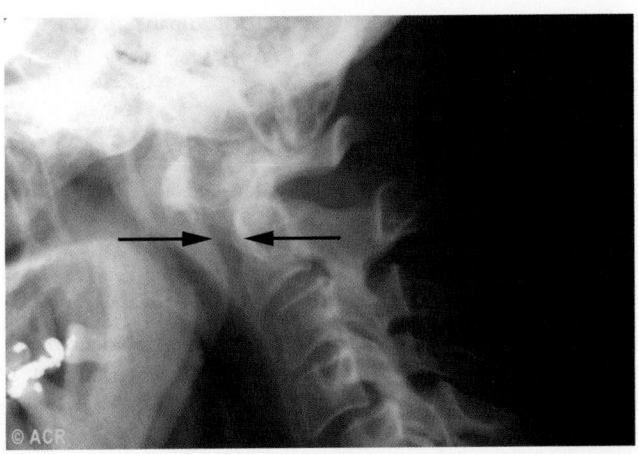

Figure 8-1. The cervical spine in rheumatoid arthritis, showing atlantoaxial subluxation. A lateral view of the upper cervical region shows posterior displacement of the odontoid process. The preodontoid space measures approximately 8 mm (*arrows*). Normally, this measurement should not exceed 2.5 to 3 mm in an adult. (Reproduced with permission from McKean SC, et al. *Principles and Practice of Hospital Medicine.* New York: McGraw-Hill; 2012.)

> *Moving the case forward a month or two at a time, or waiting for your pregnant patient to deliver, you then restart the MTX therapy.*

Which of the following is most likely to occur in the long term with RA?

a. SI joint involvement
b. Peritoneal inflammation
c. Carpal tunnel syndrome
d. Vasculitis
e. Pericarditis

Answer c. Carpal tunnel syndrome

Carpal tunnel can happen in 10% of patients. Pericardial involvement is rare (<1%) and usually clinically silent. Vasculitis is also much rarer than carpal tunnel.

> *The computer-based case simulation (CCS) and the Step 3 examination are very big on testing your ability to advise patients about prognosis. You have to know what to tell patients to expect. You should tell RA patients that they may get carpal tunnel. You do not have to tell patients to expect Felty syndrome (enlarged spleen and neutropenia).*
>
> *A year after the delivery of the baby and restarted on MTX, the patient's Interval History shows progression of joint pain and immobility.*

Which of these medications should be added next?

a. Adalimumab or etanercept
b. Rituximab
c. Abatacept
d. Tocilizumab
e. Anakinra

Answer a. Adalimumab or etanercept

These are TNF inhibitors. It is clear that you should use the TNF inhibitors first as add-on therapy to MTX if the disease progresses.

Why do TNF inhibitors reactivate tuberculosis (TB)?

a. They suppress neutrophil function.
b. They remove CD20 cells.
c. TNF maintains granulomas.
d. They block interleukin-6.
e. They block interleukin-1.
f. They inhibit T cell costimulation.

Answer c. TNF maintains granulomas.

TNF inhibitors (adalimumab, etanercept, golimumab, certolizumab) "unlock" the old TB stored away in walled-off granulomas (Figure 8-2). This is why purified protein derivative (PPD) screening is needed before they are used.

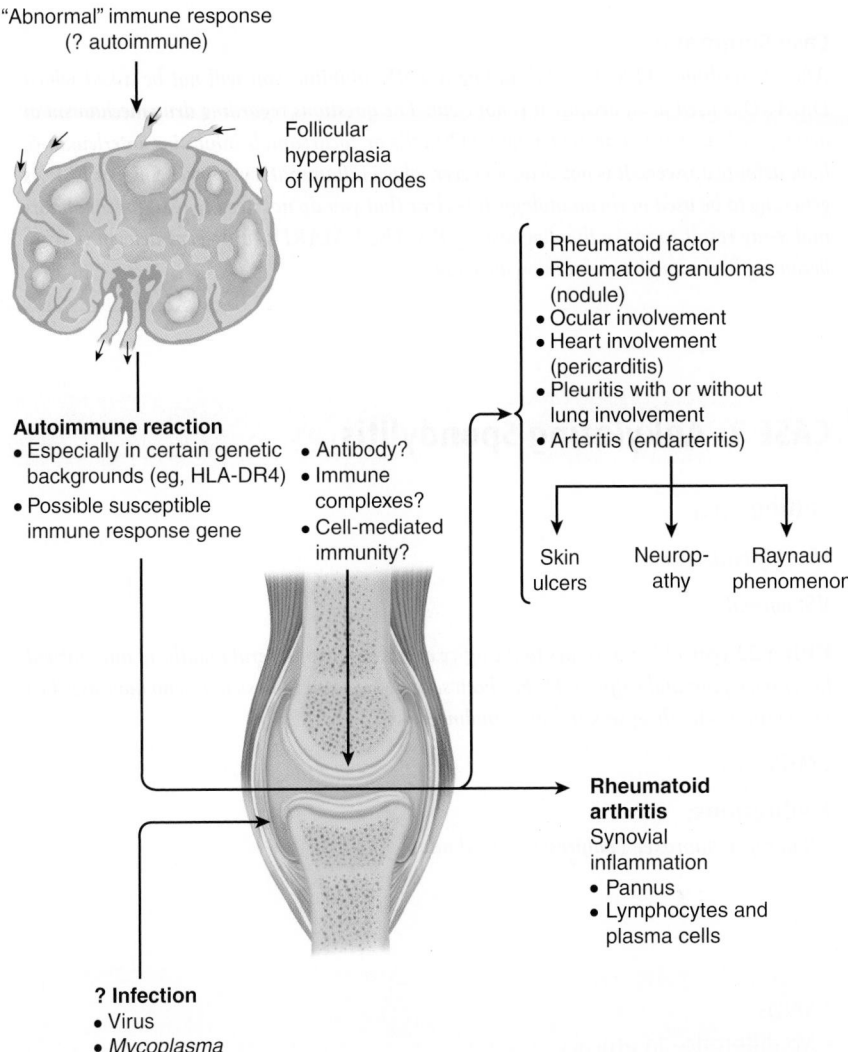

Figure 8-2. Pathophysiology of rheumatoid arthritis. HLA-DR4, human leukocyte antigen DR4. (Reproduced with permission from Chandrasoma P, Taylor CR. *Concise Pathology*, 3rd ed. Originally published by Appleton & Lange. © 1998 by the McGraw-Hill.)

Rituximab removes CD20 cells.
Anakinra suppresses neutrophil function.
Tocilizumab blocks interleukin-6.
Abatacept inhibits T-cell costimulation.

Case Summary:

After prescribing MTX first and adding a TNF inhibitor, you will not be asked which DMARD is used next, because it is not clear. The questions regarding drug mechanism of action, such as rituximab removing CD20 cells or tocilizumab inhibiting interleukin-6, have definite answers. It is not clear, however, which inflammatory marker, CRP or ESR, is generally to be used in rheumatology. It is clear that you do not need to wait for an abnormal x-ray result to make the diagnosis of RA. Use DMARDs to prevent deformity from becoming bad enough to be seen on an x-ray.

CASE 2: Ankylosing Spondylitis

Setting: *office*

CC: *"My back is sore."*

VS: *normal*

HPI: *A 22-year-old man comes to the office complaining of several months of intermittent lower back pain and stiffness. He has been seen by two other physicians who have ascribed his symptoms to "drug-seeking" and "malingering."*

PMHx: *none*

Medications:
• *Ibuprofen, naproxen (Naprosyn), or sulindac*

NSAIDs
• *No* difference in efficacy
• *No* difference in adverse effects

PE:
• *Musculoskeletal: normal*
• *Cardiovascular: normal*
• *Neurological: normal; normal reflexes; no focal neurological deficits; straight leg raise test is normal*

Initial Orders:
• *Ibuprofen as needed*

Indications for Radiologic Imaging with Back Pain
• Focal neurological defects
• Hyperreflexia
• Extensor plantar reflexes
• Bowel or bladder abnormalities (e.g., incontinence)

The straight leg raise test does *not* count as a "focal" neurological deficit.

After you educate and advise the patient on the lack of utility of imaging studies, he agrees to try only NSAIDs for a while longer, but he is frustrated.

Lower back pain: Without focal findings, spine imaging does not help 99% of patients.

Straight Leg Raise
• Cord *not* compressed
• Nerve root impingement (radiculopathy)

The patient returns in several months. His low back pain is gradually worsening. It is (1) more frequent, (2) associated with stiffness of the back, and (3) radiates into his buttocks.

Order:
• *Lumbosacral spine x-ray*   • *RF*
• *ESR*   • *Anti-CCP*

The patient returns in 2 weeks to discuss results and appears happy that you are taking his pain seriously and not dismissing him as a malingering drug-seeker. The immobility and stiffness of his back are worsening, but are distinctly better with use as the morning goes on.

An ankylosing spondylitis (AS) diagnosis is usually delayed by 2 years.

Human Leukocyte Antigen B27 (HLA-B27)
• Found in 8% of the general population
• Not a specific diagnostic test

Reports:
- *Lumbosacral spine x-ray: normal*
- *ESR: elevated*
- *RF: negative*
- *Anti-CCP: negative*

ESR is the only blood test that is positive in AS, but it is nonspecific.

The patient has had symptoms for about 18 to 24 months at this point. The SI joint and spine x-ray may be falsely normal.

What difference does it make if the diagnosis of AS is made now or later, since the disease is not curable?

a. There is no difference.

b. Pain medications can be increased.

c. TNF inhibitors delay progression of the disease.

d. You can add steroids.

e. You can add sulfasalazine.

Answer c. TNF inhibitors delay progression of the disease.

TNF inhibitors are of near miraculous benefit for patients with AS. They can stop pain in those not responsive to NSAIDs. The benefits can be of long duration, essentially delaying disease progression. Sulfasalazine has no benefit on axial disease. Steroids have no benefit in AS and worsen damage to the bone because they contribute to osteopenia and osteoporosis.

NSAIDs are not controlling the patient's back and buttock pain. The duration of morning stiffness is increasing.

Orders:
- *Magnetic resonance imaging (MRI) of SI joint*

MRI is based on tissue water content.

Report:
- *MRI: narrowing and damage of SI joint consistent with AS*

Which is most common in AS?

a. Anterior uveitis
b. Aortic regurgitation (AR)
c. Atrioventricular (AV) conduction block

d. Enthesopathy
e. Plantar fasciitis

Answer a. Anterior uveitis

All of the manifestations occur in AS. The most common is anterior uveitis (30–40%). Cardiac abnormalities (AV block, AR) occur in 3% to 4% of patients. Enthesopathy is inflammation of tendinous insertion sites. Enthesopathy can present as plantar fasciitis or "sausage digits" of the fingers and toes.

Schober Test = Immobile "Boardlike" Lower Spine

Sausage digits are more common in psoriatic arthritis than in AS.

The mechanism of eye and heart abnormalities is unknown in AS.

Which of the following is most likely in AS?

a. Obstructive lung disease
b. Restrictive lung disease

c. Apical lung fibrosis
d. Diaphragmatic paralysis

Answer b. Restrictive lung disease

As the chest wall stiffens, it becomes more and more difficult for patients to breathe in. Although apical lung fibrosis does occur, it is not as common as restrictive lung disease.

Spine and rib immobility cause restrictive lung disease.

"Bamboo Spine" = Vertebral Osteophytes

The patient is started on a TNF inhibitor and experiences a tremendous improvement in pain and mobility. AS is the only disease for which TNF inhibitors are first-line therapy. In RA and psoriasis, they are used only after the failure of other medication.

CASE 3: Sjögren Syndrome

Setting: *office*

CC: *"My eyes are always dry and my joints hurt."*

VS: *normal*

HPI: *A 50-year-old woman comes to the office with several months of increasing dryness of her mouth and eyes. Her eyes are "burning" and "itching" and sometimes feels like she has a grain of sand in them. She feels like she has "dry cotton" in her mouth. She has joint pain in her knees and ankles.*

Tear production is neutrally mediated through acetylcholine.

PMHx:
- *Primary biliary cirrhosis*
- *Hypothyroidism*

Medications:
- *Levothyroxine*
- *Artificial tears*

PE:
- *Head, ears, eyes, nose, throat (HEENT): several lost teeth, dental caries present*

What is the greatest stimulant to saliva production?

a. Acetylcholine

b. Epinephrine

c. Norepinephrine

d. Nicotinic receptors

Answer a. Acetylcholine

Saliva production is the only part of the body in which the sympathetic and parasympathetic nervous system both lead to increased production of a substance. The greatest stimulant, however, by far, is acetylcholine. The acetylcholine receptors in the salivary glands are muscarinic receptors not nicotinic receptors.

Nicotinic Receptors
- Neuromuscular junction
- Autonomic ganglia
- Central nervous system (CNS)

Which test is most likely to be positive in Sjögren syndrome?

a. Antinuclear antibody (ANA) **d.** RF

b. Anti-SSA (Ro) **e.** Anti-Jo

c. Anti-SSB (La)

Answer a. Antinuclear antibody (ANA)

Although the ANA test has no specificity for Sjögren syndrome, it is the test most commonly found to be positive. Ninety-five percent of patients with Sjögren syndrome should be positive for ANA, this means the ANA has an enormously strong negative predictive value for the disorder.

Initial Orders:

• *ANA*

• *Anti-SSA (Ro)*

• *Anti-SSB (La)*

• *RF*

• *Schirmer test*

Saliva pH is high to neutralize acid in the mouth.
Acid destroys tooth enamel.

Saliva has IgA to protect against infection.

Lactoferrin in saliva binds iron to "starve" bacteria of this essential nutrient.

Continue artificial tears and saliva. Sugar-free sour candy is useful to increase saliva production because the sour taste receptors are stronger than sweet, salt, umami, and bitter taste receptors in producing the highest volume of saliva.

Normal saliva volume is 1 to 2 *liters* a day.

More Acetylcholine = More Saliva

Acetylcholine will
- Increase bicarbonate content
- Increase volume
- Decrease sodium reabsorption

Reports:
- *ANA, anti-SSA (Ro), anti-SSB (La), RF: all positive*
- *Schirmer test: decreased tear production*

- Saliva is needed for taste and smell.
- Saliva is hypotonic.

Patients with Sjögren syndrome will lose their teeth because of multiple dental caries. Replacing saliva with artificial saliva and stimulating salivary flow is important.

Orders:
- *Artificial tears and saliva*
- *Pilocarpine*
- *Cevimeline*
- *Fluoride oral treatments*

How can salivary acetylcholine be increased?
Pilocarpine = Muscarinic Receptor Agonist
Cevimeline = Acetylcholine Analogue

What is the most specific test of Sjögren syndrome?

a. Anti-SSA

b. Lip biopsy

c. Schirmer test

d. Anti-SSB

Answer b. Lip biopsy

Lip biopsy shows the foci of lymphoid cells in salivary gland tissue in the accessory salivary glands. This is more specific than any serologic test.

The pilocarpine, cevimeline, and artificial tears improve symptoms immediately. The patient returns in a week because dry eyes still bother her.

Orders:
• *Cyclosporine eyedrops*
• *Counseling about possible development of lymphoma*

Cyclosporine:
• Inhibits lymphocyte activation
• Immunosuppressant
• Calcineurin inhibitor

Saliva
• Seventh and ninth cranial nerve control
• Slower Flow = More Sodium Reabsorption

Cevimeline is more active at the M1 and M3 receptors of the salivary and lacrimal glands.
Cevimeline is less active at the cardiac acetylcholine receptors.

Which of these impairs taste perception in Sjögren syndrome?

a. Loss of amylase and lipase
b. Loss of salivary protease

c. Increased lysozyme
d. Increased lactoperoxidase

Answer a. Loss of amylase and lipase

Salivary amylase and lipase break down enough starch and fat to increase taste perception of food. There is no normal salivary protease. Lysozyme and lactoperoxidase are decreased, but they kill bacteria and have nothing to do with taste perception.

Adverse Effects of Pilocarpine and Cevimeline
• Diarrhea
• Bronchospasm
• Bradycardia

Mechanism of Adverse Effect
• Overstimulation of muscarinic receptors

The patient's symptoms of oral dryness and eye dryness are improved. There is little therapy for the joint pain.

Orders:
• *Educate and advise the patient to avoid cola, coffee, and tea.*
• *Order a dental evaluation.*
• *Educate and advise the patient regarding diligent oral care.*

• Acid destroys teeth.
• The pH of cola is pH 2.5.
• Bacteria make acid.

CASE 4: Gout

Setting: *emergency department*

CC: *"My toe hurts real bad!"*

VS: *BP: 144/94 mm Hg; P: 96 beats/minute; T: 102°F; R: 18 breaths/minute*

Pain can cause hypertension and tachycardia.

HPI: *A 34-year-old Asian man arrives at the emergency department with the acute onset of severe pain in the great toe of his right foot that developed over a few hours. He had one episode like this before a few months ago but never went to the hospital because of being uninsured at that time. He took an over-the-counter NSAID and it got better in a day or two. Today the pain came on very suddenly, and his toe is clearly red and warm.*

PMHx/Medications: *none*

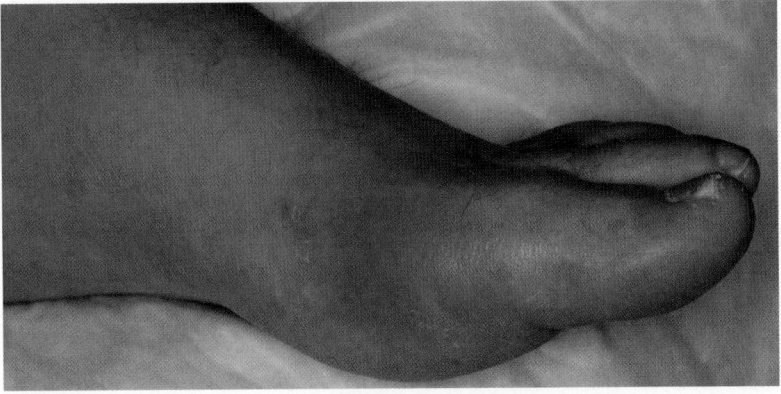

Figure 8-3. Podagra denotes gouty inflammation of the first metatarsophalangeal (MTP) joint. Note the swelling and erythema. (Reproduced with permission from Kevin J. Knoop, MD, MS.)

PE:
- *General: uncomfortable man, in pain trying to stay immobile*
- *Extremities: Great toe of right foot is warm, red, and extremely tender. Overlying skin is tense (Figure 8-3).*
- *HEENT: no tophi*
- *Skin: no tophi*

Tophi = Gout

Tophi
• Deposits of monosodium urate crystals
• Foreign body reaction

Initial Orders:
- *Arthrocentesis*
- *Ibuprofen*
- *Basic metabolic panel (CHEM-7)*
- *Uric acid level*

Acute gout and septic joints can look very similar.

Men have higher uric acid levels.
Gout is more common in men than in women.

Reports:
- *Synovial fluid cell count: WBCs 44,000/μL; 80% neutrophils; Gram-stain negative*
- *CHEM-7: blood urea nitrogen (BUN) 21 g/dL (elevated); creatinine 1.8 mg/dL (elevated)*
- *Uric acid level: 7.2 mg/dL (The normal level for men is 2.4–7.4 mg/dL.)*

- Uric acid levels are normal in 25% of acute gout attacks.
- Uric acid level decreases from precipitation as crystals in an acute attack.

The cell count is 39,000/μL, predominantly neutrophils, and the uric acid level is normal. What is the appropriate approach for this patient?

a. Treat the gout.

b. Treat the infectious arthritis.

c. Treat both the gout and infectious arthritis.

d. Wait for definitive tests to treat.

e. Give intraarticular antibiotics only.

Answer c. Treat both the gout and infectious arthritis.

The patient's cell count is in a range equivocal for gout and infectious arthritis, the Gram stain shows no organisms, and the uric acid level is normal.

Infectious arthritis:
- Cell count: usually >50,000 to 100,000/μL
- Stain: 50% to 70% sensitive
- Culture: 90% sensitive, but takes 2 to 3 days

Gout:
- Cell count: 20,000 to 50,000/μL
- Uric acid level: normal in 25% of patients

Gout attacks are extremely painful. When the diagnosis is unclear, it is best to order treatment for both infectious arthritis and gout until the crystal analysis is done. Intraarticular antibiotics are never needed for septic arthritis. All antibiotics will pass into the joint fluid.

Synovial lining has no basement membrane.
All antibiotics pass into the synovial fluid.

Orders:
• *Crystal analysis by polarized light microscopy*
• *Ceftriaxone and vancomycin IV*
• *Rheumatology evaluation*
• *Intraarticular triamcinolone*

Do not use NSAIDs in patients with renal insufficiency.

• Prostaglandins dilate the afferent arteriole.
• NSAIDs cause vasoconstriction of the afferent arteriole.
• NSAIDs cause papillary necrosis.

Report:
• *Crystal analysis: positive for negatively birefringent needle-shaped crystals*

Acute Gout
• Monocytes and synoviocytes ingest uric acid crystals.
• They get inflamed.

The patient continues to have extremely severe pain for the next 4 to 6 hours. As you move the clock forward reexamine the patient and do an "Interval History." If steroids work, they will do so after about 6 hours, the same as they do in an acute asthma exacerbation. If there is a contraindication to NSAID use such as renal insufficiency or active ulcer disease, use steroids.

Steroids and Acute Gout
• Single joint: inject
• Multiple joints: IV or oral

> *As the clock moves to 12 to 24 hours after the injection of triamcinolone, there is marked improvement in symptoms. The toe is less red, less warm, and less febrile.*

Acute gout causes fever.

When is colchicine the answer for gout?

a. Never

b. As an alternative to NSAIDs for acute gout

c. As first-line preventive therapy

d. As an alternative to xanthine oxidase inhibitors in prevention

Answer d. As an alternative to xanthine oxidase inhibitors in prevention

Colchicine is no longer used to treat acute gout. Acute gout is treated with NSAIDs, and if there is renal insufficiency or ulcer disease, with steroids. Colchicine is an alternative to xanthine oxidase inhibitors such as allopurinol or febuxostat in preventing gout attacks.

Colchicine inhibits microtubule formation.

Orders:
- *CHEM-7*
- *Uric acid level*

Never start allopurinol during an acute gout attack!

In questioning the patient about the food he's eaten, what is most likely to have caused the acute attack?

a. Milk and cheese

b. Steak and beer

c. Butter and eggs

d. Gluten (wheat)-containing foods

Answer b. Steak and beer

Red meat, beer, and seafood have the highest purine content. Dairy products decrease the risk of gouty attack. Milk, butter, and eggs are low-purine foods.

CHAPTER 8: **RHEUMATOLOGY** 363

Vegetables with rapid growth have high purine content:
· Asparagus
· Spinach
· Peas, lentils

Alcohol increases uric acid production.

Report:
· *CHEM-7: BUN 25 g/dL (elevated); creatinine 2.1 mg/dL (elevated)*
· *Uric acid level: 7.8 mg/dL (The normal level for men is 2.4–7.4 mg/dL.)*

What is the mechanism of renal dysfunction in gout?

a. Vasoconstriction of the afferent arteriole
b. Urate crystal deposition in the medulla and pyramids
c. Obstructive renal stones
d. Inhibition of filtration at the glomerulus
e. Excess filtration at the glomerulus

Answer b. Urate crystal deposition in the medulla and pyramids

Renal insufficiency is directly proportional to the height of a person's uric acid levels. The higher the uric acid level, the more uric acid will deposit in the kidney and form stones. Uric acid has no effect on filtration or on the vasculature.

Drugs That Cause Gout Attacks
· Thiazides
· Niacin

Move the clock forward. Once pain has improved, you can send the patient home and have him come back for an office visit. In several weeks, recheck the uric acid level and start uric acid–lowering medications.

Order:
· *Allopurinol orally*
· *Uric acid level*

Move the clock forward 1 week and recheck uric acid levels. Seeing the patient right after the start of allopurinol is the correct approach because

- *Allopurinol hypersensitivity (rash, renal failure) is common.*
- *Xanthine oxidase inhibitors can precipitate acute gout attacks.*
- *Colchicine to prevent an attack on starting allopurinol is an acceptable use of colchicine.*

If the uric acid level is not controlled on allopurinol, then switch allopurinol to febuxostat. If febuxostat is not controlling the patient, add an uricase medication. Pegloticase metabolizes uric acid to allantoin.

Pegloticase
- It is an uricase.
- It metabolizes uric acid to allantoin.
- Allantoin is easily excreted by the kidneys.

Probenecid
- Increases urinary excretion of uric acid
- Not effective with low urine flow or renal insufficiency

If on moving the case forward, kidney stones are described, the treatment is to alkalinize the urine. Calcium oxalate stones form in an alkaline urine, but uric acid stones dissolve in alkaline urine.

Urine acid solubility increases with urine pH >6.0.

CASE 5: Osteoarthritis

Setting: *office*

CC: *"My knees hurt."*

VS: *normal*

HPI: *A 64-year-old man comes to your office complaining of worsening pain and discomfort in his knees. This has been happening gradually over the past year. He claims "to* *hear them creaking" when he gets up from a seated position. He has pain in his hands in multiple joints. His grip strength is down and he has a hard time opening the lids of jars and twisting the knobs on water faucets. All the pain is definitely worse toward the end of the day and with increased use.*

Worsening with Use = Osteoarthritis (OA)
Better with Use = Rheumatoid Arthritis (RA)

ROS:
- *The patient has no fever and no weight loss.*
- *He denies injection drug use.*
- *Discomfort makes him avoidant of exercise.*

PMHx:
- *Hypertension*
- *Former tobacco smoker*

Medications:
- *NSAIDs*
- *Nifedipine*

Medications do not cause OA.
Medications do not prevent OA.

PE:
- *General: obese; cheerful as long as he does not move*
- *Musculoskeletal:*
  - *Prominent tuberosities of the distal interphalangeal (DIP) joints*
  - *Crepitus palpable on movement of knees*
  - *No warmth, no redness, no tenderness*

DIP Joints Affected = OA or Psoriatic Arthritis
Proximal Interphalangeal (PIP) and MCP Joints Affected = RA
Spine and SI Affected = AS
Single Large Joint Affected = Septic or Lyme

Articular cartilage is composed mostly of water.

Initial Orders:
- *X-ray*
- *ESR, RF, CRP, ANA*
- *Complete blood count (CBC)*
- *CHEM-7*

Which of these will be abnormal in OA?

a. None
b. X-ray of knees and hands
c. ESR, RF, CRP, ANA
d. CBC
e. CHEM-7

Answer a. None

You are not doing these tests because you expect anything to be abnormal in OA. Quite the opposite. You are doing these tests because if any of them is abnormal it is likely *not* OA! The reason for the CHEM-7 test is to be careful about the use of NSAIDs in those with renal insufficiency. The CBC is looking for a microcytic anemia that may have been caused by an occult ulcer. Although daily NSAID use leads to an ulcer in 10% to 20% of patients after a year, only half (5–10%) will be symptomatic and half of them (1–3%) will bleed from it.

What should all users of NSAIDs be taking along with the NSAIDs?

a. Proton pump inhibitor (PPI)
b. H$_2$-blocker
c. Misoprostol
d. None
e. Sucralfate

Answer d. None

Although daily PPI use (e.g., omeprazole) will decrease the risk of ulcers, there is no routine recommendation to put every NSAID user on a PPI. H$_2$-blockers, such as cimetidine or sucralfate, which coat the gastric lining, are even less effective. Misoprostol is never the right answer for anything in gastroenterology.

Misoprostol
- Increases prostaglandins
- Supposed to increase gastric mucous production
- Nice basic science idea
- Does not work

The patient returns to discuss his laboratory test results the following week. He has no change in symptoms.

Reports:
• *ANA, RF, CRP, CHEM-7, CBC: normal*
• *X-ray: joint space narrowing, osteophytes*

Be careful of nonspecific laboratory tests!
• ANA is positive in 5% of the population.
• RF increases with age.

CCS is more "liberal" or "forgiving" with the amount of testing you can order. In this case, getting some "extra tests" like the CHEM-7, ANA, or RF would be forgiven. On a single best answer question about OA, do not order any tests.

Joint Space Narrowing (Figure 8-4)
• There is loss of articular cartilage.
• Articular cartilage is water.
• Water is radiolucent.

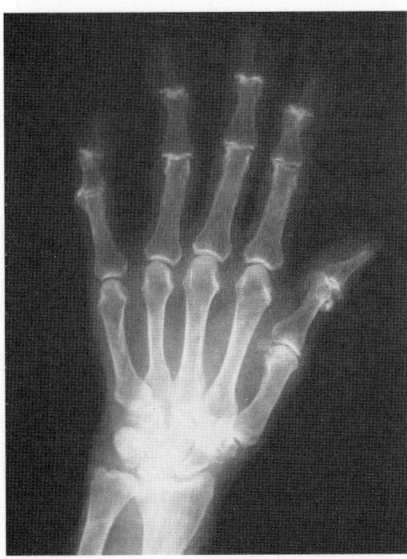

Figure 8-4. Radiograph of a hand showing osteoarthritis of the distal interphalangeal (DIP), proximal interphalangeal (PIP), and first carpometacarpal (CMC) joints. Note the joint-space narrowing of the DIP and PIP joints compared to the metacarpophalangeal joints, as well as the bony sclerosis (eburnation) of all joints involved by the osteoarthritis process. (Reproduced with permission from Imboden JB, et al. *Current Diagnosis & Treatment: Rheumatology*, 3rd ed. New York: McGraw-Hill; 2013.)

Osteophytes
• They are caused by asymptomatic widening of the articular contact area.
• They "spread the load."
• Weak bone needs more surface area.

What is the best pain medication for OA?

a. Acetaminophen

b. Ibuprofen

c. Indomethacin

d. Chondroitin sulfate

e. Glucosamine

Answer a. Acetaminophen

Acetaminophen has an equivalent analgesic capacity to NSAIDs but no adverse effects on the gastrointestinal system. Indomethacin is an NSAID that with chronic use will practically burn a hole in your stomach. Indomethacin should never be used chronically.

Glucosamine + Chondroitin = Placebo

You switch the patient from an NSAID to acetaminophen.

Orders:

• *Advise weight loss.*
• *Advise exercise and weight training.*
• *Consult physical therapy.*

Weight loss will decrease force on joints.
Strengthening muscles decreases work on joints.

The patient comes to see you every few months for blood pressure (BP) management. He comes to see you on a Monday morning after his knee becomes worse after going hiking with his grandchildren.

PE:

• *Worsening redness and crepitans of knee*

Orders:

• *Hyaluronic acid injection*
• *Intraarticular triamcinolone*
• *Orthopedic surgery evaluation*

- Hyaluronic acid and steroid injection helps relieve pain but lasts for a short time.
- Hyaluronic acid increases synovial fluid volume and buoyancy.

Move the clock forward an hour after the injections of steroids and hyaluronic acid. On the Interval History, there is significant improvement in pain and discomfort. Ultimately, there is *no medical therapy to reverse the process of OA. Losing weight decreases the stress on the knees and ankles. Exercise will strengthen the muscles around the joint to bear more of the load. Both of these interventions can slow the process of deterioration, but cannot reverse it. Eventually, more than 100,000 people a year in the United States alone need knee replacement. When the patient gets to the point where relief of pain and immobility requires steroid and hyaluronic acid injections, referral should be made for replacement of the affected joint.*

CASE 6: Scleroderma

Setting: *office*

CC: *"My face and hands are getting tight."*

VS: *BP: 152/94 mm Hg; P: 86 beats/minute; T: 98°F; R: 22 breaths/minute*

HPI: *A 43-year-old woman with progressive immobility of her fingers and tightening of her face visits you in your office. She is also somewhat short of breath but only with two to three blocks of exertion. She does not notice the dyspnea often because joint pain makes her avoid walking.*

PMHx:
- *Hypertension*
- *Raynaud disease*

Medications:
- *Nifedipine*

PE:
- *Chest: fine crepitations throughout*
- *Extremities: sclerodactyly, edema of lower extremities*
- *Skin: tightening at face and hand, no Raynaud disease now; some telangiectasia present*

Which of the following tests is most likely to be positive?

a. SCL-70

b. Anti-centromere antibody

c. ANA

d. Antineutrophil cytoplasmic autoantibody (ANCA)

e. Anti-Jo

Answer c. ANA

As with many autoimmune disorders, ANA is most likely to be positive, but has no specificity. ANA is positive in 80% to 95% of those with scleroderma, which gives it a false negative rate of only 5% to 15%. Anti-Jo reveals lung involvement in polymyositis and dermatomyositis.

	Scleroderma (%)	CREST Syndrome (%)
ANA	80–95	80–95
SCL-70	30	20
Anti-centromere	1	50
RF	30	30

ANA, antinuclear antibody; CREST, calcinosis cutis, Raynaud phenomenon, esophageal motility disorder, sclerodactyly, and telangiectasia; RF, rheumatoid factor.

Calcinosis: mechanism unknown
Sclerodactyly: mechanism unknown

Scleroderma + High BP = Angiotensin-Converting Enzyme (ACE) Inhibitors

Initial Orders:
- SCL-70
- ANA
- Chest x-ray
- Oximeter
- CHEM-7, CBC
- Enalapril

Nifedipine is best for Raynaud disease.

SCL-70 is an antibody against topoisomerase III.

See the patient as soon as possible after starting the ACE inhibitor. Chemistry should be checked to see there is no worsening of renal function.
Interval History: "Patient has epigastric pain going into chest with sore throat and bad taste in mouth."

VS: *BP: 124/84 mm Hg on enalapril*

On CCS, you cannot order medications by class. You have to write "enalapril" or "lisinopril." You cannot just order "ACE inhibitor." Do not worry about spelling. CCS automatically checks spelling and asks if you are sure that is the drug or test you wanted.

Reports:
- *SCL-70: positive*
- *ANA: positive*
- *Chest x-ray: normal*
- *Oximeter: 96% saturation on room air*
- *CHEM-7, CBC: normal except slight anemia; hematocrit 34%; mean corpuscular value (MCV) normal; no eosinophilia*

Eosinophilic Fasciitis
Thick Skin +
Orange Color +
Worse on Exertion +
Eosinophils =
Treat with Steroids

Inform the patient she likely has gastroesophageal reflux disease (GERD). Patients with scleroderma have the skin manifestations before the internal organ involvement.

What is the main difference between CREST and scleroderma?

a. GERD
b. Telangiectasia
c. Lung and heart
d. Pulmonary hypertension
e. Calcinosis and sclerodactyly

Answer c. Lung and heart

Scleroderma or progressive systemic sclerosis has all the manifestations of CREST and also has the involvement of several internal organs. Scleroderma involves the heart, lungs, and kidneys. CREST has a primary pulmonary hypertension, but the lung parenchyma itself is normal. In scleroderma, the pulmonary hypertension is secondary to lung fibrosis. Both disorders have joint pain and skin manifestations.

Scleroderma has:
- Renal
- Heart
- Lung

Orders:
- *Omeprazole*
- *Continue ACE inhibitor and nifedipine*

Although the underlying pathology and disease progression of scleroderma are not an emergency, the symptoms of GERD, elevated BP, and Raynaud disease can be controlled.

Interval History: "Epigastric pain and bad taste in mouth are improved on PPIs; BP 124/78 mm Hg."

Which manifestation of scleroderma can be slowed with treatment?

a. Calcinosis and sclerodactyly

b. Pulmonary fibrosis

c. Renal fibrosis

d. Cardiac fibrosis

Answer b. Pulmonary fibrosis

We do not have a clear treatment to stop the progression of skin calcinosis or sclerodactyly. Pulmonary fibrosis may be slowed with cyclophosphamide or mycophenolate. Although we use ACE inhibitors for renal hypertensive crisis, this is not the same as controlling the primary renal fibrosis or the cardiac fibrosis. Pulmonary hypertension can be treated with bosentan and the prostacyclin analogues epoprostenol, treprostinil, and iloprost. Overall, treatment in scleroderma is extremely frustrating. We have symptomatic therapy for Raynaud disease (i.e., calcium channel blockers) and GERD but no clear drugs to stop the underlying pathology of the skin, heart, or kidneys.

Orders:
- *Pulmonary function testing*

Penicillamine is not effective in controlling calcinosis.

Bosentan inhibits endothelin-1.

Prostacyclin dilates pulmonary vasculature.

The patient returns for discussion of her pulmonary function tests (PFTs). Symptoms of dyspnea slowly progress.

PFT Report:
- *Decreased forced expiratory volume at 1 second (FEV$_1$); decreased forced vital capacity (FVC)*
- *Decreased residual volume; decreased total lung capacity*

Which of the following is the most accurate test of lung involvement?

a. PFTs

b. Diffusing capacity of the lungs for carbon monoxide (DLCO)

c. Lung biopsy

d. Right-sided heart catheterization response to vasodilators

e. High-resolution chest computed tomography (CT)

Answer c. Lung biopsy

Pulmonary involvement is present in 70% of those with scleroderma. Lung biopsy is simply the most accurate of all these methods at establishing a diagnosis. Right-sided heart catheterization may be useful to assess response to vasodilatory treatment, but it is not a direct assessment of interstitial lung disease. This is how you are going to tell the need for cyclophosphamide.

The patient undergoes PFTs, high-resolution CT, and ultimately lung biopsy. A trial of cyclophosphamide and bosentan is made. Ultimately, scleroderma does shorten lifespan, but there is no clear therapy to reverse any manifestation on a permanent basis.

CASE 7: Polymyositis-Dermatomyositis

Setting: *office*

CC: *"I just can't get up out of a chair without using my arms."*

VS: *BP:118/74 mm Hg; P: 72 beats/minute; T: normal; R: normal*

HPI: *A 29-year-old woman comes to the office with several months of progressively worsening muscle weakness. She delayed coming to see you because she just thought it was fatigue and tiredness from working a lot. Over the past week, the weakness worsened to the point where she needs to use her arms to get up out of a chair. The muscles are not painful. Joint pain is present.*

"I can't get up from my seat without using my arms!" = Proximal Muscle Weakness

PMHx: *rash on hands and neck*

Medications: *none*

Which of these is usually *not* painful?

a. Fibromyalgia

b. Polymyositis

c. Polymyalgia rheumatica (PMR)

d. Rhabdomyolysis

Answer b. Polymyositis

Polymyositis-dermatomyositis (PM-DM) is an autoimmune myopathy characterized by weakness in nearly patient, but with pain in <25% of patients. Fibromyalgia and PMR are, by definition, pain disorders. That's what the word "fibro*myalgia*" means, "fibrous muscle *pain*." As PM-DM progresses, some people develop pain later.

PE:

- *No fever.*
- *Skin: red-purple rash around her eyes.*
- *Chest: clear to auscultation, V-shaped red rash at top of chest.*
- *Extremities: rough patches on backs of hands.*
- *Musculoskeletal: weakness of shoulders, hips, and girdle; patient cannot easily get up from a seated position without using her hands; muscles are not tender.*

Fibromyalgia:
- Focal tenderness
- "Trigger points"
- 100% normal laboratory test results

PMR
- Age >50 years
- Nontender
- ESR high, creatine phosphokinase (CPK) level normal

Initial Orders:

- *CPK*
- *Aldolase*
- *Lactate dehydrogenase (LDH), aspartate aminotransferase (AST)*
- *ESR*
- *ANA*

What is the difference between polymyositis (PM) and dermatomyositis (DM)?

a. ANA positivity
b. Aldolase
c. Skin finding

d. Response to steroids
e. LDH level

Answer c. Skin finding

On presentation, there is no difference between PM and DM. They both have positive ANA and elevated aldolase, CPK, and LDH levels, and they both respond to steroids. There is a difference on pathologic finding on biopsy, but nothing is different on physical findings or symptoms besides skin findings. DM has a vasculopathy with terminal complements C5 to C9 around the vessels. PM has lymphocytes accumulated in muscle fascicles.

Dermatomyositis: C5-C9 around vessels
Polymyositis: lymphocytes around muscle fascicles

DM Skin Effects
• Gottron papules: hands
• Shawl: neck
• Heliotrope: eyes

The patient comes in 3 days to discuss laboratory test results. Muscle weakness is interfering with her ability to navigate train station stairs and travel to your office.

Reports:
• *CPK: 2450 units/L (elevated)*
• *Aldolase: elevated*
• *ESR: 84 mm/h*
• *ANA: positive*
• *LDH, AST: elevated*

Aldolase = Muscle damage
Nonspecific

Which is the most accurate test of dermatomyositis?

a. Muscle biopsy
b. Electromyography (EMG)

c. Anti-Jo
d. Skin biopsy

Answer a. Muscle biopsy

Although skin involvement is the hallmark of dermatomyositis, the most accurate test is a muscle biopsy. EMG is generally recommended even though it is not as specific as a muscle biopsy.

CCS is more "forgiving" on ordering tests. On CCS, get the ANA, AST, ANA, EMG, and ESR.

For single-best-answer questions,

Proximal Weakness without Pain = PM-DM = CPK and Aldolase = Muscle Biopsy

Orders:
- EMG
- Prednisone orally
- Rheumatology consultation if not done

Consult rheumatology on all rheumatologic disorders except OA and gout.

Weakness + CPK and Aldolase Elevation = Enough to Start Therapy

Steroids are the mainstay of PM-DM treatment.

Which of these factors is different in comparing PM with DM?

a. Use of azathioprine

b. Incidence of cancer

c. Dysphagia

d. Lung fibrosis

Answer b. Incidence of cancer

Dermatomyositis confers the risk of cancer much more than polymyositis. Both of them are treated with azathioprine or MTX if steroids are not effective. Both confer a risk of lung fibrosis. Both of them can cause dysphagia. PM and DM are identical on muscle involvement.

On CCS, always do an Interval History a few days after the start of therapy that should improve symptoms. Always confirm symptomatic improvement.

Move the clock forward 3 to 4 days.

Interval history: "Improved muscle weakness. Able to walk up stairs and get up from a seated position without the use of her arms."

PE: *hip, shoulder, and quadriceps flexion and extension*

Report:
• *EMG: abnormal, possible inflammatory myopathy*

EMG can reveal the presence of a primary muscle disorder.
EMG cannot specify which disorder the patient has.

Orders:
• *Muscle biopsy*

Muscle biopsy is consistent with dermatomyositis. Continue the patient on steroids and follow up in a few weeks.

Order:
• *Anti-Jo antibody*

• Anti-Jo = Lung Involvement Possible
• It is not clear what to do if Anti-Jo is positive.

The patient returns in 2 weeks. She has developed dysphagia and her muscle strength is somewhat worse.

Orders:
• *Continue prednisone.*
• *Add azathioprine.*
• *Add trimethoprim-sulfamethoxazole (TMP-SMZ).*
• *Order a colonoscopy.*
• *Order a mammography.*

Dysphagia
• Muscle weakness
• Proximal third of the esophagus
• Skeletal muscle

Screen DM patients for cancer.

TMP-SMZ
- Pneumocystis prophylaxis
- For chronic steroid use
- Especially with steroid-azathioprine combination

After 2 to 4 weeks, there is an improvement in muscle strength.

What will you *add* to treatment if there is worsening on steroids and azathioprine?

a. MTX

b. Rituximab

c. Androgens

d. 6-Mercaptopurine

Answer b. Rituximab

You continue the patient on both medications for now. It is not clear what to do next. Rituximab is, at present, considered the best of the alternative immunosuppressant medications for those with steroid-resistant PM-DM. MTX is an alternative to azathioprine and would never be added. Androgens are not effective for PM-DM.

6-Mercaptopurine is a metabolite of azathioprine. It is, essentially, the same drug with the same effect. Intravenous immunoglobulin (IVIG) is an alternative to rituximab. Other alternatives to add later are:

- Cyclosporine or tacrolimus
- Cyclophosphamide

The treatment of steroid-resistant PM-DM is difficult and unclear. You would not need to know more than:

1. Steroids are given first.
2. Add azathioprine or MTX if steroids are not effective.
3. Rituximab may help later.

The extent of cancer screening is not clear.
Exclude:
- Colon
- Breast
- Ovary

CASE 8: Systemic Lupus Erythematosus

Setting: *emergency department*

CC: *"My urine is dark, and I am so tired all the time."*

VS: *BP: 160/95 mm Hg; P: 85 beats/minute; T: 101.4°F; R: 18 breaths/minute*

HPI: *A 23-year-old woman is brought by her family on a one-way ticket to New York City from out of the country because of dark urine and fatigue for the past few months. She had been told she had renal damage and needed a kidney biopsy but was not able to have it done. She is extremely fatigued with joint pain. She has had several spontaneous abortions and is very concerned about her ability to have children.*

PMHx:
- *G2 P0020*
- *Alopecia*
- *Hypertension*

Social History: *visitor from Haiti who claims to be a medical student*

Medications:
- *Ibuprofen*
- *Hydralazine*

PE:
- *General: tired, uncomfortable, sullen, and angry appearing*
- *Skin: alopecia of scalp, no facial lesions*
- *HEENT: oral ulcers present*
- *Chest: clear*
- *Cardiovascular: normal*
- *Musculoskeletal: no joint deformity*

Initial Orders:
- *Urinalysis (UA)*
- *ANA*
- *Double-stranded DNA (dsDNA)*
- *CBC*
- *CHEM-7*

Which is the most *specific* test for systemic lupus erythematosus (SLE)?

a. ANA
b. Anti-dsDNA
c. Anti-Sm
d. Complement C3 and C4 levels
e. Anti-Ro (SSA)

Answer c. Anti-Sm

The only test for lupus (SLE) that is more specific than the dsDNA is the anti-Smith or anti-Sm antibody. Anti-Sm is present in only 20% to 30% of patients, but it is very useful to diagnose SLE in those with a positive ANA whose anti-dsDNA is negative. SLE can be a very difficult diagnosis to establish in patients. There is no one single presentation or physical finding that is pathognomonic for the disorder. You must combine at least four findings to consider a person to have SLE.

Reports:
- UA: *proteinuria 300 (3+), red blood cells (RBCs) and RBC casts present*
- ANA: *positive at 1:160*
- dsDNA: *positive*
- CBC: *WBC 12,400/μL (elevated); hematocrit 32%; MCV 86 fL;*
  platelets 156,000/μL
- CHEM-7: *BUN 28 g/dL (elevated); creatinine 2.4 mg/dL*

Fever can be from lupus alone.

What is needed to confirm lupus in this patient?

a. Renal biopsy
b. Nothing
c. Bone marrow biopsy

d. Anti-Sm
e. Complement levels

Answer b. Nothing

This patient already has enough information to be diagnosed with SLE.

- Joint pain
- Renal involvement
- Oral ulcers
- ANA positive
- dsDNA positive
- Anemia

Only 4 of the 11 criteria for SLE are needed to establish a diagnosis of lupus. A renal biopsy is the most accurate test of lupus nephritis, but we already know she has renal involvement. A bone marrow biopsy is not needed. Any level of hematologic involvement is enough to be one of the criteria. It can be low levels of WBCs or platelets, or anemia.

Anti-Sm
- It is the best test when dsDNA is negative.
- It is the most specific of all SLE tests.
- It is present in only 20% to 30% of patients.

Which test is used to determine that increased disease activity (lupus flare) is present?

a. Increasing ANA
b. Decreasing complement level, increased dsDNA

c. Increasing anti-Sm
d. Rising urine protein level and decreasing hematocrit level

Answer b. Decreasing complement, increased dsDNA

Only two tests reliably determine if a sudden worsening of disease is from SLE. If the complement (C3 and C4) level is dropping or the dsDNA is increasing, this is the only clear laboratory evidence of a lupus flare.

SLE Skin Disease
• Malar rash
• Discoid lupus
• Oral ulcers
• Photosensitivity

Which is the most common hematologic manifestation of SLE?

a. Increasing WBC count
b. Anemia of chronic disease

c. Hemolysis
d. Thrombocytopenia

Answer b. Anemia of chronic disease

Anemia of chronic disease is more common than hemolysis in SLE. When there is WBC involvement, it is usually a decrease in WBC count, not an increase.

The patient is very tired and frustrated about her disease. The oral ulcers bother her, as well as her fatigue and reproductive issues.

What is next in the management of this patient?

a. Renal biopsy
b. Prednisone
c. Prednisone and cyclophosphamide

d. Belimumab
e. Hydroxychloroquine

Answer b. Prednisone

You do not need to wait for the results of a renal biopsy to give steroids. The patient will experience an immediate improvement in fatigue, cell counts, oral ulcers, and kidney involvement with steroids. You should not add additional immunosuppressive medication for lupus nephritis without a renal biopsy. Cyclophosphamide can cause hemorrhagic cystitis and bladder cancer and should not be used until you know precisely what type of renal disease you have. Hydroxychloroquine is for skin lesions only. Belimumab is an inhibitor of B-cell lymphocyte function. Belimumab is used when there is recurrent disease or the disease is refractory to steroids. Belimumab is the first new drug for SLE in nearly 50 years, but has limited efficacy.

> Belimumab inhibits B-cell activating factor.

> *The patient is started on prednisone, and a renal biopsy is requested.*

> Joint x-ray is normal in SLE.

Why get a renal biopsy?

a. To prove that lupus nephritis is present
b. To determine the extent of treatment
c. To determine that RBC casts are not from lupus nephritis

Answer b. To determine the extent of treatment

The patient has lupus renal involvement, but you do not know if steroids alone are enough therapy or if either mycophenolate or cyclophosphamide is needed. The only way to determine if there is advanced-stage disease with proliferative glomerulonephropathy is with biopsy. A biopsy determines the need for additional therapy to steroids.

> *A renal biopsy is performed. Also, anyone with multiple first-trimester or one second-trimester spontaneous abortions needs evaluation for antiphospholipid (APL) syndrome.*
>
> **Orders:**
> • *Continue prednisone*
> • *Prothrombin time (PT), activated partial thromboplastin time (aPTT)*
> • *Anticardiolipin antibodies*

> Venereal Disease Research Laboratory (VDRL) False Positive
> • Fluorescent treponemal antibody (FTA) is negative.
> • It is not needed if APL testing is to be done.
> • It is the same as anticardiolipin antibody testing.

Reports:
- *Renal biopsy: proliferative membranous glomerulonephritis*
- *PT normal; aPTT prolonged*
- *Anticardiolipin antibody present*

VDRL is a cardiolipin.

Drug-induced lupus does *not* have renal or cerebral manifestations.

What do you do for the next pregnancy?

a. Recommend an abortion.

b. Give aspirin and heparin.

c. Give warfarin.

d. Give prednisone.

e. Give belimumab.

Answer b. Give aspirin and heparin.

Aspirin and heparin therapy during the pregnancy is the standard of care for antiphospholipid syndromes such as anticardiolipin antibody or lupus anticoagulant causing spontaneous abortion. They are both treated the same way.

Prolonged aPTT
- Does *not* correct with mixing study.
- False positive results in VDRL testing.
- Russel viper venom test for lupus anticoagulant.

Drug-Induced Lupus
- Spares brain
- Spares kidney

As you move the clock forward, prednisone will have an effect in a day or two. You do not have to keep the patient in the hospital to await the results of the biopsy.

CHAPTER **9**

ONCOLOGY

CASE 1: Breast Cancer

Setting: *office*

CC: *"My mammogram showed a lump."*

VS: *normal*

HPI: *A 44-year-old woman who just had a mammogram that showed an abnormality comes to the office to find what the next step is. The patient's mother and sister both had breast cancer so when she went to a random "health fair" in her neighborhood, she was advised to get a mammogram earlier than age 50. She feels well.*

At what age is mammographic screening recommended for the general population?

a. At 35 years

b. At 40 years

c. At 50 years

Answer **c.** At 50 years

For women at average risk, screening mammography is recommended to begin by the age of 50 years. This patient should have been screened starting at least by age 40 years because of the very significant family history. A woman in the general population has a risk of 12% to 14% (1 in 9) without any family history. With two first-degree relatives, her risk is closer to 40% to 45%.

First-Degree Relatives
• Siblings
• Parents

PMHx/Medications: *none*

PE: *normal*

With her family history of breast cancer, besides starting screening early, which would be best to have prevented having breast cancer?

a. Breast cancer antigen (BRCA) testing
b. Tamoxifen
c. Breast ultrasound (US)
d. Breast magnetic resonance imaging (MRI)
e. Self-examination once a month

Answer b. Tamoxifen

Tamoxifen and raloxifene prevent breast cancer from ever occurring in the first place. These selective estrogen receptor modulators (SERMs) give a 50% reduction in the risk of breast cancer. They are used in those with two first-degree relatives who are at much higher risk of breast cancer than the general population. Breast US is used when a lump is detected in a younger, premenopausal patient and it is not clear if the lesion is solid or cystic. Breast MRI is useful in evaluating firm breasts with unusual architecture, but it is not clear that MRI is definitely better than mammogram. BRCA testing does not prevent cancer. BRCA is associated with the 10% of patients with familial breast cancer, but in this patient, we already know she is at high risk of cancer. In terms of the breast, it is not clear what BRCA offers.

SERMs stop cancer. BRCA tells risks without a clear therapeutic path.

Tamoxifen prevents breast cancer in high-risk patients.

BRCA testing benefit is not clear.

Initial Orders:
• *Needle aspiration biopsy*

SERMs
• Antagonistic at breast
• Agonistic at:
  • Bone
  • Endometrium
  • Clotting factors

What is the absolute increase in risk of endometrial cancer after using a SERM for 5 years in 1000 women?

a. 1
b. 10
c. 100
d. 200

Answer a. 1

The absolute increase in the risk of endometrial cancer is about one new cancer over 5 years in 1000 treated women. Without SERMs, 1/1000 women get endometrial cancer in 5 years. With a SERM, it is 2/1000 women.

If you have a 40% risk of breast cancer in a high-risk person, that would be 400 breast cancers in 1000 women. With a SERM (e.g., tamoxifen) the number drops to 200. So, bottom line, you have one more endometrial cancer, and 200 less breast cancers.

SERMs decrease breast cancer risk *much* more than increase endometrial cancer risk.

Tamoxifen stimulates osteoblasts.

The patient returns after the breast biopsy, which shows infiltrating ductal adenocarcinoma of the breast.

Report:
- *Estrogen receptor (ER) positive*
- *Progesterone receptor (PR) positive*
- *No cancer on mammography of other breast*
- *HER2/Neu antigen increased*

Trastuzumab
- Monoclonal antibody
- Removes HER2/Neu positive cells
- Negligible adverse effects
- Prevents metastases

Which of the following should be done next?

a. Axillary lymph node dissection
b. Sentinel node biopsy
c. Bone marrow biopsy
d. Lumbar puncture

Answer b. Sentinel node biopsy

The "sentinel" node is the first node in the operative field (Figure 9-1). If this node shows no cancer, you do not need to do an axillary lymph node dissection. There is no need to do bone marrow biopsy or lumbar puncture in the routine preoperative or prechemotherapy evaluation of breast cancer. To find the sentinel node, contrast is put into the operative field. You then remove the first node that the contrast goes to and send it for immediate histologic examination.

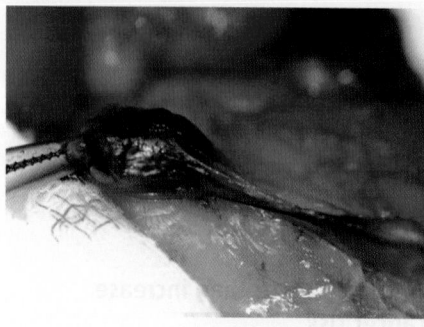

Figure 9-1. Sentinel node. (Reproduced with permission from Giuliano AE.)

On computer-based case simulation (CCS), you cannot physically transfer the patient to a location called "Operating Room." Order the procedure you feel is correct. The software will tell you if you also need a consultation to do the procedure. For example, if you order "Pap smear," the CCS software lets you do the test. If you order "Colposcopy," the software will tell you to get a gynecology consultation first.

As you have the results of the needle biopsy and mammography showing a unilateral, unifocal lesion, you should proceed to order the procedures you know are needed.

Orders:
- Surgical consultation
- Oncology consultation
- Sentinel node biopsy
- Lumpectomy
- Radiation of breast tissue

Lumpectomy = Modified Radical Mastectomy Only if Breast is Radiated!

Without radiation to the breast, cancer recurs with lumpectomy alone.

The patient undergoes the procedure and the procedure report states: "Lumpectomy performed successfully, no cancer found in sentinel node; 2-cm infiltrating ductal carcinoma removed. Frozen sections show surrounding tissue free of cancer."

The oncology and surgical consultation reports, as is usual on CCS, do not give specific recommendations or directions.

- If ER or PR is positive, give a SERM.
- SERMs and aromatase are *more* effective if both ER and PR are positive.

Which of the following will lower mortality the most?

a. Modified radical mastectomy (MRM) versus radical mastectomy

b. MRM versus lumpectomy and radiation

c. Adjuvant chemotherapy

d. Oophorectomy

Answer c. Adjuvant chemotherapy

Adjuvant chemotherapy provides a definite mortality benefit. MRM is not better than lumpectomy and radiation in most patients. Radical mastectomy is obsolete and never the right answer. Adjuvant means chemotherapy that is used to prevent metastases. It is not "prophylactic" because the person already has cancer. You will not be asked much at all about the different types of chemotherapy because it is not clear which therapy would be best for this patient.

Aromatase Inhibitors
- Anastrazole
- Letrozole
- Exemestane

Which of the following is the most common adverse effect of aromatase inhibitors?

a. Endometrial cancer

b. Osteoporosis

c. Bladder cancer

d. Ovarian cancer

Answer b. Osteoporosis

Osteoporosis occurs because aromatase inhibits estrogen production with side effects including bone loss. SERMs have an agonist effect on bone, and an antagonist effect on breast tissue, that is why tamoxifen and raloxifene are considered "selective."

Aromatase Inhibitors
- Stop the conversion of testosterone to estrogen.
- Block the removal of one carbon from steroid nucleus testosterone.
- Work at the ovary and in adipose tissue.
- Simulate oophorectomy.

The patient undergoes radiation therapy to the breast after the lump is removed surgically. Because the lesion is >1 cm, chemotherapy is given. It is not clear whether to use a SERM or an aromatase inhibitor.

Treatments That Lower Mortality
- Surgery: MRM or lumpectomy with radiation
- HER2/Neu: trastuzumab if extra HER2 present
- Adjuvant chemotherapy
- SERMs or aromatase inhibitors

Aromatase inhibitors inhibit osteoblasts.

To provide blockage of estrogen in premenopausal women, leuprolide and goserelin are sometimes given to prevent the need for oophorectomy. How do they work?

a. They block luteinizing hormone (LH) and follicle-stimulating hormone (FSH) on the ovary.

b. They decrease the release of LH and FSH from the pituitary.

c. They decrease the level of adrenal androgens.

d. They block the peripheral conversion to estrogen.

Answer b. They decrease the release of LH and FSH from the pituitary.

These medications are gonadotropin-releasing hormone (GnRH) agonists. They will block FSH and LH release.

CASE 2: Prostate Cancer

Setting: *office*

CC: *"I want a PSA!"*

VS: *normal*

HPI: *The 51-year-old chairman of medicine of your hospital comes to be screened for prostate cancer. He is asymptomatic.*

PMHx/Medications: *none*

PE: *normal*

What screening test lowers mortality for prostate cancer?

a. None

b. Prostate specific antigen (PSA) above age 40 years

c. PSA above age 50 years

d. Digital rectal examination

Answer a. None

PSA should not be routinely done. It does not lower mortality and does not improve a patient's quality of life. In fact, it worsens quality of life. The PSA has been changed to a "D" recommendation, which is "Recommend against." The PSA results in prostatectomy and radiation that damages erectile function and urinary continence without preventing metastases.

You and the patient acknowledge all this (as does the author of this book). They understand the risk of unnecessary procedures and the lack of clear efficacy, yet the patient still wants the PSA test.

Initial Orders:
• PSA

Do not forget the screening colonoscopy at age 50!

Finasteride and dutasteride have been shown to decrease the risk of prostate cancer on biopsy, but still do not lower mortality or prevent metastatic disease. What is the reason?

a. Tachyphylaxis—they wear off over time.
b. They suppress only small stage A1 cancers.
c. They only work on benign prostatic hyperplasia (BPH).
d. They cannot be used as single agents.
e. Adverse effects lead to discontinuation.

Answer b. They suppress only small stage A1 cancers.

Finasteride and dutasteride are medications that do decrease the overall number of prostate cancers. However, they have been shown to have no effect on larger cancers that have the propensity to grow and metastasize. They only suppress small, early stage A1 prostate cancer that would not have metastasized or grown.

Finasteride
• Small cancers are suppressed.
• Larger cancers present later.

The patient wants to know what to do about using finasteride. You tell him that it definitely will not help him. He still wants the finasteride to prevent prostate cancer.

What do you tell him?

a. Give him the finasteride.
b. Refuse to give it to him.

c. Refer this patient to another physician in another department such as urology to give it to him.

Answer b. Refuse to give it to him.

There is a difference between allowing the PSA, which is a subject of controversy that had been recommended before, and allowing finasteride. There is no benefit of using finasteride in preventing prostate cancer and, in fact, because it suppresses the rate of rise of PSA, can mask the diagnosis of larger prostate cancers until they are more widely spread.

Patients do not have a right to therapy you feel is useless.

Finasteride and Dutasteride
- They block 5-alpha-reductase.
- They block production of dihydrotestosterone.
- Dihydrotestosterone stimulates prostate growth.

Finasteride treats benign prostatic hypertrophy not cancer.

The patient returns in a week for results:

- *Report: PSA 8 ng/mL (normal 0–4 ng/mL)*

PE: *rectal: no masses found*

What should be done to guide therapy?

a. Computed tomography (CT) of pelvis
b. US of pelvis

c. Transrectal US
d. Sigmoidoscopy

Answer c. Transrectal US

If you see an elevated PSA, you need to be sure if there is really a prostate cancer there. Do not do a test if you do not want to know the answer. If you feel a mass on rectal examination, then biopsy the mass you feel. If you do not feel a mass, then use the transrectal US to guide a biopsy.

The patient undergoes the transrectal US, which is negative and shows no masses.

- *Repeat PSA: 8.5 ng/mL*

What should you recommend to exclude prostate cancer?

a. No further action is needed.

b. Do multiple palpation-guided biopsies.

c. Repeat the transrectal US.

Answer b. Do multiple palpation-guided biopsies.

The only way to be truly sure that there is no prostate cancer is to do multiple palpation-guided biopsies. This means if the PSA is elevated, it always results in a biopsy.

The patient declines having the multiple palpation-guided biopsies. He leaves with plans to follow up in 6 months.

On CCS, patients can refuse procedures that they do not want or do not feel are indicated.

The patient is lost to follow-up for 2 years. Two years later he comes because of symptoms of dysuria, hesitancy, and dribbling.

PE:
• Rectal: enlarged prostate with nodule palpated in one lobe

Orders:
• PSA
• Prostate biopsy

Report:
• PSA: 18 ng/mL
• Biopsy: adenocarcinoma of prostate

Prostate Cancer Treatment
• Local: prostate resection
• Metastases: hormonal manipulation

A staging evaluation with a head CT and bone scan show no metastases. The patient is reluctant to have radical prostatectomy because of the risk of incontinence and erectile dysfunction.

Which of the following indicates the likelihood of metastasis occurring?

a. Number of lobes

b. Gleason scoring on pathology

c. PSA level

d. Age of patient

Answer b. Gleason scoring of the pathology

Gleason scoring is a numerical measurement of the pathogenicity of prostate cancer (Figure 9-2). A low score of 1 is closest to normal tissue. A high score of 10 is the most anaplastic or highest likelihood of metastasizing. When you have patients who are uncertain as to whether to risk prostate surgery, you can use the Gleason scoring as a way of giving them a likelihood of spread. For example, a young man with a high Gleason score should undergo

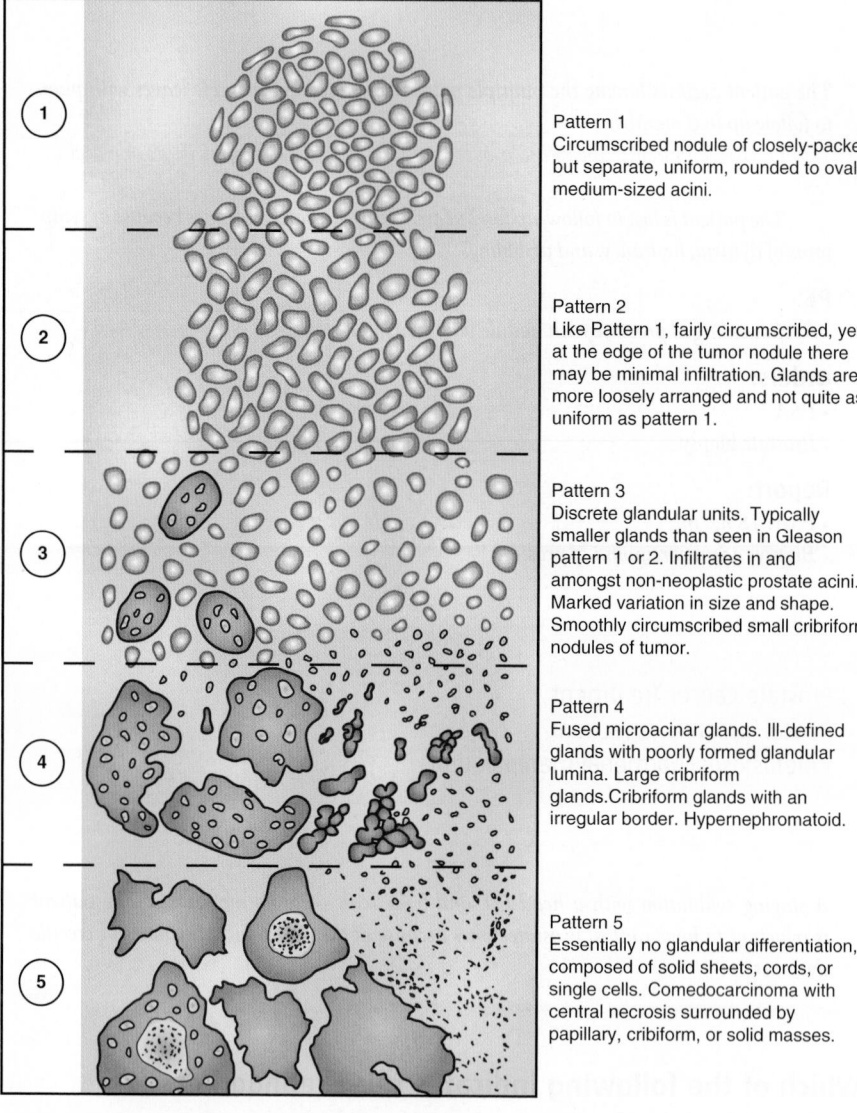

Pattern 1
Circumscribed nodule of closely-packed but separate, uniform, rounded to oval, medium-sized acini.

Pattern 2
Like Pattern 1, fairly circumscribed, yet at the edge of the tumor nodule there may be minimal infiltration. Glands are more loosely arranged and not quite as uniform as pattern 1.

Pattern 3
Discrete glandular units. Typically smaller glands than seen in Gleason pattern 1 or 2. Infiltrates in and amongst non-neoplastic prostate acini. Marked variation in size and shape. Smoothly circumscribed small cribriform nodules of tumor.

Pattern 4
Fused microacinar glands. Ill-defined glands with poorly formed glandular lumina. Large cribriform glands. Cribriform glands with an irregular border. Hypernephromatoid.

Pattern 5
Essentially no glandular differentiation, composed of solid sheets, cords, or single cells. Comedocarcinoma with central necrosis surrounded by papillary, cribiform, or solid masses.

Figure 9-2. Prostate cancer staging. (Adapted with permission from Epstein JI, et al. The 2005 International Society of Urological Pathology (ISUP) Consensus Conference on Gleason Grading of Prostatic Carcinoma. *Am J Surg Pathol.* 2005;29(9):1228–1242.)

radical prostatectomy with the intention of cure because of the high likelihood he will live a long time with a risk of spread. In an older man with a low Gleason score, it may be safe just to use radiation therapy.

The patient ultimately refuses surgery and opts for brachytherapy. Radioactive seeds are implanted into the prostate. Over the next few months, the PSA goes down and the symptoms of obstructive uropathy subside.

There is no "adjuvant" chemotherapy for prostate cancer.

There is no "modified radical prostatectomy."
There is no "lumpectomy" for prostate cancer.

One year later, the patient is brought to the emergency department (ED) with severe back pain and weakness in his legs.

PE:

• *Musculoskeletal: focal spine tenderness present*

Neurological: extensor plantar reflexes present; hyperreflexic knee jerk reflexes present; sensation in lower extremities normal

What is the next "best step" in the management of this patient?

a. Dexamethasone

b. MRI

c. Radiation

d. Flutamide

e. Goserelin (GnRH agonist)

Answer a. Dexamethasone

Cord compression needs stat intravenous (IV) glucocorticoids. The most important thing is to prevent permanent neurological damage from impingement on the spinal cord. Steroids work faster than radiation. A biopsy is unlikely to be needed in this person who has a clear history of prostate cancer. Hormonal manipulation will help stop the growth of the lesion, but it will not actually shrink the lesion that is already there. Steroids will shrink the lesion. MRI is needed. Steroids are needed more. With back pain and focal neurological deficits and hyperreflexia, this is enough information to warrant steroids. Get the MRI done afterward. If it is a CCS case, you can order all of these things at the same time, because all of them are needed. CCS is a test of understanding timing. When you have cord compression, it is a big deal to give steroids before waiting for an MRI.

Dexamethasone is given and radiation is ordered. The patient is transferred to the hospital ward because you cannot send a person home with progressive neurological damage.

Report:
• *The MRI shows compression of the spinal cord.*

After the start of steroids and radiation, which of the following is most urgent?

a. Denosumab

b. Finasteride

c. Flutamide

d. Goserelin (GnRH agonist)

Answer c. Flutamide

Flutamide and bicalutamide are testosterone receptor antagonists. In terms of hormonal therapy, it is critically important to start the target organ receptor blocker first.

GnRH agonists such as goserelin or leuprolide must never be started before flutamide in a person with metastatic prostate cancer, especially when it is on the spinal cord. The GnRH agonists initially give a burst up in LH and FSH levels. This will raise the testosterone levels and briefly increase the growth of the prostate cancer. Denosumab is a treatment for bone destruction from metastases and it is also a treatment for osteoporosis.

1. Block the testosterone target first.
2. Stop the gonadotropins (LH and FSH) after.

Finasteride and Dutasteride
• They are useless in prostate cancer.
• They block 5-alpha-reductase.
• They only decrease dihydrotestosterone.

What is the mechanism whereby goserelin or leuprolide decreases testosterone?

a. They downregulate at the pituitary gland.

b. They block testicular LH and FSH receptors.

c. They block dehydroepiandrosterone (DHEA) production at the adrenal gland.

d. They inhibit 17,20-lyase

e. They decrease the hypothalamic release of GnRH.

Answer a. Downregulation at the pituitary.

Hormones are usually made in pulsatile form. When a target organ is exposed to a constant amount of a hormone, the receptors at the target begin to involute and decrease. This is called either "downregulation" or "target organ resistance." Because the pituitary gland is the target organ of GnRH, it is the pituitary gland where the receptors downregulate.

Denosumab
- It protects bones.
- It inhibits the receptor activator of nuclear factor kappa B ligand (RANKL).
- RANKL is similar to tumor necrosis factor (TNF).

RANKL = Receptor Activator of Nuclear Factor Kappa B Ligand

The patient undergoes treatment with radiation and has flutamide started, followed by a GnRH agonist shortly after. Symptoms of back pain resolve. Weakness in the legs improves.

Orchiectomy is the fastest way to lower androgen levels.

What other therapy can be done to block androgen production?

a. Abiraterone and degarelix

b. Estrogen and progesterone

c. Tamoxifen and exemestane

d. Nothing

Answer a. Abiraterone and degarelix

Abiraterone is an inhibitor of 17-alpha-hydroxylase in the gonads and adrenal glands. This drug shuts off production of the testosterone precursor DHEA. You cannot make testosterone if you do not make DHEA first. This drug closes the precursor "pipeline" for all sex hormones.

Degarelix is a GnRH receptor antagonist. It directly blocks the effect of GnRH on the pituitary gland.

The other medications manipulate estrogen. Exemestane is an aromatase inhibitor.

Chemotherapy is poor for prostate cancer.

Prostate metastases are controlled with hormone inhibitors.

CASE 3: Myeloma

Setting: *office*

CC: *"I coughed, and my chest has been sore ever since."*

VS: BP: 112/76 mm Hg; P: 76 beats/minute; T: 98°F; R: 24 breaths/minute

HPI: *A 64-year-old man comes to the office with pain on the right side of his chest after a coughing spell a few days ago. He went to his local ED last night and an x-ray showed two fractured ribs. He has had a few episodes of bronchitis and pneumonia in the last 2 years. Old x-rays are compared and definitely showed no lesions in the past.*

PMHx:
- *Fatigue*
- *Anemia*
- *Nephrolithiasis earlier this year*

"Pathologic" Fracture
- Break during normal use

ROS:
- *Losing height, 2 inches shorter than he was*

Medications:
- *Vitamins*

PE:
- *General: tired, in visible pain when he moves*
- *Chest: focal tenderness over site where fractures were found*
- *Cardiovascular: normal*
- *Rectal: no masses*

Initial Orders:
- *Chest x-ray*
- *Rib x-ray*
- *Vertebral and spine x-ray*
- *Complete blood count (CBC)*
- *Comprehensive metabolic panel (CHEM-20)*
- *Acetaminophen*

Look for vertebral compression fractures when looking for pathological fracture.

Prostate cancer likes to metastasize to the bone.

Reports:
- *Chest x-ray: no pneumothorax; no pneumonia*
- *Rib x-ray: two fractures, three lytic lesions*
- *Vertebral and spine x-ray: compression fracture T4, T5*
- *CBC: hematocrit 32%; mean corpuscular volume (MCV) 86 fL*
- *CHEM-20: high total protein; normal albumin; calcium 11.5 mg/dL (elevated)*

What will a nuclear bone scan show in myeloma?

a. Increased uptake diffusely   **c.** No change in uptake

b. Increased uptake at lytic lesion sites

Answer c. No change in uptake

Nuclear bone scans do not pick up extra technetium isotope in myeloma. The lesions in myeloma are purely lytic (Figure 9-3). Nuclear bone scans show where there is blastic activity as well. Metastases are a mix of lytic and blastic activity and so is osteomyelitis.

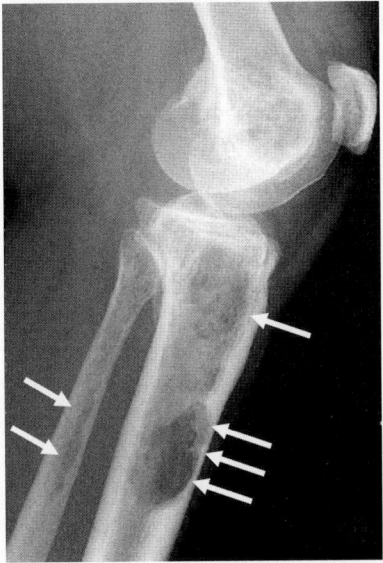 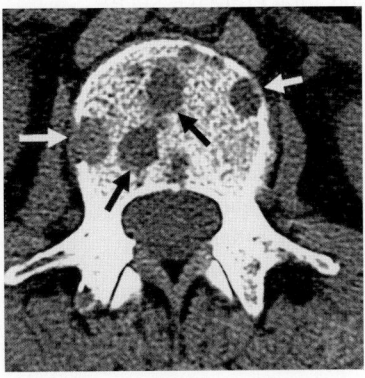

Figure 9-3. Myeloma lesions: Radiolucent or darker areas represent lytic lesions. (Reproduced with permission from Kaushansky K, et al. *Williams Hematology*, 8th ed. New York: McGraw-Hill; 2010.)

Nuclear isotope is deposited by osteoblasts.

There is no specific therapy for rib fractures beyond analgesia. You want to reduce pain so the patient does not "splint" when there is pain, reduce breathing, and develop a pneumonia.

"Splinting": reducing ventilation secondary to rib pain

Orders:
- *Bisphosphonates (pamidronate, alendronate)*
- *Serum protein electrophoresis (SPEP)*
- *Peripheral blood smear*
- *Uric acid level*
- *Urinalysis (UA)*
- *Oncology evaluation*

Bisphosphonate inhibits osteoclasts.

High Total Protein = SPEP

Report:
- *SPEP: monoclonal spike in immunoglobulin G (IgG) range*
- *Smear: rouleaux formation*
- *Uric acid: normal*
- *UA: trace protein*
- *Oncology evaluation: no specific recommendations*

Rouleaux Formation
- Red blood cells (RBCs) appear in stacks or "rolls" on the smear.
- IgG on the RBC surface makes RBCs "stick" to each other.
- Rouleaux formation is clinically meaningless.

What is the single most specific test for myeloma?

a. SPEP

b. Bone marrow biopsy

c. Urine immunoelectrophoresis

d. Bence Jones protein

e. Peripheral blood smear

Answer b. Bone marrow biopsy

Looking for >10% plasma cells on bone marrow biopsy is the single most specific test for myeloma. When combined with a monoclonal spike on SPEP and lytic lesions, this establishes the diagnosis of myeloma (Figure 9-4). Some cancers can give lytic lesions. The monoclonal gammopathy of unknown significance (MGUS) accounts for 99% of IgG spikes on SPEP. You can have Bence Jones proteinuria alone without myeloma. The only thing that gives >10% plasma cells on bone marrow biopsy is myeloma.

> MGUS = IgG spike
> · No bone lesion
> · No renal damage
> · No infections
> · Normal calcium level
> · Normal uric acid level

Why do you get hyperuricemia in myeloma, but not in hemolysis?

a. RBCs have no nuclei.

b. Neutrophils function normally.

c. Renal insufficiency makes it accumulate.

d. Haptoglobin removes uric acid from circulation.

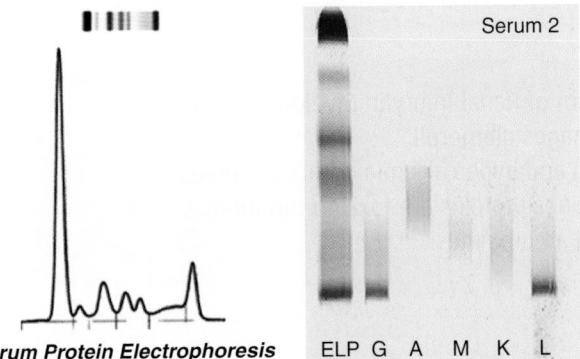

Serum Protein Electrophoresis   ELP G A M K L

Figure 9-4. Serum protein electrophoresis demonstrates an M-protein peak (*left*). Immunofixation electrophoresis confirms it to be monoclonal IgG lambda type. (Reproduced with permission from Katarjian HM, et al. *The MD Anderson Manual of Medical Oncology*, 2nd ed. New York: McGraw-Hill; 2011.)

Answer a. RBCs have no nuclei.

Uric acid increases from increased destruction of cells that have nuclei. RBCs have no nuclei. Freshly and abnormally released purines and pyrimidines come out of the nuclei. The metabolic end product of purines and pyrimidines is uric acid. Hyperuricemia generally occurs with chemotherapy of hematologic malignancy. This is why it can be normal on initial diagnosis.

> Nucleic acids are made into uric acid.

> *You explain to the patient that the lytic bone lesions, pathologic fractures, hypercalcemia, and hyperuricemia with a monoclonal IgG spike on SPEP likely indicate multiple myeloma.*
>
> **Orders:**
> - *Bone marrow biopsy*
> - *Repeat calcium and uric acid levels*
> - *Urine immunoelectrophoresis*
> - *Beta-2-microglobulin*
> - *CBC*
> - *Basic metabolic panel (CHEM-7)*

> Beta-2-Microglobulin
> - The level is elevated in myeloma.
> - It is used as a marker of response to treatment.

> Mechanism of Renal Injury in Myeloma
> - IgG damages glomeruli.
> - Uric acid and hypercalcemia damage tubules.
> - Bence Jones proteins are toxic to the tubules.
> - Amyloid accumulates.

> *The patient continues to be fatigued. He has a brief episode of pneumonia since the last time he saw you. He was treated with antibiotics and improved.*

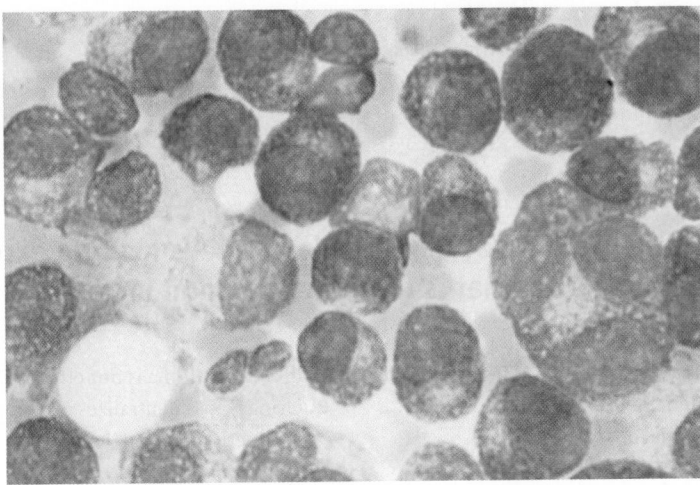

Figure 9-5. Multiple myeloma (marrow). The cells bear characteristic morphologic features of plasma cells, round or oval cells with an eccentric nucleus composed of coarsely clumped chromatin, a densely basophilic cytoplasm, and a perinuclear clear zone containing the Golgi apparatus. Binucleate and multinucleate malignant plasma cells can be seen. (Reproduced with permission from Longo DL, et al. *Harrison's Principles of Internal Medicine*, 18th ed., Vol. 2. New York: McGraw-Hill; 2012.)

Reports:
- *Bone marrow biopsy: 24% plasma cells (Figure 9-5)*
- *Calcium 11.2 mg/dL and uric acid normal*
- *Urine immunoelectrophoresis: Bence Jones protein markedly elevated*
- *Beta-2-microglobulin: elevated*
- *CBC: hematocrit 29%*
- *CHEM-7: creatinine 1.7 mg/dL*

Bence Jones Protein
- Immunoglobulin fragment
- Kappa or lambda light chains
- Toxic to kidneys
- Not detected by UA

Protein Detected on UA = Albumin

Death in myeloma is from:
- Infection
- Renal failure

In myeloma, if there are excess plasma cells making excess immunoglobulins, what is the mechanism of increased infections?

a. Myeloma switches to IgA.

b. IgE is deficient.

c. Neutrophils do not work.

d. IgG in myeloma is not effective.

e. Urinary loss neutralizes excess production.

Answer d. IgG in myeloma is not effective.

Plasma cells are made in excess amounts in myeloma, but they are not useful in producing effective immunoglobulins. Plasma cells in myeloma make large amounts of ineffective IgG. They do not make the immunoglobulins that the patient needs to fight infection.

Bence Jones protein is not functional.

Myeloma
- IgG: 50%
- IgA: 20%
- Bence Jones alone: 20%

Plasma cells secrete humoral factors that destroy bone in myeloma.

The patient returns in a week after the oncologist evaluates him.

What is the best therapy for this patient?

a. Melphalan

b. Steroids

c. Autologous stem cell transplant (ASCT)

d. Allogeneic bone marrow transplant (BMT)

e. Observation

Answer c. Autologous stem cell transplant (ASCT)

Autologous BMT can be done in patients up to age 70 years. Allogeneic bone marrow from a related, matched donor should be avoided after age 50 years. Melphalan alone is inappropriate for this patient. Melphalan by itself is little better than palliation. It will not result in a sustained remission in anyone. Steroids do have a primary antileukemia effect, but they cannot be used alone.

Allogeneic BMT kills the patient from graft-versus-host disease and from graft rejection. ASCT cannot reject the patient, because it is the patient's own marrow. Stem cell transplantation allow a shorter duration of neutropenia. The cells are already partially grown and differentiated. This allows a much shorter duration of neutropenia compared to allogeneic BMT.

Longer Duration of Neutropenia = Higher Death Rate

Allogeneic = More Chance of Cure + More Chance of Death
Autologous = Less Chance of Cure + Less Chance of Death

Collect stem cells tagged with CD34.

The patient undergoes ASCT. Move the clock forward 1 day at a time and check the CBC each day. When the patient eventually recovers his cell count, he can be sent home.

*Complex cases like chemotherapy management in leukemia or myeloma are **unlikely** to occur as CCS cases. You will never be asked which of the chemotherapy combinations is best. It is just not clear.*

As you move the clock forward, it will become clear from cell count and beta-2-microglobulin level whether the patient is recovering or needs additional chemotherapy. It is not clear which drug or set of drugs will be used for relapsed myeloma. All of the following in combination of two or three are possible:

- *Lenalidomide (or thalidomide)*
- *Melphalan*
- *Prednisone (or dexamethasone)*
- *Bortezomib*

Lenalidomide: TNF inhibitor
Bortezomib: proteosome inhibitor

CASE 4: Polycythemia Vera

Setting: *office*

CC: *"I'm itchy and my hands hurt!"*

VS: *BP: 145/88 mm Hg; P: 88 beats/minute; T: 98°F; R: 23 breaths/minute*

HPI: *A 45-year-old man comes to the office with generalized pruritus that is clearly worse after taking a bath. He is also having difficulty breathing. He has been to his local ED twice for the same problems. He was sent home because his pulse oximeter level, arterial blood gas (ABG) test, and chest x-ray were all normal.*

PMHx:
• *Peptic ulcer*

Medications:
• *Diphenhydramine*

PE:
• *General: flushed, red face with plethora*
• *Chest: clear to auscultation*
• *Abdomen: enlarged spleen palpable*
• *Extremities: nontender, red painful hands (erythromelalgia)*

Initial Orders:
• *CBC*
• *Oximeter*
• *Chest x-ray*

Borderline elevations in blood pressure (BP) have no meaning in a patient who is distressed for any reason.

This case is a good example of how the setting in which the patient is encountered makes a big difference in the diagnostic approach. If this person were in the ED, you would end up doing an urgent ABG, chest x-ray, and CT. If the office, the diagnostic pathway is much slower.

As the clock is moved forward, the patient continues to have an extremely uncomfortable generalized itching, especially after a warm shower.

Reports:
- *Oximeter 97% on room air*
- *CBC:*
  - *Hematocrit 64%; MCV 74 fL; RBCs 6.5 × 10⁶ cells/μL (increased)*
  - *White blood cells (WBCs): 18,000/μL*
  - *Platelets: 850,000/μL*
- *Chest x-ray: normal*

Routine Findings in Polycythemia Vera
- High vitamin B_{12} level
- High leukocyte alkaline phosphatase (LAP)

Increased RBC count with small MCV
- Polycythemia vera
- Hypoxia
- Thalassemia

Pruritus
- Histamine releases from basophils.
- Warmth releases it.

High Hematocrit Level + Low MCV Level – Hypoxia = Polycythemia Vera

The patient is scheduled to undergo phlebotomy because of shortness of breath.

Janus kinase 2 (JAK2) mutation is 95% sensitive for polycythemia vera.

Low Erythropoietin + High Hematocrit = Polycythemia Vera

What is the most common cause of death in polycythemia vera?

a. Bleeding

b. Thrombosis

c. Transformation to acute leukemia

d. Transformation to myelofibrosis

Answer b. Thrombosis

Blood vessels get clogged up with the increased hematocrit increasing the viscosity of the blood. Large vessel thrombosis such as deep venous thrombosis (DVT), pulmonary embolus (PE), and Budd-Chiari syndrome can kill the patient. The idea is to do phlebotomy to remove the extra RBCs before the vessels clot off.

- Ulcers are part of polycythemia vera.
- Histamine from basophils stimulates extra acid.

After phlebotomy, the patient feels much better. This is the mainstay of therapy. Radioactive phosphorus (P-32) is no longer used. Hydroxyurea is not necessary.

Decreasing blood viscosity increases blood flow.

Over the next 12 to 24 months, the patient is well maintained on regular phlebotomy. The hematocrit decreases and shortness of breath resolves. Pruritus is controlled.

What is the most likely long-term transformation?

a. Acute leukemia
b. Myelofibrosis
c. Myeloma
d. Myelodysplastic syndrome

Answer b. Myelofibrosis

Myelofibrosis can develop from polycythemia vera. You will recognize it when you see teardrop-shaped cells and nucleated RBCs appearing on the peripheral blood smear. Treat myelofibrosis with lenalidomide.

Lenalidomide
- Inhibits TNF

The patient is well maintained on intermittent phlebotomy. The redness of the hands (erythromelalgia) resolves. Splenomegaly from the polycythemia vera persists.

CHAPTER **10**

INFECTIOUS DISEASES

CASE 1: Osteomyelitis

Setting: *emergency department (ED)*

CC: *"I've got fluid coming out of an ulcer in my leg."*

VS: *BP: T: 98°F; R: 14 breaths/minute*

HPI: *A 64-year-old man with long-standing diabetes and peripheral arterial disease (PAD) comes to the ED with drainage coming out of an area of ulcer over the tibial area. He has had recurrent ulcers in this area off and on for years. Most have responded to local wound care. Occasionally he has used antibiotics. He did not go see his doctor for this one, and decided on his own to come to the ED.*

PMHx:
- *Diabetes*
- *Hypertension*
- *PAD*

Medications:
- *Aspirin, cilostazol*
- *Metformin, glyburide, and sitagliptin*

PE:
- *General: comfortable, sitting upright, no distress*
- *Chest: clear bilaterally*
- *Extremities: 2-cm ulcer over anterior surface of lower left leg, halfway between knee and ankle; modest warmth in the area, little tenderness. Draining sinus tract is visible in the center. Bone is not visible.*

Diabetes + PAD = Ulcers ± Osteomyelitis

The first question to ask yourself when confronted with a patient with a diabetic ulcer is:
- Osteomyelitis: yes or no?

Neutrophils do not function normally in diabetes.

Initial Orders:
- *X-ray of leg*
- *Complete blood count (CBC), basic metabolic panel (CHEM-7)*
- *Restart outpatient medications*

On the computer-based case simulation (CCS), if you do not order something, it is not being given or done. In this case, unless you order the PAD and diabetes medications, you should not assume they are automatically continued. Nothing is automatically continued on CCS, unless you have ordered it. You will be able to see on the order screen in front of you every medication that is ordered, and every laboratory test that is pending.

Probing straight to bone
- Highly suggestive of osteomyelitis
- Will not give specific organism

Which of these is *useless* in osteomyelitis evaluation?

a. Gallium scan

b. Indium scan

c. Swab culture of ulcer

d. Computed tomography (CT) scan

e. Technetium-99 scan

Answer c. Swab culture of ulcer

Culturing the surface of an ulcer generates irrelevant and misleading data. The ulcer will definitely grow organisms, but it will not tell you what is in the bone. That makes it distracting. The other scans are not as accurate as magnetic resonance imaging (MRI), but they can be useful to determine if there is bone involvement or if the infection is limited just to the skin.

Scan	Mechanism	Key Advantage/Disadvantage
Gallium	Tagged transferrin	Normal scan excludes osteomyelitis Needs 2–3 days to perform
Indium	Take patient's blood, remove and tag WBCs, then reinject	Nonspecific Hard to distinguish bone vs. soft tissue infection
CT	Bone calcium loss	Specific, but needs extensive damage to be abnormal
Technetium-99 (nuclear bone scan)	Incorporated into bone by osteoblasts	Normal scan = No Osteomyelitis Abnormal cannot distinguish bone versus soft tissue

CT, computed tomography; WBCs, white blood cells.

Do not give antibiotics just for a bone infection. Osteomyelitis in a diabetic patient is a chronic infection that takes weeks to months to develop, and needs weeks to months to cure. It is more important to get a specific microbiologic identification, than to start empiric therapy that might be incorrect.

Move the clock forward to get x-ray results.

- Bone loss needs 1 to 2 weeks to show as abnormal on x-ray.
- For the x-ray to be abnormal, 50% to 70% of bone calcium must be lost.

Report:
- *X-ray: no destruction of bone detected*
- *CBC: normal white blood cell (WBC) count, no anemia*
- *Chemistry: normal except glucose 138 mg/dL*

What is an abnormality shown on MRI based on?

a. Calcium

b. Water

c. Sodium and potassium

d. Nuclear isotope deposition

e. Glucose metabolism

Answer b. Water

The MRI is based on an alteration of the spin of hydrogen ions in molecules when exposed to different magnetic frequencies. The spin or "flip" in the ion occurs under different magnetic intensity based on its water content. Bone actually swells in 2 to 3 days after infection begins. The swelling of bone changes its water content very early and very clearly and this is why it shows as an abnormality on MRI so early. CT and x-ray are based on calcium content. The positron emission tomography (PET) scan is based on the metabolism of 18-fluorodeoxyglucose. Cancer generally has a higher rate of glucose metabolism than surrounding tissues and that is why it lights up with PET scan.

- MRI is based on tissue water content.
- PET is based on glucose metabolism.

Orders:
- *MRI*

Only do a nuclear bone scan if an MRI cannot be done, for example, because of the presence of a pacemaker.

Hold antibiotics until you get a bone sample.

On your clinical rotations you will see doctors treating with antibiotics before a bone sample is obtained. Do not do this on your Step 3 examination test. Advance the clock to get MRI results.

The CCS order screen will always tell you the precise time, down to the minute, when a test result will come back.

Report:
• *MRI: abnormal uptake in the tibia consistent with osteomyelitis*

The culture of the surface of an ulcer does not reveal what is in the bone.

Orders:
• *Bone biopsy*
• *Erythrocyte sedimentation rate (ESR)*

Gram-negative bacilli causes 30% of osteomyelitis in diabetes.

Only biopsy can tell if *Staphylococcus* is sensitive or resistant.

Move the clock forward until the biopsy is obtained. You do not have to wait for the results to start antibiotics. You just have to take the sample before the start of antibiotics so that you know it will be accurate.

After the bone biopsy is obtained, order antibiotics.

CCS will tell you that it will be 1 to 2 days before the culture and pathology reports are back. The culture will give you the organisms and the sensitivity. Pathology will tell you whether osteomyelitis is present on the microscopic examination of the slides.

Osteomyelitis Pathology
• Neutrophils infiltrating bone

Organisms
1. Staphylococcus: both sensitive and resistant
2. Gram-negative rods
3. Fungus, mycobacterial, mixed

Orders:
• *Vancomycin or linezolid or daptomycin*
  and
• *Piperacillin/Tazobactam or cefepime or quinolone (levofloxacin, ciprofloxacin)*

If a rash is associated with the use of penicillin, cephalosporin is safe to use.

Move the clock forward to obtain the results of the bone biopsy. Antibiotics should be continued intravenously until results are obtained.

Reports:
• *ESR: 110 mm/h*
• *Bone biopsy:*
  ◦ *Pathology shows neutrophils.*
  ◦ *The culture is* Staphylococcus aureus.
  ◦ *It is sensitive to oxacillin.*

What is the mechanism of vancomycin?

a. DNA gyrase   **c.** Cell wall
b. RNA polymerase   **d.** Ribosome

Answer c. Cell wall

Vancomycin inhibits the formation of the cell wall by a mechanism different than that of penicillin or cephalosporin (Figure 10-1). Despite them both working by inhibiting the cell wall, beta-lactam antibiotics are more effective and bactericidal at inhibiting growth of organisms that are sensitive to oxacillin. For this reason, it is imperative that you switch vancomycin to a beta-lactam antibiotic if the organism is sensitive. Vancomycin has a greater failure rate in controlling sensitive microorganisms that are oxacillin (methicillin) sensitive.

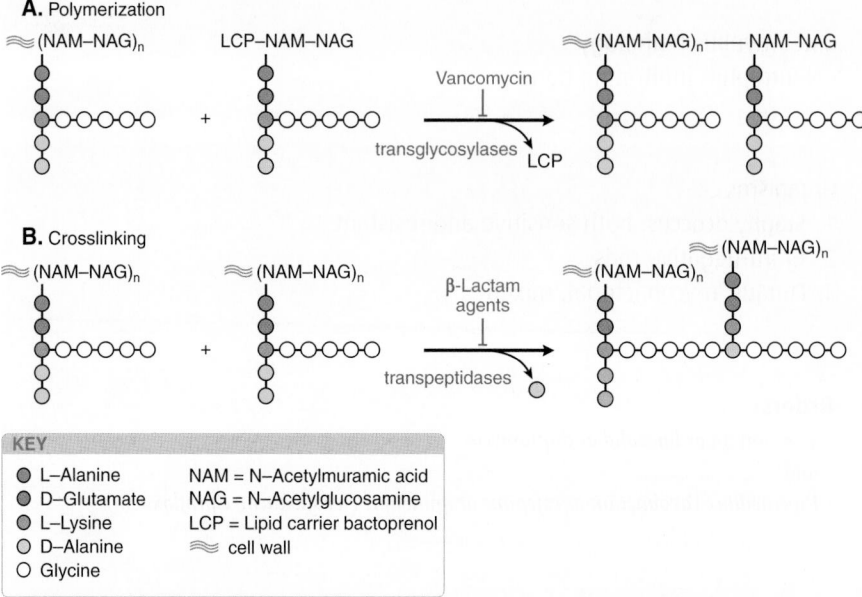

A. Polymerization

B. Crosslinking

KEY
- ● L–Alanine   NAM = N–Acetylmuramic acid
- ● D–Glutamate   NAG = N–Acetylglucosamine
- ● L–Lysine   LCP = Lipid carrier bactoprenol
- ○ D–Alanine   ≈ cell wall
- ○ Glycine

Figure 10-1. Inhibition of bacterial cell wall synthesis: vancomycin and beta-lactam agents. Vancomycin inhibits the polymerization or transglycosylase reaction (**A**) by binding to the D-alanyl-D-alanine terminus of the cell wall precursor unit attached to its lipid carrier and blocks linkage to the glycopeptide polymer (indicated by the subscript n). These $(NAM–NAG)_n$ peptidoglycan polymers are located within the cell wall. Van A-type resistance is due to the expression of enzymes that modify the cell wall precursor by substituting a terminal D-lactate for D-alanine, reducing vancomycin binding affinity by 1000 times. Beta-lactam antibiotics inhibit the cross-linking or transpeptidase reaction (**B**) that links glycopeptide polymer chains by formation of a cross-bridge with the stem peptide (the five glycines in this example) of one chain, displacing the terminal D-alanine of an adjacent chain. (Reproduced with permission from Brunton LL, et al. *Goodman & Gilman's The Pharmacological Basis of Therapeutics,* 12th ed. New York: McGraw-Hill; 2011.)

The patient can be sent home on antibiotics intravenously. Only gram-negative osteomyelitis can be reliably treated with oral antibiotics such as a quinolone. Staphylococci, whether sensitive or resistant, must be treated with intravenous (IV) antibiotics.

Orders:
- *Discontinue vancomycin.*
- *Discontinue piperacillin/tazobactam.*
- *Start IV oxacillin (or nafcillin) or ceftriaxone.*
- *Transfer the patient home.*

CCS is easier than real life in that you do not have to worry about dosing of antibiotics. Oxacillin, nafcillin, cefazolin, and ceftriaxone are all IV antibiotics that effectively cover sensitive staphylococcus. Any one of them is acceptable on CCS based on the sensitivities that are reported to you.

Move the clock forward at 1- to 2-week intervals. You should not *repeat the x-ray or MRI to follow the effect of treatment. Use the ESR. If the ESR comes down slowly over 4 weeks, you can stop antibiotics. If, at 3 weeks, the ESR is still elevated, continue IV treatment to 6 weeks. If the ESR is still elevated at 5 and 6 weeks, then repeat the MRI and evaluate for surgical debridement. Persistently high ESR may indicate necrotic bone or abscess formation.*

Bone biopsy is the *key* to osteomyelitis management!

You will feel stupid if you did not biopsy the bone, and the treatment fails at 6 weeks.

CASE 2: Endocarditis

Setting: *ED*

CC: *"I have a fever."*

VS: *BP: 110/70 mm Hg; P: 90 beats/minute; T: 102°F; R: 14 breaths/minute*

HPI: *A 43-year-old man with a history of injection drug use (IDU) comes to the ED with fever for the past several days. The last time he injected drugs was several days prior to coming to the ED. He had been sober for 2 years when he relapsed. He denies chest pain or shortness of breath.*

PMHx:
• *Alcoholism: 2 years of sobriety*
• *Three-month residential rehabilitation in past*

Medications: *none*

What valve would be involved most often with endocarditis secondary to IDU?

a. Mitral

b. Aortic

c. Tricuspid

d. Pulmonic

Answer c. Tricuspid

Because of continuously exposing the right side of the heart to infected material you should expect to have an infection of the right side of the heart. The tricuspid valve is most vulnerable. Right-sided endocarditis can spread infection to the lungs with septic emboli.

PE:
- *Cardiovascular: 3/6 systolic murmur heard best at the lower left sternal border*
- *Extremities: splinter hemorrhages found in some fingernails; no Janeway lesions, no Osler nodes*

Which lesion will increase on inhalation?

a. Mitral stenosis

b. Aortic stenosis

c. Tricuspid regurgitation

d. Mitral regurgitation

Answer c. Tricuspid regurgitation

Right-sided lesions increase with inhalation. Left-sided lesions increase with exhalation.

Inhalation Mechanism
- It expands the volume of the chest.
- The phrenic nerve stimulates the diaphragm.
- Negative intrathoracic pressure is present.
- It pulls more blood into the thorax.

The patient's murmur increases with inhalation. The lower left sternal border is the location of the tricuspid valve.

Initial Orders:
- *Blood cultures*
- *CBC*
- *CHEM-7*

Sensitivity of Blood Cultures
1. 70% to 80%
2. 90% to 95%
3. 95% to 99%

Move the clock forward 5 to 10 minutes and repeat the cultures.

On CCS, the only way to get multiple blood cultures is to move the clock forward and repeat the test. For acute endocarditis, such as from IDU, do not wait for the results of cultures or echocardiography to give the antibiotics.

Three cultures are standard when excluding endocarditis.

Mechanism of Blood Cultures
1. Media contains labeled carbon.
2. Bacteria ingest labeled carbon as they grow.
3. Labeled carbon excreted as labeled carbon dioxide (CO_2) by bacteria.
4. Machine samples air in the bottles by needle.
5. Labeled CO_2 above the cutoff indicates growth of bacteria.

After the third blood culture is obtained, start antibiotics. Waiting 15 to 30 minutes between cultures is acceptable. Sustained or continuous bacteremia is a strongly suggestive of endocarditis.

Reports:
• *CBC: normal*
• *CHEM-7: normal*

You check the patient's chemistry to guide dosing of medications. It does not matter that dosing is not possible on CCS. It matters that you know you need to estimate glomerular filtration rate (GFR) so as not to kill your patient's kidneys.

Subacute endocarditis is associated with anemia in >90% of patients.
A normal CBC in this situation suggests acute endocarditis.

Orders:
• *Vancomycin IV*
• *Gentamicin IV*

All initial laboratory tests and treatments should be ordered while in the ED before transferring the patient to the hospital ward. Never just shoot the patient to the floor or intensive care unit (ICU) without doing something for them.

Native valve endocarditis: Viridans group streptococci is the most common cause.
IDU: *S. aureus* or epidermidis is the most common cause.

What is the mechanism of aminoglycoside antibiotics such as gentamicin, tobramycin, and amikacin?

a. DNA gyrase

b. RNA polymerase

c. Cell wall

d. Ribosome

e. Unknown

Answer d. Ribosome

Aminoglycoside antibiotics inhibit messenger RNA (mRNA) translation at the ribosome. This is not the same as inhibiting the production of mRNA. Gentamicin stops the production of protein from mRNA at the ribosome. There is no difference in the mechanism or aminoglycosides.

Beta-Lactam Antibiotics
• Penicillins
• Cephalosporins
• Carbapenems
• Monobactam (aztreonam)

Why are beta-lactam antibiotics and gentamicin synergistic in effect?

a. Blocking excretion raises blood level.

b. Gentamicin increases tissue penetrance of penicillin.

c. Different mechanisms of action are complementary.

d. Gentamicin affects the cell wall when used with beta-lactam antibiotics.

Answer c. Different mechanisms of action are complementary.

Beta-lactam antibiotics inhibit the cell wall. This literally puts a hole in the bacterial cell wall. The aminoglycoside can enter the hole in the wall and disrupt the work or production of the ribosome.

Synergism = Two Drugs with Different Mechanisms of Action

Two beta-lactam antibiotics are never synergistic when used together!

Do not forget to order a diet for all admitted patients. The CCS does not expect you to starve your patient!

Why are splinter hemorrhages potentially important in this patient?

a. Changes dose of antibiotics

b. Changes duration of antibiotics

c. Establishes diagnosis of endocarditis if cultures are negative

d. Changes which echocardiogram to use

e. Antiquated and never relevant

Answer c. Establishes diagnosis of endocarditis if cultures are negative

Blood cultures are falsely negative in 1% to 5% of patients with endocarditis. This form of "culture-negative" endocarditis is diagnosed with the presence of vegetations on an echocardiogram and the presence of at least three minor criteria. Splinter hemorrhages are one of the minor criteria.

Minor criteria:

• Risk: IDU or prosthetic valve

• Fever

• Embolic or vascular phenomena: splinter hemorrhages, Osler nodes, Roth spots, Janeway lesions

This type of patient can have the clock moved forward at long intervals, for example, 12 hours is okay for a hospitalized patient. Blood culture results take 1 to 2 days to become positive.

Report:

• *Blood cultures:* S. aureus *in all three cultures*

What microbiologic feature of *S. aureus* allows it to cause acute endocarditis?

a. Routine feature of gram-positive organism

b. Coagulase

c. Absence of coagulase

d. Plasmid

e. Mutation of penicillin-binding protein

Answer b. Coagulase

Coagulase is present in the cell surface of *S. aureus.* This organism is synonymous with the term "coagulase positive staphylococci." Coagulase literally "melts" its way through intact tissue. This is why IDU causes acute endocarditis. Coagulase makes the organism able to aggressively penetrate normal tissue. Viridans group streptococci and enterococcus are relatively much less virulent. They generally can only invade damaged tissue such as prosthetic valves or those underlying native valvular disease such as mitral stenosis or regurgitation. *Staphylococcus epidermidis* is one of more than 30 types of less virulent staphylococci that are coagulase negative.

Coagulase penetrates normal tissue.

Orders:
• *Transthoracic echocardiogram (TTE)*
• *Repeat vital signs*

Report:
• *Repeat temperature 100.8°F at 2 days after start of antibiotics*

Make sure fever resolves with endocarditis.

TTE has same sensitivity for right-sided endocarditis as transesophageal echocardiography (TEE).

The right ventricle covers 75% of the anterior surface (front) of the heart.

Strongest indication for valve replacement:
• Ruptured chordae tendineae

Move the clock forward to get the sensitivity of the organism and the TTE results.

Reports:
• *Sensitivity report: sensitive to oxacillin*
• *TTE: tricuspid valve vegetation (Figure 10-2)*

**Switch vancomycin to a beta-lactam antibiotic
if it is Staphylococcus sensitive.**

Orders:
• *Stop vancomycin*
• *Start oxacillin (or nafcillin)*
• *Chest x-ray*

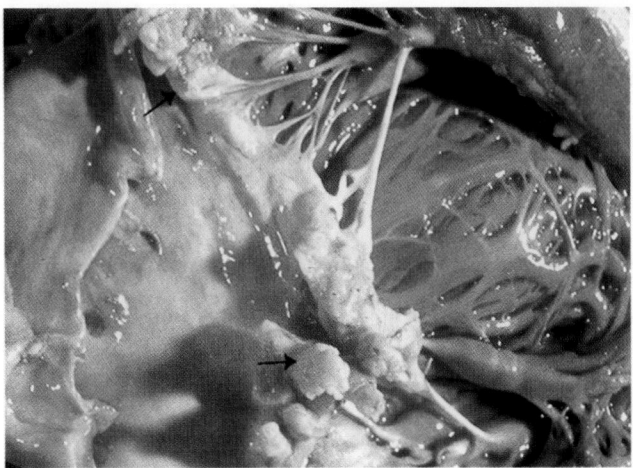

Figure 10-2. Vegetations (*arrows*) due to viridans streptococcal endocarditis involving the mitral valve. (Reproduced with permission from Longo DL, et al. *Harrison's Principles of Internal Medicine*, 18th ed., Vol. 2. New York: McGraw-Hill; 2012.)

Check for septic emboli to the lungs in patients with right-sided endocarditis.

Report:
• *Chest x-ray: normal*

Coagulase creates lung abscesses by tissue penetrance into the lungs.

Move the clock forward to day 5 of treatment. Gentamicin is only needed for synergy with the beta-lactam antibiotic for the first 3 to 5 days of therapy.

Orders:
• *Stop gentamicin*
• *Continue oxacillin (or nafcillin or cefazolin) for 4 weeks*

When the patient's treatment is finished, what will the patient need for endocarditis prophylaxis with dental procedures in the future?

a. Nothing

b. Amoxicillin with fillings

c. Amoxicillin with dental extraction

d. Quinolones with colonoscopy if biopsied

Answer c. Amoxicillin with dental extraction

Previous endocarditis is an indication for endocarditis prophylaxis if undergoing a potentially bacteremia-causing procedure. Dental extraction or cutting the mouth needs prophylaxis. Dental fillings and any form of endoscopy of either the lungs or gastrointestinal (GI) tract do not need prophylaxis.

Lesions needing prophylaxis with dental extractions:

• Previous endocarditis

• Prosthetic valves

• Unrepaired cyanotic heart disease

• Cardiac transplant recipients

CASE 3: Pyelonephritis

Setting: *ED*

CC: *"It burns when I pee."*

VS: *BP: 108/70 mm Hg; P: 104 beats/minute; T: 101.6°F; R: 14 breaths/minute*

HPI: *A generally healthy 32-year-old woman with fever, urinary frequency, and burning for several days and back pain has arrived at the ED. She had cystitis once several years ago. She has not seen a physician for a long time. She is nauseated and vomited twice.*

PMHx/Medications: *none*

PE:
• *General: sitting up in bed; uncomfortable*
• *Back: tenderness at the left flank. Costovertebral angle tenderness is present.*
• *Abdomen: nontender; normal bowel sounds*

Initial Orders:
• *Urinalysis (UA)*
• *Blood cultures*
• *CBC*
• *CHEM-7*

Escherichia coli is still most common cause of urinary tract infections.

On UA, look for white blood cells (WBCs).
Bacteria on UA is relevant only in pregnancy.

Blood cultures take 2 to 3 days to become positive on CCS.

Report:
- *UA: WBCs 400/µL; protein trace; nitrite positive*
- *CBC: WBCs 16,700/µL*
- *CHEM-7: normal*

Nitrites = Gram-Negative Bacilli
Bacteria convert nitr*ate* to nitr*ite.*

**Dysuria + UA WBCs = Urinary Tract Infection (UTI) + Flank Pain
= Pyelonephritis**

Staphylococcus saprophyticus
- UTI
- Sexually active young women

Dysuria + UA WBC + Suprapubic Pain = Cystitis

Start treatment as soon as blood cultures are obtained and the presence of WBCs is confirmed on UA.

Imaging is *not* needed prior to starting antibiotics (Figure 10-3).

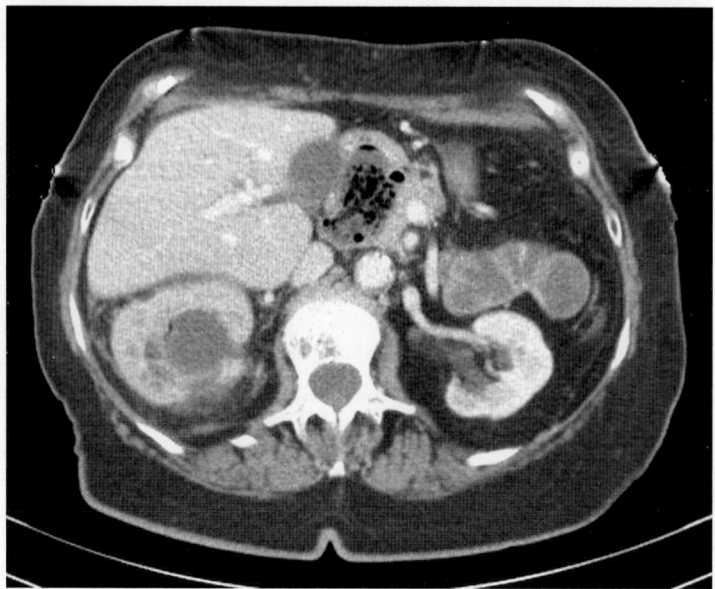

Figure 10-3. Computed tomography scan of the abdomen showing pyelonephritis in a patient with a urinary tract obstruction from a stone at the ureteropelvic junction. The right kidney is significantly enlarged, with hydronephrosis and perinephric fat stranding. (Reproduced with permission from McKean SC, et al. *Principles and Practice of Hospital Medicine.* New York: McGraw-Hill; 2012.)

Orders:
- *Ceftriaxone IV*
- *Renal ultrasound (US)*

CCS will expect you to know practical issues, such as, "Do not prescribe pills for vomiting people with pyelonephritis."

IV Pyelonephritis Therapies
- Ceftriaxone
- Ampicillin *and* gentamicin
- Aztreonam
- Ciprofloxacin
- Levofloxacin
- Ertapenem

Aztreonam
• Monobactam
• Cell wall inhibitor
• No cross reaction with penicillin

Move the clock forward to get the results of the renal US. **The US is not to diagnose pyelo-nephritis, but to identify a potential correctable etiology.**

Renal US to identify:
• Stones
• Strictures
• Tumor
• Obstruction

Report:
• *Renal US: no stones, no hydronephrosis; enlarged left kidney, edema consistent with pyelonephritis*

Advance the clock 6 to12 hours and do an Interval History. This is the only way to see if the nausea and vomiting has resolved.
    The main reason to admit a patient with pyelonephritis is:
• *Inability to take pills*
• *Hypotension and hemodynamic instability*

Nausea and vomiting are common in pyelonephritis.

Interval History: "Nausea is much improved. No further episodes of vomiting today.
    Still febrile with temperature 102°F."

Reports:
• *Blood cultures: no growth*
• *Urine culture: E. coli, sensitivity pending*

CCS will not engage in controversial or unclear practices. Oral and IV pyelonephritis treatment are nearly equal. If you are not certain, keep the patient in the hospital until the sensitivity of the organism is known.

Move the clock forward a day to get the sensitivity of the organism. You can be fully sure the pyelonephritis will resolve by that time.

Reports:
- Blood culture: *no growth at 3 days*
- Urine: *E. coli sensitive to ciprofloxacin*

Orders:
- *Stop ceftriaxone.*
- *Start oral ciprofloxacin.*
- *Transfer the patient home.*
- *Schedule a follow-up appointment in the office in 7 days.*

Quinolones
- They inhibit DNA gyrase.
- Gyrase is needed to unwind genetics so it can reproduce.
- IV and oral blood level are nearly identical.

CASE 4: Cellulitis

Setting: *ED*

CC: *"My leg is red and swollen."*

VS: *BP: 134/88 mm Hg; P: 96 beats/minute; T: 102°F; R: 18 breaths/minute*

HPI: *A 49-year-old generally healthy man with several days of increasing redness and warmth of his right lower extremity presents at the ED. The leg is painful. He has been "feeling warm" for a few days as well. He denies injury to the leg, cancer, long flights, knee surgery, or immobility. He has had no previous episode of skin infection and no recent hospitalizations.*

PMHx: *none*

Medications: *none*

PE:
- *General: well-groomed, alert, and friendly*

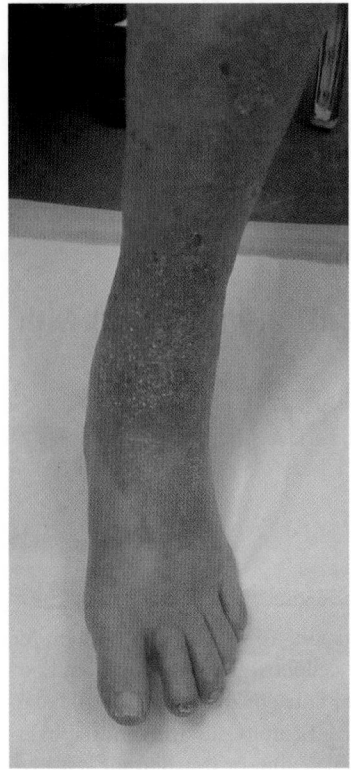

Figure 10-4. Cellulitis in an older man with venous stasis dermatitis. (Reproduced with permission from Richard P. Usatine, MD.)

- *Extremities: right leg has an area of redness in the skin over the medial half of the lower leg and the calf (Figure 10-4). Redness is warm to touch. There are no ulcerations. Tinea pedis is found in between the toes.*

CCS allows the artificial distinction between choosing tests or treatments to disappear. In this respect, CCS is similar to real life. This patient needs several things simultaneously, and it would be artificial to ask a student to choose only one of them.

Initial Orders:
- *Cefazolin IV*
- *Lower-extremity duplex US*
- *Blood cultures*

Cellulitis Organisms
Number 1 is *S. aureus.*
Number 2 is beta-hemolytic streptococci.

Sensitive and resistant S. aureus cannot be distinguished by appearance.

Exclude clot in all leg-related cellulitis.

Beta-Hemolysis = Complete Hemolysis

Which of these are considered "standard" in *this* patient with cellulitis?

a. Potassium hydroxide (KOH) prep of interdigital web space

b. Biopsy of skin

c. Infuse sterile saline into skin and aspirate for culture

d. X-ray of leg

e. Swab surface

Answer a. Potassium hydroxide (KOH) prep of interdigital web space

Skin breakdown and tinea pedis was seen on examination. You should always look for an entry point of skin breakdown in people who have cellulitis. Healthy skin should not develop cellulitis. You also need to correct any point of entry or the infection will recur. Biopsy of skin is virtually never done. Patients are treated empirically with antistaphylo-coccal and streptococcal antibiotics such as cefazolin, nafcillin, or oxacillin for sensitive organisms. If there is methicillin-resistant *Staphylococcus aureus* (MRSA) suspected, use vancomycin, linezolid, ceftaroline, or daptomycin.

Move the clock forward to obtain the results of the duplex US of the leg and the KOH prep.

Leg duplex US is >95% sensitive and specific for deep venous thrombosis (DVT).

Reports:
• *Lower extremity duplex US: negative, no clot*
• *KOH: fungal hyphae visible*

Fungi do not dissolve in KOH.

Chitin are
• In the fungal cell wall
• Not dissolvable by KOH
• Same as lobster or crab shell

Ceftaroline is the only cephalosporin to cover MRSA.

Orders:
• *Apply terbinafine topically to feet.*
• *Continue cefazolin.*

Cellulitis and tinea pedis do not have a clear length of therapy that you can determine in advance. Move the clock forward a day at a time and see if there is improvement in the temperature and examination. Most patients should markedly improve in 2 to 3 days and be discharged.

Oral MRSA Drugs
• Doxycycline
• Trimethoprim-sulfamethoxazole (TMP-SMZ)
• Clindamycin

Move the clock forward 1 day to reassess the patient's temperature and examination. Because we rarely ever aspirate and culture out a specific organism for cellulitis, we are stuck treating empirically and looking for a response in 24 to 48 hours.

Antibiotics needs at least 12 to 24 hours even to begin to work.

Interval History: *"Feet are less itchy. Leg is less painful."*

PE:
• *T: 100.6°F*
• *Extremities: less red and warm*

Molds such as *Epidermophyton* and *Trichophyton* cause tinea pedis. What is the major difference between molds and yeast?

a. Response to topical nystatin

b. Formation of spores at room temperature

c. Causing human disease

d. Nothing

Answer b. Formation of spores at room temperature

Both molds and yeast are fungi. Yeasts are organisms like *Candida*. *Candida* only grows at body temperature (98.6°F or 37°C). Yeasts do not form spores at room temperature. Molds are organisms that cause skin or nail infections. Also like *Aspergillus*, blastomycosis, and coccidioidomycosis, they form spores at room temperature that can exist at temperatures much colder than room temperature for an indefinite period of time. That is why you can inhale mold spores in the environment, but cannot obtain yeast growth such as *Candida* in the same way.

When improved, a patient with cellulitis can be sent home on an oral version of the medication used intravenously in the hospital. This is easy for cefazolin. The oral equivalent of cefazolin is cephalexin. It is essentially identical to cefazolin. Treatment with oral equivalents of antistaphylococcal medication against resistant organisms, such as MRSA, is much more difficult. There is no direct oral equivalent of vancomycin.

Oral vancomycin is not absorbed.

Orders:
- *Stop cefazolin.*
- *Transfer the patient to home.*
- *Schedule a follow-up office appointment in 7 days.*
- *Continue topical terbinafine (or clotrimazole or nystatin).*
- *Give oral cephalexin.*

Treatment of cellulitis is empiric.
No specific organism is identified.
Look for response to treatment, and switch if there is none.

CASE 5: Urethritis

Setting: *ambulatory clinic*

CC: *"It burns when I urinate."*

VS: *T: 98°F*

HPI: *A 24-year-old man comes to the clinic complaining of burning on urination for the past 3 days. He feels "when I have to go, I really have to go in a hurry" happens 10 times a day. He is sexually active with both men and women. He has a creamy yellow discharge coming from his penis.*

PMHx:
• *Herpes genital infection three times in past*
• *Human immunodeficiency virus (HIV) test negative 6 months ago*

Medications: *none*

PE:
• *Genital: discharge from urethra visible on slight pressure to glans of penis; no vesicular lesions*
• *Joints: normal*
• *Skin: normal*

Initial Orders:
• *Urethral swab for Gram stain*
• *Voided urine for nucleic acid amplification test (NAAT)*
• *Chlamydia and gonorrhea testing*

Urethral discharge tells you it is urethritis, not cystitis.

Dysuria + Urethral Discharge = Urethritis

What is the main difference between urethritis in men and cervicitis in women?

a. A urethral swab is used for Gram stain testing.

b. NAAT is required.

c. Chlamydia is the most common cause.

d. Ceftriaxone and azithromycin are used.

e. Cefixime is used.

Answer a. A urethral swab is used for Gram stain testing.

The management of urethritis in men and cervicitis in women is the same except for two points:

1. Gram stain testing for *Neisseria gonorrhoeae* is only used in men.
2. Women can do a self-administered swab into the vagina.

Otherwise, both cervicitis and urethritis are treated with ceftriaxone and azithromycin and both are most commonly caused by chlamydia. Neither should be treated with cefixime.

Neisseria gonorrhoeae
- Gram-negative diplococcus
- Chocolate agar growth medium
- CO_2 needed
- Oxidase positive

On CCS, add HIV testing for every person with an sexually transmitted disease (STD). You will never lose points for hepatitis B testing and Venereal Disease Research Laboratory (VDRL) rapid plasma reagin (RPR) for syphilis.

The patient agrees to HIV testing.

Report:
- *Gram stain of urethral discharge: gram-negative diplococci inside multiple neutrophils (Figure 10-5)*

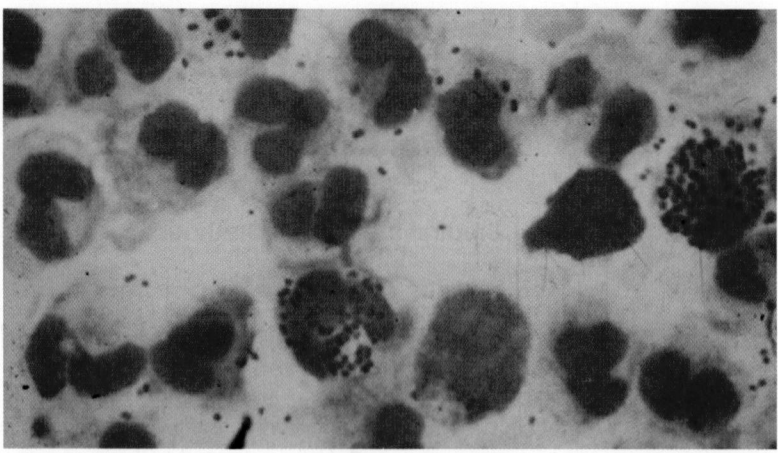

Figure 10-5. Gram stain of urethral discharge from a male patient with gonorrhea shows gram-negative intracellular monococci and diplococci. (Reproduced with permission from the Public Health Agency of Canada.)

Additional written consent is not needed for HIV testing.

Neisseria grows on **Thayer-Martin medium**
· Antibiotics in media
· Vancomycin, colistin, and nystatin
· Kills off potentially competitive bacteria

Orders:
• *Ceftriaxone intramuscularly (IM)*
• *Azithromycin orally*
• *HIV test*
• *VDRL-RPR*

Treat both chlamydia and gonorrhea at the same time.

Chlamydia trachomatis
· It is an intracellular parasite.
· NAAT is the best test.
· Use doxycycline, azithromycin, or erythromycin.
Chlamydia is present in 50% of patients with gonorrhea.

Do not forget to "counsel," "educate," or "advise" on safe sex practices for any patient with an STD, as well as to do screening and treatment of the patient's sexual partners. Without treating the partner, the patient will likely become reinfected.

The patient can leave to go home after the ceftriaxone and azithromycin are given. Directly observed therapy in the clinic for oral azithromycin is preferred. Cefixime orally is not as effective as ceftriaxone orally. The patient and his partner should return to discuss the HIV, hepatitis, and syphilis test in a week. A routine test of cure is not needed if the patient's symptoms resolve.

CASE 6: Syphilis

Setting: *ambulatory clinic*

CC: *"I have a sore on my penis."*

VS: *normal*

HPI: *A 34-year-old man with an ulcer on his penis for the past several days comes to the walk-in clinic. He had a raised papule a few days ago that started to ulcerate after 2 days. He has never had a lesion like this before, although he has had herpes simplex vesicles in the past. The lesion is not painful. He was on vacation 3 weeks ago and had multiple unprotected sexual encounters with other men.*

PMHx:
- *Herpes simplex*
- *HIV negative*

Medications: *none*

PE:
- *Genital: There is a 2-cm lesion on the shaft of the penis with raised, indurated edges. There is nontender inguinal adenopathy present and no vesicles.*

Initial Orders:
- *Darkfield microscopy*
- *VDRL or RPR*

Darkfield microscopy is the most accurate test for primary syphilis.
• Spirochetes are mobile when seen (Figure 10-6)

Treponema pallidum
• Never cultured
• Spiral gram-negative
• Spirochete

VDRL and RPR
• They are nontreponemal tests.
• They detect anticardiolipin antibodies.
• They are 75% to 80% sensitive in detecting primary syphilis.

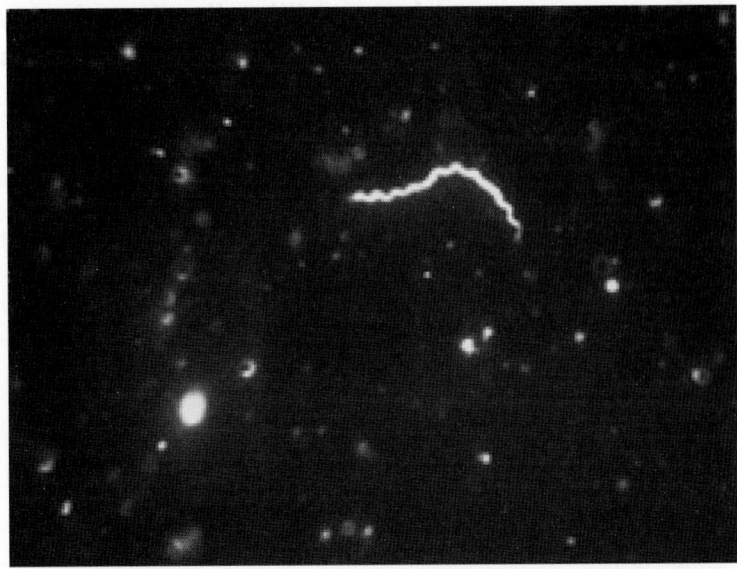

Figure 10-6. Microscopic view of *Treponema pallidum*. With darkfield microscopy, spirochetes appear as motile, bright corkscrews against a black background. (Reproduced with permission from Cox D, Liu H, Moreland AA, et al. Syphilis. In Morse S, Ballard RC, Holmes KK, et al., eds. *Atlas of Sexually Transmitted Diseases*, 3rd ed. Edinburgh: Mosby; 2003.)

Darkfield microscopy can be done on the spot in a person with a genital lesion. This test is more sensitive than the nontreponemal tests, the VDRL and RPR. Nontreponemal tests need time to become abnormal.

Report:
• *Darkfield microscopy: positive for mobile spirochetes*

Darkfield microscopy is 100% specific.

In real life, most places do not use the darkfield examination. Only the RPR or VDRL is done initially, followed by specific treponemal tests such as the fluorescent treponemal antibody absorption (FTA-ABS) test. On CCS, however, you get to be an "idealist," where every test you want is available.

What is the management of a penicillin-allergic patient with a chancre?

a. Desensitization to penicillin

b. Ceftriaxone IM

c. Doxycycline orally

d. Erythromycin

Answer c. Doxycycline orally

Oral doxycycline is more effective than erythromycin. Desensitization is not necessary for primary or secondary syphilis. Desensitization is performed in those with tertiary syphilis and those who are pregnant. Ceftriaxone is a less effective alternative to IV penicillin for tertiary syphilis.

Desensitization is not needed for genital lesions.
Doxycycline orally is enough.

Orders:
• *Benzathine penicillin: one IM injection*

Keep all patients given IM injections in the clinic for a few hours for observation postinjection. Move the clock forward at 1-hour intervals for 3 hours and do an Interval History.

Chancre
• It is the main manifestation of primary syphilis.
• They resolve spontaneously in 3 to 6 weeks.
• Twenty-five percent recur as secondary syphilis.

Interval History: (at 3 hours after IM penicillin)
• *Headache, myalgia, and rash develop (Jarisch-Herxheimer reaction)*

Mechanism of Jarisch-Herxheimer Reaction
• Release of treponemal lipopolysaccharide
• Tumor necrosis factor alpha (TNF-alpha)
• Interleukin-6
Jarisch-Herxheimer reaction is not dangerous.

Orders:
- *Transfer patient to home.*
- *Have patient use aspirin.*
- *Have patient return in 1 to 2 days for follow-up.*

The patient returns the following day.
> *Interval history: "Resolution of fever and myalgia"*

Report:
- *VDRL or RPR: positive at 1:256*
- *FTA positive*

A single IM injection of penicillin is all that is needed for primary and most secondary syphilis. Bring the patient back at 3, 6, and 12 months. Recheck the VDRL or RPR at each visit. There should be a marked reduction in the titer. The FTA will stay positive lifelong.

CASE 7: Herpes Zoster: Shingles

Setting: *office*

CC: *"My side hurts."*

VS: *BP: 142/92 mm Hg; P: 102 beats/minute; T: 99.2°F; R: 18 breaths/minute*

HPI: *A 72-year-old man comes to your office with complaints of pain in the left side of his chest for the past 5 days. The pain is continuous and increasing in intensity. He comes now because he has developed a rash at the site where the pain is.*

PMHx:
- *Benign prostatic hypertrophy*
- *Chronic obstructive pulmonary disease (COPD)—mild*
- *Former smoker—stopped 15 years ago*

Medications:
- *Tiotropium regularly*
- *Albuterol intermittently*
- *Finasteride*
- *Tamsulosin*

Pain can elevate blood pressure (BP).
Single BP elevations with pain are meaningless.

PE:
- *General: uncomfortable from pain*
- *Chest: vesicular rash in a stripe across the left side of the chest. Rash does not cross the midline. Vesicles are fluid filled. No crusting is visible.*

Herpes zoster rash does not cross the midline.

Varicella-zoster virus (VZV) is stored in the dorsal root ganglia—one side only.

Which of the following is most important to do first for this patient?

a. Tzanck prep

b. Viral culture

c. Antiviral treatment

d. Varicella serology of blood

Answer c. Antiviral treatment

When there is a clear dermatomal distribution of herpes zoster or shingles, neither the Tzanck prep nor viral culture is necessary. Nothing else besides VZV gives a vesicular rash in a dermatomal distribution. When testing is needed, the viral culture of the skin is the most accurate test. Viral culture needs to be done on specific viral media. It will not grow on blood agar. The Tzanck smear can be useful in herpes infections, particularly VZV. VZV takes 10 to 14 days to grow, so although viral culture may be the most accurate test for herpes zoster, it is most often not clinically practical because it does not allow an answer in time to affect treatment.

Tzanck Smear
- Swab or smear of lesion
- Pathologic and cytologic test on a slide
- Like a Papanicolaou (Pap) smear of the cervix
- Multinucleated giant cells in positive test
- Cannot distinguish herpes zoster from herpes simplex

Herpes Virus Family
- Simplex 1 and 2
- VZV

- Cytomegalovirus (CMV)
- Epstein-Barr virus (EBV)
- Human herpes virus 6,7, 8

Initial Orders:
- *Give valacyclovir orally.*
- *Keep vesicles covered.*

Herpes Zoster = Shingles = Varicella Reactivation

Can varicella spread to others?

a. Never
b. Only adults who have not had shingles

c. Only persons who never had chicken pox or the vaccine
d. Children yes, adults no

Answer c. Only persons who never had chicken pox or the vaccine

It is possible for VZV that causes shingles reactivation to spread to others. It is highly unlikely if the shingles is only on one or two dermatomes, but it is possible. The patient should not be allowed near patients who are immunocompromised and have never had chicken pox or the vaccine.

- VZV can spread to nonimmune persons.
- VZV is spread by airborne transmission.

Valacyclovir = Acyclovir = Famciclovir Equal Efficacy

Steroids in Zoster
- *Not* clearly beneficial

Move the case forward to be sure that there is no spread to other dermatomes and that it does not disseminate. In addition, you want to be sure that there is crusting of the lesions, indicating that healing has occurred and that there is no possibility of transmission.
Interval History: "Lesions are crusting, but there is still some pain."

> **PE:**
> • *No fever*
> • *Chest: crusting of vesicular lesions*

> Transmissibility stops when the lesions dry and crust.

What is the mechanism of valacyclovir?
a. Protein inhibition
b. Cell wall
c. Thymidine kinase
d. Reverse transcriptase

Answer c. Thymidine kinase

Acyclovir, famciclovir, and valacyclovir work by inhibition of thymidine kinase. Without an effective thymidine kinase, the genetic material of the herpes virus cannot reproduce. These agents are effective against herpes simplex and VZV. They are not effective against CMV.

What is the best postexposure prophylaxis for a pregnant woman exposed to shingles or chicken pox?
a. Varicella-zoster immune globulin (VZIG)
b. VZIG and varicella vaccine
c. Varicella vaccine

Answer a. Varicella-zoster immune globulin (VZIG)

VZIG offers some protection against acquiring new varicella infection. The persons most in need of postexposure prophylaxis are those who are pregnant and those who are immunocompromised, such as those undergoing chemotherapy and those using steroids. Pregnant women should not receive varicella vaccine because it is a live-attenuated vaccine. Live vaccines should be avoided in pregnancy because of concern that they might spread to the fetus.

> Varicella vaccine is a live-attenuated virus.
> Avoid in varicella vaccine immunocompromised or pregnant persons.

> **VZIG**
> • Immunoglobulin G (IgG)
> • Intercepts VZV before it infects lymphocytes

Move the clock forward 1 to 2 weeks to see if postherpetic neuralgia has developed. Neither steroids nor tricyclic antidepressants (TCAs) will prevent the development of postherpetic neuralgia (PHN). If PHN does develop, acceptable treatments are pregabalin, gabapentin, or TCAs.

    Interval History: "The patient's lesions have fully healed, and there is no pain at this time."

Which of the following is most likely to benefit the patient?

a. Chronic valacyclovir use

b. Zoster vaccine

c. Prednisone

Answer b. Zoster vaccine

Zoster vaccine in a person such as this is not to prevent the primary varicella infection. Zoster vaccine is to prevent the reactivation of shingles. It is the same type of vaccine, but at much higher dose. Zoster vaccine should be given to all persons at the age of 60 years to prevent shingles from occurring.

Five percent of people older than age 60 years get shingles.

Give zoster vaccine to those older than age 60 routinely!

CASE 8: Infectious Diarrhea

Setting: *ED*

CC: *"I have diarrhea."*

VS: *BP: 104/62 mm Hg; P: 94 beats/minute; T: 101.6°F; R: 18 breaths/minute*

HPI: *A 30-year-old resident in internal medicine comes to the ED at his own hospital with 1 day of watery brown diarrhea with blood in it and abdominal pain. He is generally a very healthy person and this is the first time this has happened to him. He does not recall an exposure to infected or contaminated food. None of his friends have diarrhea nor does anyone in his family with whom he has recently eaten.*

PMHx/Medications: *none*

PE:
- *General: very weak and tired appearing*
- *Abdomen: soft, but diffusely tender; no masses found*
- *Chest: clear bilaterally*

Initial Orders:
- *Orthostatic blood pressure measurement*
- *CHEM-7*
- *CBC*
- *Blood cultures*
- *Stool culture, ova/parasite examination*

Stool WBCs
- Detect invasive diarrhea
- Sign of inflammation
- Not needed if blood visible in stool

Use methylene blue to detect WBCs in stool.

Orthostasis
- Detects >15% to 20% volume loss
- Pulse rate increase by 10 beats/minute
- Systolic BP decrease by 20 mm Hg

It is not always clear whether to use IV fluids in a person with diarrhea. Most infectious diarrhea is not severe enough to need IV fluids or antibiotics. Use orthostasis as an indicator of how severe diarrhea is as you move the clock forward.

Move clock forward 5 minutes to get results of orthostatic BP and pulse rate measurement:

- *Systolic BP drops to 86/52 mm Hg; pulse rate rises to 118 beats/minute*

Orthostasis = Severe Diarrhea = IV Saline Needed

Volume Depletion Detection
1. Mechanoreceptors ("stretch" receptors) respond in the aorta and carotid sinuses.
2. Decreased stimulation results.
3. Cranial nerves IX and X transmit to the medulla.
4. Vasoconstriction and tachycardia result.

Orders:
• *Normal saline bolus, then continuously*
• *Ciprofloxacin orally*

Antibiotics for Diarrhea
Fever + Blood + Orthostasis
Pain + Tenderness

What is the most likely organism?

a. Campylobacter
b. Shigella
c. Yersinia
d. Viral
e. Staphylococcus

Answer a. Campylobacter

Viruses and staphylococci do not cause blood in the stool with diarrhea. The rest of the answer relies on statistical data. *Campylobacter* is more common than *Salmonella*, *Shigella*, *Yersinia*, or *E. coli* as a cause of infectious diarrhea, especially from food poisoning.

When bolusing with fluids, move the clock forward only 5 minutes to detect an improvement in BP and pulse rate. These effects will be nearly instantaneous on CCS.

• The carotid baroreceptor transmits to the brainstem by glossopharyngeal nerve.
• The aortic baroreceptor transmits to the brainstem by the vagus nerve.

Move the clock 5 minutes. Repeat vital signs

VS: *P: 100 beats/minute; BP 106/70 mm Hg*

Yersinia
- Gram-negative bacillus
- Siderophilic (likes iron to grow)
- Can grow in the cold
- Invades Peyer patches in ileum
- Simulates appendicitis

Reports:
- *CHEM-7:*
  - *Bicarbonate: 18 mEq/L (low)*
  - *Potassium: 3.0 mEq/L (low)*
  - *Chloride: 115 mEq/L (high)*
  - *Sodium: 140 mEq/L (normal)*
- *CBC: WBCs 14,000/μL*

**Diarrhea = Normal Anion Gap Diarrhea = High Chloride Level
+ Low Bicarbonate Level**

Metabolic Acidosis in Diarrhea
- There is a normal anion gap.
- The colon excretes bicarbonate.
- The colon excretes potassium.

*Once you find potassium level abnormalities, you should replace potassium immediately
and recheck the potassium level.*

Orders:
• *Oral potassium*
• *Continue IV saline and oral ciprofloxacin*

Shigella
• It is resistant to stomach acid.
• A very small number of organisms can cause infection (10–100).
• It does not ferment lactose.
• *Shigella* toxin causes hemolytic uremic syndrome (HUS).

Move the clock forward 1 hour and repeat the potassium level and vital signs.

VS: *BP 110/72 mm Hg; P: 92 beats/minute; T: 101°F*

Report:
• *Potassium 4.0 mEq/L*

Move the clock forward 12 hours. Most infectious diarrhea will show improvement in 12 to 24 hours and is self-limited. Give antibiotics for infectious diarrhea by mouth, because the gastrointestinal (GI) tract is where the infections is.

On the second hospital day, do an Interval History to see if the diarrhea is improving. Look at the fever curve to see if the temperature is coming down with the use of antibiotics.

Antibiotics need 12 to 24 hours to start working.

Interval History: "Frequency of diarrhea is decreasing. Temperature is 99.8°F."

Orders:
• *CHEM-7*

Campylobacter (Figure 10-7)
• Gram-negative bacillus
• Helical shape
• Grows at 42°C (higher than usual body temperature)

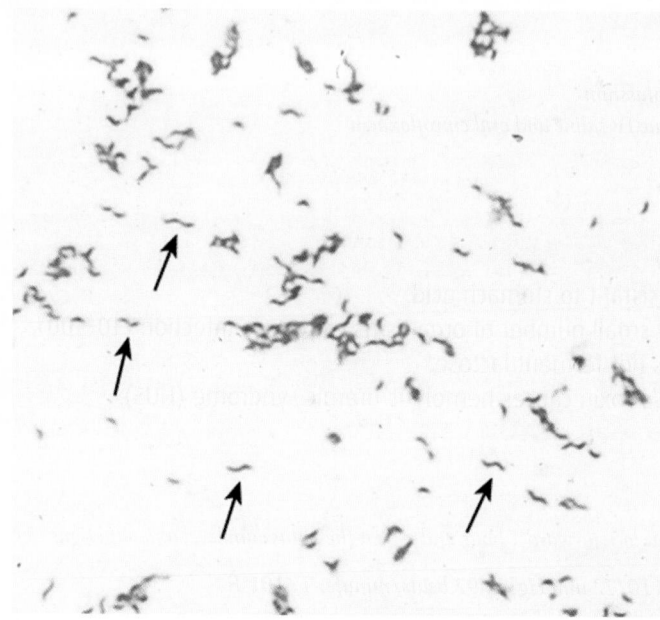

Figure 10-7. Gram stain of *Campylobacter jejuni* showing "comma"- or "gull wing"–shaped gram-negative bacilli (*arrows*). Campylobacters stain faintly and can be difficult to visualize. Original magnification ×1000. (Reproduced with permission from Brooks GF, et al. *Jawetz, Melnick, & Adelberg's Medical Microbiology,* 25th ed. New York: McGraw-Hill; 2010.)

Move the clock to the third hospital day. **Fever and diarrhea resolve.**

Reports:
- *CHEM-7: normal*
- *Stool Culture:* Campylobacter
- *Blood Culture: no growth*

You can discharge the patient and send him home. No further antibiotics are needed past 3 days for campylobacter.
This is a follow-up "as needed" type of case on the clock at the end.

CASE 9: Malaria and Travel Medicine

Setting: *office*

CC: *"I'm going on a trip to Africa for three weeks."*

VS: *normal*

HPI: *A 24-year-old healthy medical student is going on a 3-week trip to Africa as part of a medical mission and vacation. She is here seeking advice about vaccinations and prophylaxis.*

PMHx/Medications: *none*

PE: *normal*

Which of the following is not an appropriate preventive therapy for this type of traveler?

a. Ciprofloxacin daily

b. Hepatitis A vaccine

c. Malaria prophylaxis

d. Typhoid vaccine

Answer a. Ciprofloxacin daily

It is not necessary to use daily prophylactic antibiotics to prevent diarrhea. It is inappropriate to use antibiotics in advance of developing diarrhea, and if asked, you should specifically refuse to do so. The traveler should be careful to eat foods that are fully cooked or can be peeled, such as bananas or oranges. She should avoid street food as well. Hepatitis A and typhoid fever vaccinations are routine where the water supply is not safe. Malaria prophylaxis is advised in many places around the world.

CCS will not require you to memorize which specific countries need specific malaria regimens. No one will expect you to remember the chloroquine sensitivity or resistance levels in 190 separate countries in the world.

Which of these is not appropriate for malaria prophylaxis?

a. Mefloquine

b. Artemisinin

c. Atovaquone/Proguanil

d. Doxycycline

e. Netting

Answer b. Artemisinin

Artemisinin-containing combination therapy is used as a drug of choice in acute malaria. It is not a prophylactic medication. The two most commonly used preventive malaria treatments are mefloquine and atovaquone/proguanil. Both of these are equal in efficacy. Doxycycline is used in areas of mefloquine resistance in Southeast Asia. Doxycycline is not the best first choice because there is a risk of photosensitivity reaction. Chloroquine can be used in areas where there is clear chloroquine sensitivity. All of these kill blood schizonts of malaria. Mosquito netting at night is one of the most effective preventive measures you can do for malaria.

Trophozoites = Red Blood Cell (RBC) "Ring" Seen in Malaria Smear (Figure 10-8)

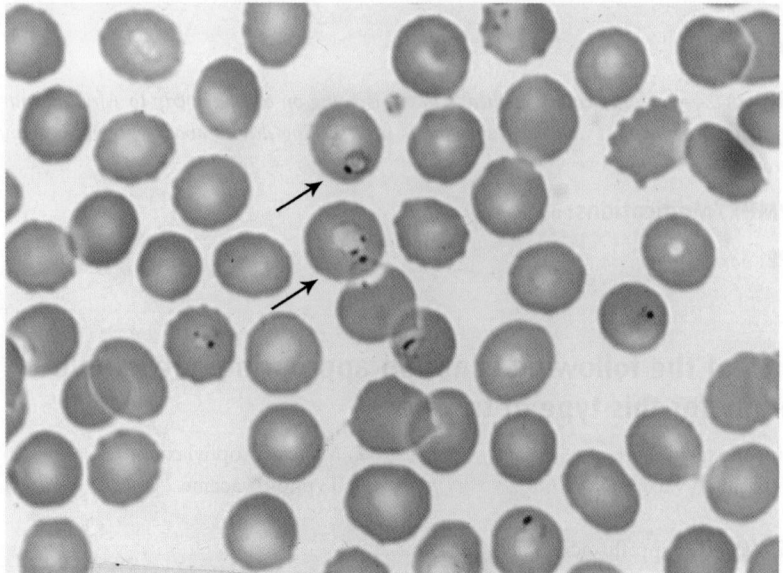

Figure 10-8. Malaria. *Plasmodium falciparum*. Blood film. Several red cells contain trophozoites (ring forms). The *arrows* point to a ring form and double-dot ring form. (Reproduced with permission from Lichtman MA, et al. *Lichtman's Atlas of Hematology*, www.accessmedicine.com.)

Trophozoites develop into schizonts in RBCs.

Schizonts = RBCs "Pregnant" with Malaria = Burst = Spread

All of these kill blood schizonts of malaria.

Initial Orders:
- *Hepatitis A vaccine*
- *Typhoid fever vaccine*
- *Mefloquine*

Mefloquine
- Must start 3 weeks before departure
- Safe in pregnancy
- Not for use with severe psychiatric illness
- Not for use with history of seizures

Atovaquone/Proguanil
- Active against liver schizonts of falciparum
- Prevent blood schizont release

Primaquine
- Kills liver schizonts of all species
- Kills blood schizonts of all species *except Plasmodium falciparum*

The patient is vaccinated against hepatitis A and is given the typhoid fever vaccine to take at home over several days. The prescription for mefloquine (or atovaquone/proguanil) is also given to her.

Genetic Protective Factors against Malaria
- No Duffy antigen on RBC
- Sickle cell trait
- Thalassemia trait

The patient calls you 2 months later. She returned from her trip 2 weeks ago and now has a fever. She did not remember to take preventive therapy for malaria.

Orders:
- *Transfer to ED*
- *Thick and thin smear for malaria*

> • *Fingerstick for glucose on arrival*
> • *CBC*
> • *CHEM-7*

All patients with malaria have some GI distress.
It is not dangerous.

Which of these indicates severe malaria?

a. Positive thick smear with elevated bilirubin

b. Positive rapid diagnostic test with enlarged spleen

c. Ten percent of cells with plasmodia present with hypoglycemia

d. Temperature 104°F and hematocrit 32%

Answer c. Ten percent of cells with plasmodia present with hypoglycemia

Malaria is complicated or dangerous when parasitemia goes above 5% to 10% of cells. At this parasite level, hypoglycemia develops as well as dangerous signs of disease, such as:

• Cerebral involvement

• Renal failure

• Metabolic acidosis

• Respiratory distress

Mechanism of Hypoglycemia in Severe Malaria
• There is decreased gluconeogenesis.
• There is decreased glycogen level.
• Parasites consume the glucose.

Hypovolemia + Hemoglobinuria = Renal Failure = Blackwater Fever

Mechanism of Acidosis
• There is increased lactate level from the parasite.
• There is decreased liver and renal clearance of the lactate.
• Parasites block the blood flow, which increases anaerobic glycolysis.

The patient comes to the ED. She has a temperature of 103°F with chills.

PE:
• *Neurologic: normal*
• *Chest: normal, no respiratory distress*

Reports:
• *Fingerstick: glucose 80 mg/dL*
• *CHEM-7: total bilirubin 2.4 mg/dL (slight elevation); indirect bilirubin elevated*
• *CBC: hematocrit 34%; platelets 128,000/μL*
• *Reticulocytes 4%*
• *Normal blood urea nitrogen (BUN) and creatinine levels*
• *Thick and thin smear: positive for P. falciparum, 2% parasitemia*

The thick smear detects malaria.
The thin smear speciates.

Rapid Diagnostic Tests for Malaria
• Antibody tests
• Detect histidine-rich protein
• Detect plasmodium antigens

Which of these is *not* appropriate for treating this patient?

a. Artemether/Lumefantrine
b. Atovaquone/Proguanil
c. Mefloquine and doxycycline
d. Quinine and doxycycline
e. Chloroquine

Answer e. Chloroquine

It is inappropriate to use chloroquine alone to treat malaria acquired in Africa, even if it is uncomplicated. The Center for Disease Control and Prevention (CDC) recommends artemisinin-containing regimens such as:
• Artesunate and amodiaquine or
• Artemether/Lumefantrine

However, any of the other regimens can be safely used.

On CCS, this patient has mild malaria. After treatment, she can be seen "as needed."

CASE 10: Human Immunodeficiency Virus and Acquired Immunodeficiency Syndrome

Setting: *office*

CC: *"Here for the results of my HIV test."*

VS: *normal*

HPI: *A 34-year-old man comes to your office for a discussion of his HIV test, which he took when he had an episode of urethritis 1 week ago. He has been asymptomatic. You have just informed the patient that his test is positive.*

PMHx:
- *Urethritis: finished treatment with ceftriaxone and azithromycin*
- *Herpes simplex: 1 to 2 episodes a year*

Medications: *none*

PE: *normal*

Initial Orders:
- *Lymphocyte subsets (CD4 count)*
- *Polymerase chain reaction (PCR) HIV RNA viral load assay*
- *Genotype of HIV virus*
- *CBC, lipid panel*
- *RPR*
- *Purified protein derivative (PPD) skin test*
- *Hepatitis B serology (surface antibody, core antibody, surface antigen)*
- *Hepatitis C antibody*

CCS and Step 3 examination, in general, very much want you to know the routine health maintenance and preventive medicine of diseases such as diabetes and HIV. It does not matter that the patient is asymptomatic with a normal physical examination. The tests listed here are needed. They are not extra or unnecessary. Students often ask, "Are you penalized for unnecessary tests?" The answer is: Absolutely you are! However, testing for latent tuberculosis (TB), hepatitis, and syphilis are not unnecessary in HIV.

Why get genotyping if there is no previous drug treatment?

a. All patients have some resistance.

b. Resistance to even one drug can be damaging at the start of therapy.

c. You are documenting the baseline. It has no effect on therapy.

Answer b. Resistance to even one drug can be damaging at the start of therapy.

If the patient is resistant to one of the medications you plan to start, it can be damaging to treatment. There is a <5% chance of resistance in a treatment-naïve person, but it is critical to be sure that your patient is sensitive to all three medications at the start of therapy.

The patient returns in a few days to discuss results. It is important to see the patient frequently at the beginning of therapy to form a bonded doctor-patient relationship that encourages adherence to medications.

Do not forget to take a thorough sexual history and to advise partner notification. Although you have the legal right to notify the partners yourself, Step 3 examination will always want you to encourage the patient to notify the partners themselves.

Reports:
- *Lymphocyte subsets (CD4 count): 335 cells/mm³*
- *PCR HIV RNA viral load: 140,000 copies (<20 undetectable)*
- *Genotype of HIV virus: no resistance detected*
- *CBC, Lipid panel: normal*
- *RPR: Nonreactive*
- *PPD skin test: no reaction*
- *Hepatitis B serology (surface antibody, core antibody, surface antigen): negative*
- *Hepatitis C antibody: positive*

All patients with CD4 counts <500 cells/mm³ should be on antiretroviral therapy.

PPD >5 mm is positive in HIV.

Discuss the need to take antiretroviral therapy with the patient. Make sure he understand the need for essentially 100% adherence to medication to assure control of the virus. There is no point in starting antiretroviral medications to which the patient will not adhere.

Orders:
- *Emtricitabine*
- *Tenofovir*
- *Efavirenz*
- *Hepatitis C RNA viral load*

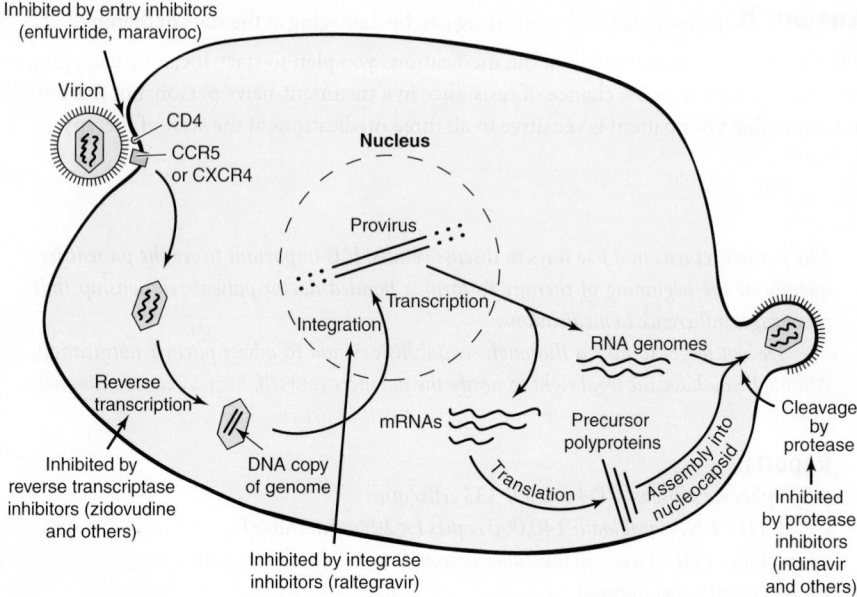

Inhibited by entry inhibitors
(enfuvirtide, maraviroc)

Virion

CD4

CCR5
or CXCR4

Nucleus

Provirus

Transcription

Integration

RNA genomes

Reverse
transcription

mRNAs

Precursor
polyproteins

Cleavage
by
protease

Inhibited by
reverse transcriptase
inhibitors (zidovudine
and others)

DNA copy
of genome

Translation

Assembly into
nucleocapsid

Inhibited
by protease
inhibitors
(indinavir
and others)

Inhibited by integrase
inhibitors (raltegravir)

Figure 10-9. Replicative cycle of human immunodeficiency virus (HIV). The sites of action of the important antiviral drugs are indicated. (Modified and reproduced with permission from Ryan K, et al. *Sherris Medical Microbiology*, 3rd ed. New York: Mc-Graw Hill; 1994. Copyright 1994, McGraw-Hill.)

- Emtricitabine and tenofovir inhibit reverse transcriptase (Figure 10-9).
- Reverse transcriptase
  - Converts RNA of HIV into DNA
  - Prepares for entry into the HIV nucleus

Protease Inhibitors
- Prevent packaging of HIV
- Prevent protein covering of RNA
- Stop infection of next HIV virus

Have the patient return in 1 week to discuss adherence to medications. Antiretroviral medication is a lifelong commitment. It is important not to just hand someone a prescription and ask the patient to show up in 3 months for testing.

Interval History: No adverse effects of medications."

Adherence <95% = Resistance Developing

Reports:
• *Hepatitis C RNA viral load: 850,000 units/mL*

Viral load changes first in response to therapy.

Half-life of HIV
• In CD4 cell: 1.2 days
• In plasma: 6 hours

Orders:
• *Interferon*
• *Ribavirin*
• *Boceprevir*
• *Gastroenterology evaluation*

Three Drugs for Hepatitis C
• Sustained viral response 70% to 80%

Have the patient return in 4 weeks.
Interval History: "No adverse effects of therapy."

Orders:
• *PCR HIV RNA viral load assay*
• *CD4 count*
• *Hepatitis C RNA viral load*

Report:
- *Both HIV and hepatitis C viral load are reduced by 90%*
- *CD4: 425 cells/mm³*

Treat the hepatitis C for 6 to 12 months depending on the genotype. If the HIV viral load rebounds up, recheck the genotype to see if there is resistance. Otherwise, just continue life-long therapy.

On CCS, it can be difficult to tell how long to manage the case. Just keep moving the clock forward. Seeing "this case will end in 5 minutes of real time" can be jarring to some people. It does not mean you made a mistake.

CHAPTER 11

EMERGENCY MEDICINE

CASE 1: Tricyclic Antidepressant Overdose

Setting: *emergency department (ED)*

CC: *"I feel confused and my mouth is dry."*

VS: *BP: 104/68 mm Hg; P: 112 beats/minute; T: 99.8°F; R: 22 breaths/minute*

HPI: *A 23-year-old man with a history of depression is brought to the ED because of confusion developing over the past several hours. He has been drinking alcohol and taking a number of unknown substances. He became more disoriented and obtunded just as he passed through the triage process in the ED and went to the bathroom. The staff were concerned that he had taken something in the bathroom.*

The ED is the most "time-sensitive" part of the hospital. It is where the computer-based case simulation (CCS) is meant to evaluate your proper understanding of the right order in which to give treatments and do tests. It is not being "picky" to insist you know the right timing and sequence of patient management.

Which of these is most important to do *first*?

a. Give naloxone, thiamine, and dextrose.

b. Test acetaminophen and aspirin levels.

c. Do a urine or blood toxicology screen.

d. Order gastric emptying (lavage).

e. Give oxygen.

f. Do an endotracheal intubation.

Answer a. Give naloxone, thiamine, and dextrose.

Prescription opiate overdose is markedly increasing. Patients are far more likely to die of a prescription opiate overdose than an illegal opiate such as heroin. Naloxone works instantly, and if the patient's altered mental status is from opiates, you will know immediately. Naloxone works before you even leave the patient's bedside. There is no significant danger from acute opiate withdrawal. Dextrose and thiamine are routinely given to every person with acute mental status changes of unclear etiology.

Diagnostic testing with toxicology screening is important, but not as important as instantly reversing opiate intoxication or hypoglycemia. Oxygen is not important in the absence of hypoxia or respiratory distress.

Do not intubate, when you might be able to just wake the person up with naloxone.

Fast reversal with naloxone is better than lavage.

Get aspirin and acetaminophen levels on every overdose.

PMHx:
• *Depression*
• *Anxiety*

Medications:
• *Alprazolam*
• *Amitriptyline*

PE:
• *General: lethargic, increasingly sleepy*
• *Neurologic: stuporous; incomplete examination because of inability to follow commands*
• *Head, ears, eyes, nose, throat (HEENT): dilated pupils*
• *Abdomen: decreased bowel sounds*
• *Cardiovascular: tachycardia only*
• *Skin: hot, dry, flushed*

Initial Orders:
• *Naloxone, thiamine, dextrose*
• *Urine toxicology screen*
• *Aspirin and acetaminophen levels*
• *Comprehensive metabolic panel (CHEM-20)*

Patients often ingest aspirin or acetaminophen in conjunction with the drug overdose.

Move the clock forward only 5 minutes and do an "Interval History." If naloxone is going to work, it will take immediate effect.

Interval History: "There is no effect with naloxone, dextrose, or thiamine. The patient remains confused and delirious. The urine toxicology, chemistry, and drug levels have been collected and sent to the laboratory."

On CCS, medications are considered as administered or given instantly. You must move the clock forward, however, to see the effect.

Why not give flumazenil to patients (such as this one) with altered mental status of unclear etiology?

a. Benzodiazepine overdose is rare.

b. Acute benzodiazepine withdrawal causes seizures.

c. Benzodiazepine overdose is not fatal.

d. Flumazenil is ineffective.

e. You should give it.

Answer b. Acute benzodiazepine withdrawal causes seizures.

Flumazenil is an immediate antagonist of benzodiazepines, which should result in an immediate reversal of benzodiazepine effect. That is why it causes seizures. In this case with potential tricyclic antidepressant (TCA) overdose evident from the first sentence, it is even more likely to cause seizures. TCA overdose produces seizures. Being on benzodiazepines protects against those seizures.

> Flumazenil creates benzodiazepine withdrawal.

> *The case is moved forward* and there is no improvement in altered mental status.
>
> **PE:**
> - HEENT: *dilated pupils*
> - Neurological: *lethargic, disoriented*
> - Skin: *dry, warm*

> TCA antihistamine effect creates disorientation and lethargy.

What is the most urgent step?

a. TCA level

b. Electrocardiogram (ECG)

c. Calcium chloride

d. Pyridostigmine

Answer b. Electrocardiogram (ECG)

ECG is the most urgent step because it detects the most common cause of death in TCA overdose, which is cardiac arrhythmia (Figure 11-1). TCA level is important, but not as important as seeing if we have life-threatening TCA toxicity.

Pyridostigmine does increase ACh, but this will have no effect on TCA overdose.

> *The patient continues to be lethargic.*
>
> **ECG:** *wide QRS (>120 msec)*

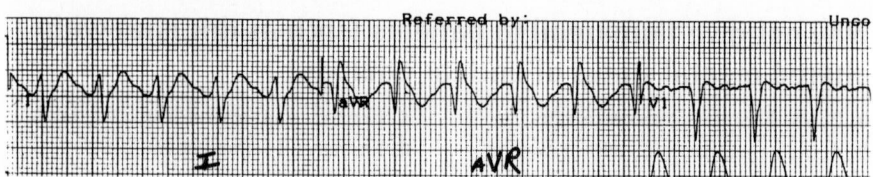

Figure 11-1. Electrocardiogram (ECG) with manifestations of cyclic antidepressant toxicity. The right axis deviation of the terminal 40 msec of the QRS complex is because of cyclic antidepressant toxicity. Note the large R wave in lead aVR and S wave in lead I. (Reproduced with permission from Tintinalli JE, et al. *Tintinalli's Emergency Medicine, A Comprehensive Study Guide*, 7th ed. New York: McGraw-Hill; 2011.)

With this additional information, what is the most urgent step?

a. Bicarbonate

b. Atropine

c. Lidocaine

d. Amiodarone

Answer a. Bicarbonate

Bicarbonate administration will protect the heart. This is the fastest way to reverse the effect of TCAs on the heart. Bicarbonate is not given to increase excretion of TCA. There will be no effect on the blood level of TCAs. It is given entirely to reverse the possibility of an imminent arrhythmia.

Lidocaine and amiodarone are used when there actually is an arrhythmia that has developed. We never use these agents prophylactically.

> Always test acetaminophen and aspirin levels with drug overdose! Co-ingestion is common.

> *The patient is given a stat dose of intravenous (IV) bicarbonate. Move the clock forward. A repeat ECG shows the QRS duration has gone back to 100 msec.*

> TCAs have a quinidine-like effect on the heart.
> TCAs inhibit fast sodium ion (Na$^+$) channels in phase 0.

> *Transfer the patient to the intensive care unit (ICU).*
>
> **Orders:**
> - *Repeat ECG in 1 hour*
> - *Telemetry monitoring*
> - *Repeat dose of bicarbonate*

What is the mechanism of decreased bowel sounds in this patient?

a. Increased ACh

b. Decreased ACh

c. Decreased norepinephrine

d. Increased serotonin

Answer b. Decreased ACh

TCAs inhibit the effect of ACh throughout the body. The anticholinergic effect of TCAs causes constipation and it also explains the diminished bowel sounds with a TCA overdose.

The anticholinergic effect of TCAs can also cause dilated pupils and dry skin.

Sweat production is stimulated by ACh.

The only effect that ACh has on the sympathetic system is in the production of sweat.

After the administration of bicarbonate and transfer of the patient to the ICU, there is an improvement in the ECG. Over the next few hours, the patient's mental status starts to improve.

- TCAs cause death by:
  - Wide QRS and arrhythmia
  - Seizures
- TCAs cause seizures by:
  - Increasing central nervous system (CNS) norepinephrine levels
  - Decreasing the inhibitory effect of gamma-aminobutyric acid (GABA) on neurons

Over the next 12 to 24 hours, the patient starts to wake up.

Reports:
- *Amitriptyline level elevated*
- *Chemistries normal*
- *Repeat ECG (second hospital day): normal QRS*

When the ECG and QRS are normal without the use of bicarbonate, the patient can be safely transferred to regular hospital floor. If there is a question of possible intentional overdose, always get a psychiatric evaluation. For a patient like this with a history or depression and anxiety, psychiatric evaluation is beneficial as well.

Adverse Effects of TCA
• Dry mouth
• Constipation
• Urine retention
• Dry eyes

Adverse Effect Mechanism
• Inhibition of ACh

CASE 2: Acetaminophen Overdose

Setting: *ED*

CC: *Vomiting*

VS: *BP: 110/70 mm Hg; P: 108 beats/minute T: 98°F; R: 12 breaths/minute*

HPI: *A 46-year-old man comes to the ED after intentionally trying to end his life by taking a bottle of acetaminophen pills within the last hour. He took 30 extra-strength 500-mg pills. He is extremely nauseated. He has not vomited yet.*

What is the single most important thing to do *first*?

a. Test acetaminophen level now.

b. Test acetaminophen level in 4 hours.

c. Give *N*-acetylcysteine (NAC) and charcoal.

d. Give *N*-acetylcysteine (NAC) alone.

e. Order a psychiatry consultation.

f. Do gastric lavage.

Answer c. Give *N*-acetylcysteine (NAC) and charcoal.

NAC is a specific antidote for acetaminophen. Charcoal blocks absorption, but does not interfere with NAC. A level of the drug is important, but not as important as preventing toxicity of the drug. Gastric lavage has no utility in acetaminophen overdose ever. Charcoal and NAC are superior to any attempt at gastric emptying. Acetaminophen level reaches its peak in 4 hours after ingestion, but is still not as important as preventing toxicity. On CCS, do not expect a consultant to do anything for you.

Knowing the *amount* of acetaminophen ingested is more than enough reason to give NAC and charcoal. You do *not* have to wait for the blood level of acetaminophen.

• Do not wait for blood level.
• Give the NAC and charcoal.

PMHx:
- *Alcoholism*

Medications: none
Acetaminophen overdose: Quick administration of NAC and charcoal is essential to protect the liver. Do not wait for time it takes to do the physical examination.

Orders:
- *NAC IV or oral depending on the presence of vomiting*
- *Charcoal*
- *CHEM-20*

Make sure you get baseline liver function tests (LFTs)!

PE:
- *General: nauseated, no abnormalities seen*
- *Chest, Heart, Abdomen: normal*
- *Neurological: no focal deficits; normal mental status*

Lavage removes:
- Fifty percent at 1 hour
- Fifteen percent at 2 hours
- Less than NAC and charcoal

Giving ipecac on an empty stomach is always wrong.

When *is* gastric emptying the right answer?

a. Never
b. For caustic ingestions (e.g., lye, drain cleaner)
c. For pills with no antidote within the hour of ingestion
d. For more than 2 hours after ingestion

Answer c. For pills with no antidote within the hour of ingestion

Gastric emptying is almost never the correct thing to do. It is rarely done. Gastric emptying with an Ewald gastric tube is done only within 1 to 2 hours of ingestion of a pill that has no other antidote. Lavage is absolutely contraindicated with the ingestion of caustics. When you lavage out caustics, all you do is increase the chance of burning the mouth and upper gastrointestinal (GI) tract on its way out of the stomach. Emptying is absolutely useless when more than 2 hours have passed since the ingestion.

Normal gastric emptying time:
• For pills without food, 30 to 60 minutes
• With most foods, 2 hours

Initial Orders:
• *NAC*
• *Charcoal*
• *Repeat CHEM-20 and LFTs*
• *Repeat acetaminophen level*

Once you administer NAC and charcoal, there is nothing more that can be actively done to reverse or prevent hepatic toxicity from acetaminophen. Acetaminophen is metabolized into an end product that is a profound oxidant stress to the liver. Acetaminophen metabolites deplete the body of glutathione reductase.

• NAC restores glutathione reductase.
• Charcoal, microscopically, has an enormous surface area to bind drugs.

Reports:
• *CHEM-20 and LFTs: normal*
• *Acetaminophen level: elevated*

Drug Toxicity = Aspartate Aminotransferase (AST)

What in this patient's history makes it more likely for him to have liver damage or toxicity?

a. Time from ingestion to arrival
b. Use of NAC at same time as charcoal
c. History of alcoholism

d. Not doing gastric emptying
e. Age >30 years
f. Gender

Answer c. History of alcoholism

Alcoholics need less acetaminophen to result in toxicity. The liver is already partially damaged in alcoholics. Alcoholics have already undergone a significant degree of oxidant stress to the liver. In an average-sized person, toxicity begins above 10 g of acetamino-phen. Fatality from the depletion of glutathione reductase begins around 15 g of inges-tion. In an alcoholic, toxicity may occur from 6 to 8 g of ingestion and fatality at 10 to 12 g of ingestion.

Alcoholism decreases the toxic dose needed to hurt the liver.

As you move the clock forward, remember to give repeated doses of oral charcoal and NAC. Repeat the chemistry level every day to be sure there is no liver toxicity. There is nothing more you can do in therapy besides NAC and charcoal, but it will be expected on CCS that you should know that you need to check LFTs and prothrombin time (PT). *If toxicity does occur and it is severe, all you can do is try to get a liver transplantation.*

Orders:
- *LFTs*
- *PT*

NAC is only effective if used within 24 hours after the ingestion.

NAC is given for 1 to 2 days. Charcoal is given for the first 24 hours. Charcoal will not only block the absorption of acetaminophen, it will remove it from the bloodstream after it has been well absorbed through the small bowel. You need 2 to 3 days to be sure there is no liver toxicity.

CASE 3: Aspirin Overdose

Setting: *ED*

CC: *"I'm puking, my head hurts, and my ears are ringing."*

VS: *BP: 124/82 mm Hg; P: 114 beats/minute; T: 101°F; R: 24 breaths/minute*

HPI: *A 54-year-old man come to the ED because shortness of breath, headache, and ring-ing in his ears. He is your former roommate in medical school, who took a bottle of aspirin in the bathroom at the twenty-fifth reunion. He usually takes an aspirin a few times a day for his joint pain. He comes to the ED the day after the overdose.*

PMHx:
- *Rheumatoid arthritis*
- *Depression*
- *Recovering alcoholic—10 years sober*

Medications:
- *Aspirin*
- *Etanercept*
- *Methotrexate*

PE:
- *General: uncomfortable, sitting up on edge of bed holding his head*
- *Cardiovascular: no murmur, no gallops*
- *Abdomen: soft, nontender*
- *Neurological: confused*

Which of the following is the most urgent test?

a. Salicylate level

b. Acetaminophen level

c. Arterial blood gas (ABG)

d. Liver function tests

e. Blood urea nitrogen (BUN) and creatinine

Answer c. Arterial blood gas (ABG)

All of these tests are important. Your job is to understand which is the most important. Metabolic acidosis and respiratory alkalosis are the most likely causes of death, as well as seizure and pulmonary edema.

Respiratory alkalosis happens first!

Initial Orders:
- *Salicylate level*
- *Acetaminophen level*
- *ABG*
- *LFTs*
- *Basic metabolic panel (CHEM-7)*
- *Charcoal*

Charcoal can remove absorbed poisons and lower blood level.

Respiratory Alkalosis
First: direct stimulation to the brainstem

Salicylates stimulate brainstem respiratory centers.

Move the clock forward only 10 to 20 minutes to see what the results of the tests are.

Reports:
- *Salicylate level: 70 μg/mL (markedly elevated)*
- *Acetaminophen level: none detected*
- *ABG: pH 7.42; partial pressure of carbon dioxide (PCO_2) 22 mm Hg; partial pressure of oxygen (PO_2) 68 mm Hg*
- *Serum bicarbonate 18 mEq/L (decreased)*
- *LFTs: normal*
- *BUN 22 g/dL (elevated); creatinine 1.9 mg/dL (elevated)*
- *Anion gap 20 mmol/L (normal 6–12 mmol/L)*

Always get salicylate and acetaminophen levels on all pill overdoses because of high rates of co-ingestion.

Salicylates directly stimulate the medulla, causing hyperventilation.

The mechanism of tinnitus is unknown.

What is the mechanism of the metabolic acidosis?

a. Renal insufficiency
b. Lactic acidosis
c. Oxalic acid accumulation
d. Unknown
e. Ketoacids (beta-hydroxybutyric acid, acetoacetic acid)

Answer b. Lactic acidosis

Salicylate intoxication produces metabolic acidosis with increased anion gap. The source of the lactic acidosis is the loss of oxidative phosphorylation. Oxidative phosphorylation or the Krebs cycle is the aerobic method whereby large amounts of adenosine triphosphate (ATP) are produced from each molecule of glucose. Salicylate intoxication poisons this activity in the mitochondria. Poisoned mitochondria cannot make ATP from glucose and the body is dependent on glycolysis. The end product of glycolysis is lactic acidosis.

> Nausea and Vomiting
> • Stimulation of chemoreceptor trigger zone
> • Located in the medulla: no blood–brain barrier

> *Now that salicylate poisoning is clearly diagnosed, you should try to lower the level as quickly as possible. Also, because death can be from pulmonary edema, you should look at the chest.*
>
> **Orders:**
> • *Bicarbonate IV*
> • *Dextrose 5% in water (D5W) (or any IV fluid with glucose)*
> • *Urinalysis (UA): check urine pH*
> • *Chest x-ray*

Why is bicarbonate use beneficial?

a. It corrects acidosis on ABG.

b. It increases urinary excretion.

c. It reverses cardiac effect.

d. It reverses CNS effect.

e. It restores oxidative phosphorylation in the mitochondria.

Answer b. It increases urinary excretion.

Bicarbonate prevents reabsorption of salicylates after they have been filtered at the glomerulus. Bicarbonate use in aspirin overdose is entirely about lowering the blood level as quickly as possible by increasing urinary excretion. It has nothing to do with protecting the heart. That is how it works with TCA overdose.

> 1. Salicylates filter at the glomerulus.
> 2. Bicarbonate charges salicylates in the tubule.
> 3. Charged molecules cannot be reabsorbed.

> *IV bicarbonate is started. The patient is transferred to the ICU.*
>
> *If a test and a treatment are ordered at the same time on CCS, the test will not reflect the treatment. UA and IV bicarbonate ordered at the same time will not reflect the IV bicarbonate. To see that effect, you would have to move the clock forward and recheck the UA.*

Reports:
- *UA: no cells, pH 5.4 (before bicarbonate)*
- *Chest x-ray: pulmonary edema and acute respiratory distress syndrome (ARDS)*

Weak acids lose hydrogen ions (H⁺) and get charged in the basic environment. Charged molecules do not pass biological membranes easily.

Salicylates cause fever by their effect on the brain.

Mechanism of Confusion
- Direct CNS toxicity of salicylates
- Decreases CNS glucose from salicylates
- Cerebral edema

Why is there lung damage in salicylate poisoning?

a. It is from vasoconstriction.
b. It is from renal failure.
c. Salicylates cause capillary leak directly.

d. It is from hyperventilation from metabolic acidosis.

Answer c. Salicylates cause capillary leak directly.

Salicylate poisoning causes direct toxicity to the lungs resulting in ARDS. No one knows precisely why people have ARDS. The noncardiogenic pulmonary edema does not occur as an effect of respiratory compensation for metabolic acidosis. If the hyperventilation were compensation for metabolic acidosis, the chest x-ray would be normal.

Always give glucose-containing IV fluids for aspirin overdose.

No one knows why CNS glucose level is low in aspirin overdose. Serum glucose is *normal*, but CNS glucose is *low*.

The patient's mental status starts to improve with the start of IV glucose-containing fluids. Dyspnea improves as well. Repeat the salicylate level measurement every 2 hours and do an Interval History to check mental status.

Salicylate Metabolic Acidosis = Lactate

Orders:
- *UA*
- *Salicylate level*
- *ABG*

ATP Molecules per Molecule of Glucose
- Aerobic: 30 to 36
- Glycolysis: 2

Salicylate Poisoning = Glycolysis Only = Lactate Overproduction

Reports:
- *UA: pH 7.8*
- *Salicylate level: 60 μg/mL*
- *ABG: pH 7.46; PCO$_2$ 28 mm Hg; PO$_2$ 78 mm Hg*

Keep the patient in the ICU until several salicylate level measurements show that the level is decreasing. Also, bicarbonate drip is something best done in the ICU. An ICU stay of 1 to 2 days should be sufficient.

Transfer the patient out of ICU when:
- Pulmonary edema and CNS effects resolve
- Salicylate level drops
- Bicarbonate drip not needed

Move the case forward 12 hours and do an Interval History.
    Interval History: "Confusion, tinnitus, and shortness of breath have resolved and the patient feels much better."

Indications for Dialysis with Salicylates
- Seizures and coma
- Pulmonary edema
- Severe confusion

Salicylic acid becomes charged by basic urine.
Charged molecules cannot reenter the tubule to go back into the blood.

The patient is transferred to the hospital floor. Stop the bicarbonate drip as the patient is moved out of the ICU.

CASE 4: Carbon Monoxide

Setting: *ED*

CC: *Patient brought in unresponsive from a fire*

VS: *BP: 118/82 mm Hg; P:114 beats/minute T: 98°F; R: 32 breaths/minute*

HPI: *A 78-year-old man is brought to the ED after having been found on the floor of his home during a fire. The patient is barely conscious and not able to offer a clear history. He arrives in the ED within half an hour of being found. Another part of the house was on fire. The neighbors called the police and fire department and they broke down the door. The patient did not sustain burns himself, but several others from the next room sustained significant burn injury.*

What is the most common cause of death in fires?

a. Volume depletion and hypovolemic shock
b. Sepsis
c. Carbon monoxide (CO) poisoning
d. Renal failure
e. Hyperkalemia and arrhythmia
f. Respiratory burn

Answer c. Carbon monoxide (CO) poisoning

Sixty percent of deaths on the first day in a fire are from smoke inhalation and CO poisoning. All of the answer choices can cause death in fires. CO poisoning is just the most common one. Sepsis or infection from a skin source is the most common cause of late death several days or weeks after a fire. When respiratory burn occurs, it is extremely lethal, but it is just not as common a cause of death as the others.

Smoke kills at a distance: Burn needs contact.

Smoke spreads easier than fire.

PMHx: (from medical alert bracelet)
• *Hypertension*
• *Aortic stenosis*

Medications: unknown

Fires = Smoke Inhalation = CO Poisoning

Fires and smoke inhalation are reasons to write orders before doing the physical examination. There is a cookbook of standard orders to do before anything. No matter what you see on the physical, in a fire you need to administer oxygen and to measure oxygenation; 100% oxygen is what is needed, but there is no way on CCS to order dosing, including the dosing of oxygen.

Orders:
• *Oxygen*
• *ABG*
• *Carboxyhemoglobin (COHb) level*
• *CHEM-7*

PE:
• *General: lethargic man lying on stretcher*
• *Chest: clear bilaterally*
• *Cardiovascular: 3/6 murmur radiating to carotid arteries*
• *Neurological: disoriented, lethargic, unable to assess focal findings because of disorientation*

How do you die from CO poisoning?

a. Stroke
b. Myocardial infarction
c. Lung infarction
d. Renal failure
e. High output failure

Answer b. Myocardial infarction

Although disorientation and possible coma are apparent from severe smoke inhalation and CO poisoning, the organ that receives fatal damage is the heart. The heart cannot physiologically distinguish between hypoxia, coronary artery stenosis, anemia, and CO poisoning.

For Myocardium: CO = Anemia = Stenosis = Hypoxia

On CCS, if you forget to write an order, such as the ECG in a person with CO poisoning, just add it on as soon as you remember. If you have not moved the clock forward, there will be no points lost.

Orders:
• *ECG*

Repeating the ABG would reflect oxygen use in this patient because doing the physical examination moved the clock forward.

Half-Life of COHb Breathing:
• Room air: 4 to 6 hours
• One hundred percent oxygen: 60 to 90 minutes
• Hyperbaric oxygen: 20 to 30 minutes

Standard pulse oximetry *cannot* detect CO.

Reports:
• *ABG: pH 7.32; PCO_2 28 mm Hg; PO_2 90 mm Hg; 98% saturation*
• *COHb level: 42%*
• *CHEM-7: normal*
• *ECG: ST depression in V2 to V4*

What is the mechanism of metabolic acidosis?

a. Decreased perfusion of tissues
b. Lactate from tissue hypoxia
c. Rhabdomyolysis
d. Sepsis

Answer b. Lactate from tissue hypoxia

COHb does not release oxygen to tissues. The tissues become hypoxic. Hypoxic tissues produce lactate. See the previous discussion about lactate buildup from anaerobic glycolysis. The tissues are perfused, but oxygen is not delivered. Without oxygen delivery, the metabolic acidosis that develops would look identical to decreased tissue perfusion or sepsis.

Normal respiratory rate is 8 to 14 breaths/minute.
This patient, at 32 breaths/minute, should have pH >7.4.

Hyperventilation should produce alkalosis.

COHb Elevation + pH <7.4 = Massive Tissue Acidosis

What is the mechanism of cardiac ischemia?

a. Decreased coronary perfusion

b. Increased CO release to tissues

c. Decreased oxygen release from hemoglobin at tissues

d. Decreased oxygen pickup by hemoglobin at lungs

Answer c. Decreased oxygen release from hemoglobin at tissues

CO does not interfere with hemoglobin picking up oxygen at the lungs. CO interferes with the release of oxygen at tissues. That is why the blood is red. Methemoglobinemia interferes with oxygen pickup at lungs.

Move the clock forward 5 to 10 minutes and reevaluate the patient. You will not lose points if you repeat the ABG on oxygen or repeat the ECG. After starting 100% oxygen, your main issues in management are:

1. *Does the patient need hyperbaric oxygen?*
2. *Has respiratory burn occurred and is intubation needed?*

Which of the following is the strongest indication to use hyperbaric oxygen in this patient?

a. pH 7.32

b. ST depression on the ECG

c. Confusion

d. COHb level 42%

Answer b. ST depression on the ECG

All of these indicate serious CO poisoning, but the worst one is the myocardial ischemia.

Severe metabolic acidosis with pH <7.2 is an indication, as well as coma. The high COHb level (>25%) is certainly dangerous, but the most dangerous is the ischemia.

Oxygen on hemoglobin (Hb) with COHb will not release to tissues.

COHb = Effects of Anemia
COHb 42% = Effects of Loss of 42% of blood

Transfer the patient to the ICU and order hyperbaric oxygen. Continue 100% oxygen in the meantime.

Orders:
- *Hyperbaric oxygen*
- *Troponin level*

What is the most common presentation of aortic stenosis, which this patient has?

a. Angina

b. Syncope

c. Congestive heart failure (CHF)

Answer a. Angina

Fifty to seventy percent of patients with aortic stenosis have coronary disease. That is what makes this patient's COHb level so dangerous. If this patient bled and lost a third of his blood volume, he would have myocardial ischemia as well. COHb is the same in its effect on tissues.

Your patient is lucky enough to be in a hospital with a hyperbaric chamber. Move the clock forward 1 hour and recheck the laboratory test results.

Orders:
- *ECG*
- *COHb*
- *ABG*

Remember that a COHb level and hyperbaric oxygen ordered at the same time will not show the effects of the hyperbaric oxygen.

Move the clock forward a half hour and do an Interval History. **Hyperbaric oxygen will reduce half of COHb within a half hour.**

Interval History: "The patient is more alert and awake. He denies chest pain."

One hundred percent inspired oxygen should give PO_2 >700 mm Hg.

Reports:
- *ECG: ST segment has normalized.*
- *COHb level is 18%.*
- *The pH is 7.37 and PO_2 680 mm Hg on 100% oxygen in the hyperbaric chamber.*
- *The troponin level is elevated.*

The patient's symptoms improve, but the myocardial ischemia should be treated as it would be in a person who had a myocardial infarction (MI) from coronary disease unmasked by the CO poisoning. He should undergo investigation to determine the need for revascularization when stable. The point of the case is understanding that CO poisoning leads to tissue hypoxia from a failure to release oxygen to tissues. This leads to ischemia of every tissue. It is just that the heart and brain are the most vulnerable.

Methemoglobin
- Oxidized blood
- Brown
- Does not pick up oxygen in the lungs

COHb
- Hb picks up 200 times more than oxygen
- Red
- Picks up oxygen in the lungs
- Does not release in tissues

CASE 5: Ethylene Glycol and Methanol

Setting: *ED*

CC: *"I feel drunk."*

VS: *BP: 110/70 mm Hg; P: 84 beats/minute; T: 100.2°F; R: 24 breaths/minute*

HPI: *A 28-year-old man is brought to the ED by his friends because he tried to kill himself with something he drank in the garage. The patient is clearly drunk and unable to provide a clear history. It is not clear how much vodka he may have drunk as well.*

PMHx:
- *Depression*

Medications:
- *Alprazolam*
- *Paroxetine*

Orders:
- *Naloxone, thiamine, dextrose*

PE:
• *General: disoriented, visibly intoxicated*
• *HEENT: red eyes, hard to visualize retinas*
• *Neurologic: unable to complete the examination because of inability to cooperate*
• *Abdomen: soft, nontender*

Interval History: "No response to naloxone/dextrose. Patient remains disoriented with mental status changes."

Initial Orders:
• *CHEM-7*
• *UA*
• *Complete blood count (CBC)*
• *Urine toxicology screen*
• *Serum osmolarity*

Delirium Etiology
• Sodium level up/down
• Glucose level down
• Calcium level up
• Osmolar changes
• Liver or renal failure
• Hypoxia

Altered mental status is one of those symptoms for which treatment is started before getting tests.

The worst form of confusion is a seizure.

On CCS, do not get a neurology consultation until after these simple tests have been done. You are not supposed to need a neurology consultation to know to check the levels of calcium, glucose, oxygen, sodium, and to test for liver or renal failure.

Move the clock forward only far enough to get the test results. You will not know what type of hospital admission you need for this patient until you know the severity of his illness.

Reports:
- *CHEM-7:*
  - *Sodium 140 mEq/L*
  - *Glucose 90 mg/dL*
  - *Chloride 100 mEq/L*
  - *BUN 9 g/dL*
  - *Bicarbonate: 16 mEq/L (normal 22–26 mEq/L)*
- *UA: No white blood cells (WBCs), "envelope-shaped" crystals present*
- *CBC: WBCs 14,200/μL; 78% neutrophils*
- *Urine toxicology screen: no cocaine, opiate, marijuana, benzodiazepines*
- *Serum osmolarity 360 mOsm/kg*

Serum Osmolarity = 2 × Sodium + Glucose/18 + BUN/2.8

Which laboratory test result tells you that there must have been a toxic ingestion?

a. WBC count elevation

b. Osmolar gap

c. Metabolic acidosis

d. Decreased anion gap

Answer b. Osmolar gap

The measured osmolarity is 360 mOsm/kg.

The calculated osmolarity is 287 mOsm/kg.

The difference between the osmolarity you measure and the osmolarity you calculate means that there must be an additional toxic substance in the bloodstream. A mild elevation in WBC could mean very little. Any form of "stress" for the body can lead to a mild elevation in WBC count. Fifty percent of WBCs are in circulation and 50% are on the "margins" or edges of the blood vessels. It is easy to double the WBC count just from "stress." Also, this patient has an increased anion gap of 24 mmol/L, not a decreased anion gap. The normal gap is 6 to 12 mmol/L. Ethylene glycol leads to the increase in osmolar gap.

Envelope crystals are calcium oxalate.

Stress Leukocytosis
- Epinephrine
- Cortisol

Both pull WBCs off the endothelial lining.

Which of these would *not* be a cause of this metabolic acidosis?

a. Diarrhea

b. Sepsis

c. Hypotension

d. Methanol

e. Ethylene glycol

Answer **a.** Diarrhea

Diarrhea causes a GI tract loss of bicarbonate with an increased serum chloride. This is why diarrhea and renal tubular acidosis (RTA) have normal anion gaps. An increased anion gap in metabolic acidosis results from the insertion, or addition, of a new substance into the body. This decreases the bicarbonate and does not allow the chloride to rise.

Any form of hypoperfusion or hypotension increases lactate production. Methanol increases formic acid and is the insertion of a new anion.

Methanol Poisoning
- Increased anion gap
- Toxic to the eye and retina
- "Blind drunk"
- Fomepizole for drug therapy
- Dialysis to remove

Isopropyl alcohol: normal anion gap acidosis

Alcohol dehydrogenase metabolizes methanol to formic acid (Figure 11-2). Formic acid burns the eye.

Metabolic Acidosis + Elevated Gap + Envelope Crystals = Ethylene Glycol

All patients who have metabolic acidosis need an ABG assay to determine the severity of decrease in pH. You should wait for the ABG results and ethylene glycol level to start treatment.

Orders:
- *ABG*
- *Ethylene glycol level*
- *Calcium levels*
- *Repeat CHEM-7*

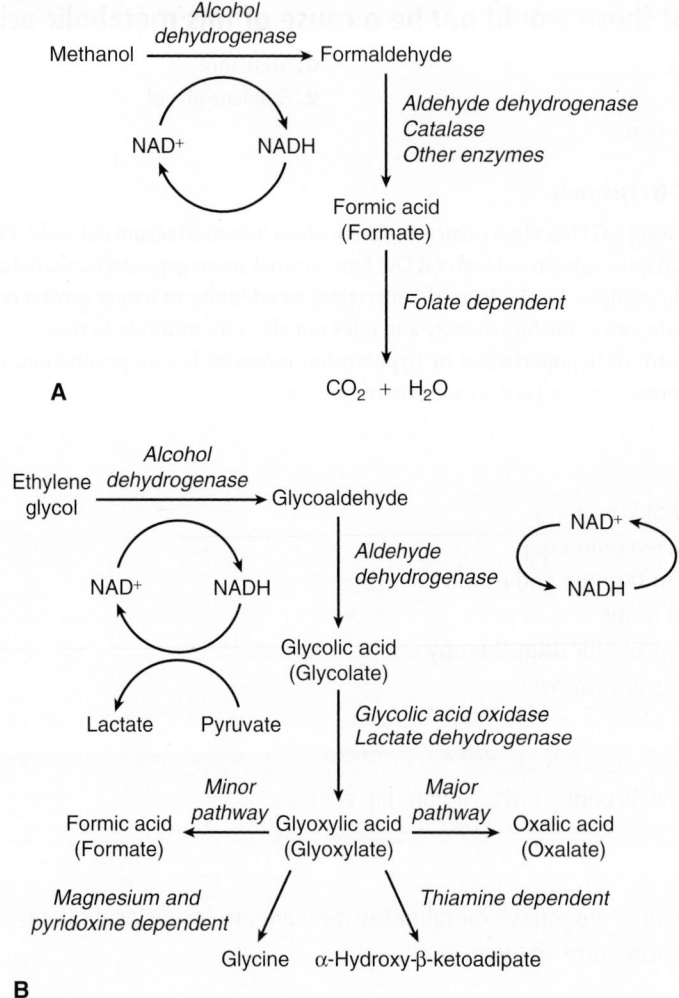

Figure 11-2. A. Metabolism of methanol. **B.** Metabolism of ethylene glycol. NAD⁺, oxidized form of nicotinamide adenine dinucleotide; NADH, reduced form of nicotinamide adenine dinucleotide. (Reproduced with permission from Tintinalli JE, et al. *Tintinalli's Emergency Medicine, A Comprehensive Study Guide*, 7th ed. New York: McGraw-Hill; 2011.)

Why is ethylene glycol toxic to renal function?

a. Hydrogen ions damage the glomerulus.
b. Ethylene glycol causes sloughing of the proximal tubule cells.

c. Oxalic acid and glycolic acid have direct cytotoxic effects.
d. Ethylene glycol lowers calcium levels.
e. The mechanism is unknown.

Answer c. Oxalic acid and glycolic acid have direct cytotoxic effects.

The entire point of the basic science correlate of this case is knowing that it is the metabolite of ethylene glycol and methanol that causes their toxic effects. Ethylene glycol is not directly toxic to the kidney. Ethylene glycol is metabolized to glycolic acid and oxalic acid. It is the metabolites that are dangerous to the kidney tubules by their direct cytotoxic effects.

Gastric lavage is never the correct treatment for toxic alcohols.

The patient remains intoxicated and difficult to interview.

Reports:
- *ABG: pH 7.34; PCO_2 24 mm Hg; PO_2 90 mm Hg*
- *Ethylene glycol level: elevated*
- *Calcium levels: 6.5 mg/dL (decreased)*
- *Repeat chemistry: serum bicarbonate 18 mEq/L; creatinine 1.7 mg/dL*

Renal toxicity takes 1 to 2 days after the ingestion of ethylene glycol.

Calcium complexes with oxalic acid
- Lowers blood calcium levels
- Precipitates in the kidneys

Orders:
- *Fomepizole*
- *Bicarbonate drip if pH <7.2*
- *Transfer to ICU*

Fomepizole
- Blocks alcohol dehydrogenase
- Prevents production of oxalic acid from ethylene glycol
- Prevents formic acid production from methanol

> *The patient is moved to the ICU if there is severe metabolic acidosis (pH <7.2) or an overdose bad enough to need:*
> - *Bicarbonate drip*
> - *Fomepizole*
> - *Dialysis*

- Fomepizole inhibits alcohol dehydrogenase.
- Alcohol dehydrogenase makes toxic metabolites.
- Only dialysis removes toxic alcohol from the blood.

CASE 6: Organophosphates

Setting: *ED*

CC: *"I got splashed with insecticide; now I can't breathe."*

VS: *BP: 92/72 mm Hg; P: 56 beats/minute; T: 98°F; R: 36 breaths/minute*

HPI: *A 57-year-old farmer comes to the ED after a bag of insecticide was accidentally splashed on his face while working on his farm. He had diarrhea, vomiting, and difficulty breathing. He is spitting continuously since the exposure occurred. He asks for a urinal twice while giving the history. There is no burning with urination. He denies fever or cough.*

PMHx/ Medications: *none*

What is the most common cause of death from insecticide poisoning?

a. Aspiration pneumonia
b. Diarrhea
c. Heart block

d. Respiratory failure
e. Infection

Answer d. Respiratory failure

Insecticides contain organophosphates, which markedly increase ACh levels. Massive increases in ACh levels cause death from respiratory distress, bronchospasm, and diaphragmatic paralysis. Although there is diarrhea, heart block, urinary frequency, and excess salivation, these do not cause death.

ACh increases salivary volume.
Normally, 1 to 2 L/day of saliva are made.

What is the most important thing to do first?

a. Remove the clothes.

b. Wash the patient.

c. Give atropine.

d. Intubate and begin mechanical ventilation.

e. Give pralidoxime.

Answer c. Give atropine.

All of these efforts, except intubating the patient, should be done. Decontamination with removing the clothes and washing the patient is important, but not as important as stopping the effects of the extra ACh already inside the body. No matter how much you wash the skin, it will not stop the effects of the organophosphate already inside it.

The emergency medicine section of CCS has the largest number of cases where treatment before the physical examination is done. Correct timing or the right order of testing and treatment is the essence of CCS.

Saliva
• Muscarinic receptors stimulate secretion.
• Secretions are serous.
• ACh increases the bicarbonate content of saliva.

Orders:
• *Atropine IV*
• *Oxygen*
• *Decontamination of patient's skin (Wash the patient's skin.)*

PE:
• *General: uncomfortable man on stretcher in an isolation room*
• *Chest: bilateral wheezing*
• *HEENT: constricted pupils*
• *Cardiovascular: slow heart rate, no murmurs*
• *Abdomen: hyperactive bowel sounds*

ACh constricts the pupils.

What is the mechanism of the patient's current respiratory distress?

a. ACh constricts bronchial smooth muscle.

b. The central (medullary) drive is decreased.

c. The pulmonary vasculature is constricted.

d. The pulmonary vasculature is dilated.

e. The peripheral chemoreceptors are blocked.

Answer a. ACh constricts bronchial smooth muscle.

ACh is increased from insecticide exposure by blocking its metabolism. ACh in the lung has a direct effect on:

• Constricting bronchial smooth muscle

• Increasing bronchial gland secretions

ACh has no effect at all on the medullary respiratory centers or smooth muscle in the vasculature. Although the autonomic nervous system is usually paired in opposite directions, with ACh increasing GI tract motility and norepinephrine (NE) decreasing it, or ACh decreasing heart rate and NE increasing it, this is not true of vascular smooth muscle. NE will constrict smooth muscle by alpha-1 stimulation. ACh has no effect on vascular smooth muscle to either constrict it or dilate it.

Central Chemoreceptors
• Increasing carbon dioxide
• Acid

ACh slows heart rate
• Decreased sinoatrial (SA) and atrioventricular (AV) node automaticity

---

ACh
• Flattens the slope of phase 4 depolarization
• Increases the time to achieve threshold for depolarization
• Slows conductance through Funny sodium channels

Ordering a physical examination moves the clock forward. Atropine is considered to be done instantly on CCS, so if there is an effect of atropine, you will see it right away.
Interval History: "Breathing improved somewhat. Feeling better."

Orders:
- *Repeat IV atropine*
- *Pralidoxime*
- *CHEM-7, CBC*
- *ECG*
- *Chest x-ray*

ACh
- Constricts intestinal smooth muscle
- Leads to diarrhea
- Constricts stomach smooth muscle
- Leads to vomiting

Which is the mechanism of excess ACh with insecticides?

a. Increased release from neuron

b. Prevention of splitting into acetic acid and choline

c. Blockade of neuromuscular junction

d. Increased calcium flow into presynaptic neuron

Answer b. Prevention of splitting into acetic acid and choline

Acetylcholinesterase ends the effect of ACh at the neural junction. This happens by splitting ACh into acetic acid and choline. This effect is most apparent at muscarinic receptors, which are:

- Salivary and lacrimal glands
- GI tract smooth muscle: distal esophagus, stomach, and, intestine
- Urinary bladder smooth muscle (detrusor muscle)

Pralidoxime reactivates acetylcholinesterase.

Move the clock forward at increments of 15 minutes at first. You should expect to re-dose atropine numerous times. The half-life of atropine is short and the half-life of organophosphate insecticides is long. You should see all the effects resolve within minutes if you have given enough.

You do not have to do anything to get reports of tests ordered on CCS except to move past the time that it says "report available." The report will pop up automatically as you pass the time. You can cancel a test at any time before it becomes available by double clicking on it.

Reports:
- CHEM-7, CBC: normal
- ECG: sinus bradycardia (timed before repeat dose of atropine)
- Chest x-ray: normal

After repeated doses of atropine, there is no effect on muscular strength. What accounts for this?

a. Atropine does not penetrate muscles.

b. The neuromuscular junction is nicotinic.

c. Muscles are stimulated by calcium in the junction, not atropine.

d. The mechanism is unknown.

Answer b. The neuromuscular junction is nicotinic.

Atropine only effects muscarinic receptors such as are found in saliva, GI, bowel, and bladder tissue.

*Move the clock forward at 30- to 60-minute intervals for the first 12 hours because of the short half-life of atropine. **The management of nerve gas such as sarin gas is identical to the management of insecticides.***

Nerve gas attack presents the same way:
- Salivation
- Lacrimation
- Urination
- Defecation
- Respiratory distress

CASE 7: Spider Bite

Setting: ED

CC: "There was a spider in my shoe, and I stepped on it."

VS: normal

HPI: A 62-year-old man was getting up in the morning in his beach house on the Jersey shore when he put his foot into a shoe and experienced a sudden sharp pain. He originally thought that he stepped on a nail or piece of glass. He found a dead spider in the shoe. Over the next few hours, he developed waves of abdominal pain so severe he came to the ED.

PMHx/Medications: *none*

PE:
- *General: very uncomfortable; clearly in pain*
- *Chest: clear*
- *Abdomen: rigid, not tender; no rebound.*
- *Cardiovascular: normal*

Initial Orders:
- *Antivenin*
- *CHEM-7*
- *Calcium level*
- *Upright chest x-ray*
- *Abdominal x-ray*

Brown Recluse Spider Bite
- Local necrosis of skin
- No specific test
- Wound debridement
- Dapsone or steroids (sometimes help)

Black Widow Spider Bite
- Red hourglass on belly of spider
- Calcium chelation
- Abdominal pain

As you move the clock forward, **consult poison control or toxicology on spider, snake, and insect bites.**

If you remember a test or treatment you forgot to order before you move the clock forward, just order it and you will lose no points at all. The "penalty" on your score for forgetting to order a test or treatment is based on how long you move the clock forward before ordering it.

Reports:
- *CHEM-7: normal*
- *Calcium level: 6.4 mg/dL (low)*
- *Upright chest x-ray: normal; no air under diaphragm*
- *Abdominal x-ray: normal; no ileus, no air or fluid levels*

Perforation of GI Organs and Intestines
• Free air is detected on chest x-ray.
• Chest x-rays always show the top of the diaphragm.

Abdominal X-ray
• Only for ileus or small bowel obstruction

Orders:
• *IV calcium*
• *Antivenom if not already ordered*
• *Transfer patient to ICU*

Use ICU observation in black widow spider bites (Figure 11-3). Observe for:
• Seizures
• Prolonged QT on ECG
• Worsening tetany
• Laryngospasm

Low Calcium Level = Abnormal Excess Muscle and Neural Depolarization

Move the clock forward, do an Interval History, and reexamine the abdomen.
    Interval History: "Patient still in severe abdominal pain."
    Abdomen: rigid, tight, not tender; no change

Figure 11-3. Black widow spider (with offspring). *Latrodectus mactans*, with characteristic hourglass marking on its abdomen. (Photograph by Lawrence B. Stack, MD, reproduced with permission from Knoop KJ, et al. *The Atlas of Emergency Medicine*, 3rd ed. New York: McGraw-Hill; 2010.)

Black widow spider venom chelates calcium.

Low calcium level causes tetany.

Low serum calcium level decreases the threshold for depolarization.

After giving the calcium, the abdominal pain starts to improve. Antivenin has been administered. When the calcium level normalizes and abdominal pain has resolved, the patient can be transferred back to the hospital floor.

CASE 8: Digoxin Toxicity

Setting: *ED*

CC: *"I feel nauseated and I vomited twice."*

VS: *BP: 104/68 mm Hg; P: 50 beats/minute; T: 98°F; R: 24 breaths/minute*

HPI: *An 84-year-old man comes to the ED with 1 to 2 days of increasing nausea and vomiting as well as diarrhea and some abdominal pain. The patient has been having visual disturbance and palpitations. His family says he has grown somewhat confused over the last several days.*

PMHx:
- *Atrial fibrillation*
- *Hypertension*

Medications:
- *Chlorthalidone*
- *Digoxin*
- *Nifedipine*

PE:
- *General: old man mumbling on a bed*
- *Chest: clear to auscultation bilaterally*
- *Cardiovascular: slow, irregularly irregular rate*
- *Neurological: disoriented to time, examination incomplete secondary to lethargy*

Initial Orders:
- CHEM-7
- ECG
- Abdominal x-ray
- Oximeter

Altered Mental Status
- Sodium level
- Glucose level
- Hypoxia
- Calcium level
- Liver or renal failure
- Intoxications

Potassium Disorders
- Cause arrhythmias
- Do not cause neurological problems

Move the clock forward to get the laboratory test results. Elderly patients can become disoriented with disorders that would be very minor for a younger person, such as cystitis or sleep disturbance. In an older person, just staying awake too much at night is enough to disorient them. You cannot diagnose "sundowning" like that until you have excluded the other "organic" problems listed in the box.

Report:
- Oximeter: 97% saturation

What is the point of getting the abdominal film?

a. Perforation

b. Ileus or small bowel obstruction

c. Gallstones

d. Nephrolithiasis

Answer b. Ileus or small bowel obstruction

Abdominal x-ray or computed tomography (CT) is the only way to detect an ileus. Any electrolyte abnormality, such as abnormal levels of potassium, calcium, or magnesium, can paralyze the bowel. The intestines are a long muscular tube. These electrolytes make this muscle nonoperative.

Report:
- *CHEM-7: potassium 5.8 mEq/L (normal 3.5–5.2 mEq/L); BUN 38 g/dL (elevated); creatinine 2.0 mg/dL*
- *ECG: atrial fibrillation, curved downsloping of ST segments, premature ventricular contractions; heart rate 50 beats/minute*
- *Abdominal x-ray: multiple air fluid levels diffusely*

What is the downsloping ST segment from?

a. Potassium

b. Digoxin

c. Dehydration

d. Renal insufficiency

Answer b. Digoxin

Digoxin can give downsloping of ST segments even at normal levels (Figure 11-4). This is not considered a sign of toxicity. Dehydration is present based on a BUN-to-creatinine ratio of 20:1. This is not surprising in an elderly person using a diuretic to control blood pressure (BP), although it is more common with a loop diuretic.

Dehydration is a good reason for the patient's disorientation. Potassium disorders do not cause cognitive dysfunction. Both dehydration and potassium elevation can cause an ileus. There is no specific therapy to reverse a small bowel obstruction. You have to correct the underlying cause, such as electrolyte problems, and wait for it to start moving again.

Orders:
- *IV normal saline*
- *Stop digoxin and stop diuretics if not already done*
- *Digoxin level*

What is the most common toxicity associated with digoxin?

a. Cardiac

b. Neurological

c. Vision changes

d. GI tract

e. Electrolyte

Answer d. GI tract

Digoxin toxicity is rare because CHF is managed with angiotensin-converting enzyme (ACE) inhibitors, beta-blockers and spironolactone first. When it occurs, the most common symptoms are nausea, vomiting, and abdominal pain. These are nonspecific. The GI tract manifestations of digoxin toxicity have nothing unique to them. The most dangerous complication is cardiac arrhythmia. Virtually any rhythm disorder can occur. Yellow "halos" around objects are seen. This is part of neurological toxicity.

Altered mental status can be from digoxin toxicity.

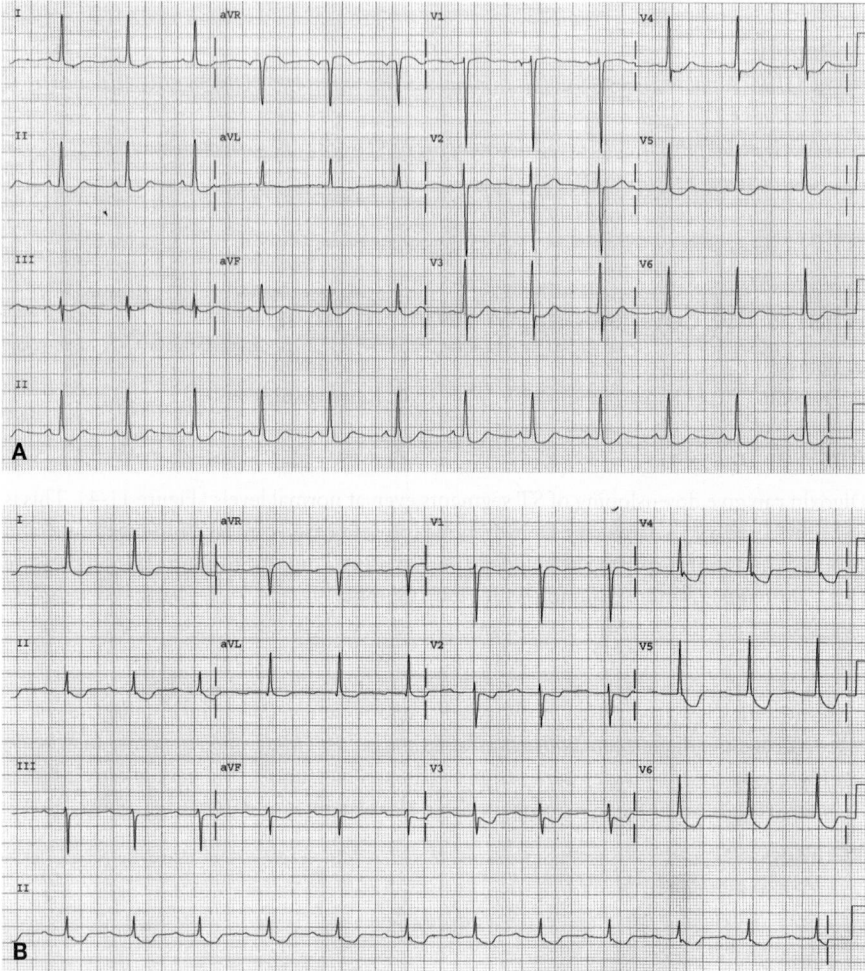

Figure 11-4. Electrocardiogram (ECG) demonstrating findings seen with therapeutic digoxin concentrations. **A.** ECG shows scooping of ST segments and small U waves with a serum digoxin level of 0.9 ng/mL. **B.** ECG shows scooping of ST segments, flattening of T waves, and first-degree atrioventricular block with a serum digoxin level of 1.2 ng/mL. (Reproduced with permission from Tintinalli JE, et al. *Tintinalli's Emergency Medicine, A Comprehensive Study Guide,* 7th ed. New York: McGraw-Hill; 2011.)

Digoxin toxicity causes confusion

HypOkalemia (low potassium [K]) = Digoxin Toxicity

Digoxin toxicity leads to hypERkalemia.

Hyperkalemia Etiology
• Digoxin inhibits sodium- and potassium-activated adenosine triphosphatase (NaK ATPase)

What is the most common arrhythmia from digoxin toxicity?

a. Atrial fibrillation

b. Premature ventricular contractions

c. Ventricular tachycardia

d. Bradycardia

Answer b. Premature ventricular contractions

Any arrhythmia is possible with digoxin toxicity. Premature ventricular contractions (PVCs) are the most common. Supraventricular tachycardia (SVT) with variable block is extremely common. This patient's bradycardia is definitely a manifestation of digoxin toxicity as is the abdominal distress, yellow halos around objects, and confusion.

Advance the clock and repeat the neurological examination.

PE:

• *Neurological: lethargic and confused*

Vomiting causes hypokalemia.
Hypokalemia causes digoxin toxicity.

Digoxin and potassium compete for the same binding site on NaK ATPase.

Digoxin increases contractility by:
• Stimulating the ryanodine receptors
• Releasing calcium from the sarcoplasmic reticulum

Report:

• *Digoxin level: 3.2 ng/mL (elevated)*

The patient has persistent neurological symptoms, an abnormal ECG, and hyperkalemia. All of these are indications for giving digoxin-binding antibodies.

Orders:
- *Digoxin-binding fragment antigen binding (Fab) antibodies*
- *CHEM-7*
- *Telemetry cardiac monitoring*
- *Transfer to ICU if not already done*

Digoxin-Binding Antibodies
- Fab portion of immunoglobulin G (IgG)
- Derived from sheep
- Excreted bound to digoxin renally

There should be an immediate effect of the digoxin-binding Fab portions. Bradycardia, confusion, and arrhythmias should quickly resolve.

Digoxin-Binding Fab
- It splits off the Fc portion.
- Papain splits into two pieces Fab and Fc.

Strongest Indications for Digoxin-Binding Fab
- Arrhythmia
- Symptomatic bradycardia
- Lethargy and confusion
- Hyperkalemia

As you move the clock forward, repeat the ECG, neurological examination, and potassium level. When these have normalized, move the patient out of the ICU. Because the indication for digoxin in this case is just rapid atrial fibrillation, switch digoxin to metoprolol or diltiazem or both. Both beta-blockers and diltiazem will control the heart rate and the BP.

CASE 9: Drowning and Hypothermia

Setting: *ED*

CC: *"We found him in the water off side of the boat."*

VS: *BP: 92/60 mm Hg; P: 45 beats/minute; T: 88°F; R: 32 breaths/minute*

HPI: *A 52-year-old man was at a party on his boat when he was noticed missing. The boat was on the dock in only about 12 feet of water. The patient has been drinking alcohol for several hours before what seemed to be slipping off the side of the boat and falling into the water. It is not clear how long he was in the water before his friends called 911.*

PMHx/Medications: *none*

What is the cause of death in hypothermia?

a. Seizure

b. Arrhythmia

c. Rhabdomyolysis

Answer b. Arrhythmia

The cardiac conduction system is made extremely irritable by hypothermia. The ECG will show bradycardia or "Osborn J waves," which look similar to ST-segment elevation. Although hypothermia decreases cerebral functioning, it does not cause seizures. Hypothermia causes coma. Cold can cause muscle breakdown and rhabdomyolysis, but this is not as common a cause of death as interfering with cardiac conduction.

Orders:
- *Oxygen*
- *Oximeter*
- *ABG*
- *Chest x-ray*
- *ECG*

PE:
- *General: lethargic, intoxicated and short of breath*
- *Neurologic: incomplete examination*
- *Chest: rhonchi bilaterally*
- *Cardiovascular: no murmurs*

Saltwater
• The osmolarity is 2700 mOsm/kg.
• It draws water into the lungs from the vasculature.
• It washes away surfactant.

Freshwater
• High volume causes hemolysis.
• It creates hypotonic blood.
• It washes away surfactant.

Move the clock forward only 1 to 2 minutes to get the results of oximeter.

Hypothermia: Lethargy + Dyspnea = Endotracheal Intubation

Hypothermia
• Decreases oxygen consumption
• Decreases CO_2 production
• Protects heart and brain from hypoxia
• Slows heart rate (diving reflex)

Report:
• *Oximeter: 88% saturation*

Orders:
• *Endotracheal intubation*
• *Transfer to ICU*
• *Warmed, humidified air*
• *External rewarming: blankets, heating pads, warm IV fluids*
• *CHEM-7, CBC*
• *Urine toxicology screen, alcohol level*

Most drowning and hypothermia deaths
• Are related to intoxication
• Happen in less than 12 feet of water

Report:
- *ABG: pH 7.32; PCO_2 48 mm Hg; PO_2 55 mm Hg*
- *Chest x-ray: ARDS, atelectasis*
- *ECG: Osborn J waves (Figure 11-5)*

Remember that on CCS, the tests are considered done instantly, so even though the report is available after rewarming has started with warm IV fluids, blankets, and heating pads, the ECG does not reflect the use of these treatments yet.

Atelectasis
- It causes the loss of airway volume.
- It can be caused by loss of surfactant.
- The small airways collapse first.

Ineffective Therapies in Drowning
- Steroids
- Antibiotics

Move the clock forward 10 minutes to see the effect of rewarming and mechanical ventilation. Both of these will have an immediate effect.

PE:
- *VS: BP: 104/64 mm Hg; P: 58 beats/minute; T: 94°F; R: 24 breaths/minute*
- *Neurological: The patient is much more alert.*
- *Chest: rales/rhonchi diffusely bilaterally*

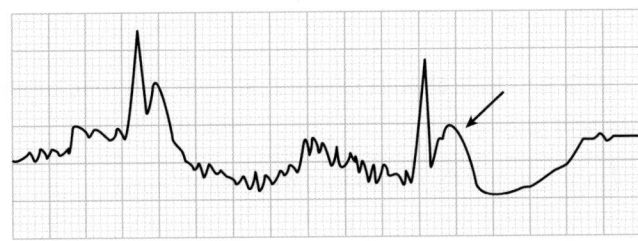

Figure 11-5. Electrocardiogram (ECG) strip from a patient with a temperature of 25°C (77°F) showing atrial fibrillation with a slow ventricular response, muscle tremor artifact, and Osborn (J) wave (*arrow*). (Reproduced with permission from Tintinalli JE, et al. *Tintinalli's Emergency Medicine, A Comprehensive Study Guide*, 7th ed. New York: McGraw-Hill; 2011.)

Both saltwater and freshwater create noncardiogenic pulmonary edema.

Reports:
- CHEM-7, CBC: BUN 24 g/dL (increased); hematocrit 50% (increased)
- Urine toxicology screen: negative
- Alcohol level: 340 mg/mL (legally "drunk" >100 mg/mL)

Saltwater aspiration draws free water into the lungs.
- Hemoconcentration raises hematocrit concentration.
- BUN level is increased (pre-renal azotemia).

- Decreased volume increases antidiuretic hormone (ADH).
- ADH stimulates urea transporters in the kidney.
- More urea is absorbed.

As you move the clock forward, there is no way to predict the amount of recoverability of the neurological status of the patient. *The benefit of rewarming will become clear right away, but the degree of recovery from the hypoxia of drowning is impossible to predict.*

Orders:
- Vital signs
- ECG

On CCS, the end notice—"This case will end in 5 minutes of real time"—is the same no matter how well or badly you manage the patient. This can be very disconcerting because you do not know precisely how you did. The closest thing you will get to feedback is the "Interval History."

Reports:
- VS: BP: 112/74 mm Hg; P: 68 beats/minute; T: 98°F; R: 18 breaths/minute

The patient is more alert.

ECG: *normal sinus rhythm at 68 beats/minute; resolution of J waves*

There is no maximum rate of rewarming.

CASE 10: Neuroleptic Malignant Syndrome

Setting: *ICU*

CC: *Unexpectedly high carbon dioxide level during surgery*

VS: *BP: 94/62 mm Hg; P: 120 beats/minute; T: 98°F; R: 30 breaths/minute*

HPI: *A 34-year-old woman with a history of Crohn disease, who has just been in the operating room for her third surgery to relieve obstruction, is now brought to the ICU because of a rise in PCO_2 to 65 mm Hg that cannot be explained. The patient had induction of anesthesia with midazolam then an inhalational anesthetic by face mask. Despite increasing the respiratory rate on the ventilator to 30 breaths per minute, the increased PCO_2 persists.*

PMHx:
- *Crohn disease*
- *Surgery to relieve obstruction from stricture in past*
- *Nephrolithiasis*

Medications:
- *Mesalamine (Pentasa)*
- *Infliximab intermittently*

PE:
- *General: muscle rigidity*
- *Chest: clear to auscultation; normal lung examination*
- *Cardiovascular: normal*
- *HEENT: normal*

Initial Orders:
- *ABG*
- *Chest x-ray*
- *CHEM-20*
- *Creatine kinase (CK)*

CCS sometimes gives unexpected "Nurses Notes" that have updates on the patient's condition. The updates can be either positive or negative in terms of improvement or worsening of the patient's condition.

While moving the clock forward on CCS to get the results of ABG, you get a "Nurses Note," which says, "The patient's muscles have become more rigid." You think that the increased carbon dioxide is from muscular rigidity and decide to give a neuromuscular blocking agent to relax the muscles and decrease carbon dioxide production.

Order:
- *Succinylcholine administration IV*

On CCS, medications are considered administered instantly, but you cannot see the effects of them until you move the clock forward.

What is the mechanism of succinylcholine?

a. It inhibits the release of ACh.

b. It blocks nicotinic receptor depolarization.

c. It prevents repolarization of the nicotinic receptors.

d. It cleaves ACh prematurely.

e. It prevents the release of calcium from the sarcoplasmic reticulum.

Answer C. It prevents repolarization of the nicotinic receptors.

Succinylcholine causes persistent depolarization of the nicotinic receptors, which results in neuromuscular blockade. It works exclusively at nicotinic receptors. Succinylcholine is not hydrolyzed by acetylcholinesterase, so its effect cannot be ended. Flaccidity of the muscles occurs because intramuscular calcium is taken up by the calcium ATPase of the muscle into the sarcoplasmic-endoplasmic reticulum calcium adenosine triphosphatase (SERCA). When all the calcium is removed from the cytoplasm, muscle contraction ends.

Succinylcholine prevents repolarization of the neuromuscular junction.

No Repolarization = Block of Next Depolarization

You move the clock forward 5 minutes to see the effects of the neuromuscular blocking agent.

PE:

• *Markedly increased muscle rigidity; masseter rigidity is severe.*

Reports:

• *ABG: pH 7.24; PCO$_2$ 64 mm Hg; PO$_2$ 74 mm Hg*

• *Chest x-ray: normal*

• *CHEM-20: potassium 5.4 mEq/L (elevated)*

• *CK: 7400 units/L (normal 40–175 units/L)*

Anesthesia + Unexpected Rise in PCO$_2$ = Malignant Hyperthermia

Malignant Hyperthermia (MH)

• Genetic predisposition

• Third or fourth exposure

• Inhalational anesthetics *plus* succinylcholine

Move the clock forward to recheck the laboratory test results and confirm MH.

Repeat Laboratory Tests:
- *ABG: pH 7.22; PCO_2 68 mm Hg; PO_2 74 mm Hg*
- *Potassium 6.0 mEq/L (elevated)*
- *CK: 16,300 units/L (normal 40–175 units/L)*

Succinylcholine makes MH worse.

Depolarizing blockade massively increases CO_2 production by the muscles.

The patient's muscular rigidity persists.

VS: *P: 112 beats/minute; T: 104°F*

Increased PCO_2 precedes temperature elevation in MH.

Which of the following is most effective for MH?

a. Dantrolene
b. Cooling blanket
c. Iced IV fluids
d. Bromocriptine
e. Spraying with water and evaporation

Answer a. Dantrolene

Dantrolene reorders the heat-generating mechanisms of skeletal muscle in both MH and neuroleptic malignant syndrome (NMS). NMS is specifically treated with bromocriptine because we think NMS has to do with the antidopaminergic qualities of neuroleptics.

Cooling blankets and especially the power of heat removal through evaporation are what is used in heat stroke. Heat stroke is entirely a problem of exertion of the body with high outside temperatures. MH and NMS have nothing to do with the outside temperature. They have to do with an idiosyncratic reaction of the body to either inhalational anesthetics and succinylcholine (MH) or neuroleptics. Iced IV fluids are always wrong. Iced IV fluids can stop the heart.

Orders:
- *Dantrolene*
- *Stop anesthetics and stop succinylcholine if not already done*
- *IV normal saline*
- *UA*
- *Urine myoglobin*

Massive CO_2 overproduction is always first in MH!
It cannot be compensated by hyperventilation.

After administering dantrolene and stopping exposure to anesthetics, the treatment of MH is similar to management of rhabdomyolysis with fluids and monitoring potassium, CK, calcium, and phosphate levels.

Rhabdomyolysis
- Potassium (K) level increased
- Phosphate level increased from muscles
- Calcium level down

Damaged muscles bind calcium.

Masseter Muscle Rigidity = Succinylcholine-Induced Malignant Hyperthermia

Report:
- *UA: dipstick positive blood, no red blood cells seen*
- *Urine myoglobin: elevated*

CK and urine myoglobin levels peak at about 24 hours after the use of inhalational anesthetics and neuromuscular blockers.

MH Mechanism
• Abnormal calcium release from SERCA
• Abnormal muscle contraction and rigidity

Dantrolene Mechanism
• Binds ryanodine receptors
• Inhibits calcium release from SERCA

Expect dark urine in MH.

If your case describes severe hyperkalemia and rhabdomyolysis, move the clock forward 30 to 60 minutes after administering insulin and glucose and recheck the potassium level. If your case describes only rhabdomyolysis with a normal potassium level, move the clock forward 4 to 6 hours and recheck the CK and potassium. Vital signs in an ICU are measured every 2 hours.

MH kills by
• Hyperkalemia
• Seizures from high temperature

VS: at 2-hour intervals

• T: 104°F, 103°F, 102.8°F, 103.4°F

You should not expect CK and temperature to peak for 24 hours. Both will come down after that.

Orders:
• Dantrolene—continue for 48 hours
• IV saline
• Repeat potassium, calcium, and CK levels at 6- to 12-hour intervals in ICU
• Repeat ABG

On CCS, you can get notes saying, "Are you sure you want to continue?" on any case. It does not mean you did anything wrong or made a mistake. It is simply giving you an opportunity to cancel orders or make changes.

The patient should stay in the ICU until mental status and temperature have normalized. If the hydration and correction of ventilatory support and potassium and calcium levels are well monitored, the patient will leave the ICU in 48 hours.

INDEX

Page numbers followed by *f* or *t* indicate figures or tables, respectively.